PRACTICAL GUIDE TO EVIDENCE

FOURTH EDITION

Christopher Allen,
LLM, MA, PhD, Barrister

Formerly Senior Lecturer, Inns of Court School of Law

Routledge·Cavendish
Taylor & Francis Group
LONDON AND NEW YORK

Fourth edition first published in Great Britain 2008
by Routledge-Cavendish
2 Park Square, Milton Park, Abingdon, Oxon OX14 4RN

Simultaneously published in the USA and Canada
by Routledge-Cavendish
270 Madison Ave, New York, NY 10016

Previous editions published by Cavendish Publishing

Routledge-Cavendish is an imprint of the Taylor & Francis Group, an informa business

© 2008 Christopher Allen

Typeset in Adobe Garamond and Helvetica Neue by
RefineCatch Limited, Bungay, Suffolk
Printed and bound in Great Britain by
MPG Books Ltd, Bodmin, Cornwall

British Library Cataloguing in Publication Data
A catalogue record for this book is available from the British Library

Library of Congress Cataloging in Publication Data
Allen, C. J. W. (Christopher J. W.), 1944–
    Practical guide to evidence / Christopher Allen. – 4th ed.
        p. cm.
    1. Evidence (Law)–England. 2. Evidence (Law)–Wales. I. Title.
    KD7499.A855 2008
    347.42′06–dc22   2008001049

ISBN13: 978–0–415–45719–4 (pbk)
ISBN10: 0–415–45719–X (pbk)

PRACTICAL GUIDE TO EVIDENCE
Fourth Edition

Practical Guide to Evidence provides a clear and readable account of the law of evidence, acknowledging the importance of arguments about facts and principles as well as rules.

The fourth edition has been revised and updated to address the radical changes brought about by the Criminal Justice Act 2003, particularly in relation to hearsay, character evidence and opinion evidence and to expand coverage of the Human Rights Act 1998.

Particular attention is given to changes made by the revised Codes of Practice, and to the growing body of case law on topics such as reverse burden of proof, the cross-examination of rape victims, evidence obtained by entrapment, and silence in the face of police questioning.

Now including enhanced pedagogical support such as further reading advice and self-test questions, this leading textbook can be used on both undergraduate and professional courses.

Christopher Allen, LLM, MA, PhD, Barrister, was formerly Senior Lecturer at the Inns of Court School of Law, City University. He continues to teach evidence at University College London and on London University's programme for external students.

To Tom and Minnie

Rules capable of rendering right decisions secure are what the nature of things denies. To the establishment of rules by which misdecision is rendered more probable than it would otherwise be, the nature of man is prone. To put the legislator and the judge upon their guard against such rashness is all that the industry of the free inquirer can do in favour of the ends of justice.

Jeremy Bentham

It may safely be laid down as an universal position, that the less the process of inquiry is fettered by rules and restraints, founded on extraneous and collateral considerations of policy and convenience, the more certain and efficacious will be its operation.

Thomas Starkie

······ PREFACE TO THE FOURTH EDITION ······

The last edition of this book was finished at a time when the evidence provisions of the Criminal Justice Act 2003 had not been brought into force. The courts since then have been engaged in interpreting and applying the new legislation, and their work is reflected in this edition. I have paid particular attention to cases on the definition of 'evidence of bad character' such as *Machado* (2006), *Brummitt* (2006) and *McNeill* (2007); to the guidelines laid down by the Court of Appeal in *Hanson* (2005); and to other decisions on the various 'gateways' under s 101 of the Act such as *Renda* (2005), *Highton* (2005), *Wilkinson* (2006), *M (Michael)* (2006), *Singh* (2007), *Mustapha*, (2007) and *Campbell* (2007).

Decisions on the new hearsay law have not been so numerous, but I have taken the opportunity to provide an account of the decision in *Maher v DPP* (2006) which, while breaking no new ground, seemed to be useful as an example of how several provisions of the Act were applied to a not uncomplicated set of facts. Among other topics that have required attention are reverse burdens of proof, section 41 of the Youth Justice and Criminal Evidence Act 1999, the judgment of the House of Lords on the definition of a confession in *Hasan* (2005), the decision of the Court of Appeal in *O* (2006) on previous consistent statements, and developments in the law relating to opinion evidence. I have also said rather more than in previous editions about the influence of the European Convention on Human Rights on evidence law.

Innovations in this edition are the reading lists and exercises that follow each chapter. Their object is to help students, particularly those working on distance learning courses, to broaden their understanding of the subject and to test their progress.

Christopher Allen
January, 2008

EXTRACT FROM PREFACE TO THE FIRST EDITION

With evidence, it is easy to miss the wood for the trees. One of the main reasons for this is that the subject is as much about reasoning with facts, the use of language, and the application of principles as it is about rules of law. I have tried to write a book that will make this clear. My experience of teaching and examining has shown that many students find it hard to understand evidence outside the context of factual situations, and even harder to apply what has been learned to different sets of facts in problem questions. I have tried to cope with these difficulties by providing detailed illustrations from the cases. Where a point has seemed particularly important I have provided several examples of the law at work, in the hope that if one example fails to make things clear another may succeed. I have tried to keep particularly in mind the needs of students who are studying part time or for an external degree. In a full time class any obscurities or ambiguities in a text can be resolved quickly before they develop into difficulties with the subject, but for the part time or external student it is vital to get things as clear as possible from the start. I cannot claim to have achieved this completely, but I have tried to do so. I owe a special debt of gratitude to Stephen Guest, who has read much of my manuscript. It has benefited greatly from his comments. Of course, he must not be taken to endorse all the opinions here, and any errors that remain are mine alone. Many of the chapters have their origins in lectures and seminars given at the Inns of Court School of Law, at University College London and on London University's External Programme. I am grateful to my students for helping me to clarify my ideas about how to present this subject.

Christopher Allen
Gray's Inn
April 1998

CONTENTS

CONTENTS

TABLE OF CASES

TABLE OF STATUTES

┄┄ TABLE OF STATUTORY INSTRUMENTS ┄┄

TABLE OF EUROPEAN LEGISLATION

1

INTRODUCTION

INTRODUCTION

Law cannot be properly understood without some knowledge of the context in which it operates. Just as the student of commercial law needs to understand something of what is involved in ordinary commercial transactions, so the student of evidence needs some understanding of what is involved in ordinary processes of proof.

Those processes will therefore be my first concern in this chapter. I shall then turn to a more traditional topic: the definition of 'evidence'. This will be followed by a short glossary of some technical terms commonly encountered in studying evidence law. The fourth section covers the concepts of relevance, weight and admissibility. These are fundamental to the consideration of all aspects of our subject. The fifth section discusses three characteristics of evidence law which it is helpful to appreciate at the outset. The sixth section is concerned with a particular contextual topic: the functions of judge and jury in a Crown Court trial. The last provides a brief introduction to the European Convention on Human Rights and its influence on evidence law.

EVIDENCE AND PROOF

A useful way of approaching this topic is by looking at a case which was notorious at the beginning of the 20th century and for some decades afterwards. The defendant was Dr Crippen, who was charged in 1910 with the murder of his wife.[1] According to the prosecution, Crippen had fallen in love with his young secretary, Ethel Le Neve, and had decided to kill his wife to leave himself free to marry Ethel. One night, therefore, he put poison in a glass of stout – his wife's regular nightcap. The poison might have been sufficient to kill her, or it might merely have made her unconscious. At any rate, by the time Crippen had finished with her she must have been dead, because he drained the blood from the body, dissected it, and separated the flesh from the bones. He buried the pieces of flesh in the cellar of the house where they lived. The bones and the head were never found; it was assumed that they had been burned. To explain his wife's absence, Crippen at first told her friends that she was staying with her sister in America; later he said that she had died there. When the police began to make inquiries, he told them that his wife had left him and that he had been too embarrassed to tell the truth to friends and neighbours. Crippen had not yet been arrested, and shortly after his interview with the police he hurriedly left the country with Ethel Le Neve. Meanwhile, the police dug up the cellar floor and discovered the human remains buried there. Crippen was followed and brought back to England to stand trial.

Imagine yourself now in the position of a lawyer for the prosecution in that case. You know, of course, what constitutes murder in English law but, given these facts and that law, what had to be established before a jury could find Crippen guilty of murder? The first thing that had to be proved was that Mrs Crippen was dead. Crippen maintained when questioned by the police and later at trial that his wife had left him and that he knew nothing of the remains in the cellar, so it was necessary for the prosecution to establish that the remains were those of Mrs Crippen. They also had to show that it was her husband who had killed her and that he had done so intentionally. This meant they had to prove that Mrs Crippen had died from poison administered by the accused with the intention of causing her death.[2]

The task faced by the prosecution is illustrated by Figure 1.1. Item 1 represents 'the thing that has ultimately to be proved'. This expression can be shortened by adopting a term used by JH Wigmore:[3] the *ultimate probandum*. In this case, it is

---

1   See Cullen, 1988.

2   To keep this analysis as simple as possible, I have ignored the possibility that she did not die until Crippen dismembered her body.

3   Wigmore (1863–1943) was a Professor of Law at Northwestern University in Chicago from 1893 until his death 50 years later. He was the author of many works, including a famous *Treatise on*

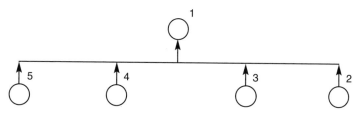

Figure 1.1

Key list
1   Dr Crippen murdered his wife (*ultimate probandum*).
2   Mrs Crippen was dead.
3   Poison had caused her death.
4   Dr Crippen had administered the poison.
5   He had done so with the intention of causing death.

expressed by the proposition 'Crippen murdered his wife.' Items 2 to 5 inclusive represent what Wigmore called *penultimate probanda.*[4] These are the propositions which, taken together, go to prove the ultimate probandum. Unless there was some evidence to support each one of the penultimate probanda, a defence submission that there was no case to answer would have been likely to succeed.

It is not necessary, for the purpose of understanding the process of proof, to show how all the *penultimate probanda* were proved in the *Crippen* case. It is enough to concentrate on the first of these, which appears as item 2 in Figure 1.1. The proof of this item is illustrated by Figure 1.2.

The following points should be observed:

(a)   Proof is made by establishing several sets of inferences which ultimately converge on item 2.

(b)   Each set of inferences rests on a foundation, which is marked in Figure 1.2 either by a diamond shape or by the letter G.

(c)   There are three types of foundation on which sets of inferences can be based:

   ■   the testimony of a witness at trial, represented by a square with a diamond beneath it. Examples are the testimony of the forensic scientists on each side (items 6 and 12);

   ■   an item of 'real evidence', ie, something which the jurors can examine for themselves. An example is a piece of flesh collected with the other

---

Evidence (1st edn, 1909–15; 3rd edn, 1940) and *The Principles of Judicial Proof* (1913, 1931; later *The Science of Judicial Proof*, 1937). His system for analysis of evidence, described in the latter work, is best studied today in Anderson, Schum and Twining, 2005. See also Twining, 1985.

4   Note the plural form. The singular is *penultimate probandum.*

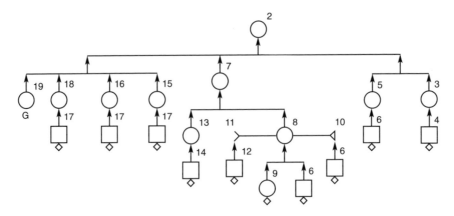

Figure 1.2

Key list
2 Mrs Crippen was dead.
3 Some remains were found in the cellar.
4 Police testimony to this effect.
5 The remains came from a human body.
6 Prosecution expert's testimony to this effect.
7 The body was that of Mrs Crippen.
8 A piece of the abdomen bore the mark of an operation scar.
9 Item of real evidence.
10 The shape of the mark was more consistent with a scar than with a fold.
11 The mark may have been caused by folding.
12 Defence expert's testimony to this effect.
13 Mrs Crippen had an operation scar on her abdomen.
14 Her sister's testimony to this effect.
15 No one had seen Mrs Crippen since 31 January 1910.
16 Mrs Crippen had friends and relations.
17 Prosecution testimony to this effect.
18 Mrs Crippen had a friendly, outgoing personality.
19 Someone with such a personality who has not communicated with any friends or relations
   for some months may be dead.

pieces from the cellar and said by the prosecution to bear an identifying scar. This type of foundation is represented by a circle with a
diamond beneath it (item 9);

■ a generalisation about the way things are in the world, for example,
item 19, represented by a circle with the letter G beneath it.

(d) All three types of foundation have in common the fact that the members
of the jury rely on their own perception for experience of them. The
jurors can see and hear the witnesses giving oral evidence in the witness
box. They are able to see the items of real evidence. They rely on their
own previous perceptions, that is, their experience, when deciding
whether or not to accept the truth of a proposed generalisation. If they

recognise it as something that is either already part of the way in which they understand the world, or as something that at least fits with their understanding, they are likely to accept it; otherwise, it is likely to be rejected. In these ways, members of a jury are in direct touch with all foundational items, but they are in direct touch with nothing else. Every item not foundational has to be inferred, and every process of inference is open to error and so apt to produce a false conclusion. The majority of items in Figure 1.2 are, like the majority of items of evidence in any case, non-foundational and therefore to be regarded with particular care before their truth is accepted. Direct perceptions are open to error too, of course, but inferences about events in the past provide additional scope for error.

(e) Just as a set of inferences is based on a foundation, so each inference in the set is based on those immediately below it. This basing relationship is hard to define, but for these purposes it will be enough to say that a basing item, often taken in conjunction with other items of evidence, makes another item in the chain of proof to some degree likely. For example, you probably feel instinctively that once it is established that a piece of the abdomen bore the mark of an operation scar (item 8) and that Mrs Crippen had an operation scar on her abdomen (item 13), it is likely that the remains came from the body of Mrs Crippen (item 7). How likely you feel any particular inference to be will depend on how cautious you are in forming beliefs and what weight you think ought to be attached to the data on which you base the inference in question. Someone who wishes to prove something will ideally be able to rely on an accumulation of different items of evidence from different witnesses. So here, if items 15 to 19 (relating to Mrs Crippen's disappearance) stood alone, we might be willing to accept Mrs Crippen's death as no more than a remote possibility, but the likelihood that she is dead becomes much stronger when evidence of the discovery in the cellar is added. 'Likelihood' in this context is often referred to as 'probability', meaning probability of any degree, however slight. This sense of 'probability' is different from the more colloquial one where it stands for something with a greater than 50% chance of being the case – a probability rather than a possibility.[5]

(f) The significance of an item of evidence lies in the fact that it makes a particular inference either more or less likely to be true. Look at the inference represented by item 8 in Figure 1.2. The prosecution needed to show that the remains found in the cellar were those of Mrs Crippen.

---

5   See generally Eggleston, 1983, Chapter 2.

They hoped to establish this by proving that Mrs Crippen had an operation scar on her abdomen and that an identical scar was to be found on one of the pieces of flesh found by the police. The defence countered this argument by calling expert evidence to the effect that the mark on the flesh was not a scar, but a fold that had developed after burial. Items 10 and 11 represent the experts' evidence on this question. Whether the jury accepted the truth of the inference represented by item 8 was going to depend on which expert they found the more persuasive.

Wigmore's chart system is one way of thinking methodically about the facts of any case in which you may be instructed. As an advocate and a lawyer, you must be able to ensure, so far as possible, that your client has available all the evidence needed to establish or rebut a claim. You have to be aware of the weaknesses in your own case and in that of your opponent. Does too much depend on the evidence of one witness? What grounds might there be for questioning that person's reliability? It will very rarely be the case that one particular inference must inevitably be made from certain facts; what other possible inferences might be made which would do your client less damage or your opponent more harm? To what extent are you or your opponent relying on the truth of hidden and hitherto unconsidered generalisations about the way things are in the world as the basis for making inferences? We shall return to these questions, but at this stage, having already used the word 'evidence' in several contexts, it is desirable to break off in order to say something about attempts to define this word.

DEFINING EVIDENCE

Wigmore thought it 'of little practical consequence to construct a formula defining what is to be understood as "evidence"', and he may well have been right. He nevertheless attempted a definition[6] and writers of textbooks on evidence have traditionally taken this to be one of their first tasks. The most satisfactory attempt was probably made in the 19th century by WM Best, who, influenced by Jeremy Bentham, defined evidence as 'any matter of fact, the effect, tendency, or design of which is to produce in the mind a persuasion, affirmative or disaffirmative, of the

---

6   'What we are concerned with is the process of presenting evidence for the purpose of demonstrating an asserted fact. In this process, then, the term Evidence represents: any knowable fact or group of facts, not a legal or a logical principle, considered with a view to its being offered before a legal tribunal for the purpose of producing a persuasion, positive or negative, on the part of the tribunal, as to the truth of a proposition, not of law or of logic, on which the determination of the tribunal is to be asked.' (Wigmore, 1983, Vol I, section 1.)

existence of some other matter of fact'.[7] More recent attempts at defining 'evidence' have included: 'that which makes evident a fact to a judicial tribunal';[8] 'information by which facts tend to be proved';[9] 'any material which has the potential to change the state of a fact-finder's belief with respect to any factual proposition which is to be decided and which is in dispute';[10] and 'something which may satisfy an inquirer of [a] fact's existence'.[11] This sort of thing is helpful up to a point, but the word 'evidence' can be used in different ways, depending on the context. Take, for example, the following:

(a) 'In August of last year, Bywaters, according to the evidence, made a statement to his mother about the unhappy life of Mrs Thompson.'

(b) 'The damp mud on his boots was evidence that he had left the house earlier that evening.'

(c) '"You must not tell us what the soldier, or any other man, said, sir," interposed the judge, "it's not evidence".'

In the first of these examples, 'evidence' was used to refer to what had been said in court by one or more witnesses. In the second, 'evidence' referred to a relationship of relevance between the fact of there being damp mud on boots and the fact that he had left the house earlier that evening. In the third example, 'evidence' was used in a restricted sense to cover only those legally admissible things that a witness could say in court.

As lawyers, you will be concerned with evidence in all these senses. You may have to advise on what information should be obtained from potential witnesses to substantiate or rebut a claim at trial. You may have to challenge the evidence of an opponent's witness on the basis that it is irrelevant, or construct an argument to demonstrate the relevance of what your own witnesses have to say. You may have to consider whether the law permits an admittedly relevant item of information to be given in evidence, or whether the item is caught by some rule or principle of exclusion.

RELEVANCE, WEIGHT AND ADMISSIBILITY

THE CONCEPTS DISTINGUISHED

It will help you to analyse problems and to develop arguments if I begin with a brief outline that distinguishes between these three concepts, even though we shall see later

---

7   Best, 1870, p 10. Cf Bentham, 1838–43, Vol 6, p 208.

8   Nokes, 1967, p 1.

9   Keane, 2006, p 1.

10   Murphy, 2005, p 2.

11   Tapper, 2007, p 1.

that judges have sometimes appeared to erode their boundaries so that one concept merges with another.

Let us suppose that Charlie is being prosecuted for burglary of a shop in London. The likelihood that he committed the crime can be expressed by means of a scale running from 1 to −1 thus:

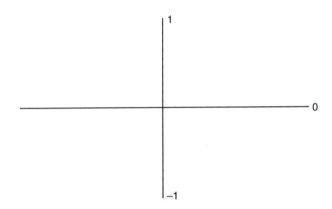

Figure 1.3

At the top of the scale, the point marked '1' represents the mental condition of being certain that it was Charlie who did the burglary. At the bottom of the scale, the point marked '−1' represents the mental condition of being certain that Charlie did not commit the burglary. Any item of evidence that makes it either more or less likely that Charlie did what the prosecution allege will have a place on the scale at some point between 0 and 1 or between 0 and −1, and will, in principle, be relevant at Charlie's trial. So, for example, if a prosecution witness says that he saw Charlie near the shop shortly before the burglary, that will be relevant and will have a place somewhere between 0 and 1. If Charlie produces a witness who says that she was with him several hundred miles away at the time the offence was committed, that piece of information will be relevant and will have a place somewhere on the scale between 0 and −1.

An item of evidence that makes neither the Crown's case nor Charlie's case more likely to be true will be *irrelevant* and will have no place on the scale.

The *extent* to which a piece of evidence makes the case of one of the parties more likely to be true is not a matter of relevance but of *weight*. It is relevance that gets the item onto the scale in the first place, but it is weight that dictates the position it takes there. The weightier the evidence, the nearer it will be to one or other extremity. Generally, while questions of relevance are for the judge to decide, questions of weight are left to the jury.

Although an item of evidence may be relevant, sometimes its legal *admissibility* may be in doubt. Problems of this kind are decided by the judge.

RELEVANCE

The principal way in which evidence is relevant is 'if it is logically probative or disprobative of some matter which requires proof'.[12] This does not mean that evidence has to be *conclusive* before it can be relevant. A popular fallacy is that an item of evidence is not relevant to the prosecution case if an innocent explanation can be found for it. If that were so, little if any evidence would ever be adduced in support of a prosecution, for an innocent explanation can probably be given for any item of potentially incriminating evidence. It would be absurd, for example, if the defendant's possession of a murder weapon were to be held irrelevant to the charge against him merely because the defendant said that he found it lying in the street, and picked it up out of curiosity or a desire to keep the street tidy. All that is required for an item of evidence to be relevant is that it should have *some* tendency in logic and common sense to advance (or defeat) the proposition in issue.[13] Accordingly, relevant evidence is that which makes the matter requiring proof more or less probable.[14] It may be important to be able to establish by argument the relevance of a contested item of evidence. The reason for this is that, although relevance does not always, because of the way the law works, make an item of evidence admissible, any item of evidence that *is* admitted *must* be relevant.[15] So one way of excluding an item of an opponent's evidence is to argue that it is irrelevant, hence the need to be able to make convincing submissions on this subject. But how are we to know what is, in Lord Simon's words, logically probative or disprobative? The question can almost never be answered by reference to a rule of law. In the vast majority of cases the law furnishes no test of relevance but refers, tacitly, to logic and general experience.[16] This can be seen, for example, in the study of a group of cases in which the Court of Appeal had to consider the relevance of the possession of cash, or of a lavish life style, where the charge concerned the possession of drugs. All these cases were decided at a time when evidence of propensity to commit a particular kind of offence was generally inadmissible as evidence for the prosecution. Evidence of propensity is now more freely admitted,[17] and what was said in these cases about instructions to the jury on the use of cash to establish past dealing is likely now to be out of date. The cases are still useful, though, as an example of the way in which the courts have felt their

---

12   *DPP v Kilbourne* [1973] AC 729, 756, *per* Lord Simon.

13   *R v A (No 2)* [2002] 1 AC 45, para 31, *per* Lord Steyn.

14   Cf Stephen: the word 'relevant' means that 'any two facts to which it is applied are so related to each other that according to the common course of events one either taken by itself or in connection with other facts proves or renders probable the past, present, or future existence or non-existence of the other' (1877, p 4).

15   *R v Turner* [1975] QB 834, p 841. See also *R v Sandhu* [1997] Crim LR 288; *R v Byrne* [2002] 2 Cr App R 311.

16   Thayer, 1898, p 265.

17   See s 101(1) Criminal Justice Act 2003, and Chapter 12 below.

way towards regarding logical relevance as dependent on the facts of particular situations.[18]

In *R v Batt*[19] the defendant was charged with possession of 500 grams of cannabis resin, with intent to supply. There was evidence that £150 in cash had been found in an ornamental kettle that he possessed. The Court of Appeal held that this was not probative of the offence, because the cash could have had nothing to do with intent to supply in the future the cannabis that had been found. (Because of the general rule against evidence of propensity, the jury was not entitled to infer from the presence of the cash that the defendant had been engaged in earlier dealings, and was therefore likely to have been in possession of the cannabis with the intention of supplying it to other customers in the future.) But in *R v Wright*,[20] where the defendant was charged with possession of cocaine with intent to supply, evidence was admitted to show that he also had in his possession £16,000 in cash and a gold necklace worth about £9,000. The Court of Appeal held that this evidence was relevant and had been properly admitted, Beldam LJ observing that supplies of cash were essential to enable a dealer to purchase new stock.

In *R v Grant*[21] the defendant was charged with possession of crack cocaine with intent to supply. When arrested he had just over £900 in cash in his possession. He admitted possession of the drug; the only issue was whether he intended to supply it to others. The Court of Appeal held that the finding of cash in conjunction with a substantial quantity of drugs is capable of being relevant to the intent to supply. It is for the jury to decide if possession of the cash is evidence of a continuing trade in drugs. However, a proper direction should be given as to the use that can be made of such evidence. Any innocent explanation for possession of the cash must be rejected before its possession can be relied on as relevant to the offence. If there is any possibility of the money being in the accused's possession for reasons other than drug dealing, the evidence would not be probative. If the presence of the money indicates not merely past dealing, but a continuing dealing in drugs, possession of the money can be considered in determining whether the necessary intent has been proved.

In *R v Halpin*[22] the Court of Appeal said that evidence of a lavish lifestyle would only rarely be relevant to intent to supply, and could not be relevant at all where the issue was simply one of possession. But *Halpin* was distinguished in *R v Guney*.[23] In this case the defendant was charged with possession of heroin with intent to supply. When his premises were searched it was discovered that he had £25,000 in cash in a wardrobe and, in the top of the wardrobe, heroin with a street value of about

---

18   Further examples can be found in Chapter 12.
19   [1994] Crim LR 592.
20   [1994] Crim LR 55.
21   [1996] 1 Cr App R 73.
22   [1996] Crim LR 112.
23   [1998] 2 Cr App R 242.

£750,000. The defendant said that the money was his savings, and that he knew nothing about the heroin. He claimed that he had been 'set up'. It was argued that evidence of the cash was irrelevant to the question of possession. The Court of Appeal said that the observations in *Halpin* had been made *obiter*. Evidence of a lavish life-style, or of possession of a large sum in cash, does not on its own prove very much, and certainly not possession of drugs. But the relevance of any particular piece of evidence should be decided on a case by case basis. Where the charge is simple possession, cash and lifestyle can be relevant. In this case the defendant had said that he was ignorant of the presence of drugs in his wardrobe. The physical proximity of the cash was relevant to that claim. Would he have left such a sum lying around in a house so insecure that people could enter and plant drugs there? Another consideration was the fact that both drugs and cash had been poorly concealed. How had he missed the drugs when he put the cash in the wardrobe, according to him, on the evening before his arrest?

This line of cases, culminating in *Guney*, shows that relevance will very often be determined by the facts of the particular case under consideration, and that it is unwise to say that in no circumstances will a particular item of evidence be relevant.[24]

The key to relevance is an understanding of the importance of *generalisations about the way things are in the world*: the sort of things exemplified by item 19 in Figure 1.2. That item was needed to make sense of items 15, 16 and 18. You will remember that the immediate object was to prove that Mrs Crippen was dead. To this end, the prosecution wished to adduce evidence to show that she had not been seen by anyone since 31 January 1910, that she had friends and relations, and that she possessed a friendly, outgoing personality; but those facts are meaningless if you do not accept that item 19 says something true about the way things are in the world. If you do not accept that someone with a friendly, outgoing personality who has failed for some time to communicate with any friends or relations may be dead, it follows that it is irrelevant to prove those facts about Mrs Crippen. The tentative form of the generalisation in this instance, that someone in those circumstances *may* be dead, illustrates the fact that generalisations will rarely take the form of a universally true proposition.

An advocate needs to be familiar with the structure of arguments about relevance. It follows that, as part of your preparation of a case, you will have to think through matters that you might hitherto have accepted instinctively so that, if necessary, you can justify or challenge a claim that something is relevant. If your object is to exclude a particular item of evidence, a denial of relevance may be an effective weapon. If you can show that your opponent must rely on a generalisation that is absurd, or at least questionable, in order to establish relevance, that evidence is likely to be excluded.

---

24   See, however, the topic of 'legal relevance', below. A trial judge's decision on logical relevance is unlikely to be upset by the Court of Appeal, but for an instance where this occurred, see *R v Ilomuanya* [2006] Crim LR 422.

An example of this approach can be seen in *R v Bracewell*.[25] Two men, Bracewell and a man named Lockwood, were charged with burglary and murder. The case for the prosecution was that they had agreed to burgle a house occupied by a man named Blakey, that in the course of the burglary Blakey had been killed, and that both men were responsible for his death. Both defendants admitted burglary, but each said the other was solely responsible for Blakey's death. The deceased had suffered death from a violent attack. One of the witnesses for the prosecution was Lockwood's mistress, a Mrs Firth. Her statement to the police referred to the fact that Lockwood was a very violent man. She described occasions when he had been violent to her and added: 'Once he started these assaults he did not appear to be able to stop himself.' This part of her statement was inadmissible as evidence for the prosecution because at that time evidence of an accused's general criminal disposition was inadmissible to show that he had committed the crime for which he was being tried. Although the prosecution could not use this evidence, the question arose whether Bracewell could. His counsel, in order to support Bracewell's defence that Lockwood had been the sole cause of the death, applied to cross-examine Mrs Firth with a view to making these matters known to the jury. The trial judge refused to allow this, and in due course Bracewell was convicted of murder. He appealed, arguing that the judge's decision had been wrong.

Counsel for Bracewell argued before the Court of Appeal that Mrs Firth's evidence on these matters was relevant to his client's case, and so admissible. In order to establish relevance he relied on the generalisation that: 'A man who, when he uses violence to his mistress, does not know when to stop, is more likely to have been guilty of a violent assault on a man in the course of a burglary than a man who has not used violence to his wife or mistress.' Of this generalisation, Ormrod LJ said that opinions on its validity might differ widely. Without the benefit of statistical evidence, it could only be a matter of opinion. The onus of satisfying the judge as to the relevance of evidence was on the party tendering it. The Court of Appeal clearly thought that this burden had not been satisfied and that the decision of the trial judge to exclude the evidence had been correct.

The decision shows several things. First, counsel and judges recognise the significance of generalisations in establishing relevance. Secondly, the burden is on the party who tenders evidence to show that it is relevant; it is not for the party challenging relevance to show that the evidence is irrelevant. Thirdly, a judge may be unwilling to accept the truth of an appropriate generalisation without the support of expert evidence.[26]

I said at the beginning of this section that the *principal* way in which evidence is relevant is if it is logically probative or disprobative of some matter requiring proof.

---

25   (1978) 68 Cr App R 44.

26   On generalisations, see further Tapper, 2007, pp 69–70; Twining, 1985, pp 142–46.

Another way in which evidence can be relevant is where it describes the 'background' to the evidence primarily relied on. Criminal charges, in particular, cannot always be fairly judged in a factual vacuum. It may be necessary, in order to assess the primary evidence relating to a charge, to admit evidence describing the context and circumstances in which the offence is alleged to have been committed.

A good example of this occurred in *R v Sawoniuk*.[27] The defendant was charged, by virtue of the War Crimes Act 1991, with the murder in 1942 of two Jewish women in Domachevo, Belorussia, in circumstances constituting a violation of the laws and customs of war. The prosecution case was that the defendant, a member of the local police force, had shot and killed two unidentified Jewish women as part of a 'search and kill' operation, which had been conducted by local police following the massacre by special task forces of the German security police of many of the Jewish population of Domachevo. The defendant admitted that he had joined the local police force in Domachevo after the German invasion and had remained in that occupation until July 1944, when he had fled westward to escape the advancing Red Army. He denied taking part in the massacre, saying that he had been visiting a friend in a neighbouring village when it took place. He further denied that there had been a search and kill operation after the massacre, or that he had taken part in one.

At trial, the judge admitted evidence, including evidence of criminal actions not covered by the indictment, to show the participation of the defendant in a 'search and kill' operation carried out by the local police after the massacre. The trial judge held that although evidence of this operation did not relate to specific counts on the indictment, it was nevertheless relevant to the issues that they raised. The defendant was convicted on the counts relating to the two women. On his appeal, the prosecution supported the trial judge's decision by arguing that proof of the defendant's participation in the search and kill operation was relevant because it identified him as the member of a group to which the killer had belonged, and to that extent supported identifications of the defendant made by witnesses who, when children, had seen the killings referred to in the indictment. The evidence had been called not to prove the defendant's propensity for misconduct, which at the time would have been inadmissible, but his participation in a police operation that included the matters referred to in the indictment. The Court of Appeal upheld this argument, but also said that the trial judge had been correct to admit the evidence because without it the eye-witness evidence in the case that directly related to the deceased women would have been incomplete or incomprehensible. This was particularly important in a case in which a jury was being asked to assess the significance of evidence relating to events that took place many years ago in a distant country, and in very unusual circumstances.

---

27   [2000] 2 Cr App R 220.

There was a similar ruling in the very different case of *R v Phillips*.[28] The defendant was charged with the murder of his wife. There was evidence that he had previously threatened to kill her on several occasions, extending over a period of some years. The defence accepted that evidence of recent incidents could be adduced, but objected to evidence relating to earlier periods. The judge held that it was unrealistic to exclude the evidence of earlier incidents because it was all part of the continuing history of the relationship between the defendant and the deceased. The Court of Appeal upheld his ruling, adding that all the evidence was relevant because it rebutted the claim made by the defendant in his police interview that the marriage had been happy, and that he therefore had no motive to kill his wife.

IS THERE A CONCEPT OF LEGAL RELEVANCE?

Everything that I have written so far suggests that any arguments about relevance are going to be about facts, not law. This is a view that has been challenged in the past and on which two great American evidence scholars, JB Thayer and JH Wigmore, were divided. Thayer defined the law of evidence as 'a set of rules and principles affecting judicial investigations into questions of fact',[29] but he thought that these rules and principles did not regulate the process of reasoning, save to the extent of helping to select the factual material on which the processes of reasoning were to operate. The principle forbidding the reception of irrelevant evidence was not so much a rule of evidence as a presupposition involved in the very conception of a rational system of evidence.[30] According to Thayer, the law furnished no test of relevance. Instead, the law tacitly referred to logic and general experience, the principles of which were presumed to be known.[31]

Wigmore accepted that relevance had originally been a matter of logic and common sense, but he argued that there were so many instances in which the bearing of particular facts on particular issues had been ruled upon by courts that the united logic of a great many judges and lawyers furnished evidence of the sense common to a great many individuals, and so acquired the authority of law. It was therefore proper, he argued, to talk of legal relevance.[32]

It is certainly the case that, in some instances, judges have laid down rules about what is relevant or irrelevant. For example, in *DPP v Camplin*,[33] it was decided that

---

28   [2003] 2 Cr App R 521.

29   Thayer, 1898, p 263.

30   Thayer, 1898, pp 264–65. Cf the *dicta* of Lawton LJ in *R v Turner* [1975] QB 834, p 841; *Sourcebook*, 1996, p 401.

31   Thayer, 1898, p 265.

32   Wigmore, 1983, Vol 1, section 12.

33   [1978] AC 705. But a more usual approach is that of the Court of Appeal in *R v Guney* [1998] 2 Cr App R 242, p 265, where it was emphasised that questions of relevance do not depend on 'abstract legal theory but on the individual circumstances of each particular case'.

age and sex were always relevant when considering the defence of provocation. Further, in ss 41–43 of the Youth Justice and Criminal Evidence Act 1999, Parliament has provided a statutory framework for determining the relevance of a complainant's previous sexual history where the defendant is on trial for a 'rape offence'.[34] But in addition to specific rules like this, it is also necessary to take into account the courts' practice of rejecting evidence of minimal weight on the ground that it is 'irrelevant'.[35] Judges have pragmatic reasons for not admitting every item of logically relevant evidence, however slight its weight. The best reason is that if the field of judicial inquiry is too wide, confusion leading to misdecision may result. Another reason is that concessions have to be made to the shortness of life, as well as to the financial resources of the litigants or the legal aid fund.

An old case illustrating an approach of this kind is *Hollingham v Head*.[36] The plaintiff sold a quantity of guano to the defendant. When he sued the defendant for the price, the defendant alleged that he was entitled, by the terms of the contract, to refuse payment. He alleged that the guano, which had been sold under the name of 'Rival guano', was of a new kind and that in order to persuade him to place an order, the plaintiff had sold it at £7 per tonne on the condition that if it was not equal to Peruvian guano, the price of which was £14 per tonne, the defendant was not to pay for it. The plaintiff denied that this had been a condition of the contract. The question arose whether, in order to prove the existence of the condition, the defendant could cross-examine the plaintiff about sales of Rival guano to other customers on the same condition, and whether evidence could be called as part of the defendant's case to this effect. The Court of Common Pleas held that such evidence and cross-examination were inadmissible as not being relevant to the issue between the parties. The judgments of Willes and Williams JJ, however, showed that the court was mainly concerned with the need to save time and ensure that the jury was not distracted from the point in issue.

Willes J appeared to base his judgment on the ground of relevance by saying: 'I do not see how the fact that a man has once or more in his life acted in a particular way makes it probable that he so acted on a given occasion.' But this is unconvincing. There may be circumstances where the fact that someone has done X in the past *does* make it more likely that, where X has been committed, he, rather than someone who has not done X before, committed X on this occasion. That was not the type of problem found in *Hollingham v Head* but, even so, the conclusion seems odd. It seems likely – the report has insufficient detail for the reader to be sure – that the defendant wanted to show that the contract he had made with the plaintiff was part of something like a promotion campaign for Rival guano. It would surely have been

---

34   *Hansard*, HL Deb, 23 March 1999, col 1216. See below, Chapter 6.

35   Judges often achieve this by using a concept of 'sufficient relevance', thereby eroding the boundary between relevance and weight. See, eg, *R v Byrne* [2002] 2 Cr App R 311.

36   (1858) 27 LJCP 241.

relevant to the existence of the alleged condition to prove that the contract with the defendant had been part of such a campaign, during which contracts had been made on identical terms with other purchasers. The real reason for exclusion seems to have been the fear of inconvenience if the inquiry had to be extended in this way.

Another move which appeared to limit the concept of relevance in law was made by the House of Lords in *R v Blastland*.[37] The body of a boy who had been buggered and strangled was found and in due course the defendant was charged with buggery and murder. He denied murder, but admitted some sexual activity with the boy not far from where the body was later found. According to the defendant, after having oral sex with the boy he noticed another man nearby, whereupon he panicked and ran home. He gave a description of the other man which corresponded closely to that of a man referred to throughout the proceedings as 'Mark'. The case for the defence was that it was Mark, and not the accused, who had committed buggery and murder. In order to support this, the defence wished to call evidence of persons to whom Mark had spoken after the murder had taken place. It was hoped that this evidence would show that Mark knew things about the murder that only the murderer could have known.

The House of Lords held that this evidence was inadmissible because, amongst other reasons, it was irrelevant. What the defence witnesses could say would amount to evidence of Mark's knowledge, and so of his state of mind. However, said Lord Bridge, for that state of mind to be relevant, it had to be itself directly in issue in the trial, which it clearly was not, or it had to be 'of direct and immediate relevance' to an issue arising in the trial. The issue at the trial was whether it was proved that the defendant had buggered and murdered the deceased, but Mark's knowledge was not, *per se*, of any relevance to this issue. What was relevant was not the fact of Mark's knowledge but how he had come by that knowledge. He might have done so in a number of ways, but the two most obvious possibilities were either that he had witnessed the commission of the murder by the appellant or that he had committed it himself. The statements which it was sought to prove that Mark made, indicating his knowledge of the murder, provided no rational basis whatever on which the jury could be invited to draw an inference as to the source of that knowledge. To admit the evidence would have been a mere invitation to speculate.[38] Accordingly, the evidence was irrelevant and therefore inadmissible.

A problem arising at once is what we are to understand by the qualifying words 'direct and immediate' in relation to relevance. What the prosecution had to prove in this case was, as Lord Bridge said, that Blastland had buggered and murdered the

---

37   [1986] AC 41; Carter, 1987, pp 108–13.

38   [1986] AC 41, p 54. The idea that inconclusive evidence may be irrelevant is a potential weapon in the defence armoury. It could be used to exclude prosecution evidence on the basis that a jury could only speculate about its significance. For another case recognising the impropriety of jury speculation, see *R v Woodward* (1994) *The Times*, 7 December.

deceased. It was devastatingly clear that anything tending to prove or disprove that proposition was relevant to the issue with which the trial court was concerned. What did the requirement that the relevance be 'direct and immediate' add? Nothing. Some things, of course, point more clearly to a particular conclusion than others, but this is a matter of weight, not relevance. Ought we to take Lord Bridge as stipulating that, for evidence to be relevant, it must have some minimum weight? But while 'weight' in relation to evidence can usually be understood, the metaphor cannot be pressed too far. A requirement of a minimum weight presupposes an ability to measure exactly. At this point the metaphor breaks down. While physical objects may be capable of exact measurement, items of evidence are not.

Another way of reading what Lord Bridge said is to stress the inconclusiveness of the information tendered. Mark's knowledge was relevant because it opened up a possibility that he had come by it in a way that was inconsistent with the defendant's guilt, but because the jury had no means of telling whether that possibility was likely to be right or not, it was 'irrelevant'. Lord Bridge appears to have assumed that an ambiguity which is incapable of resolution can never, to any significant degree, tend to the disproof of a fact in issue. But it is absurd to suggest that an ambiguity which cannot be resolved is incapable of providing a reasonable doubt, and if there was a reasonable doubt the accused was entitled to a verdict of not guilty.

The unsatisfactory nature of *Blastland* is underlined when that decision is compared with the decision of the Court of Appeal in *R v Greenwood*.[39] The defendant had been charged with the murder of a young woman. The case against him was based entirely on confessions that he had made to the police and to others. At trial he said that these confessions were untrue, and there was medical evidence to show that he suffered from a depressive illness that might have led him to make false confessions. The defence wanted to adduce evidence about a man named Parkinson, to the effect that he had been a boyfriend of the victim and had been violent towards her. There was further evidence that he had been in the vicinity at the time when she was killed, and that he had in his possession her bloodstained underwear. The trial judge ruled that all this evidence was irrelevant and therefore inadmissible. He said that there was no evidence to link Parkinson to the events of the night in question, and that in the absence of such evidence the jury could do no more than speculate about his involvement. The Court of Appeal held that this ruling was wrong. In particular, the fact that Parkinson had been in the vicinity, had been known to the victim, and might be considered to have a motive were relevant to the question of the defendant's guilt. The Court said that if it is accepted that there has been a murder, but the defendant is saying simply that he did not do it, he must by inference be asserting that someone else did. There is no *obligation* on a defendant to establish that someone else committed the offence, but if he has evidence to show that

---

39   [2004] EWCA Crim 1338.

someone else did, he must be able to adduce it. In particular, he must clearly be entitled to show that someone else had a motive to commit the murder. The Court concluded that it was wrong to exclude from the jury's consideration all information about Parkinson, especially his relationship with the victim, his violence towards her, and his presence in the vicinity at the time when the offence was committed.

The evidence in *Greenwood* that someone other than the defendant had committed the murder was circumstantial, but so was the evidence in *Blastland*. And in that case the House of Lords had been prepared to say that *some* circumstantial evidence relating to Mark was admissible: namely, the fact that he had been investigated by the police, the results of his medical examination, and his movements on the evening of the murder. It is difficult to justify the exclusion of evidence that he knew about the boy's death on the basis that it could lead only to speculation. How did it differ from the other circumstantial evidence?[40]

There have been other suggestions that relevance may be a matter of law. In *Vernon v Bosley*,[41] Hoffmann LJ appeared to acknowledge a concept of legal relevance that in some cases would involve qualifying a party's right to choose how to present his case by reference to other public or private interests. For example, in any litigation, the general public and the party's opponent would have an interest in keeping down the length and cost of the proceedings. To defend this interest a judge might have to rule inadmissible the exploration of side issues which, though probably having potential relevance, did not appear sufficiently relevant to justify the time and expense needed to investigate them. Relevance might also have to be balanced against other interests where a question involved a witness breaking a confidence imposed by his religion, profession or conscience. Hoffmann LJ insisted that as a matter of legal analysis this was not an exercise of a discretion but the application of the law: the concept of relevance employed by the law would sometimes involve the need to carry out such balancing exercises. The other members of the Court of Appeal did not adopt Hoffmann LJ's views. The practical problem has now been solved in civil proceedings by the Civil Procedure Rules, which give the court a broad discretion to exclude evidence that is in principle admissible. Rule 32.1 gives power to a civil court to control the evidence by giving directions as to the issues on which it requires evidence, the nature of the evidence required to decide those issues, and the way in which the evidence is to be placed before the court. It is explicitly stated in r 32.1(2) that the court may use these powers to exclude evidence that would otherwise be admissible. One of the ways in which this power can be used is to exclude evidence obtained by improper methods,[42] but the fact that evidence has been improperly

---

40   See, further, the commentary on *Greenwood* in [2005] Crim LR 60–61.

41   (1994) *The Times*, 8 April. A full transcript of the judgment has been relied on for the passage in the text.

42   There is a power to do this in criminal trials also. See the discussion of s 78 of the Police and Criminal Evidence Act 1984 in Chapter 11.

obtained will not lead to automatic exclusion under r 32.1(2). The court can admit the evidence but discourage improper conduct by orders as to costs. In *Jones v University of Warwick*,[43] the defendants in a personal injury claim wanted to adduce in evidence some video tapes that had been taken of the claimant without her knowledge.[44] A private inquiry agent had been employed by the defendants' insurers to take secret films of the claimant, and in order to carry out his task he had committed trespass and had been in breach of the claimant's right to privacy contained in Art 8 of the European Convention on Human Rights. The district judge had ruled that the video tapes should be excluded. This order was overturned on appeal to the judge, and the judge's order was then itself the subject of an appeal. The Court of Appeal acknowledged that it was concerned with two competing public interests: the interest of the public that in litigation the truth should be revealed, and the interest of the public that the courts should not acquiesce in, let alone encourage, the use of unlawful means to obtain evidence. The court said that a judge should consider the effect on litigation generally when exercising his discretion under the Civil Procedure Rules.[45] The fact that the defendants' insurers had been responsible for trespass and a breach of Art 8 was therefore a relevant circumstance to be considered when deciding what orders to make for the management of the proceedings, including, possibly, the exclusion of the video evidence under r 32.1(2).[46]

The question whether it is desirable to recognise a concept of 'legal relevance' that is stricter than 'logical relevance' may still be a live issue in criminal proceedings, just as it was in civil proceedings before the Civil Procedure Rules came into force.

Two principal difficulties stand in the way of such a development. The first is that a concept of this kind would be impossible to define. The second is that, since each case would depend so much on its own facts, there would be considerable difficulty in developing a body of case law about what was legally relevant. Cases where a court has made a general rule about the relevance in certain circumstances of a particular kind of evidence, such as *DPP v Camplin*, are better seen as defining substantive law than as saying something about a concept called 'legal relevance'. Cases where relevance has been used as a cloak for pragmatic decisions should simply be marginalised in favour of greater openness.

There are other potential disadvantages in acknowledging a concept of legal relevance. There is a danger that such a concept would exclude logically relevant evidence unless legal precedent authorised its admission. Further, if, despite

---

43   [2003] 3 All ER 760.

44   The object was to try to establish that the claimant had exaggerated the extent of her disabilities.

45   This is clear from the Civil Procedure Rules themselves. For example, judges who exercise their discretion under r 32.1 are required to ensure, *inter alia*, that a case uses only its appropriate share of the resources of the court (r 1.1(2)(e)).

46   On the facts, the court held that it would not be right to exclude the evidence, but that disapproval of the insurers' conduct could be adequately reflected in orders for costs.

difficulties, a body of case law were to develop, it would give rise to a large number of cumbersome rules and exceptions. However, perhaps the greatest disadvantage arises from the fact that, since the decisions of judges about relevance tend to reflect the prevailing value judgments of the society in which they live, relevance can become a useful instrument for discarding arguments and evidence that challenge important, but perhaps unexpressed, values. To fix relevance in a straitjacket of case law would make it even more difficult than it already is to adapt the law to changing circumstances.[47]

Sometimes courts avoid a full challenge to the relevance of an item of evidence, but attempt to distinguish between evidence with a 'direct' relevance to the principal question in dispute and evidence relevant to 'collateral facts',[48] which will, if established, tend to elucidate that question. It is then said that, while it is the right of the party tendering evidence of the former kind to have it admitted, there is not the same absolute right when a party tenders evidence of facts collateral to the main issue. In order to entitle him to give such evidence, he must first satisfy the court that the collateral fact which he proposes to prove will, when established, be capable of affording a reasonable inference as to the matter in dispute. He is also bound to satisfy the court that the evidence will be reasonably conclusive, and will not raise a difficult and doubtful controversy of precisely the same kind as that which has to be determined on the main issue.[49] The reasons for this approach are the practical ones that have already been shown to affect decisions about relevance itself: collateral inquiries can confuse a jury and lengthen trials. The investigations undertaken in any trial have to be kept within reasonable limits, so as to secure 'promptitude, precision and satisfaction in the administration of justice'.[50]

The application in practice of this distinction may not be easy, as was shown by *Managers of the Metropolitan Asylum District v Hill and Others*.[51] In that case the plaintiffs, who were landowners in Hampstead, brought an action for nuisance, allegedly caused by the construction and maintenance in the vicinity of a hospital for smallpox patients. The trial judge had rejected their application to call evidence as to the effect of other similar hospitals on their surrounding neighbourhoods. Although this was not the main issue in the appeal, various observations about this ruling were made by members of the House of Lords. The Lord Chancellor, Lord Selborne, said:

---

47 See James, 1941; Trautman, 1952; Weyrauch, 1978.

48 'Collateral facts' are facts relating to some subsidiary matter which itself affects the question of whether a 'fact in issue' will be established or not. See below under 'Some Terminology'.

49 *Managers of the Metropolitan Asylum District v Hill and Others* (1882) 47 LT 29, p 35, *per* Lord Watson.

50 *Ibid*, p 31, *per* Lord O'Hagan.

51 *Ibid*. This case was decided at a time when the law relating to collateral facts was of importance in civil and criminal trials. The discussion remains of significance for criminal trials, but it is far less likely to be of importance now for civil trials because of the power to exclude relevant evidence under the Civil Procedure Rules.

'If evidence could be given of any similar or other facts, from which the effect (or absence of effect) of other hospitals ... on the surrounding neighbourhoods, could either positively or approximately be ascertained, it would ... be admissible and material.'[52]

Lord O'Hagan was not prepared to say that the trial judge had been wrong in rejecting the evidence. Even supposing there to have been proof as to the state and management of the other hospitals, so as to establish a similarity between them and the hospital at Hampstead, he thought that such evidence would not have been pertinent. It would, he said, 'have involved the jury in a multitude of collateral inquiries, calculated to confuse and embarrass them; and it might have been endlessly prolonged by an indefinite multiplication of objects of comparison'.[53]

Lord Blackburn thought that the plaintiffs could derive no benefit from evidence that other hospitals had led to the spread of the disease in the surrounding neighbourhood unless they could show that the disease had spread despite the taking of those precautions that had been taken at the Hampstead hospital. The defendant, on the other hand, should be able to give evidence that, in the case of other hospitals, the disease had not been communicated to the neighbourhood, so as to show that a hospital did not inevitably lead to the spread of disease. He added, however, that he was aware that such inquiries might make the trial of such an issue by a jury impracticable, and so declined to say whether the evidence was properly rejected or not. Lord Watson also declined to decide the point.

The problem whether facts were collateral or directly relevant to facts in issue arose more recently in *R v Funderburk*.[54] The defendant was charged with having unlawful sexual intercourse with a girl aged 13, the daughter of a woman who was lodging with him and his partner, a Miss Potts. The girl's evidence made it clear to the jury that she had been a virgin before her first act of intercourse with the defendant. The defence case was that she was lying in order to support her mother, who had a grudge against the defendant. A difficulty the defence had to meet was the detailed account that the girl gave of the alleged acts of intercourse. One answer suggested by the defence was that, despite her age, she was sexually experienced, and had transposed experiences that she had had with other men onto the defendant. In order to substantiate this theory, the defence wished to call Miss Potts to give evidence that, before the first alleged act of intercourse with the defendant, the girl had had a conversation with Miss Potts. During this conversation, she had told Miss Potts that she had had sexual intercourse with two named men, and consequently wanted a pregnancy test. The trial judge refused to permit either evidence or questions in cross-examination on the subject of this conversation. He ruled that whether or not the girl was a virgin at

---

52   *Managers of the Metropolitan Asylum District v Hill and Others* (1882) 47 LT 29, p 30.
53   *Ibid*, p 31.
54   [1990] 1 WLR 587. Cf *R v Neale* [1998] Crim LR 737.

the time of the first incident was irrelevant to the charge of unlawful sexual intercourse.

The Court of Appeal accepted that in order to keep criminal trials within bounds, and to assist the jury to concentrate on what mattered without being distracted by doubts about marginal events, it was necessary wherever possible to avoid a multiplicity of issues. But was the evidence that Miss Potts would have given directly relevant to a fact in issue, or was it evidence of collateral facts that were relevant, if at all, only to the girl's credibility? The court said that the answer to a question of this kind must be 'an instinctive one based on the prosecutor's and the court's sense of fair play, rather than any philosophic or analytic process'.[55] On the facts of this case, the challenge to the girl's loss of virginity was sufficiently closely related to the subject matter of the indictment for justice to require evidence to be called to substantiate the challenge. The defence should therefore have been allowed to cross-examine the girl about her conversation with Miss Potts, and to call Miss Potts to rebut any denial.[56]

WEIGHT

Although relevance and weight are distinct concepts, the weight of an item of evidence may still be connected to relevance. Even if it is accepted that there is no separate concept of legal relevance and that a clear distinction exists between relevance and weight, there remains at least some connection between relevance and weight, because the weight of an item of evidence may be affected by the form of any generalisation that is relied on to make it relevant. The bolder the generalisation, the weightier the evidence is likely to be, but the trouble with bold generalisations is that they are less likely than cautious ones to be true. When arguments about weight are addressed to juries, an overly analytical approach by an advocate is likely to be inappropriate, but further analysis can be required for purely practical reasons: arguments about weight are addressed to judges in civil trials, and in criminal trials weight may be of importance when a judge has to consider admissibility. The reason for this is that judges in criminal cases have a discretion to exclude evidence presented by the prosecution against the defendant if they think its probative worth will be outweighed by any improperly prejudicial effect it is likely to have on the jury.[57]

An example will illustrate the connection between relevance-supporting generalisations and the weight of evidence. Suppose Ronnie is charged with theft. The prosecution can show, among other items of evidence, that at a time immediately before the theft Ronnie was badly in debt. What line are you going to take about this if you are defending him? My own view is that it would be better if the jury

---

55   [1990] 1 WLR 587, p 598.

56   Whether a matter is collateral or directly relevant to an issue in the case also affects rules about cross-examination and calling evidence in rebuttal: see below, Chapter 6.

57   *R v Sang* [1980] AC 402.

• 22 •

heard nothing of this. There is always a danger of speculation – of some unjustified assumption being made. It will therefore be tempting to challenge the admissibility of this evidence on the basis that it is irrelevant. The prosecution will then have to defend its relevance. They may do so by saying: 'Of course it's relevant. It provides a motive for committing theft.' Pressed further, this may be elaborated by a generalisation on these lines: 'Persons who are in debt are highly likely to commit theft to relieve themselves of their burdens.' This, if true, would certainly make the evidence of debt relevant and weighty. But is this generalisation true? Surely not. Another, more acceptable, generalisation is needed. This time the prosecution come up with: 'Persons who are in debt are fairly likely to commit theft to relieve themselves of their burdens.' Most people would probably agree that this was still too sweeping a generalisation to be accepted as true. So the prosecution try again: 'Persons who are in debt are more likely than those who are not to commit theft.' This might be accepted as true. By now, however, the generalisation has become so weak that the value of the evidence of debt is highly questionable. In particular, the generalisation says nothing about *how much more likely* are persons in debt to commit theft than those who are not in debt.

At this stage, a different line will be taken by the defence in their attempt to get the evidence of debt excluded. 'Your Honour, I do not concede that this item of evidence is relevant. But even if it is, the weight of the evidence must be very slight because of the weak, inconclusive nature of the generalisation needed to make it so. That in itself is a reason for exclusion, because the probative worth of the evidence is very small when set against its possible prejudicial effect.' More will be said about the judge's discretion to exclude evidence later.[58] The important thing at this stage is to see that the defence have available an argument for exclusion based on weight, which itself is founded on the form of the argument relied on to establish relevance.

ADMISSIBILITY

I have been discussing admissibility so far mainly in connection with relevance. However, it is possible to have an item of evidence which is clearly relevant but which is nevertheless inadmissible because of some rule of law. You might think that this situation, at least, could be dealt with merely by knowing the law, but you would be mistaken. The reason for this, as we shall see in more detail in later chapters, is that the application of some of the most important rules of exclusion is governed by the probative job that the questioned item of evidence has to do.[59] It is wise, therefore, when considering the possibility of exclusion on legal grounds, to clarify first the way in which the questioned item of evidence is relevant; that is, in effect, to discover its probative job. Failure to do this is likely to lead to misapplication of the law. In

---

58   See below, Chapter 11.
59   See, in particular, the law relating to hearsay.

particular, any argument based on a previous judicial decision is foolhardy unless you are satisfied that the analogy between your own case and the earlier one is proper. And it is unlikely to be proper if the probative jobs done by the evidence in the two cases are different.

An example will show what I mean. Suppose in your present case you want to call Charlie. If permitted, he will say, 'Danny told me that he saw Edward breaking into the bank'. Now suppose that you had doubts about the admissibility of this. You have done some research and you have found a Court of Appeal decision which has not been overruled and which held on its facts that Gerald could say in evidence, 'Harry told me that he saw Jim breaking into the post office'. If you were interested in the *form* of the words rather than in their *function in the case as a whole* you might well conclude that there was no significant difference between these two statements and that by virtue of the earlier decision Charlie should be able to give evidence of what Danny told him.

But suppose you check the *probative job* of the evidence in each case. In the present case you are prosecuting Edward for burglary, but the Court of Appeal case concerned a civil action for defamation brought by Jim against Harry. The probative job is different in each case. In the civil action, Jim wanted to prove that Harry had made a defamatory allegation of robbery against him. The last thing he wanted to prove, if he were to recover damages for defamation, was that what Harry said was true. The function of the evidence was solely to prove that the particular allegation had been made. In the present criminal case, however, the function of the evidence is to prove that Edward is guilty of burglary. The words are being relied on for the truth of what they allege, not just for the fact that they were uttered. The result of the difference in function is that the earlier piece of evidence was admissible but the later is not. The evidence in the criminal case is inadmissible because it offends the rule against hearsay. Put simply, this is a rule which forbids calling evidence of what was asserted by someone outside court in order to establish *the truth of the matters asserted*, as opposed to *the fact of assertion*.

It is clear from this example that the form of words alone will not reveal the probative job of the item of evidence in question. This will be revealed only when you look at what the parties are trying to prove in the case and see what is the relevance of the particular item of evidence to one or more of those objectives. In other words, until you know what is the relevance of the proposed evidence, you do not know the probative job and you cannot apply the law.

SOME TERMINOLOGY

It may be helpful at this stage to provide simple explanations of some of the technical terms most commonly encountered in this subject. They are arranged alphabetically.

Usage varies to some extent and what I have provided should be regarded as a guide, not as a set of closed definitions.

BEST EVIDENCE RULE

This was an old rule of evidence requiring that the best evidence that the nature of the case allowed should always be presented to the jury. It did not require the greatest quantity of evidence that could possibly be given of any fact; the object of the rule was to prevent the introduction of any evidence which, from the nature of the case, suggested that better evidence was in the possession of the party producing it. So, for example, oral evidence of the physical condition of certain objects was rejected when the objects could have been produced in court.[60] The best evidence rule was also one of the traditional justifications for rejecting hearsay evidence.[61] The rule has long since fallen into abeyance.[62]

CIRCUMSTANTIAL EVIDENCE

Suppose x is a fact that has to be proved. It can be proved in two different ways. You may be able to prove it by producing a witness who, with his own senses, perceived x: such evidence is sometimes called 'direct' evidence of x. If you cannot do this, you may be able to prove x by producing a witness who, though he did not perceive x, did perceive directly facts y and z, from which x can be inferred: such evidence is called 'circumstantial' evidence of x. Suppose, for example, that Cameron is charged with robbing a jeweller's shop. Direct evidence that he did so might be provided by a customer who was present when the robbery took place and who recognised Cameron as the robber, but in the absence of such evidence there may still be enough circumstantial evidence to secure a conviction. Suppose the prosecution can prove the following: jewellery from the shop was discovered shortly after the robbery hidden in Cameron's house; Cameron possessed an unlicensed gun similar to that used in the robbery; Cameron gave a false alibi in an interview with the police; and shortly before the robbery took place Cameron had been heard boasting to acquaintances in a wine bar that he knew of a jeweller's shop where he could find 'some pretty things that won't cost me anything'. A conclusion of guilt would not follow inevitably, but it would not follow inevitably from direct evidence either: the identifying witness might be mistaken or lying.

It is sometimes suggested that circumstantial evidence is inferior to direct evidence. It might be said that there are only two possibilities of error where the proof is direct: mistake or perjury on the part of the witness. With circumstantial evidence there is always a third possibility of error: a mistaken inference. But there has been

---

60   *Chenie v Watson* (1797) Peake Add Cas 123.

61   See below, Chapter 8.

62   *Garton v Hunter* [1969] 2 QB 37, p 44. But see Nance, 1988. In *AG's Reference (No 1 of 2003)* 2 Cr App R 453, p 458, the Court of Appeal said that if such a rule exists, it applies only to documents.

judicial recognition of the persuasive force that circumstantial evidence can produce. In *R v Exall*[63] Pollock CB said that 'there may be a combination of circumstances, no one of which would raise a reasonable conviction, or more than a mere suspicion; but the whole, taken together, may create a strong conclusion of guilt, that is, with as much certainty as human affairs can require or admit of'. And in *R v Taylor, Weaver and Donovan*[64] Lord Hewart CJ emphasised that 'it is no derogation of evidence to say that it is circumstantial'.[65]

COLLATERAL FACTS

These are facts relating to some subsidiary matter which itself affects the question of whether a fact in issue will be established or not. Examples are facts affecting a witness's competence,[66] or the weight to be attached to a witness's evidence. For example, evidence about a witness's bias would generally be held to fall within this category.

DOCUMENTARY EVIDENCE

This expression refers to evidence of the contents of documents. Obvious examples of documentary evidence are written contracts, correspondence and memoranda. 'Documentary evidence' refers to anything in which information of any description is recorded, and may therefore include such items as films, tapes and video recordings.[67] The contents of documents may be proved by either 'primary' or 'secondary' evidence. 'Primary evidence' refers to the original document itself, produced for the inspection of the court. 'Secondary evidence' refers to evidence of the contents of the original document which comes by report, or in some other second hand or derivative way. Examples would be a copy of the original document, or oral evidence from a person who has seen the original and can recall its contents.

FACTS IN ISSUE

In a civil action, this expression refers to those facts alleged in the statements of case by the parties, including facts necessary to establish pleaded defences, that are either denied or not admitted by the other party. In criminal cases the effect of a plea of not

---

63   (1860) 4 F&F 922, p 929.

64   (1928) 21 Cr App R 20, p 21.

65   For an example of a conviction for murder where the alleged victim's body was never recovered, and which was based solely on circumstantial evidence, see *R v Rose (NT)* [2006] EWCA Crim 1720.

66   Some writers call these 'preliminary facts'.

67   Criminal Justice Act 2003, s 134(1) and Civil Evidence Act 1995, s 13. In fact, the common law included within the class of documentary evidence 'all material substances on which the thoughts of men are represented by writing, or any other species of conventional mark or symbol'. So, eg, the wooden tally sticks used as receipts in the Exchequer counted as documentary evidence: Best, 1870, pp 297–98.

guilty is to declare everything that the substantive law makes material to the offence a fact in issue.[68] In practice today, this statement of the effect of a plea of not guilty does not represent the whole picture. There are informal procedures for clarifying issues in any complex criminal case at a pre-trial hearing. There are also statutory procedures for the same purpose where a criminal case involves serious or complex fraud, or where the indictment reveals a case of such complexity or length that a preparatory hearing would be of substantial benefit.[69] There is also a duty of defence disclosure under s 5 of the Criminal Procedure and Investigations Act 1996.

HEARSAY

According to the rule against hearsay, an assertion other than one made by a person while giving oral evidence in the proceedings is inadmissible *as evidence of any fact asserted.*[70] Thus, the rule operates if, and only if, the object of reporting an out-of-court assertion is to establish the truth of what was asserted. Take, for example, a prosecution under the Public Order Act 1986, which makes it an offence in certain circumstances for a person to use threatening, abusive or insulting words. Evidence of what was said can be given without any infringement of the rule against hearsay because the object of giving the evidence is to show that threatening, abusive or insulting words were uttered by the defendant. It is no part of the prosecution case that what was said was true. Evidence that does infringe the rule is often referred to as 'hearsay evidence' and is sometimes contrasted with 'direct evidence'. In this context, the term 'direct evidence' is used to refer to evidence given by a witness who perceived for himself the relevant act.[71] So if Adam is charged with theft of a frozen chicken from a supermarket, prosecuting counsel, unless a relevant exception applies, cannot call Ben to say that the store detective told him that she saw Adam take the chicken and leave the store without paying for it. Counsel must call the store detective herself to give 'direct' evidence of what she saw Adam doing.

ORIGINAL EVIDENCE

A distinction has traditionally been drawn between evidence which is 'original' and evidence which comes before the tribunal at second hand or in some other derivative way. An example of this distinction is the division of documentary evidence into primary and secondary categories. The expression 'original evidence' is also used to refer to evidence of words uttered by someone other than the testifying witness, where the object of adducing such evidence is not to prove the truth of anything asserted by

---

68   *R v Sims* [1946] KB 531, p 539, *per* Lord Goddard CJ.

69   *Practice Direction (Criminal: Consolidated)* [2002] 3 All ER 904, paras 41.2, 41.13; Criminal Justice Act 1987, ss 7–11; Criminal Procedure and Investigations Act 1996, ss 29–31.

70   *R v Sharp* (1988) 86 Cr App R 274, p 278. See also Chapter 8, below.

71   Note that the term 'direct evidence' can be used to refer to different concepts, depending on whether a contrast is being expressed with circumstantial evidence or with hearsay evidence.

the person who first uttered the words, but merely to prove the fact that the assertion was made.

REAL EVIDENCE

This term is used to refer to items of evidence which are presented to the senses of the tribunal and which may be examined by it. A good example was the piece of scarred flesh in the Crippen case. Original documents such as letters, contracts or memoranda may also become items of real evidence if they are adduced to show their condition rather than the truth of their contents. In the latter case, it would be more appropriate to refer to them as documentary evidence. The use of real evidence as a means of persuasion can be most effective. A famous American trial lawyer once observed that 'jurors learn through all their senses, and if you can tell them and show them, too, let them see and feel and even taste or smell the evidence; then you will reach the jury'.[72]

TESTIMONY

'Testimonial evidence', or 'testimony', was traditionally defined as the sworn statements of witnesses in court.[73] There are several difficulties with this definition today. First, not all statements in court are sworn. The evidence of children under 14, for example, cannot be given on oath in criminal trials.[74] Secondly, evidence today can be given in certain circumstances by video-link. Thirdly, the old definition tended to obscure the fact that in some civil proceedings, especially at pre-trial applications, the sworn statement of the witness was in writing. Such statements were called 'affidavits' (from the medieval Latin *affidare*, meaning 'to declare on oath'). Under the new Civil Procedure Rules, at pre-trial applications, written, unsworn, witness statements are generally used instead, and these now constitute the evidence on which the court will base its decision at that stage. Perhaps 'testimony' is ceasing to be a useful term.

VOIR DIRE

The *voir dire* is a trial within a trial, in which the court determines disputed facts that have to be established before certain items of evidence can be admitted. Examples are disputed questions of fact in relation to the competence of a witness, or in relation to the admissibility of a confession or a tape recording. The name of the procedure comes from the old form of a special oath taken by witnesses on such occasions. In trials on indictment, the *voir dire* is held in the absence of the jury, as the decision on the question is one for the judge alone.

---

72   See the obituary of Melvin Belli (1996) *The Times*, 11 July, p 19.

73   See, eg, Stone and Wells, 1991, p 84.

74   See below, Chapter 5.

THREE IMPORTANT CHARACTERISTICS OF EVIDENCE LAW

There are three characteristics of evidence law that it is useful to bear in mind at the outset.

- ■ Evidence law has only a limited application.
- ■ Evidence law is a mixture of principles, rules and discretions.
- ■ Evidence law is about more than admissibility.

EVIDENCE LAW HAS ONLY A LIMITED APPLICATION

Evidence law applies in its fullest form only in contested Crown Court cases. Whatever the historical origins of rules of exclusion, the fact remains that, since the 19th century at least, they have been justified as a way of controlling the supposedly erratic reasoning of juries. In civil cases, which are only very exceptionally tried by a jury, there is virtually no need for this protective approach. Gradually, this has had its effect on the law of evidence, and now many of the restrictions on admissibility which still operate in criminal cases have been abolished in civil cases. For example, the Civil Evidence Act 1995 has abolished the operation, in civil proceedings, of one of the most entrenched of the exclusionary rules – the rule against hearsay.[75] In magistrates' courts, the strict rules of evidence apply in the hearing of criminal cases, but arguments about evidence law are less frequent than in Crown Court trials because the magistrates are judges of both law and fact. There can be no question of keeping them in ignorance, as a jury can be kept in ignorance, of an item of evidence whose admissibility is contested. Further, because there is no summing up in a trial before magistrates, arguments about directions on evidence cannot arise. In practice, a law of criminal evidence that has been developed by appellate courts in the context of Crown Court trials may not always be easy, or even possible, to apply in magistrates' courts.[76]

In addition, much dispute resolution goes on outside courts. Arbitrators and tribunals of various kinds have, from the beginning, adopted a much more flexible approach to the admissibility of evidence. Even within the criminal process, important pre-trial decisions are made which affect citizens, but which are governed only very loosely, if at all, by evidence law. For example, evidence law has little or nothing to say that will affect decisions to arrest or charge a suspect.

EVIDENCE LAW IS A MIXTURE OF PRINCIPLES, RULES AND DISCRETIONS

Our starting point must be the distinction between rules and principles, which is a common feature of any developed legal system and which has been made familiar

---

75   See below, Chapter 8.
76   See Darbyshire, 1997a; Darbyshire, 1997b.

since the 1960s by Ronald Dworkin.[77] The distinction is this: rules are applicable in an all-or-nothing fashion. If the facts are those stipulated in the rule, then the rule applies. A rule can have exceptions, but an accurate statement of the rule will take these into account. For example, it is a rule that, in criminal proceedings, the evidence of a child aged under 14 shall be given unsworn.[78] So if little Johnnie, aged 13, has to give evidence in a criminal trial, he must do so unsworn, however intelligent or religious he may be. There are no two ways about it.

Principles, on the other hand, do not necessitate a particular decision in the way that rules do; they do not apply in an all-or-nothing way. All we mean when we say that something is a principle of our law is that it is something which officials, including judges, must take into account if it is relevant in a particular situation. For example, it is a principle applicable to evidence law that in the determination of a criminal charge, a defendant is entitled to a fair trial.[79] This, like every other legal principle, has a dimension that rules lack. That dimension is one of weight, or importance. We cannot say that, within a system of rules, one rule is more important than another, so that when two rules conflict one supersedes the other because of its greater weight. If two rules conflict, one of them must be an invalid rule. The position is entirely different with principles: because a principle is simply something that must be taken into account if relevant, it does not point conclusively to a particular result in the way that a rule does. Nor can it, strictly speaking, conflict with other principles. The existence of another, different, principle does not entail that the first one should be ignored because it is irrelevant. Both principles are to be taken into account, but, on the facts of a particular case, the judge will give greater weight to one principle rather than the other. For example, it is also a principle of evidence law that, subject to some exceptions, relevant evidence should be admissible.[80]

To illustrate the application of principles, let us suppose that Charlie is charged with possession of drugs with intent to supply. The drugs were discovered in Charlie's house, but only because the police entered unlawfully, albeit in good faith, on an unconnected matter. Charlie's counsel, relying on Charlie's right to a fair trial, argues that, because of the way in which the discovery was made, to admit this evidence would have such an adverse effect on the fairness of the proceedings that it ought to be excluded.[81] No rule of law *compels* the judge to exclude this evidence, so both principles are relevant, and the judge will have to give greater weight to one than to the other if the prosecution argues that such clear evidence of Charlie's guilt is relevant, of substantial weight, and should be admitted.[82]

---

77   See, eg, Dworkin, 1977a, pp 38–65.

78   Youth Justice and Criminal Evidence Act 1999, s 55(2)(a).

79   Article 6(1) ECHR.

80   Stone and Wells, 1991, pp 129–30.

81   See s 78 Police and Criminal Evidence Act 1984.

82   Cf *R v Veneroso* [2002] Crim LR 306.

The difference between rules and principles is of the utmost importance when considering whether, or to what extent, a previous case should be used in arguing a point of evidence law. If the earlier case is at appellate level and *defines or modifies a rule*, the ratio of the case becomes part of the rule and therefore binding in relevantly similar circumstances. But if the earlier case involves *the application of a principle* to a particular situation, that decision will reinforce the principle, but is not likely to be of much help in deciding a later case. There are two main reasons for this. The first is that the application of the principle in the first case does not make irrelevant other competing principles in the later case. The second reason is that, when principles have to be chosen and applied, courts are more sensitive to the facts of the particular case under consideration and less likely to be influenced by the preferences made in earlier cases where the facts inevitably were different. At best, an earlier decision will be only persuasive; at worst, it will be irrelevant.

It is clear that if a principle-based approach is adopted rather than one that is rule-based, the court is less constrained. Where a principle has to be chosen and applied, argument will be about the facts of the particular case rather than about other cases. A principle-based approach to the law inevitably gives the trial judge greater discretion than does a rule-based approach to admit or exclude evidence. The Court of Appeal recognises this, and has on several occasions said that it will not interfere with decisions about admissibility made in exercise of a discretion except on the familiar public law grounds.[83] The effect of this is that the advocate will often have to argue about admissibility at trial *on the facts* and without the assistance of binding precedents. This will generally be the only opportunity for his submission to succeed; in the absence of public law grounds he is unlikely to have a second chance in the Court of Appeal.

There is a strong argument in favour of a principle-based approach to evidence law, since an overly rule-based approach is likely to lead to frustration from attempts to reconcile the irreconcilable. If, for example, you adopted a rule-based approach towards the cases on the admissibility of evidence about finding cash when a defendant is charged with possession of drugs with intent to supply, not only would you have to memorise the particular facts of all the cases where such evidence was allowed or disallowed, but you would have to try to construct from the cases a system of rules without any contradictions. It is much simpler, and it makes far more sense, to regard these cases as attempts, more or less successful, to apply basic principles of relevance, without in themselves establishing any binding rules about admissibility.

---

83   See, eg, *R v Rankin* (1995) *The Times*, 5 September; *R v Khan and Others* [1997] Crim LR 508. Those grounds are that the person with a power of decision took into account something that should have been ignored, failed to take into account something that should have been considered, or reached a decision that no reasonable person could have reached.

Nevertheless, there are quite a few decisions of appellate courts on points of evidence law that can still properly be described as 'authoritative', in the sense either that they establish binding rules of law or that they provide *dicta* having persuasive authority. Examples of both types will be found throughout this book and it is unnecessary to give examples here. It is necessary, however, to become aware at this stage of the problems caused by conflicting decisions. Conflicts arise because there are probably now more reported decisions than ever before, because access to unreported decisions is easier than ever before, and because pressure of judicial work in the Criminal Division of the Court of Appeal limits the amount of time available for delivery of reserved judgments. Conflicts cannot always be easily resolved, but some limited assistance can be obtained from *R v Simpson*,[84] where the Court of Appeal, Criminal Division, sitting with five judges, held in a reserved judgment that the court has a 'degree of discretion' to decide whether or not one of its previous decisions should be treated as a binding precedent when there are grounds for saying that the decision in question was wrong.[85] The court added that it is not safe to rely on a decision given in the absence of relevant information if it is at least probable that, if that information had been known, the decision would have been affected by it.[86] 'Relevant information' clearly refers to information of a legal nature, so a decision may be vulnerable if it can be shown that not all the relevant authorities were cited to the court.

EVIDENCE LAW IS ABOUT MORE THAN ADMISSIBILITY

Judges have traditionally been free to advise juries, if they think it would be helpful to do so, about the weight to be given to individual items of evidence in a particular case. Provided they make it plain that juries are free to reject their views, they are still largely free to do so. Gradually it came to be thought that there might be categories of witness or evidence which a jury might find particularly difficult to assess; for example, evidence of former accomplices who testified as witnesses for the prosecution, or evidence of a defendant's good character. At first, what a judge said about such evidence, or whether he said anything at all, was entirely a matter for his discretion. In time, some judicial consensus began to develop about what should be said concerning particular categories of evidence; but it did not have the force of law, and if a judge chose not to follow it he could not be faulted. Later, however, the desire for uniformity led to a movement from consensus to binding rules. Although some of these have been modified to take into account different perceptions of the risk from

---

84   [2003] 3 All ER 531, pp 538–41.

85   In considering whether to exercise that discretion it is relevant to take into account the constitution of the court. The discretion is not to be exercised lightly. See *ibid, per* Lord Woolf CJ, p 541.

86   See *ibid, per* Lord Woolf CJ, p 540.

certain categories of witness, judges are now increasingly bound by rules, founded on case law, about what a judge should say to a jury concerning various kinds of evidence. For example, what a judge has to say about the significance of a defendant's good character is now governed by rules established by case law. The same is true concerning evidence of identification, or evidence that a defendant failed to mention to the police facts later relied on in his defence. There are many other examples, some of which will appear from time to time in this book. The importance of these rules is that if a judge does not follow them, the defendant will generally have a good ground for an appeal. It follows that these rules are as much a part of evidence law as rules about the admissibility of evidence. If, therefore, in an examination question you are given a set of facts and asked to 'advise on the evidential issues arising', or are given some similarly broad direction, you should realise that this may require you to point out that a judge has an obligation to give a particular direction to a jury in respect of some item of admissible evidence.[87]

THE FUNCTIONS OF JUDGE AND JURY

In jury trials the judicial function is divided between the judge, whose decision on matters of law is (subject to the right of appeal) final, and the jury, who are in principle the sole judges of fact. Every summing up should contain a direction to the jury about these separate functions. The specimen direction prepared by the Judicial Studies Board encourages the judge to explain to the jury that the law is his responsibility and that they must follow his directions on that subject, but that it is the jurors' responsibility to judge the evidence. If in the course of the judge's review of the evidence he appears to express any views concerning the facts, or to emphasise a particular aspect of the evidence, they should not adopt those views unless they agree with them. If the judge fails to mention something which they think is important, they should have regard to it and give it such weight as they think fit. When it comes to the facts of the case, it is the jury's judgment alone that counts.[88]

It is particularly important that this division of functions be made clear to juries, because the law permits the trial judge to comment on the evidence in his summing up. Subject to an overriding obligation to be fair, a judge is entitled to give his opinion to the jury on a question of fact and to express it strongly, so long as he makes

---

87   You should know the content of the more important directions. It is not enough, for example, to say that a judge should give a *Turnbull* direction in relation to a witness's evidence of identification. You must be able to spell out what this requires. For particulars, see below, Chapter 10.

88   Judicial Studies Board specimen directions, June 2007. Accessed at www.jsboard.co.uk.

it clear that this is advice, rather than a direction that must be followed.[89] In *R v Sparrow*, Lawton LJ recommended a robust approach by trial judges:

> [I]n our experience a jury is not helped by a colourless reading out of the evidence as recorded by the judge in his notebook. The judge is more than a mere referee who takes no part in the trial save to intervene when a rule of procedure or evidence is broken. He and the jury try the case together and it is his duty to give them the benefit of his knowledge of the law and *to advise them in the light of his experience as to the significance of the evidence* . . .[90]

More recently, the Court of Appeal has said that in a trial where the prosecution case is strong, the judge should present it as such to the jury, and he should treat a strong defence case similarly.[91]

There are, however, at least two important situations where, despite the general principle, the judge in a criminal trial makes rulings that involve decisions about facts. In the first place, it is sometimes necessary to establish the existence of certain facts before a particular witness's evidence, or a particular item of evidence, can be admitted. Here it is for the judge to decide whether the condition is satisfied. For example, it is for the judge to decide whether a witness is competent to give evidence.[92] It is also for the judge, not the jury, to decide whether the prosecution has proved those matters which have to be established before evidence can be given of a confession by an accused person.[93]

Secondly, it is the judge's task to decide, on a defence submission that there is no case to answer, whether there is sufficient evidence to allow the case to proceed or whether the jury should be instructed to return a verdict of not guilty without waiting to hear the case for the defence. The approach of a trial judge to such a submission was set out in *R v Galbraith*[94] and approved in *R v Fulcher*. If there is no evidence that the alleged crime has been committed by the defendant, the judge should stop the case by directing the jury at that stage to return a verdict of not guilty. Where there is some evidence of a tenuous character, for example because of an inherent weakness or vagueness, or because it is inconsistent with other prosecution evidence, he should stop the case if he decides that it is not such as would allow a properly directed jury to convict. But where the strength or weakness of the prosecution case depends on the view to be taken of a witness's reliability, and where on one possible view of the facts

---

89   *Chandler v DPP* [1964] AC 763, p 804, *per* Lord Devlin. Cf the summing up of Devlin J, as he then was, in the trial of Dr Bodkin Adams in 1957: Devlin, 1986, p 177. But the Court of Appeal has said that a judge should not give his own views about whether witnesses have told the truth or not: *R v Iroegbu* (1988) *The Times*, 2 August. See also *Mitchell v R* [1998] 2 Cr App R 35, p 42.

90   [1973] 1 WLR 488, p 495, emphasis added.

91   *R v Bryant (P)* [2005] EWCA Crim 2079.

92   Youth Justice and Criminal Evidence Act 1999, s 54(1), (4).

93   Police and Criminal Evidence Act 1984, s 76(2) and (3).

94   [1981] 1 WLR 1039.

there is evidence on which a jury could properly conclude that the defendant was guilty, the case should be allowed to proceed.[95]

Finally, it should be noticed that, although the judge's directions on the law are his responsibility, it has become increasingly common for the judge to invite prosecution and defence advocates to address him on the content of those directions where there is room for more than one view about what that should be. In *R v N*,[96] the Court of Appeal observed that it had frequently said that difficulties would be avoided, and cases conducted with clarity, if discussion took place between judge and counsel at the end of the evidence about points of law and, more particularly, about the points of evidence that had arisen. (Such discussion should, of course, be in open court, but in the absence of the jury.) The effect of this development has been to increase the amount of preparation required for a criminal jury trial. Not only must advocates prepare arguments for or against the admissibility of problematic items of evidence; arguments will also have to be prepared about the directions which the judge should give to the jury on admissible items of evidence that may call for special guidance.

THE EUROPEAN CONVENTION ON HUMAN RIGHTS

The United Kingdom was a party to the Convention when it was first signed in Rome in 1950. It was ratified by the United Kingdom in 1951 and came into force in 1953. Before 1998 its provisions were regarded as relevant to statutory interpretation but they formed no part of English domestic law. This position was altered by the Human Rights Act 1998, which came into force in 2000. The effect of the Act is to make the European Convention on Human Rights directly enforceable by English and Welsh courts.[97] By s 2(1)(a), a court determining a question which has arisen in connection with a Convention right must take into account judgments of the European Court of Human Rights. These are not binding authorities, but it is expected that English

---

95 These are not the only, or even the only important, instances when a judge makes a decision about facts in a criminal trial. Other instances include the balancing between probative value and likely prejudicial effect when a judge is asked to exercise his common law discretion to exclude evidence: see below, Chapter 11; see also the discussion of relevance in this chapter, above. If there is no special concept of legal relevance, it looks very much as if a judge's decision on this subject is a decision about facts rather than law.

96 [1998] Crim LR 886. See also *R v Islam* [1999] 1 Cr App R 22, p 23.

97 Strictly speaking, the Act does not 'incorporate' the convention into English law. Instead, all the substantive rights recognised by the Convention are re-enacted as provisions of English law known as 'convention rights' (Roberts and Zuckerman, 2004, p 33).

courts will not depart from them unless constrained to do so, either by statute or by existing binding case law.[98] The importance of these judgments for legal argument was emphasised by Schiemann LJ in *Barclays Bank plc v Ellis*,[99] where he said that if counsel wish to rely on provisions of the Human Rights Act it is their duty to have available the relevant decisions of the European Court of Human Rights. A mere reference to an article in the Convention will not be helpful. By s 3(1), so far as it is possible to do so, legislation must be read and given effect in a way that is compatible with Convention rights. It has already been shown that this provision can be very flexibly applied.[100] The Act does not go so far as to invalidate legislation that is clearly incompatible with a Convention right. In such a case the court must apply the law as it stands, but it may make a declaration of incompatibility under s 4. It is expected that this will lead to amendment of the offending legislation. Section 6 makes it unlawful for public authorities, which include courts, to act in a way that is incompatible with Convention rights unless obliged to do so by primary legislation. Several of the Articles in the Convention have a bearing on the Law of Evidence. The most important ones are set out below.

Article 3

This short Article provides that no one shall be subjected to torture or to inhuman or degrading treatment or punishment. The admission of evidence obtained in breach of this article is capable of infringing the accused's right under Art 6 (see below) to a fair trial. In *Jalloh v Germany*[101] the European Court of Human Rights held that the admission of evidence obtained by inhuman or degrading treatment not amounting to torture was *capable* of rendering a trial unfair so as to constitute a breach of Art 6. The Court observed that where evidence had been obtained by torture it should *never* be relied on as proof of the victim's guilt, irrespective of its probative value.[102]

Article 6

This Article provides as follows:

1.   In the determination of his civil rights and obligations or of any criminal charge against him, everyone is entitled to a fair and public hearing within a reasonable time by an

---

98   *R (on the application of Alconbury Developments Ltd) v Secretary of State for the Environment* [2001] 2 All ER 929, 969, *per* Lord Slynn; *R v Togher* [2001] 3 All ER 463, 472, *per* Lord Woolf CJ. Because the obligation is simply to take judgments of the European Court into account, it would be possible for English courts to develop a wider protection of Convention rights than that given by the European Court.

99   (2000) *The Times*, 24 October.

100   See, eg, *R v Lambert* [2001] 3 All ER 577; *R v A (No 2)* [2001] 2 Cr App R 351.

101   [2006] 20 BHRC 575.

102   See also *A and Others v Secretary of State for the Home Department (No 2)* [2005] UKHL 71, [2006] 2 AC 221.

independent and impartial tribunal established by law. Judgment shall be pronounced publicly but the press and public may be excluded from all or part of the trial in the interest of morals, public order or national security in a democratic society, where the interests of juveniles or the protection of the private life of the parties so require, or to the extent strictly necessary in the opinion of the court in special circumstances where publicity would prejudice the interests of justice.

2.   Everyone charged with a criminal offence shall be presumed innocent until proved guilty according to law.

3.   Everyone charged with a criminal offence has the following minimum rights:

(a)   to be informed promptly, in a language which he understands and in detail, of the nature and cause of the accusation against him;

(b)   to have adequate time and facilities for the preparation of his defence;

(c)   to defend himself in person or through legal assistance of his own choosing or, if he has not sufficient means to pay for legal assistance, to be given it free when the interests of justice so require;

(d)   to examine or have examined witnesses against him and to obtain the attendance and examination of witnesses on his behalf under the same conditions as witnesses against him;

(e)   to have the free assistance of an interpreter if he cannot understand or speak the language used in court.

The effect of para 1 is to provide a right to a fair trial. In *Delcourt v Belgium*[103] the European Court of Human Rights said that a restrictive interpretation of this provision would be inappropriate. The Court also acknowledged that it might be difficult to define exactly its field of application. Its application is clearly not confined to the features described in para 1, nor to the 'minimum' rights described in para 3. Several decisions show that the European Court is prepared to extend the list of rights that make up a fair trial. These have tended to reinforce the importance of fairness as a feature of pre-trial proceedings. For example, in *S v Switzerland*[104] the Court held that an accused's right to communicate with his advocate without being overheard by a third person was part of the basic requirements of a fair trial, and followed from para 3(c). If a lawyer were unable to confer with his client and receive confidential instructions his assistance would lose much of its usefulness. In *Edwards v United Kingdom*[105] the Court held that it was a requirement of fairness under para 1 that prosecution authorities should disclose to the defence all material evidence, both for

---

103   (1979–80) 1 EHRR 355, para 25; see also the dissenting opinion of Judge Martens, para 4.4, in *Borgers v Belgium* (1993) 15 EHRR 92, where the concept of a fair trial was said to be vague, open-ended, and in need of filling in by developing case law.

104   (1992) 14 EHRR 670, para 48.

105   (1993) 15 EHRR 417, para 36; see also *Rowe and Davis v United Kingdom* (2000) 30 EHRR 1.

and against the accused. In *Saunders v United Kingdom*[106] the Court held that, although not specifically mentioned in Art 6, the right to silence and the right not to incriminate oneself were generally recognised international standards lying at the heart of the notion of a fair procedure under para 1. And in *T and V v United Kingdom*[107] the Court held that Art 6, read as a whole, guarantees the right of an accused person to participate effectively in his criminal trial. It followed that where a child was charged with an offence, he had to be dealt with in a way that took full account of his age, level of maturity, and intellectual and emotional development.[108]

Paragraph 2 has already had a substantial impact on statutory provisions that purport to impose a burden of proof on an accused person. Before the Human Rights Act 1998 a provision requiring a defendant to prove a particular matter was routinely held to impose on him a legal burden of proof: that is to say, in relation to that matter he had to satisfy the court or jury on the balance of probabilities of the existence or non-existence, depending on the terms of the statute, of the matter in question. If he failed to do so, he would be convicted. This is no longer so. Cases since the passing of the Act have shown that sometimes what appears to be the imposition of a burden of proof amounts to no more than a requirement that there be sufficient evidence to make the existence or non-existence of the matter in question a live issue in the trial.[109]

Breaches of the right to a fair trial are likely to make a conviction unsafe.[110] But the courts have a good deal of flexibility in determining whether the right has in fact been violated. For example, where evidence, other than that of a confession, has been improperly obtained, a consideration by the trial judge of whether he should exercise his discretion to exclude it under s 78 Police and Criminal Evidence Act 1984 can be sufficient to comply with Art 6(1).[111]

Article 8

The Article provides as follows:

1. Everyone has the right to respect for his private and family life, his home and his correspondence.

2. There shall be no interference by a public authority with the exercise of this right except such as is in accordance with the law and is necessary in a democratic society in the

---

106 (1997) 23 EHRR 313, para 68; see also *Funke v France* (1993) 16 EHRR 297, para 44.

107 (2000) 30 EHRR 121, paras 83–84.

108 It is not yet clear what implications this decision might have for the trial of adults who are suffering from mental disability or who simply possess low intelligence. See the partly dissenting opinion of Judge Baka.

109 See Chapter 7 for further details.

110 See, eg, *R v Togher* [2001] 3 All ER 463; *R v Forbes* [2001] 2 WLR 1; *R v Lyons* [2002] 2 Cr App R 210.

111 *Khan v United Kingdom* (2001) 31 EHRR 45. For the operation of s 78, see below, Chapter 11.

> interests of national security, public safety or the economic well-being of the country, for
> the prevention of disorder or crime, for the protection of health or morals, or for the
> protection of the rights and freedoms of others.

The Article is typically invoked where evidence has been improperly obtained by the police.

At various stages throughout this book the influence of the Convention is considered in relation to specific topics. However, it will be helpful at the outset to have some understanding of the general approach of the European Court of Human Rights to its interpretation. A fundamental point to grasp is that the Court adopts a flexible approach, despite the apparently absolute character of some of the articles. Convention rights tend to be regarded as principles to be applied in the particular circumstances of individual nation states.[112]

In *Brown v Stott*, Lord Steyn observed that the preambles to the Convention reveal two basic aims. The first is to maintain and realise human rights and fundamental freedoms. The second is to foster effective political democracy. The makers of the Convention, he said, realised that from time to time the fundamental right of one individual may conflict with the rights of others. For example, the principles of free speech and privacy may be in conflict in a particular set of circumstances. A single-minded concentration on the pursuit of individuals' fundamental rights, to the exclusion of the interests of the wider public, might be subversive of the ideal of a tolerant liberal democracy. So, the Convention requires that where difficult questions arise, a balance must be struck.[113]

Some applications of Art 6 can be used to illustrate this. The right to be presumed innocent of a criminal offence until proved guilty under Art 6(2) appears to be an absolute requirement. But it has been held that it does not prohibit rules that transfer the burden to the accused to establish a defence, provided the overall burden of proof remains on the prosecution.[114] The admissibility of evidence has been recognised as generally a matter for national systems to regulate. Unlawfully obtained evidence may be admissible without affecting the fairness of the trial as a whole.[115] The right of silence is not absolute.[116] Lord Hope has summarised a three-step approach, based on

---

112   *Brown v Stott (Procurator Fiscal, Dunfermline)* [2001] 2 All ER 97 PC, p 115.

113   *Ibid*, p 118. See also Lord Bingham at p 115. But see also *Heaney and McGuinness v Ireland* [2001] Crim LR 481, where the European Court of Human Rights held that in some circumstances the very essence of a Convention right may be destroyed, and so give rise to a violation. See further Ashworth, 2001, which questions the reasoning in *Brown v Stott* in the light of *Heaney and McGuinness*.

114   *Ibid, Brown v Stott*, p 105.

115   *Ibid*, pp 107–08.

116   *Ibid*, p 119.

decisions of the European Court, to be followed when issues are raised about an alleged incompatibility with a right under Art 6:

- Is the right in question an absolute right, or is it a right that is open to modification or restriction?
- If it is not absolute, does the modification or restriction contended for have a legitimate aim in the public interest?
- If so, is there a reasonable relationship of proportionality between the means employed and the aim sought to be realised?[117]

FURTHER READING

—Allen, *Sourcebook on Evidence*, 1996, Chapter 1, 'Basic Concepts'; repr in University of London, *Evidence Study Pack*, 2007, pp 129–47.

—Anderson, Schum and Twining, *Analysis of Evidence*, 2nd edn, 2005, pp 112–22; 262–80; 290–98.

—Choo, 'The Notion of Relevance and Defence Evidence' [1993] Crim LR 114.

—Redmayne, 'Drugs, Money and Relevance' (1999) 3 E&P 128.

—Roberts and Zuckerman, *Criminal Evidence*, 2004, Chapter 3, 'Relevance, Admissibility and Fact-Finding'.

—Twining, *Rethinking Evidence: Exploratory Essays*, 2nd edn, 2006, pp 41–45; 61–65.

—James, 'Relevancy, Probability and the Law' (1941) 29 *California LR* 689.

—Trautman, 'Logical or Legal Relevancy – A Conflict in Theory' (1952) 5 *Vanderbilt LR* 385.

EXERCISES

1. In what ways can the word 'evidence' be used in the context of a criminal trial?
2. What is the difference between the relevance of an item of evidence and its weight?
3. What part is played by generalisations in arguments about relevance?
4. To what extent do criminal courts recognise a concept of legal relevance?
5. Explain the following terms:

   (a) the best evidence rule;

   (b) circumstantial evidence;

   (c) collateral facts;

   (d) facts in issue;

   (e) hearsay;

   (f) original evidence;

   (g) real evidence;

   (h) the *voir dire*.

6. Why is *Blastland* an unsatisfactory decision?

---

117   *Ibid*, p 130.

7. Explain the distinction between principles and rules.

8. In what ways can the judge in a Crown Court trial be a judge of fact as well as of law?

9. What rights have been recognised by the European Court of Human Rights as elements of a fair criminal trial?

10. What, according to the JSB specimen direction, are the main points to be made in summing up about the functions of judge and jury in a criminal trial?

2

DEVELOPMENT AND CURRENT OBJECTIVES

INTRODUCTION

The purpose of this chapter is to provide an outline of the way in which evidence law has developed, and to say something about its possible objectives today. Some knowledge of the development of a legal subject is useful because it can make the present law easier to understand. It can also be helpful in practice if you have to argue a point of law. An opponent will sometimes try to rely on an earlier decision that appears to be against you. It may not be possible to show that it has been overruled, and it may be difficult to distinguish it from your case on the facts. What you may be able to do, though, is show that the legal context in which it was decided was different from that of today; the law moves on, and your opponent's 'authority' is no more than a relic of an outdated approach.[1] Thinking about the possible *objectives* of evidence law can have a use beyond that of answering examination questions. In a subject that is increasingly governed by discretion and based on principles as well as rules, a wide perspective can be useful in argument, as the statute and case law on improperly obtained evidence shows.[2]

---

1   See, eg, *R v Butler* (1987) 84 Cr App R 12.
2   See below, Chapter 11.

DEVELOPMENT

In 1983, Dennis Butler was tried for raping and indecently assaulting two women, each on a separate occasion. Various sexual activities were alleged against him. In an interview with the police Mr Butler denied everything. He refused to take part in an identification parade, so confrontations were arranged between him and the complainants. One failed to recognise him. The other was rather doubtful about his appearance but recognised him more definitely by his voice. No doubt because it was clear that identification would be an issue at trial, the prosecution wished to rely on evidence of 'similar facts' to strengthen the case against the accused. Leave was requested to call a woman who had previously had a sexual relationship with Mr Butler. She, it was hoped, would describe a variety of sexual practices in which they had freely indulged, but which closely resembled those that the complainants said their attacker had forced them to perform. The defence objected to the admissibility of this evidence. Later, in the Court of Appeal, Sir Ralph Kilner Brown described the way in which this question had been determined:

> At the trial, and to some extent before us, there was an unnecessary citation of lengthy extracts from numerous authorities, one or two of which go back nearly a hundred years. Encouraged by the very full and detailed treatment of the subject in *Archbold* (42nd edn), Chapter 13 and Chapter 14, para 12, application to call the evidence took a long time and went into a second day. The argument before the judge occupied no less than 15 pages of transcript, and the ruling by the judge another 13 pages of the transcript.[3]

Even a decade earlier, such an extensive citation of cases would probably have attracted no comment because evidence of 'similar facts' had, for much of the 20th century, been regarded as governed by a detailed system of *rules*, established by binding decisions of appellate courts. But Sir Ralph Kilner Brown observed that the leading case of *DPP v Boardman*[4] and other authorities had established *principles* that were well known, and that within those principles, every case was to be decided *on its own particular circumstances*.

A year after Dennis Butler's trial, Parliament emphasised the place of principle and discretion in evidence law. In s 78 of the Police and Criminal Evidence Act 1984, it was enacted that a judge might exclude evidence on which the prosecution proposed to rely if it appeared that its admission would have such an adverse effect on the fairness of the proceedings that it ought to be excluded.[5] This more flexible approach

---

3   *R v Butler* (1987) 84 Cr App R 12, p 16.
4   [1975] AC 421.
5   See also the Criminal Justice Act 2003, ss 101(3); 103(3); 114(1)(d); 116(4); 121(1)(c).

is not a complete novelty: courts for much of the 18th century adopted a far less restricted approach than they did later towards the evidence of competent witnesses. For example, although the leading treatise stated that 'a mere hearsay' was 'no evidence', such evidence was nevertheless widely admitted.[6] From quite early in the 19th century, however, this approach gave way in civil cases to an increasingly rule-based system. A study of the development of modern evidence may therefore conveniently begin in the 18th century and try to follow the ways in which a more rigid system became established, from which we have only fairly recently begun to be released.

Counsel in the 18th century regularly appeared in civil cases in the superior courts of common law and at *nisi prius*,[7] and in doing so followed a well established practice. This is reflected in the work on evidence by Gilbert, which was published posthumously in 1754 and was the leading work on the subject for about 50 years.[8] Gilbert's *Law of Evidence* was not primarily a work of theory: it was a practical work, in which the longest section was taken up with a consideration of the evidence admissible to prove or disprove issues arising in different forms of action. Gilbert shows us what evidential matters were important to lawyers acting for parties in 18th century civil proceedings.

Apart from the large section dealing with substantive law, two features indicate a way of looking at evidential problems that was strikingly different from the way we look at it today. The first is a substantial body of rules excluding not classes of *evidence*, but classes of *witnesses*. Two major groups were affected. Those who would not give evidence on oath were generally excluded, whether their refusal was due to religious scruples or to lack of any religious belief. In addition, anyone with a financial or proprietary interest in the outcome of a case was incompetent to testify as a witness in it, however small the interest might be. One of the effects of this rule was, of course, to bar the parties to the litigation from testifying. In addition, some potential witnesses might be excluded because of past criminal convictions. Some idea of the reasons for these exclusions can be gathered from arguments that were raised against subsequent proposals for reform. Evidence had to be given on oath because it was thought that people with the wrong sort of religious belief – or, worse, no religious belief at all – could not be trusted as

---

6   Gilbert, 1791, Vol 1, p 279. For the admissibility in practice of hearsay, see Langbein, 1978; Langbein, 1983; Langbein, 1996.

7   Juries in civil cases were traditionally summoned to appear on a fixed day at Westminster, but it became the practice to add to the summons, 'unless before then [*nisi prius*] the King's justices should have come' into the county as commissioners of assize and gaol delivery. Baker, 1990, pp 24–25; Milsom, 1981, p 49.

8   See above, and see also Twining, W, 'The rationalist tradition of evidence scholarship', in Twining, 2006, pp 35–41; Landsman, 1990a.

responsible members of society. The oath was a fundamental safeguard of truth; to make it optional would be to encourage infidelity and irreligion.[9] Treatise writers tended to justify the exclusion of interested persons from testifying on the basis of their supposed lack of integrity or impartiality.[10] However, when reform was mooted a different argument was put forward: people ought not to be put in a position where they might be tempted to commit perjury.[11] This argument may in fact have been closer to the original purpose of the rule than that suggested by the treatise writers. Steven Shapin has shown the importance of truthfulness as a characteristic of gentility in the 17th century;[12] it may be that the exclusion of interested witnesses in the superior courts of common law was not to protect the courts from being misled, but to protect the gentry from the embarrassment of being found to be liars. In inferior courts, where small claims were heard, the ban did not apply.[13]

The second feature of Gilbert's treatise that marks it out from later writings on evidence is the emphasis placed on written testimony. Gilbert's basic principle was that proof should be by the best available evidence. In his hierarchy of sources, written evidence was preferred because he thought it less likely to be fallible than mere oral testimony. This preference is reflected in the amount of space devoted to the two subjects: written evidence was given about three times as much space as oral evidence. He first considered sealed public records, then other public documents such as affidavits and depositions, and then private documents such as deeds. Only afterwards did he turn to the subject of oral evidence.[14]

In criminal courts, the position was very different. Research by John Langbein has thrown light on the conduct of criminal trials in the 18th century.[15] In the early decades of the century, it appears that anything like modern adversary procedure was entirely absent. Adversary procedure has been described as containing three fundamental elements. In the first place, the decision maker remains neutral and passive during the trial. Secondly, the litigants themselves are responsible for the production and quality of the proof upon which the case will be decided. The third element is the existence of an elaborate set of rules to govern the trial and the actions of the advocates.[16] Langbein concluded that in relation to criminal trials:

---

9   See the comment by Taylor, 1872, Vol II, para 1248, in which he regretted the reforms that had by then been made.

10   See, eg, Phillipps, 1829, Vol I, p 45; Starkie, 1842, Vol I, p 17.

11   See, eg, Lowndes, 1843.

12   Shapin, S, 1994; see especially pp 3–125.

13   Winder, 1936.

14   Cf Landsman, 1990a, p 1153.

15   See above. See further Langbein, 2003.

16   Landsman, 1990b, pp 500–01. See also Damaska, 1986, Chapter 4.

> . . . adversary procedure cannot be defended as part of our historic common law bequest. The criminal lawyer and the complex procedures that have grown up to serve him are historical upstarts.[17]

This was so of necessity. In situations where it was rare for the prosecution to be represented by a lawyer, let alone the defence, the evidence had to be obtained from a mixture of judicial questioning and confrontation between the accused and his accusers. It is clear that, although the prisoner could not be sworn, he was expected to answer questions and make out the facts relied on in his defence.[18] Further, in the absence of counsel, there was a much greater opportunity for informal judicial control of the jury. Not only could the judge provide advice and comment throughout the trial, but it was rare for a jury to retire from court in order to discuss its verdict. Most verdicts were discussed by jurors while remaining in the jury box, and this also allowed a judge to give guidance where he thought it necessary. Nothing like our modern system of evidence could have grown in those circumstances. Then, as Langbein has shown, from about the mid-1730s counsel began to appear on behalf of some accused persons. At first they were allowed only to examine and cross-examine witnesses. It was not until 1836 that counsel for persons accused of felony were given statutory authority to address the jury on their clients' behalf. The extent of their participation until then depended on the discretion of the trial judge and the practices of the various circuits. There was clearly a great variety of modes of trial in the early 19th century. Here, for example, is an attorney's account, published in 1833, of trials at the Old Bailey:

> For several sessions I made a calculation of the average time which each trial occupied; I never found it exceed eight and a half minutes, notwithstanding many cases engage the court a whole day . . . The rapidity with which the trials are dispatched throws the prisoners into the utmost confusion. Fifty or sixty of them are kept in readiness in the dock under the court, to be brought up as they may be called for. These men, seeing their fellow prisoners return tried and found guilty in a minute or two after being taken up, become so alarmed and nervous, in consequence of losing all prospect of having a patient trial, that in their efforts at the moment to rearrange their ideas and plan of defence, and put the strongest features of their cases before the court as speedily as possible, they lose all command over themselves, and are then, to use their own language, taken up to be knocked down like bullocks, unheard . . . The evident anxiety of all the city judges to proceed with indecent and unjudicial haste with the business of this court makes them frequently petulant at any interruption or impediment to their usual dispatch, which manifests itself in much acrimony between themselves and counsel . . .[19]

---

17   Langbein, 1978, p 316.

18   See, eg, the fictional account of a criminal trial in Fielding, H, *The History of Tom Jones*, 1963 [1749], Book VIII, Chapter 11.

19   Anon, 1833, pp 276–77.

As a contrast, we have a description of what a French observer, Charles Cottu, saw when he was a guest of the Bench and Bar on the Northern Circuit in the early 1820s. The judge remained 'almost a stranger' to what was going on. He took notes of examination-in-chief and cross-examination. Sometimes he would ask questions of a witness, but his object was 'more to obtain an explanation of the witness's depositions than to establish any additional circumstance against the prisoner'. At the end of each deposition the prisoner was told to ask the witness whatever questions he pleased, but, since an accused person was generally represented by counsel, Cottu concluded that the prisoner did so little in his own defence that 'his hat stuck on a pole might without inconvenience be his substitute at the trial'. According to Cottu, prisoners in London were only very rarely represented by counsel, and this, rather than any cynical attempt to impress a foreign visitor, probably accounts for the vivid differences between these two descriptions from the early 19th century.[20]

The intervention of counsel in criminal trials may have been accepted initially because judges were aware of imperfections in criminal procedure, especially the use of accomplices who volunteered to give evidence for the prosecution in the hope of obtaining a pardon for themselves. However, adversary procedure probably came to be established in criminal trials chiefly as the result of a population explosion at the Bar during roughly the first half of the 19th century.[21] In these circumstances, young barristers would have been eager to break into work wherever they could, and it is likely that criminal work, especially on circuit, appeared an attractive new market.[22]

The growth of adversary procedure in criminal trials was a large step towards the development of our modern law of evidence, but one important element remained lacking: until 1907, there was no effective system of criminal appeals. Without such an appellate system, a rule-based system of law could scarcely develop to match the one that was growing rapidly in the civil courts.

Before the 19th century the common law was generally regarded as being in a continuous process of growth, flexible enough to operate as an instrument of reform and better suited to that task than Parliament. These views depended on the belief that common law was essentially a *system of reasoning*, which might be partially expressed by way of maxims, and of which the decisions of the judges were only evidence.[23] There was little scope for binding authority because the three common

---

20   Cottu, 1822, pp 88–90.

21   Duman, 1980.

22   In addition to the works cited on the growth of adversary procedure in criminal trials, see Baker, 1977; Post, 1984; Beattie, 1991; Cairns, 1998.

23   Baker, 1990, pp 226–29; Lieberman, 1989, pp 43–46, 84–86, 102; Lobban, 1991, pp 2–15, 47–49; Postema, 1986, Chapter 1.

law courts developed separately, and law reporting was inadequate.[24] However, a line of authority might be strong enough to be considered binding, and in this situation there was room for the idea to develop that decisions of the courts formed the *substance* of the law, and were not merely *evidence* of it. The 19th century saw a change in attitude to case law,[25] and this affected the way in which evidence law developed. In this development treatise writers, law reporters and judges all played a part.

Treatise writers attempted to present their subject as a rule-based system derived from case law.[26] Passages in the works of WM Best and of other writers show that the authors regarded their subject as having been recently developed by the judges, although based on older principles.[27] The treatise writers' increasingly rule-based approach left less room for judicial discretion in the admission of testimony. The writers themselves appear to have realised that this was a novel development. Several of them argued in favour of exclusionary rules, relying on the supposed lack of weight possessed by certain types of testimony, the difficulties experienced by jurors in assessing evidence, and the need for clear, general rules in the interests of certainty. There was a perception that uncertainty was a great defect in English law[28] and, for various reasons, this could not be remedied by codification. Not least of these reasons was the fact that, in criminal evidence, the case law was underdeveloped through lack of an effective appellate system. In addition, Members of Parliament were unwilling to allow significant changes in the law to be made without thorough examination, for which there was insufficient parliamentary time. Among the judges, codification was supported only by a minority.

Any increase in the certainty of the common law had therefore to be made by the judges. In the law of civil evidence, they tried to achieve this by developing an increasingly rule-based system of exclusions. In this they were assisted by institutional changes that made for a more uniform approach to civil appeals.[29] However, because the criminal courts lacked an effective appellate structure until 1907, the judges were unable to develop rules of criminal evidence to anything like the same extent. There were informal common practices, but no more. On the formation of the Court of Criminal Appeal in that year, criminal evidence law began to develop in the same way. Only in recent decades have the benefits of a more discretionary approach to admissibility been appreciated. The result is that modern criminal evidence law is a mixture of statute law, of common law rules (mainly developed after 1907), and more

---

24   On law reporting, see Megarry, 1973, pp 117–33.

25   Evans, 1987, pp 35–72.

26   Simpson, 1981; Sugarman, 1986, pp 26–61.

27   Best, 1870, pp 146–47. For other treatise writers, see Twining, 2006, pp 45–75.

28   Daniel, undated, p 32.

29   Evans, 1987, p 64; Allen, 1964, pp 219–21.

recent discretionary powers. As for civil evidence, the rule-based, exclusionary system that had developed during the 19th century could no longer be justified after the virtual abolition during the 20th century of trial by jury in civil actions. Gradually it was demolished by statute, and today comparatively little of importance remains.

The other great change in evidence law during the 19th century was the gradual abolition of the old restrictions on competence, which was a long and piecemeal process. The religious bars were removed in two stages. Attention was focused during the first on the relief of those who, like Quakers, had religious scruples against taking an oath. After some partial reforms, complete success was achieved for civil proceedings when the Common Law Procedure Act 1854 made an affirmation an acceptable replacement for a religious oath. This reform was extended to criminal trials in 1861. Attention then turned to the relief of those who refused to take an oath because they subscribed to no religious belief. These attempts succeeded with the passing of the Evidence Further Amendment Act 1869.

The 19th century also saw the removal of witness disqualifications based on criminal convictions and financial interest in the outcome of the litigation. Three main stages can be seen. The first was reached in 1843: in that year, Lord Denman's Act abolished the rule whereby persons with certain criminal convictions had been disqualified from giving evidence. The Act also made a substantial inroad on the rule that an interested witness could not testify. The second stage was reached in 1851, when the Evidence Amendment Act (also known as Lord Brougham's Act) made competent the parties to most civil proceedings in the superior courts of common law. The third stage was reached only in 1898, when the Criminal Evidence Act permitted the accused to give evidence in all criminal cases.

The traditional view, represented for example by Holdsworth,[30] was that these statutory reforms were largely inspired by the critique of Jeremy Bentham, many of whose writings on evidence were published during the 1820s. There is no doubt that, for the student of jurisprudence or intellectual history, Bentham is a formidable figure.[31] It is likely, however, that the traditional view exaggerates Bentham's role in the story of evidence law reform. Debates in Parliament, as well as in pamphlets, journals and newspapers, show that those supporting the various proposals for reform had widely different concerns from those expressed by Bentham. He had wanted competence to be extended as part of a grand campaign for reform, which was aimed at the destruction of what he called the 'sinister interests' of Church and State. The statutory reforms were achieved for pragmatic reasons that had nothing to do with such a radical programme. Success depended on convincing enough lawyers and politicians that increased social stability made change both safe and desirable, and, so far as the 1898 reforms were concerned, that what was proposed involved no threat to

---

30   Holdsworth, 1903–72, Vol XIII, p 42; Vol XV, pp 138, 307. See also Hart, 1982, p 31.

31   For his work on evidence, see Twining, 1985.

the relatively new balance of power in criminal trials between judge, counsel and the accused.[32]

More recently, statute has played an increasingly large part in the development of evidence law. Concern about police misconduct, and an increasing awareness of wrongful convictions, led ultimately to the provision of important safeguards for suspects in the Police and Criminal Evidence Act 1984. But within a relatively short period of time, concerns that the scales of justice had tipped too much in favour of defendants led to the passing of further legislation that tended to favour the prosecution. The old rules about the corroboration of suspect witnesses had already been abolished.[33] Now, by the Criminal Justice and Public Order Act 1994, the defendant's right of silence was significantly weakened by allowing his exercise of that right to be taken into account, subject to certain conditions, when assessing guilt.[34] The scope for cross-examination of complainants where a sexual offence was alleged had already been restricted by the Sexual Offences (Amendment) Act 1976. The Youth Justice and Criminal Evidence Act 1999 went considerably further, and seemed at one stage to put at risk a defendant's right to a fair trial.[35] Further statutory development of evidence law was provided by the Criminal Justice Act 2003, which substantially revised the former law relating to evidence of bad character and hearsay evidence.[36]

CURRENT OBJECTIVES

Evidence law has been regarded as part of what is known as 'adjective' law, at least one of the purposes of which is to enforce 'substantive' rights and duties.[37] One of the aims of evidence law, sometimes referred to as 'rectitude of decision', will be to help courts to make accurate findings of fact, to which the relevant substantive law will then be applied. Many rules of evidence were originally aimed at securing rectitude of decision in the context of an adversary trial. For example, rules about the competence of witnesses excluded those who could not testify on oath and be cross-examined. Rules excluding hearsay evidence ensured, subject to some exceptions, that juries should not use evidence unless there had been an opportunity to test it by cross-

---

32   Allen, 1997.

33   See below, Chapter 10.

34   See below, Chapter 11.

35   *R v A (No 2)* [2001] UKHL 25; [2002] 1 AC 45.

36   See below, Chapters 8, 9 and 12.

37   See, eg, Nokes, 1967, p 30; Carter, 1990, p 3. Some scepticism has been expressed about this distinction. See Alexander, 1998, where it is argued that 'procedural rights just *are* substantive rights, albeit rights of a special (but quite numerous) kind: rights against risks.'

examination. The object of rules about corroboration was to protect defendants in criminal trials from conviction solely on the basis of evidence that was, of its nature, particularly subject to unreliability.[38] But to claim rectitude of decision as the sole aim of evidence law is too simple.

The main function of civil process in the English legal system today is conflict resolution. According to this theory, civil proceedings are primarily a method of achieving peaceful settlement of private disputes. The aim of adjective law must therefore be to encourage parties to litigation to accept the adjudication (subject to a right of appeal), and to encourage others to resort to litigation rather than self-help as a means of dispute resolution.[39] These aims require that adjective law should be efficient and should provide procedures that are accepted as fair by actual and potential litigants. Such procedures will include a right to be heard, a right to legal representation (at public expense, if need be), an impartial hearing, a reasoned judgment, and a right of appeal. Efficiency requires procedures that, so far as possible, achieve accuracy of outcome but also avoid waste of time and delay. Justice that is delayed harms the litigants in the case in question, who must pay increased costs, and other litigants, who have to wait longer for a hearing. In addition, delayed justice harms those parties whom it continues to keep out of their rights while they await adjudication.[40]

Criminal trials, in particular, have wider objectives that must be reflected in the law of evidence and procedure. Two of the most obvious are the satisfaction of victims and the protection of society. Behind both objectives lies the need for a system of criminal justice to be able, among other things, to justify its verdicts so as to have the confidence of society. The usual way to achieve this will be to show that verdicts are reached by means that inspire confidence. English courts recognise this fact. For example, in *Connelly v DPP*[41] Lord Devlin said that it was the duty of the courts to conduct their proceedings so as to command the respect and confidence of the public. In *R v Latif* Lord Steyn referred to the danger of bringing the criminal justice system into disrepute.[42] Rules of evidence and procedure will, on this basis, aim at

---

38   Jackson in *Trials on Trial*, Vol 1, p. 135.

39   There may, of course, be acceptable alternatives to litigation in the courts, such as arbitration.

40   Another way of regarding the civil process is to see it as a means of altering behaviour by imposing costs on people. On this view, the court is not so much concerned with the resolution of the immediate dispute as with its effect on others' future conduct. The imposition of legal liability is then a way of making individuals take into account the costs of their actions. In this way the State encourages appropriate attitudes of care towards others as well as compliance with obligations. See Scott, 1974–75. Something of this approach can occasionally be found in English procedure (eg, in cases where a plaintiff is entitled to exemplary damages), but it is too rare to have much, if any, effect on procedural objectives.

41   [1964] AC 1254, 1353.

42   [1996] 1 WLR 104, 112.

rectitude of decision. But no system of justice can get things right all the time; sometimes the guilty will go free, and on other occasions the innocent will be convicted. A system in which it was known that either happened with more than acceptable frequency would fail to inspire confidence.

It is likely that there is quite a high risk of erroneous conviction in criminal cases that varies, probably, with the tribunal and the nature of the offence charged.[43] A major reason for this is almost certainly that there is regularly a substantial imbalance of resources between the prosecution and the defendant. Imbalance may occur in civil proceedings also, as where a major corporation and a private individual are in dispute, but such imbalance is a matter of chance. It is not, as it is in criminal prosecutions, a built-in feature.[44] Because of this imbalance, there is a permanent danger that a defendant will be wrongly convicted because he is unable through lack of resources to gather the evidence he needs to combat the case put forward by the State. This is not to say that the State always uses its power efficiently. The point is that, when it comes to the crunch, the State can pull out all the stops; most defendants cannot. The imbalance is particularly dangerous because of the temptation for police to pursue only those lines of investigation that support their preconceived theories of the case. Nor is this a temptation confined to members of the police. The State's scientific experts may also be partisan, ignoring lines of inquiry that might assist the defendant and even suppressing evidence that weakens the prosecution case. The prosecution has a duty to disclose evidence that may assist the defence, but this is now governed by the Criminal Procedure and Investigations Act 1996, and some scepticism has been expressed about the effectiveness of this legislation to protect defendants.

Another reason why there is a risk of wrongful conviction is the special difficulty of evaluating evidence in criminal trials. Problems may arise both from the nature of the evidence itself and from the way in which it is presented. Evidence of previous misconduct provides a classic example of the difficulties of evaluation.[45] Suppose Bertie is charged with committing a robbery in London. His defence is that he was on holiday with his girlfriend in Plymouth at the time. Bertie has been convicted of a number of robberies in the recent past; on each occasion, he gave evidence of a similar alibi defence. Or suppose Freddie, a married man, is charged with indecently assaulting the family's babysitter. Part of the prosecution case is that just before the alleged assault, Freddie tried to get the babysitter to look at pornographic photographs with him. Freddie vigorously denies this, but the prosecution have statements from two other women who did babysitting for his family and

---

43   In the nature of things this has to be guesswork, but see, eg, Woffinden, 1989, p 485; Baldwin and McConville, 1979.

44   Most criminal prosecutions are against individuals. It is possible that where a corporation is prosecuted, the imbalance may be less pronounced.

45   See below, Chapter 12.

who say that, although Freddie never assaulted them, he did try to get them to look at pornographic photographs. If the jury hear the supporting evidence in the cases of Bertie and Freddie, there is a danger that they may give it too much weight, and so convict the defendants. Alternatively, they may decide that the defendants are such anti-social characters that even if they did not commit the offence charged, they are likely to have committed others for which they were not caught. They therefore convict.

Problems of evaluation may arise if evidence is not given by an eye witness, but by someone who heard an earlier account from an eye witness. The testifying witness can obviously be questioned about whether he heard the eye witness accurately, but there will generally be little point in asking questions designed to discover how reliable the eye witness was. The evidence of what the testifying witness heard may be relevant because it makes a fact in issue to *some* degree more or less likely to be true. But how is that degree to be assessed?

A more general problem arises from the way evidence is presented in an adversary system. Under such a system, evidence may have a built-in risk of misleading, because the parties, not the court, are responsible for producing evidence, and neither party is likely to be willing for the whole truth to emerge. An advocate who examines his own witness in court will be doing so on the basis of a statement of facts which have already been selected during the pre-trial stage. He knows that he will move outside that framework at his peril, because if he asks the witness a question on a topic not covered in the statement he will risk getting an answer that damages his client's case. Cross-examining counsel is likely to rely substantially on questions to which a plain 'yes' or 'no' answer is appropriate, and he will generally try to deny the witness any chance of providing wider explanations for fear that the witness may say something that damages the party on whose behalf he is conducting the cross-examination.[46] Where evidence is presented in so partial and restricted a way, there is a risk that truth will suffer. One result of that may be a wrongful conviction.

It appears that those responsible for the administration of justice in the broadest sense, such as government ministers, members of Parliament and judges, must do their best when developing rules of evidence and procedure to assess what is an acceptable level of error. But there are difficulties in making such an inquiry. To what extent do the very public reactions of politicians and mass media reflect public opinion? What weight should be given to the opinions of well-organised and vociferous pressure groups? Do reliable research methods exist for assessing a general public opinion? Even if one could be found, what guarantees would there be that it was not based on incomplete information, misconceptions, failure to consider relevant arguments, or on prejudice?[47]

---

46   See Stone, 1988, pp 106–07; Boon, 1993, p 88; Law Commission Consultation Paper 138, 1995, paras 6.42–6.49.

47   Ashworth, 2003, p 111.

There is another difficulty in making public confidence in verdicts, sometimes referred to as the 'legitimacy' of verdicts, the sole standard by which rules of evidence and procedure should be assessed. On this consequentialist test, all that can be said about the wrongfulness of convicting innocent persons is that if enough wrongful convictions are publicised that in itself will lead to loss of confidence in the criminal justice system. Some would say that this fails to understand the nature of the wrong in question. Dworkin, for example, has argued that '[p]eople have a profound right not to be convicted of crimes of which they are innocent'.[48] If this is so, truth is of intrinsic, not just instrumental, value in a criminal trial. It would follow that certain constraints should be placed on the criminal process, so that while a trial might not establish the truth about a defendant's guilt or innocence, at least it should avoid establishing, by a wrongful conviction, a particularly unjust falsehood. This would encourage more protections against erroneous convictions than might be justified by a purely consequentialist theory.[49] These might be given effect by side constraints in a system that was primarily consequentialist in its search for truth. Alternatively, due process values could be seen as having a bearing on the ends of the trial process, and not just as side constraints in a search for rectitude of decision. This would be the case, for example, if defendants were to be treated as rational, autonomous agents in a process that called them to account for their actions, rather than as the subjects of a merely factual enquiry.[50] The basis of this approach is the Kantian principle that persons exist as ends in themselves, and not merely as means, to be arbitrarily used by the will of some other persons or institutions.[51] Moreover, this is a principle that appears to be reflected in the European Convention on Human Rights, especially in Arts 3, 5, 6, 8 and 10.

It is against this background that rules of evidence and procedure must be assessed. The legal process should take rectitude of decision into account not just because truth is valuable in itself, but because it is instrumental in securing fundamental rights. Process values such as fairness and human dignity should also be taken into account, because the law ought to treat citizens as rational autonomous agents – to be persuaded, if possible, not merely coerced. Just as the criminal *law* needs to be justified to those on whom it is binding, so a criminal *verdict* needs to be justified to the defendant and to others. It must carry moral authority, and it cannot do this if the criminal process concentrates solely on factual accuracy, to the exclusion of all other considerations. Truth finding is, then, a major means by which the legitimacy of the verdict is secured, but it is not an end in itself. If this is the case, there may, for example, be circumstances where evidence should be excluded because, although reliable, it was obtained by iniquitous means. Suppose that vital evidence used in the

---

48   Dworkin, 1986, p 72.
49   Jackson, 2004, pp 21–22.
50   Ibid, pp 24–25.
51   Scruton, 1982, pp 69–71; Sullivan, 1994, pp 67–70.

trial of a dangerous robber had been obtained by torturing his wife and children. Could the verdict against him be morally justifiable?[52]

FURTHER READING

Development

—Baker, 'Criminal Courts and Procedure at Common Law 1550–1800,' in Cockburn, (ed), *Crime in England 1550–1800*, 1977.

—Duff and Others, *The Trial on Trial*, Vol 3, 2007, Part I, 'The Criminal Trial and Its History'.

—Langbein, *The Origins of Adversary Criminal Trial*, 2003.

—Twining, *Rethinking Evidence: Exploratory Essays*, 2nd edn, 2006, pp 35–98.

Current Objectives

—Ashworth, 'Exploring the Integrity Principle in Evidence and Procedure,' in Mirfield and Smith, (eds), *Essays for Colin Tapper*, 2003, pp 107–25.

—Ashworth and Redmayne, *The Criminal Process*, 2005, pp 19–58.

—Dennis, 'Reconstructing the Law of Criminal Evidence' (1989) CLP 21.

—Duff, *Trials and Punishments*, 1986, especially Chapter 4.

—Duff and Others, *The Trial on Trial*, 2004–07, Vol 1, pp 1–28; 121–45; Vol 2, pp 37–64; Vol 3, Part II, 'The Criminal Trial and Its Values', pp 55–161, 225–57.

—Dworkin, 'Is Law A System of Rules?' in Dworkin (ed), *The Philosophy of Law*, 1977.

—Dworkin, *Taking Rights Seriously*, 1977, Chapter 4, 'Hard Cases'.

—Dworkin, *A Matter of Principle*, 1986, Chapter 3, 'Principle, Policy, Procedure'.

EXERCISES

1. What are the fundamental features of adversary procedure?

2. What part has the legal profession played in the development of evidence law?

3. What part has legislation played in the development of evidence law?

4. Explain the following terms:

    (a) adjective law;

    (b) rectitude of decision;

    (c) the legitimacy of the verdict;

    (d) consequentialist theories;

    (e) process values.

5. What factors contribute to the risk of wrongful conviction in a criminal trial?

6. Should evidence obtained by torture ever be admissible? Give reasons for your answer.

---

52   See Dennis, 1989 and Duff, 1986, especially Chapter 4. On evidence obtained by torture, see *A and Others v Secretary of State for the Home Department (No 2)* [2005] UKHL 71, [2006] 2 AC 221; *Jalloh v Germany* [2006] 20 BHRC 575.

3

DOCUMENTARY AND REAL EVIDENCE

DOCUMENTARY EVIDENCE

A party who wishes to rely on a statement contained in a document as evidence supporting his case needs to consider, in addition to any other relevant evidence law, at least one further matter: proof of the contents of the document. In some cases, proof of due execution may have to be considered also.[1] So far as criminal cases are concerned, the basic provision that deals with proof of a document is s 133 of the Criminal Justice Act 2003. This provides that where a statement in a document is admissible as evidence in criminal proceedings, it may be proved either by the production of that document, or, whether or not the document is still in existence, by the production of a copy. A copy may be authenticated in whatever way the court may approve. A 'copy' means anything onto which information recorded in a document has been copied, by whatever means and whether directly or indirectly.[2] The number of removes between a copy and the original is therefore immaterial for the purposes of admissibility, though it may, of course, affect the weight of the evidence. A 'statement' is 'any representation of fact or opinion made by a person by whatever means, and it includes a representation made in a sketch, photofit or other pictorial form'.[3]

---

1   This chapter deals only with proof of the contents of private documents; there are special rules for the proof of various public documents, details of which may be found in standard practitioners' works.

2   Section 134(1).

3   Section 115(2).

'Document' means anything in which information of any description is recorded.[4] The effect of these provisions is that proof of the contents of a document is now essentially the same in both civil and criminal proceedings.[5] Given the broad terms of the present law, it is likely that the special provisions of the Bankers' Books Evidence Act 1879, regulating proof of the contents of such books by a system of examined copies, will fall into disuse, and the rather complex provisions of that Act are therefore not considered further.

It will be noted that where an original document is not available, s 133 of the Criminal Justice Act 2003 and s 8 of the Civil Evidence Act 1995 do not go so far as to allow proof of the contents of the original by oral evidence. In civil proceedings, although s 8 of the 1995 Act does not sanction the admission of oral evidence, oral hearsay evidence of the contents of a document that would itself be admissible if it were available can be given under the general provision for the admission of hearsay evidence contained in s 1. In criminal proceedings, oral proof of the contents of a document would be subject to the hearsay provisions in Pt 11, Chapter 2 of the Criminal Justice Act 2003.

The party who adduces a document in evidence must usually, in the absence of an admission by his opponent, prove that it was duly executed. This obligation may simply require evidence that the document was signed by the person whose signature it purports to bear. Sometimes it may be necessary to prove the handwriting of the whole of a disputed document. Proof of execution may also require proof of attestation.

Proof of a signature or of handwriting may be made in one or more of the following ways:

(a) By evidence of the writer, or of someone else who saw the maker of the document write it or put his signature on it.

(b) By evidence of opinion, given by an ordinary witness. Such evidence is admissible even where the evidence of the writer is available. Thus, on a charge of forgery, it is not necessary to call the person whose signature is alleged to have been forged.[6] Such an opinion will be based on the witness's recollection of having seen a particular person's writing or signature before, as was described by Coleridge J in *Doe d Mudd v Suckermore*:

> Either the witness has seen the party write on some former occasion, or he has corresponded with him, and transactions have taken place between them upon the faith that letters purporting to have been written or signed by him have been so

---

4   Section 134(1).
5   Cf Civil Evidence Act 1995, ss 8 and 13.
6   *R v Hurley* (1843) 2 Mood&Ry 473.

> written or signed. On either supposition, the witness is supposed to have received into his mind an impression, not so much of the manner in which the writer has formed the letters in the particular instances, as of the general character of his handwriting; and he is called on to speak as to the writing in question by a reference to the standard so formed in his mind . . . The test of genuineness ought to be the resemblance, not to the formation of the letters in some other specimen . . . but to the general character of writing, which is impressed on it as the involuntary and unconscious result of constitution, habit, or other permanent cause, and is therefore itself permanent.[7]

(c)   By an actual comparison, often aided by expert opinion evidence. Section 8 of the Criminal Procedure Act 1865 applies to both civil and criminal proceedings and provides that:

> Comparison of a disputed writing with any writing proved to the satisfaction of the judge to be genuine shall be permitted to be made by witnesses; and such writings, and the evidence of witnesses respecting the same, may be submitted to the court and jury as evidence of the genuineness or otherwise of the writing in dispute.

In civil proceedings, the judge has to be satisfied on the balance of probabilities as to the genuineness of the writing that is to be used as a standard for comparison. In criminal proceedings, he must be satisfied beyond reasonable doubt.[8] The statute does not expressly require the evidence of witnesses. Once a document has been proved to the judge's satisfaction to be a genuine sample of handwriting from the person who is alleged to have written the disputed document, it may apparently simply be compared with the disputed document, but it has been held that, in criminal cases, expert evidence should also be available. Thus, in *R v Harden*,[9] where the defendant was charged with obtaining money by false pretences, the prosecution alleged that he had sent fictitious agreements to a finance company, and the jury were invited by the trial judge to compare peculiarities in the handwriting of various documents. The defendant was convicted, but his appeal was allowed; the Court of Criminal Appeal held that the jury should have had the assistance of expert evidence.[10]

In *Lockheed-Arabia v Owen*[11] the Court of Appeal held that s 8 was wide enough to allow an expression of opinion to be based on a photocopy of the disputed writing to be given in evidence. In the course of his judgment Mann LJ said:

---

7   (1837) 3 A&E 703, p 705.

8   *R v Ewing* [1983] 2 All ER 645.

9   [1963] 1 QB 8.

10   See also *R v Tilley* [1961] 1 WLR 1309, *R v Smith (Michael Graham)* (1968) 52 Cr App R 648.

11   [1993] QB 806.

Mr. Cowan, for the defendant argued that an opinion formed after consideration of a photocopy was not admissible under the section. He referred us to the deficiencies of a photocopy as a comparison source. Thus, a photocopy will not reveal pressure marks, overwritten words or pen lifts. I acknowledge the force of those points but they relate to the credibility of an opinion. They are not persuasive against admissibility. The legislators in 1854 knew of the daguerreotype and their successors in 1865 knew of photography. Neither could have foreseen the facsimile reproduction which now we both suffer and enjoy and which doubtless will be the subject of yet further improvement. The legislative language can accommodate an expression of opinion based upon a facsimile of a disputed writing and I think there is no reason why the court should hold such an opinion to be inadmissible. An ongoing statute ought to be read so as to accommodate technological change: see *Bennion, Statutory Interpretation*, 2nd ed. (1992), p. 627.

'Attestation' refers to the signature of a document by a person who is not a party to it, but who is a witness to the signature of one of the parties. By s 3 of the Evidence Act 1938, any document required by law to be attested, with the exception of a will or other testamentary document, 'may, instead of being approved by an attesting witness, be proved in the manner in which it might be proved if no attesting witness were alive'. The effect of this provision is that non-testamentary documents required by law to be attested may now be proved by showing that the signature is in fact that of the attesting witness. Where the court is asked to pronounce for a will in solemn form, the general practice is for at least one of the attesting witnesses to be called to give evidence of execution, but a will can be pronounced for where both attesting witnesses are proved to be dead, or even if the evidence shows merely that they cannot be traced, if the court is satisfied in all the circumstances that the will was duly executed.[12]

There is said to be a presumption that a document was made on the date that it bears.[13] In any proceedings, proof of execution may be dispensed with in the case of 'ancient documents', which, by s 4 of the Evidence Act 1938, are documents more than 20 years old. For this rule to apply, the document must appear to be regular on the face of it, and must be produced from proper custody. 'Proper custody' is any custody that is consistent with the genuineness and legitimate origin of the document. Thus, in *Bishop of Meath v Marquess of Winchester*,[14] documents that had belonged to a deceased bishop by virtue of his office, which had been found among his private papers in the possession of his family, were held to have been produced

---

12   *Re Lemon's Estate* (1961) 105 SJ 1107.

13   *In the Goods of Adamson* (1875) LR 3 P&D 253, 256. This is no more than a presumption of fact – an inference that may be drawn. See *Anderson v Weston* (1840) 6 Bing NC 296, where Bosanquet J referred to the date as prima facie evidence of the date of execution, pp 300–01.

14   (1836) 3 Bing NC 183.

from proper custody, even though they should have been in the custody of his successor as bishop. As Tindal CJ said: 'It is not necessary that they should be found in the best and most proper place of deposit.'[15]

STATEMENTS IN DOCUMENTS PRODUCED BY COMPUTERS

There are now no special conditions to be satisfied before admitting in evidence documents produced by a computer. The provisions contained in Pt I of the Civil Evidence Act 1968 were repealed by s 15(2) and Sched 2 to the Civil Evidence Act 1995. The provisions contained in s 69 of the Police and Criminal Evidence Act 1984 were repealed by s 60 of the Youth Justice and Criminal Evidence Act 1999.

REAL EVIDENCE

'Real evidence' is an ill-defined concept. There is general agreement that it includes physical objects produced for the inspection of the court. If a document is adduced in evidence, the question whether it is 'real' or 'documentary' evidence depends on the purpose for which it is adduced. If the purpose is to establish its contents, it is classed as an item of documentary evidence; if the purpose is to establish its condition or appearance (for example, to show that it has been damaged, or to show its size or shape), it is classed as an item of real evidence. The distinction was formerly of some importance because of the rule that the original of an item of documentary evidence had to be produced (or the foundation laid for the admission of secondary evidence), whereas it was not essential to produce items of real evidence in court. At the risk of reducing the weight of the evidence, oral evidence could be given about the state of a physical object. As was shown earlier, statutes have now removed almost completely the requirement to produce original documentary evidence, and one result is that the question whether a piece of evidence is to be classified as 'real' or 'documentary' has lost much of its former importance.

Beyond physical objects produced for the inspection of the court there was room for argument about what else might count as 'real evidence'. The arguments about classification are of limited importance now; indeed, their major significance is probably to provide a useful checklist of occasions when direct perception by a trier of fact can be part of the evidence in the case.

DEMEANOUR OF THE WITNESS

The traditional view of demeanour is that it may be relevant to credibility. One of the standard arguments against the admissibility of hearsay evidence has been that the

---

15   (1836) 3 Bing NC 183, p 200.

court is unable to see the demeanour of the person making the original statement.[16] The weight attached to demeanour can also be perceived in the reluctance of appellate courts to interfere with the conclusions of trial judges who have seen and heard the witnesses.[17]

PHYSICAL APPEARANCE OF A PERSON OR ANIMAL IN COURT

In *Line v Taylor*,[18] a dog was brought into court to display its good temper. More recently, a parrot's display of affection in court towards a particular person was used as evidence that the parrot belonged to that person.[19] In another case, in which the plaintiff was suing for damages and for the return of cats which she claimed belonged to her, the judge agreed that the cats should be present in open court when the case was heard so that their reactions to the plaintiff and her children could be observed.[20]

It appears that before defendants in criminal trials are allowed to give evidence, the jury might take into account their reactions in the dock at various stages of the trial. In *AG for New South Wales v Bertrand*,[21] the Privy Council had to consider a case where there had been a re-trial after a jury had disagreed. At the second hearing, the trial judge had attempted to shorten the proceedings by reading back to the prosecution witnesses the notes of their evidence at the first trial and asking them if what he had read was true. After that, he had permitted fresh oral examination-in-chief and cross-examination. The Privy Council, allowing the appeal, disapproved of this course and emphasised the value of 'open oral examination of the witness in the presence of prisoner, judge, and jury'. According to Sir John Coleridge:

> The most careful note must often fail to convey the evidence fully in some of its most important elements . . . It cannot give the look or manner of the witness: his hesitation, his doubts, his variations of language, his confidence or precipitance, his calmness or consideration; *it cannot give the manner of the Prisoner, when that has been important, upon the statement of anything of particular moment.*[22]

The resemblance of a child, produced to the court, to a person alleged to be its father has in some cases been held to be evidence, albeit slight, of parentage.[23]

16　*Teper v R* [1952] 2 AC 480, p 486. But see Stone, 1991; Law Commission No 245 (1997), paras 3.9–3.12.

17　*SS Hontestroom v SS Sagaporack* [1927] AC 37, pp 47, 48; *Hvalfangerselskapet Polaris A/S v Unilever Ltd* (1933) 46 LlL Rep 29; *Yuill v Yuill* [1945] P 15; *In the Estate of Bercovitz (Decd)* [1962] All ER 552, p 558.

18　(1862) 3 F&F 731.

19　(1995) *The Times*, 16 February, p 5.

20　(1995) *The Times*, 26 April, p 3.

21　(1867) LR 1 PC 520.

22　*Ibid*, p 535, emphasis added.

23　*Slingsby v AG* (1916) 33 TLR 120, p 122; *Russell v Russell and Mayer* (1923) 129 LT 151, p 153; *C v C and C* [1972] 1 WLR 1335.

VIEWS

Things and places outside court may be inspected during the course of a trial. For example, members of a jury in one case viewed reconstructions of events, enacted outside court in a Range Rover motor car, to assist them in determining whether police had seen an act of oral intercourse in a similar car on an earlier occasion.[24] In a trial for murder, a jury inspected a house, where the bodies of nine victims had been unearthed, to determine whether the wife of a man living there might have failed to notice her husband's activities on the premises.[25] During the course of hearing *Tito v Waddell*,[26] the trial judge visited Ocean Island in the Pacific Ocean, which was the subject of the litigation.

The legal status of a view was settled by the Court of Appeal in *Buckingham v Daily News Ltd*.[27] The case concerned an employee of the defendants who had been injured when cleaning one of his employer's machines. During the course of an action for negligence against the employers, the judge inspected the machine and watched a demonstration by the plaintiff of how he cleaned it. The Court of Appeal held that the inspection was part of the evidence in the case: it was as if the machine had been brought into court and the plaintiff had there demonstrated what took place. In the course of his judgment, Birkett LJ referred to occasions when, as a judge of first instance, he had visited factories, workshops, shops and cinemas in order to see the nature of the place where an accident had occurred.[28] The parties, their legal representatives and the judge (or judge and jury) should all be present at the view.[29]

AUTOMATIC RECORDINGS

Where the recording device operates as no more than a calculator, the print-out or other reading is an item of real evidence. An obvious example is the print-out produced by a breathalyser.[30] In *R v Spiby*,[31] the Court of Appeal had to consider whether the rule against hearsay applied to the print-out from a device which monitored telephone calls and recorded the numbers to which calls were made and their duration. The court held that the print-out was an item of real evidence, and not caught by the hearsay rule, because the recording was entirely automatic and did not depend on anything that had passed through a human mind.

---

24   (1994) *The Times*, 13 January, p 3.
25   (1995) *The Times*, 20 October, p 5.
26   [1975] 3 All ER 997.
27   [1956] 2 QB 534.
28   *Ibid*, p 542.
29   *Salusbury v Woodland* [1970] 1 QB 324, p 343; *R v Hunter* [1985] 1 WLR 613; *R v Ely JJ ex p Burgess* [1992] Crim LR 888.
30   *Castle v Cross* [1984] 1 WLR 1372.
31   (1990) 91 Cr App R 186.

In other circumstances a tape recording will be treated as documentary evidence. For example, the contents of tape recordings may be admitted as evidence of what was said on a particular occasion. In *R v Maqsud Ali*, where a conversation between defendants had been surreptitiously obtained, Marshall J said:

> For many years now photographs have been admissible in evidence on proof that they are relevant to the issues involved in the case and that the prints are taken from negatives that are untouched. The prints as seen represent situations that have been reproduced by means of mechanical and chemical devices. Evidence of things seen through telescopes or binoculars which otherwise could not have been picked up by the naked eye have been admitted, and now there are devices for picking up, transmitting, and recording, conversations. We can see no difference in principle between a tape recording and a photograph.[32]

The voices recorded must, of course, be identified by admissible evidence and, if there is a challenge to the authenticity of the recording, the court must be satisfied on this matter before admitting it. However, it seems that it is enough merely to establish a prima facie case for authenticity.[33] The recording is a document within the meaning of s 134 of the Criminal Justice Act 2003, and a transcript of the recording will be admissible as a copy under s 133.

In *R v Rampling*,[34] the Court of Appeal gave guidance on the use in court of tape recordings of police interviews:

(a) The tape can be produced and can be proved by the interviewing officer or any other officer present when it was taken.

(b) The officer should have listened to the tape before the trial so that he can, if necessary, deal with any objections to authenticity or accuracy.

(c) The transcript of the recording can be produced by the officer. He should have checked this against the recording for accuracy before the trial.

(d) The defendant is entitled to have any part of the tape played to the jury.

(e) If any part of the tape is played, it is for the judge to decide whether the jury should have a transcript to enable them to follow more clearly.

Subject to any necessary editing to remove inadmissible evidence, a jury in retirement may, on request, be allowed to hear a tape recording of a police interview with the defendant, where the tape has been made an exhibit, even though the tape has not been played earlier during the trial.[35] Any playing of the tape after the jury has retired should be in open court, with judge, counsel and the defendant present.[36] A jury may

---

32   [1966] 1 QB 688, p 701. See also *R v Senat and Sin* (1968) 52 Cr App R 282.

33   *R v Robson and Harris* (1972) 56 Cr App R 450.

34   [1987] Crim LR 823.

35   *R v Riaz and Burke* (1991) 94 Cr App R 339.

36   *R v Hagan* [1997] 1 Cr App R 464, p 470.

also want, after retirement, to see once again a video tape of an interview with a child admitted under s 27(1) of the Youth Justice and Criminal Evidence Act 1999. It is a matter for the judge's discretion whether this should happen. He must have in mind the need to avoid unfairness from replaying only the complainant's evidence-in-chief. Usually, if the jury simply wish to be reminded of what the witness said, it will be sufficient for the judge to remind them of this from his own notes. A jury should only rarely be permitted to retire with a transcript of a child complainant's video interview. Where that does happen, the judge should give warnings to the jury which would prevent their giving disproportionate weight to the transcript,[37] but if the question of how the words were spoken is important to the jury, the judge may allow the video, or the relevant part of it, to be replayed. If there is a replay, the following rules apply:

(a)   It must be in court, with judge, counsel and defendant present.

(b)   The judge should warn the jury that because they are hearing the evidence-in-chief of the complainant a second time, well after all the other evidence, they should guard against the risk of giving it disproportionate weight simply for that reason, and should bear well in mind the other evidence in the case.

(c)   To assist in maintaining a fair balance, when the video has been replayed the judge should remind the jury from his own notes of the cross-examination and re-examination of the complainant, whether the jury ask him to do so or not.[38]

A film or photograph may be admitted to prove the commission of an offence and the identity of the offender. For example, in *R v Dodson*,[39] photographs taken at half second intervals by a security camera at a building society office were held admissible to show an offence being committed. It is necessary, of course, in such a case to adduce oral evidence to authenticate the video recording or still photographs. In *The Statue of Liberty*,[40] Sir Jocelyn Simon P admitted a cinematograph film of radar echoes, recorded mechanically by a shore radar station. Films or photographs are treated as if they are extensions of human perception.[41] In *Taylor v Chief Constable of Cheshire*,[42] police officers saw a video recording made by a security camera of someone picking up an item in a shop and putting it in his jacket. The police identified the man as Taylor. The film was later accidentally erased, but the Divisional Court held that the officers' evidence of what they had seen on the tape had been properly

---

37   *R v Morris* [1998] Crim LR 416.

38   *R v Rawlings and Broadbent* [1995] 2 Cr App R 222, pp 227–28; cf *R v Horley* [1999] Crim LR 488.

39   [1984] 1 WLR 971.

40   [1968] 1 WLR 739.

41   See the judgment of Marshall J in *R v Maqsud Ali* [1966] 1 QB 688, referred to above.

42   [1986] 1 WLR 1479.

admitted: they were in effect in the position of bystanders who had witnessed the event.

FURTHER READING

—Ormerod, 'A Prejudicial View' [2000] Crim LR 452.

EXERCISES

1. How can a document be proved in criminal proceedings?
2. Which of the following are documents for the purpose of criminal proceedings?

    (a) A letter from one defendant to another.

    (b) A sketch by a witness of a suspect.

    (c) A tape recording of an interview.

    (d) A gravestone recording the date of death of the deceased.

    (e) All of the above.

3. In what non-statutory ways can proof of handwriting be made?
4. What is the standard of proof required under Criminal Procedure Act 1865, s 8?
5. What is an attestation?
6. What special conditions, if any, have to be satisfied before admitting in evidence documents produced by a computer (a) in civil proceedings, and (b) in criminal proceedings?
7. How can you tell whether a hand-written letter produced in evidence is produced as documentary or real evidence?
8. What is the legal status in a trial of a 'view'?
9. Why is a computer print-out from a breathalyser classified as an item of real evidence?
10. Which of the following is *not* a rule to be followed when using in court a tape recording of a police interview?

    (a) The tape can be produced by any officer concerned in the case.

    (b) The officer producing the tape should have listened to it before the trial.

    (c) Any transcript of the recording should be checked for accuracy before trial.

    (d) The defendant is entitled to have any part of the tape played to the jury.

4

FACTS NOT REQUIRING PROOF

INTRODUCTION

The general rule is that if a party wants to rely on a particular fact in support of his case, that fact must be formally proved by providing evidence of it at trial. To this rule, there are two important exceptions: formal admissions and judicial notice.

FORMAL ADMISSIONS

If one party admits the existence of a fact on which the other proposes to rely, he will do so because his legal advisers see that the fact is not in contention, and that it would be pointless and time wasting to insist that it be proved by evidence. *Formal* admissions, however, must be distinguished from *informal* admissions. The latter are frequently referred to simply as 'admissions' (or, in criminal cases, as 'confessions') and the facts to which they refer require proof like any other item of evidence. The reason for this is the difference between formal and informal admissions. A formal admission is made deliberately, for the purpose of the proceedings, and is binding on the party who makes it (unless he is allowed to withdraw it). An informal admission is not deliberately made for the purpose of the proceedings. Even if proved, it is not binding on the maker, who is entitled to explain it away if he can. There is quite likely, also, to be a dispute about whether an informal admission was made at all, or about its terms, or about the sense in which it should be understood. Formal admissions, which are recorded, are far less likely to give rise to these problems. Of course, the fact that someone has said something contrary to his interest will generally increase the probability that what he said was true. For example, in an action for negligence based on a road traffic accident the claimant might adduce evidence that immediately after the accident the defendant said to him, 'I'm terribly sorry; that was entirely my fault. I was distracted by my children in the back of the car'. That clearly constitutes an admission of liability, but unless (as is extremely unlikely) it is *formally* admitted by the defendant, the claimant will have to prove by evidence that it was the defendant who was solely responsible for the collision. The fact that an admission was made can, of course, be used to prove this. Similarly, in a criminal case, a defendant who was charged with murder might say during an interview with the police, 'All right; I admit I used the dead man's credit card'. That would almost certainly be a confession within the meaning of s 82(1) of the Police and Criminal Evidence Act 1984, but unless the defence formally admitted that the defendant *did* use the dead man's card, that fact would need to be proved by evidence at trial. How, then, are formal admissions made?

IN CIVIL TRIALS

By r 14.1 of the Civil Procedure Rules, a party may admit the whole or any part of another party's case. He may do this by giving notice in writing, for example, in a statement of case or by letter. Admissions can also be made in other ways:

- by default, where a defendant fails to deal in his defence with an allegation made by a claimant;[1]
- in response to a notice to admit facts;[2]
- in response to a written request or court order to give additional information.[3]

IN CRIMINAL TRIALS

At common law, the rule was that there could be no formal admissions, at least by a defendant, in criminal proceedings. The basis of this was that it was contrary to public interest to waive the rules of evidence by consent in criminal cases. As Sir John Coleridge said in *AG for New South Wales v Bertrand*:

---

1   CPR, r 16.5(5).
2   CPR, r 32.18.
3   CPR, rr 18.1 and 26.5(3).

The object of a trial is the administration of justice in a course as free from doubt or chance of miscarriage as merely human administration of it can be – not the interests of either party. This remark very much lessens the importance of a prisoner's consent, even when he is advised by counsel, and substantially, not of course literally, affirms the wisdom of the common understanding in the profession, that a prisoner can consent to nothing.[4]

A change in this respect was proposed by the Criminal Law Revision Committee in its 9th Report on Evidence.[5] The Committee thought that if one party was willing to treat something as proved, it was unnecessary for the other party to have the burden of proving it. The existing law could lead to considerable waste of time and money, as, for example, in a conspiracy trial mentioned by the Committee, in which it had been necessary to bring a witness from Los Angeles to England in order to prove a receipt that the defendant did not dispute. (This was before the time when proof could be made by an agreed written statement, a reform that the Ninth Report also recommended.) Effect was given to the Committee's proposals in s 10 of the Criminal Justice Act 1967, which provided as follows:

(1) Subject to the provisions of this section, any fact of which oral evidence may be given in any criminal proceedings may be admitted for the purpose of those proceedings by or on behalf of the prosecutor or defendant, and the admission by any party of any such fact under this section shall as against that party be conclusive evidence in those proceedings of the fact admitted.

(2) An admission under this section:

    (a) may be made before or at the proceedings;

    (b) if made otherwise than in court, shall be in writing;

    (c) if made in writing by an individual, shall purport to be signed by the person making it and, if so made by a body corporate, shall purport to be signed by a director or manager, or the secretary or clerk, or some other similar officer of the body corporate;

    (d) if made on behalf of a defendant who is an individual, shall be made by his counsel or solicitor;

    (e) if made at any stage before the trial by a defendant who is an individual, must be approved by his counsel or solicitor (whether at the time it was made or subsequently) before or at the proceedings in question.

(3) An admission under this section for the purpose of proceedings relating to any matter shall be treated as an admission for the purpose of any subsequent criminal proceedings relating to that matter (including any appeal or re-trial).

---

4   (1867) LR 1 PC 520, p 534.

5   Cmnd 3145, 1966.

(4)   An admission under this section may with the leave of the court be withdrawn in the proceedings for the purpose of which it is made or any subsequent criminal proceedings relating to the same matter.

Where there is a plea of not guilty at a plea and directions hearing, both prosecution and defence are expected to inform the court of facts which are to be admitted and which can be reduced into writing under s 10(2)(b).[6]

JUDICIAL NOTICE

Broadly speaking, 'judicial notice' refers to the acceptance by a judicial tribunal of the truth of a fact without formal proof, on the ground that it is within the knowledge of the tribunal itself.[7] Beyond this, statements of a general nature are hard to make. Judges and writers have commonly referred to 'the doctrine of judicial notice', but this is not an apt expression because it suggests a unity and coherence that the topic does not possess. It is not even possible to say whether, in all circumstances, a judge has a duty rather than a discretion to take judicial notice of a particular fact. As will be shown, there are some statutory provisions that require judicial notice to be taken; in those cases a duty will obviously exist, but beyond that the position is unclear. For example, in *R v Aspinall*, Brett JA said that 'judges are entitled *and bound* to take judicial notice of that which is the common knowledge of the great majority of mankind and of the great majority of men of business',[8] but according to Cross and Tapper,[9] a judge has a discretion whether or not to take judicial notice of any fact, and there is support for this contention in Commonwealth authority. For example, in *R v Zundel*,[10] a decision of the Ontario Court of Appeal, the defendant was charged with an offence, contrary to s 177 of the Criminal Code, of spreading false news by publishing a pamphlet denying that the Holocaust occurred. His defence was, in part, his belief in the truth of what he had published. Among a number of issues raised on appeal was a submission by the prosecution that the trial judge had erred in failing, at the prosecution's request, to take judicial notice of the fact that the Holocaust did occur. The court upheld his refusal to do so, and stated, relying on works by Thayer and Phipson,[11] that judges have a wide discretion as to matters of which they will take

---

6   *Practice Direction (Criminal: Consolidated)* [2002] 3 All ER 904, para 41.13.

7   Nokes, 1967, p 54.

8   (1876) 2 QBD 48, pp 61–62, emphasis added. See also the judgment of Clauson LJ in *McQuaker v Goddard* [1940] 1 KB 687.

9   Tapper, 2007, p 82.

10   (1987) 35 DLR (4th) 338. In *Mullen v Hackney London Borough Council* [1997] 1 WLR 1103 the Court of Appeal assumed without argument that a discretion existed.

11   Thayer, 1898, p 309; *Phipson on Evidence*, 13th edn, p 26.

judicial notice, and *may* notice matters which they cannot be *required* to notice. The court pointed out that the generally accepted modern view was that where a court takes judicial notice that is final, in the sense that the court declares that it will find that a fact exists or will direct the jury to do so. The effect of such a direction in this case would have been to tell the jury that they must conclude the fact of the Holocaust to be so notorious as to be indisputable by reasonable men and women. From that they might have inferred that the defendant knew that what he had published was false, and so the operation of judicial notice would have been gravely prejudicial to the defence. Accordingly, the trial judge had exercised his discretion properly.

The idea of taking judicial notice of facts has been familiar to English lawyers for over 650 years.[12] Various rationales for the practice have been suggested, and a writer's favoured rationale tends to affect his view of the scope and effect of judicial notice. It has been suggested, for example, that the purpose of judicial notice is to save the time and expense involved in adducing formal evidence of matters that are simply *likely to be true*.[13] Another, rather different, view is that the practice reduces the risk of diversion and confusion that would result from disputing what is really *indisputable*. This view was best expressed by EM Morgan:

> In the practical operation of our adversary system, where so much does in fact depend upon the financial resources of the respective parties and the comparative diligence, skill and other qualities of contending counsel, it is especially important that a party be prevented from perverting the true function of the court by presenting a moot issue or securing a wrong result by disputing what is demonstrably indisputable among reasonable persons.[14]

Yet another justification is that judicial notice can make for consistency between cases, in particular by operating as a form of judicial control over the jury. For example, courts take judicial notice of the fact that flick knives and butterfly knives are offensive weapons in themselves for the purposes of s 1 of the Prevention of Crime Act 1953, and juries are to be directed accordingly.[15]

Judicial notice may be applied to facts which a judge can be called upon to accept *either* from his general knowledge of them, *or* from inquiries to be made by him for his own information from sources to which it is proper for him to refer.[16] In addition, statutes have sometimes provided that judicial notice be taken of certain matters. I shall therefore consider this topic under the following heads:

---

12   Nokes, 1958, p 61, citing *Botton v Wilton* (1302) YB 30 & 31 Edw I (RS), pp 256, 258.

13   Thayer, 1898, p 309.

14   Morgan, 1956, p 42.

15   *R v Simpson* [1983] 3 All ER 789; *DPP v Hynde* [1998] 1 All ER 649. For the definition of a butterfly knife, see the schedule to the Criminal Justice Act 1988 (Offensive Weapons) Order 1988 (SI 1988/2019).

16   *Commonwealth Shipping Representative v P & O Branch Service* [1923] AC 191, p 212.

(a)   Facts judicially noticed without inquiry.

(b)   Facts judicially noticed after inquiry.

(c)   Some examples of statutory provisions for judicial notice.

(d)   Problems associated with judicial notice.

FACTS JUDICIALLY NOTICED WITHOUT INQUIRY

These are facts that are regarded as matters of common knowledge. Thus, in *R v Luffe*,[17] the question arose as to a child's legitimacy. The evidence was that the husband did not have access to the wife until a fortnight before the birth, and the court took judicial notice of the fact that he could not have been the father. Lord Ellenborough CJ remarked:

> Here . . . in nature the fact may certainly be known that the husband, who had no access until within a fortnight of his wife's delivery, could not be the actual father of the child. Where the thing cannot certainly be known, we must call in aid such probable evidence as can be resorted to, and the intervention of a jury must, in all cases in which it is practicable, be had to decide thereupon; but where the question arises as it does here, and where it may certainly be known from the invariable course of nature, as in this case it may, that no birth could be occasioned and produced within those limits of time, we may venture to lay down the rule plainly and broadly, without any danger arising from the precedent . . .[18]

Similarly, courts have taken judicial notice of the fact that the nature of an opera singer's work differs from that of an ordinary hired labourer;[19] that cats are kept for domestic purposes;[20] that boys have mischievous natures;[21] that there are large numbers of motor cars and motor buses in the streets of London, and that a boy employed to ride a bicycle through London traffic runs the risk of injury by collision with other vehicles;[22] that people who go to hotels do not like having their nights disturbed;[23] and that the reception of television has become a very common feature of domestic life, and is enjoyed almost entirely for recreational purposes.[24]

More recently, judicial notice has been taken of the fact that stripes are often used on football shirts to identify teams;[25] that Elvis Presley was resident in the USA and performed mainly there;[26] that more men than women leave surviving

---

17   (1807) 8 East 193.

18   *Ibid*, pp 201–02.

19   *Lumley v Gye* (1853) 2 E&B 216, pp 266–67.

20   *Nye v Niblett* [1918] 1 KB 23.

21   *Clayton v Hardwicke Colliery Co Ltd* (1915) 85 LJKB 292.

22   *Dennis v AJ White and Co* [1916] 2 KB 6; [1917] AC 479, p 491.

23   *Andreae v Selfridge and Co Ltd* [1938] Ch 1.

24   *Bridlington Relay Ltd v Yorkshire Electricity Board* [1965] Ch 436, p 446.

25   *Cook & Hunt's Design Application* [1979] RPC 197.

26   *RCA Corp v Pollard* [1982] 2 All ER 468.

spouses;[27] that a higher proportion of women than men are secondary earners and that, accordingly, a higher proportion of women than men would find it impossible in practice to comply with a direction of their employer which involved moving house;[28] that there has been a huge expansion of hiring and hire purchase, especially of motor vehicles, since World War II;[29] and that lintels above windows are an extremely common feature of twentieth-century houses.[30]

What is common knowledge differs, of course, according to time and place. Thus, the common knowledge of Aesop's fables that was assumed in 1848 would not be assumed today.[31] A fact may be common knowledge only among a class of the community, such as those interested in a particular sport or other form of entertainment, and where that is likely to be the case it is best not to assume that judicial notice will be taken.

FACTS JUDICIALLY NOTICED AFTER INQUIRY

Whenever the meaning of words arises, however technical or obscure, then, unless there is some dispute about it, it is common practice for the court to inform itself by any means that is reliable and ready to hand. Counsel usually give any necessary explanation, or reference may be made to a dictionary.[32] For the purposes of more complicated inquiries, reference may be made to such sources as reports of earlier cases, certificates from responsible officials, letters from Secretaries of State or statements made in court by counsel on their behalf, works of reference and the oral statements of witnesses. The cases show that such inquiries have generally been made in at least three types of case: where information is required about current political or diplomatic matters; about historical facts; and about customs, including professional practices.

Current political and diplomatic matters

If a court needs information about matters of this kind, it may formally ask a government minister to provide it. The answer will be regarded as conclusive in relation to the matters with which it deals. A leading case that illustrates this approach is *Duff Development Co Ltd v Government of Kelantan*.[33] In 1912, the Government of Kelantan, which was situated in the Malay Peninsula, granted the appellant company certain mining and other rights by an agreement containing an arbitration clause.

---

27   *Turner v The Labour Party* [1987] IRLR 101.

28   *Meade-Hill and Another v British Council* [1995] ICR 847.

29   *Salford Van Hire (Contracts) Ltd v Bocholt Developments Ltd* [1995] CLC 611.

30   *Eden v West & Company* [2002] EWCA Civ 991.

31   *Hoare v Silverlock* (1848) 12 QBD 624.

32   *Baldwin & Francis Ltd v Patents Appeal Tribunal* [1959] AC 663, p 691.

33   [1924] AC 797.

Disputes later arose. These were referred to an arbitrator, who made an award in favour of the company. The company subsequently obtained a court order giving it leave to enforce the award. The Government applied to set aside the order on the ground that Kelantan was a Sovereign independent State, and so entitled to immunity from legal process. Before setting aside the order, the master asked the Secretary of State for the Colonies for information as to the status of Kelantan. He received in reply an official letter stating that Kelantan was an independent State and its Sultan the sovereign ruler. It was ultimately held by the House of Lords that this letter was conclusive of the question of sovereignty. Viscount Cave stated:

> It has for some time been the practice of our courts, when such a question is raised, to take judicial notice of the sovereignty of a State, and for that purpose (in any case of uncertainty) to seek information from a Secretary of State; and when information is so obtained the court does not permit it to be questioned by the parties.[34]

Judicial notice has similarly been used in determining the extent of the monarch's territorial sovereignty;[35] whether a person was entitled to diplomatic immunity;[36] and whether a state of war existed between this country and a foreign State.[37]

Historical facts

It was held by the Judicial Committee of the Privy Council in *Read v Bishop of Lincoln*[38] that when it is important to ascertain ancient facts of a public nature, the law permits historical works to be referred to. In the opinion delivered by Lord Halsbury LC, reference was made to earlier occasions when such works had been referred to, and in order to resolve questions concerning Church ritual raised by the *Read* case, Lord Halsbury himself referred in his opinion to the first prayer book of King Edward VI, Wither's *Hymns and Songs of the Church*, which had been licensed by James I and Charles I, and to the writings of Plutarch and St Paul.[39]

The view was formerly taken that while judicial notice might be taken of ancient facts of a public nature, it would not extend to facts of a contemporary, or nearly contemporary kind. Thus, in *Commonwealth Shipping Representative v P & O Branch Service*,[40] Viscount Cave LC said that he knew of no authority for the proposition that the date of a particular event in a modern war might be stated without proof and an inference based on it. A more liberal approach was, however,

---

34   (1924) AC 797, pp 805–06.

35   *The Fagernes* [1927] P 311.

36   *Engelke v Musman* [1928] AC 433.

37   *R v Bottrill ex p Kuechenmeister* [1947] 1 KB 41.

38   [1892] AC 644.

39   *Ibid*, pp 656, 658, 660.

40   [1923] AC 191, p 197. See also Lord Atkinson at p 206.

suggested by Lord Dunedin, who stated that although he would not feel justified in resting any conclusion on such things as the particular dates when certain operations of war were begun or were in progress, when those dates had not been proved but had to be supplied from his own knowledge, nevertheless:

> ... it is settled by authority that a judge may be aware that there is a state of war; and by that I do not understand a vague consciousness such as may have been felt by an ancient Roman when he noticed that the Temple of Janus was open, but an intelligent apprehension of the state of war as it is and the theatre of the operations thereof.[41]

More recent authority suggests that judicial knowledge may be taken of contemporary, or near contemporary, events. In *Monarch Steamship Co Ltd v Karlshamns Oljefabriker (A/B)*,[42] the question arose of whether British shipowners who were parties to a charterparty made in April 1939 should have foreseen that war might break out, with the resulting loss or diversion of the vessel. In the House of Lords, Lord du Parcq said that it was not necessary that the outbreak of war should have been contemplated as something certain and unavoidable; it was enough if the parties might reasonably be assumed to have contemplated a war and the likelihood that it would lead to such an embargo as in fact occurred. He continued, 'Your Lordships are entitled ... to take judicial notice of the facts of history, whether past or contemporaneous with ourselves'. Several of the Law Lords did so. Lord du Parcq himself referred to the Prime Minister's announcement on 31 March 1939 of the guarantee given to Poland, and Lord Wright said:

> There was indeed in 1939 the general fear that there might be war. Munich, the Sudetenland, the invasion by Germany of Czechoslovakia, the difficulty about the Polish Corridor, were matters of common knowledge.[43]

Customs

Judicial notice may be taken of general customs that have been proved in earlier cases, despite the rule[44] that a court cannot treat a fact as proved on the basis of evidence heard in a previous case. For example, in *George v Davies*,[45] the plaintiff, a domestic servant, had entered the defendant's service on 3 November 1910 at yearly wages, payable monthly, without an express agreement as to notice. On 17 November, she gave notice to leave at the expiration of the first month of her service. She left on

---

41   (1923) AC 191, p 205.
42   [1949] AC 196. See also *Cornelius v Banque Franco-Serbe* [1941] 2 All ER 728; *R v Birkenhead Borough JJ ex p Smith* [1954] 1 WLR 471.
43   [1949] AC 196, pp 222, 234. See also pp 214, 215.
44   See, eg, *Roper v Taylor's Central Garages (Exeter) Ltd* [1951] 2 TLR 284.
45   [1911] 2 KB 445.

3 December. The defendant refused to pay her wages for the month during which she had been in service on the ground that she had left without giving one month's notice. The plaintiff brought an action in the county court to recover the wages, alleging a custom that either party to the contract of hire of a domestic servant was entitled, in the absence of an express agreement, to determine the service at the end of the first month by notice given at or before the expiration of the first fortnight. She called no evidence in support of the custom, but the county court judge said that he had taken judicial notice of the custom in previous cases and would do so again in this one. Accordingly, he gave judgment for the plaintiff. On appeal, the Divisional Court[46] held that he had been entitled to do so. Bray J declared, 'A time must come when a county court judge, having had the question of the existence of this custom before him in other cases, is entitled to say that he will take judicial notice of it, and will not require it to be proved by evidence in each case'.[47] Of course, what is judicially noticed is the existence of the custom; this does not preclude evidence that there was a departure from the custom on a particular occasion. Among other customs judicially noticed have been the practice of the Ordnance Survey Office in compiling ordnance survey maps[48] and, it seems, good accountancy practices.[49]

STATUTORY PROVISIONS

Several Acts of Parliament direct the courts to take judicial notice of various matters. For example, the Interpretation Act 1978 provides (re-enacting earlier provisions) that every Act passed after 1850 shall be a public Act and judicially noticed as such unless the contrary is expressly provided.[50] By s 3(2) of the European Communities Act 1972, judicial notice is to be taken of various treaties,[51] of the Official Journal of the Communities, and of any decision of, or expression of opinion by, the European Court on questions concerning the meaning or effect of any of the treaties or Community instruments. There is no express provision for taking judicial notice of statutory instruments, but some have been so frequently relied on that judicial notice will be taken of them.[52] Judicial notice will not, however, be taken of foreign law; expert evidence is required on this subject.[53]

PROBLEMS ASSOCIATED WITH JUDICIAL NOTICE

The ground covered so far may appear misleadingly simple. In fact, the topic of judicial notice gives rise to a number of problems, which may be grouped together

---

46   The Divisional Court at that time heard appeals from county courts.

47   [1911] 2 KB 445, pp 447–48.

48   *Davey v Harrow Corp* [1958] 1 QB 60, p 69.

49   *Heather v P-E Consulting Group Ltd* [1973] 1 Ch 189, pp 218, 224.

50   Interpretation Act 1978, ss 3, 22(1) and Sched 2, para 2.

51   European Communities Act 1972, ss 1(2) and Pt 1 of Sched 1.

52   See, eg, *R v Jones* [1969] 3 All ER 1559 (SI approving the breathalyser Alcotest R 80 device).

53   *R v Ofori* (1994) 99 Cr App R 223; *R v Okolle* (2000) *The Times*, 16 June.

in four categories. These include: the relationship of judicial notice and evidence; the effect of judicial notice; the scope of judicial notice; and the use of personal knowledge by judges, jurors, and others exercising a judicial function.[54]

Relationship between judicial notice and evidence

It has been suggested in the past that judicial notice is a form of proof. Sir JF Stephen changed his mind on the matter. He originally included judicial notice in a chapter of his *Digest of the Law of Evidence* headed 'Facts Which Need Not be Proved – Judicial Notice'.[55] In the 3rd edition, he changed the heading to 'Facts Proved Otherwise than by Evidence' and this was followed in later editions.[56] The current view, however, is that judicial notice is not properly regarded as a form of *proof*, rather, it is a *substitute* for proof.[57]

Where judicial notice is taken without inquiry, it is clear that no process of proof is involved, because no material containing information is produced by either party. But is judicial notice *after* inquiry based on a process of proof? It has been shown already that the court may accept information as part of its inquiry from such diverse sources as written statements from a minister of the Crown, statements made in court by counsel on behalf of a minister, a court's earlier decision about the existence of a custom, and historical or other works of reference. The opinions of judges on whether judicial notice is a form of proof have not been consistent. In *Duff Development Co Ltd v Government of Kelantan*, Lord Finlay said of cases where a minister of the Crown provides information about the sovereignty of a foreign State, 'Such information is not in the nature of evidence; it is a statement by the sovereign of this country through one of his ministers upon a matter which is peculiarly within his cognisance'. However, in the same case, Lord Sumner said that the minister's statement was the 'best evidence', and that where such a statement was provided, 'other evidence' was neither admissible nor needed.[58] However, in *Commonwealth Shipping Representative v P & O Branch Service*, Lord Sumner described the taking of judicial notice as involving that 'at the stage when evidence of material facts can be properly received, certain facts may be *deemed* to be established, although not proved by sworn testimony, or by the production, out of proper custody, of documents which speak for themselves'.[59]

---

54   As well as Nokes, 1958; Morgan, 1956; and Thayer, 1898, see also Davis, 1955; Manchester, 1979; McConville, 1979; Carter, 1982, pp 88–99.

55   Stephen, 1877, Chapter VII.

56   See, commenting on the change, Thayer, 1890, p 288, fn 1.

57   See, eg, Carter, 1990, p 123.

58   [1924] AC 797, pp 813, 824.

59   [1923] AC 191, p 212, emphasis added.

The position was scarcely clarified by the Court of Appeal in *McQuaker v Goddard*.[60] In that case, the plaintiff had been bitten by a camel at Chessington Zoo. As the law then stood, it was necessary to determine, for purposes of liability, whether camels were wild or tame animals. The trial judge concluded that they belonged to the latter class. He reached this conclusion after he had consulted books about camels and had heard witnesses from each party on the nature and habits of camels. The Court of Appeal upheld his decision. The evidential status of the information presented to him was discussed in the judgment of Clauson LJ. He said of the evidence given by the witnesses about camels:

> That evidence is not, it must be understood, in the ordinary sense evidence bearing upon an issue of fact. In my view the exact position is this. The judge takes judicial notice of the ordinary course of nature, and in this particular case of the ordinary course of nature in regard to the position of camels among other animals. The reason why the evidence was given was for the assistance of the judge in forming his view as to what the ordinary course of nature in this regard in fact is, a matter *of which he is supposed to have complete knowledge* . . . When that evidence was given and weighed up with the statements in the books of reference which were referred to, the facts became perfectly plain; and the learned judge was able without any difficulty whatever to give a correct statement of the natural phenomena material to the matter in question, of which he was bound to take judicial notice.[61]

Only Clauson LJ relied explicitly on judicial notice as the basis for his judgment. The key to understanding what he said is to realise that he was adopting an old legal fiction that judges have complete knowledge of the ordinary course of nature, and that witnesses and reference books are no more than devices for refreshing the judge's memory.[62] MacKinnon LJ said nothing on the subject, concluding only: 'The learned judge has held, upon overwhelming evidence, that the camel is within the class of tame animals, and not within the class of wild animals.'[63] However, Scott LJ seems to have adopted what Clauson LJ said on the subject, saying in the course of his judgment:

> [I]t is also well to remember that it is the function of the judge and not of the jury to decide whether an animal belongs to the class of domestic animals or to the class of wild animals. I need say no more for the moment on this head – I think Clauson LJ will probably add a few words on that aspect of the case.[64]

---

60 [1940] 1 KB 687.

61 *Ibid*, pp 700, 701, emphasis added. See also *Behrens v Bertram Mills Circus Ltd* [1957] 2 QB 1.

62 Cf Schiff, 1963, p 348.

63 [1940] 1 KB 687, p 699.

64 *Ibid*, p 696.

But it seems as if Scott LJ did accept that taking judicial notice involved a process of proof. When all three judgments had been delivered, counsel for the appellant asked for leave to appeal to the House of Lords. Scott LJ responded:

> I do not think we ought to give that leave. *On the facts proved, of which the learned judge and this court are entitled to take judicial notice,* there is nowhere in the world a camel which is wild and not domesticated and used in the service of man, and the law is clear that in England, as elsewhere, the camel is a domesticated animal. It is not open to you to contend that the camel is a wild animal anywhere.[65]

What is clear from *McQuaker v Goddard* is that where judicial notice is taken after inquiry, that inquiry is not limited by the ordinary rules of evidence. No member of the Court of Appeal, for example, suggested that the trial judge had improperly referred to books of reference on the subject of camels. However, where inquiry is made, and particularly where witnesses are heard, it is artificial to regard judicial notice as being wholly divorced from proof.

Effect of taking judicial notice

When judicial notice is taken, is the matter noticed conclusive and indisputable, or is the effect merely to establish a fact that may be rebutted by other evidence? Certainly in some cases judicial notice will be conclusive, as the cases in relation to political and constitutional affairs have shown.[66] The problem arises where judicial notice is taken of facts that are supposed to be part of common knowledge. The answer appears to be that, despite some occasional statements to the contrary,[67] judicial notice is final. It follows that a judge who has taken judicial notice of a fact must instruct a jury, if the case is being tried with one, that they must accept as a fact the matter noticed, and he should not admit evidence to show anything to the contrary.[68] Misunderstanding on this point can arise if the fact of which judicial notice is taken is not defined with sufficient clarity. For example, if a court takes judicial notice that a particular custom exists, that settles that *at the time of the court's decision* the custom did exist, but that will be no bar to proving in a later case that the custom was not in fact followed[69] or, where sufficient time has passed, that the custom has changed or has ceased to exist.

---

65   [1940] 1 KB 687, p 701, emphasis added.

66   See above, p 58.

67   See, eg, Thayer, 1898, pp 308–09.

68   McConville, 1979, p 72; Nokes, 1958, pp 70–75.

69   It is in this sense that Lord Goddard CJ's observation in *Davey v Harrow Corp* [1958] 1 QB 60, p 69, is best understood. He said that the courts could in future take notice of a practice of the Ordnance Survey Office as 'at least *prima facie* evidence' of what a line on an ordnance survey map represents. (See Carter, 1982, p 94.)

Scope of judicial notice

Two main views have been taken of the scope of judicial notice. On one view, which may be called the broad view, judges are taking judicial notice of facts all the time, without any overt reference to the matter. The reason for this is that when conducting a process of judicial reasoning, as of any other reasoning, not a step can be taken without assuming something that has not been proved.[70] This is particularly true, as we have seen above in Chapter 1, when assessing the relevance or weight of a given item of evidence. The process has been vividly described by Davis:

> When a judge or an officer starts to write findings of fact and conclusions of law, every paragraph necessarily contains facts that have not been proved with evidence. When the judge or officer looks at the testimony of the first witness, he uses extra-record information about the meaning of words in the English language, and this is so whether or not he consults the dictionary, and whether or not the meaning of a word is at issue between the parties. His knowledge of the meaning of the word 'the' comes from beyond the record. He assumes that a man is not 30 ft tall, that trains run on rails, that automobiles are not flying machines, that France is outside the United States, and that coal is a fuel. He assumes the existence of human beings, of organised government, of a legal system, of courts, of businesses, of corporations. Every simple case involves the assumption of hundreds of facts that have not been proved.[71]

If this view is right, then, as Cross and Tapper have stated, 'the tacit applications of the doctrine of judicial notice are more numerous and more important than the express ones'.[72]

There are those, however, who have preferred to maintain a more restrictive view. Sir Richard Eggleston, for example, has acknowledged that a judge or jury must make use of general knowledge to interpret the evidence. However, he continued, 'This is not a question of judicial notice, but of the tribunal relying on its own experience as to the ordinary course of human affairs'.[73] In *Burns v Lipman*,[74] the High Court of Australia observed that while a juror or judge might take into account in a road traffic negligence case what usually occurs on a highway, that knowledge is not properly to be regarded as judicial notice.

But it is difficult to see how this distinction can be maintained, because there seems to be no difference between notorious facts (of which judicial notice will be taken) and general knowledge (which can be used only to help the judge interpret the evidence). As Lord Sumner said in *Commonwealth Shipping Representative v P & O*

---

70   Thayer, 1898, pp 270, 279.

71   Davis, 1955, p 975.

72   Tapper, 1999, p 77. Another effect is that it makes the word 'doctrine' even less appropriate if it refers to such a variety of circumstances.

73   Eggleston, 1983, pp 143–44. See also Carter, 1982, p 94.

74   (1974) 132 CLR 157.

Branch Service, 'Judicial notice refers to facts, which a judge can be called upon to receive and to act upon, *either from his general knowledge of them*, or from inquiries to be made by himself for his own information from sources to which it is proper for him to refer'.[75] Nor is the distinction always made in practice, as can be seen from the speeches in *Monarch Steamship Co Ltd v Karlshamns Oljefabriker (A/B)*.[76]

The division of opinion about the scope of judicial notice is probably a result of different rationales that have been suggested for the practice. If, like Morgan, you regard judicial notice as a device for filtering out evidence about matters that are really unarguable, you will tend to favour restricting its scope to notorious or readily ascertainable facts, making its application mandatory instead of discretionary, and the effect of its application conclusive. If, like Thayer, you prefer to see judicial notice as a labour saving device in litigation, its scope can be wider and its application discretionary. Its effect might even be defeasible in the light of further evidence.[77]

USE OF PERSONAL KNOWLEDGE

While it seems clear that a tribunal may make use of its *general* knowledge by virtue of judicial notice, or as part of its interpretation of the evidence if a narrow view of judicial notice is taken, it is also said that neither judges nor jurors can make use of their purely *personal* knowledge in reaching a decision.[78] A line of cases suggests that a county court judge may take into account his own knowledge of labour conditions in the area where he sits, but these cases were all decided under the Workmen's Compensation Acts, under which the judge's function was that of an arbitrator. Even in those cases, a judge was expected to apply the common knowledge of everyone in the district, and was not supposed to rely on his personal knowledge of highly specialised matters.[79]

The Divisional Court has on several occasions held that magistrates have properly applied their own knowledge of local conditions. In *Ingram v Percival*,[80] the

---

75   [1923] AC 191, p 212, emphasis added.

76   [1949] AC 196.

77   Thayer, 1898, p 309.

78   Formerly, jurors were entitled and expected to use personal knowledge: see *Bushell's Case* (1670) Vaugh 135. But by the early 19th century, the position had changed: *R v Sutton* (1816) 4 M&S 532; *R v Rosser* (1836) 7 C&P 648.

79   *Roberts & Ruthven Ltd v Hall* (1912) 5 BWCC 331; *Peart v Bolckow, Vaughan and Co Ltd* [1925] 1 KB 399; *Keane v Mount Vernon Colliery Co Ltd* [1933] AC 309; *Reynolds v Llanelly Associated Tinplate Co Ltd* [1948] 1 All ER 140. Cf *Mullen v Hackney LBC* [1997] 1 WLR 1103, where these matters were apparently not drawn to the attention of the Court of Appeal. See further Allen, 1998.

80   [1969] 1 QB 548.

defendant was convicted of an offence under s 11 of the Salmon and Freshwater Fisheries Act 1923, which made it an offence to place a 'fixed engine' of any description for taking salmon or migratory trout in any inland or tidal waters. The justices found that the defendant had used a net for taking salmon and migratory trout in waters near the North Pier at Sunderland, and that the net was a fixed engine within the meaning of the statute. They also found that the net was fixed in the sea about 100 yds from the shore, and that the location was in tidal waters. The sole question in the Divisional Court was whether the justices had been entitled to find that at the position where the net was found there was 'a perceptible, a real, ebb and flow of the tide, notwithstanding that it was fixed . . . below low water mark'. The justices in the case said:

> We considered that tidal waters consist of waters affected by a lateral or horizontal flow of water as distinct from a vertical rise and fall and it is within our knowledge that such a flow extends beyond low water mark and is experienced at more than 100 yds from the shore. We therefore hold that in this case the net was in tidal waters.

Lord Parker CJ held that the justices were fully entitled to make use of that knowledge which they said they had. 'It has always been recognised,' he said, 'that justices may and should – after all, they are local justices – take into consideration matters which they know of their own knowledge, and particularly matters in regard to the locality, whether it be on land, as it seems to me, or in water.'[81]

This decision has been criticised on the ground that the tidal nature of the waters was apparently not notorious in the locality, and that in this case the justices were not using background knowledge to interpret evidence about the matter because there was no evidence on the question whether the waters were tidal or not. They were therefore using their own private knowledge in the place of evidence in order to find a fact in issue.[82] A better example of justices taking their knowledge of local conditions into account can be found in *Paul v DPP*.[83] The defendant was alleged to have been 'kerb crawling' in his car and to have stopped a woman who was a known prostitute. It was said that after a short conversation she got into his car. Although he was observed by police officers, who followed the car and arrested him, there were no other vehicles or pedestrians in the area at the time. He was charged under s 1(1) of the Sexual Offences Act 1985 with soliciting a woman in a street for the purposes of prostitution in such manner or circumstances as to be likely to cause a nuisance to other persons in the neighbourhood. In reaching their decision that the defendant's actions were likely to cause a nuisance of this kind, the justices took into account their own knowledge that the area had a heavily residential population, and that it was a frequent haunt of prostitutes, who attracted a constant procession of cars at

---

81   [1969] 1 QB 548, p 555.
82   Carter, 1982, pp 98–99.
83   (1990) 90 Cr App R 173.

night. The Divisional Court held that the justices had been right to take their local knowledge into account. In this case, of course, it was clear that the justices had the common knowledge of anybody living in that locality; it is at best unclear that the justices in *Ingram v Percival* were in that position.

Other cases suggest that it may be difficult, if not impossible, for magistrates to disregard their own private knowledge, but that their use of it will be legitimate if confined to their interpretation of evidence in the case. In *R v Field and Others ex p White*,[84] a grocer had been prosecuted under s 6 of the Sale of Food and Drugs Act 1875 for selling a packet of cocoa which, when analysed, had been found to contain 80% starch and sugar. Under the statute, an offence was not committed where any ingredient not injurious to health had been added if it was required for the production or preparation of the food or drug as an article of commerce. The justices had all served in the navy, and this had apparently made them experts in the constitution of cocoa. They concluded that it was a matter of common knowledge that cocoa, as an article of commerce, must necessarily contain a large proportion of other ingredients. They therefore dismissed the complaint. Their decision was upheld. In delivering judgment, Wills J said that the justices had:

> . . . decided the case as they did upon their own knowledge; and in the nature of things, no one in determining a case of this kind can discard his own particular knowledge of a subject of this kind. I might as well be asked to decide a question as to the sufficiency of an Alpine rope without bringing my personal knowledge into play.[85]

The use by justices of their personal knowledge was considered by the Divisional Court in *Wetherall v Harrison*.[86] The defendant was charged with failing to provide a specimen of blood without reasonable excuse, contrary to s 9(3) of the Road Traffic Act 1972. He had reacted abnormally and struggled when a doctor had tried to take the specimen. The doctor gave evidence to the effect that the defendant's reaction had not been genuine, and that he had been pretending to have a fit. The defendant in evidence stated that he had been apprehensive in the past when required to have an injection, and that on this occasion he had felt hot and faint and had had difficulty in breathing. He called no expert medical evidence. Among the justices was a doctor who gave his fellow justices his professional opinion as to the genuineness of the defendant's reaction. The justices also had a layman's experience of wartime inoculations and the fear that they could create in certain individuals. They concluded that the defendant had suffered a hysterical reaction from his fear of the needle, and that he therefore had a reasonable excuse for failing to provide the sample. The prosecutor appealed. In dismissing the appeal, Lord Widgery CJ said:

---

84   (1895) 64 LJMC 158.
85   *Ibid*, p 160. The judge was a distinguished mountaineer.
86   [1976] 1 QB 773.

I do not think the position of a justice of the peace is the same, in this regard, as the position of a trained judge. If you have a judge sitting alone, trying a civil case, it is perfectly feasible and sensible that he should be instructed and trained to exclude certain factors from his consideration of the problem. Justices are not so trained. They are much more like jurymen in this respect. I think it would be wrong to start with the proposition that justices' use of their own local or personal knowledge is governed by exactly the same rule as is laid down in the case of trained judges. I do not believe that a serious restriction on a justice's use of his own knowledge or the knowledge of his colleagues can really be enforced. Laymen (by which I mean non-lawyers) sitting as justices considering a case which has just been heard before them lack the ability to put out of their minds certain features of the case. In particular, if the justice is a specialist . . . it is not possible for him to approach the decision in the case as though he had not got that training, and indeed I think it would be a very bad thing if he had to. In a sense, the bench of justices are like a jury, they are a cross-section of people, and one of the advantages which they have is that they bring a lot of varied experience into the court room and use it.[87]

Lord Widgery CJ emphasised, however, that although such special knowledge could be used to *interpret* the evidence given in court, it must not be used to *contradict* it. The same point was made by O'Connor J, who said that a justice with specialised knowledge 'must not start substituting what he might have said in evidence, as opposed to using his knowledge to assess the evidence which is available'.[88] Whether such a distinction can be maintained in practice may well be doubted. Perhaps for this reason it was stated by the Divisional Court in *Bowman v DPP*[89] that justices must be extremely circumspect in using their own local knowledge. They should inform the parties if they are likely to use such knowledge, so as to give an opportunity for comment on the knowledge that they claim to have. Another result of what was said in *Wetherall v Harrison* appears to be that a *judge* who has expert knowledge is expected to put that knowledge entirely to one side, so that someone in the position of Wills J would have to forget, for the purposes of the trial, his knowledge of Alpine ropes.[90]

The position of members of industrial tribunals was dealt with by the Employment Appeal Tribunal in *Dugdale v Kraft Foods Ltd*,[91] where Phillips J said that members of such tribunals are appointed because of their special knowledge and experience. They are entitled to draw on it in assisting the tribunal as a whole to reach a decision. However, he added that while the main use of such knowledge will be to explain and understand the evidence that they hear, members are also entitled to use their knowledge to fill gaps in the evidence about matters which will be obvious to

---

87 [1976] 1 QB 773, pp 777–78.
88 *Ibid*, pp 778, 779.
89 [1990] Crim LR 600.
90 See *R v Field and Others ex p White* (1895) 64 LJMC 158, p 160.
91 [1977] 1 All ER 454.

them, but might be obscure to a layman. If evidence is given that appears to be contrary to their knowledge, they ought to draw the witness's attention to the fact so as to give the witness an opportunity to deal with it. Provided, however, that such an opportunity has been given, it seems that they may prefer their own knowledge to that of the witness.[92]

FURTHER READING

—Carter, 'Judicial Notice: Related and Unrelated Matters', in Campbell and Waller (eds), *Well and Truly Tried*, 1982, pp 88–99.

—Davis, 'Judicial Notice' (1955) 55 Col LR 945.

—Manchester, 'Judicial Notice and Personal Knowledge' [1979] 42 MLR 22.

—McConville, 'The Doctrine of Judicial Notice and Its Relation to Evidence' (1979) 1 Liverpool LR 62.

—Morgan, *Some Problems of Proof under the Anglo-American System of Litigation*, 1956, pp 36–69.

—Nokes, 'The Limits of Judicial Notice' [1958] 74 LQR 59.

—Thayer, *A Preliminary Treatise on Evidence at the Common Law*, 1898, pp 277–312.

EXERCISES

1. What is the difference between formal and informal admissions?
2. How may parties make formal admissions in civil trials?
3. How may a formal admission be made in criminal proceedings?
4. What is judicial notice?
5. Give some examples of facts that have been judicially noticed without inquiry.
6. How does a court take judicial notice of current political and diplomatic matters?
7. What matters other than current political and diplomatic matters can be judicially noticed after inquiry?
8. Which of the following could *not* be the subject of judicial notice?

   (a) Acts of Parliament passed after 1850.
   (b) Decisions of the European Court on questions concerning EC treaties.
   (c) The domestic law of Germany.
   (d) The date of the execution of Louis XVI.

---

92   [1977] 1 All ER 454, p 459.

5
COMPETENCE AND COMPELLABILITY

What persons are permitted by law to give evidence? This question is considered in the topic known as *competence*. This is a technical term and should not be used to refer to the question whether a witness who does give evidence is *reliable* or not. What persons may be compelled by law to give evidence, or risk punishment for contempt of court if they refuse? This question is considered in the topic known as *compellability*.

All evidence must generally be given on oath or affirmation unless a witness in a criminal trial is aged under 14.[1] The Oaths Act 1978 requires that the oath be administered in the manner provided in s 1, unless the witness objects or is physically incapable of taking the oath in the prescribed way. Persons who wish to affirm, or to swear in the manner prescribed by a religion other than Judaism or Christianity, may do so.[2] An oath administered otherwise than in accordance with s 1 will be administered in a lawful manner, provided it appears to the court to be binding on the witness's conscience, and provided the witness himself considers it to be binding on his conscience.[3] However, the effect of s 4(1) is to make binding any oath that has been administered in a form that the witness has declared to be binding. By s 4(2),

---

1   See the Youth Justice and Criminal Evidence Act 1999, s 55.
2   Oaths Act 1978, ss 1(3) and 5(1).
3   *R v Kemble* [1990] 1 WLR 1111.

the validity of an oath is not affected if the person swearing has no religious belief. By s 5(4), an affirmation has the same force and effect as an oath. It follows that it would be improper for a judge to make any distinction in summing up between witnesses who gave evidence on oath and witnesses who affirmed. Evidence given on affirmation is subject to the law against perjury in the same way as evidence on oath.

Inability to testify has always been regarded as the exception rather than the rule. When the modern law of evidence was beginning to develop in the 18th century, the exception was a wide one whose rationale was probably twofold: a desire to keep people away from a situation where they might be tempted to commit perjury, and the view that certain types of people were so unreliable that any testimony from them would be worthless. Those excluded from testifying were: the parties to civil actions and their spouses, and any other persons with a financial interest in the outcome of the proceedings; the accused and their spouses in criminal cases; certain persons with criminal convictions; and many people who would not, or could not, take a Christian oath before giving evidence. This last category included those, such as children, who were unable to satisfy the court that they understood the nature and significance of an oath.

Subject to some exceptions, a witness who was competent was also compellable. The primary rule of universal competence and compellability was stated by Willes J in *Ex p Fernandez*:[4]

> Every person in the kingdom except the sovereign may be called upon and is bound to give evidence to the best of his knowledge upon any question of fact material and relevant to an issue tried in any of the Queen's courts, unless he can shew some exception in his favour . . .

The principle is an old one, and was vividly illustrated by Bentham, in his *Draught of a new plan for the Organisation of the Judicial Establishment in France*, at the end of the eighteenth century:

> Were the Prince of Wales, the Archbishop of Canterbury, and the Lord High Chancellor to be passing in the same coach, while a chimney-sweeper and a barrow-woman were in dispute about a halfpenny worth of apples, and the chimney-sweeper and the barrow-woman were to think proper to call upon them for their evidence, could they refuse it? No! most certainly not.[5]

In civil actions, this primary rule applies to the parties themselves and their spouses. The Evidence Act 1851 allowed the parties to a civil action in the superior courts of

---

4   (1861) 10 CBNS 3, p 39. See also *Hoskyn v Commissioner of Police for the Metropolis* [1979] AC 474, pp 484, 500–01.

5   Quoted in Best, 1870, p 172.

common law to give evidence, but left their spouses incompetent as witnesses. This state of affairs was clearly unsatisfactory. A contemporary critic noted:

> Among the middle classes matters of business are often conducted by [the wife] for her husband. Yet in such cases we have the practical absurdity that the husband, who knows *nothing* about it, *may* be called, while the wife, who knows *all* about it, *may not.*[6]

The Evidence Amendment Act 1853 was passed to meet this sort of criticism. Section 1 provided that on the trial of any matter, husbands and wives of the parties were to be both competent and compellable as witnesses. This section remains in force. The result is that, if thought appropriate, one party can compel the other, or the other's spouse, to testify. Of course, although the witness can be compelled to testify, he or she cannot be compelled to co-operate by giving a witness statement in advance. A party would need to have a strong reason for calling somebody without knowing for sure what that person might say in the witness box; nevertheless, it can be done.

For the last two centuries the tendency has been to increase the scope of competence while maintaining a few cases where a competent witness is not compellable. Four classes of witness require special consideration:

(a) defendants in criminal cases;
(b) spouses of defendants in criminal cases;
(c) children;
(d) persons of defective intellect.

DEFENDANTS IN CRIMINAL CASES

Accused persons as a general class were not allowed to give evidence at their trials until the Criminal Evidence Act 1898. It is a mistake, however, to state that they were always unable to testify in their own defence prior to this Act. During and after the 1860s, statutes from time to time created new offences and specifically allowed defendants charged under the statute in question to testify in their own defence. This gave rise to some curious anomalies which in the end helped to ease the path of the 1898 Act.[7]

By s 1 of the Criminal Evidence Act 1898, all defendants were made competent, but not compellable, witnesses in their own defence. An accused person is also

---

6   (1851–52) *Law Times* 18, p 122.

7   The Criminal Law (Amendment) Act 1885 produced particularly blatant anomalies. This Act created a number of new sexual offences, and a person charged with any of these was allowed by the statute to give evidence in his own defence, but a person charged with the common law offence of rape was incompetent to testify.

a competent, but not compellable, witness for any co-accused.[8] This assumes that two or more persons who have pleaded not guilty are being tried together on the same indictment. Once one of the defendants has been separated from the others (for example, by changing his plea to guilty, or by being discharged at the end of the prosecution case on a submission of no case to answer, or by severance of the indictment), he will become compellable, as well as competent, for any of the remaining defendants.[9]

Accused persons are incompetent as witnesses for the prosecution.[10] In a case where several persons are charged, and the prosecution wish to use the evidence of one of them against the other, it is necessary to separate the potential witness from his companions, so that he is not, or is no longer, liable to be convicted of any offence in the proceedings.[11] This may be done in several ways. The prosecution may discontinue proceedings against their potential witness. A more usual way of obtaining an accomplice's evidence is to persuade the accomplice to plead guilty when his co-defendant pleads not guilty. Because of his plea, the accomplice will no longer be *liable to be convicted* of any offence in the proceedings, and will thus be available as a witness for the prosecution. The question has arisen whether, in such circumstances, the accomplice should be sentenced before giving evidence at his former companion's trial. Judicial practice has varied, but it is clear that whether sentence has been passed or not has no effect on the competence of an accomplice. It may, of course, affect the weight that a jury attaches to his evidence.

THE EFFECT OF A DEFENDANT'S GIVING EVIDENCE

Where a defendant gives evidence, he must do so on oath or affirmation and he will be liable to cross-examination.[12] His testimony will be evidence at the trial *for all purposes*. Thus, he may incriminate himself in the witness box and anything he says there may be used as evidence against any co-defendant.[13] Counsel for the prosecution is entitled to cross-examine with a view to incriminating not only the defendant giving evidence but a co-defendant also.[14] The defendant who gives evidence may also be cross-examined on behalf of any co-defendant.

---

8   *R v Macdonnell* (1909) 2 Cr App R 322; Criminal Evidence Act 1898, s 1(1).

9   *R v Boal* [1965] 1 QB 402; *R v Richardson* (1967) 51 Cr App R 381; *R v Conti* (1973) 58 Cr App R 387.

10   Youth Justice and Criminal Evidence Act 1999, s 53(4).

11   *Ibid*, s 53(5).

12   Criminal Justice Act 1982, s 72. This is subject to the Youth Justice and Criminal Evidence Act 1999, ss 55 and 56, which provide for unsworn evidence to be given in criminal trials by persons under the age of 14, and by those older persons who do not satisfy the conditions for taking an oath or affirming.

13   *R v Rudd* (1948) 32 Cr App R 138.

14   *R v Paul* [1920] 2 KB 183.

THE EFFECT OF A DEFENDANT'S FAILURE TO GIVE EVIDENCE

Under the 1898 Act, the judge and counsel for any co-accused were always permitted to comment on a defendant's failure to testify. The judge, however, had a duty to warn the jury that they were not entitled to infer guilt from silence at trial.[15] In certain cases, provided this basic point had been made, some criticism was regarded as acceptable. For example, in *R v Brigden*,[16] the accused's case, put to the appropriate witnesses in cross-examination, was that the police had planted incriminating evidence on him. The accused himself did not testify. The Court of Appeal approved the trial judge's comment to the effect that the jury had not heard from the accused, and that this might help them in deciding whether there was any truth in the allegation against the police.

Similar criticism was permitted where the accused did not testify, but relied on facts that must have been within his knowledge. Thus, in *R v Martinez-Tobon*,[17] the accused was charged with the illegal importation of cocaine in a packet. The defence was that he had thought the packet contained emeralds, but the accused chose not to testify. The trial judge commented in his summing up that if the defendant had thought the drugs were emeralds, one might have thought that he would be very anxious to say so. On appeal against conviction it was argued that the judge's comment had gone beyond what was permissible, but the Court of Appeal disagreed. Provided the judge made the basic point that guilt should not be inferred from silence, it might be appropriate to make a stronger comment where the defence case involved alleged facts which: (a) were at variance with the Crown's evidence or were additional to it and exculpatory; and (b) must, if true, be within the defendant's knowledge.

The law was changed by s 35 of the Criminal Justice and Public Order Act 1994. The court or jury, in determining whether the accused is guilty of the offence charged, may now draw such inferences as appear proper from the accused's failure to give evidence at trial, or his refusal without good cause to answer any question when giving evidence.[18]

Certain conditions have to be satisfied for this provision to apply. The defendant must:

- have pleaded not guilty;[19]
- be physically and mentally fit to testify;[20] and,
- be aware of the risks attached to silence.[21]

---

15   *R v Wickham* (1971) 55 Cr App R 199; *R v Bathurst* [1968] 2 QB 99.

16   [1973] Crim LR 579.

17   (1993) 98 Cr App R 375.

18   Criminal Justice and Public Order Act 1994, s 35(3).

19   Section 35(1)(a).

20   Section 35(1)(b).

21   Section 35(2). For the procedure to ensure that the defendant is aware of these risks, see *Practice Direction (criminal: consolidated)* [2002] 3 All ER 904, para 44.

The requirement that the defendant be physically and mentally fit to testify pre-supposes, of course, that he is fit to plead. If the defence wishes to argue that s 35 does not apply because of the defendant's physical or mental condition, there must be some admissible evidence to support this contention.[22] It will be for the judge to decide whether or not this condition is satisfied. In *R v Friend*[23] the defendant was charged with murder. At the date of the offence he was aged fourteen. He was fifteen by the time of the trial. There was evidence that he had a mental age of a child of nine at the time of the offence, and that he could not do himself justice in giving evidence because of his poor ability to concentrate and express himself. Nevertheless, the trial judge ruled that he was physically and mentally fit to testify. In due course, the defendant having failed to testify, a s 35 direction was given to the jury. The defendant was convicted. One of the grounds of appeal was that the trial judge had erred in ruling as he did. The Court of Appeal dismissed the appeal, but in doing so Otton LJ, delivering the judgment of the Court, made some observations on s 35(1)(b). He said, first, that it would be only in very rare cases that a judge would have to consider whether it was undesirable for a defendant to give evidence because of his mental condition. In the majority of cases there would be evidence that he was 'unfit to plead'. In the present case that issue had not been raised. Secondly, it could not be said that the trial judge had applied the wrong test in considering the application of s 35(1)(b) because there was no right test. The statutory provision was clear, and it was inappropriate to supplement the statute by spelling out a specific test to be applied in such a situation; nor were any formal guidelines called for. However, he suggested that a physical condition might include a risk of an epileptic attack; and a mental condition might include latent schizophrenia where the experience of giving evidence might trigger a fully developed state.[24]

This appeal had an interesting sequel. Some years later the Criminal Cases Review Commission referred the defendant's conviction to the Court of Appeal under s 9 of the Criminal Appeal Act 1995. Among the grounds for doing so was availability of fresh evidence that could not have been made available at trial because of the state of medical knowledge at that time. This was to the effect that at the time of the trial the defendant had been suffering from attention deficit and hyperactivity disorder (ADHD), the symptoms of which include inattention, impulsiveness and poor behavioural controls. A medical report stated that at trial the defendant would have become easily distracted and might have missed completely some parts of the process. Had he given evidence he would have had problems with concentration and might have blurted out the first thing that came to mind. He might have given inconsistent evidence. These vulnerabilities were likely to have been misinterpreted by a jury. At the second appeal, following the Commission's referral, the prosecution

---

22   *R v A* [1997] Crim LR 883.
23   [1997] 1 WLR 1433.
24   See pp 1442–43.

conceded that had this evidence been available at trial, the prosecution then would not have invited the court to allow an adverse inference to be drawn under s 35. The result was that, in the light of the fresh evidence, the Court of Appeal allowed the appeal and quashed the conviction.[25]

This decision suggests that it may be wrong to allow a s 35 direction to be given where a defendant's mental condition sufficiently impairs his ability to follow the proceedings and give coherent evidence. This would mean that a judge might have to consider the defendant's mental condition in relation to s 35 more often than on the 'very rare' occasions envisaged earlier by Otton LJ. At the same time, the decision shows that there may now be an overlap between a condition that would render a defendant unfit to plead and a condition that would allow a judge to rule that no inferences should be drawn from failure to testify. The reason for this is that the test of unfitness to plead is whether the defendant will be able to understand the proceedings and make a proper defence.[26] It looks as if someone suffering from ADHD might well fall into this category.

Where an accused gives evidence but fails to answer a certain question, no inferences can be drawn if he is entitled to refuse to answer the question by virtue of any enactment, or on the grounds of privilege, or where the court in the exercise of its general discretion excuses him from answering it.[27] For example, the defendant might be entitled to refuse to answer a question about his previous convictions under the Criminal Justice Act 2003, or he might be able to claim legal professional privilege,[28] or the judge might excuse him from answering a question because it was oppressive or likely to produce information whose probative worth would be outweighed by its likely prejudicial effect on the jury.[29]

In *R v Cowan*,[30] Lord Taylor CJ, in delivering the judgment of the Court of Appeal, accepted that it would be open to a court to decline to draw any adverse inference from silence at trial and for a judge either to direct or merely to advise a jury against drawing such an inference if the circumstances of the case justified it. But for either course to be taken, at least one of two conditions would have to be satisfied. There would have to be some evidential basis for taking that course: it would not be proper for a defence advocate to give to the jury reasons unsupported by evidence for his client's silence at trial. Alternatively, there would have to be some exceptional factors in the case, making it fair not to draw any adverse inferences. As the Court of Appeal emphasised in *R v Napper*,[30a] the general rule is that it should be open to a jury

---

25   *R v Friend* [2004] EWCA Crim 2661.

26   *R v Pritchard* (1836) 7 C&P 303; *R v Berry* (1977) 66 Cr App R 156.

27   Criminal Justice and Public Order Act 1994, s 35(5).

28   See below, Chapter 15.

29   See below, Chapter 11.

30   [1996] QB 373.

30a   [1996] Crim LR 591.

to draw adverse inferences when a defendant fails to testify. Attempts to minimise or marginalise the operation of the section are contrary to the spirit of its provisions.

In any direction under s 35, the judge must direct the jury on certain matters.[31]

(a) The defendant is entitled to remain silent.

(b) The jury must not convict solely or mainly on the strength of an inference from silence.[32]

(c) The jury may draw an inference against the defendant only if they think it is fair and proper to do so.

(d) An inference may be drawn only if the case for the prosecution is so strong that it clearly calls for an answer by him.[33] The importance of this requirement has been emphasised by the Court of Appeal. For example, in *El-Hannachi and Others* and in *R v Birchall*[34] convictions were quashed because the trial judge had omitted this direction in his summing-up.

(e) If the jury concludes that the only sensible explanation for the defendant's silence is that he has no answer, or none that would bear examination, an adverse inference may be drawn.

SPOUSES AND CIVIL PARTNERS OF DEFENDANTS IN CRIMINAL CASES

The current law is to be found in s 80 of the Police and Criminal Evidence Act 1984 (PACE), as amended, and in s 53(1) of the Youth Justice and Criminal Evidence Act 1999.

---

31 The principal authority is the judgment of Lord Taylor in *Cowan*, but the influence of later authorities is also noted.

32 Criminal Justice and Public Order Act 1994, s 38(3); *Murray v United Kingdom* (1996) 22 EHRR 29, para 47.

33 According to *Cowan*, an adverse inference can be drawn only if the jury finds 'a case to answer'. This is potentially confusing because the decision about whether there is a case to answer is one generally associated with the judge. The point is that a judge may decide that there is a case to answer if the prosecution witnesses, or some of them, are believed. But the jury may decide that they do not believe those witnesses, in which case they could properly say that the defendant did not have a case to answer. Other expressions have been used instead of the one adopted in *Cowan*. See, eg, *R v Birchall* [1999] Crim LR (a case 'sufficiently compelling to call for an answer'); *Murray v United Kingdom* (a situation which 'clearly calls for an explanation'). The reference to a case for the prosecution 'so strong that it clearly calls for an answer' is the currently approved specimen direction from the Judicial Studies Board.

34 [1998] 2 Cr App R 226, [1999] Crim LR 311.

Section 53(1) provides that at every stage in criminal proceedings, *all* persons (whatever their age) are *competent* to give evidence. It follows that an accused's husband or wife (spouse) is always competent for the prosecution. The only possible exceptions to this would occur where the spouse failed to satisfy the requirements for competence contained in s 55(3), or where he or she was a defendant in the same proceedings. In that case, the spouse would be incompetent for the prosecution by virtue of s 53(4). It follows from the very wide terms of s 53(1) of the 1999 Act that an accused's spouse will also be competent for the accused and for any co-accused.

By s 80(2) of PACE, the accused's spouse or civil partner is always compellable as a witness for the accused, but this provision is subject to s 80(4), which provides that no person who is charged in any proceedings shall be compellable under s 80 to give evidence in those proceedings. For example, if a husband and wife are both charged in the same proceedings, the husband cannot compel the wife under s 80(2) to give evidence for him, and she cannot compel him to give evidence for her.

The accused's spouse or civil partner will, again subject to sub-s (4), be compellable for the prosecution and for any co-accused, but only in relation to offences that are 'specified'.[35] In other words, the accused's spouse or civil partner is compellable for a co-accused only in those circumstances where he or she would be compellable for the prosecution. The reason for this is that since the prosecution cannot compel the spouse or civil partner to give evidence in trials for offences that are not 'specified', it would be wrong for someone jointly charged with the accused to be able to do so, because the result would be to give the prosecution an indirect advantage through the opportunity for cross-examination.[36] For example, if the husband and a co-accused are charged with handling, the wife would not be a compellable witness for the prosecution because handling is not a 'specified' offence. But if the co-defendant could compel the wife to give evidence in his defence, she could be cross-examined by the prosecution, and during the course of that cross-examination she might have to provide answers that would support the case against her husband.

The 'specified' offences are set out in s 80(3) of PACE. They are offences where:

(a)   the offence charged involves an assault on, or injury or a threat of injury to, the spouse of the accused or a person who was at the material time under the age of 16;

(b)   the offence charged is a sexual offence alleged to have been committed in respect of a person who was at the material time under the age of 16;

---

35   See PACE, s 80(2A).

36   May, 2004, paras 17–33.

(c) the offence charged consists of attempting or conspiring to commit either of the above, or being a secondary party to or inciting either of the above.

There is at least one problem with the interpretation of these provisions. It concerns what is referred to in sub-s (3)(a) as an offence which '*involves* an assault on, or injury or a threat of injury to' the spouse of the accused or a person who was at the material time under the age of 16. The sub-section clearly covers an offence such as robbery, where violence or the threat of it is an essential element of the offence, but it is unclear whether 'involves' covers an offence where this is not the case, and the violence is only an incidental element.[37] In *R v McAndrew-Bingham,*[38] the same wording in s 32(2)(a) of the Criminal Justice Act 1988 was given the broader inter-pretation, but this was in the context of a provision for the use of video and live-link TV wherever a child witness was likely to be traumatised by confrontation with the accused. The court adopted a purposive construction, but it is by no means clear that a purposive construction of s 80(3) of PACE would have the same result.

In any proceedings, a person who has been, but is no longer, married to the accused shall be competent and compellable to give evidence as if that person and the accused had never been married.[39] Marriage persists until grant of decree absolute.

By s 80A of PACE, the failure of an accused's spouse to give evidence shall not be made the subject of any comment by the prosecution. The judge, and counsel for any co-accused, can comment. In *R v Naudeer,*[40] the Court of Appeal said that, save in exceptional circumstances, a judge should exercise a great deal of circumspection if he chooses to make any comment. (The reason for this is that, as with any other potential witness, there may have been some good reason why that person was not called.) But counsel for a co-accused may, presumably, comment as strongly as he thinks fit.

Finally, it should be noted that unmarried partners, other than civil partners, are not at present given any protection by s 80; nor are a defendant's children. In *R v Pearce*[41] the defendant was charged with murder. His unmarried partner, with whom he had lived for nineteen years, and his daughter, aged about sixteen, were both called as prosecution witnesses. It was argued on appeal that they were not compellable witnesses, but the argument was directed primarily towards the position of the unmarried partner. It was submitted that in 2001 whether such a person was com-pellable should not depend on the existence of a marriage certificate. The reason why

---

37   Andrews and Hirst, 2001, p 232; Creighton, 1990, pp 38–39.

38   (1998) *The Times,* 28 December.

39   PACE, s 80(5). The same principle applies to civil partners: see s 80(5A).

40   (1984) 80 Cr App R 9, p 13.

41   [2001] EWCA Crim 2834, [2002] 1 WLR 1553.

a wife was not compellable was to protect relationships within the family, and in recent years courts both in this country and in other European countries had looked at the substance of a relationship rather than the form in order to decide whether a family relationship existed. But the Court held that the words of s 80 were clear and were not capable of being expanded to cover a relationship to which they clearly did not apply. In delivering the judgment of the Court, Kennedy LJ said that this was an area where the interests of the family must be weighed against those of the community at large. He continued:

> There may be much to be said for the view that with very limited exceptions all witnesses who are competent should also be compellable, and certainly the material before us does not enable us to conclude that because a concession has been made to husbands and wives proper respect for family life requires that a similar concession should be made to those in the position of a husband or a wife. As [counsel for the prosecution] points out, if the concession were to be widened it is not easy to see where logically the widening should end.[42]

He added that it would plainly require primary legislation to extend the s 80 concession to children.[43]

CHILDREN

A distinction is drawn between civil and criminal cases.

CIVIL CASES

The first question that will arise is whether the child is competent to give sworn evidence. The test is the one which used to govern both civil and criminal cases and which was laid down in *R v Hayes*:[44] does the child understand *the solemnity of the occasion* and *the special duty to tell the truth*, over and above the ordinary social duty to do so? Belief in a divine sanction is unnecessary. If the child does not satisfy these conditions, the court must then rely on the Children Act 1989. Section 96 applies to a child (defined in s 105 as a person under the age of 18) who is called as a witness in

---

42   Paragraph 12. By the Civil Partnership Act 2004, s 80 of PACE was amended to cover civil partners as well as husbands and wives. But it is unlikely that this would give additional strength to the appellant's argument were it to be presented again in another case. Civil partners can be readily identified as such, but unmarried partners cannot always be readily identified as members of a family relationship. Further, a court would be likely to hold that since it was Parliament that extended the benefit of s 80 to civil partners, so it should be Parliament that decided whether any more extensions should be made.

43   Paragraph 13.

44   [1977] 1 WLR 234.

any civil proceedings and who does not, in the court's opinion, understand the nature of an oath. Such a child's evidence may be heard if, in the court's opinion, the child understands that it is his duty to speak the truth and he has sufficient understanding to justify his evidence being heard.

CRIMINAL CASES

The current law is contained in ss 53–57 of the Youth Justice and Criminal Evidence Act 1999. The fundamental provision is contained in s 53(1): at every stage in criminal proceedings, all persons are, *whatever their age*, competent to give evidence.

By sub-s (3), a person is *not* competent to give evidence if it appears to the court that he is not a person who is able to:

(a)   understand questions put to him as a witness; and

(b)   give answers to them which can be understood.

Section 53(3) is concerned simply with understanding: can the witness understand what is being asked, and can the jury understand the witness's answers? The words 'put to him as a witness' in s 53(3)(a) refer to those questions being asked of him in court. There is, apparently, no necessity that the person giving evidence should understand his status as a witness, or have any awareness of a need to tell the truth, or even any understanding of the difference between truth and falsehood. The witness's credibility and reliability are relevant to the weight to be given to his evidence, and might well form the basis of a submission of no case to answer, but they are not relevant to competence.[45] In delivering the judgment of the Court of Appeal in *R v Sed*,[46] Auld LJ pointed out that s 53 does not expressly provide for 100 per cent comprehension by either the witness or the jury. Depending on the length and nature of the questioning, and the complexity of its subject matter, s 53 may not always require even nearly 100 per cent comprehension. Allowance should be made for the fact that the witness's performance and command of detail may vary according to the importance to him of the subject matter of the questions, on the length of time between the events referred to by the witness and the date of the questioning, and on any strong feelings that those events may have caused. He continued:

> It is thus for the judge to determine the question of competence almost as a matter of feel, taking into account the effect of the potential witness's performance as a whole, whether there is a common and comprehensible thread in his or her responses to the questions, however patchy – bearing always in mind that if, on critical matters, the witness can be seen and heard to be

---

45   *R v MacPherson* [2005] EWCA Crim 3605, [2006] 1 Cr App R 30.

46   [2004] EWCA Crim 1294, [2004] 1 WLR 3218.

intelligible, it is for the jury and no one else to determine matters of reliability and general cogency.[47]

Competence relates to the whole of a witness's evidence and not just to part of it. A child who may appear at first to be competent (for example, in a recorded interview) may during the trial (for example, when cross-examined) prove to be incompetent. In appropriate cases the judge should keep the question of competence under review during the trial.[48]

Any question of whether a witness in criminal proceedings is competent may be raised either by a party to the proceedings, or by the court of its own motion (that is, by the judge, even if none of the parties raises the issue). If such a question arises, the procedure set out in s 54 will be followed. It is for the party calling the witness to satisfy the court that, *on a balance of probabilities*, the witness is competent.[49] It should be noted that this civil standard applies to both the defence and the prosecution. The issue must be determined in the absence of the jury, if there is one.[50] Expert evidence may be received on the question.[51] Any questioning of the witness, where the court considers that necessary, shall be conducted by the court in the presence of the parties.[52] In other words, the potential witness will not be submitted to examination and cross-examination by counsel, but may be questioned by the judge.

Assuming a child is competent to give evidence, will that child's evidence be sworn or unsworn? By s 55(2), no witness may be sworn unless:

(a) he has attained the age of 14; and

(b) he has a sufficient appreciation of the solemnity of the occasion and of the particular responsibility to tell the truth which is involved in taking an oath.

This is, in essence, the test applied in *R v Hayes*,[53] so belief in a divine sanction is unnecessary. However, witnesses aged 14 and over are likely to take the oath without further question, because sub-s (3) provides that if the witness is able to give intelligible testimony, he shall be presumed to have satisfied condition (b) if no evidence tending to show the contrary is adduced by any party. The effect of this is that children aged 14 and over will be treated as adults, and no inquiry will be made

---

47   Paragraphs 45–46. Where there is a danger that a complainant may be incompetent, the judge will usually, before the trial, have seen a video recording of the complainant's interview with the police, and so will be in some position to make a decision about competence after hearing submissions from prosecution and defence. See Youth Justice and Criminal Evidence Act 1999, s 27.

48   *R v Powell* [2006] EWCA Crim 3.

49   Youth Justice and Criminal Evidence Act 1999, s 54(2).

50   *Ibid*, s 54(4).

51   *Ibid*, s 54(5).

52   *Ibid*, s 54(6).

53   [1977] 1 WLR 234.

into their capacity to take the oath unless an objection, supported by evidence, is made. If any question as to the satisfaction of either of the conditions in sub-s (2) arises, it is for the party wishing to have the witness sworn to satisfy the court that, on a balance of probabilities, those conditions are satisfied.[54] Again, the standard is the same for both defence and prosecution, and the proceedings to determine the question will be conducted under the same rules as proceedings to determine competence.[55]

If a person is competent to give evidence, but fails to satisfy the tests for giving sworn evidence, his evidence may be given unsworn.[56]

PERSONS OF DEFECTIVE INTELLECT

Here, also, a distinction is drawn between civil and criminal cases.

CIVIL CASES

The old common law, formerly applicable to both criminal and civil cases, still applies: a person who is mentally disordered or defective will not inevitably be incompetent to testify. Competence depends on the nature and severity of the disability, which may be investigated in open court before testimony is received. If there is a doubt about the ability of a witness to give reliable evidence because of his mental condition, expert evidence should be called on the *voir dire* to deal with the matter. It should not normally be necessary at that stage to call the witness whose mental condition has given rise to the problem.[57]

The crucial test is whether the potential witness understands the nature of the oath in the light of the test stated in *R v Hayes*. Thus, in an old case, the prosecution wished to call an inmate of a lunatic asylum. One of the attendants was called first and gave evidence that the man in question had the delusion that spirits continually conversed with him. However, he added, he believed that the inmate was capable of giving an account of anything that had happened before his eyes. The man was allowed to testify because the court found that he had a clear understanding of the obligation of an oath and was rational on all subjects except his particular delusion.[58]

More recently, in *R v Bellamy*,[59] a rape complainant aged 33 had a mental age of 10. The Court of Appeal held that she should have been allowed to give sworn

---

54   Youth Justice and Criminal Evidence Act 1999, s 55(4).
55   *Ibid*, s 55(5)–(7).
56   *Ibid*, s 56.
57   *R v Barratt and Sheehan* [1996] Crim LR 495.
58   *R v Hill* (1851) 2 Den 254.
59   (1985) 82 Cr App R 222.

evidence because it had been clear from her answers to initial questions from the trial judge that she had satisfied the *Hayes* test. The Court of Appeal was particularly impressed by the fact that she had realised that if she told a lie when she gave evidence she could, as she had said, be 'put away'.

CRIMINAL CASES

Sections 53–57 of the Youth Justice and Criminal Evidence Act 1999 constitute a code governing the competence and capacity to be sworn of all persons tendered as witnesses in criminal cases. Where a potential witness has a defective intellect, therefore, the tests to be applied and the procedure for determining them are the same as have already been described in relation to children. It follows that a person with defective intellect may be able to give evidence in criminal, but not in civil, proceedings. In criminal proceedings, provided he satisfies the basic test for competence, he will be able to give evidence – if not sworn, then unsworn. In civil proceedings, an adult witness with defective intellect must be able to satisfy the *Hayes* test and be sworn; if he cannot do so, there is no provision enabling him to give unsworn evidence.

FURTHER READING

—Allen, *The Law of Evidence in Victorian England*, 1997, Chapter 5, 'The Incompetency of the Accused'.

—Birch, 'Children's Evidence' [1992] Crim LR 262.

—Brennan, 'The Battle for Credibility' [1993] NLJ 623.

—Munday, '*Cum Tacent Clamant*: Drawing Proper Inferences from a Defendant's Failure to Testify' [1996] CLJ 32.

—Spencer and Flin, *The Evidence of Children: The Law and the Psychology*, 2nd edn, 1993.

EXERCISES

1. Aidan and Benedict are co-defendants in a criminal trial. How can Benedict become competent and compellable as a witness for the prosecution against Aidan?

2. When can an adult witness in a criminal trial give unsworn evidence?

3. What conditions have to be satisfied before a direction under s 35 of the Criminal Justice and Public Order Act 1994 (CJPOA) can be given?

4. What are the essential elements of a direction to the jury under s 35 CJPOA?

5. Cyril and Damian are charged with attempting to rape Ellen, aged 15. Which of the following are compellable as defence witnesses for Damian?

   (a) Cyril's employer.

   (b) Cyril.

    (c) Cyril's civil partner.

    (d) Cyril's daughter, aged 13.

    (e) Cyril's former wife.

6. In what circumstances will a child aged 14, but with a mental age of 7, be competent to give evidence:

    (a) In a civil trial?

    (b) In a criminal trial?

6

THE COURSE OF TESTIMONY

There are three golden rules which, if followed faithfully, will ensure that you understand this part of evidence law:

(a)   leave your books and go into a court;

(b)   once there, watch and listen carefully; and

(c)   repeat this process frequently.

If you do these things, the rather dry topics covered in this chapter will make more sense, and so will be more easily remembered. Watching films of trials, whether fictional or not, is no substitute. Nearly all are American, or influenced by American procedure. American and English procedures and terminology differ, and it is indiscreet to confuse the two.

Behind the rules governing the way in which evidence is given, there exist certain assumptions, listed below. An understanding of these can be useful, because they go some way towards giving shape to an otherwise amorphous topic. These are ideas that have shaped the way the law developed; whether they are good ideas or not is, for present purposes, immaterial:

(a)   It is the responsibility of the parties, not the court, to produce the evidence. It follows from this that the examination of witnesses is the job of the advocate, not the judge.

(b) Testimony is best evaluated when it is fresh, and this is taken to mean when it emerges orally from the witness at trial. There was originally, therefore, reluctance to rely on pre-trial accounts from witnesses of the events in question. In civil cases this reluctance has substantially diminished, and even in criminal cases the courts today adopt a more relaxed attitude than in the past.

(c) The credibility of a witness is one of the relevant facts in any trial. One of the most important guides to a person's credibility is his moral character. A conviction for any criminal offence is relevant to moral character, and so to credibility.

(d) Trials, and criminal trials in particular, should be over quickly. If they are not, the wheels of justice will grind to a halt. There must therefore be a limit to the number of issues that can be pursued in a trial.

I have divided this chapter into eight sections. The first three deal with the various stages of witness examination: examination-in-chief, cross-examination and re-examination. I then turn to four particular problems: the rules governing the way in which a witness may refresh his memory before and during testimony; the admissibility of a witness's previous statements to support or contradict his testimony in court; hostile witnesses; and questions on collateral matters. Finally, I deal in outline with procedural measures that have been adopted for the protection of vulnerable or intimidated witnesses.

EXAMINATION-IN-CHIEF

This is the first stage in the examination of a witness at trial, and is conducted on behalf of the party who has called him. In civil actions a witness's pre-trial written statement may stand as the evidence-in-chief.[1] Where this happens, the witness will usually be called and sworn, asked for his name and address and whether the contents of his statement are true, and then tendered for cross-examination. However, before tendering the witness for cross-examination, it may be necessary to ask some questions about matters that have become relevant since the statement was served, or to apply for leave to ask questions about matters that should have been included in the statement but were omitted. In all cases the trial judge has an unfettered discretion to require a witness to give oral evidence-in-chief and, in *Cole v*

---

1   Civil Procedure Rules, r 32.5(2).

Kivells,[2] the Court of Appeal said that this discretion might usefully be exercised in relation to evidence about matters where there are conflicts on the facts.

A witness will very frequently be favourable to the cause of the party who has called him. Because of this, two rules that are peculiar to examination-in-chief have developed. These are the rules against leading questions and against discrediting one's own witness.

THE RULE AGAINST LEADING QUESTIONS

The best account of leading questions that I know was given in 1813 by Lord Ellenborough CJ in a speech in the House of Lords:

> I have always understood, after some little experience, that the meaning of a leading question was this, and this only, that the judge restrains an advocate who produces a witness on one particular side of a question, and who may be supposed to have a leaning to that side of the question, from putting such interrogatories as may operate as an instruction to that witness how he is to reply to favour the party for whom he is adduced. The counsel on the other side, however, may put what questions he pleases, and frame them as best suits his purpose, because then the rule is changed, for there is no danger that the witness will be too complying.[3]

A leading question, then, is one that suggests to the witness the answer that is wanted, and an advocate must not ask leading questions of his own witness.[4] Obviously, if an advocate does obtain evidence from his own witness by a leading question, that evidence is likely to have less weight than evidence adduced without such assistance.

It is, of course, necessary to a certain extent to 'lead' the mind of the witness to the subject of the inquiry, but this is permissible provided the answer is left open to the witness. It is not always easy in practice to decide how far to go. Suppose you want the witness to say, 'I was in Trafalgar Square on 1 December 2007'. A clearly leading question would be, 'You were in Trafalgar Square on 1 December 2007, weren't you?' but what about, 'Where were you on 1 December 2007?' or, 'Have you been in Trafalgar Square recently?' or, 'Were you in Trafalgar Square on 1 December 2007?'. It could be argued that the last of these questions suggests neither a negative nor affirmative reply, and is therefore not a leading question. On the other hand, it clearly directs the witness's attention to a particular time and place, both of which may be contested, and it could be argued that for that reason it falls under the ban on leading questions. Whether the other questions are permissible will depend on the extent to which the assertion is contested. If, for example, the witness is an alibi witness, the

---

2   [1997] EWCA Civ 1323.

3   *Campbell*, 1849–57, Vol III, pp 209–10.

4   The rule was established by at least the late 17th century: see *R v Rosewall* (1684) 10 St Tr 147, col 190.

date will be all-important. The prosecution may be ready to accept that at some time the witness was in Trafalgar Square, but will vigorously contest that it was on 1 December 2007. In those circumstances, the examination should be conducted on these lines:

Q: Do you remember a time when you were in Trafalgar Square?

A: Yes.

Q: When was that?

Suppose instead that the witness is appearing for the prosecution, and the case against the defendant is that he attempted to drown his girlfriend in one of the fountains in Trafalgar Square on 1 December 2007. The defence is self-defence. The date of the contested events will not be in issue, but their nature most certainly will. If the prosecution witness has been called to give an account of what he saw on that date, the accuracy of his perception is very likely to be contested. In that case, the place from which he observed what was happening will be important. The examination should then go like this:

Q: Do you remember 1 December 2007?

A: Yes.

Q: Where were you on that day?

In both cases, a leading question has been avoided *on a matter in contention.*

This suggests an exception to the rule against leading questions during examination-in-chief. Questions on non-controversial matters, which will frequently include matters of an introductory nature, may be the subject of leading questions. Leading questions are also permissible where a witness proves to be 'hostile' to the party calling him.[5]

A less usual, but always illegitimate, form of leading question is one that assumes that something has already been established by evidence when that is not the case. Thus, if it is in issue that a particular custom existed, and the witness has not yet given evidence of that fact, it is improper to ask whether certain conduct was in accordance with the custom, because that question assumes the custom to exist.[6]

THE RULE AGAINST DISCREDITING ONE'S OWN WITNESS

A witness called by a party will have been chosen as a witness by that party and put forward by him as a truthful witness. If a party has reason to think a particular person is not to be believed on his oath, that party ought not to try to support his case by the testimony of such a witness. So if a witness's evidence unexpectedly turns out to be against the interest of the party who has called him, the latter cannot repair the

---

5   See below.

6   *Curtis v Peek* (1864) 29 JP 70.

damage by trying to show that the witness is of bad character. As Lord Denman CJ said in *Wright v Beckett*,[7] 'You shall not prove that man to be infamous whom you endeavoured to pass off to the jury as respectable'. However, the party who called the witness may call other witnesses to contradict the damaging testimony and, in certain circumstances, he may to some extent discredit the witness by cross-examining him about a former statement of the witness that is inconsistent with his testimony in court.[8]

CROSS-EXAMINATION

The object of cross-examination is to complete and correct the story told by the witness during evidence-in-chief. The business of the cross-examiner is therefore to test the accuracy and honesty of that evidence and to give an opportunity to the witness to bring out matters that are favourable to the case of the party on whose behalf the cross-examination is being conducted. If, for example, you are defending someone charged with burglary and your defence is an alibi, you must give the prosecution witnesses who identified your client at the scene of the crime an opportunity to concede that they may have been mistaken. In addition, of course, you will try to bring out those facts, such as poor lighting and short periods of observation, that you hope will lead the jury to have a reasonable doubt about the accuracy of the witnesses' identifications. Because the object of cross-examination is to complete and correct a witness's story, the right to cross-examine can be exercised by anyone whose interests have been affected by the testimony in question. If co-claimants or co-defendants have conflicting interests, the evidence of one may affect others, and it is only fair that those affected should have the right to cross-examine.[9] Another rule that follows from the objects of cross-examination is that its scope is not confined to those matters that have been covered by evidence-in-chief, but extends to all relevant matters.[10]

Counsel conducting the defence in a criminal trial must also remember that there is a duty to 'put the defendant's case' to those prosecution witnesses with whose evidence the defendant disagrees. It is often at this stage that the jury will first become aware of the nature of the defence. 'Putting the defendant's case' is achieved by asking the prosecution witness leading questions based on the instructions given by the defendant to his advisers about the nature of his defence. Suppose, for example, that Jack is charged with raping Emily. Jack has told his solicitor and counsel that,

---

7   (1834) 1 M&Rob 414, p 425.
8   See Criminal Procedure Act 1865, s 3.
9   *Lord v Colvin* (1855) 3 Drew 222; *R v Hadwen* [1902] 1 KB 882.
10   *Berwick-upon-Tweed Corp v Murray* (1850) LJ Ch 281, p 286.

although he had sexual intercourse with Emily, it was at her suggestion and with her entire consent. Jack will say this in due course when he himself gives evidence, but English criminal procedure does not allow him to do this without having given Emily an opportunity to deal with these allegations. Thus, in very abbreviated form, cross-examination of Emily will at some stage go something like this:

Defence Counsel:	You suggested to my client that he should have sex with you, didn't you?
Emily:	No, I didn't.
Defence Counsel:	You were keen on having sex with him, weren't you?
Emily:	The thought never entered my head.
Defence Counsel:	And it was only after your suggestion that he made any move of a sexual nature towards you; isn't that so?
Emily:	Certainly not!
Defence Counsel:	And when sex did take place you were fully consenting, weren't you?
Emily:	That's a wicked lie!

Unlike examination-in-chief, cross-examination operates on the assumption that the witness does not favour the cause of the party on whose behalf it is conducted. There is no danger that such a witness will simply follow the questioner's lead and accept without thinking the suggestions put to him, and the reason for excluding leading questions from examination-in-chief is therefore absent in cross-examination. Further, since the cross-examining party has not been responsible for bringing the witness before the court, he cannot be understood to vouch for that witness's character, and so is free to discredit him by all proper means at his disposal. There may be another reason why leading questions are permitted in cross-examination. Counsel appearing for accused persons in trials for felony were allowed to cross-examine prosecution witnesses, but were not allowed to address the jury until 1836. Sir James Stephen's theory was that while counsel were confined to cross-examination alone, 'the cross-examination tended to become a speech thrown into the form of questions', and that it retained that character afterwards to a greater or lesser extent.[11]

But there are limits to what can be done in cross-examination. Its purpose to complete and correct evidence-in-chief is to be achieved by eliciting evidence, not by indulging in argument. The advocate who is cross-examining should therefore avoid questions that invite argument. In *R v Baldwin* Lord Hewart CJ said:

> One so often hears questions put to witnesses by counsel which are really of the nature of an invitation to an argument. You have, for instance, such questions as this: 'I suggest to you that . . .' or 'Is your evidence to be taken as suggesting that . . .?' If the witness were a prudent

---

11   Stephen, 1973 [1883], Vol I, p 431. See also Cairns, 1998, p 48.

person he would say, with the highest degree of politeness: 'What you suggest is no business of mine. I am not here to make any suggestions at all. I am here only to answer relevant questions. What the conclusions to be drawn from my answers are is not for me, and as for suggestions, I venture to leave those to others.' An answer of that kind, no doubt, requires a good deal of sense and self-restraint and experience . . . It is right to remember in all such cases that the witness in the box is an amateur and the counsel who is asking questions is, as a rule, a professional conductor of argument, and it is not right that the wits of the one should be pitted against the wits of the other in the field of suggestion and controversy. What is wanted from the witness is answers to questions of fact.[12]

Cross-examination should consist of questions only, and never statements of fact. The time for statements such as 'The defendant will say that . . .' is during an opening speech, not during cross-examination.[13] The way to avoid such expressions is to put your allegations in the form of a question. So, if it is your case that the police planted the gelignite on your client, you ask: 'You planted the gelignite on my client, didn't you?'[14]

Another restriction that must be borne in mind is that, although the methods of obtaining evidence are wider in cross-examination than in examination-in-chief, the evidence that is obtained must still be admissible under the ordinary rules of evidence. Hearsay, for example, does not suddenly become admissible just because it is obtained during cross-examination. This presents a special problem in criminal trials where there are several defendants, because evidence may be admissible in relation to some of the defendants but not to others. The judge must tell the jury in his summing up to ignore such evidence when considering those defendants against whom it is inadmissible. It follows from this that a defendant must not be cross-examined about evidence that is inadmissible in relation to the case against him, even though it has been held admissible in relation to some other defendant.

In *R v Windass*,[15] for example, the appellant was one of several persons charged with conspiracy to steal. He had been stopped in a motor car carrying a quantity of stolen clothes. His girlfriend, a Miss Findlay, was a co-defendant; more stolen clothing was found at her flat. A diary was also found in her possession. This contained material that showed her complicity in the conspiracy, but the trial judge held

---

12   (1925) 18 Cr App R 175, pp 178–79.

13   *Archbold: Criminal Pleading, Evidence and Practice 2008*, para 8–116.

14   In my view this is preferable to 'Did you plant the gelignite on my client?'. The leading question (permissible, remember, in cross-examination) gives an impression of quiet confidence, suggesting that you know the truth of the matter, and if only the police were honest, they would come clean and agree with you. I once heard an elegant variation on this from a very distinguished QC, thus: '[In world weary tones] I suppose, officer, if I suggested that you'd planted the gelignite on my client, you'd disagree with me, wouldn't you?' But this style is probably not suitable for beginners.

15   (1989) 89 Cr App R 258.

it to be admissible only against her, because it was no more than a private record and was not a document created to further the conspiracy.[16] Despite the fact that the diary was admissible only in relation to the girlfriend, the prosecution were allowed to use it in their cross-examination of the appellant. His attention was drawn to an entry for 27 May, which read: 'Finished with Knocky for good now, he's found other new shoplifters, so let him get on with it.' It was admitted that the appellant's nickname was 'Knocky'. He was asked whether he had any idea of what the entry meant, and he attempted an explanation. Prosecuting counsel was even allowed to give copies of the diary entry to the jury so that they could follow the cross-examination better.

The Court of Appeal held that this line of cross-examination had been improper for two reasons:

(a)   It was wrong to ask a witness what a third party meant in a document written, without any contribution from that witness, by the third party.

(b)   It was even more wrong for counsel to take a statement that was inadmissible in relation to the witness he was cross-examining, and then to ask the witness to explain the inadmissible, but highly damaging, statements that the maker of the document had written.

R v Windass was applied in *R v Gray and Evans*,[17] where the Court of Appeal held that one defendant should not have been cross-examined by the prosecution about statements relating to him that a co-defendant had made in a police interview.

Sometimes it may initially be unclear whether an item of evidence is admissible or inadmissible against a particular defendant. It is necessary then to establish the conditions that will make it admissible before proceeding to ask any questions about it. This applies to cross-examination as well as examination-in-chief. For example, in *R v Cooper*[18] the defendant was charged with an offence involving the importation of cannabis concealed in a television set. As part of its case, the prosecution relied on two letters, which had not been posted and which had been found in a room occupied by the defendant with his wife. They were written by the wife, but in the joint names of herself and the defendant. The prosecution argued that the jury could infer from what had been written that the defendant was expecting the arrival of a consignment of drugs. For example, one letter said: 'We have been hashless for a couple of weeks (all the houses) and the strain was showing. There was a sharp increase in the consumption of alcohol and general erratic behaviour. But, Ali's contact came thru [*sic*] for us last Friday and had us all smiling.'

The trial judge held that the letters were admissible. In evidence, the defendant said that he did not know that his wife had written the letters; he was not aware of

---

16   See also below, Chapter 9.
17   [1998] Crim LR 570.
18   (1985) 82 Cr App R 74.

their contents and was not responsible for them. The judge in summing up told the jury that unless they were satisfied that the defendant knew of the contents of the letters, they should ignore them. It was argued on appeal that the letters should never have been admitted. They were inadmissible as hearsay, and were an attempt to get round the general rule under which one spouse was not a compellable witness against the other. The Court of Appeal made it clear that before a defendant can be cross-examined on a third party's account of events, he must have accepted that account as true. The prosecution should have proved as part of their case the finding of the letters in the place where they were found, so as to give notice to the defendant of the use that might eventually be made of them. But initially there should have been no indication to the jury of their contents. Then, at an appropriate stage in the cross-examination of the defendant, the letters should have been placed before him, and he should have been asked if he was aware of their contents. Only if he had said that he was aware of their contents could he have been asked about the passages suggesting drug shortages in the past.[19]

The scope of cross-examination can be limited by common law or statute. An example of a common law limitation is the restrictive approach adopted towards attempts to cross-examine police witnesses about their conduct in other cases. Important statutory restrictions are contained in the Youth Justice and Criminal Evidence Act 1999.

CROSS-EXAMINING THE POLICE ON OTHER CASES

In *R v Edwards*,[20] the defence at trial had been that alleged admissions had been concocted by the police, who were members of the West Midlands Serious Crimes Squad. By the time of the appeal, police officers involved in the case were the subject of a large number of allegations, which were being investigated by the Police Complaints Authority. One of the officers had been charged with perjury, and it was known that other trials involving members of this squad had resulted in acquittals or the quashing of convictions on appeal. The Court of Appeal said that if that information had been available to the defence at trial, the court would have had to consider what questions could properly have been asked of the police witnesses in cross-examination.

The court said that it would be unwise to lay down hard and fast rules as to how a trial judge should exercise his discretion to secure a balanced picture of a witness's reliability. The court went on to say that it would not have been proper to ask the appropriate officers about either an untried charge of perjury or complaints not yet ruled on by the Police Complaints Authority. Nor should police witnesses have been asked about allegedly discreditable conduct by other officers, whether serving in the

---

19   See also *R v Cross* (1990) 91 Cr App R 115.
20   [1991] 1 WLR 207.

same squad or not. There was no legal basis on which the defence could adduce evidence of an habitual course of conduct, designed by police to defeat the provisions of the Police and Criminal Evidence Act 1984.[21]

In relation to other cases where the same police officer had given evidence 'unsuccessfully', the court laid down the following propositions:

(a) The acquittal of a defendant in case A, where the prosecution case depended largely or entirely on the evidence of a police officer, does not normally render that officer liable to cross-examination as to credit in case B.

(b) However, where a police officer, who has allegedly fabricated an admission in case B, has also given evidence of an admission in case A, where there was an acquittal, *by virtue of which his evidence is demonstrated to have been disbelieved*, it is proper that the jury in case B should be made aware of the fact.

(c) However, where the acquittal in case A does not 'necessarily' indicate that the jury disbelieved the officer, such cross-examination should not be allowed. A verdict of not guilty may mean no more than that the jury had some doubt about the prosecution case, not that they believed any witness was lying.[22]

What appears to be required is a verdict that *entails* perjury by a police officer, rather than a verdict that is merely *consistent with* perjury, but in the absence of any reasons for a jury's verdict this is an impossible test to satisfy. The Court of Appeal suggested as much in *R v Meads*.[23] In this case, counsel for the appellant and counsel for the prosecution both accepted that, where the circumstances of an earlier acquittal *pointed to* fabrication of evidence by a police officer, cross-examination should be permitted.

It was accepted by both sides that cross-examination about unproved allegations against a police officer should not be permitted, nor should cross-examination about the misconduct of other officers. The Court of Appeal observed that it might be necessary on another occasion to consider whether an acquittal could ever demonstrate that the evidence of a prosecution witness should be disbelieved.

The problem was indirectly considered in *R v Guney*,[24] where one of the issues raised on appeal related to the disclosure of relevant material by the prosecution. The

---

21   See also *R v Clancy* [1997] Crim LR 290.

22   [1991] 1 WLR 207, p 217.

23   [1996] Crim LR 519. And see *R v D* [2007] EWCA Crim 4, where the question arose whether evidence of the acquittal of a third party on a charge of indecent assault showed that the complaint against him had been false. The Court said that the fact of acquittal demonstrated nothing more than that the jury had not been sure that the third party was guilty.

24   [1998] 2 Cr App R 242.

Court of Appeal said that the defence were entitled to be informed of convictions of any officers in the case or of disciplinary findings against any of them. However, the court said that it would be wholly unrealistic for the prosecution to attempt to maintain records of every occasion when any police officer gave evidence that was 'successful or unsuccessful (whatever that may mean)'. In the court's opinion, 'the records available to the Crown Prosecution Service should include transcripts of any decisions of the Court of Appeal Criminal Division in which convictions have been quashed on the express basis of misconduct or lack of veracity of identified police officers as well as with cases which have been stopped by the trial judge or been discontinued on the same basis'.[25] The court took *R v Edwards*[26] as the starting point for the contemporary approach to the problem of discreditable behaviour by a police witness. The court went on to consider the problem that arose where the witness had given evidence 'unsuccessfully' in earlier cases. In relation to successful appeals, the court endorsed an earlier statement by Lord Lane CJ. He had said that the fact that the Court of Appeal 'was not satisfied' about aspects of the police evidence could not be the subject of cross-examination. From this, it followed that the quashing of a conviction 'should be less likely to found a proper basis for cross-examination than an acquittal by the jury, not least because the witness whose conduct is impugned has not normally had any opportunity to give evidence'.[27]

Thus, the Court of Appeal envisaged circumstances when an earlier acquittal in a different case *might* be the subject of cross-examination, but said nothing about the nature of those circumstances. On the other hand, because the court clearly considered itself bound by *R v Edwards*,[28] it could be argued that the test in that decision has been endorsed, with all its difficulties. However, the point did not arise directly, and *R v Meads*[29] appears not to have been cited. But in delivering the judgment of the Court in *R v Twitchell*,[30] Rose LJ identified four principles from the line of authority started by *Edwards*. First, the evidence must be relevant. Secondly, cross-examination relating to a criminal conviction or an adverse disciplinary finding is permissible. Thirdly, where an acquittal in one case indicates that the jury must have 'entirely rejected' the evidence of the police officer, that officer can be cross-examined about it in a subsequent case. Fourthly, it is not permissible to cross-examine an officer about complaints made against him which did not result in a criminal conviction or adverse disciplinary finding; nor is it permissible to cross-examine one officer about discreditable conduct by others.

---

25   [1998] 2 Cr App R 242, p 258.
26   [1991] 1 WLR 207.
27   *Ibid*, p 262.
28   [1991] 1 WLR 207.
29   [1996] Crim LR 519.
30   [2000] 1 Cr App R 373, p 382.

Cross-examination of particular officers about unresolved allegations of impropriety seems, however, to have been accepted as a possibility in *R v Edwards (Maxine)*.[31] In that case the Court of Appeal had to consider the safety of a conviction after a trial in which evidence had been given by members of the Stoke Newington Drugs Squad. The defence had been that officers in the case had fabricated incriminating evidence. After the trial, an investigation into this squad had begun, and the officers in the defendant's case were among those investigated. At the end of the investigation, no charges were made, or disciplinary proceedings taken, against them. At one stage, however, the degree of suspicion as to the trustworthiness of one of these officers was such that the Crown Prosecution Service had offered no evidence in two cases in which he had been involved and had not resisted an appeal in another. The Court of Appeal held the defendant's conviction to be unsafe. Beldam LJ said that it was impossible to be confident that there would have been a conviction had the jury known the facts and circumstances of the other cases in which this officer had been involved. Thus, the court assumed that information about the unresolved investigations in other cases would have been admissible at the defendant's trial if it had been available.[32]

On the other hand, in *R v Guney*[33] Judge LJ said that cross-examination about unresolved criminal charges or complaints was not permitted and, that rule was endorsed by the Court of Appeal in *Twitchell*. Although the law cannot be regarded as entirely settled, it seems likely that those statements of the law will be followed in future.

Finally, it should be noted that cross-examination of police officers about alleged misconduct in other cases would have to comply with s 100 of the Criminal Justice Act (CJA) 2003, which governs the admissibility of evidence of a non-defendant's bad character.[34]

CROSS-EXAMINATION OF COMPLAINANTS IN TRIALS FOR SEXUAL OFFENCES

The credibility of a witness is a relevant fact in any case because it is something that makes that witness's testimony about other relevant matters more or less likely to be true. At common law, cross-examination of a witness may be relevant either solely to credibility, or solely to an issue in the case, or to a mixture of both. For some centuries, moral character was regarded as relevant to credibility, and witnesses in any type of case could therefore be cross-examined about sexual promiscuity (amongst other things) with a view to showing that their evidence was not worthy of belief.

---

31   [1996] 2 Cr App R 345.

32   A similar decision was reached in *R v Whelan* [1997] Crim LR 353, in which *R v Edwards (Maxine)* was approved.

33   [1998] 2 Cr App R 242, p 260.

34   See below, Chapter 12.

Thus, in *R v Castro* (1874)[35] the question was whether the defendant committed perjury in swearing that he was Sir Roger Tichborne. A witness, Lord Bellew, stated that he had made tattoo marks on the arm of Roger Tichborne when they were at school together. No such marks were on the defendant's arm. It was held that Bellew could be asked and compelled to answer the question whether, many years after the alleged tattooing and many years before the occasion on which he gave evidence, he had committed adultery with the wife of one of his friends. The position was no different in cases where a complainant alleged rape or a similar offence. So a complainant could be cross-examined about being a prostitute, or about indiscriminate promiscuity, simply in order to show that she was not to be trusted. Such evidence might, on the facts of a particular case, be thought relevant not merely to her credit, but to the issue of guilt itself. This was particularly likely to be so where the act of intercourse was admitted by the defendant, but was alleged to have been with the complainant's consent. Whatever might be the position today, it is probably true that for much of the 20th century jurors would quite readily accept that a woman who was in the habit of committing fornication or adultery with different men was more likely than one who did not have that habit to have consented to sexual intercourse with a man to whom she was not married. On that basis, her sexual habits would have been relevant not only to her credit but to the issue of the defendant's guilt as well. Even today, where consent is in issue, a woman's previous sexual relations with *the defendant* are likely to be thought relevant, on the basis that a habit of consensual intercourse with a particular man makes another act of intercourse with that man more likely to have been consensual than if there had been no previous history of sexual relations between them. It will, of course, be remembered that an item of evidence does not have to be conclusive, or even very weighty, to be *relevant*.[36]

The common law was first changed by the Sexual Offences (Amendment) Act 1976, which applied where the defendant was charged with a 'rape offence'. Broadly speaking, this included rape, attempted rape, and aiding and abetting rape. It did not include other sexual offences, such as indecent assault. Section 2 of the Act provided that the defendant could not call any evidence, or ask any questions in cross-examination, about any 'sexual experience' of the complainant with a person *other than* the defendant unless the judge gave leave. On an application for leave, the judge was bound to grant it if he was satisfied that it would be unfair to the defendant to refuse.

In *R v Viola*,[37] the Court of Appeal said that leave should be given if the evidence or questions might reasonably lead the jury to take a different view of

---

35   *Charge of the Lord Chief Justice of England in the Case of The Queen against Thomas Castro . . . printed from the shorthand writer's notes*, 1874, Vol II, p 4764.

36   See above, Chapter 1.

37   [1982] 1 WLR 1138.

the complainant's evidence. It said that the Act was aimed primarily at protecting the complainant from questions that were relevant only to credibility, so if the proposed line of questioning was relevant to an issue in the trial in the light of the way the case was being run, it was likely to be admitted. The court acknowledged that there was a grey area in such cases between relevance to credit and relevance to an issue in the case. Evidence of promiscuity might be so strong, or so closely contemporaneous to the event in issue, as to reach the border between credit and issue. Conversely, relevant evidence might have such slight weight that it would not be unfair to exclude it. Later cases showed that the complainant's sexual history might become relevant because her evidence of circumstances surrounding the alleged offence had a 'ring of truth' that gave credibility to her story as a whole. For example, if, during her evidence, she claimed or gave evidence suggesting that the encounter had led to the loss of her virginity, a jury might think in relation to a particular defendant, 'It's not likely she'd have chosen him for a first experience; it must have been rape'.[38]

The relevant provisions of the 1976 Act have now been repealed by ss 41–43 of the Youth Justice and Criminal Evidence Act 1999. Section 41(1) puts a significant restriction on the way the defence can conduct its case where the defendant is charged with what the Act calls a 'sexual offence'. This is defined in s 62 of the 1999 Act and includes, among other offences, rape, indecent assault, unlawful sexual intercourse and any attempt to commit these offences. The new Act applies to a wider range of offences than the Act of 1976.

The restriction imposed by s 41(1) is that, except with the leave of the court, no evidence may be adduced by the defence, nor any questions asked in cross-examination, 'about any sexual behaviour of the complainant'. 'Sexual behaviour' is defined in s 42(1)(c) as:

> . . . any sexual behaviour or other sexual experience, whether or not involving any accused or other person, but excluding (except in s 41(3)(c)(i) and (5)(a)) anything alleged to have taken place as part of the event which is the subject matter of the charge . . .

The scope of exclusion in s 41(1) is significantly wider than in the 1976 Act. In particular, the 1976 Act expressly allowed questions about a complainant's previous sexual experience with the defendant, but this is now subject to the general ban. The expression 'sexual behaviour' appears to be wider than 'sexual experience', which was used in the earlier Act. For example, it seems capable of including flirtatious conduct or conversation. In many cases it will be very easy to say what is or is not sexual behaviour, but there will also be borderline cases. For example, the trial judge in *R v Mukadi*[39] held the expression to include the complainant's getting into an expensive-looking car in Oxford Street after the male driver, whom she apparently did

---

38   See *R v SMS* [1992] Crim LR 310.
39   [2003] EWCA Crim 3765, [2004] Crim LR 373, paras 14, 17.

not know, had slowed down to speak to her. But the Court of Appeal did not find it necessary to decide whether this was right in order to dispose of the appeal, and did not express any view on the matter. In *R v T, R v H*,[40] the Court of Appeal held that 'sexual behaviour' does not include false accusations of sexual offences made on earlier occasions. But the Court said that defence counsel who wishes to question a complainant about such an accusation should obtain a ruling from the judge that s 41 does not apply. For questions to be justified, the defence must have a proper evidential basis for asserting not only that the accusation was made, but also that it was false. If these conditions are not satisfied, the questions will be treated as questions about sexual behaviour, to which s 41 will apply.[41]

By s 41(2), the court may give leave to adduce evidence of the complainant's sexual behaviour, or to allow cross-examination about it if, and only if, it is satisfied of two matters: first, that either sub-s (3) or sub-s (5) applies; *and*, secondly, that a refusal of leave might have the result of rendering unsafe a conclusion of the trier of fact on any relevant issue in the case. These are not *alternative* conditions; for leave to be given, *both* must apply. It has been argued, notably by Lord Ackner,[42] that the Act creates, potentially, a situation where refusal of leave might render a conclusion of fact unsafe, but where leave must still be refused because the conditions laid down for admissibility in sub-s (3) or (5) are not satisfied. The government answer to that criticism, given by Lord Williams of Mostyn in the House of Lords, was that the provisions allowed enough scope for all *relevant* evidence about a complainant's sexual behaviour to be introduced. However, he immediately qualified this by claiming that the provisions now contained in s 41 provided a statutory framework for determining relevance.[43] He repeated this later in his speech, adding that the government believed that, in the past, the law had not been sufficiently balanced between respective interests.[44] It looks very much as if the government is accepting that some facts may be *logically* relevant, but, to preserve a 'balance' between the interests of the complainant and the defendant, they are not allowed to be *legally* relevant. On the other hand, if either sub-s (3) or (5) applies, it is difficult to imagine circumstances in which a refusal of leave would not render a conclusion on an issue in the case unsafe.

---

40   [2001] EWCA Crim 1877, [2002] 1 WLR 632.

41   This has been emphasised in a number of other cases. See, eg, *R v E* [2004] EWCA Crim 1313, [2005] Crim LR 227; *R v W* [2004] EWCA Crim 3103, [2005] Crim LR 965; *R v W* [2006] EWCA Crim 1292.

42   *Hansard*, 23 March 1999, col 1209.

43   *Ibid*, col 1216.

44   *Ibid*, col 1220. The European Court of Human Rights has recognised that this kind of balancing act is legitimate. Although the interests of victims and witnesses are not expressly taken into account by Art 6, they are regarded as protected by other Articles of the Convention. See *Oyston v UK* [2002] Crim LR 497.

The expression 'any relevant issue in the case' is defined by s 42(1)(a) as 'any issue falling to be proved by the prosecution or defence in the trial of the accused'. In a rape trial, of course, the defence has no burden of proof, but this is not the case with all the sexual offences covered by the Act. See, for example, the offence created by s 128 of the Mental Health Act 1959, which makes it unlawful for a member of hospital staff to have sexual intercourse with a woman receiving treatment for mental disorder at that hospital.

In *R v F*[45] the Court of Appeal pointed out that s 41 does not provide for the exercise of a judicial discretion, although it is sometimes 'loosely suggested' that it does. Under this provision the trial judge makes a judgment whether certain evidence should be admitted or excluded. If the evidence is relevant, then, subject to s 41(4) and assuming one or more of the statutory criteria for admission to have been satisfied, the court has no discretion to limit or refuse to admit it. This was a case where the defendant was charged with the rape of his stepdaughter. Although the allegations related to incidents that took place when the complainant was between 7 and 16 years of age, she made no complaint until she was nearly 30. Between the ages of 18 and 24 she had lived with the defendant in a sexual relationship. The defendant denied the allegations relating to her childhood, saying that they had been falsely made out of a desire for revenge when he ended the adult relationship. It was clear that the existence of the adult relationship was relevant to the question whether the defendant had sexually abused the complainant when she was a child, and the judge allowed evidence of the adult relationship to be given under s 41. The claimant's explanation for the adult relationship was that she had been in fear of, and dominated by, the defendant. The defence wished to counter these assertions by adducing evidence of photographs and videotapes, which, it was alleged, showed the enthusiastic part played by the complainant in the adult relationship. The trial judge refused to admit this evidence, but the Court of Appeal held that it was relevant, satisfied the s 41 criteria, and there was no discretion to exclude it.

The scope of sub-s (3)

The sub-section distinguishes between cases where the evidence or question in cross-examination relates to a relevant issue, but that issue is *not* one of consent, and those cases where the relevant issue *is* one of consent. The expression 'issue of consent' is defined in s 42(1)(b) as 'any issue whether the complainant in fact consented to the conduct constituting the offence with which the accused is charged (and accordingly does not include any issue as to the belief of the accused that the complainant so consented)'. So, if the defence is not that the complainant consented, but that the defendant *believed that she was consenting*, the sole test is whether the evidence or

---

45   [2005] EWCA Crim 493, [2005] 1 WLR 2848, para 29.

question relates to a relevant issue in the case, and the restrictions imposed by s 41(3)(b) and (c) will not apply.

However, the test of relevance where such a defence is put forward has been strictly applied. In *R v Barton*,[46] the defence to a rape charge was mistaken belief that the complainant had consented. The defendant wanted to call evidence of the complainant's sexual experiences with other men to establish the foundation for that belief, but the trial judge refused leave. The Court of Appeal upheld this decision and drew a distinction between belief that a woman *would consent if asked*, and belief that a woman *is consenting* to a particular act of intercourse. If a defendant wishes to establish that he was getting the wrong message from a complainant's responses, the evidence will have to be relevant to that issue. It will be no good establishing that the woman is promiscuous; that would be relevant only to a belief that she *would consent if asked*, not to a belief that she *was consenting on a particular occasion*. To establish the latter, evidence would be needed of the defendant's knowledge of her idiosyncratic behaviour on other occasions that might have led him to believe, for example, that when she said 'no', she meant 'yes'.

Another consideration in assessing the relevance of sexual history is the nature of the defence. The courts are likely to look at this realistically. Of course, a defendant who alleges consent will presumably have believed that the complainant was consenting. But this does not mean that the issue of belief in consent will automatically become a live issue in the trial. In many cases there will be diametrically opposite accounts of the circumstances in which the relevant acts took place; for example, where the complainant alleges that there was violence, and the defendant denies this, saying that she was the instigator and at all times participated enthusiastically.[47] Where the defendant's belief in the complainant's consent is not the central issue, a court is unlikely to allow cross-examination under s 41(1)(a). In *R v W*[48] the complainant's account was 'unequivocally of indecent assault and rape'. The defendant said that she had not only consented to the acts complained of, but had instigated them. The trial judge had excluded cross-examination about her sexual history, and it was argued on appeal that she should have permitted it because of its relevance to belief in consent. The Court of Appeal held that it had been right to exclude this line of cross-examination. The primary issue before the jury had been whether the complainant had consented. 'Honest but mistaken belief in consent was at best a secondary issue.'[49]

Sub-section 41(3) applies if the evidence or question in cross-examination relates to a relevant issue in the case *and either*:

---

46 (1987) 85 Cr App R 5.
47 *R v A (No 2)* [2001] UKHL 25, [2002] 1 AC 45, paras 35, 130.
48 [2004] EWCA Crim 3103, [2005] Crim LR 965.
49 Paragraph 15.

(a) that issue is not an issue of consent; *or*

(b) it is an issue of consent, and the sexual behaviour of the complainant to which the evidence or question relates is alleged to have taken place at or about the same time as the event which is the subject matter of the charge; *or*

(c) it is an issue of consent and the sexual behaviour of the complainant is alleged to have been, in any respect so similar:

   (i) to any sexual behaviour of the complainant which the defendant alleges took place *as part of the event* which is the subject matter of the charge, *or*

   (ii) to any other sexual behaviour of the complainant which the defendant alleges took place *at or about the same time as* that event,

that the similarity cannot reasonably be explained as a coincidence.

Sub-sections (3)(b) and (c) are sometimes misunderstood. It is essential to appreciate that they specify two quite different tests for admissibility. Sub-section (3)(b) is a test based on *contemporaneity*, sub-s (3)(c) is a test based on *similarity*.

Sub-section (3)(b) allows the court to look, but only to a limited extent, at the context in which the event which is the subject matter of the charge is alleged to have taken place. The bill originally provided for a 24 hour framework on either side of the alleged offence. If the complainant's sexual behaviour did not fall within that period, it was automatically excluded. Section 41(3)(b) is more flexible, but only slightly so. Lord Williams, speaking for the government, said that anything that happened more than 24 hours before or after the alleged offence should only rarely be considered to have taken place 'at or about the same time' as the event giving rise to the charge. He referred to the possible inclusion of events happening 'a few minutes – or at the very most, a few hours – outside the 24 hour limit'. (Conversely, if something had occurred just within 24 hours of the alleged offence, the court might not consider it to have taken place 'at or about the same time'.) In particular, Lord Williams said, the sub-section was not intended to include evidence of behaviour three, four or five days before the alleged offence. So if a complainant had had sexual intercourse with four different men a few days before the alleged offence, that evidence would not be admissible to support a defence of consent.[50]

The expression 'at or about the same time' occurs in s 41(3)(c) as well, and in *R v A*[51] the House of Lords considered its interpretation in that provision. It was alleged that the defendant had raped the complainant on 14 June 2000. The defendant's case was that the complainant had consented. He wished to adduce

---

50   *Hansard*, 23 March 1999, col 1217.

51   [2001] 3 All ER 1.

evidence that they had had consensual intercourse over a period of time that began approximately three weeks before 14 June, and that the last instance of consensual intercourse before that date had taken place approximately one week earlier. One of the questions that arose was whether any of those acts of intercourse could be said to have taken place 'at or about the same time as' the incident on 14 June. All the Law Lords were clear that none could, but some observations were made about the interpretation of the words in s 41(3)(c), on which the defendant had relied. Lord Steyn said that the words could not be extended to cover a period of several days. Lord Hope construed the words without reference to the debates in Parliament, but did rely on the explanatory notes to the Act prepared by the Home Office. The relevant note stated that it was expected that the words 'at or about the same time' would generally be interpreted no more widely than 24 hours before or after the offence. Lord Hope merely observed that the use of the words 'or about' in s 41(3)(c) avoided the trap of placing a straitjacket around a matter that had to be determined according to the facts and circumstances of each case.[52] What was said by Lords Steyn and Hope suggests that any event taking place more than, at most, a few hours outside the 24 hour periods before and after the alleged offence will be inadmissible. Lord Clyde left the question more open. In his view, how far backwards or forwards one might go beyond the borders of the event remained for the trial judge to determine. Even so, he thought it might be 'difficult' to extend that period to one of several days.[53]

A case where evidence was admitted under s 41(3)(b) is *R v Mukadi*.[54] The defendant was a security guard employed in the Oxford Street branch of Tesco. One day, the 23-year-old complainant went into the supermarket. Her appearance attracted the attention of the defendant, who fell into conversation with her. They agreed to go out together when the defendant came off duty, which he very shortly did. After stopping in Green Park to drink some wine, they proceeded by underground to the complainant's flat, which was a considerable distance away. The complainant's evidence was that she went with the defendant in order to get to know him and see if they might become friends. Once in the flat, sexual activities short of full intercourse took place, but this, according to the complainant, was not what she

---

52   [2001] 3 All ER 1, pp 15, 28.

53   *Ibid*, p 44. An example of evidence that passed the test under s 41(3)(b) is *R v Mukadi* [2004] Crim LR 373. The decision is particularly interesting because of the difference of opinion between the trial judge and the Court of Appeal about the relevance of the evidence in question.

54   [2003] EWCA Crim 3765, [2004] Crim LR 373. The judgment does not refer explicitly to sub-s (3)(b), but the facts indicate that this must have been the provision that the Court of Appeal had in mind. Care has to be taken when reading cases on s 41. Quite often the courts do not make clear which part of the sub-section is relied on; in some cases both (3)(b) and (c) could be a basis for admissibility; and sometimes the judgment, either of the trial judge or of the Court of Appeal, refers to an inappropriate provision in the section.

had had in mind, although she did reluctantly agree to it. According to her, there came a time when full sexual intercourse took place; to this she did not consent. The defendant's account was different. He said that she had been eager and encouraging in the early stages of sexual activity and had consented to full intercourse.

In order to support the defendant's evidence, defence counsel sought leave to cross-examine the complainant about an incident in Oxford Street, involving the complainant, that had taken place shortly before she went into Tesco's supermarket. She had been standing on the pavement in Oxford Street when a large, expensive-looking car pulled up beside her. There was only the driver, who was a good deal older than the complainant, in it. He spoke to her, whereupon she entered the car and the driver took her to a filling station. The complainant left the car at that stage, but before she did so, she and the driver exchanged telephone numbers.

The trial judge took the view that the complainant's act of getting into the car constituted sexual behaviour, and did not fall within any of the exceptions in s 41. He therefore refused leave to cross-examine on this matter. The Court of Appeal held that even if he had been correct in reaching this conclusion, the evidence should still have been admitted. Hearing about the car incident might have put in a different light the complainant's evidence about giving reluctant consent to the sexual activity with the defendant that had preceded full intercourse. And if the jury had disbelieved or doubted her account of that, they might well not have been sure that she was telling the truth when she said that she gave no consent, reluctant or otherwise, to full intercourse.

The Court could have been thinking only of admissibility under s 41(3)(b). There was no suggestion of similarity between the incident involving the driver and the events that took place with the defendant, but the incident with the driver clearly took place 'at or about the same time' as the event which was the subject matter of the charge against the accused.[55]

Sub-section (3)(c) allows the court to look at the sexual behaviour of the complainant on other occasions where that behaviour is so similar to the behaviour of the complainant on the occasion under investigation that the similarity cannot be explained as a coincidence. The behaviour may match either some element alleged by the defendant to have been part of the event that has led to the charge, or some feature of its surrounding circumstances within the limitations just described. It

---

[55]   It is worth reading the Commentary on this case in [2004] Crim LR 373, which is critical of the Court of Appeal's decision. Even under the new legislation, admissibility in cases of this kind is likely to remain largely unpredictable, because so much turns on the particular facts and the balance that is struck by the court, in the light of those facts, between the interests of the defendant and those of the witness. A useful comparison, in a case that also concerned sexual behaviour with someone other than the defendant, is *R v Harrison* [2006] EWCA Crim 1543. See, particularly, the observations of Hughes LJ at para 13.

appears to cover behaviour either before or after the alleged offence. It should be carefully noted that under sub-s (3)(c), the events in the complainant's sexual history that are relied on do not themselves have to take place at or about the same time as the alleged sexual offence. They can take place at any time, provided they are not so remote in time as to be irrelevant.[56] The defendant in *R v A*,[57] in an answer to an allegation of rape, said that the complainant had consented to sexual intercourse and further, if he was wrong about that, he had believed that she was consenting. In support of these alternative defences he wished to cross-examine the complainant about a sexual relationship between them that had lasted for approximately three weeks shortly before the alleged rape. It was accepted by all counsel in the appeal that the sub-s (3)(c) exception was not available on the facts. Nevertheless, there was some discussion about how the provision should be interpreted. On one view, the test was effectively that of 'striking similarity'. This concept emerged during the development of the law relating to 'similar fact' evidence, which, exceptionally, allowed the prosecution to adduce evidence of bad character in order to support its case against the defendant.[58] In *Boardman v DPP* Lord Salmon said that if the crime charged was committed 'in a uniquely or strikingly similar manner to other crimes committed by the accused, the manner in which the other crimes were committed may be evidence on which a jury could reasonably conclude that the accused was guilty of the crime charged'.[59] It seems clear, therefore, that such evidence must be of an unusual and specific nature.

Lord Williams appears to have had this test in mind during the debate on the bill in the House of Lords. According to him, evidence admissible under s 41(3)(c) could not include 'evidence of a general approach towards consensual sex', such as a taste for 'one night stands' or for having sex on a first date. It certainly could not include the fact that the complainant had previously consented to sex with people of the same race as the defendant. Nor could it include, where the allegation was of rape in a car, the fact that the complainant had previously had consensual sex in a car. He said that to be admitted under this provision, behaviour had to be 'the sort of behaviour that is so unusual that it would be wholly unreasonable to explain it as coincidental'. As an example, he took a complaint alleging gang rape where one of the defendants alleged consent. If the defence had 'specific factual evidence' that the complainant had previously engaged in consensual group sex in similar circumstances, this might be relevant for the jury to consider.[60] An example given by Lord Steyn in *R v A* was that of a defendant who alleged consent and also stated that after

---

56   *R v Tahed* [2004] EWCA Crim 1220, [2004] 2 Cr App R 551, especially paras 10–12.
57   [2001] 3 All ER 1.
58   See below, Chapter 12.
59   [1975] AC 421, p 462.
60   *Hansard*, 23 March 1999, col 1218.

intercourse the complainant tried to blackmail him by alleging rape. Evidence that on a previous occasion she had similarly tried to blackmail him would be admissible under this exception.[61]

Lord Clyde took the view that the standard set by s 41(3)(c) was 'something short of striking similarity'. It was not necessary that the similarity should be in some rare or bizarre conduct.[62] Lord Hutton pointed out, as had Lord Clyde, that s 41(3)(c) did not contain the expression 'strikingly similar', but used less stringent words.[63] He added, however, that some weight must be given to the word 'so', which was intended to emphasise that mere similarity was not sufficient. It may be, therefore, that in practice there is little difference between the approach of Lord Steyn and that of Lords Clyde and Hutton.

An example of the operation of s 41(3)(c) can be found in *R v Tahed*.[64] The defendant was charged with indecent assault and rape. He had previously had an intermittent sexual relationship with the complainant for between two and three years. The prosecution alleged that on a day in July 2002 the defendant telephoned the complainant, visited her home, and invited her to go with him to a nearby park. She agreed to do so. In the park there was a children's play area which contained a climbing frame. The defendant and the complainant went inside the frame and took part in sexual activities there. According to the complainant, she consented to none of them. The defendant alleged that she did, and asked for leave to adduce supporting evidence of a number of incidents that had taken place during their earlier relationship. These included evidence that they had had consensual intercourse inside the same climbing frame approximately three to four weeks before the date of the alleged offences. He wished to adduce further evidence to the effect that on that earlier occasion they had adopted the same respective sexual positions as they had done on the date of the alleged offences (both standing, with the complainant facing away from the defendant). The trial judge excluded all evidence relating to the earlier incident in the climbing frame. By the time the matter came before the Court of Appeal, the prosecution was ready to concede that the evidence of earlier intercourse within the climbing frame fell within s 41(3)(c)(i). Waller LJ, delivering the judgment of the Court, said that the concession had been properly made. He added that it was clearly arguable that evidence of the sexual positions on both occasions was similarly admissible.

By s 41(4), no evidence or question shall be regarded as relating to a relevant issue in the case if it appears to the court to be reasonable to assume that the sole or main purpose of the defence is to impugn the credibility of the complainant as a

61   *R v A* [2001] 3 All ER 1, p 16.
62   *Ibid*, p 44.
63   *Ibid*, p 52.
64   [2004] EWCA Crim 1220, [2004] 2 Cr App R 551.

witness. Of course, in one sense, evidence and questions about a complainant's sexual behaviour are bound to be designed to impugn the credibility of the complainant: the whole purpose of such questioning and evidence will be to create a reasonable doubt about whether the complainant is telling the truth when he or she says that sexual intercourse took place without consent. This can hardly be what the sub-section refers to. It presumably refers to the old common law rule, originally abolished for complainants in rape offences under the 1976 Act, that permitted evidence of immorality to be adduced to discredit generally what a witness said on oath.

This interpretation is supported by the decision of the Court of Appeal in *R v Martin (Durwayne)*,[65] where it was held that questioning about a complainant's previous sexual behaviour was not permitted if the main purpose was to impugn her credibility, but that it could be permitted if the main purpose was to strengthen the defence case. So, for example, if it is the defendant's case that sexual intercourse was by consent, and that it took place only after the complainant had pestered him for sex on a number of previous occasions, a court would almost certainly hold that the main purpose of the evidence about the earlier occasions was to strengthen the defence of consent, and not simply to shake the complainant's credibility.[66]

Sub-section (5)

This exception to the general prohibition applies if the evidence or question relates to any evidence adduced *by the prosecution* about any sexual behaviour of the complainant. The evidence admissible under this provision is not restricted by any time limit. For example, in *R v Rooney*[67] the complainant claimed during evidence-in-chief to have had no sexual experience before a particular incident with the defendant. It was held that in order to rebut this statement she could be cross-examined under sub-s (5) about her sexual activity with persons other than the defendant that had taken place approximately a year before the alleged incident. So, if during examination-in-chief the complainant states that she was a virgin before she was raped, the defence may cross-examine with the object of rebutting that assertion, and call evidence to do so if need be. But what is the position where the complainant makes a statement about her sexual behaviour during cross-examination? Suppose that when counsel for the defendant puts it to her that she consented, she replies,

---

65   [2004] 2 Cr App R 354. See also *R v F* [2005] 1 WLR 2848, para 27.

66   There would be two possible arguments open to the defence on these facts. (1) A woman who has sex with a man is more likely to have done so by consent if she has previously pestered him for sex. (2) A woman who has pestered a man for sex is less likely to tell the truth than one who has not. Argument (1) strengthens the defence case. Argument (2), even if true, relates only to the complainant's general credibility. If the defence relies wholly or mainly on (1), the questioning may be permitted, but not if it relies only on (2).

67   [2001] EWCA Crim 2844.

'That's a lie! I'd never have sex with anyone but my husband!'. The defence know that the complainant has in fact had sexual relations with at least three other men in the last six months. But can this be put to her? It does not appear to be evidence *adduced by the prosecution*, unless you regard everything said by a prosecution witness as such. If it was adduced by anyone, it was by defence counsel. More probably, it is wrong to think of it as adduced by anybody; rather, it has been volunteered by the witness. But in neither case could the statement, on a literal construction of sub-s (5), be rebutted. Yet the statement with nothing to contradict it could powerfully influence the jury.

Sub-section (6)

This provides that, for the purposes of sub-ss (3) and (5), the evidence that is permitted to be called must relate to *specific* instances of alleged sexual behaviour by the defendant. The question is, how specific? Would it be sufficiently specific to refer to an adulterous relationship with Charlie during summer last year? Or must there be greater particularity, stating, for example, the date and place of every act of adultery relied upon?

Procedure

By s 43, an application for leave under s 41 shall be heard in private and in the absence of the complainant. Nothing is said of the defendant's presence; *presumably* Parliament did not intend to exclude him, and the application will be made to the court after members of the press and public have been excluded. Where such an application has been determined, the judge must state in open court, but in the absence of the jury if there is one, his reasons for giving or refusing leave, and, if leave is granted, the extent to which evidence may be adduced or questions asked. Presumably, this also will take place in the presence of the defendant, but in the absence of the complainant, who would otherwise be alerted to questions she or he would face in cross-examination.

An escape hatch

I have already suggested that s 41 of the 1999 Act makes it possible for probative evidence to be excluded, to the disadvantage of the defendant. For example, a long standing sexual relationship between the complainant and the defendant could be concealed from the jury. Another example of potential injustice was given in the House of Lords by Lord Thomas of Gresford. Suppose, he said, a man and a woman live happily together for a period of time, but that the woman subsequently goes to live with another man. In due course that man leaves her and she returns to her first partner. A little later she has a row with that partner about having left him for another man. After the row she goes to the police and complains that her first partner has raped her. At the trial for rape, counsel for the defendant wants to put to the complainant that she made the complaint because of the row she had over her going away with the other man. Naturally, the defendant wants to give evidence explaining what the row was about. However, the effect of s 41 is to exclude both cross-examination and defence evidence on that matter.[68]

It was inevitable that the provisions of s 41 would be challenged by reference to the European Convention on Human Rights, and this is what happened in *R v A*, the facts of which have already been outlined. At a preparatory hearing in the Crown Court the defendant's counsel applied for leave to cross-examine the complainant about the alleged sexual relationship between her and the defendant. The judge held that such cross-examination was excluded by s 41. The defendant appealed. The Court of Appeal held that evidence of the alleged relationship was admissible in relation to the defendant's belief in consent, but not in relation to the issue of consent itself. The prosecution appealed to the House of Lords, which considered, as we have seen, the interpretation of s 41(3)(c), but also considered the effect on that provision of s 3 of the Human Rights Act 1998. Section 3 requires the court, so far as it is possible to do so, to read and give effect to primary legislation in a way that is compatible with human rights. The relevant right here was, of course, the right to a fair trial under Art 6. The House of Lords applied this rule of interpretation to s 41 and held that where the evidence relied on by a defendant was so relevant to the issue of consent that to exclude it would endanger the fairness of the trial, it should be admitted, as should cross-examination based on it. The decision has been criticised on the basis that it was not possible to interpret s 41 in this way, and that the appropriate course would have been to make a declaration under s 4 of the 1998 Act that s 41 was incompatible with the European Convention. Be that as it may, it is now clear that defence counsel who wishes to refer to a complainant's sexual history now has two lines of approach. First, he can try to show that the evidence falls within an exception to the basic rule of inadmissibility imposed by s 41. If that fails, it may be possible to argue that the questioning and evidence should nevertheless be admissible on the principle established in *R v A*. This is likely to be easier where the defence wishes to show the existence of a previous sexual relationship with the defendant. Sexual relations with other men are most unlikely to be regarded as relevant.[69] Even where there has been previous sexual intercourse with the defendant, its relevance may be open to question. For example, 'an isolated episode distant in time and circumstances' would almost certainly be excluded.[70] On the other hand, a recent close and affectionate relationship would probably be regarded as relevant.[71]

---

68   *Hansard*, 23 March 1999, col 1214.

69   See, eg, *R v A* [2001] 3 All ER 1, p 11, *per* Lord Steyn, and p 41, *per* Lord Clyde. See also *R v White* [2004] EWCA Crim 946, para 35, where Laws LJ said that it would take 'a very special case' to bring the complainant's sexual acts with other men within the *R v A* exception.

70   *Ibid*, p 18, *per* Lord Steyn.

71   *Ibid*, p 50, *per* Lord Hutton.

RE-EXAMINATION

The object of re-examination is to clarify and complete matters which were referred to in cross-examination, but which were left in an ambiguous or incomplete state. Re-examination should not be used merely as an opportunity to repeat evidence-in-chief. An advocate is not allowed, in re-examination, to ask questions that do not arise from the matters covered in cross-examination. If a subject was raised during examination-in-chief but not covered in cross-examination, it cannot be referred to in re-examination. Still less can a wholly new subject be raised in re-examination. For example, in *R v Fletcher and Others*,[72] the defendant's cross-examination of a prosecution witness was limited to the witness's credit only. The prosecution was not allowed, in re-examination, to ask their witness further questions so as to incriminate the defendant.

REFRESHING MEMORY

A witness may want to refresh his memory in the witness box about the events to which he is testifying. Typically, such a witness is a police officer, but the same rules apply if any other person wants to use a memory-refreshing note. Formerly, such a note had to be 'contemporaneous' before it could be used. This was interpreted to mean that it must have been made as soon as possible after the events recorded, at a time when the matters were still fresh in the witness's memory.[73] The conditions for memory-refreshing have now been relaxed by s 139(1) of the CJA 2003, which provides as follows:

> A person giving oral evidence in criminal proceedings about any matter may, at any stage in the course of doing so, refresh his memory of it from a document made or verified by him at an earlier time if –
>
> (a) he states in his oral evidence that the document records his recollection of the matter at that earlier time; and
>
> (b) his recollection of the matter is likely to have been significantly better at that time than it is at the time of his oral evidence.

The practical effect of s 139 is likely to be that prosecution and defence witnesses will, while giving evidence, be allowed to refresh their memories from witness statements that they made earlier, either to the police or to the defence solicitors. Unlike a police

---

72   (1829) 1 Lewin 111.

73   *R v Richardson* [1971] 2 QB 484.

officer's notes, such statements are usually made too late after the event to count as contemporaneous notes.[74]

Refreshing memory *outside* court was discussed in *R v Richardson*.[75] The defendant was being tried for offences committed about 18 months earlier. The civilian witnesses called for the prosecution were told outside court before giving evidence that they might refresh their memories, if they wished, by reading the statements they had made to the police a few weeks after the offences were committed. Each of the witnesses did so. On appeal, the question arose whether this had been proper. The court accepted that the statements were not sufficiently 'contemporaneous' to have been used as memory-refreshing documents while giving evidence. The Court of Appeal approved of what had happened and made several points:

(a) The court recognised the difference in approach towards documents used in the witness box and those used outside it, but there was no compulsion to aim for consistency in what was only a matter of practice, if that would produce results that would hinder the course of justice.

(b) To refuse to offer a chance of reading their statements to witnesses would tend to hinder justice: it would make testimony a test of memory rather than truthfulness. It would create difficulties for honest witnesses but do little to hamper dishonest ones.

(c) It would be wrong if several witnesses were handed statements in circumstances enabling one to compare with another what each had said.

Since the requirement of contemporaneity has now gone, point (a) has lost its significance, and there is even less reason to prevent witnesses from seeing their witness statements before giving evidence. As for the other points, the changes brought about by s 139 were presumably inspired by (b), and (c) is obviously still sound.

In *R v Westwell*,[76] the Court of Appeal said that there was no rule that witnesses *must* be allowed to see their statements before giving evidence. There might be cases where there was reason to suppose that the witness had an improper purpose in wishing to see it; in those circumstances he should be denied the opportunity. The court also said that it was desirable, though not essential, for the prosecution to tell the defence if witnesses had been shown their statements. In *R v Thomas*,[77] the Court

---

74 Section 139(2) allows a witness to refer for the same purpose to the transcript of an earlier sound recording of his account of any matter. If the document, including a sound recording, had been made when the matter was in fact fresh in the witness's memory, it might also be possible to admit it as evidence of the truth of its contents under s 120(4) and (6). See below.

75 [1969] 1 QB 299.

76 [1976] 2 All ER 812.

77 [1994] Crim LR 745.

of Appeal approved a trial judge's decision that a child aged eight should not be shown her statement before giving evidence. Presumably this was on the basis that so young a child might not appreciate that her testimony had to be about what she remembered of the day in question, and not about what she had read.

Where a note is relied on to refresh a witness's memory, the advocate who cross-examines may wish to look at it. May he do so? What use may he make of the document? And in what circumstances can the document itself become an item of evidence in the trial? In order to understand how the rules about these matters work, three things must be appreciated. The first is that if a memory-refreshing document becomes an item of evidence, or 'exhibit', in the case, it is evidence of the truth of the matters stated in it.[78]

Secondly, a document used to refresh a witness's memory may cover a variety of matters, not all of which will be obviously relevant to the trial of any particular defendant. The police officer's original notes in *R v Cheng*,[79] for example, contained records of observations involving other suspects who were not being tried with Cheng.

Thirdly, for a document to become an exhibit in the case, application must be made to the judge by the party who wants this. In the sort of situation under discussion, that party will often be the one whose witness has been cross-examined. Talk about a document 'becoming an exhibit' is a shorthand device that I use to refer to a procedure of this sort where the judge allows the application. It does not mean that the document becomes an exhibit *automatically*.

The rules about the use of memory-refreshing documents were summarised as follows by Sir Jocelyn Simon P in *Senat v Senat*:[80]

(a) Where a document is used to refresh a witness's memory, cross-examining counsel may inspect the document in order to check it. This will not make the document an exhibit. (Where a witness has given evidence without referring to notes, but has used notes to refresh his memory before going into the witness box, counsel may call for and inspect those notes and cross-examine on them.)[81]

(b) Counsel may cross-examine on the contents of such a document without making it an exhibit, provided the cross-examination does not go beyond the parts that are being used to refresh the witness's memory. For example, if counsel finds among the memory-refreshing parts something favourable to his client that has not yet been mentioned in evidence by

---

78   CJA 2003, s 120(3), reversing the common law.
79   (1976) 63 Cr App R 20.
80   [1965] P 172.
81   *Owen v Edwards* (1983) 77 Cr App R 191.

the witness, he can cross-examine about it, and the document will not become an exhibit.

(c)   However, where cross-examination is on parts of the document that have not been used to refresh the witness's memory, there is a risk that the document *will* be made an exhibit.

The effect of all this is that you may sometimes have to balance the possible advantage to be gained from cross-examination on the non-memory-refreshing parts of a document against the disadvantage of having the document put in as an exhibit, and becoming a permanent reminder to the jury of a witness's testimony.

The operation of these rules can be seen in *R v Britton*.[82] The defendant had been charged with assault during a political demonstration. After he was released from the police station, he typed out his recollection of events. At trial he was allowed to use this note, because it was regarded as sufficiently contemporaneous to refresh his memory while giving evidence of what happened prior to his arrest. On cross-examination, counsel for the prosecution inspected the note and asked questions about matters in it that had not been relied on to refresh the defendant's memory while giving evidence-in-chief. The defence applied to have the typed note made an exhibit, but the trial judge refused. The Court of Appeal held that this was wrong. Cross-examining counsel had gone beyond the parts used to refresh the witness's memory, and the defence were therefore entitled to have the whole document put in as an exhibit.

PREVIOUS STATEMENTS OF A WITNESS

To what extent can reference be made at trial to a witness's earlier out-of-court statements that are either consistent or inconsistent with the evidence that he gives in court?

PREVIOUS INCONSISTENT STATEMENTS

Any witness can be cross-examined about an earlier statement of his that is inconsistent with his testimony in court. If the witness then admits that his earlier account is the correct one, no problem arises. But what if he does not? In civil proceedings the previous inconsistent statement will be evidence of the truth of its contents,[83] so the trial judge can choose between the earlier and the later accounts. This was formerly not the case in criminal trials. The previous inconsistent statement was not evidence of the truth of its contents, and could be used only to challenge the credibility of the

---

82   [1987] 2 All ER 412.
83   Civil Evidence Act 1995, ss 1, 6(3) and 6(5).

witness. This distinction was criticised, and the law was changed by s 119 of the CJA 2003. Such statements are now evidence of the truth of their contents.

It follows from this change in the law that it is possible for a defendant to be convicted on the strength of a prosecution witness's earlier written statement, even though the witness's oral testimony does not repeat the matters set out in that statement. This could be important where a witness's oral evidence is affected by intimidation or bribery.[84]

An example of the operation of this provision is *R v Joyce (RJ) and Joyce (JP)*,[85] in which the defendants were charged with possessing a firearm with intent to cause fear of violence. The case for the prosecution was that they drove to the complainant's house, where one of them got out of the car and fired at the windows. They then drove away. The prosecution relied on witness statements identifying the defendants made by the complainant and two other witnesses. At trial all three witnesses retracted their statements and said that they had been mistaken. They were treated as hostile witnesses and cross-examined about their previous statements. The judge admitted the statements under s 119 and was upheld by the Court of Appeal. Rose LJ said that it would have been an affront to the administration of justice if the jury had not been able to rely, if they thought fit, on the original statements.

The manner in which a witness should be cross-examined about previous inconsistent statements is governed by provisions in the Criminal Procedure Act 1865.[86] Section 4 applies to both oral and written statements[87] and provides as follows:

> If a witness, upon cross-examination as to a former statement made by him relative to the subject matter of the indictment or proceeding, and inconsistent with his present testimony, does not distinctly admit that he has made such statement, proof may be given that he did in fact make it; but before such proof can be given the circumstances of the supposed statement, sufficient to designate the particular occasion, must be mentioned to the witness, and he must be asked whether or not he has made such statement.

Section 5 applies to written statements only and provides as follows:

> A witness may be cross-examined as to previous statements made by him in writing or reduced into writing relative to the subject matter of the indictment or proceeding, without such writing being shown to him; but if it is intended to contradict such witness by the writing, his attention must, before such contradictory proof can be given, be called to those parts of the writing which are to be used for the purpose of so contradicting him: provided always, that it shall be competent

---

84   For other practical consequences, see Law Com No 245, 1997, para 10.98.

85   [2005] EWCA Crim 1785.

86   This Act, which applies to civil as well as to criminal proceedings, re-enacted the Common Law Procedure Act 1854, ss 23 and 24, which applied only to civil proceedings.

87   *R v Derby Magistrates' Court ex p B* [1996] AC 487.

for the judge, at any time during the trial, to require the production of the writing for his inspection, and he may thereupon make such use of it for the purposes of the trial as he may think fit.

These provisions are intended to protect a witness against being unfairly surprised during cross-examination. Under s 4, the 'circumstances' which are to be mentioned to the witness include such details as the time of the earlier statement, the place where it was made, and particulars of other persons present when it was made.[88] The section applies if the witness does not 'distinctly admit' the earlier statement, and can therefore be used if the witness says simply that he does not remember, or if he refuses to answer. Under s 5, the witness can be shown the earlier statement, asked to read it silently, and then asked if he still stands by what he has just said in the witness box. That may be enough for the witness to change his testimony. If he does not, the advocate must decide whether he wants to use the writing to establish the inconsistency. If he does, the document must be put in evidence. The disadvantage of this is that it will then be available to the court in its entirety, and its overall effect may be to show far more consistency than inconsistency between what the witness said at first and what he has later said in the witness box.

PREVIOUS CONSISTENT STATEMENTS

The common law rule is that evidence may not be given of the fact that a witness, on some occasion before the trial, made a statement that was consistent with his later testimony at trial. Such statements are usually referred to as 'previous consistent statements' and the rule is sometimes referred to as 'the rule against narrative'. The purpose of the rule is to avoid a situation in which a potential witness might be tempted to manufacture evidence, and artificially increase the weight of what he says in court, by telling the same story to any number of people before the trial takes place. The application of this rule is illustrated by the decision of the Court of Criminal Appeal in *R v Roberts*.[89] The defendant was tried for the murder of his former girlfriend by shooting her with a rifle. His defence was that the death had been an accident. At trial, the defence wished to call evidence from the defendant's father to the effect that his son, shortly after being arrested, had told him that there had been an accident. The trial judge held this evidence inadmissible and was upheld by the Court of Criminal Appeal. Humphreys J said that the law was well settled: a party is not permitted to make evidence for himself.

Despite the decision in *R v Roberts*, it has been the practice to admit in evidence all unwritten and most written statements made by an accused person to the police,

---

88   *Angus v Smith* (1829) Mood&M 473; *Carpenter v Wall* (1840) 11 A&E 803. Section 4 very largely reflected the common law (Tapper, 2007, p 341), and earlier decisions can therefore be used to show how the section should be applied.

whether they contained admissions of guilt or denials. But in *R v Pearce*,[90] the trial judge excluded two voluntary statements and part of an interview on the ground that they were self-serving statements, and so inadmissible under the general rule.[91] The Court of Appeal held that this was wrong, and summarised the law as follows:

(a) A statement containing an admission is evidence of the facts admitted.

(b) A statement that is not an admission is admissible to show the attitude of the accused at the time when he made it. This should not be limited to statements made on first encounter with the police, though the longer the time that has elapsed since the first encounter, the less weighty the denial is likely to be. It is the duty of the prosecution to present the case fairly to the jury, and it would be unfair to give evidence of admissions but exclude answers favourable to the defendant.

(c) Although, in practice, most statements to the police are given in evidence even when they are largely self-serving, there may be a rare occasion when a defendant produces a carefully prepared written statement to the police with a view to making it part of the evidence in the case. The trial judge would plainly exclude such a statement as inadmissible.[92] (This was said before the passing of ss 34, 36 and 37 of the Criminal Justice and Public Order Act 1994. Since the change in the law effected by these sections, it is unlikely that even a statement of the sort described would be ruled *inadmissible*, though the weight to be attached to it would probably not be great.)[93]

Suppose the defendant makes a statement containing a mixture of inculpatory and exculpatory matters. For example, he admits that he drove his co-defendants to the scene of the crime and drove them away afterwards, but says that he did so only because they threatened to kill him if he refused. What should the jury be told about the evidential status of that? On the basis of the law just described, it seems that the inculpatory part is evidence of the truth of its contents but the exculpatory part is not – it is evidence only of the defendant's reaction when questioned by police. However, in *R v Sharp*,[94] the House of Lords accepted that it was unrealistic to expect a jury to

---

89   [1942] 1 All ER 187.

90   (1979) 69 Cr App R 365.

91   Confessions would have been admissible as an exception to the rule against hearsay: see below, Chapter 9.

92   (1979) 69 Cr App R 365, pp 369–70.

93   A document of this kind, produced by a defendant 'on being questioned' by the police, is admissible to show that a defendant 'mentioned' facts relied on in his defence, and so can avoid the drawing of inferences under s 34 of the Criminal Justice and Public Order Act 1994 (*R v Ali and Others* (2001) 151 NLJ 1321; *R v Knight* [2004] 1 Cr App R 117). See Chapter 11.

94   (1988) 86 Cr App R 274. The decision was followed by the House of Lords in *R v Aziz* [1996] AC 41.

understand the distinction, and said that the jury should be told to consider the whole statement in deciding where the truth lies. However, the judge should usually point out that the excuses are unlikely to have the same weight as the incriminating parts.

There are other exceptions to the rule against admitting previous consistent statements. If, in cross-examination, a witness's account is challenged as being a recent invention, he may support his account by reference to earlier statements to the same effect as his evidence. A case in point is *R v Oyesiku*.[95] The defendant had been arrested and taken into custody for assaulting a police officer. About two days later, before he was given bail, his wife went to his solicitors and made a written statement. The effect of it was that the policeman, who had been in plain clothes, was the aggressor, and that her husband did not realise that he was dealing with a police officer. At that stage the wife had not seen her husband. At trial she gave evidence on these lines in his defence. She was cross-examined on the basis that she had invented her evidence to help her husband. To rebut this suggestion, the defence asked for leave to put her statement to the solicitors before the jury. The trial judge refused, but the Court of Appeal held that he had been wrong. Following an Australian case,[96] the court said that if the credit of a witness is attacked on the ground that his testimony is a recent invention or has been recently devised or reconstructed, even though not with conscious dishonesty, evidence of an earlier statement will be admissible to rebut the suggestion made in cross-examination. If, however, the prosecution alleges that the defendant's story was fabricated from the outset, rather than at a later date, the usual rule applies: a previous consistent statement will be inadmissible.[97]

By s 120(2) of the CJA 2003, a statement admitted in this way is evidence of the matters stated, and not simply of the witness's credibility.

Section 120(2) may be too narrow. In *R v Ali*,[98] the Court of Appeal held that although there is no general rule that allows a witness who has been cross-examined about his previous inconsistent statements to be re-examined about previous statements that were consistent, there is a residual discretion to permit re-examination on these lines to correct an impression left by cross-examination that would otherwise be misleading. The difficulty with applying s 120(2) in such a case is that the sub-section refers to admissibility of a previous statement to rebut a suggestion of fabrication. Cross-examining counsel will in many cases not wish to go so far, and will allege only that the witness's honest testimony is mistaken. The witness in such a case might be re-examined on the basis of the discretion recognised in *R v Ali*, but the previous consistent statements revealed would be evidence only of consistency, not of their contents.

---

95   (1971) 56 Cr App R 240. See also *R v Tyndale* [1999] Crim LR 320.

96   *Nominal Defendant v Clements* (1961) 104 CLR 476.

97   See, eg, *R v Williams* [1998] Crim LR 494.

98   [2004] 1 Cr App R 501.

By s 120(3) of the CJA 2003, a statement made by a witness in a document, which he uses to refresh his memory while giving evidence, on which he is cross-examined, and which as a consequence is received in evidence in the proceedings, is admissible as evidence of any matter stated of which oral evidence by him would be admissible. It should be recalled that a memory-refreshing document will become evidence in the case only if cross-examination goes beyond those matters that are used to refresh the witness's memory.[99] Where such a document is admitted as evidence, the effect of s 120(3) is probably to make the document evidence of all the matters contained in it of which oral evidence could have been given.

By s 120(4) of the CJA 2003, a previous statement by a witness is admissible as evidence of any matter stated of which oral evidence by him would be admissible, if any one of three conditions is satisfied, and, while giving evidence, the witness indicates that to the best of his belief he made the statement, and that to the best of his belief it states the truth.

The first condition is that the statement identifies or describes a person, object or place.[100] This elaborates somewhat the old rule that allowed evidence to be given of a previous identification made by a witness. It allows, for example, a witness to an incident (W1) to tell someone who did not see the incident (W2) the registration number of a car that W1 saw taking part in the incident. If W2 makes a note of this, he will be able to give evidence at trial of the number that W1 indicated to him.[101]

The second condition is that the statement was made by the witness when the matters stated were fresh in his memory, but he does not remember them, and cannot reasonably be expected to remember them, well enough to give oral evidence of them in the proceedings. The scope of this provision is potentially very wide. Provided the witness is called to give evidence in the proceedings,[102] his earlier written witness statement could effectively be used as his evidence-in-chief if he says that he does not now remember the matters in question, and the court is satisfied that he cannot reasonably be expected to remember them. A witness who is forgetful or muddled in relation to part of his evidence would similarly be able to rely on his witness statement, at least in relation to the part of his evidence that was affected.[103]

The third condition, set out in s 120(7), is that:

(a) the witness claims to be a person against whom an offence has been committed;

(b) the offence is one to which the proceedings relate;

---

99   See above.

100   Section 120(5).

101   Cf Law Commission Consultation Paper No 138, 1995, para 13.35. W2 will, on ordinary principles, be able to use the note to refresh his memory.

102   Section 120(1).

103   It is not clear what would be the status under s 120(4) of those parts of the witness statement on which he did not need to rely in order to give a clear account.

(c)   the statement consists of a complaint made by the witness (whether to a person in authority or not) about conduct which would, if proved, constitute the offence or part of the offence;

(d)   the complaint was made as soon as could reasonably be expected after the alleged conduct;

(e)   the complaint was not made as a result of a threat or a promise; and

(f)   before the statement is adduced the witness gives oral evidence in connection with its subject matter.

For the purposes of sub-s (7) the fact that the complaint was elicited (for example, by a leading question) is irrelevant unless a threat or promise was involved.[104]

Sub-sections (4) and (7) cover an area very similar to that dealt with by common law rules governing the admissibility of a 'recent complaint' relating to the commission of a sexual offence. But the new provisions are not limited to sexual offences, and, unlike recent complaints at common law, statements admissible under sub-ss (4) and (7) are evidence of the truth of their contents, and not merely evidence of the complainant's consistency. At common law, a complaint elicited by a leading question was inadmissible. This is no longer the case, unless a threat or promise was involved, but the weight to be attached to a complaint produced in this way could be greatly reduced, and the defence might well make a successful application to have it excluded, either in the court's general common law discretion, or under s 78 of the Police and Criminal Evidence Act 1984.[105]

Since the main value of the complaint at common law was to show consistency in a complainant's account, no evidence of a recent complaint could be given if the complainant did not give evidence. Where s 120 is relied on, the position is the same because, for the section to apply, the witness must be called to give evidence,[106] and before evidence of the complaint can be given, the witness while giving evidence must indicate that to the best of his belief he made the statement and it states the truth.[107] In *White v R*,[108] the Privy Council held that a complainant could not give evidence of making a complaint unless the person to whom it was made was called to prove its terms. It remains to be seen whether this rule will be applied under the new law.

The requirement, under s 120(7)(d), that the complaint must have been made 'as soon as could reasonably be expected after the alleged conduct' was a requirement of the common law in relation to recent complaints in sexual cases. The trend during the last century was to make it easier to admit complaints. The first reasonable

---

104   Section 120(8).
105   See below, Chapter 11.
106   Section 120(1).
107   Section 120(4)(b).
108   [1999] 1 Cr App R 153.

opportunity did not have to be the first opportunity. As Roch LJ said, in *R v Valentine*:[109]

> We now have greater understanding that those who are victims of sexual offences, be they male or female, often need time before they can bring themselves to tell what has been done to them; that some victims will find it impossible to complain to anyone other than a parent or member of their family, whereas others may feel it quite impossible to tell their parents or members of their family.

This approach will no doubt be adopted under the new law in relation to the victims of sexual offences. It is less likely that victims of other offences will have good reasons for delaying a complaint.[110]

However, at common law the fact that the complaint was made at the first reasonable opportunity was not by itself sufficient; it had also to be 'recent' in relation to the offence. In *R v Birks*,[111] the defendant was charged with offences of indecent assault and indecency with a child based on events alleged to have taken place some 14 years earlier, when the complainant was very young. She gave evidence that she had first made a complaint to her mother approximately two months after the last incident on which the prosecution relied. In cross-examination she said that the gap in time could have been six, rather than two, months. Her mother's evidence was that at the time of the complaint she had understood her daughter to be referring to a sequence of events that had finished a year earlier. The trial judge ruled the complaint admissible, on the basis that it had been made at the first reasonable opportunity. On appeal against conviction, it was argued that this evidence should not have been admitted because the complaint had not been made within a reasonable time of the offence. Counsel for the prosecution acknowledged that they knew of no case of recent complaint where there had been a delay of more than a week from the alleged incident, but argued that it was enough that the complaint had been made as soon as reasonably possible in the circumstances. But the Court of Appeal felt unable to develop the law in this way. The test that the complaint had to be made within a reasonable time of the alleged offence could not be taken to mean 'within a reasonable time of the alleged offence *whether the complaint is recent or not*'.[112]

---

109   [1996] 2 Cr App R 213, p 224.

110   Less likely, but not inconceivable. Suppose Jezebel, a female student living with her parents, is robbed as she tries to pick up men in the red light district of her home town. She might well not want to disclose anything of the incident to her parents lest they discover the nature of her irregular source of income.

111   [2003] 2 Cr App R 122.

112   *Ibid*, p 131. The court added that it would be preferable if the law could be developed in the way suggested. It was undesirable for juries to be kept in the dark as to what had happened between the time, sometimes distant, of the alleged abuse and the time when the trial was taking place: *ibid*, p 132.

The effect of s 120(7) is to develop the law in the way that the Court of Appeal felt unable to follow in *R v Birks*. This appears from the decision of the Court of Appeal in *R v O*,[113] where it was alleged that the complainant had been subjected to sexual abuse by her stepfather between the ages of nine and seventeen. When the complainant was seventeen she left the family home to stay with a school friend and her mother. While she was away from home she told both her friend and her friend's mother of sexual abuse by her stepfather. The trial judge admitted evidence of these complaints under s 120. He also admitted evidence of a complaint to her brother, which she made about four months later. Was this a complaint made 'as soon as could reasonably be expected' after the alleged conduct?

The trial judge held that s 120 allowed evidence of more than one complaint to be admitted. The Court of Appeal agreed, saying that the statutory provisions were free-standing and provided their own criteria of admissibility. There was no limitation in the Act on the number of complaints that could be adduced in evidence, nor was there any reason to import one. Obviously there was a need in fairness to restrict evidence of 'complaint upon complaint', which might be merely self-serving. But where a later complaint was made in different circumstances, to a different party, and against a different background, it could be admitted. On the facts, these conditions were satisfied. Apparently, the distance in time between the end of the period of abuse and the complaint to the brother was no bar to admissibility.

In *R v Islam*[114] the Court of Appeal said that, as a matter of law, juries should be directed that the fact of a recent complaint cannot be independent confirmation of a complainant's evidence because the complaint does not come from an independent source. Although the old common law rules about corroboration of complainants in sexual cases had been abolished by the time *Islam* was tried, the Court of Appeal clearly took the view that a jury might nevertheless be looking for independent supporting evidence, and so needed to be warned against treating a complaint as if it were independent evidence. At the time of this decision, evidence of a recent complaint was evidence only of the complainant's consistency, and not of the truth of the facts stated. But the change in the evidential status of a complaint has not altered the fact that both complaint and oral testimony will have come from the same source. The case for the warning to be given is as strong as it was when the appeal in *Islam* was decided, and there seems to be no reason why the rule then laid down should cease to be followed.

It is convenient to note at this stage that in cases involving sexual assaults, evidence of a complainant's distress at about the time when the complaint is made can also be given. This is not evidence of any previous statement by the complainant,[115] and its admissibility is still governed by the common law, according to

---

113   [2006] EWCA Crim 556, [2006] 2 Cr App R 405.

114   [1999] 1 Cr App R 22.

115   It is unlikely to be regarded as a 'representation' within s 115(2).

which it is admissible to show consistency with the description of the incident given in evidence by the complainant, but it cannot be regarded as confirming that evidence from an independent source.[116] In *R v Romeo*[117] the Court of Appeal said that the weight to be given to evidence of distress varies infinitely, and that in appropriate cases the judge should warn the jury of the risk that distress may have been fabricated.

There is a final point to make about admissibility of previous consistent statements under the exceptions contained in s 120 of the Criminal Justice Act 2003. Even if relevant conditions are not satisfied, it is open to the court to admit such statements under s 114(1)(d) of the Act.[118] This provision allows a court in criminal proceedings to admit a statement not made in oral evidence in the proceedings as evidence of any matter stated, if it is satisfied that it is in the interests of justice for it to be admissible.

HOSTILE WITNESSES

An advocate who calls a witness in support of his client's case will not, save in exceptional circumstances, conduct his examination-in-chief in ignorance of what the witness is expected to say: he will have with his papers a written statement of that witness's evidence about the matters in issue. However, sometimes a witness fails to say what is expected of him; he may even say the contrary of what is expected. Reasons for this may be that he is honest but muddled, or that his recollection of events has genuinely changed. Such a witness is described as 'unfavourable', but the advocate can do nothing to discredit him, and his only remedy will be to call other witnesses to give a different account of events.[119]

Sometimes, however, a witness will fail to say what is expected of him, or say the contrary, because he is *not desirous of telling the truth to the court at the instance of the party calling him.* Such a witness is described as 'hostile' and may be discredited to a limited extent. This definition of a hostile witness by Sir James Fitzjames Stephen[120] is the most useful one to remember, because it makes no assumption about the motive for the witness's lack of co-operation. Some writers have stated that a witness is

---

116   *R v Keast* [1998] Crim LR 748; *R v Islam* [1999] 1 Cr App R 22, p 27.

117   [2003] EWCA Crim 2844, [2004] 1 Cr App R 417.

118   See, eg, *R v Xhabri* [2005] EWCA Crim 3135, [2006] 1 All ER 776, para 36. And see Chapter 9, below.

119   *Ewer v Ambrose* (1825) 3 B&C 746; *Greenough v Eccles* (1859) 5 CBNS 786.

120   Stephen, 1936, Art 147. It was adopted by the Court of Appeal in *R v Prefas* (1988) 86 Cr App R 111.

hostile 'when he shows animus against the party calling him',[121] but this is misleading. If Freddie is due to appear as a witness for the prosecution against Charlie, but is warned by Charlie's sisters, cousins and aunts of the unspeakable things they will do to him if he testifies, he may very well lack the desire to tell the truth when prosecuting counsel examines him. But this will be because he wants to save his skin, not because he has an 'animus' against the prosecution; he will be 'hostile', nevertheless. The key to avoiding confusion on this topic is to remember that 'unfavourable' and 'hostile' are technical terms and are not to be given their ordinary meanings.

A witness ruled hostile by the judge may be cross-examined by the party calling him with a view to showing that he said something different on an earlier occasion. But he may not be cross-examined with a view to discrediting him generally, for example, by asking him questions about any previous convictions he may have.[122] The power to cross-examine hostile witnesses can be found in both statute and common law. The statutory provision is contained in s 3 of the Criminal Procedure Act 1865. Like ss 4 and 5, this applies in civil proceedings also. The advocate calling such a witness may, by leave of the judge, 'prove that he has made at other times a statement inconsistent with his present testimony'.

Sometimes a problem may arise because the hostile witness fails to provide enough 'present testimony' to be inconsistent with the previous statement. Such a person may be treated as hostile and cross-examined by virtue of common law. For example, in *R v Thompson*,[123] the daughter of the defendant, who was charged with incest, took the oath and gave her name and address, but then refused to testify against her father. The Court of Appeal decided that the judge had power at common law, as well as under the 1865 Act, to allow her to be cross-examined by the prosecution, who had called her.

The object of cross-examination will very often be to put to a hostile witness his earlier statement, in hope that the witness will revert to his original story. According to s 3 of the 1865 Act, the witness must first be reminded of the occasion when he made the statement, and asked whether he did in fact make such a statement on that occasion. It is useful to remember that if a witness is hostile through fear, it is possible to put in his statement to the police as evidence under provisions in the Criminal Justice Act 2003.[124] If an unimportant witness is hostile it may be better tactics to stop questioning the witness, rather than make it obvious to the jury that he is giving evidence unwillingly.

A judge may conclude that a witness is hostile without a *voir dire*; it is in his discretion to hold one or not.[125]

---

121 Nokes, 1967, p 143.
122 See above, Chapter 6, for references to the rule against discrediting one's own witness.
123 (1976) 64 Cr App R 96.
124 See s 116(2)(e) of the Act and below, Chapter 9.
125 *R v Honeyghon and Sales* [1999] Crim LR 221.

One of the effects of s 119 of the CJA 2003 is that if a hostile witness admits making a previous inconsistent statement, or his previous inconsistent statement is proved under the provisions of the Criminal Procedure Act 1865, the statement is admissible as evidence of the matters stated.

COLLATERAL QUESTIONS AND EVIDENCE IN REBUTTAL

A multiplicity of issues in a case will lengthen the proceedings and is likely to confuse a jury. For this reason there is a rule that a witness's answers to questions on collateral matters (for example, matters that are relevant only to credit and not to an issue in the case) are 'final'. In other words, evidence may not subsequently be adduced by the party who asked the question to rebut the answer given by the witness. Unfortunately, it is not always easy to determine what is relevant to an issue in the case, and what is relevant only to a collateral matter.[126] The rule can create an artificial situation. For example, the complainant in one rape case had made allegations earlier that two other prosecution witnesses had been guilty of cruelty to children. The reaction of those other witnesses was to say that the complainant's allegations were untrue and malicious. Obviously, the jury's conclusion about the complainant's general truthfulness depended on whether her allegations about the other witnesses were true or not. The Court of Appeal said that in those circumstances it would have been the duty of defence counsel to put the untruthfulness of her allegations to the complainant in cross-examination, as relevant to her credit. However, it was said, if the complainant had insisted that they were true, evidence to the contrary from the other prosecution witnesses would have been collateral to the rape allegation and so inadmissible.[127] There are some exceptions to the rule that answers to questions on collateral matters are 'final':

(a)   Section 6 of the Criminal Procedure Act 1865 allows previous convictions (usually relevant only to credit) to be proved where the witness denies them or refuses to answer.

(b)   If a witness denies that he is *biased*, either for or against a party, evidence may be called to disprove him. Thus, in *R v Phillips*,[128] where

---

126   For further discussion, see the references to *Managers of the Metropolitan Asylum District v Hill and Others* (1882) 47 LT 29 and to *R v Funderburk* [1990] 1 WLR 587, above, Chapter 1. See also *R v Nagrecha* [1997] 2 Cr App R 401; *R v Neale* [1998] Crim LR 737; *R v Somers* [1999] Crim LR 744.

127   *R v Colwill* [2002] EWCA Crim 1320.

128   (1936) 26 Cr App R 17.

the defendant was charged with incest, his daughters denied in cross-examination that they had been 'schooled' in their evidence by their mother. The Court of Criminal Appeal held that the defendant should have been allowed to call witnesses to say that the daughters had told them that their mother had done this.[129]

(c) Evidence may be given of a witness's general reputation for untruthfulness. If Q is the witness whose reputation for truth is challenged, another witness, R, may be asked whether he has knowledge of Q's general reputation for truthfulness and whether, from such knowledge, he would believe Q's sworn testimony. R may also express his own opinion, based on personal knowledge, as to whether Q is to be believed upon his oath. In either case, however, R may not, during examination-in-chief, refer to facts forming the basis of his opinion, although he may be cross-examined about them.[130]

(d) Evidence may be given of a physical or mental disability affecting a witness's reliability.[131] So, for example, if an identifying witness denies in cross-examination that he is short sighted or suffers from delusions, evidence may be called to prove that he does suffer from those disabilities.

PROTECTING VULNERABLE OR INTIMIDATED WITNESSES

Sections 16–33 of the Youth Justice and Criminal Evidence Act 1999 provide special measures to protect vulnerable or intimidated witnesses. Witnesses may be eligible for assistance either on the grounds of age or incapacity, under s 16, or on grounds of fear or distress about testifying, under s 17. A witness is eligible under s 16 if he is under the age of 17 at the time of the hearing, or if the court considers that the quality of evidence given by the witness is likely to be diminished because the witness suffers from a mental disorder or otherwise has a significant impairment of intelligence and social functioning, or if the witness has a physical disability or is suffering from a physical disorder. Under s 17, a witness other than the accused is eligible for assistance if the court is satisfied that the quality of evidence given by the witness is likely to be diminished by reason of fear or distress on the part of the witness in connection with testifying in the proceedings. A complainant in respect of a sexual

---

129 See also *Thomas v David* (1836) 7 C&P 350; *R v Yewin* (1811) 2 Camp 638n; *R v Shaw* (1888) 16 Cox CC 503.

130 *R v Richardson* (1968) 52 Cr App R 317. The common law rules about evidence of reputation concerning a person's character are preserved by Criminal Justice Act 2003, s 118(1), para 2.

131 *Toohey v Metropolitan Police Commissioner* [1965] AC 595.

offence is also eligible for assistance in relation to proceedings in respect of that offence.

The court may make 'special measures directions' in respect of eligible witnesses under s 19. It also has powers under s 21 to make special provisions for child witnesses, that is, witnesses under the age of 17 at the time of the hearing, if the trial is for one of the offences specified in s 35, which includes, *inter alia*, sexual offences and kidnapping. The primary rule in such a case is that evidence-in-chief must be video recorded, and any evidence not given in that way must be given by means of a live-link.

As well as video recorded evidence and evidence by live-link, the special measures available to the court include screening the witness from the accused, excluding the public from court (but only where the proceedings relate to a sexual offence or it appears to the court that there are reasonable grounds to fear intimidation of the witness), removal of wigs and gowns and examination through an interpreter or some other intermediary. As a final sweeping-up provision, s 30 provides that a special measures direction may provide for 'such device as the court considers appropriate with a view to enabling questions or answers to be communicated to or by the witness despite any disability or disorder or other impairment which the witness has or suffers from'.

By s 32, where on a trial on indictment evidence has been given in accordance with a special measures direction, the judge must give the jury such warning (if any) as he considers necessary to ensure that the accused is not prejudiced by that fact.

Sections 34–39 of the Act protect certain witnesses, such as complainants in trials for sexual offences and some child witnesses, from cross-examination by the accused in person.

In *R v Camberwell Green Youth Court*[132] the House of Lords had to consider whether the scheme governing the way in which children are to give evidence in criminal cases was compatible with the defendant's right to a fair trial under Art 6 of the European Convention on Human Rights. It was held that the scheme is compatible. What matters is that the defence should have a proper opportunity to challenge and question the witnesses against the accused. Although, in principle, all the evidence must be produced in the presence of the defendant at a public hearing, this does not mean that a witness's evidence must invariably be produced in this way. The Convention does not guarantee a face-to-face confrontation between the defendant and the witness. By s 51(1) of the Criminal Justice Act 2003, a witness other than the defendant may, if the court so directs, give evidence in criminal proceedings through a live link. So far, this provision has been brought into effect only in relation to Crown Court proceedings for certain specified offences, which include rape.[133]

---

132   [2005] UKHL 4, [2005] 1 All ER 999.
133   SI 2007/3451.

The YJCEA was amended by the Police and Justice Act 2006 to enable a court to direct that any oral evidence from the accused should be given through a live link.[134] The court must be satisfied that such a course is in the interests of justice and that certain conditions are satisfied.

Where the accused is aged under 18 when the application is made, the conditions are that:

(a) his ability to participate effectively in the proceedings as a witness giving oral evidence in court is compromised by his level of intellectual ability or social functioning, and

(b) use of a live link would enable him to participate more effectively in the proceedings as a witness (whether by improving the quality of his evidence or otherwise).

Where the accused has attained the age of 18 at that time, the conditions are that:

(a) he suffers from a mental disorder (within the meaning of the Mental Health Act 1983) or otherwise has a significant impairment of intelligence and social function,

(b) he is for that reason unable to participate effectively in the proceedings as a witness giving oral evidence in court, and

(c) use of a live link would enable him to participate more effectively in the proceedings as a witness (whether by improving the quality of his evidence or otherwise).

FURTHER READING

— Birch, 'Rethinking Sexual History Evidence: Proposals for Fairer Trials' [2002] Crim LR 531.

— Hoyano, 'Variations on a Theme by Pigot: Special Measures Directions for Child Witnesses' [2000] Crim LR 250.

— Kibble, 'Judicial Perspectives on the Operation of s 41 and the Relevance and Admissibility of Prior Sexual History Evidence: Four Scenarios' [2005] Crim LR 190.

— Kibble, 'Judicial Discretion and the Admissibility of Prior Sexual History Evidence under section 41 of the Youth Justice and Criminal Evidence Act 1999' [2005] Crim LR 263.

— McEwan, 'In Defence of Vulnerable Witnesses: the Youth Justice and Criminal Evidence Act 1999.' (2000) 4 E&P 1.

— McEwan, ' "I Thought She Consented": Defeat of the Rape Shield or the Defence That Shall Not Run?' [2006] Crim LR 969.

— Redmayne, 'Myths, Relationships and Coincidences: The New Problems of Sexual History' (2003) 7 E&P 75.

— Spencer, 'The Evidential Status of Previous Inconsistent Statements' [2006] 65 CLJ 518.

---

134   See YJCEA, s 33A. The provision came into force on 15 January 2007: see SI 2006/3364, art 2(h).

EXERCISES

1. What is a leading question?

2. What is the reason for the rule against discrediting your own witness?

3. A and B are jointly charged with murder. In his interview with the police, A incriminates B. Can B, if he gives evidence, be cross-examined by the prosecution about what A said concerning him?

4. What rules were laid down in *R v Edwards* (1991) about the cross-examination of police officers on other cases in which they gave evidence for the prosecution, but in which the defendant was acquitted? Are there difficulties in applying any of these rules?

5. In what respects does s 41 YJCEA extend the protection given to complainants in sexual cases by the Sexual Offences (Amendment) Act 1976?

6. In what circumstances can the complainant in a sexual case be cross-examined about her sexual history, (a) when the issue raised by the defence is not one of consent; and, (b) where the issue is one of consent?

7. What is the significance of the decision of the House of Lords in *R v A (No 2)* (2001)?

8. Give an example of a situation in which the defence could rely on s 41(5) YJCEA as the basis for cross-examination on a complainant's sexual history.

9. What limitations, if any, apply to re-examination of a witness?

10. What did *Senat v Senat* (1965) establish concerning the use in court of a memory-refreshing document?

11. What is the evidential status in a criminal trial of a witness's previous inconsistent statement?

12. When can evidence be given of a witness's previous consistent statements?

13. What direction should a judge give to the jury about evidence of the distressed condition of a complainant in a sexual case?

14. What is the difference between a hostile and an unfavourable witness?

15. What exceptions are there to the rule that answers to questions on collateral matters are 'final'? What is meant in this context by 'final'?

7

BURDEN AND STANDARD OF PROOF AND PRESUMPTIONS

SUMMARY

INTRODUCTION

Every contested case, civil or criminal, must give rise to at least one contested issue of fact, but many cases of both kinds give rise to several issues of fact to be decided between the parties. This is particularly frequent in civil cases, because a defendant against whom a claim is made will often not only defend that claim but raise one of his own against the claimant (formerly the 'plaintiff') – called a 'counterclaim' – to be decided in the same action. This chapter deals with two questions which arise in relation to every issue of fact:

(a) Who has the 'legal burden' of proof, that is, the burden of adducing evidence to prove the fact in question?

(b) What test will be applied to determine whether sufficiently weighty evidence has been called to discharge that burden?

Before considering these questions, however, it is necessary to say something about what is called the 'evidential burden'. This must not be confused with the 'legal burden'. It is particularly important to understand the nature of the evidential burden because the effect of the Human Rights Act 1998 in some cases has been to reduce a statutory legal burden on a defendant in a criminal case to an evidential burden only.

THE EVIDENTIAL BURDEN

The evidential burden is not strictly a burden of *proof* at all.[1] It is best seen as a *rule of common sense* which says that there must be *some* evidence for a particular issue to become a live one so as to be fit for consideration by a jury or other tribunal of fact. It is sometimes said that an evidential burden is on a party 'to adduce' some evidence to support a particular issue. This can be misleading; it is not essential that the evidence be adduced by the party who has the evidential burden. The evidence could come from witnesses on the other side, either in cross-examination or even when giving evidence-in-chief. All that a party with an evidential burden needs to be able to do is to *point to* some evidence making the issue in question a live one.[2]

Whether an evidential burden has been satisfied is a matter for the judge alone. It follows that there should never be any reference to it in a summing up. The evidential burden governs what the judge *does*, in leaving the question to the jury or withdrawing it from them. The legal burden governs what he *says* when directing the jury about how they are to reach their verdict.[3]

The effect of having an evidential burden can be seen in an illustration. Suppose, first, that Mr Whitewig is defending Charlie on a charge of assault. Charlie has decided not to give evidence and there is no suggestion from the prosecution witnesses or anyone else that he might have been acting in self-defence when he struck his victim. In an impassioned closing speech to the jury, Charlie's counsel says: 'Members of the jury, you cannot convict my client because there is always the possibility that he might have been acting in self-defence. And so long as that possibility remains, how can you be satisfied so that you are sure of his guilt?' At that stage the judge would be likely to interrupt and say: 'Mr Whitewig, there is not a scrap of evidence to support the suggestion that the accused might have been acting in self-defence and I shall have to tell the jury in due course that that issue is not open for their consideration.'

In practice, the question of whether an evidential burden has been satisfied is more likely to arise on a defence submission, at the end of the prosecution case, that there is no case to answer. As well as having the legal burden of proof, the prosecution also have an evidential burden to adduce some evidence fit to go to a jury of every element necessary to establish their case against the accused. If, at the end of their case, there is no evidence of an essential element of the offence, the judge will allow

---

1   See *Jayasena v R* [1970] AC 618, p 624; *L v DPP* [2002] 2 All ER 854.
2   See *L v DPP* [2002] 2 All ER 854, p 861; *Sheldrake v DPP* [2003] 2 All ER 497, pp 510, 511, 530.
3   Williams, 1977b.

the submission and direct the jury to return a verdict of not guilty without hearing the case for the defence.[4]

Questions are sometimes asked about the weight of evidence required to satisfy an evidential burden. Judges have occasionally referred to this, but what they have said has not been very helpful and it can be misleading if it encourages students to think of the evidential burden as a burden of *proof.* It would, for example, be wholly wrong to suggest that the evidential burden has to be discharged 'on the balance of probabilities' or 'beyond reasonable doubt'. The simplest line to take is that, because the evidential burden is not a burden of proof, it does not make sense to talk of a standard of proof in relation to it. The only qualification to this is that where non-insane automatism is relied on as a defence, a judge is unlikely to leave that defence to the jury in the absence of medical or scientific evidence in support.[5]

When does an evidential burden rest on the defence? The answer is that the defence will have such a burden *in relation to any issue that the prosecution are not required to raise.* One obvious case is where the defence have a *legal* burden to satisfy in relation to a particular issue. However, even where the defence has no legal burdens, it may still, in relation to some issues, have an evidential burden. Where a defendant in a criminal trial has an evidential burden in relation to a particular issue and has satisfied it by identifying sufficient evidence to raise the issue, the prosecution has the legal burden of negating that issue and must satisfy that burden before the defendant can be convicted.[6] General defences (such as self-defence, duress, and non-insane automatism), which are applicable to more than one offence, will place an evidential burden on the defendant.[7] The same is true of the defence of provocation as a defence to a murder charge.[8] These 'defences' operate by way of what, in a civil action, would be called 'confession and avoidance': they admit certain facts, but raise a new issue to avoid the likely consequence of what has been admitted. The placing of an evidential burden on a defendant is compatible with Art 6(2) of the European Convention on Human Rights because it does not breach the presumption of innocence.[9] An example of a defence that does *not* work in this way is the defence, where rape is alleged, that the complainant consented to the act of sexual intercourse. The absence of consent in rape is an essential element of the offence, in respect of which

---

4   See *R v Galbraith* [1981] 1 WLR 1039, approved in *R v Fulcher* [1995] 2 Cr App R 251; see above, Chapter 1.

5   *Hill v Baxter* [1958] 1 All ER 193, p 197; *Bratty v AG for Northern Ireland* [1963] AC 386, pp 413–14.

6   *R v Lambert* [2001] 3 All ER 577, p 635, *per* Lord Hutton.

7   *R v Lobell* [1957] 1 QB 547; *R v Gill* [1963] 1 WLR 841; *Bratty v AG for Northern Ireland* [1963] AC 386.

8   *Mancini v DPP* [1942] AC 1.

9   *R v DPP ex p Kebilene and Others* [2000] 1 Cr App R 275, p 324.

the prosecution has both a legal and evidential burden.[10] It should be remembered that an evidential burden, like a legal burden, can rest on only one party in respect of one issue. There is therefore no evidential burden on the defendant in a rape trial to show consent, though obviously a defendant is likely to be convicted if that is the defence and there is not at least *some* evidence of consent.

Where an alibi defence is raised, there is no legal burden of proof on the defendant. The judge must tell the jury in summing up that it is for the prosecution to disprove the alibi beyond reasonable doubt before there can be a conviction.[11]

THE BURDEN OF PROOF

The 'burden of proof' is the obligation which rests on a party in relation to a particular issue of fact in a civil or criminal case, and which must be 'discharged', or 'satisfied', if that party is to win on the issue in question. This burden is often referred to as 'the legal burden'. It is to be distinguished from what is called 'the evidential burden' which, as we shall see, is something completely different. Unfortunately for students of this subject, there are several synonyms for 'legal burden'. This concept can also be referred to by any of the following expressions: 'persuasive burden', 'probative burden', 'ultimate burden', 'burden of proof on the pleadings' and 'risk of non-persuasion'. Remember, though, that 'evidential burden' does *not* refer to the same concept.

Remember also that talk about the burden of proof in any given case makes no sense *unless you relate that burden to a particular issue of fact.* It is dangerous to talk of the burden of proof in relation to a case as a whole, because in many civil cases, and in some criminal cases also, one party will bear the burden of proof on some issues and another party will bear it on others. For example, in a simple case of negligence arising from a road traffic accident there are quite likely to be at least two fundamental issues. The claimant will say that there was a collision between the defendant's car and his own, that this was caused by the negligence of the defendant, and that as a result the claimant suffered injury, loss and damage. In response to this, the defendant may admit that there was a collision, but deny that he was guilty of any negligence, saying that the only person guilty of negligence was the claimant. And he may go on to say that as a result of the claimant's negligence, he, the defendant, suffered injury, loss and damage. He will have, in other words, a counterclaim against the claimant.

How many issues are there here? To establish his claim the claimant will have to prove that:

---

10   *DPP v Morgan* [1976] AC 182.
11   *R v Popat (No 2)* [2000] 1 Cr App R 387.

(a)   there was a collision between the two cars;

(b)   the collision was caused by the defendant's negligence; and

(c)   as a result of the collision, he suffered loss.

The defendant admits the collision, but to establish his counterclaim he must then go on to prove that:

(d)   the collision was caused by the claimant's own negligence; and

(e)   as a result, he (the defendant) suffered injury, loss and damage.

So there are five issues, four of which are disputed. (The collision is admitted.) Who has the burden of proof in this case? An answer to this question can be given only by reference to the issues. In fact, the claimant has the burden of proof on issues (b) and (c), and the defendant has the burden of proof on issues (d) and (e).

It is very important to remember that, in relation to any particular issue, the burden of proof can rest on only *one* party. Thus, in relation to a single issue, you cannot have a burden on one party to prove the existence of a state of affairs and a burden on the other party to prove its non-existence. In particular, you should note that a counterclaim raises issues that are entirely separate. If the claimant fails to satisfy the judge that the accident was caused by the negligence of the defendant, the claimant will not recover damages from the defendant, but this does not mean that the defendant will recover from the claimant. To do so, the defendant must satisfy the judge that the accident was the claimant's fault, and he may fail to achieve this. It might be a perfectly rational result for both claim and counterclaim to fail, because on neither side was the evidence strong enough to persuade the judge that one party was at fault rather than the other.

In *Rhesa Shipping Co SA v Edwards*[12] Lord Brandon said that the judge is not always bound to make to make a finding one way or the other with regard to the facts averred by the parties.

> He has open to him the third alternative of saying that the party on whom the burden of proof lies in relation to any averment made by him has failed to discharge that burden. No judge likes to decide cases on burden of proof if he can legitimately avoid having to do so. There are cases, however, in which, owing to the unsatisfactory state of the evidence or otherwise, deciding on the burden of proof is the only just course for him to take.

However, a judge cannot avoid his duty to resolve conflicts of evidence by resorting to the burden of proof as a means of deciding a case. Before dealing with a disputed issue in this way, he must be in the exceptional situation of being unable reasonably to make a finding in relation to a disputed issue, despite having striven to do so.[13]

---

12   [1985] 1 WLR 948, pp 955–56.

13   *Sewell v Electrolux Ltd* (1997) *The Times*, 7 November; *Stephens v Cannon* [2005] EWCA Civ 222.

DECIDING BURDENS OF PROOF IN CIVIL CASES

In some cases the point may already be covered by case law or statute. Many commercial transactions are undertaken according to a standard form of contract. For example, standard forms of contract are in use for building and construction works and for the carriage of particular commodities. Where your client entered into a standard form of contract, the contract may already have been the subject of appellate decisions which will bind a subsequent court on points of interpretation. However, such decisions will be binding *only* if you are dealing with a contract which is of the standard form in question. Just because a particular form of words was used in *one* type of contract, it does not follow that a decision about the interpretation of *that* contract will be persuasive, let alone binding, where the court has to interpret a *different* contract. Interpretation takes place *in a context*; words and phrases do not have immutable meanings wherever they may appear.

Statutes sometimes impose burdens of proof in civil proceedings. Suppose, for example, an insolvent debtor has preferred one creditor over others (as by paying that creditor in full while others went completely unpaid). The Insolvency Act 1986 provides that if the debtor is subsequently made bankrupt, the trustee in bankruptcy may apply to the court for an order restoring the position to what it would have been if that preference had not been made.[14] The court cannot make such an order unless the debtor who gave the preference was influenced in deciding to give it by a desire to put the creditor into a better position than he would otherwise have had in the event of the debtor's bankruptcy. Ordinarily, therefore, the burden will be on the trustee in bankruptcy to prove that desire. However, where the preferred creditor was an 'associate'[15] of the debtor, the Act provides that the appropriate desire shall be presumed 'unless the contrary is shown'. The effect of this is to put onto the preferred creditor the burden of proving that at the time the preference was made, the debtor did *not* have the appropriate desire.

In the absence of precedent or statutory provision, resort must be had, in doubtful cases, to general guidelines. At least two can be perceived, but unfortunately they are only of the most tenuous kind. The first is that the burden should lie on the party who affirms a proposition rather than on the party who denies it.[16] The second is that 'the burden of proof in any particular case depends on the circumstances under which the claim arises'.[17]

Quite properly, the courts have avoided a mechanical approach to the 'affirmation or denial' test. In particular, the court's decision will not be determined

---

14   Insolvency Act 1986, s 340.

15   Defined in the Insolvency Act 1986, s 435.

16   *Constantine (Joseph) SS Line Ltd v Imperial Smelting Corp Ltd* [1942] AC 154, p 174, *per* Viscount Maugham.

17   *Ibid.*

by the form of words used in the statements of case, formerly known as 'pleadings'. In *Soward v Leggatt*,[18] a landlord claimed against his tenant under a repairing covenant in a lease. In his pleading he alleged that the defendant 'did not repair' and 'did not paint' the premises. To this the defendant pleaded that he 'did . . . well and sufficiently repair' and that he 'did paint' the premises. Thus, on paper, it looked as if the plaintiff was making denials and the defendant the positive assertions.

At trial, the defendant's counsel claimed that he had the burden of proof and so the right to open the case. Lord Abinger CB said:

> Looking at these things according to common sense, we should consider what is the substantive fact to be made out, and on whom it lies to make it out. It is not so much the form of the issue which ought to be considered, as the substance and effect of it. In many cases, a party, by a little difference in the drawing of his pleadings, might make [his allegation] either affirmative or negative, as he pleased. The plaintiff here says, 'You did not repair'; he might have said, 'You let the house become dilapidated.' I shall endeavour by my own view to arrive at the substance of the issue, and I think in the present case that the plaintiff's counsel should begin.[19]

In other words, despite the form of the pleadings, the burden of proof was on the plaintiff to prove breach by the defendant of the covenants in the lease.

It may be particularly difficult to predict how a judge will allocate the burdens of proof in a case where contractual provisions exclude or limit liability. The cases often referred to on this topic in the books show no more than the application in differing circumstances of the second guideline referred to above: that where the burden of proof lies will depend on the circumstances of the particular claim.

A case often cited is *The Glendarroch*.[20] The plaintiffs had bought a consignment of cement, which was to be carried to them by the defendant shippers. But the ship carrying the cement became stranded and the cement was so damaged as to be worthless. No bill of lading had in fact been signed, but the trial judge found that the contract was governed by the terms of an ordinary bill of lading. Under a contract of this type, shippers were exempt from liability for damage caused by perils of the sea unless the damage was due to the shippers' own negligence.

The shippers denied liability on the ground that the ship had become stranded and the cement damaged by reason of perils of the sea. The trial judge ruled that in order to excuse themselves they had to show not just a peril of the sea, but that the peril had not been occasioned by their negligent navigation. The shippers thereupon called no evidence and the plaintiffs were awarded judgment. Had the trial judge been right?

---

18 (1836) 7 C&P 613.
19 (1836) 7 C&P 613, p 615.
20 [1894] P 226.

In the Court of Appeal, Lord Esher MR dealt first with the contractual structure. He agreed with the trial judge that the case had to be treated as if the contract had been on the ordinary terms of a bill of lading. Such a bill of lading expressly excluded the shippers from liability caused by perils of the sea. The next question was whether a term was to be implied in an ordinary bill of lading that the perils of the sea should not have been occasioned by the shippers' negligence. Lord Esher thought that such a term did exist by necessary inference. Further, it was to be read into the contract as an exception to an exception. The contract had to be read as if it stated that the shippers would be liable *unless* the loss was caused by perils of the sea, *unless that loss was the result of the negligence of the shippers.*

In those circumstances, it was for the plaintiff to prove the contract and non-delivery. The defendants had the burden of showing that the loss had been caused by perils of the sea, so as to exclude them from liability. It was then for the plaintiffs to make out the exception to that exception by proving that the shippers had been negligent.

What swayed Lord Esher was the way in which actions of that kind had for many years been pleaded. The plaintiff would allege the existence of a bill of lading and the fact of non-delivery under it. The defendant would then plead that the loss had been by perils of the sea. No plea that could be found in the books had ever gone on to say that the loss by perils of the sea was not caused by negligence. However, if the contention were true that the burden of proof to that extent lay on the defendant, every one of those pleas without that allegation had been no answer to the plaintiff's pleading and had thus been open to demurrer,[21] but in no such case had a demurrer been pleaded. From this it could be inferred that there was no burden on shippers in such circumstances to prove that the perils of the sea had not been caused by their own negligence. Instead, a long succession of similar cases showed the plaintiff setting out a replication[22] saying in effect, 'True, there was a loss by perils of the sea within the *prima facie* exception, but that was brought about by the negligence of the shippers'. This practice of pleading reflected where, as a matter of law, the burdens lay. The judge had been wrong. The onus had been on the plaintiffs to prove negligence; it had not been for the shippers to prove absence of negligence on their part.

In this case, the Court of Appeal reached its decision by treating the contract as

---

21   A demurrer was a written plea to the effect that the facts pleaded failed as a matter of law to establish a cause of action or a defence, as the case might be.

22   Another technical term from the old forms of pleading. The first pleading, in which the plaintiff stated his case, was the 'declaration'. The defendant would reply with either a demurrer or a 'plea'. Various pleas could be used to avoid liability. The type used by a defendant in this sort of case was a 'confession and avoidance', ie, the defendant *confessed* that the goods had been lost, but hoped to *avoid* liability by relying on the fact that the loss had been caused by perils of the sea: Holdsworth, 1903–72, Vol III, pp 629–30.

one in a standard form and by looking to see where the burdens had been placed in other contracts of the same nature. In adopting this approach, the judges were no doubt influenced by the need felt by commercial men for legal predictability in their dealings with each other.

However, later cases showed that *The Glendarroch* was not to be used blindly as a precedent in different contractual circumstances. In *Hurst v Evans,*[23] the defendants had insured the plaintiff, a jeweller, against loss of or damage to his jewellery and other property, 'arising from any cause whatsoever . . . except breakage . . . and except loss by theft or dishonesty committed by any servant . . . in the exclusive employment' of the plaintiff. Those were the only two exceptions.

A robbery was committed at the plaintiff's premises and jewellery was stolen. The plaintiff had two employees, Brown and Mason. There was no suggestion that Brown had had any part in the crime, but the insurers called evidence to show that, about the date of the offence, Mason had been associating with notorious and highly skilled safe breakers.

Counsel for the jeweller argued that the burden was on the insurers, if they wished to avoid liability, to show that Mason had been either the actual perpetrator of the crime or an accomplice. The insurers argued that this was wrong, and that the burden was on the plaintiff to show that his servant Mason had not been dishonest.

Lush J relied on a long established rule for pleading claims on policies of marine insurance which required that the plaintiff should state the contract accurately, with all exceptions to the defendant's liability, and should allege that the defendants did not come within any of those exceptions. *The Glendarroch* had been cited, but Lush J said that there was nothing in that case to show that the rule on which he relied should not apply. However, what was Lush J thinking of to rely on standard form contracts of *marine* insurance in a claim on insurers for loss of a jeweller's goods? The answer lies later in the report and shows that the legal justification was simply a support for a decision that turned on the facts.

'Looking at the policy,' the judge said, 'it is impossible to hold that the onus is on the defendant. To do so would produce absurd results.' It was not a case of insurance against loss by some specified peril such as fire or theft. The insurance was against *any* loss due to *any* cause, except the two specified – breakage and servants' dishonesty. If the plaintiff was right, he would only have to prove a loss of jewellery and it would be for the defendants to prove that amongst the multitude of possible causes the actual cause was either breakage or servants' dishonesty. To avoid such a situation, the burden was on the plaintiff to prove that the loss was one against which the insurers had agreed to indemnify him. In other words, he had the burden of proving that the loss had not been occasioned by the dishonesty of his servant Mason.

---

23   [1917] 1 KB 352. Cf *Munro Brice and Co v War Risks Association Ltd* [1918] KB 78.

Although Lush J did not explicitly say so, his decision was clearly influenced by the consideration that it would be easier for the plaintiff to prove that his servant had not been involved than for the insurers to prove that he had.

Another case in which reliance was placed on *The Glendarroch* was *Constantine (Joseph) SS Line Ltd v Imperial Smelting Corp Ltd.*[24] The appellants were owners of a steamship which had been chartered to the respondents to carry a cargo from Australia to Europe. The ship duly sailed to pick up the cargo, but before it could do so there was an explosion on board which utterly disabled it from carrying out the charterparty. The respondent charterers claimed damages from the owners for failure to load the cargo. The owners relied on the doctrine of frustration to excuse them from performance. The charterers argued that this would not work unless the owners could show that the explosion had occurred without any fault on their part. But the owners argued that once the frustrating event was proved, the burden was on the charterers to prove negligence by the owners so as to bar them from relying on frustration as a defence.

The arbitrator was unable to make a finding as to the cause of the explosion. At that point the allocation of burdens of proof became decisive.

The speeches in the House of Lords showed that the desire to achieve a just result was uppermost in the Law Lords' minds. Viscount Simon LC observed that if the party relying on frustration had to show that the event happened without his default, he would often fail in his action because of the difficulty of proving a negative:

> Suppose that a vessel, while on the high seas, disappears completely during a storm. Can it be that the defence of frustration of the adventure depends on the owner's ability to prove that all his servants on board were navigating the ship with adequate skill and that there was no 'default' which brought about the catastrophe? Suppose that a vessel in convoy is torpedoed by the enemy and sinks immediately with all hands. Does the application of the doctrine require that the owners should affirmatively prove that those on board were keeping a good lookout, were obscuring lights, were steering as directed, and so forth?[25]

Viscount Simon added that frustration depended on whether, from the express terms of the particular contract, a further term should be implied which, its conditions fulfilled, would end the contract. Such an implied term in this case might well be: 'This contract is to cease to be binding if the vessel is disabled by an overpowering disaster, provided that disaster is not brought about by the default of either party.' Having drafted the notional clause in this way, Viscount Simon was then able to draw an analogy with 'perils of the sea' clauses like the one in *The Glendarroch* and say that the implied clause should affect the burden of proof in a similar way. The effect of

---

24   [1942] AC 154.
25   [1942] AC 154, pp 161–62.

this analogy was to place a burden on the charterers to prove negligence by the owners in order to defeat the owners' reliance on frustration as an excuse for their failure to load the goods.

But the implied clause might equally well have said: 'This contract is to cease to be binding if the vessel is disabled by an overpowering disaster *for which neither party is responsible.*' If a form of words was to dictate where the burden lay, this would have produced a different result. But the result was not based on a form of words; the case was not, despite superficial appearances, decided by a piece of notional drafting and a precedent. Instead, notional drafting and the precedent were brought in to support a decision that was justifiable on pragmatic grounds. As Lord Wright said in the same case: 'The court is exercising its powers, when it decides that a contract is frustrated, in order to achieve a result which is just and reasonable.' Once again, the crucial consideration appears to have been ease of proof: to make the party relying on frustration in such circumstances prove absence of fault would have been unreasonable.

Ease of proof was the determining consideration in *Levison v Patent Steam Carpet Cleaning Co.*[26] In this case the plaintiffs had sent an expensive Chinese carpet to the defendants for cleaning. The defendants failed to return it and ultimately concluded that it had been stolen. They relied on a clause in their contract with the plaintiffs limiting their liability for loss, the effect of which was to make them liable for only £44 rather than £900 – the value of the carpet. A clause like this could be relied on only if the party relying on it had carried out the substance of the contract and had not been guilty of a fundamental breach of it. But was it for the plaintiffs to prove fundamental breach or for the defendants to negative it?

Lord Denning MR thought that it should be for the cleaners to prove that they had not been guilty of fundamental breach. The plaintiffs did not know what had happened to the carpet. The cleaners were the ones who knew, or should have known, what had happened. The burden should therefore be on them to show that they had used proper care in their handling of the carpet; it was not for the plaintiffs to prove that the defendants had been guilty of negligence. The legal hook on which Lord Denning hung this result was a point about bailment. This transaction had been a bailment for reward, and the cases showed clearly that, in such circumstances, the bailee was absolutely liable for loss of or damage to the goods which were the subject of the bailment. He could avoid his liability only by proving that he had used all due care when handling the goods.[27]

Orr LJ agreed: the bailee in such circumstances was more likely to know the facts and be in a better position to ascertain them than the bailor. Sir David Cairns added that, however difficult it might sometimes be for a bailee to prove a negative,

---

26   [1978] 1 QB 69.
27   [1978] 1 QB 69, pp 81–82.

he was at least in a better position than the bailor to know what happened to the goods while they were in his possession.

These cases show that the courts' approach to problems about the burden of proof in civil actions is likely to be determined on the basis referred to by Viscount Maugham in the *Constantine* case: it depends on 'the circumstances under which the claim arises'.[28] The only hard and fast conclusion that can be made is that 'where the burden of proof should rest is merely a question of policy and fairness based on experience in the different situations'.[29] In looking at those situations it is likely that a court will be chiefly concerned with the question of which of the parties will find it easier to discharge a burden of proof, even if sometimes that may involve proving a negative.

That 'he who asserts must prove' may involve having, in effect, to prove a negative can be seen from the decision of the House of Lords in *Pickford v Imperial Chemical Industries plc*.[30] In this case, the plaintiff had been employed by the defendants as a secretary. She developed a disease in both hands, which was recognised by the DHSS for the purposes of industrial injury benefit and which was known as 'PDA4'. It consisted of cramp caused by repetitive movements. She sued the defendants for negligence, claiming that the disease was organic in origin and so had been reasonably foreseeable by them. The defendants said that it was psychogenic in origin, and so could not have been reasonably foreseen. (A disease that is organic has its origin in the physical body; one that is psychogenic has its origin in the mind.) Both sides produced medical experts. The plaintiff's expert said that her disease was organic in origin. The defendants' expert said that it was psychogenic, and gave a particular reason for this conclusion. The trial judge said that he was not satisfied that the defendants' explanation was correct, but he said also that he was not satisfied that the disease was organic in origin. He therefore found for the defendants.

The Court of Appeal allowed the plaintiff's appeal by a majority. Stuart-Smith LJ said that all the judge had to do was decide on the evidence which of the two explanations actually advanced was the more probable. He had therefore approached the burden of proof wrongly. Waite LJ agreed. He asked this question: why should a plaintiff who has established PDA4, and who has satisfied the court that the only psychogenic explanation relied on against her did not apply, be under any duty to prove a negative and show by positive evidence that her complaint had no psychogenic origin?

However, a majority of the House of Lords held that the trial judge's approach had been right. The basis of the plaintiff's claim was that her disease was organic in origin, and so foreseeable. The Court of Appeal had effectively reversed the burden of

28   *Constantine (Joseph) SS Line Ltd v Imperial Smelting Corp Ltd* [1942] AC 154, p 174.

29   *Rustad v Great Northern Railway Co* 122 Minn 453, 142 NW 727 (1913), opinion by Dibell J, quoted in Morgan, 1956, p 76.

30   [1998] 3 All ER 462.

proof. It had, of course, been open to the defendants to adduce evidence to rebut the plaintiff's claim about the cause of her disease, but they did not have to prove any particular psychogenic explanation. Failure to prove the explanation that they did put forward still left open the question of whether the plaintiff had proved that her disease was organic in origin. The burden of proving this remained with her and, since she had failed to discharge it, the trial judge's decision in favour of the defendants had been correct.

THE BURDEN OF PROOF IN CRIMINAL CASES

The basic *rule* was laid down by Viscount Sankey LC in *Woolmington v DPP*.[31] 'Throughout the web of the English criminal law one golden thread is always to be seen, that it is the duty of the prosecution to prove the prisoner's guilt.' That is the rule, but is it supported by any *principle*?

It would be possible to justify the rule as part of a policy to avoid embarrassing criticisms of the administration of justice by minimising wrongful convictions. These are more likely to be avoided if the burden is fixed in this way than if an accused person has to prove his innocence. It is also possible to justify the rule by appeal to principle. For example, it would be a necessary feature of the law if it were accepted that, in Dworkin's words, 'people have a profound right not to be convicted of crimes of which they are innocent'.[32] Do our politicians, or even our judges, recognise a basis of principle rather than policy for this rule? The story of the exceptions to it does not provide an encouraging answer.

Viscount Sankey said that the rule was subject to exceptions in the case of the defence of insanity and subject also to any statutory exception. But there have been challenges to the idea that it is ever just to place a legal burden of proof on defendants.

The best starting point is that put forward by Paul Roberts: placing the burden of proof on the prosecution restricts 'the power of the State to intervene in the lives of individuals and their families in the far-reaching and sometimes catastrophic ways sanctioned by the machinery of criminal justice'.[33] But where a burden of proof rests on a defendant in relation to any issue, he must be convicted even though the magistrates or jury are left undecided about facts that are relevant to that issue. The Criminal Law Revision Committee, in their 11th Report, were strongly of the opinion that burdens on the defence should be evidential only. They pointed out that in the typical case under the existing law, where the essence of the offence is that the offender has acted with blameworthy intent and the defence that the defendant must

---

31   [1935] AC 462, p 481. For the importance of a correct direction to the jury on the burden of proof, see *R v Bentley (Decd)* [2001] 1 Cr App R 307, p 326.

32   Dworkin, 1986, p 72.

33   Roberts, 1995, p 785.

prove is that he acted innocently, it was 'repugnant to principle' that a court, left in doubt as to the defendant's intent, should be bound to convict.

Statute has already adopted this principle to a limited extent. Under the pre-Theft Act 1968 law, a person charged with the statutory offence of possession of housebreaking implements had the legal burden of proving lawful excuse.[34] But s 25(3) of the Theft Act 1968 provides that proof that the accused had with him any article made or adapted for use in committing a relevant offence shall be merely evidence that he had it with him for such use. In other words, the legal burden of proving the offence remains with the prosecution. Consistency suggests that existing statutory provisions placing a legal burden on defendants should be amended so as to place on them an evidential burden only. Such a change would also be in general accordance with the common law, which, with the sole exception of insanity, has not found it necessary to impose any legal burden on the defence.

The Criminal Law Revision Committee thought that the real purpose of casting burdens on the defence in criminal cases was to prevent the defendant from submitting that he had no case to answer in a situation where, as a matter of common sense, his conduct called for explanation, but where the prosecution had not adduced evidence to negative the possibility of an innocent explanation. This applied especially to cases where the defence related to a matter peculiarly within the knowledge of the defendant. The Committee thought it entirely justifiable to impose a burden on the defence for this purpose, but said that the purpose was sufficiently served by making the burden an evidential one. Further, a change would remove the existing need for the judge to give a complicated direction to the jury on the different standards of proof.[35]

Another reason for placing only an evidential burden on the defence is that it is easier for the prosecution to discharge the legal burden of proof. The prosecution dictates the nature of the proceedings, and it has far greater resources than the defendant to further them and bring them to a successful conclusion. The prosecution employs professional investigators to detect crime and gather evidence; it has scientific resources unavailable to most defendants and the manpower to conduct detailed and lengthy inquiries. It has legal advisers to shape the charges to fit the evidence. Innocent people are not generally concerned to prove their innocence until called upon to do so, and by then it may be too late to collect the necessary evidence. The defendant's access to physical evidence may be restricted, as where the prosecution has destroyed all available samples during testing or has failed to collect samples at all. To *know* that your state of mind was an innocent one is not the same as being able to *prove* that that was the case.

---

34   Section 28(2) of the Larceny Act 1916.
35   Criminal Law Revision Committee, 11th Report, 1972, para 140. See also Williams, 1988, pp 263–67.

Legal burdens on defendants must be considered in the light of the European Convention on Human Rights, which is now incorporated into English law under the Human Rights Act 1998. By Art 6(2), 'Everyone charged with a criminal offence shall be presumed innocent until proved guilty according to law'. The effect of this provision was considered by Lord Hope in *R v DPP ex p Kebilene and Others*.[36] After noting that Art 6(2) is wholly consistent with the common law as stated by Viscount Sankey in *Woolmington*, he added that, as Viscount Sankey had recognised, it has always been open to Parliament, by way of a statutory exception, to transfer the burden of proof on a particular issue from the prosecution to the defendant. Until recently, the only check on Parliament's freedom to do so was political. However, the Human Rights Act changes this, and it applies to *all* legislation, whether before or after the Act.

To see if a statutory provision is incompatible with Art 6(2), it is necessary to see what the provision says. Some encroach more on the presumption of innocence than others. Broadly speaking, three kinds are possible:

- A mandatory presumption of guilt as to an essential element of the offence. This is a presumption that *must* be applied if the basis of fact on which it rests is established. This will be inconsistent with the presumption of innocence.
- A discretionary presumption of guilt as to an essential element of the offence. Here the court may or may not rely on the presumption, depending on its view as to the weight of the evidence.
- Presumptions that relate to an exemption or proviso which the defendant must establish if he wishes to avoid conviction, but which is not an essential element of the offence. Examples are the provisions that the courts had to consider in *R v Edwards* and *R v Hunt*.[37]

However, Lord Hope emphasised that even if the court decides that a particular provision breaches the presumption of innocence, this will not lead inevitably to incompatibility with Art 6(2). The decisions of the European Court of Human Rights show that other factors have to be considered. By what is known as the 'margin of appreciation', the European Court has acknowledged that national authorities are better placed to evaluate local needs and conditions than an international court. For this reason, the Convention does not have to be applied uniformly by all States. Instead, its application may vary according to local needs and conditions. National courts should see the Convention as an expression of fundamental principles rather than as a set of rules. Application of these principles will involve balancing competing

---

36   [2000] 1 Cr App R 275, pp 321–33.
37   [1975] QB 27, [1987] AC 352: see below.

interests: those of the individual and those of society. In some circumstances, the courts should recognise that there is an area of judgment within which they should defer, on democratic grounds, to the considered opinion of the elected body or person whose act or decision is said to be incompatible with the Convention, and this will be the case *even where the Convention states a right in unqualified terms*. The cases decided by the European Court show that although Art 6(2) is expressed in absolute terms, it is not regarded as imposing an absolute prohibition on reverse burden provisions. In order to consider whether a provision is reasonable in balancing the interests of the individual and those of society, it may be useful to consider these questions:

- What does the prosecution have to prove in order to transfer the burden to the defendant?
- What is the nature of the burden on the defendant? Does it relate to something that is likely for him to be difficult to prove? Or does it relate to something that is likely to be within his knowledge, or to which he readily has access?
- What is the nature of the threat faced by society that the provision is designed to combat?

The potential effect of the Human Rights Act 1998 on reverse burdens in criminal cases was first shown in *R v Lambert*,[38] a decision of the House of Lords. Lambert had been arrested in possession of a bag containing cocaine. He was charged with possession of a controlled drug with intent to supply, contrary to s 5(3) of the Misuse of Drugs Act 1971. He relied on a defence provided by s 28 of that Act, claiming that he had not believed or suspected, or had reason to suspect, the existence of a fact which it was necessary for the prosecution to prove if he was to be convicted, namely that the bag contained a controlled drug. On the traditional interpretation of the 1971 Act, where a defendant was in possession of a package that in fact contained drugs, the burden was initially on the prosecution to prove that the defendant had, and knew that he had, a package in his control and that the package contained something. That was enough to prove possession. Once those matters were proved, there was a legal burden on the defendant to bring himself within the defence available under s 28(2). The trial judge directed the jury on this basis and Lambert was convicted. His appeal against that direction ultimately reached the House of Lords, where it was argued that to interpret s 28 in this way violated the presumption of innocence contained in Art 6(2) of the European Convention on Human Rights. The main question to be decided on the appeal was whether the Human Rights Act 1998, which gave statutory force to the Convention, operated retrospectively. The House of

---

38   [2001] 3 All ER 577.

Lords held that it did not. Nevertheless, the Law Lords took the opportunity to discuss the effect of the Act on s 28.

The majority, relying on s 3(1) of the Human Rights Act 1998, held that it was possible to read s 28(2) as imposing only an evidential burden, and that it should be read in this way because to read it as imposing a legal burden would be to violate the presumption of innocence contained in Art 6(2) of the Convention. *Lambert* obviously has significance for anyone who has to study the Misuse of Drugs Act 1971, but the particular decision on that Act is of relatively minor interest to the student of evidence. What is more important from the latter's standpoint is the wider significance of *Lambert* in other cases, as yet unlitigated, where Parliament appears to have imposed a legal burden on a defendant in criminal proceedings. To appreciate the full significance of *Lambert* it is, of course, necessary to study the speeches of the Law Lords in one of the law reports, but it may be helpful when doing so to bear in mind the following summary of points that were made:

- The 1998 Act was accepted as being potentially radical in its effect. As Lord Slynn said, it is clear that it must be given its full import and that 'long or well entrenched ideas may have to be put aside, sacred cows culled'.[39]
- The imposition of a legal burden on a defendant will not inevitably be incompatible with Art 6(2).[40] It is vital to remember this. *Lambert* is emphatically not authority for the proposition that in future wherever a statute appears to have imposed a reverse burden, it should always be read as imposing only an evidential burden.
- A reverse burden may be justified where it is directed towards a clear and proper public objective, and where it is a reasonable or 'proportionate' response to the mischief at which it is directed. In deciding whether this condition is satisfied, it is necessary to strike a balance between the general interest of the community and the fundamental rights of the defendant.[41] According to Lord Steyn, the burden is on the State to show that the legislative means adopted were not greater than necessary, and there must be 'pressing necessity' to impose a legal burden on the accused.[42]
- A reverse burden may be acceptable where a statute prohibits the doing of an act except in specified circumstances, or by specified persons, or with some licence or permission. This is particularly likely to be the case where the statute has been enacted to regulate a particular activity in the public interest, for example, to promote health and safety or to avoid pollution. Such

---

39 *R v Lambert* [2001] 3 All ER 577, p 581.
40 *Ibid,* pp 590, 606, 625.
41 *Ibid,* pp 590, 606, 625, 638.
42 *Ibid,* pp 591, 592.

offences are to be distinguished from those which are truly criminal and involve moral fault.[43]

A case producing a different interpretation was *L v DPP*.[44] The defendant was charged with having a lock-knife in his possession in a public place, contrary to s 139 of the Criminal Justice Act 1988. This provision makes it unlawful for a person to have with him in a public place 'any article which has a blade or is sharply pointed except a folding pocket knife'. Section 139(4) provides that 'It shall be a defence for a person charged with an offence under this section to prove that he had good reason or lawful authority for having the article with him in a public place'. The district judge held that this sub-section imposed a legal burden of proof on the defendant, but that this did not infringe Art 6(2) of the Convention. On appeal, the Divisional Court accepted the principles laid down in *Lambert*, but the Court regarded s 139 of the 1988 Act as readily distinguishable from s 28 of the 1971 Act in six respects:

- Section 28, on the traditional interpretation, required the defendant to prove on a balance of probabilities that he did not know that a package proved to be in his possession contained controlled drugs, but under s 139 it is for the prosecution to prove that the defendant *knowingly* had the offending article in his possession.[45]
- There is a strong public interest in bladed articles not being carried in public without good reason. Respect should be given to the way in which a democratically elected legislature has sought to strike the right balance between the interests of the individual and those of the public at large.[46]
- Under the 1988 Act the defendant is required to prove something that is within his own knowledge.
- A defendant is entitled, by virtue of Art 6(2), to expect the court to scrutinise the evidence with a view to deciding if a good reason existed; this applies whether the defendant gives evidence or not.
- In the great majority of cases the fact-finding tribunal will be able to make a judgment about the existence or non-existence of a good reason without having to depend on the allocation of the burden of proof.
- Sentencing powers in relation to the s 139 offence are narrower than in relation to the offence under s 5 of the 1971 Act, although only limited weight should be given to this consideration.[47]

---

43 *R v Lambert* [2001] 3 All ER 577, pp 590–91, 627. See also *Sheldrake v DPP* [2003] 2 All ER 497, p 516. For an example, see *Davies v Health and Safety Executive* [2003] IRLR 170.

44 [2002] 2 All ER 854.

45 'Has with him' means 'knowingly has with him'. See *Archbold*, para 24–110 and *Blackstone's Criminal Practice,* paras B12.92, B12.97 and the cases cited there.

46 See also the observations on this point of Lord Woolf CJ in *R v Lambert* [2001] 1 All ER 1014, CA, p 1022. These appear to be unaffected by the subsequent decision of the House of Lords.

47 See *L v DPP* [2002] 2 All ER 854, pp 862–63, 864.

The Divisional Court therefore concluded that the imposition of a legal burden did not infringe Art 6(2). Its reasoning is not wholly uncontroversial; for example, it could be objected that the threat posed to society by the sale of cocaine and similar drugs is at least as great, if not greater, than the threat posed by the carrying of bladed or pointed articles in public places. Nevertheless, in *R v Matthews*[48] the Court of Appeal reached the same conclusion on the interpretation of s 139.[49]

The most recent leading authorities on the compatibility of reverse burden provisions with Art 6(2) of the European Convention on Human Rights are two decisions of the House of Lords: *R v Johnstone*[50] and *Sheldrake v DPP*.[51]

In *Johnstone* the defendant was charged with an offence under s 92 of the Trade Marks Act 1994. It was alleged that he had had in his possession, in the course of a business, goods or their packaging to which he had applied a sign identical to, or likely to be mistaken for, a registered trademark. The defendant relied in part on s 92(5), which provides as follows:

> It is a defence for a person charged with an offence under this section to show that he believed on reasonable grounds that the use of the sign in the manner in which it was used, or was to be used, was not an infringement of the registered trademark.

The House of Lords dismissed the prosecution's appeal without relying on this provision. But, since there were conflicting Court of Appeal decisions on whether s 92(5) imposed on defendants a legal burden or merely an evidential one, the House of Lords took the opportunity to resolve the issue, albeit *obiter*, in favour of the imposition of a legal burden.

Lord Nicholls, in observations on statutory provisions that prima facie reverse the burden of proof, made the following points, with which the other law lords agreed.

■ Presumptions of fact or law are not prohibited by the European Convention. But the effect of Art 6(2) is that they must be confined within reasonable limits, which take into account the importance of what is at stake and maintain the rights of the defence. Here, as elsewhere in the Convention, a

---

48   (2003) 153 NLJ 635.

49   For further examples of cases where a reverse burden was upheld, see *R v Drummond* [2002] 2 Cr App R 352; *AG's Reference (No 4 of 2002)* [2004] 1 All ER 1. See also *R v Lambert* [2001] 1 All ER 1014, CA. Two other appeals were heard at the same time as Lambert's appeal. These concerned the defence of diminished responsibility under s 2 of the Homicide Act 1957. The Court of Appeal held that the legal burden imposed on defendants by that provision did not infringe Art 6(2). Those decisions were not appealed to the House of Lords, and the law on the burden of proof in relation to diminished responsibility is therefore currently as stated by the Court of Appeal.

50   [2003] UKHL 28, [2003] 1 WLR 1736.

51   [2004] UKHL 43, [2005] 1 AC 264.

reasonable balance has to be held between the public interest and the interests of the individual. But in each case the State must show that the balance held in the legislation is reasonable; derogation from the presumption of innocence requires justification. Lord Nicholls added, a little later in his speech, that for a reverse burden to be acceptable, there must be a 'compelling reason' that makes its existence fair and reasonable.

■ A difficulty in striking the required balance is that the more serious the crime and so the greater the public interest in securing convictions, the more important the constitutional protection of the accused becomes.

■ When considering whether a reverse burden is fair and reasonable, a sound starting point is to remember that if an accused is required to prove a fact on the balance of probability in order to avoid conviction, this will permit a conviction despite the existence of a reasonable doubt as to his guilt.

■ The more serious the punishment that may follow conviction, the more compelling must be the reason for a reverse burden.

■ The extent and nature of the facts to be proved by the accused, and their importance relative to those required to be proved by the prosecution, are to be taken into account. So does the ease or difficulty that the accused will have in discharging his burden. For example, are the facts within his own knowledge, or does he have ready access to them?

■ Parliament, not the court, has the primary responsibility for deciding, as a matter of policy, what should be the constituent elements of the criminal offence. The role of the court is one of review only. It should reach a different conclusion from the legislature only when it is apparent that the legislature has attached insufficient importance to the presumption of innocence.[52]

In the next year, the House, again considered the problem presented by reverse burdens in two conjoined appeals: *Sheldrake v DPP* and *Attorney General's Reference (No 4 of 2002).*[53] Lord Bingham set out some general matters, with which Lord Steyn and Lord Phillips agreed. The remaining members of the House, Lord Rodger and Lord Carswell, expressed neither agreement nor disagreement, but confined their speeches to the particular legislation that formed the subject matter of the two appeals. The main points made by Lord Bingham were as follows:

■ The overriding concern is that a trial should be fair, and the presumption of innocence is a fundamental right directed to that end. The Convention does not outlaw presumptions of fact or law, but requires that they should be kept within reasonable limits. Relevant to any judgment about reasonableness

---

52   Paragraphs 44–51.
53   [2004] UKHL 43, [2005] 1 AC 264, paras 21–22, 29–31.

or proportionality will be the opportunity given to the accused to rebut the presumption,[54] maintenance of the rights of the defence, flexibility in application of the presumption, retention by the court of a power to assess the evidence, the importance of what is at stake, and the difficulty that a prosecutor may face in the absence of a presumption.

■ The justifiability of any infringement of the presumption of innocence cannot be resolved by any rule of thumb, but only on examination of all the facts and circumstances of the particular provision as applied in the particular case.

■ The task of the court is never to decide whether a reverse burden should be imposed on a defendant, but always to assess whether a burden enacted by Parliament unjustifiably infringes the presumption of innocence. However, it is doubtful whether it would be right for a court to assume that Parliament would not have reversed the burden without good reason. That approach might lead the court to give too much weight to the enactment under review, and too little to the presumption of innocence.

Lord Bingham also observed that in *Attorney General's Reference (No 1 of 2004)*,[55] an enlarged Court of Appeal had detected a 'significant difference in emphasis' between the approach of Lord Steyn in *Lambert* and that of Lord Nicholls in *Johnstone*, and had made plain its preference for the latter. Lord Bingham disapproved of these opinions. He emphasised that both decisions were binding on all lower courts 'for what they may decide'. Nothing said in *Johnstone* suggested an intention to depart from or modify the decision in *Lambert*, which was not to be treated as superseded or implicitly overruled. Any differences of emphasis were accounted for by the difference in subject matter of the two cases.

Prediction of outcome in cases where, prima facie, there is a burden of proof on the defendant is clearly not going to be easy. Nevertheless, Ian Dennis has identified six elements that may be taken into account in reaching a decision where the court is faced with legislation that apparently reverses the burden of proof.[56]

The first element is based on a classification of offences that distinguishes, in the traditional terminology, between *mala in se* and *mala prohibita*. For example, in

---

54 The presumption referred to here is the presumption of guilt that is created where a defendant has a reverse burden to satisfy. For example, if a piece of legislation says that it shall be an offence to carry a knife in a public place, unless the defendant has a lawful excuse, the proof of which lies on him, there is prima facie a burden on the defendant to prove that he had a lawful excuse, once it is proved that he was in possession of a knife in a public place. Another way of putting this is to say that once the defendant is proved to have had possession of a knife in a public place, he is presumed to be guilty of the offence unless he proves that he had a lawful excuse for his possession.

55 [2004] EWCA Crim 1025, [2004] 1 WLR 2111.

56 Dennis, 2005.

R v Lambert[57] Lord Clyde said that a strict responsibility might be acceptable in the case of statutory offences that were concerned to regulate the conduct of a particular activity in the public interest. A licence could be required to carry out certain activities, or controls might be imposed to promote health and safety and avoid pollution. Such cases, he said, could properly be seen as not truly criminal. Many might be relatively trivial and carry no real social disgrace.[58] This approach was adopted by the Court of Appeal in *R v Davies*,[59] where the Court upheld s 40 of the Health and Safety at Work Act 1974. This provision imposed a legal burden on a defendant to prove that it had not been reasonably practicable to do more than he had done to ensure that employees were not exposed to risks to their health and safety. The difficulty with classification of offences as a criterion for reverse burdens of proof is, as Dennis pointed out, that the moral quality of regulatory offences is variable. For example, where a regulatory offence leads to someone's death, as was the case in *R v Davies*, it might not be easy to maintain that the breach involved no real social disgrace. The same could also be true of a regulatory offence that led to widespread pollution of the environment.

A second consideration is the deference that should be shown to Parliament's decision. In *Lambert* Lord Steyn said that the burden is on the State to show that the legislative means adopted were not greater than necessary. He added that there must be a 'pressing necessity' to impose a legal burden on the accused.[60] But other judges have been more inclined to give weight to the decision of the elected body that passed the legislation. For example, in *R v DPP, ex parte Kebilene*[61] Lord Hope said that such deference would be particularly appropriate where the issues involved questions of social or economic policy. In *R v Johnstone*[62] Lord Nicholls pointed out that Parliament had the primary responsibility for deciding, as a matter of policy, what should be the constituent elements of a criminal offence, and courts should reach a different conclusion from the legislature only where it was apparent that the latter had attached insufficient importance to the individual's fundamental right to be presumed innocent until proved guilty.

However, in *Sheldrake*, Lord Bingham doubted whether there should be an assumption that Parliament would not have made an exception to the basic rule without good reason. Such an approach might lead the court to give too much weight to the enactment under review, and too little to the presumption of innocence. Dennis has suggested that the court's approach should depend on drawing a clear

---

57   [2001] UKHL 37, [2002] AC 545.

58   Paragraph 154.

59   [2002] EWCA Crim 2949.

60   Paragraphs 34, 38.

61   [2000] 2 AC 326.

62   [2003] UKHL 28, [2003] 1 WLR 1736.

distinction between the two criteria referred to in *Salabiaku v France*.[63] Deference to the democratic body should be due when considering whether it was in fact pursuing a legitimate aim; less deference should be due when considering whether a reverse onus was a proportionate method of achieving that aim.

A third consideration is based on drawing a distinction between elements of the offence and available defences. For example, in *AG of Hong Kong v Lee Kwong-Kut*,[64] a decision of the Privy Council, Lord Woolf said that if the prosecution retains responsibility for proving the essential ingredients of the offence, a reverse burden is more likely to be acceptable. But, recognising the difficulty of isolating the essential ingredients, he added that the substance and reality of the language creating the offence should be regarded, rather than its form.

However, the distinction between elements of an offence and defences has often been criticised. Lord Steyn in *Lambert* said that the distinction would sometimes be 'unprincipled and arbitrary', and he observed that it could be based simply on drafting technique.[65] A constituent element of an offence can be removed from the definition and cast as a defensive issue. Further, any definition of an offence can be reformulated so as to include all possible defences within it. A good example of the difficulty in applying this criterion is *R v Hunt*,[66] where an element of the offence was found in what appeared at first sight to be a list of exceptions contained in a statutory instrument that had been made pursuant to powers contained in the primary legislation.

Maximum penalties are another consideration. In *Davies* Tuckey LJ said that the absence of any risk of imprisonment was 'undoubtedly an important factor' in determining whether there was a legitimate reverse burden of proof.[67] Conversely, in *Lambert* Lord Steyn was clearly influenced by the fact that the maximum sentence was life imprisonment.[68] In *Johnstone* Lord Nicholls said that the more serious the punishment, the more compelling must be the reasons for imposing a reverse burden. But in *Sheldrake* the House of Lords upheld a reverse onus where the maximum penalty for the offence was only six months' imprisonment. Dennis has noted that maximum penalties are a very uncertain guide, and that the nature of the penalty, whether custodial or pecuniary, is not conclusive either way.

The ease of proof and the defendant's peculiar knowledge can also be taken into account. For example, in *ex parte Kebilene* Lord Hope said that one of the considerations was the nature of the burden on the accused. Did it relate to something that it was likely to be difficult for him to prove, or to something likely to be

---

63   (1988) 13 EHRR 379.
64   [1993] AC 951, pp 969–70.
65   Paragraph 35.
66   [1987] AC 352.
67   Paragraph 19.
68   Paragraph 38.

within his knowledge or to which he had access? The same point was made by Lord Nicholls in *Johnstone*. On the other hand, as Dennis has pointed out, there are very many cases where the accused's state of mind is of crucial importance, but where the burden of proving it is on the prosecution.

A final consideration is the presumption of innocence itself. As Lord Bingham said in *Sheldrake*, the underlying rationale of the presumption is that it is repugnant to ordinary notions of fairness for a prosecutor to accuse a defendant of crime and for the defendant to be then required to disprove the accusation, on pain of conviction and punishment if he fails to do so. The closer a legislative provision is to that situation, the more objectionable it is likely to be.[69] Approaching the problem from a slightly different angle, Lord Nicholls in *Johnstone* said that a sound starting point for considering a reverse burden in the light of Art 6(2) is to remember that if a defendant is required to prove a fact on the balance of probability in order to avoid conviction, a conviction can follow in spite of the fact-finding tribunal having a reasonable doubt as to his guilt.

It will be seen that there can be no straightforward answer to the question whether a statute imposes a legal or merely an evidential burden. It is possible to identify a number of considerations, but the weight the court will give to them in any particular case is unlikely to be readily predictable. The problem is substantial. In 1996 40 per cent of offences triable in the Crown Court appeared to violate the presumption of innocence.[70]

Subject to the Convention, there is at least no problem in seeing where the burdens lie if a statute provides, for example, that an accused person shall be guilty of an offence 'unless the contrary is proved'.[71] However, the question whether Parliament in any given case has *impliedly* overridden the *Woolmington* principle is more difficult to resolve.

A convenient starting point for discussion of this topic is s 101 of the Magistrates' Courts Act 1980 (formerly s 81 of the Magistrates' Courts Act 1952). It provides that where the defendant relies for his defence on any 'exception, exemption, proviso, excuse or qualification', whether or not it is part of the description of the offence, the burden of proving such a defence shall be on him. In *R v Edwards*,[72] the Court of Appeal held that this principle was not confined to cases heard in magistrates' courts; the provision was a statutory statement of a common law rule applicable in *all* criminal courts.

---

69   Paragraph 9.

70   Ashworth and Blake, 1996, p 314.

71   See, eg, the Prevention of Corruption Act 1916, s 2. For further examples with slightly different wording, see the Prevention of Crime Act 1953, s 1; the Sexual Offences Act 1956, s 30; the Homicide Act 1957, s 2; the Misuse of Drugs Act 1971, s 28; the Criminal Justice Act 1988, s 139.

72   [1975] QB 27.

Lawton LJ spoke of the need, when applying this principle, to 'construe the enactment under which the charge is laid' in determining where the burden of proof lay.[73] This task of interpretation was subsequently emphasised by the House of Lords in *R v Hunt*.[74] In that case, the prosecution proved that the defendant was in possession of powder containing morphine, but their evidence did not prove whether or not this powder was of a type covered by a provision in the relevant legislation that exempted preparations containing not more than 0.2% of morphine. There was a submission of no case to answer, which the trial judge rejected. The defendant then changed his plea to guilty and appealed against his conviction on the basis that the trial judge had erred in law in rejecting the submission. The Court of Appeal dismissed the appeal on the basis that the effect of the Act was to place the burden of proving that the powder fell within the exception on the defendant, and he had failed to discharge it. The House of Lords allowed the appeal on the ground that the rule about exceptions contained in s 101 of the Magistrates' Courts Act 1980 did not apply. The 0.2% provision was part of the definition of the essential ingredients of the offence, which the prosecution had to prove to make out a case against the defendant.

In reaching this conclusion, the House of Lords said that the classification of defences for s 101 purposes is not constrained by the form of words used or their location in the statute creating the offence. A more subtle approach to interpretation was required, one which would pay regard to the wording of the Act, but would also take into account the mischief at which it was aimed, as well as practical matters affecting the burden of proof. Some guidelines were suggested by Lord Griffiths:

(a) Courts should be 'very slow' to classify a defence as falling within s 101, because Parliament can never lightly be taken to have intended to impose an onerous duty on a defendant to prove his innocence in a criminal case.

(b) Ease and difficulty to be encountered by the parties in discharging the legal burden are of great importance.

(c) The gravity of the offence must be considered. Offences involving the misuse of hard drugs were 'among the most serious in the criminal calendar' and, subject to certain special defences where the burden of proof was specifically placed on the defendant, they were absolute offences. In those circumstances any ambiguity should be resolved in favour of the defendant.[75]

The task of interpretation is a difficult one. There are at least four reasons for this. First, the question whether a given statutory provision falls within the class of 'any

---

73   [1975] QB 27, p 40.

74   [1987] AC 352.

75   [1987] AC 352, pp 374, 378.

exception, exemption, proviso, excuse or qualification' is inherently problematic, as *Nimmo v Alexander Cowan and Sons Ltd*[76] shows.

This case was concerned with the interpretation of s 29(1) of the Factories Act 1961, which provided: 'There shall, so far as is reasonably practicable, be provided and maintained safe means of access to every place at which any person has at any time to work and every such place shall, so far as is reasonably practicable, be made and kept safe for any person working there.' The House of Lords had to decide whether, under this provision, the defendant employers had a burden of proving that it was *not* reasonably practicable for them to make the workplace safe, or whether the plaintiff employee had to prove that it *was* reasonably practicable for his employers to make the workplace safe. As the section also created a summary offence, the same question could have arisen in a prosecution.

The House divided, three to two, on the construction of the section. The minority held that it required the plaintiff or prosecution to prove that it was reasonably practicable to make the workplace safe. The majority held that, once the plaintiff or prosecution had proved that the workplace was not safe, it was for defendants to excuse themselves by proving that it was not reasonably practicable to make it safe. All agreed that if the words of a statute did not clearly state on whom the burden should lie, the court should look to other considerations to determine the intention of Parliament, such as the mischief at which the Act was aimed, and at practical considerations affecting the burden of proof: in particular, the ease or difficulty the respective parties would have in discharging the burden.

A second difficulty of interpretation arises from the fact that s 101 has been only haphazardly applied. In cases involving offences on highways, for example, two very similar statutory provisions have been differently construed. *Gatland v Metropolitan Police Commr*[77] was concerned with s 140 of the Highways Act 1959, which made it an offence 'if a person, without lawful authority or excuse, deposits any thing whatever on a highway'. The Divisional Court held that the effect of s 101 of the Magistrates' Courts Act was that it was for the accused to prove that he had lawful authority or excuse. *Nagy v Weston*[78] was concerned with s 121(1) of the Highways Act 1959. This made it an offence 'if a person without lawful authority or excuse, in any way wilfully obstructs' a highway. In this case, the Divisional Court held, without reference to the Magistrates' Courts Act, that it was for the prosecution to prove the absence of lawful authority or reasonable excuse.[79]

---

76 [1967] 3 All ER 187.

77 [1968] 2 QB 279.

78 [1965] 1 All ER 78.

79 The decision was subsequently approved by the Court of Appeal and the Divisional Court. See *Hirst and Agu v Chief Constable of West Yorkshire* (1987) 85 Cr App R 143; *Carey v Chief Constable of Avon and Somerset* [1995] RTR 405.

Cases involving criminal damage constitute another anomaly. Definitions of various offences under the Criminal Damage Act 1971 begin with the words 'A person who, without lawful excuse . . .'. Neither the Law Commission nor, in one case, the Divisional Court, thought that these provisions were covered by the principle in s 101 of the Magistrates' Courts Act.[80] Other legislation has imposed a burden of proof on defendants, even though this would have been unnecessary if s 101 had been regularly enforced.[81]

A third reason for difficulty in interpretation is that the project of distinguishing between rules and exceptions for s 101 purposes may be logically flawed. Glanville Williams has argued that the courts have allowed themselves to become ensnared by words. There is no intrinsic difference between the elements of an offence and an exception, or defence, to that offence. All the exceptions or defences can be stated in negative form as part of the definition of an offence instead of as something outside the offence. A rule that is subject to an exception is only partly true if stated without the exception.[82] The exception is, rationally regarded, part of the rule. There are no characteristic features of exceptions – they are just linguistic constructs.

An example will illustrate the point. Suppose some future government in the UK wishes to gratify citizens who pay tax at the higher rate. It decides to do so by conferring on them a privilege of a trivial nature and accordingly enacts a statute, s 1 of which provides: 'Only citizens who pay tax at the higher rate shall be permitted to wear gold watches.' The statute also provides in s 2 that it shall be an offence for any person to wear a gold watch in breach of s 1. The parliamentary draftsman might equally well have provided: 'No citizen shall wear a gold watch unless he pays tax at the higher rate.' Now suppose that Tim has been discovered wearing a gold watch and is prosecuted under the Act. If the distinction between rules and exceptions can be maintained, the allocation of the burden of proof will depend entirely on the whim of the draftsman. If the first formula is used, the burden will be on the prosecution to prove that Tim did not pay tax at the higher rate. But if the second formula is used, the burden will be on Tim to show that he does pay tax at the higher rate and so comes within the exception.

On a true analysis of the situation, you have in either case an offence package which consists of the offence elements and the negative of any defences or exceptions.

---

80 Law Commission No 29, 1970, para 48; *Jaggard v Dickinson* [1981] QB 527, 530.

81 Prevention of Crime Act 1953; Sexual Offences Act 1956. See, generally, Smith, 1987.

82 Williams, 1988. Cf Dworkin: 'Of course a rule may have exceptions (the batter who has taken three strikes is not out if the catcher drops the third strike). However, an accurate statement of the rule would take this exception into account, and any that did not would be incomplete. If the list of exceptions is very large, it would be too clumsy to repeat them each time the rule is cited; there is, however, no reason in theory why they could not all be added on, and the more that are, the more accurate is the statement of the rule.' Dworkin, 1977a, pp 45–46. See also *R v Lambert* [2001] 3 All ER 577, p 590, *per* Lord Steyn.

It is an indivisible whole and should be treated as such. Section 101 rests on a false premise.

Finally, the reliance on policy that was authorised by the Law Lords in *Nimmo* and *R v Hunt* makes for uncertainty in interpretation. There are pointers: for example, the ease or difficulty that the respective parties would encounter in discharging the burden may be significant. But this is a question of fact on which there may be different opinions in different cases. In *R v Hunt* itself the Court of Appeal, unlike the House of Lords, thought that the burden should be on the defendant to prove that a preparation of morphine in his possession was in a form permitted by the statute. Their reason was that sometimes it would be easier for a defendant to discharge that burden than for the prosecution to prove that the preparation was in a form not permitted by the statute, for example, where there was evidence that the defendant had possessed the substance but where he had refused to surrender it for examination.[83]

Although a just result appears to have been reached on the facts in *R v Hunt*, the decision has been criticised for the effect that it may have had on the *Woolmington* principle. One problem is its assumption that an implied allocation of an issue to the defendant involves a legal, rather than an evidential, burden. But the main thrust of the criticism is that it failed to establish a clearly defined rule of limited application to allow for implied statutory exceptions to *Woolmington*. Instead, it established a broad rule that allows an uncertain range of policy criteria to be adopted by the courts in their interpretation of legislation. The effect has been to authorise judicial policy making under the guise of statutory interpretation. This significantly undermines *Woolmington*, because it makes it possible for judges to adopt utilitarian policies that ignore, or at any rate give less weight to, the principles that justify placing the burden of proof on the prosecution.[84]

The strength of this criticism has been weakened by the way in which the European Convention has been interpreted. The European Court of Human Rights, the House of Lords and the Court of Appeal have accepted that where a reverse burden question arises, judges may have to take into account such considerations as the threat faced by society that the legislation was designed to correct, and the right balance to be struck between the interests of the individual and those of society.[85] The suggestion that judges ought not to concern themselves with public policy sounds increasingly like an argument from another world, but there is at least one argument that can be used to enforce the principle contained in Art 6(2). The effect of s 35 of the Criminal Justice and Public Order Act 1994 has been to put defendants under greater pressure to offer an explanation where prima facie evidence of an offence has been adduced. The former disadvantage of the prosecution where the defendant had

83   [1986] 1 All ER 184, p 191.
84   See particularly Healy, 1987. A more optimistic view was taken in Birch, 1988.
85   See the references to *Ex p Kebilene* and *Lambert*, above.

special knowledge may now have been substantially reduced, if not removed altogether. If a reverse burden is thereby made unnecessary, it is difficult to see how it could be supported if a breach of Art 6(2) is alleged.[86]

THE STANDARD OF PROOF

STANDARD OF PROOF IN CRIMINAL CASES

Two formulas are traditional. Jurors may be told, 'You must be satisfied so that you are sure', or 'You must be satisfied beyond reasonable doubt' of the accused's guilt. *But it is the effect of the summing up as a whole that matters.* A direction that does not follow one of these formulas exactly may still be a good one.[87] The overall effect of the summing up may be particularly important where the judge refers to the standard of proof several times. A single reference which, taken alone, would be insufficient, may be cured by the presence in other parts of the summing up of accurate statements of the law.

Some directions will be obviously wrong and, if they stand alone, may cause a conviction to be quashed on appeal. For example, it is not enough for the judge to tell the jury merely that they must be 'satisfied' that the prosecution has proved its case, because this would allow the jury to convict if satisfied to the civil standard on a mere balance of probabilities.[88] Where there is a legal burden on a defendant in a criminal case in respect of any issue, that burden will be discharged by proof on the balance of probabilities – the civil standard.[89]

Why should there be two different standards of proof? Having two standards reflects a fundamental assumption that our society makes about the comparative costs of erroneous factual decisions. In any judicial proceeding in which there is a dispute about the facts of some earlier event, the fact-finder can never acquire unassailably accurate knowledge of what happened. All he can acquire is a belief about what *probably* happened. The strength of this belief can vary. A standard of proof represents an attempt to instruct the fact-finder about the degree of confidence our society thinks he should have in the correctness of factual conclusions for a particular type of adjudication. The expressions 'proof on the balance of probabilities' and 'proof beyond reasonable doubt' are quantitatively imprecise. Nevertheless, they do communicate to the fact-finder different ideas concerning the degree of confidence he is

---

86 For a discussion of this in relation to the Prevention of Corruption Act 1916, s 2, see Law Commission Consultation Paper 145, 1997, Pt XI. See also s 34 of the Act, referred to below in Chapter 11.

87 *Walters v The Queen* [1969] 2 AC 26.

88 *R v Hepworth and Fearnley* [1955] 2 QB 600; *R v Gourley* [1981] Crim LR 334.

89 *R v Carr-Briant* [1943] KB 607.

expected to have in the correctness of his conclusions. Any trier of fact will some-times, despite his best efforts, produce a decision about facts that is wrong. In a law suit between two parties, a factual error can make a difference in one of two ways. First, it can result in a judgment in favour of the claimant when the true facts warrant a judgment for the defendant. The corresponding result in a criminal case would be the conviction of an innocent man. On the other hand, a factual determination that is wrong can result in a judgment for the defendant when the true facts justify a judgment in the claimant's favour. The result corresponding to this in a criminal trial would be the acquittal of a guilty man.

The standard of proof influences the relative frequency of these two types of erroneous outcomes. If the standard of proof in a criminal trial was proof on a balance of probabilities rather than proof beyond reasonable doubt, there would be a smaller risk of factual errors resulting in the release of guilty persons, but greater risk of factual errors resulting in conviction of the innocent. The standard of proof in a particular type of litigation therefore reflects society's assessment of the harm attach-ing to each kind of error. It is this that explains the difference between criminal and civil standards of proof. In a civil suit we generally regard it as no more serious for there to be an erroneous verdict in the defendant's favour than for there to be such a verdict in the claimant's favour. Proof on the balance of probabilities therefore seems the appropriate standard, but in a criminal case we do not view the harm that results from the conviction of an innocent man as equivalent to the harm that results from acquitting someone who is guilty. The defendant in a criminal trial generally has more at stake than a defendant in a civil trial, and so the margin of error must be reduced in his favour by placing on the prosecution the burden of proving guilt beyond reasonable doubt.[90] As Lord Woolf CJ has stated:

> At the heart of our criminal justice system is the principle that while it is important that justice is done to the prosecution and justice is done to the victim, in the final analysis the fact remains that it is even more important that an injustice is not done to a defendant. It is central to the way we administer justice in this country that although it may mean that some guilty people go unpunished, it is more important that the innocent are not wrongly convicted.[91]

STANDARD OF PROOF IN CIVIL CASES

The criminal courts have produced many decisions which have attempted to clarify the criminal standard of proof, because judges have to instruct the jury correctly about both burden and standard in summing up.[92] Idiosyncratic approaches, or ones that were plainly wrong, headed straight for the Court of Appeal in the event of a conviction. But because very few civil cases are heard with a jury, the opportunity to

---

90   *In Re Samuel Winship* 397 US 358 (1970), pp 369–72, opinion of Harlan J.

91   *R v B* [2003] 2 Cr App R 197, p 204.

92   See, eg, *R v Hay* (1983) 77 Cr App R 70.

define the civil standard has not often arisen. An attempt sometimes referred to is that of Denning J in *Miller v Minister of Pensions*.[93] There he said that, in a civil case, the evidence 'must carry a reasonable degree of probability, but not so high as is required in a criminal case. If the evidence is such that the tribunal can say: "We think it more probable than not," the burden is discharged, but, if the probabilities are equal, it is not'.[94]

The application of this standard has sometimes given rise to difficulty where an allegation has been made in civil proceedings of exceptionally bad conduct. Examples in the past have included allegations of adultery, of fraud, or of conduct which would have amounted to a criminal offence. More recently the problem has arisen in connection with allegations of child abuse in care proceedings or in matrimonial disputes. The problem can be put in this way: where a particularly serious allegation has been made, is it still the case that the burden of proof can be satisfied on a mere balance of probabilities? The courts have tended to answer this question in two ways. One approach is to say that, although the standard in all civil cases is proof on the balance of probabilities, there may be different degrees of probability within that standard. The other approach is not to emphasise degrees of probability, but the weight of evidence required to satisfy a court that a particular allegation has been proved.

A useful starting point is *Hornal v Neuberger Products Ltd*.[95] In this case, the question arose of whether one party to a contract had made a representation about the contract goods to the other. The representation, if it had been made, was false. The trial judge was prepared to hold that, on the balance of probabilities, the representation had been made. But if it had been made, it followed that the person who had made it was guilty of fraud and could in theory have been prosecuted for the offence of obtaining money by false pretences. The judge said that if he had to be satisfied to the criminal standard that the representation had been made, the evidence was insufficient and the plaintiff had not proved his case. But he then went on to hold that, as it was a civil case, the civil standard applied, and according to *that* standard he *was* satisfied that the representation had been made. He therefore gave judgment for the plaintiff.

On appeal it was argued that the criminal standard should have been applied, since the allegation was of conduct amounting to a criminal offence. The Court of Appeal rejected this argument. Denning LJ said that the more serious the allegation, the higher the degree of probability required, but it need not, in a civil case, reach the very high standard required by the criminal law. Hodson LJ said simply that in a civil case, the balance of probability standard was correct. Morris LJ said that the gravity of

---

93   [1947] 2 All ER 372.

94   [1947] 2 All ER 372, p 374.

95   [1957] 1 QB 247.

the allegation was part of the whole range of circumstances which have to be weighed in the scale when deciding on the balance of probabilities.

Current opinion favours the approach of Morris LJ rather than that of Denning LJ. In *Re H and Others,*[96] a majority of the House of Lords supported the opinion that 'the more serious the allegation, the less likely it is that the event occurred and, hence, the stronger should be the evidence before the court concludes that the allegation is established on the balance of probability'.[97] As Lord Nicholls put it: 'Fraud is usually less likely than negligence. Deliberate physical injury is usually less likely than accidental physical injury.'[98] He added that, although the result was much the same, this did not mean that where a serious allegation was in issue the standard of proof required was higher. It meant only that the inherent probability or improbability of an event was itself a matter to be taken into account when weighing the probabilities and deciding whether, on balance, the event had occurred. If a third standard were substituted in some civil cases, it would be necessary to identify what that standard was and when it applied. The formulation of such a standard would risk causing confusion and uncertainty; it was better to stick to 'the existing, established law on this subject'. Contrary observations were not an accurate statement of the law.[99] Strictly, the Law Lords' opinion on this point was *obiter*, but this had been the view of the Court of Appeal[100] and it had been assumed without argument by counsel for all parties in the House of Lords.[101]

PRESUMPTIONS

It is possible for both legal and evidential burdens to be affected by *presumptions*. Nevertheless, presumptions fit awkwardly into an evidence course. When lawyers in

---

96   [1996] AC 563, pp 586–87.

97   *Ibid*, p 586. Followed in *In Re U* and *In Re B* (2004) *The Times*, 27 May, CA.

98   [1996] AC 563, p 586.

99   *Ibid*, p 587. Lord Goff and Lord Mustill agreed with Lord Nicholls. Lord Browne-Wilkinson dissented on a different point.

100   [1995] 1 FLR 643.

101   Lord Lloyd said that, in the absence of argument and in the light of earlier decisions, including some in the House of Lords, he was not prepared to say that, contempt of court apart, it was never necessary to prove facts in a civil case beyond a balance of probabilities. (A person who disobeys a court order in civil proceedings will be guilty of contempt of court and may be sent to prison as punishment. Since *Re Bramblevale Ltd* [1970] Ch 128, it has been clear that an alleged contempt must therefore be proved beyond reasonable doubt, and this was accepted by the House of Lords in *Re H and Others* [1996] AC 563.) In *R (McCann) v Crown Court at Manchester* [2002] 4 All ER 593 the House of Lords held that proceedings under s 1(1) of the Crime and Disorder Act 1983 for an anti-social behaviour order are civil rather than criminal, but that the criminal standard of proof is to be applied in them.

the 18th century first started to write books on evidence, they used to include large amounts of substantive law on such subjects as trespass, nuisance, bailment, actions on the case and so forth. Their object was to include not only what we should recognise as rules or principles of evidence, but rules about what had to be proved in order to establish particular claims or defences. There was no unifying principle other than the convenience of the arrangement for practitioners. Evidence textbooks today have sections entitled 'presumptions', and this at first glance looks like a suitable topic to cover. In fact, apart from the impact of presumptions on evidential and legal burdens, it is not. These bits and pieces are simply a survival from the older style of writing. No successful attempts have been made to find an all-embracing theory that would make 'presumptions' a true part of evidence law. What you see are several quite distinct chunks of substantive law, selected for no other reason than habit, which have little or no connection with each other and which are apt to mislead, because they can obscure the fact that there are many other similar devices in statutory sources of law that never get mentioned in evidence textbooks.

Because this is an area where attempts to find unifying features have been made so unsuccessfully, you may find classification confusing. When a writer refers to a presumption, you need to be sure how the word is being used. The sort of presumption that you will be trying to learn about because it appears in an examination syllabus – for example, of marriage, legitimacy and death – is usually what is often called a *rebuttable presumption of law*. Talk of any other type of presumption is unnecessary and leads to confusion. A 'presumption of fact' is merely *an inference* from facts, which is part of an ordinary reasoning process. For example, it would be possible, though unhelpful, to say that where the fingerprints of the accused are found at the scene of a crime, there is a presumption of fact that the accused was at some time present there.

Another 'presumption' of this kind is an inference that may be drawn from the possession of property that has recently been stolen. Judges and writers have quite often referred to this as 'the doctrine of recent possession', thereby inflating even more its apparent importance. As will be seen, there are good reasons for thinking that this part of the law has become obsolete since ss 34 and 35 of the Criminal Justice and Public Order Act 1994 came into force. The rule affected cases of handling and theft, and worked as follows:

(a) there had to be proof, or an admission, of the fact that the defendant was found in possession of stolen property; and

(b) the defendant's possession was so soon after the property had been stolen that it could fairly be described as 'recent'. (This was a question of fact, depending on the circumstances of each case.)

If those conditions were satisfied, the jury were to be directed that:

(a) such possession called for explanation; and

(b)   if the defendant gave no explanation, or gave an explanation that the jury were sure was untrue, they were entitled to infer that the defendant was guilty of either handling or theft.

The burden of proof remained on the prosecution, so that if the defendant's explanation left the jury in doubt as to his dishonesty, they were bound to acquit.[102]

In *R v Raviraj*,[103] the Court of Appeal said that this rule was only a particular aspect of a general proposition that where suspicious circumstances appear to demand an explanation, the lack of a credible explanation may warrant an inference of the defendant's guilty knowledge. This proposition was itself only part of a wider proposition that guilt may be inferred from the unreasonable behaviour of a defendant when confronted with facts that seem to accuse him. That is one line on which the common law was developing some years before the Criminal Justice and Public Order Act, and it was a controversial one. It differed significantly from the later legislation, in that no inference could be drawn from a suspect's silence after he had been cautioned.[104] The effect of s 34 of the 1994 Act changed that position because, while retaining the right to silence, it removed much of its usefulness by allowing inferences to be drawn from its exercise.[105] Thus, if a defendant provides no explanation to the police for his possession of property that has recently been stolen, and produces one for the first time only at trial, inferences may be drawn under s 34. If no explanation is provided even at trial, inferences can be drawn under s 35.[106] For this reason, it is likely that the common law 'doctrine of recent possession' will fall into disuse.

Another 'presumption of fact' is that people intend the natural consequences of their acts. This was formerly a common law 'presumption' and was put on a statutory basis by s 8 of the Criminal Justice Act 1967, which provides as follows:

A court or jury, in determining whether a person has committed an offence –

(a)   shall not be bound in law to infer that he intended or foresaw a result of his actions by reason only of its being a natural and probable consequence of those actions; but

(b)   shall decide whether he did intend or foresee that result by reference to all the evidence, drawing such inferences from the evidence as appear proper in the circumstances.[107]

---

102   *R v Schama* (1914) 84 LJKB 396; *R v Garth* [1949] 1 All ER 773; *R v Aves* [1950] 2 All ER 330.
103   (1986) 85 Cr App R 93, p 103.
104   *R v Raviraj* (1986) 85 Cr App R 93.
105   See below, Chapter 11.
106   See above, Chapter 5.
107   The section was inserted in the Act to overrule the decision of the House of Lords in *DPP v Smith* [1961] AC 290, which had the effect of making the presumption irrebuttable in some circumstances.

If someone refers to an 'irrebuttable presumption of law', that is just the same as referring to some principle or rule of substantive law. So, for example, the 'presumption of innocence' refers to the principle that the burden of proof generally rests on the prosecution in a criminal case.

When dealing with true presumptions – rebuttable presumptions of law – we shall not understand them unless we realise that they serve different purposes. One purpose is to save judicial time and effort. For example, according to the presumption of legitimacy it is presumed that a child born in lawful wedlock is legitimate in the absence of evidence to the contrary. Given the fact of birth in those circumstances, it would be unreasonable and time wasting not to presume the legitimacy of the child. But another, quite different, function is to resolve a dilemma which arises from the complete lack of evidence about a fact in issue. For example, according to the presumption of death a person will be presumed to have died if it is proved that:

(a) there is no acceptable evidence that he has been alive at some time during a continuous period of at least seven years;

(b) there are persons likely to have heard of him, had he been alive, who have not heard of him during that period; and

(c) all due inquiries have been made with a view to finding the person in question, but without success.[108]

The presumption in this case operates by artificially increasing the probative value of the basic facts – absence for seven years, etc – in the absence of any contrary evidence. So far as probative worth goes, there is nothing special about seven rather than six years' absence. But seven years gives rise to a rebuttable presumption of law, while six years gives rise only to a possible inference of fact. The reason is that it would be inconvenient to suspend indefinitely the rights of someone who has disappeared. What the law has done is to provide, by a rule affecting the burden of proof, a limitation period. Another example of a presumption that has been created to resolve a dilemma in the absence of evidence is s 184(1) of the Law of Property Act 1925. This provides that where two or more persons have died in circumstances where the order in time of the deaths is uncertain, then for all purposes affecting title to property the deaths shall be presumed to have occurred in order of seniority, with younger persons surviving older ones.[109]

A dilemma-resolving presumption is only needed if a dilemma truly exists. The existence of this sort of presumption should not blind you to the fact that a court may make the inference you want from the facts that are available. So if you can prove that X took a flight on an aeroplane that exploded in mid-air, you are not going to have to wait for seven years to pass before a court can find as a fact that X is dead.

---

108   *Chard v Chard* [1956] P 259, p 272.

109   See further Tapper, 2007, p 147; Zuckerman, 1989, pp 110–21.

Because presumptions are creatures of substantive law, the best place to find out about them is in books about the relevant substantive law and not in books of evidence. The fact that presumptions are creatures of substantive law can be seen from the fact that by far the most important of them are statutory and behave according to the provisions of the legislation in which they are to be found. The lack of any unifying feature, even among the common law presumptions, is emphasised by the fact that the same common law presumption can operate differently in civil and criminal contexts. For example, in *Dillon v The Queen*,[110] the Privy Council held that the common law presumption of regularity[111] could not be relied on by the prosecution to establish a central element of the offence alleged in that case against the accused. It is unlikely that the prosecution would be able to rely on the presumption of legitimacy in a case of incest.[112]

Some examples of statutory presumptions have already been mentioned. It may be convenient at this stage to describe briefly some common law examples.

PRESUMPTION OF MARRIAGE

Where a man and a woman have gone through a ceremony of marriage followed by cohabitation, there is a presumption that the ceremony was valid. It has been said that to rebut the presumption evidence is required that is 'strong, distinct, satisfactory and conclusive', or at least 'clear, distinct and satisfactory'. The presumption is not to be shaken by 'a mere balance of probability',[113] but this test was applied at a time when concern for status was greater than it is today. In *Piers v Piers*, for example, Lord Campbell referred to the 'tremendous responsibility' borne by a court having to decide the validity of a marriage and the peril of holding that a woman was a concubine and the children bastards.[114] Further, in *Re H and Others*[115] the House of Lords favoured a single standard of proof in civil cases and, in the unlikely event of a litigant's having to rely on the presumption today, rebuttal on the balance of probabilities would almost certainly suffice.

Even where there is no evidence that a ceremony of marriage has been performed, a presumption that a man and woman were lawfully married will arise from evidence of cohabitation, coupled with their reputation as man and wife.[116]

PRESUMPTION OF LEGITIMACY

There is a presumption that a child born or conceived during wedlock is the child of the woman's husband. The presumption applies not only where the husband and

---

110 [1982] AC 484.
111 See below, p 141.
112 Tapper, 2007, p 148.
113 *Piers v Piers* (1849) 2 HLC 331, pp 362, 370, 379–80.
114 *Ibid*, p 381.
115 [1996] AC 563.
116 *In Re Taylor (Decd)* [1961] 1 WLR 9.

wife are living together, but also where they are living apart, whether by virtue of a formal or informal agreement. The presumption does not apply where the parties are separated under a court order, but it will apply after the presentation of a petition for divorce or nullity and even after the granting of a decree nisi, as opposed to a decree absolute, of divorce or nullity. The reasoning behind this is that 'the law contemplates spouses as fulfilling their marital duties to each other unless there has been an actual order of the court dispensing with the performance of such duties'. So long as the law presumes the parties to a marriage to be performing their duties to each other, so long also will the law presume that if the woman bears a child she will be bearing it as the result of intercourse with her husband.[117]

The presumption of legitimacy may be rebutted by evidence which shows that it is more probable than not that the person in question is legitimate or illegitimate, as the case may be.[118] This presumption, therefore, affects the legal burden of proof.

PRESUMPTION OF DEATH

Some statutory provisions require a court to presume the death of a person in certain circumstances.[119] In matters where no statute lays down an applicable rule, the question of whether a person is to be presumed dead or not is generally simply a question of fact. However, from a long line of judicial statements, it appears to be accepted that there is a common law presumption of death in certain cases where a person has been absent for seven years.

The presumption operates as follows. Where as regards a certain person there is no acceptable evidence that he was alive at some time during a continuous period of seven years or more, then he will be presumed to have died at *some* time during that period if it can be proved that:

(a) there are persons who would be likely to have heard of him during that period;

(b) those persons have not heard of him; and

(c) all due inquiries have been made appropriate to the circumstances.[120]

The presumption is merely that death occurred *at the latest* by the end of seven years. It says nothing as to when during that period death occurred.[121]

---

117   *Knowles v Knowles* [1962] P 161, pp 166–67.

118   Family Law Reform Act 1969, s 26.

119   See, eg, Matrimonial Causes Act 1973, s 19(3), in relation to proceedings on a petition for presumption of death and dissolution of marriage; Offences Against the Person Act 1861, s 51, in relation to prosecutions for bigamy.

120   *Chard v Chard* [1956] P 259, p 272.

121   *In Re Phene's Trusts* (1870) 5 Ch App 139, pp 144, 152.

A presumption casts a burden on the party against whom it operates. That burden may be 'evidential' or 'persuasive'. If evidential, the presumption may be rebutted by evidence sufficient to show that the question which the presumption was meant to resolve is still a live issue. It has been suggested that the common law presumption of death is merely evidential.[122] If that is correct, once *some* evidence has been adduced sufficient to raise an issue whether or not the person in question is alive, the presumption is rebutted and the party who wishes to rely on the fact of death must prove that fact on the balance of probabilities. If, however, a presumption is 'persuasive', it affects the legal burden of proof so that the fact presumed must be found to exist, once the foundational facts have been proved, unless the court is satisfied by the evidence on the balance of probabilities that it does not. There is no satisfactory authority on the effect of the presumption of death, but this is hardly surprising, because any evidence showing a person to be alive is likely to prevent the presumption from arising at all since one or more of the conditions referred to in *Chard v Chard* will remain unsatisfied. In practice, problems posed by a person's unexplained disappearance allow room for a good deal of judicial manoeuvre. Where there is no direct evidence of either life or death, a judge sitting alone will be able to reach a conclusion which he thinks desirable on the facts of the case. The result is that the common law presumption of death has now little practical effect in litigation, and this is shown by the undeveloped state of the law on this subject.[123]

RES IPSA LOQUITUR

This maxim, meaning 'the thing speaks for itself', was traditionally regarded as giving rise to some kind of presumption in actions for negligence. Where something which had caused an accident was shown to have been under the management of the defendant or his servants, and the accident was such as in the ordinary course of things did not happen if those who had management used proper care, the accident itself led to an inference of negligence.[124]

More recently, in *Lloyde v West Midlands Gas Board*,[125] approved by the Privy Council in *Ng Chun Pui v Lee Chuen Tat*,[126] the maxim was described as 'no more than an exotic, although convenient, phrase' to describe a common sense approach, not limited by technical rules, to the assessment of evidence. It means that a claimant prima facie establishes negligence where:

(a) it is not possible for him to prove precisely what was the relevant act or omission that set in train the events leading to the accident; but

---

122 Stone, 1981, p 519, citing *Cross on Evidence*, 1974, p 126.

123 Stone, 1981, p 519.

124 *Scott v London and St Katherine's Docks Co* (1865) 3 H&C 596; *Moore v R Fox and Sons* [1956] 1 QB 596. See further Witting, 2001.

125 [1971] 1 WLR 749, p 755.

126 [1988] RTR 298, p 301.

(b)   on the evidence as it stands at the close of the claimant's case it is more likely than not that the cause of the accident was some act or omission of the defendant, or of someone for whom the defendant is responsible, involving failure to take proper care for the claimant's safety.

The effect of the maxim was formerly uncertain. Some judges thought that it affected the legal burden of proof so that, once the accident had been proved, the defendant could avoid liability only by showing that he had not been negligent, or at least by providing a reasonable explanation of the accident which was consistent with the absence of any negligence on his part.[127] Others took the view that the legal burden of proof was not affected and that only an evidential burden was created.[128]

The latter view received the approval of the Privy Council in *Ng Chun Pui v Lee Chuen Tat*. In an advice delivered by Lord Griffiths, the Privy Council said that it was misleading to talk of the burden of proof shifting to the defendant in a case where *res ipsa loquitur* applied. In any action for negligence the burden of proof rests throughout on the claimant. In an appropriate case the claimant will establish a prima facie case by relying on the fact of the accident. If the defendant adduces no evidence, there will be nothing to rebut the inference of negligence and the claimant's case will have been proved. However, if the defendant *does* adduce evidence, that evidence must be evaluated to see if it is still reasonable to draw the inference of negligence from the mere fact of the accident.[129]

PRESUMPTION OF REGULARITY

This is a loose expression which appears at present to refer to two different presumptions. One is the presumption that official appointments have been properly and formally made, and that official acts have been properly and formally performed.[130] According to one writer, the reasons for making these presumptions are that it is improbable that any person would carry out public functions unless he had been duly appointed, and it is improbable that somebody who had been properly appointed would be guilty of a dereliction of duty by carrying out one of his tasks improperly.[131] A more realistic view is that it is simply a rule of convenience.

So, for example, in *R v Verelst*,[132] where the defendant was charged with committing perjury while giving evidence in an ecclesiastical court, Lord Ellenborough CJ held that the prosecution did not have to prove that the court official who

---

127   See, eg, *Woods v Duncan* [1946] AC 401, p 419; *Barkway v South Wales Transport Co* [1948] 2 All ER 460, p 471; *Colvilles Ltd v Devine* [1969] 2 All ER 53, pp 56–57.

128   See, eg, *Colvilles Ltd v Devine* [1969] 2 All ER 53, p 58; *Henderson v Henry E Jenkins and Sons* [1970] AC 282, p 301.

129   [1988] RTR 298, pp 300–01.

130   It is sometimes referred to by the Latin maxim '*Omnia praesumuntur rite esse acta*'.

131   Nokes, 1967, p 70.

132   (1813) 3 Camp 432.

administered the oath had been properly appointed. The fact of his having acted in that capacity for some years was 'sufficient *prima facie* evidence that he was duly appointed and had competent authority to administer the oath', because it was 'a general presumption of law that a person acting in a public capacity is duly authorised so to do'.[133]

The status of the presumption is less clear. After Lord Ellenborough's initial ruling in *R v Verelst*, the defendant adduced evidence that, in fact, the official in question had not been properly appointed (and so had had no authority to administer an oath). In the face of this evidence, Lord Ellenborough said that the presumption stood only 'till the contrary is proved'. On the evidence, he found that the official's lack of authority had been proved. The question that arises is whether the presumption is a persuasive presumption, or merely an evidential one: must the defendant rebut it by proving on the balance of probabilities that the contrary is the case, or merely by adducing *some* evidence that that is so, with the result that the party relying on the presumption must prove the proper appointment to the appropriate civil or criminal standard?

R v Verelst suggests that the presumption is persuasive. Support can be found in the decision of the Court of Appeal in *Harris v Knight*,[134] in which it was held that, just as the presumption is not needed where due observance of the formalities has been proved, so it has no place 'where such observance is proved'.[135] However, in the same case, Lopes LJ said that the presumption 'applies with more or less force according to the circumstances of each case', which suggests that in some cases its effect might be to place an evidential burden only on the party against whom it is used. A further complication arises from the decision of the Privy Council in *Dillon v The Queen*.[136] In this case the defendant was a police officer charged with negligently permitting the escape of prisoners in his lawful custody. No formal proof was provided at trial of the lawfulness of the prisoners' custody. The Privy Council held that this was fatal to the prosecution case and allowed the defendant's appeal against conviction. Both the trial magistrate and the Jamaican appeal court had relied on the presumption of regularity to support the conviction, but the Privy Council said that a central element of an offence could not be established in this way.[137] It is likely that this decision would now be preferred to that in *R v Verelst* in a criminal trial, but the effect of the presumption in a civil action is unclear.

The second presumption under this head is that a mechanical instrument, provided it is of a kind that is usually in working order, was in working order at a particular time that is relevant in the litigation. Its effect is to place an evidential

---

133   (1813) 3 Camp 432, p 433.

134   (1890) 15 PD 170.

135   *Ibid*, p 180.

136   [1982] AC 484.

137   See also *Swift v Barrett* (1940) 163 LT 154; *Scott v Baker* [1969] 1 QB 659.

burden on the party against whom the presumption is used. The justification is its convenience. In *Nicholas v Penny*,[138] for example, the Divisional Court said that the courts will presume, in the absence of contrary evidence, that a watch or speedometer was in working order at the material time. And in *Tingle Jacobs and Co v Kennedy*,[139] in a *dictum* with which the other members of the Court of Appeal agreed, Lord Denning MR said, in relation to a set of traffic lights, 'when you have a device of this kind set up for public use in active operation, I should have thought that the presumption should be that it is in proper working order unless there is evidence to the contrary'. Evidence from computers, formerly regarded as suspect, is no longer subject to special provisions to ensure reliability, either in civil or criminal proceedings.[140] It seems to follow that the presumption of 'working order' now applies to computers, as well as to such instruments as watches, speedometers and traffic lights.

FURTHER READING

—Criminal Law Revision Committee, 11th Report, paras 137–42.

—Dennis, 'Reverse Onuses and the Presumption of Innocence: In Search of Principle' [2005] Crim LR 901.

—Dworkin, 'Principle, Policy, Procedure,' in Dworkin, *A Matter of Principle*, 1986.

—Laudan, *Truth, Error, and Criminal Law*, pp 29–114.

—Roberts, 'Taking the Burden of Proof Seriously' [1995] Crim LR 783.

—Smith, 'The Presumption of Innocence' (1987) 38 NILQ 223.

—Stone, 'The Presumption of Death: A Redundant Concept?' [1981] 44 MLR 516.

—Williams, 'The Evidential Burden: Some Common Misapprehensions' (1977) 127 NLJ 156.

—Williams, 'Evidential Burdens on the Defence' (1977) 127 NLJ 182.

—Williams, 'The Logic of "Exceptions" ' [1988] CLJ 261.

EXERCISES

1. What is the difference between a legal burden of proof and an evidential burden?

2. To what extent is ease of proof a determining factor in deciding where a legal burden of proof lies in civil cases?

3. In *L v DPP* (2002) the Divisional Court accepted the principles laid down in *Lambert* (2001), but upheld an argument that s 139 of the Criminal Justice Act 1988 imposed a legal burden on defendants. How was this conclusion reached?

4. Why is it difficult to determine whether a statute has impliedly placed a legal burden on a defendant?

---

138   [1950] 2 KB 466.

139   [1964] 1 All ER 888, p 889.

140   Civil Evidence Act 1995, Sched 2 ;Youth Justice and Criminal Evidence Act 1999, s 60.

5. What guidelines were suggested in *Hunt* (1987) for deciding whether a legal burden has been placed on defendants?

6. What six elements were identified by Dennis as liable to be taken into account when a court is considering a statute that appears to reverse the burden of proof in a criminal case?

7. What is the standard of proof in civil trials? How, if at all, is the position changed where a criminal offence is alleged in a civil action?

8. What is an 'irrebuttable presumption of law'?

9. What presumptions are there in relation to marriage, and in what circumstances do they arise?

10. What is the presumption of legitimacy? When does it *not* apply?

11. What conditions give rise to the common law presumption of death?

12. To what does the 'presumption of regularity' refer?

8

THE RULE AGAINST HEARSAY

SCOPE OF THE RULE

Section 1(2) of the Civil Evidence Act 1995 defines hearsay, for the purposes of that Act, as 'a statement made otherwise than by a person while giving oral evidence in the proceedings which is tendered as evidence of the matters stated'. That definition is, in effect, adopted in s 114(1) of the Criminal Justice Act (CJA) 2003, which states, 'In criminal proceedings a statement not made in oral evidence in the proceedings is admissible as evidence of any matter stated if, but only if . . .', and then goes on to set out the circumstances in which such evidence will be admissible.[1]

Although a strict system of exclusionary rules and exceptions did not develop before the 19th century, by the end of the 17th century there appears to have been a recognition that the admission of hearsay evidence was generally undesirable, and this was sometimes expressed by statements to the effect that hearsay was not evidence.[2] The principal reasons for its undesirability were that the original

---

1   See also s 121(2), which defines 'hearsay statement' for the purposes of that section as 'a statement, not made in oral evidence, that is relied on as evidence of a matter stated in it'. The common law expression of the rule was not significantly different. In *R v Sharp* (1988) 86 Cr App R 274, p 278, Lord Havers LC adopted the rule then stated in *Cross on Evidence*: 'An assertion other than one made by a person while giving oral evidence in the proceedings is inadmissible as evidence of any fact asserted.'

2   See, eg, *R v Charnock* (1696) 12 St Tr 1377, col 1454.

statement was not on oath, and the person making it was not available for cross-examination.[3]

Different approaches to the rule against hearsay have been taken in civil and criminal proceedings. The Civil Evidence Act 1995 boldly enacts in s 1(1) that, 'in civil proceedings evidence shall not be excluded on the ground that it is hearsay'. In criminal proceedings the law is governed by Pt 11, Chapter 2 of the CJA 2003. This does not abolish the rule against hearsay. Instead, it defines the rule and codifies the exceptions, but it achieves the latter task in a half-hearted way by preserving a number of existing common law exceptions. Section 114(1) of the Act provides:

> In criminal proceedings a statement not made in oral evidence in the proceedings is admissible as evidence of any matter stated if, but only if–
>
> (a)   any provision of this Chapter or any other statutory provision makes it admissible,
> (b)   any rule of law preserved by section 118 makes it admissible,
> (c)   all parties to the proceedings agree to it being admissible, or
> (d)   the court is satisfied that it is in the interests of justice for it to be admissible.

Section 118(2) of the Act provides:

> With the exception of the rules preserved by this section, the common law rules governing the admissibility of hearsay evidence in criminal proceedings are abolished.

The effect of these provisions is to abolish the common law hearsay rules, save those expressly preserved by s 118(1), and to create a new rule against hearsay.[4] At least for criminal trials it is necessary to understand the scope of the rule, because it would be absurd to develop an argument that evidence should be included as a hearsay exception if the rule does not apply in the first place.[5] The scope of the rule is best understood by concentrating on two features: the definitions of 'statement' and 'a matter stated', and the purpose for which evidence of an out-of-court statement is being adduced.

'STATEMENT' AND 'A MATTER STATED'

Section 115(2) of the Criminal Justice Act 2003 defines a statement as 'any representation of fact or opinion made by a person by whatever means; and it includes a representation made in a sketch, photofit or other pictorial form'. The representation

---

3   Morgan, 1956, pp 109–14. Justifications for the exclusion of hearsay evidence are more fully considered below.

4   *R v Singh* [2006] EWCA Crim 660, [2006] 1 WLR 1564.

5   Cf Stone and Wells, 1991, p 314: 'A matter not within the hearsay rule is not an exception to the rule, any more than the proposition that dogs have four legs is an exception to the proposition that human beings have two legs.'

can therefore be made by any method. In *Chandrasekera v R*[6] the victim of an attack, unable to speak because of her injuries, made signs indicating that it was the defendant who was responsible. This was treated by the Privy Council as a statement, to which the rule against hearsay in principle applied, and would be treated in the same way today. So, for example, would representations made by semaphore or morse code. Under the common law, sketches and photofit images were held to be unaffected by the rule.[7] This was illogical, and the Act now brings them, and representations by any other pictorial form, within the rule.

Section 115(3) provides as follows:

> A matter stated is one to which this Chapter applies if (and only if) the purpose, or one of the purposes, of the person making the statement appears to the court to have been–
>
> (a)   to cause another person to believe the matter; or
>
> (b)   to cause another person to act or a machine to operate on the basis that the matter is as stated.

The common law rule against hearsay covered non-assertive utterances, such as questions, commands and greetings, where the maker did not intend to communicate any information at all, but where inferences as to the existence of some fact could be drawn from what was said. The leading case establishing this was *R v Kearley*.[8] Drugs had been discovered on the defendant's premises; he was charged, among other things, with possessing them with intent to supply. In the hours following his arrest and subsequent detention at a police station, police officers remaining at his house answered 15 telephone calls. Ten of those calls were for the defendant and were made by persons who asked for drugs. According to the police, there were also nine persons who called at the house asking for the defendant, seven of whom indicated that they wanted to buy drugs. At trial, the police officers were allowed to give evidence of all the calls, including evidence of what had been said by the callers. With one irrelevant exception, the callers themselves did not give evidence. The question for the House of Lords was whether that police evidence should have been given. It was accepted that the purpose of adducing the evidence had not been to establish the truth of any fact narrated by the words. Instead, the purpose had been to invite the jury to infer from the fact that the words were uttered that the defendant had been supplying drugs. A majority of the House of Lords held that the evidence should not have been admitted, because such 'implied assertions' were caught just as much as express assertions by the rule against hearsay.[9]

---

6   [1937] AC 220.

7   *R v Cook* [1987] QB 417; *R v Constantinou* (1990) 91 Cr App R 74.

8   [1992] 2 AC 228.

9   Another reason was that the belief of the callers that drugs were available at that address was irrelevant to the question of whether the defendant was dealing in drugs. For a powerful criticism of this view, see the dissenting speech of Lord Griffiths ([1992] 2 AC 228, p 238).

The concept of an 'implied assertion' and its use to extend the scope of hearsay was much criticised,[10] and the Law Commission recommended that this development should be reversed. However, the Commission recognised that to formulate a rule against hearsay in terms of a speaker's intention to assert something could give rise to difficulty. Admissibility would depend on the chance of how the speaker expressed himself. If one of the callers in *Kearley* had said, 'Can I have my usual stuff?', that would have been admissible because of the absence of a factual assertion. But if a caller had said, 'The stuff you sold me last week was bad', that would have been inadmissible. The Commission concluded that the crucial question should not be how a person happened to express himself, but should usually be whether his purpose was to cause someone else to believe the particular fact that the party adducing the evidence wanted to infer from his words or conduct. On this test, 'Can I have my usual stuff?' would be admissible to prove that the defendant had supplied drugs before, because the caller's purpose was simply to request drugs. It was not to cause the person to whom he was speaking to believe that he (the person receiving the call) was a drug dealer. On this test, 'The stuff you sold me last week was bad', would be admissible to prove that the defendant had supplied drugs to the caller on at least one earlier occasion. It would be that fact which the prosecution would want the jury to infer from what was said, but it would not have been the caller's purpose to cause the defendant to believe that that fact was true. The purpose of the caller would have been to cause the defendant to believe that the drugs he had supplied were bad. Of course, the prosecution would not be interested in establishing that the drugs were of good or bad quality, only that the defendant had earlier supplied the caller with some drugs.[11]

Section 115(3) corresponds to cl 2(3) in the bill drafted by the Law Commission to achieve this result. Its effect is to remove 'implied assertions' from the scope of the hearsay rule by making it essential, for the operation of the rule, that the person whose words or actions are reported should have had as at least one purpose: that of causing another person to believe the matter that he stated.[12] It follows from this that if a person writes a private document that is intended to be read by no one else, the matters stated are not statements within s 115, because it was never the purpose of the writer to cause another person to believe the matters stated, or to act on the basis that matters were as stated. If relevant, therefore, what was written will be admissible simply as facts from which inferences can be drawn. This was the position in *R v*

---

10   See, eg, Law Commission No 245, 1977, paras 4.19–4.25.

11   In different circumstances the fact of supply by a particular person could be something that the speaker wants to assert. For example, an impoverished law lecturer might say to the manager of the wines section in a supermarket, 'It was you who sold that disgusting claret to me last week, wasn't it?'.

12   See sub-s (3)(a).

KN,[13] where the defendant was charged with sexual offences against his niece at a time when she was under 16 years of age. She had kept, solely for her own purposes, a private diary containing a reference to having sexual intercourse with the defendant. In the Court of Appeal McCombe J dealt with the admissibility of the relevant entry in this way:

> If, as the appellant contends, the diary was never intended to be read by anyone, it was not hearsay because it did not fall within section 115. But that does not mean it is not admissible. On the contrary, if relevant it is admissible. It is real or direct evidence outside the hearsay rule. The statutory restrictions upon the admissibility of hearsay have no occasion to apply to an action by the complainant which never had as its purpose, principal or supplementary, that any other person should believe or act upon it. It is simply a fact from which the jury is entitled, but not bound, to infer that [the defendant] had had intercourse with her. It is a fact from which that may, but not necessarily will, be inferred, in exactly the same way as if she had been observed by other people kissing him, for example, passionately, or making a booking of a hotel room for an afternoon in his name.[14]

The circumstances envisaged by sub-s (3)(b) might seem to be obscure. What the Law Commission had in mind was a situation where a statement is made with the purpose of ensuring that another person, while not necessarily *believing* the matter stated, should act on the basis that it is true. Suppose the prosecution wants to prove that X travelled to Manchester on 1 April. Reliance is placed on a claim for expenses made out by X and handed to Y, a clerk in the finance department at the office where X works, on 2 April. Probably all that concerned Y was whether the paperwork was in order; he was unlikely, as a result of processing it, to form a belief that X went to Manchester, and X was unlikely to want to create that belief in the mind of Y. So X has not made any representation 'to cause another person to believe the matter', but he has made it 'to cause another person to act . . . on the basis that the matter is as stated'. It is therefore caught under s 115(3)(b), in principle, by the rule against hearsay. The Law Commission thought it should make no difference that X fed his information about expenses, for example, into a computer instead of giving it to Y; hence the alternative of causing a machine to operate contained in sub-s (3)(b).[15]

Two problems that arose under the old law of hearsay can now be looked at again in the light of these statutory provisions.

Statements produced by machines

The old rule against hearsay did not exclude tapes, films or still photographs that had directly recorded an incident under investigation as it was taking place. So, for

---

13 [2006] EWCA Crim 3309.

14 Paragraph 21.

15 Law Commission No 245, 1997, paras 7.17–7.41.

example, in *R v Dodson*,[16] film from a security camera that had been operating during a robbery was admitted in evidence. In *Taylor v Chief Constable of Cheshire*,[17] witnesses who had watched a video recording of an offence while it was being committed were allowed to give evidence of what they had seen where the tape itself had been accidentally erased; the court took the view that they had been in exactly the same position as someone watching the commission of a crime through a pair of binoculars.

The rule did not apply to documents produced by machines that automatically recorded some process or event, such as a print-out from a computer recording telephone calls made from a given number,[18] or from an Intoximeter recording the level of alcohol in breath.[19] Nor were readings from a machine that simply carried out arithmetical procedures caught by the hearsay rule.[20] In none of these cases was the court being asked to accept the truth of an assertion made by a *person*, so the hearsay rule was inapplicable. The courts acknowledged that it made no sense to insist on rules devised to cater for human beings where humans had been replaced by machines.[21]

The position was different, however, where there had been some human intervention in the process: for example, where an employee had previously compiled records and someone else had transferred them to a computer. Thus, in *R v Coventry JJ ex p Bullard*,[22] a computer print-out stating that a person was in arrears with a local tax was held to be inadmissible hearsay because it must have been based on information which someone had fed into the computer, but which had not been properly proved.

This distinction is preserved by the new law. A 'statement' is confined, by s 115(2), to a representation made by a person. It follows that information which has been generated by a machine, but which is not based on information provided by a person, is not a 'statement', and thus not caught by the hearsay rule. Section 129(1) provides:

> Where a representation of any fact—
>
> (a)   is made otherwise than by a person; but

---

16   (1984) 79 Cr App R 220.

17   [1987] 1 All ER 225.

18   *R v Spiby* (1990) 91 Cr App R 186. See also *R(O) v Coventry Magistrates' Court* (2004) *The Times*, 22 April, DC.

19   *Castle v Cross* [1984] 1 WLR 1372. In *Owens v Chesters* (1985) 149 JP 235, the machine reading was held to be outside the hearsay rule, and so was the oral evidence of the officer as to what the reading had been. Cf *Taylor v Chief Constable of Cheshire* [1987] 1 WLR 80.

20   *R v Wood* (1982) 76 Cr App R 23.

21   See *The Statue of Liberty* [1968] 2 All ER 195, p 196, *per* Sir Jocelyn Simon P: 'The law is bound these days to take cognisance of the fact that mechanical means replace human effort.'

22   (1992) 95 Cr App R 175.

(b)   depends for its accuracy on information supplied (directly or indirectly) by a person,

the representation is not admissible in criminal proceedings as evidence of the fact unless it is proved that the information was accurate.

It is provided by sub-s (2) that this provision 'does not affect the operation of the presumption that a mechanical device has been properly set or calibrated'. Despite the rather narrow wording, this appears to preserve the common law presumption of regularity as applied to mechanical instruments.[23] The effect of this is that it will not ordinarily be necessary, where information is generated solely by a mechanical device, to prove that the device in question was in proper working order.

'Negative hearsay'

Sometimes the prosecution or the defence will wish to prove that an event did *not* occur. The only way to do this may be to examine records to see if there is an entry to show that the event occurred and, in its absence, to infer that it did not. Under the old law such an inference could be made in certain circumstances without amounting to 'negative hearsay' – an infringement of the hearsay rule to establish a negative rather than a positive fact.

In *R v Patel*[24] the prosecution had to prove that a man named Ashraf was an illegal immigrant. It called an immigration officer to say that Ashraf's name did not appear in the Home Office records, and that it could be inferred from this that he was an illegal immigrant. The Court of Appeal held this evidence to be hearsay, but Bristow J said that if an officer with personal knowledge of the compilation and custody of the records had been called, he could have given non-hearsay evidence of the absence of the name and its significance.

This approach was followed in *R v Shone*.[25] A stock clerk and sales manager were called to give evidence that entries would have been made on record cards if certain vehicle parts had been properly disposed of rather than stolen, that there were no such entries, and that therefore the parts had been stolen. The Court of Appeal held this evidence to be not hearsay but 'direct evidence' of those matters.

It is likely that the same results would now be achieved by the application of s 115(3). Where someone has not recorded an event, it will often be clear that the omission to record was not intended to give the impression that a particular event had *not* occurred. As the Law Commission expressed it:

Either the event did not occur, or that person did not realise that it had: in either case, it will not have been his or her purpose to cause anyone to believe that it had not happened, because it will

---

23   See above, Chapter 7.

24   [1981] 3 All ER 94.

25   (1983) 76 Cr App R 72.

not have crossed his or her mind that anyone might think it had. And therefore the record will be *direct* evidence that the event did not occur.[26]

Patel and *Shone* were authority under the old law to the effect that evidence of the absence of an entry in a record must be given by someone who has personal knowledge of the compilation and custody of the records. It is likely that this requirement, adapted no doubt to the practicalities of computerised records, will remain. It is essential that the court should be able to draw the appropriate inference from the absence of an entry, and it is unlikely to be able to do this without evidence from someone with first hand knowledge of the circumstances enabling such an inference to be made.

THE PURPOSE OF ADDUCING THE STATEMENT

The rule against hearsay excludes an item of evidence *only if the purpose of adducing that evidence is to establish the truth of the facts stated*. It follows that in relation to any item of evidence that you suspect may be caught by the rule, you need first to ask, '*What is the job of proof* that this item of evidence is being put forward to do?'. Only when you know what this is can you see whether the evidence is caught by the hearsay rule, which is brought into operation not by any particular form of words, but by the use that is going to be made of them. Putting it another way, you need to know the *relevance* of the evidence being considered. Difficulties sometimes arise because it is not appreciated that in relation to an alleged out-of-court statement there are two different questions that can be asked. The first is, 'Is it true that the statement was made?'. The second is, 'Given that the statement was made, is what was stated true?'. Only if you are interested in the answer to the second question, as well as the first, will a hearsay problem arise. Whether you are interested in the answer to the second question will depend on the way in which the evidence about the statement is relevant to what is in issue at trial.

A clear example of the operation of the rule is *Sparks v R*.[27] The defendant was charged with indecently assaulting a girl who was just under four years of age. The mother, when giving evidence before the examining magistrate at a preliminary hearing, said that her daughter had told her that she had been taken out of the car by the person who had assaulted her. The mother continued, 'I then asked her what did the person look like, and she said that it was a coloured boy'. The girl herself did not

---

26   Law Commission No 245, 1997, para 7.41. But it will not always be true that someone making a record will lack the purpose of causing people to believe that a certain event has not happened. It is at least arguable, eg, that when a list of successful examination candidates is produced, one of the purposes is to cause those who sat the examination, but whose names or numbers have not appeared, to believe the fact that they have failed.

27   [1964] AC 964.

give evidence at the subsequent trial because she was too young, and the mother's evidence of what her daughter had said was ruled inadmissible because it infringed the hearsay rule. The defendant, who was white, was convicted and appealed. He argued that it was unjust for the jury to be left throughout the whole trial with the idea that the child could not give any clue as to the identity of her assailant. But obviously the only relevance of the girl's statement was to make it less likely that the defendant had done what was alleged. He was therefore relying on the girl's statement for the truth of what she had asserted, and the hearsay rule applied. The Privy Council upheld the trial judge's ruling.[28]

Another case where the defence wanted to rely on the truth of something that had been asserted by someone not giving evidence at trial was *R v Turner*.[29] In this case, one of the defendants, Donald Barrett, appealed against his conviction for robbery. He argued that the trial judge had wrongly excluded evidence that a man called Saunders had told the police that he, and not Barrett, had taken part in the robbery. The Court of Appeal held that evidence of what Saunders had said to the police was caught by the rule. Obviously, the defence was relying on what Saunders had said to establish the truth of his assertions. The Court of Appeal emphasised that the rule applied to both prosecution and defence equally.

In some instances, however, a party wants to adduce evidence of something that was said out of court, not to establish the truth of what was stated, but for some other reason. In that case the statement will not be caught by the rule against hearsay. Such a statement is sometimes said to be admissible as 'original' evidence, because what is relevant is not the truth of what was stated but the fact that the statement was made. A good example of this occurred in *Subramaniam v Public Prosecutor*.[30] The defendant was prosecuted for possession of ammunition contrary to emergency regulations. His defence was that he had been captured by terrorists and had been acting under duress. He gave evidence describing his capture and how he had been forced to accompany the terrorists. However, the trial judge ruled inadmissible as hearsay any evidence that he might want to give about conversations that he had had with the terrorists. He was convicted and appealed. The Privy Council held that the trial judge had been wrong, and allowed the appeal. They emphasised that:

> Evidence of a statement made to a witness by a person who is not himself called as a witness may or may not be hearsay. It is hearsay and inadmissible when the object of the evidence is to establish the truth of what is contained in the statement. *It is not hearsay and is admissible when it is proposed to establish by the evidence, not the truth of the statement, but the fact that it was*

---

28   The appeal was allowed on other grounds.
29   (1975) 60 Cr App R 80.
30   [1956] 1 WLR 965.

made. The fact that the statement was made, quite apart from its truth, is frequently relevant in considering the mental state and conduct thereafter of the witness or of some other person in whose presence the statement was made.[31]

In *Subramaniam*, statements could have been made to the defendant by the terrorists which, whether true or not, might have affected his mind by causing him to believe that he would suffer death if he disobeyed their orders. Such evidence would have supported his defence of duress. The judge had been wrong, therefore, to exclude all evidence of conversations with the terrorists.

Another case where the rule was inapplicable was *Mawaz Khan v The Queen*,[32] in which two defendants were prosecuted for murder. Circumstantial evidence connected them both with the scene of the crime, but the prosecution also relied on the fact that each defendant had made a statement to the police setting up the same false alibi for both of them. The prosecution relied on these statements as evidence from which the jury could infer a joint attempt to set up a false alibi, and so joint guilt. Evidence of the statements was given by the police as part of the prosecution case, and the trial judge ruled that each statement was admissible in relation to both defendants. The Privy Council upheld this ruling. The hearsay rule catches only those assertions that are adduced to prove the *truth* of the facts asserted. These statements were adduced by the prosecution, not to show that their contents were *true*, but to show that they were *false*. Accordingly, they did not come within the hearsay rule.

The interest shown by a party in a statement may be probative, regardless of the truth of its contents. This appears from *R v Lydon*.[33] In 1985, a robbery was carried out by two men at a post office in Oxfordshire. The question was whether Lydon had been one of the robbers. There was substantial identification evidence, but the prosecution also relied on the discovery, about a mile from the scene of the robbery, of a gun on a grass verge by the edge of a road that had been used by the getaway car. The gun was in four pieces. Two pieces of rolled up paper were found immediately nearby, which had written on them, 'Sean rules' and 'Sean rules 85'. The defendant's first name was Sean. On an inside surface of the broken gun barrel there was a heavy smear of blue ink, which experts said was similar to that on the pieces of paper, so that the ink could have come from the same pen.

It was argued for the defendant that the references to 'Sean' were hearsay, but the trial judge admitted the evidence. The Court of Appeal held that he had been right to do so. The writing was relevant not as an assertion of the state of facts expressed by the words, but as itself a fact providing circumstantial evidence on the

---

31   [1956] 1 WLR 965, p 970, emphasis added.
32   [1967] 1 AC 454.
33   (1987) 85 Cr App R 221.

basis of which the jury might reach relevant conclusions. Here the conclusions they were invited to reach were that the paper had been in the possession of someone wishing to write 'Sean rules', and that that person was someone either named Sean himself or associated with a person of that name. It was not the prosecution's concern to prove that someone called Sean ruled anyone.

Similar reasoning can be found in *R v McIntosh*.[34] In that case the defendant was charged with being concerned in the importation of cocaine. At a house where he had been living before his arrest, police found hidden in the chimney a piece of paper on which were written calculations of the price and weight of a quantity of drugs. The handwriting was not, however, that of the defendant. The Court of Appeal held that this was admissible evidence for the prosecution. The document was not being adduced for the truth of its contents, but it had probative value because its possession by the defendant showed that he had an interest in the information contained in it. This fact was relevant because it tended to strengthen the prosecution case that he had been involved in the importation of drugs. But for this probative job to be done, it was not necessary to prove that the calculations contained in the paper were accurate.[35]

A problem that can arise concerns the extent to which identifying marks on articles can be used as evidence without infringing the rule against hearsay. A clear case where such use was illegitimate was *Patel v Comptroller of Customs*.[36] The defendant was convicted of making a false declaration in a customs import document. The case against him was that he had made a customs declaration stating that five bags of coriander seed had come from India, when in fact they had come from Morocco. The prosecution relied in support of its allegation on labels fixed to bags of the seed which stated 'produce of Morocco'. The Privy Council held that this was hearsay evidence, and inadmissible to prove the country of origin.[37] Similarly, in *R v Brown*[38] the Court of Appeal held that the rule against hearsay was infringed where the prosecution relied on the names of hospital patients in shoes to establish the identities of the owners of the shoes.

Now consider this problem case. The police have found the body of a man, neatly strangled, concealed in a ditch. Nearby they find a hat with the name 'Tom Ripley' marked inside it. The police suspect that Ripley was the murderer of the unknown man. They argue that this second discovery is relevant to the issue of Ripley's guilt because it is possible to infer from it that Ripley was present when the

---

34   [1992] Crim LR 651. Cf *R v Balogun* [1997] Crim LR 500.

35   Similarly, ownership of books about the Second World War, written by historians whose theories had been discredited, would be capable of showing their owner's interest in that period of history, despite the fact that his ideas about it would in all likelihood be wrong.

36   [1965] AC 356.

37   See also *Comptroller of Customs v Western Lectric Co Ltd* [1966] AC 367.

38   [1991] Crim LR 835.

body was concealed, from this that he was the person who concealed it, and from this that he was the murderer.[39] But is the name marked inside the hat caught by the rule against hearsay? On one view it is, because the object of putting a name inside a hat is to make a statement about the ownership of the hat. The name in the hat should be treated in the same way as the names in the shoes in *R v Brown*, or the declaration of the place of origin in *Patel v Comptroller of Customs*. On another view, however, the name is not caught by the hearsay rule. The prosecution is not concerned to prove ownership of the hat: it is concerned only to prove how the hat arrived at its position near the concealed body. The name shows no more than a probability that the hat had been dropped by a person of that name.[40] The hat should be treated in the same way as the pieces of paper in *R v Lydon*.[41] It might be objected that in *Lydon* the truth of the statement (that Sean ruled) was of not the slightest use to the prosecution, whereas in this case it would help the prosecution considerably to establish that the hat was owned by Tom Ripley. It might further be objected that to ask the jury to infer that the hat had been dropped by a man named Tom Ripley is virtually no different from asking them to believe that the statement of ownership constituted by the name inside the hat is true.

In answer, however, the prosecution might cite *R v Rice*.[42] Rice and another man called Moore were convicted on two counts of conspiracy to steal. It was alleged that, in furtherance of the conspiracy, Rice had gone to Manchester by air. Evidential problems arose at trial in connection with an airline ticket that was produced to prove this. The trial judge's treatment of the ticket was later the basis of Rice's unsuccessful appeal against conviction. The ticket was for two seats on a flight from London to Manchester in the names of 'Rice' and 'Moore' for 10 May 1961. The ticket was produced by an airline representative whose job it was to deal with flight tickets returned after use, and was produced from the file where such used tickets would ordinarily be found. Rice said that he had never flown to Manchester and knew nothing of the ticket or of how it had come to be booked.

The Court of Criminal Appeal held that the document could not be treated as 'speaking its contents', because what it said would be hearsay, so it could not be treated as saying, 'I was issued to Rice and Moore'. But the court nevertheless held that the ticket was admissible as an item of original evidence, because a used airline ticket with a name on it is likely to have been used by someone with that name. This decision has been the subject of much criticism, but it has never been expressly overruled, and it is possible that an argument on these lines could be used to avoid the

---

39   None of these inferences follows inevitably, but remember (see Chapter 1) that evidence does not have to be conclusive to be relevant.

40   The reason for this is that, in the normal course of events, only a person with that name would have a reason to inscribe it in his hat.

41   (1987) 85 Cr App R 221.

42   [1963] 1 QB 857.

unsatisfactory situation that would arise if, in the problem case proposed, an item of evidence that most people would regard as relevant and of some weight were to be excluded.[43] Whether this is legitimate avoidance of the rule against hearsay or illegitimate evasion is less important now than before the Criminal Justice Act 2003. The reason for this is the 'safety-valve' exception to the rule provided by s 114(1)(d), which makes a hearsay statement admissible where the court is satisfied that it is in the interests of justice for it to be admissible.

Sometimes the fact that a statement has been made is relevant because it was a 'performative utterance'; in other words, making that statement in its particular context amounted to the performance of a legally significant act. Such cases were not caught by the rule against hearsay under the old law, nor would they be now. For example, words can constitute a criminal offence or the tort of defamation; they can constitute the granting of a permission that may be required before another act is lawful; they can be used to make or accept offers. A vivid example is *Woodhouse v Hall*.[44] The charge against the defendant was that she had acted in the management of a brothel, contrary to the Sexual Offences Act 1956. The premises in question were a sauna in Wanstead and the defendant was the manageress. Two other women were also employed there with her. Four police officers kept observation over a period of time. They also entered the premises, pretending to be genuine customers. There they were massaged by the defendant and by the two other women. They were prepared to give evidence that while being massaged they had been offered masturbation, referred to as 'hand relief', by the defendant and by the two other women. They had, apparently, been quoted prices of £6 for 'hand relief' and £10 for what was called 'topless hand relief'. It was said that none of the officers had accepted.

The question arose whether the police evidence about the offers made by the two other women was admissible. Those other women were not called by the prosecution. The magistrates held that this evidence was caught by the hearsay rule and so was inadmissible. The prosecution accepted that, in the absence of this evidence, they could not establish that the sauna satisfied the common law definition of a brothel: an establishment at which two or more persons were offering sexual services. The Divisional Court had to consider whether the magistrates had been right.

---

43   For a favourable account of the decision in *R v Rice*, see Dennis, 2002b, p 563. See also *R v Lilley* [2003] EWCA Crim 1789, where the Court of Appeal held that the words 'Sharon's book' on the cover of an exercise book, which had been used to practise forging signatures, were not caught by the rule against hearsay. They operated simply as evidence of the defendant's connection with a conspiracy to defraud.

44   (1980) 72 Cr App R 39. See also *R v Chapman* [1969] 2 QB 436. Language used in this way is also referred to as 'operative words' or a 'verbal act'. See further Austin, 1975, pp 1–24; Austin, 1979, pp 233–52.

It was held that they had not; the hearsay rule did not apply. The relevant issue, because of the common law definition of a brothel, was whether the women had made these offers. The police officers had been entitled to give evidence of them. The key to understanding this decision lies in the concept of performative utterances. The women who told the men that they could have 'hand relief' for £6 and 'topless hand relief' for £10 were not concerned simply to describe the way of the world in Wanstead. Their purpose was not to describe offers of sexual services, but to *make* them.

JUSTIFICATIONS FOR A RULE AGAINST HEARSAY

Several justifications have traditionally been given.[45]

HEARSAY IS NOT THE BEST EVIDENCE[46]

According to this objection, hearsay is inferior to direct evidence and should therefore be inadmissible in criminal proceedings. In many cases this is a persuasive argument, but in some cases hearsay will be the best evidence *available*, and in some cases hearsay may actually be more reliable than direct evidence. An example of the latter situation occurred in *Myers v DPP*,[47] where a contemporaneous record made by workers in a motor car factory of cylinder block and chassis numbers was held to be inadmissible hearsay. Even if it had been possible to trace the workers who had stamped the parts with numbers and then recorded them, their recollection several years later of parts and numbers must have been non-existent.

HEARSAY EVIDENCE WOULD BE EASY TO INVENT[48]

In *R v Kearley*,[49] one of Lord Ackner's reasons for excluding evidence of the telephone calls was that evidence of that kind could be easily invented by the police. It would, of course, be equally open to a defendant to manufacture hearsay statements with a view to creating a reasonable doubt about the prosecution case. The risk of manufacture does increase if the original source of information is unavailable for cross-examination. However, the Law Commission has suggested that this risk could be reduced by limiting new exceptions to the rule to first hand hearsay, by imposing requirements for admissibility such as giving advance notice of any hearsay evidence,

---

45   See, eg, *Teper v R* [1952] AC 480, p 486, *per* Lord Normand.
46   Law Commission No 245, 1997, paras 3.2–3.4.
47   [1965] AC 1001.
48   Law Commission No 245, 1997, paras 3.5–3.8.
49   [1992] 2 AC 228.

and by the exclusion of the hearsay evidence of unidentified witnesses. 'First hand' hearsay evidence is hearsay at one remove from the original speaker. For example, A makes an assertion to B, who then wishes to repeat it in court to establish the truth of what A asserted. 'Multiple' hearsay occurs when the evidence is at more than one remove from the original speaker. For example, A makes an assertion to B, who reports it to C. C then wishes to repeat it in court to establish the truth of what A originally asserted. (Multiple hearsay is sometimes referred to by the number of removes from the original speaker: second hand hearsay, third hand hearsay, and so on.)[50]

THE RISK OF ERRORS IN TRANSMISSION[51]

Someone who reports the words of another person may have misheard or misinter-preted them, but the old hearsay rule could exclude statements, such as those in letters or tape-recordings, where there was no doubt about what was said. The Law Commission's view was that this was an objection to multiple hearsay only.[52]

THE DEMEANOUR OF THE ORIGINAL SOURCE IS LOST[53]

The appearance and unconscious behaviour of a witness while giving evidence have traditionally been thought to help in assessing the weight of his testimony. Today, when 'body language' has assumed the kind of significance formerly attached to phrenology or numerology, this opinion may still be widely held. But some persons, including some judges, have disagreed, and psychological research suggests that they are right. It seems that demeanour is an unreliable guide to sincerity and is even more unreliable in relation to accuracy.

HEARSAY STATEMENTS ARE NOT ON OATH[54]

Historically, this was the main reason for rejecting hearsay evidence, but it seems improbable that nowadays an oath is any guarantee that the witness will tell the truth. It is more to the point that people are likely to be less careful about the accuracy of what they say in private conversations than in court, where they can be cross-examined publicly.

THE ABSENCE OF CROSS-EXAMINATION[55]

The fact that the maker of the original statement cannot be cross-examined is the chief objection today to the admission of hearsay evidence. It depends on an

---

50   These recommendations are largely reflected in the Criminal Justice Act 2003. See ss 116(1)(a), (b), 121, 132.

51   Law Commission No 245, 1997, paras 3.5–3.8.

52   Law Commission No 245, 1997, para 3.7.

53   Law Commission No 245, 1997, paras 3.9–3.12.

54   Law Commission No 245, 1997, paras 3.13–3.14.

55   *Ibid*, paras 3.15–3.18.

assumption that the weaknesses in such evidence will not be apparent to juries or magistrates in the absence of cross-examination. Since almost no research has been done into the ways in which juries or magistrates assess evidence, the assumption is difficult to accept or reject.

There are four potential defects in direct (non-hearsay) testimony which cross-examination may be able to expose:

(a) insincerity – the witness may be lying;
(b) ambiguity – the testimony may be unclear and so misunderstood;
(c) faulty perception – the witness may be honest but mistaken;
(d) faulty memory – the witness may no longer accurately recall what he perceived.

If a witness (W) purports to repeat in court what he has been told about an event by an out-of-court speaker (S), the possible sources of error are doubled. Either W or S could be lying. S's original statement may have been misunderstood by W and/or W may himself give unclear testimony. S may have been mistaken in what he thought he saw. W may be mistaken in what he thought S said. The memories of both W and S may be at fault.[56]

But in cases where the witness's truthfulness and accuracy of observation are not in issue, and where there is no ambiguity, little can be gained from cross-examination.[57] The Law Commission's view was that absence of cross-examination did not justify the *whole* of the old rule.[58]

THE DEFENDANT'S RIGHT OF CONFRONTATION[59]

Although not part of the common law,[60] there is a view that it is fundamental to justice that an accused person should be able to confront the witnesses who accuse him, and that to bring the witness and the accused together makes the accused and the public feel that justice is being done.[61] The Law Commission's view was that,

---

56   Where W purports to narrate in court a non-hearsay statement made by S to W – ie, a statement whose relevance depends not on the fact that it is true, but only on the fact that it was made – the possible sources of error are not doubled. Since the court is not concerned with the truth of what S said to W, questions about S's sincerity, perception and memory do not arise. Only ambiguity remains as a possible source of error. See, generally, Tribe, 1974; Choo, 1996, Chapter 2.

57   And although cross-examination may be effective in exposing faulty perception or memory, or ambiguity in narration, it is less likely to be effective at exposing insincerity (Choo, 1996, pp 32–33).

58   See now the CJA 2003, s 124 for provisions relating to the credibility of the maker of the hearsay statement.

59   Law Commission No 245, 1997, paras 3.34–3.35; Friedman, 1998.

60   *R (D) v Camberwell Green Youth Court* [2005] UKHL 4, [2005] 1 WLR 393, para 14; *Grant v The Queen* [2006] UKPC 2, [2007] 1 AC 1, para 20.

61   See also Choo, 1996, pp 37–42.

although it is desirable that witnesses should give their evidence in the presence of the accused if possible, other factors, such as the impossibility of obtaining evidence directly from a witness in court, may outweigh this consideration, and this is reflected in the new legislation.

FURTHER READING

—Austin, *How To Do Things with Words*, 2nd edn, 1975, pp 1–24.

—Austin, *Philosophical Papers*, 3rd edn, 1979, pp 233–52.

—Birch, 'The Criminal Justice Act 2003; Hearsay: Same Old Story, Same Old Song?' [2004] Crim LR 556.

—Choo, *Hearsay and Confrontation in Criminal Trials*, 1996, Chapter 2, 'The Rationales for the Rule'.

—Friedman, 'Thoughts from across the Water on Hearsay and Confrontation' [1998] Crim LR 697.

—Langbein, *The Origins of Adversary Criminal Trial*, 2003, pp 233–47.

—Law Com No 245, *Evidence in Criminal Proceedings: Hearsay and Related Topics*, 1997.

—O'Brian, 'The Right of Confrontation: US and European Perspectives' [2005] 121 LQR 481.

EXERCISE

1. When is a statement affected by the rule against hearsay?
2. In what circumstances does s 114(1) CJA 2003 provide that hearsay statements shall be admissible?
3. What did the House of Lords understand by 'implied assertions' in *R v Kearley* (1992)? How did CJA 2003 overrule their decision?
4. What do you understand by 'negative hearsay'?
5. Give some examples from decided cases of circumstances in which an out-of-court statement was adduced for a purpose other than that of proving the truth of its contents.
6. What justifications have been put forward for having a rule against hearsay? How convincing are they?
7. If the facts in *R v Lilley* [2003] EWCA Crim 1789 were to recur today, how should the case be decided?

9
HEARSAY EXCEPTIONS

SUMMARY

INTRODUCTION

The scope of the rule against hearsay has been much reduced. The Civil Evidence Act 1995 has abolished the rule completely for civil proceedings. In 1995 the Law Commission published a Consultation Paper on the subject of hearsay in criminal cases,[1] and in 1997 published a report.[2] The recommendations of the Commission have been very largely incorporated in Pt 11, Chapter 2 of the Criminal Justice Act (CJA) 2003, which has created four principal categories of admissibility:

- hearsay admissible by statute;
- hearsay admissible under any preserved common law rule;
- hearsay admissible by agreement;
- hearsay admissible in the interests of justice (the 'safety-valve').

---

1   Law Commission Consultation Paper 138, 1995.
2   Law Commission No 245, 1997.

This chapter considers each of these in turn with the exception of hearsay by agreement, as this topic is not likely to give rise to difficulties in practice.[3]

HEARSAY ADMISSIBLE BY SECTIONS 116 AND 117

By s 114(1)(a) of the CJA 2003, hearsay is admissible if made so by any provision contained in Chapter 2 of the Act, or by any other statutory provision. The main provisions in Chapter 2 are s 116, which makes admissible the statements of unavailable witnesses in certain circumstances ('the unavailability exception'), and s 117, which makes certain types of business and other documents admissible.[4] Various other statutes make hearsay statements of a particular kind admissible in criminal trials, but these are not considered here.[5]

THE UNAVAILABILITY EXCEPTION

Section 116(1) provides:

In criminal proceedings a statement not made in oral evidence in the proceedings is admissible as evidence of any matter stated if –

(a)   oral evidence given in the proceedings by the person who made the statement would be admissible as evidence of that matter;

(b)   the person who made the statement (the relevant person) is identified to the court's satisfaction; and

(c)   any of the five conditions mentioned in sub-section (2) is satisfied.

It is clear that the sub-section applies to both prosecution and defence witnesses, and that the hearsay statement can be oral or written. However, the effect of sub-s (1)(a) is that no statement will be admissible as evidence of any matter of which the relevant person could not himself have given oral evidence if he had been available. So, for example, if the statement was one of opinion from a non-expert, and so inadmissible

---

3   By s 132 a power is given for rules of court to be made to govern criminal procedure for the purposes of these provisions.

4   Sections 119 and 120 affect the evidential status of a witness's previous inconsistent or consistent statements. These have already been considered in the context of the course of testimony: see above, pp 99–106.

5   Examples are referred to in the Consultation Paper, paras 3.0–3.60 and Appendix C.

under the rules governing such evidence,[6] it will not become admissible simply because it is a hearsay statement. More importantly, if the relevant person could not have given oral evidence of the matter stated because his evidence fell within the general rule excluding hearsay, the statement will not be admitted under s 116.

Suppose, however, that the relevant person could have given oral evidence of a fact, but only by virtue of a hearsay exception. Could second hand hearsay evidence of the fact be given under s 116? This depends on s 121, which limits multiple hearsay to three circumstances.[7] The first is where either of the statements is admissible under s 117 (business documents), s 119 (previous inconsistent statements) or s 120 (other previous statements of a witness); the second is where it is agreed that the multiple hearsay statement should be admitted; the third is where the court uses its discretion to admit the statement.[8] Thus, in the absence of agreement or the exercise of judicial discretion, s 116 is confined to first hand hearsay.

By s 116(1)(b), the relevant person must be 'identified to the court's satisfaction'. This follows a recommendation of the Law Commission. The reason was to enable an opposing party to challenge the relevant person's credibility and reliability. In the Commission's opinion, 'the party tendering the statement should be required to attribute the statement to a particular individual, with sufficient detail of that person's identity for the court to be satisfied that the individual exists, and for the other party to have enough information to enable it to make enquiries' about that person. There was also concern that the admission of a statement by an unidentified person, whom the defence had had no chance to question, could be in breach of Art 6(3)(d) of the European Convention on Human Rights.[9] Section 124 gives the person against whom hearsay evidence has been admitted a right to adduce evidence to discredit the maker of the original statement, or to show that he has contradicted himself. Obviously, this right cannot be exercised if the maker of the original statement remains wholly unidentified. Equally obviously, s 116(1)(b) gives the court a fairly wide scope for deciding how much information is necessary to satisfy this requirement in any particular case.

By s 123(1), a statement will not be admissible under s 116 if it was made by a person who did not have 'the required capability' at the time when he made the statement. By sub-section (3), a person has 'the required capability' if he is capable of

---

6   See below, Chapter 13.

7   Hearsay is said to be 'multiple', or 'second hand', 'third hand', etc, where information presented to a court is at more than one remove from the person making the original observation. For example, X sees Q. He later tells Y that he saw Q. If Y gives evidence of what X said to him in order to establish the truth of Q, his testimony will be first hand hearsay evidence of Q. If X tells Y that he saw Q, and Y then tells Z of what X said to him in order to prove Q, Z's testimony of what Y said to him would be second hand hearsay evidence of Q.

8   Section 121 is discussed further below.

9   Law Commission No 245, 1997, paras 8.5–8.8. Article 6(3)(d) gives everyone charged with a criminal offence the right to examine or have examined witnesses against him.

understanding questions put to him about the matters stated, and giving answers that can be understood. The burden of proving capability, should this be in issue, is on the party wishing to adduce the statement. Whether this is the prosecution or the defence, the standard is proof on the balance of probabilities.[10] The test is very like that for competence in Youth Justice and Criminal Evidence Act 1999, s 53. In *R v Sed*[11] the Court of Appeal said that s 53 does not expressly provide for 100 per cent comprehension by either the witness or the jury. Depending on the length and nature of the questioning, and the complexity of the subject matter, s 53 may not always require even nearly 100 per cent comprehension.[12] Probably the same flexibility will be shown in applying s 123(3).

The sub-s (2) conditions

In order to use the unavailability exception, at least one of the five conditions set out under sub-s (2) must be satisfied. Condition (a) is that the person who made the statement (referred to in all five conditions as 'the relevant person') is dead. Condition (b) is that that person is unfit to be a witness because of bodily or mental condition.

Condition (c) is that the relevant person is outside the UK, and it is not reasonably practicable to secure his attendance. The test of *reasonable* practicability was recommended by the Law Commission on the basis that it would require the party wishing to adduce the evidence to make reasonable efforts to bring the witness to court, but that the court would be able to take into account factors such as the expense involved, the seriousness of the case, and the importance of the information contained in the statement.[13] An identical condition appeared in s 23(2)(b) of the Criminal Justice Act 1988, which allowed documentary hearsay to be adduced in certain circumstances.[14] In *R v Castillo and Others*[15] the Court of Appeal held, in considering this condition, that the mere fact that it was *possible* for the witness to attend was not enough. Among factors to be considered were the importance of the evidence the witness could give, and how prejudicial it would be if he did not attend; the expense and inconvenience of securing the witness's attendance, although this should not be a major consideration where the witness was 'part of the prosecution team'; and the reasons given for saying that it was not reasonably practicable for the witness to attend.

Section 116(2)(c) was considered by the Court of Appeal in *R v C*.[16] The

---

10   Section 123(4).

11   [2004] EWCA Crim 1294, [2004] 1 WLR 3218.

12   See above, Chapter 5.

13   Law Commission No 245, 1997, para 8.39.

14   These provisions are repealed by the CJA 2003, Sched 37, Pt 6.

15   [1996] 1 Cr App R 438.

16   [2006] EWCA Crim 197.

witness was a resident of South Africa, who had originally agreed to give evidence for the prosecution at a trial in the UK. He later changed his mind; he also refused to give evidence via a video link. At a preparatory hearing the judge held that it was not reasonably practicable for the prosecution to secure his attendance, and ordered that his evidence should be read under s 116(2)(c). The Court of Appeal set aside the order. It said that the expression 'reasonably practicable' has to be judged on the basis of the steps taken, or not taken, by the party seeking to secure the attendance of the witness. The court must also consider whether to exercise its powers under s 126 of the 2003 Act[17] and s 78 of PACE. Whether it is fair to admit the statement depends in part on what efforts should reasonably be made to secure the attendance of the witness or, at least, to arrange a procedure whereby the contents of the statement can be clarified and challenged. In this case there should have been further inquiries as to why the witness had changed his mind and also refused to give evidence by video link.

Condition (d) is that the relevant person cannot be found, although such steps as it is reasonably practicable to take to find him have been taken.

Condition (e) is that through fear the relevant person does not give (or does not continue to give) oral evidence in the proceedings, either at all or in connection with the subject matter of the statement, and the court gives leave for the statement to be given in evidence. By s 116(4), leave may be given under sub-s (2)(e) only if the court considers that the statement ought to be admitted in the interests of justice, having regard:

(a)   to the statement's contents,

(b)   to any risk that its admission or exclusion will result in unfairness to any party to the proceedings (and in particular to how difficult it will be to challenge the statement if the relevant person does not give oral evidence),

(c)   in appropriate cases, to the fact that a direction under section 19 of the Youth Justice and Criminal Evidence Act 1999 (special measures for the giving of evidence by fearful witnesses etc.) could be made in relation to the relevant person, and

(d)   to any other relevant circumstances.

In *R v Doherty*[18] Tuckey LJ, delivering the judgment of the Court of Appeal, said that whether a witness's fear was objectively justified is a matter that can be considered as part of the question of unfairness under sub-s (4)(b). If this were not so, he said, any genuine but irrational fear would justify the admission of important and potentially decisive hearsay evidence. He went on to say that, in considering whether to grant leave under s 116(2)(e), a judge is required to perform a balancing exercise. Broadly, the risk of unfairness to the defence, because the evidence cannot be challenged by cross-examination, has to be set against the risk of unfairness to the prosecution,

---

17   The court seems to have considered that s 126 provides a broad power to exclude hearsay evidence, not just a power to be exercised to avoid wasting time.

18   [2006] EWCA Crim 2716, paras 26, 28.

because it cannot put before the jury all available evidence. This is 'not strictly the exercise of a discretion but something similar to it. It is evaluative and fact sensitive and the sort of exercise which the trial judge is in the best position to perform'. It follows that the Court of Appeal will interfere only if satisfied that the judge's conclusion was obviously wrong.

The Law Commission was repeatedly told that a major problem in the administration of criminal justice was that many witnesses were too frightened to give evidence. The problem was not limited to prosecution witnesses: defendants sometimes had great difficulty in ensuring that their witnesses attended court, because the witnesses were afraid that they would antagonise the police or others involved or interested in the prosecution.

Section 23(3) of the 1988 Act provided that a statement contained in a document was admissible, with leave of the court, if it had been made by a person who did not give evidence through fear, or because he was 'kept out of the way'. There were two principal difficulties with this provision. The first was that the exception applied only to statements made to the police or others charged with the duty of investigating offences or charging offenders. The interests of defendants were ignored. The Law Commission recommended that this be remedied, and condition (e), like the rest of s 116, applies equally to defence and prosecution, and to statements that are oral or written.

The second difficulty was that it was initially unclear what counted as 'fear' for the purposes of the exception, although the courts ultimately settled for a liberal interpretation. In *R v Acton JJ ex p McMullen*,[19] it was argued that those relying on the sub-section had to satisfy the court that the maker of the statement was in fear owing to attempts made *after* the making of the statement to put him in fear. It was also argued that the fear had to be based on reasonable grounds. The Divisional Court rejected both arguments, saying that it was wrong to introduce a concept of 'reasonable grounds', and that it was sufficient for the court to be sure that the witness was in fear as a consequence of the commission of the offence, or of something said or done subsequently in relation to that offence. The decision of the Court of Appeal in *R v Martin*[20] showed that although it was *sufficient* that the witness's fear was a consequence of the commission of the offence, or of something said or done subsequently in relation to that offence, it was not *necessary* that the fear should arise in either of these ways. Provided fear was established, there was no need for the court to inquire into the basis of it. So if, for example, a witness's fear arose from a mistaken belief that he was being followed in the streets, the sub-section would still apply. It was enough that the witness was afraid and failed to testify as a result.

---

19   (1990) 92 Cr App R 98.
20   [1996] Crim LR 589.

The Law Commission concluded that a rigid categorisation of the circumstances in which fear could be claimed should not be attempted,[21] but the Commission thought that it would not be enough to refer to 'fear' without even a partial definition. This was because, in the absence of any definition, it would be open to a court to hold that a particular kind of fear was not what Parliament had intended. The Commission concluded that amending legislation should make it clear that the discretion was a wide one. The report added: 'Indeed, we find it hard to envisage a situation where a court would be minded to admit the statement if it had power to do so, but where it ought to be precluded from doing so because the particular kind of fear from which the witness was suffering was not the kind that ought to suffice.'[22]

Section 116(3), based on cl 5(7) of the draft bill in the report, provides that '[f]or the purposes of sub-section (2)(e) "fear" is to be widely construed and (for example) includes fear of the death or injury of another person or of financial loss'.

Under the 1988 Act, it was held that the court had to be satisfied that the witness was in fear at the time when he was expected to give evidence, and s 116 will doubtless be interpreted in the same way. In some cases it may be fairly easy to infer that a state of fear springing up at one point in time has continued, but this will not always be so. In *R v H, W and M*,[23] a complainant in November 1998 made statements to the police containing evidence against the defendants. On 29 June 1999 the complainant made a further statement, saying that he intended to 'disappear' because he feared that he would be killed, and that he would not testify at the defendants' trial because of this. The trial began on 1 September 1999. No one from the prosecution service or the police had seen the complainant after 29 June to find out if his attitude had changed, despite the fact that two months after making the further statement he had been arrested for drugs offences while still in the locality. The trial judge nevertheless unhesitatingly accepted the police evidence that the complainant was afraid, and ruled that his statement could be admitted. The Court of Appeal, quashing the convictions, held that this was wrong. The relevant date for considering whether the complainant did not give evidence through fear was the date when the trial began. The evidence that had been given was out of date, and thus insufficient to establish the necessary condition.

Sometimes proof of fear can present problems. The old law was in a state of uncertainty, and this has not been removed by the new legislation. In *Neill v North Antrim Magistrates' Court*,[24] the House of Lords held that evidence of fear which itself

---

21   One of the reasons was that if the rules were too precise it would make it easier for those wanting to intimidate witnesses to do so without having the witness statement admitted. The mental image of rival gangs queuing to buy copies of the new legislation to see how far they could go provided one of the lighter moments in writing this chapter.

22   Law Commission No 245, 1997, para 8.64.

23   [2001] Crim LR 815.

24   [1992] 4 All ER 846.

offended the rule against hearsay was inadmissible. However, in *R v Greer*,[25] the Court of Appeal said that there was no reason why a judge should not hear 'unsworn evidence' from the witness who was in fear; and in *R v H, W and M*,[26] the Court of Appeal suggested that a witness might provide information about his fear during a recorded interview. A certain flexibility is suggested by the observation of Moses LJ in *R v Davies (Anita Elizabeth)*,[27] where he said that courts are ill-advised to attempt to test the basis of fear by calling witnesses before them, since that may undermine the very thing that s 116 was designed to avoid. He added, however, that 'judges must be astute not to skew a fair trial by a too ready acceptance of assertions of fear, since it is all too easy for witnesses to avoid the inconvenience and anxiety of a trial by saying they do not want to come'.

This raises a general question in relation to the sub-s (2) conditions: do they have to be strictly proved? It is tempting to say that they do, with the possible exception of condition (e), because that was the way in which the courts interpreted very similar conditions in s 23 of the Criminal Justice Act 1988. For example, in *R v Case*,[28] the Court of Appeal held that a trial judge should not have inferred from the addresses appearing on the statements of two witnesses that they lived outside the UK. Before the statements could be used as evidence for *any* purpose, it was necessary to establish the relevant condition by admissible evidence. This could not be done by using the statements themselves, because they were inadmissible until the condition had been proved. In this respect the s 23 conditions differed from those in s 24, relating to business documents, because it was thought that documents of that kind had been intended by Parliament to 'speak for themselves'.[29] But this similarity between the conditions in s 23 of the 1988 Act and those in s 116 of the CJA 2003 is no guarantee that the earlier approach to proof will be adopted, and for the present it cannot be said with certainty whether the sub-s (2) conditions have to be strictly proved.

Reliance on the exception by a party responsible for the unavailability

The Law Commission recommended that the s 116 exception should not apply where the unavailability of the maker of the statement is caused by the person seeking to put the statement in evidence, or by someone acting on that person's behalf. Clause 5(9) of the draft bill in the Report was designed to achieve this, and now appears as s 116(5), which provides as follows:

> A condition set out in any paragraph of sub-section (2) which is in fact satisfied is to be treated as not satisfied if it is shown that the circumstances described in that paragraph are caused –

---

25   [1998] Crim LR 572.

26   [2001] Crim LR 815.

27   [2006] EWCA Crim 2643, [2007] 2 All ER 1070, paras 14–15.

28   [1991] Crim LR 192.

29   *R v Foxley* [1995] 2 Cr App R 523.

(a)   by the person in support of whose case it is sought to give the statement in evidence; or

(b)   by a person acting on his behalf,

in order to prevent the relevant person giving oral evidence in the proceedings (whether at all or in connection with the subject matter of the statement).

The effect of the words 'if it is shown that' is to place the burden of proof on the party opposing admission of the evidence where reliance is placed on s 116(5). This could put the defence in difficulties. On the other hand, the defence would need to prove the allegation only on the balance of probabilities.[30] Further, if the prosecution were to tender the statement under sub-s (2)(d), on the basis that its maker cannot be found after taking reasonably practicable steps to do so, it would be for the prosecution to prove (beyond reasonable doubt) that condition (d) was satisfied. Section 116(5) begins to operate only after it has been shown that the maker of the statement is unavailable for one of the recognised reasons. Thus, if there is a suggestion that the police are deliberately keeping the maker of the statement out of the way, this would have to be disproved beyond reasonable doubt before the prosecution could rely on condition (d).[31]

BUSINESS AND OTHER DOCUMENTS

Under ss 23 and 24 of the Criminal Justice Act 1988, documentary hearsay statements were admissible under certain conditions. However, the interpretation of ss 23 and 24 gave rise to difficulty,[32] and the powers to admit hearsay statements under them were the subject of a wide judicial discretion, contained in ss 25 and 26, that gave rise to accusations of inconsistency and uncertainty.[33] These provisions were repealed by Sched 37, Pt 6 of the CJA 2003, and replaced by an exception in favour of 'business and other documents' in s 117.

By sub-s (1), a statement contained in a document is admissible in criminal proceedings as evidence of any matter stated if oral evidence given in the proceedings would be admissible as evidence of that matter,[34] and if the requirements of sub-s (2) (and sub-s (5) also, if necessary) are satisfied. By s 134(1), 'document' is broadly interpreted as 'anything in which information of any description is recorded'.[35]

---

30   The invariable standard where a defendant in a criminal trial has to prove anything.

31   Law Commission No 245, 1997, paras 8.31–8.32, 8.42.

32   See, eg, *R v Field* (1992) 97 Cr App R 357; *Brown v Secretary of State for Social Security* (1994) *The Times*, 7 December; *R v Derodra* [2000] 1 Cr App R 41.

33   Law Commission Consultation Paper 138, 1995, paras 9.14–9.18.

34   So evidence that would be inadmissible for a reason other than the hearsay rule does not become admissible just because it is in documentary form.

35   The expression would include, for example, a film, tape recording or computer disk.

By sub-s (2):

The requirements of this sub-section are satisfied if –

(a)   the document or the part containing the statement was created or received by a person in the course of a trade, business, profession or other occupation, or as the holder of a paid or unpaid office;

(b)   the person who supplied the information contained in the statement (the relevant person) had or may reasonably be supposed to have had personal knowledge of the matters dealt with; and

(c)   each person (if any) through whom the information was supplied from the relevant person to the person mentioned in paragraph (a) received the information in the course of a trade, business, profession or other occupation, or as the holder of a paid or unpaid office.

By sub-s (3), the persons mentioned in paras (a) and (b) of sub-s (2) may be the same person.

It is possible that while the s 116 conditions will have to be strictly proved,[36] satisfaction of the s 117(2) conditions can be inferred from the document that is tendered in evidence. This was the position in relation to business documents under s 24 of the Criminal Justice Act 1988. In *R v Foxley*,[37] it was argued that for documents to be admissible under s 24 it must be separately proved that the conditions set out in that section, which were similar to those contained in s 117(2), were satisfied. But the Court of Appeal rejected this argument, holding that the purpose of s 24 was to enable a document to speak for itself. The court was influenced by the reference in s 24(1) to a person 'who may reasonably be supposed to have had personal knowledge of the matters dealt with'. In the court's view, these words showed that Parliament expected courts to draw inferences as to the personal knowledge of the person supplying the information, and, by implication, other inferences as to the satisfaction of conditions could also be drawn. This approach was followed in *R v Ilyas and Knight*.[38] A diary had been found on a counter at a business premises containing, the Court of Appeal said, the sort of entries one would expect to find in a document created by a person in the course of a business, and in circumstances where the information would have been supplied by a person who might reasonably be supposed to have had personal knowledge of the matters dealt with. It was held admissible without further explanation as a document created in the course of a business, although the court did say that there might be circumstances in which a document would have to be explained in evidence before it could be admitted under s 24.

An example may help to show how s 117(2) is likely to operate. Suppose that X plc manufactures pottery. Each item receives an individual mark from employee 1

---

36   See above.
37   [1995] 2 Cr App R 523.
38   [1996] Crim LR 810.

after its completion. At the end of each day, employee 2 sends the items to various shops. Before doing so, he fills in a form for each item showing its number and destination. On the next day, employee 3 copies the information contained in these forms into a register. At the end of each week, employee 4 copies the contents of this register onto a computer file. The prosecution wants to prove that a particular item was sent to a particular shop. In order to do so, it wishes to rely on a statement contained in the relevant computer file, which is now the only record left. Can the prosecution do so?

The computer file is something 'in which information of any description is recorded', and is therefore a 'document' for the purposes of s 117. The document containing the statement was created in the course of a business, so sub-s (2)(a) is satisfied. The person who supplied the information contained in the statement (employee 2) may reasonably be supposed to have had personal knowledge of the matters dealt with, because he was responsible for dispatching the goods and filling in the forms showing where they were sent, so sub-s (2)(b) is satisfied. Employee 4, who created the statement in the computer file, was supplied with the information by employee 3, whose daily register he copied. Employee 3 received that information from employee 2 in the course of a business, so sub-s (2)(c) is satisfied. The computer file is therefore admissible to prove where the item in question was sent.[39]

By s 117(4), if the statement contained in the document was prepared for the purposes of pending or contemplated criminal proceedings, or for a criminal investigation (but was not obtained pursuant to certain provisions relating to overseas evidence), the requirements of s 117(5) must be satisfied, in addition to those in s 117(2). This will be the case if any of the five conditions for the application of the unavailability exception, contained in s 116(2), is satisfied by the person who supplied the information contained in the statement; or if that person cannot reasonably be expected to recollect the matters dealt with in the statement, having regard to the length of time since he supplied the information and all other circumstances.

Again, an example may help.[40] Suppose that the police are investigating a bank robbery. In the course of their investigation a search is made of a house owned by one of the defendants. Various items, taken from several rooms, are sent for scientific analysis. Detective 1 puts each item in a plastic bag. He also puts a label on each bag showing the address, the nature of the item, and the room from which the item was taken. Detective 2 inspects these bags and labels and makes from them a written list of rooms and items taken from them. He passes this list to detective 3, who records the information on a computer file. Nobody has any independent recollection of what was found during the search, and the prosecution wants to use this file, which is

---

39 The reason for allowing multiple hearsay in these circumstances is that the conditions are thought to provide a guarantee of greater reliability than usual.

40 It is not suggested that this reflects actual police procedure. The sole purpose of the example is to show in a simple way how s 117 is likely to work.

the only evidence now available, to prove that a sledgehammer was taken from the kitchen. The computer file (a 'document') was created in the course of an occupation (that of police officer). The person who supplied the information contained in the statement (detective 1) had personal knowledge of the matters dealt with because he was responsible for taking the items from each room, placing them in a plastic bag, and labelling the bag. The information was supplied to detective 3, who created the document, by detective 2, who received it in the course of his occupation. The sub-s (2) conditions are therefore all satisfied. The statement was prepared for the purposes of pending or contemplated criminal proceedings, or of a criminal investigation, and was not obtained in the circumstances set out in sub-s (4)(b). The additional requirements of sub-s (5) must therefore be satisfied. It is some time since detective 1 (the person who supplied the information contained in the statement) supplied the information to detective 2, and he has been involved in many similar investigations since then. Therefore, he cannot reasonably be expected to have any recollection of the matters dealt with in the statement, having regard to the length of time since he supplied the information and all other circumstances. Sub-section (5) is therefore satisfied and the computer file is admissible.

We have seen that one of the criticisms of the 1988 Act provisions was that they left too much room for judicial discretion.[41] The Law Commission recommended that there should be a very limited scope for the exercise of discretion once a business document had been held admissible. While such documents could be assumed generally to be reliable, this would not always be so. For example, a letter would qualify as a business document as soon as it was posted,[42] but there might be reasons in a particular case to suspect that the contents of the letter were unreliable. It would be undesirable for business documents to be automatically admissible, and the Commission made recommendations that are now contained in s 117(6) and (7). These provide as follows:

(6) A statement is not admissible under this section if the court makes a direction to that effect under sub-section (7).

(7) The court may make a direction under this sub-section if satisfied that the statement's reliability as evidence for the purpose for which it is tendered is doubtful in view of –

(a) its contents;

(b) the source of the information contained in it;

(c) the way in which or the circumstances in which the information was supplied or received; or

(d) the way in which or the circumstances in which the document concerned was created or received.

---

41 Law Commission No 245, 1997, para 2.18.

42 Because it would have been received by postal workers in the course of the business or occupation of the postal service. The example appears at Law Commission No 245, 1997, para 8.74.

The words 'if satisfied that' in sub-s (7) suggest that the burden of proof is on the party asserting that the reliability of the statement is doubtful; it is not for the party putting forward the document to prove that it is reliable.

A practical point that may arise is how the contents of a document should be proved. By s 133, where a statement in a document is admissible as evidence in criminal proceedings, the statement may be proved by producing either the document, or (whether or not the document exists) a copy of the document or the material part of it, authenticated in whatever way the court may approve.[43] The section makes no express provision for proof of the contents of a document by oral evidence. A very similar provision was contained in s 27 of the 1988 Act. It was held, in relation to that provision, that proof of the contents of a document was not governed exclusively by the statute, and that common law exceptions allowing secondary evidence of the contents of a document could also be relied on.[44]

PRESERVED COMMON LAW EXCEPTIONS

With the exception of the rules preserved by s 118, the common law rules governing the admissibility of hearsay evidence in criminal proceedings are abolished.[45] Minor exceptions preserved by the section are:

- published works dealing with matters of a public nature (such as histories, scientific works, dictionaries and maps) as evidence of facts of a public nature stated in them;
- public documents (such as public registers, and returns made under public authority with respect to matters of public interest) as evidence of facts stated in them;
- records (such as the records of certain courts, treaties, Crown grants, pardons and commissions) as evidence of facts stated in them;
- evidence relating to a person's age or date or place of birth;
- reputation as evidence of a person's good or bad character;[46]
- reputation or family tradition as evidence of pedigree or the existence of a marriage, the existence of any public or general right, or the identity of any person or thing;
- informal admissions made by an agent.

---

43 By s 134(1), ' "copy", in relation to a document, means anything on to which information recorded in the document has been copied, by whatever means and whether directly or indirectly'.

44 *R v Nazeer* [1998] Crim LR 750.

45 See s 118(2). The effect is to abolish, *inter alia*, the rules relating to dying declarations and declarations against pecuniary interest.

46 See, further, below Chapter 12.

The section also preserves any rule of law under which an expert witness may draw on the body of expertise relevant to his field,[47] and any rule of law relating to the admissibility of confessions or mixed statements.[48] In addition, two major common law exceptions are preserved: *res gestae* and statements in furtherance of a common enterprise.

RES GESTAE STATEMENTS

The Latin expression *res gestae* may be loosely translated as 'events occurring' or 'things happening', and statements falling under this head are sometimes said to be 'part of the *res gestae*'. The Law Commission described this exception in its report as having 'four separate strands to it, each with its own precondition for admissibility and individual justifications for existence'.[49] It was said that these four strands consisted of spontaneous statements made by way of reaction to a relevant act or event, statements accompanying and explaining relevant acts, statements describing states of mind, and statements describing physical sensation. These four strands remain, although the division is slightly different in s 118(1), para 4, which preserves:

Any rule of law under which in criminal proceedings a statement is admissible as evidence of any matter stated if –

(a)   the statement was made by a person so emotionally overpowered by an event that the possibility of concoction or distortion can be disregarded;

(b)   the statement accompanied an act which can be properly evaluated as evidence only if considered in conjunction with the statement; or

(c)   the statement relates to a physical sensation or a mental state (such as intention or emotion).

In preserving the common law the Act, as will appear below, has preserved some uncertainties.

Excited utterances

These are the spontaneous exclamations of the victim of an offence or of an observer. Most of the cases are about victims' utterances, but this exception is not confined to them. Earlier civil cases are still relevant for the law relating to this exception and there are, for example, collision cases where the words came not from one of the parties to the litigation, but from a passenger or bystander.[50]

---

47   See below, Chapter 13.

48   See below, Chapter 11.

49   Law Commission No 245, 1997, para 8.114.

50   Stone and Wells, 1991, p 381, n 1. In *R v Fowkes* (1856) *The Times*, 8 March, it was a witness to a murder who made the excited utterance.

The leading case is *R v Andrews*,[51] in which the test for admissibility under this head was laid down by Lord Ackner. It is as follows:

(a) The primary question that the judge must ask is whether the possibility of concoction or distortion can be disregarded.

(b) To answer that question, the judge must first consider the circumstances in which the particular statement was made, in order to satisfy himself that the event was *so unusual, startling or dramatic* as to dominate the thoughts of the speaker to the extent that *his utterance was an instinctive reaction to the event*, giving no time for reasoned reflection. In such a situation the judge would be entitled to conclude that the involvement or pressure of the event excluded the possibility of concoction or distortion, provided the statement was made in conditions of approximate contemporaneity.

(c) For the statement to be sufficiently spontaneous, it must be *so closely associated with the event that excited it* that the mind of the speaker was still dominated by that event. The fact that a statement was made in answer to a question is only a factor to be taken into consideration under this head.

(d) Quite apart from the time factor, there may be *special features* in the case that relate to the *possibility of concoction or distortion*; for example, the speaker may have had a motive for fabrication, such as malice. The judge must be satisfied that, having regard to any such special feature, there was no possibility of any concoction or distortion to the advantage of the speaker or the disadvantage of the defendant.[52]

(e) The ordinary fallibility of human recollection goes to the *weight* to be attached by the jury to the original statement, not to its *admissibility*. But there may be special features that give rise to the possibility of error; for example, where the original speaker has drunk to excess, or where he made an identification in particularly difficult circumstances. If there are special features such as these, the judge must consider whether he can still exclude the possibility of error before admitting the evidence.

(f) Where the trial judge has properly directed himself as to the correct approach to the evidence, and there is material that entitles him to reach his conclusions, his decision will not be interfered with on appeal.

Lord Ackner also said, *obiter*, that he would deprecate any attempt to use the *res gestae* doctrine as a device to avoid calling the witness if he or she were available. However,

---

51   [1987] AC 281.

52   Note that this refers to the possibility of concoction or distortion on the part of the person making the excited utterance, not on the part of the person reporting it. See *R v Jamieson* [2003] EWCA Crim 3755, para 35.

in *AG's Reference (No 1 of 2003)*,[53] the Court of Appeal held that there is no rule of law that *res gestae* evidence is not to be admitted merely because the maker of the statement is available and could give evidence. Such evidence is in principle admissible, although it could be excluded under s 78(1) of the Police and Criminal Evidence Act 1984 in the exercise of the judge's discretion.[54] In this case, the defendant had been charged with a serious assault on his mother. The prosecution did not wish to call her, because it was believed that she would support her son by giving untruthful evidence. Instead, the prosecution wished to call evidence from other witnesses about excited utterances, such as 'He threw me downstairs and set me on fire', made by the mother at the time when she sustained her injuries. The Court of Appeal held that the evidence was admissible, but could, and should, have been excluded under s 78(1).

Obviously, an 'excited utterance' argument cannot succeed where the utterance precedes the dramatic event. In *R v Newport*,[55] the appellant's wife left their house after an argument. The case for the prosecution was that the appellant pursued her with a bread knife. At some stage during the flight, the wife suffered a stab wound which caused her death. The prosecution said that she had been murdered; the defence said that there had been an accident. The prosecution applied for evidence to be admitted that the wife had made a telephone call to a friend that evening. The friend said that she had sounded agitated and frightened, and had asked if she could come to the friend's house if she had to leave her own in a hurry. This evidence was admitted on the basis that what the wife had said was part of the *res gestae*, but the submission and the judge's ruling were made under a misconception that the call had been made immediately before the wife left the house, whereas in fact it had been made 20 minutes earlier. In the light of this new evidence, the Court of Appeal held that the wife's utterance was plainly not part of the immediate incident and should have been excluded. It was in no sense a spontaneous and unconsidered reaction to an immediately impending emergency.

The nature of the event itself, and the lapse of time between the event and the utterance, are likely to feature in arguments about admissibility. The less dramatic the event and the greater the lapse of time, the less likely it is that the speaker's mind was still dominated by the event so as to rule out any opportunity for concoction or distortion. For example, in *Tobi v Nicholas*,[56] this *res gestae* exception was held not to apply where a statement was made 20 minutes after a relatively undramatic traffic accident.

Tobi v Nicholas may be contrasted with *R v Carnall*,[57] where the defendant was

---

53   [2003] 2 Cr App R 453.

54   For s 78(1), see below, Chapter 11.

55   [1998] Crim LR 581.

56   (1987) 86 Cr App R 323.

57   [1995] Crim LR 944.

charged with the murder by beating and stabbing of a man who had known him well. Part of the evidence against the defendant was what the victim had said between the attack and his subsequent death. Two witnesses had seen him in the street outside their house. He was bleeding and asking for help. He said that he had been attacked with knives and baseball bats and that it had taken him about an hour to crawl to the house. The witnesses asked him who his attacker had been, and he named the defendant. A policeman went with the victim to hospital. In reply to the officer's questions, the victim again named the defendant and gave details of the background to the attack. The judge ruled that both items of evidence formed part of the *res gestae*. On appeal it was argued that this had been wrong. Reliance was placed mainly on the length of time that had elapsed between the attack and the statements by the victim.

The Court of Appeal held that the trial judge had applied the *Andrews* principles and that there had been material entitling him to reach his decision. In those circumstances the court would not interfere. The crucial question was whether there was any real possibility of concoction or distortion, or whether the judge felt confident that this could be ruled out because the speaker's thoughts were so dominated by what had happened. In answering this question, the judge had taken into account the nature of the attack, the injuries inflicted, the pain suffered by the victim, and his obsession with trying to get help and stay alive. The time factor was not conclusive.

Statements relating to the maker's performance of an act

A statement at the time of performing a relevant act is admissible to explain the act, provided it is made contemporaneously by the person who performs the act,[58] but the act has to be relevant to the facts in issue apart from the statement accompanying it. In *Wright v Doe d Tatham*,[59] Coltman J said:

> Where an act done is evidence *per se*, a declaration accompanying that act may well be evidence if it reflects light upon or qualifies the act. But I am not aware of any case, where the act done is, in its own nature, irrelevant to the issue, and where the declaration *per se* is inadmissible, in which it has been held that the union of the two has rendered them admissible.

In *R v Bliss*,[60] evidence was tendered, to prove the nature of a certain road, that someone had planted a tree at a particular point, saying simultaneously that it marked the boundary between his land and the highway. It was held that the mere planting of the tree was irrelevant apart from the declaration. Accordingly, neither evidence of the planting nor of the accompanying declaration could be given.

---

58 *Rawson v Haigh* (1824) 2 Bing 99; *Walters v Lewis* (1836) 7 C&P 344; *R v Bliss* (1837) 7 A&E 550; *Howe v Malkin* (1878) 40 LT 196.

59 (1837) 7 A&E 313, p 361.

60 (1837) 7 A&E 550.

Statements relating to a physical sensation or mental state

The rationale for these exceptions is that of necessity: such evidence will be the best, and usually the only, way of proving the fact in question.[61] As Mellish LJ said in *Sugden v Lord St Leonards*,[62] 'Wherever it is material to prove the state of a person's mind, or what was passing in it, and what were his intentions, there you may prove what he said, because that is the only means by which you can find out what his intentions were'.

The usefulness of statements relating to physical sensation is limited because, while they are admissible as evidence of the existence of the sensations, such statements are inadmissible to prove the their *cause*. In *R v Gloster*,[63] for example, statements made by a woman who was dying from the effects of an illegal abortion, and who named the person responsible, were held inadmissible. Charles J held that, to be admissible, such statements had to be confined to contemporaneous symptoms and should not include any sort of narrative about how the symptoms had been brought about. It is possible that 'contemporaneous' may be flexibly interpreted. During argument in *R v Black*,[64] Salter J said that the expression should not be confined to feelings experienced at the actual moment when the statement was made, but should include statements such as, 'Yesterday I had a pain after meals'.

In criminal cases, the exception in favour of statements relating to the maker's contemporaneous state of mind or emotion has been applied only erratically. Several old decisions at first instance can be cited in support, but the argument in them was virtually non-existent. For example, in *R v Dixon*,[65] a soldier had killed a corporal. The jury were directed that his statement immediately afterwards, 'I know what I have done and am not sorry for it', was admissible to prove an intent to kill. It was presumably thought that those words showed his state of mind very shortly after the event, and from his state of mind at that stage could be inferred his state of mind at the earlier stage, just before the killing.

In *R v Vincent, Frost and Edwards*,[66] the defendants were charged in relation to a number of political meetings where they had spoken. One of the counts in the indictment alleged that they had conspired to procure large numbers of persons to assemble for the purpose of inciting terror and alarm in the minds of the Queen's subjects. Evidence having been given of several meetings at which the defendants had been present, it was proposed to ask a superintendent of police whether people had complained to him of being alarmed by these meetings. It was argued for the defence that the prosecution should have called those who had been alarmed, but Gurney B

---

61 Law Commission No 245, 1997, paras 8.125–8.127.
62 (1876) LR 1 PD 154, p 251.
63 (1888) 16 Cox CC 471.
64 (1922) 16 Cr App R 118.
65 (1869) 11 Cox CC 341.
66 (1840) 9 C&P 275.

held the superintendent's evidence admissible. Again, it seems necessary to spell out the reasoning. It had to be shown that the defendants had encouraged persons to assemble for the purpose of inciting terror and alarm among others, who were present but not participating. Let us call the latter 'law-abiding citizens'. To prove this, it was helpful, though not essential, to show that the assembly had actually caused terror and alarm to some law-abiding citizens. To establish that fact, the police superintendent was allowed to give evidence of the complaints he had received, because these reflected the states of mind of a number of law-abiding citizens when they made the complaints.

In *R v Edwards*,[67] the defendant was charged with the murder of his wife. A neighbour was allowed to testify that, a week before her death, the wife had come to the neighbour's house with a carving knife and a large axe, which she had asked the neighbour to keep. She explained her action by saying, 'My husband always threatens me with these and when they're out of the way I feel safe'. But the decision can be criticised on at least two grounds. First, it is arguable that the statement was not one of her *contemporaneous* mental state; it was, rather, a description of an habitual state of mind that prevailed under certain conditions. Secondly, if declarations of contemporaneous mental states are to be treated in the same way as declarations about bodily sensations, and there would seem to be no good reason not to do so, it was surely wrong to admit her explanation for the way she felt.[68]

A more obvious case of admissibility would occur where a defendant charged with murder had expressed feelings of antipathy towards the deceased shortly before the death. During the course of argument in *R v Ball*, Lord Atkinson said:

> Surely in an ordinary prosecution for murder you can prove previous acts or words of the accused to shew he entertained feelings of enmity towards the deceased, and that is evidence not merely of the malicious mind with which he killed the deceased, but of the fact that he killed him. You can give in evidence the enmity of the accused towards the deceased to prove that the accused took the deceased's life.[69]

An expression of intention to do something has sometimes been relied on to prove that the speaker carried out the act in question. An expression of intention is, of course, an expression of the speaker's state of mind at the time he announces his intention. That state of mind is one of having decided to act in some way at some time in the future. Precisely what inference, if any, can be drawn from an expression of intention depends on the facts of the particular case. This is not a problem that is

---

67   (1872) 12 Cox CC 230.
68   Cf *R v Gloster* (1888) 16 Cox CC 471. The statement could not have been admitted as one accompanying and explaining a relevant act, because the act of handing over the knife and the axe had no relevance in isolation from the words spoken. See above, *R v Bliss* (1837) 7 A&E 550.
69   [1911] AC 47, p 68.

likely to be resolved by appeals to precedent, but some examples can be given by way of illustration.

In *R v Buckley*,[70] the defendant was charged with the murder of a police constable. A year earlier the constable had been the principal witness against him in a prosecution that had led to the defendant's imprisonment. Evidence was adduced, apparently without objection by the defence, that after the defendant had been released from prison he was heard to mutter threats of vengeance against the constable. The prosecution also wanted to prove that, on the night when he had met his death, the constable had gone to keep watch on the defendant. The only evidence of this was a statement of that intention made by the constable to his superior officer earlier in the day. Lush J, after consulting with Mellor J, held the superior officer's evidence to this effect admissible, but gave no reasons for his decision.

In *R v Wainwright*,[71] two brothers were tried for the murder of a woman named Harriet Lane. Evidence was available from a witness who had seen Lane as she was leaving her lodgings on the afternoon of 11 September 1874, the date alleged by the prosecution to have been the date of her murder. The witness was ready to say that Lane had told her that she was going to a certain address, which turned out to be that of premises occupied by one of the defendants. The prosecution appears to have argued that Lane's statement about where she was going was admissible as part of the act of leaving her own lodgings, and so admissible as a statement accompanying and explaining a relevant act rather than an expression of contemporaneous state of mind. But it could be argued that the words of the trial judge were relevant to the latter exception, for, in excluding the evidence as hearsay, he said that it 'was only a statement of intention which might or might not have been carried out'.

In *R v Thomson*,[72] the defendant was charged with using an instrument on a woman for the purpose of procuring a miscarriage. The woman died before trial, but not as a result of the miscarriage. The defence was that the defendant had done nothing and that the woman had performed the operation on herself. At trial, counsel for the defence wanted to cross-examine a prosecution witness in order to prove that the deceased had stated earlier that she intended to perform an operation on herself to procure a miscarriage. The trial judge ruled this evidence inadmissible. The defendant was convicted and appealed. It was argued before the Court of Criminal Appeal that an accused person is entitled to adduce any evidence in support of his defence, regardless of the strict rules of evidence. This got short shrift from the court, which dismissed the appeal. But no attempt was made to argue on the narrower ground that the deceased's words were admissible as an expression of her intention, and *R v*

---

70   (1873) 13 Cox CC 293.
71   (1875) 13 Cox CC 171.
72   [1912] 3 KB 19.

Buckley[73] was not cited. The prosecution did cite *R v Wainwright*,[74] but, as shown above, it is not clear that in that case the court had this particular exception in mind.

More recently, however, the Court of Appeal upheld the proposition that a statement of intention may be admissible under this exception. In *R v Moghal*,[75] the defendant and his mistress, who was called Sadiga, were jointly charged with the murder of a man named Rashid. Separate trials were ordered, and Sadiga was tried first. Her defence was that Moghal had been solely responsible, and she was acquitted. Moghal was then tried. His defence was that Sadiga had been solely responsible. On appeal from his conviction, the Court of Appeal considered *obiter* whether evidence could have been given at Moghal's trial, in support of his defence that Sadiga had been solely responsible, of Sadiga's state of mind at times before and after the killing.

The killing took place on 30 October 1975. Evidence was available that, at a family conference in March 1975, Sadiga had declared her intention to kill Rashid and had prophesied his death within months. There was also available evidence of a confession made by Sadiga to police who had investigated the crime. The trial judge excluded evidence of her confession, on the basis that what Sadiga had told police about her previous murderous state of mind was hearsay. This decision was upheld by the Court of Appeal. Scarman LJ accepted the statement in *Cross on Evidence* that, to be admitted, such statements must relate to the maker's *contemporaneous* state of mind or emotion. He added that although contemporaneity was a matter of degree, what Sadiga had said to the police was far too long after the event to be admitted as evidence of her state of mind before and at the time of the killing. But the Court disapproved of the judge's view that what Sadiga had said at the family conference was also inadmissible. The words uttered by her on that occasion had reflected her state of mind and feelings at that time. Her words and mental state had been contemporaneous, and were therefore admissible.

It should be noted that the evidence of what was said at the family conference was not held admissible because it was thought to be contemporaneous with the *murder*. It is the state of mind and the utterance expressing it that have to be contemporaneous, not the state of mind and the event under investigation. It does not, of course, follow from this decision that a statement of intention made seven months before a crime will now invariably be regarded as relevant evidence. As we have seen in Chapter 1, previous decisions do not generally determine relevance. It may be significant that in this case it was the defence that wanted to use the statement of intention; a similar statement might not be so readily admitted for the prosecution.

A difficult case where evidence relating to a person's state of mind was discussed is *R v Gilfoyle*.[76] The defendant, Norman Gilfoyle, was charged with the murder of his

---

73   (1873) 13 Cox CC 293.
74   (1875) 13 Cox CC 171.
75   (1977) 65 Cr App R 56.
76   [1996] 1 Cr App R 302.

wife, Paula. He had produced to the police a suicide note in her handwriting after she had been found hanging from a beam in their garage. Nevertheless, in due course he was convicted. On appeal, the Court of Appeal made observations about witness statements that had been available to the prosecution, but had not been used at trial because it had been thought that they infringed the hearsay rule.

A friend of the deceased woman had stated that Paula, some time before her death, had informed her that Norman was doing a project on suicide as part of his work as an auxiliary nurse, and had asked for her help in writing examples of suicide notes. In the view of the Court of Appeal, this was relevant to the state of mind of the deceased when she wrote the suicide note produced by her husband. Accordingly, it should have been admitted under this exception to the hearsay rule.

While this might have been an attractive result, it seems to have extended the scope of the exception significantly. As *R v Moghal*[77] shows, the declaration has to relate to the condition of the speaker's mind *at the time of making the declaration*. What the court in *Gilfoyle* did was to use the evidence of the earlier conversation because it was thought to be relevant to the state of mind of the deceased, not at the time when the words were spoken, but at the stage when she wrote the suicide note. There was therefore a break in the connection between the utterance and the state of mind under investigation. More than that, the utterance in question, though clearly relevant to the speaker's state of mind at the time when she wrote the suicide note, was not in itself a direct expression of a state of mind at all; it was an assertion about something that the defendant had done. However, it is clear that these observations were made *obiter*, and it may well be that they will not be followed.

Another difficult decision is *R v Callender*.[78] Callender and another man were tried for conspiracy to commit arson. Callender was convicted; his co-defendant was acquitted. The prosecution case was that Callender, an animal rights activist, had conspired with others to make incendiary devices. These were to be placed in various locations, but principally at premises where factory farming was carried on. In May 1994 Callender and his co-defendant had taken a lease of a house where, according to the prosecution, they planned an arson campaign. Police kept watch on the house until mid-October, when both men were arrested. On the premises was equipment designed, according to the prosecution, for the making of incendiary devices. There were kitchen timers, theatrical maroons, containers, flammable liquid, cotton wool, nails and fire lighters. An explosives expert gave evidence that, although each of these items could have had an innocent use, their combination indicated an intention to construct incendiary devices. Callender's defence was that he had not intended to commit arson, but to make dummy devices. These were to have been left at various premises to attract publicity in a campaign to oppose factory farming. Callender's

---

77   (1977) 65 Cr App R 56.
78   [1998] Crim LR 337, LEXIS 6 November 1997.

co-defendant gave evidence. He said that Callender, whatever he in fact intended, had told him that the intended devices were specifically designed not to ignite.

Although Callender did not himself give evidence, he called several witnesses. One of them, a Mrs Hammond, was also concerned with animal rights. She said that she and Callender had met on 2 October 1994. During this meeting, Callender told her that he was planning a campaign against a particular company, against which Mrs Hammond was herself planning a lawful protest. He told her that he intended to remove files from the company's premises and place dummy incendiary devices in lorries at the back of the premises in order to gain publicity for his cause. He explained to her that the devices were not dangerous. Another witness gave evidence of a similar conversation.

The trial judge held that Callender's purpose in adducing evidence of what he had said to Mrs Hammond and the other witness was to support the assertion that he had been intending to assemble dummies, not incendiary devices. He then ruled that this evidence was prima facie hearsay in relation to Callender, and that although the statements were made during the period when the conspiracy was alleged to have been taking place, they did not form part of the *res gestae* because they lacked any element of spontaneity. The evidence was admissible only in relation to the co-defendant, because the fact that Callender had made statements about dummy devices to others tended to support the co-defendant's case that that was what Callender had said to him.

It was argued on appeal that the evidence of these statements was admissible for Callender's defence because admissibility was not governed on these facts by the principles set out in *R v Andrews*.[79] It was submitted that there were at least two other categories of *res gestae*. One contained 'statements concerning the maker's frame of mind or the maker's emotions'. Where the knowledge or emotions of a person were in issue in a trial, evidence of statements made by that person would be admissible to prove his state of mind. This category appears not to have been relied on for the admissibility of Callender's statements, nor does it appear that anything was said about statements of *intention*. Instead, counsel for Callender relied on the exception for statements accompanying and explaining relevant acts. He argued that the relevant acts were Callender's visits to the witnesses, and that these were explained by what Callender had said on those occasions. The trial judge had been wrong to apply the *Andrews* test to this category.

For the prosecution, it was submitted that *res gestae* was 'a single doctrine' and that the *Andrews* test applied in all categories. In reply, Callender's counsel made a significant concession. If, he said, there were grounds for a judge to think that a statement in any of the categories of *res gestae* had been concocted, that statement should not be admitted. This concession, said Roch LJ when delivering the judgment

---

79   [1987] AC 281.

of the Court of Appeal, concluded Callender's appeal. However, he went on to say that the *res gestae* principle was a single one, and that, for evidence to come within that exception, the trial judge must be satisfied that there had been no opportunity for concoction or distortion by the speaker.

The decision is unsatisfactory, not least because the appeal was argued on the wrong basis. As has been shown, for a statement accompanying and explaining an act to be admissible, the act must be relevant in itself, quite apart from the statement.[80] But Callender's visits to Mrs Hammond and the other witness were irrelevant to any fact in issue apart from what he said on those occasions. A better argument would have been that Callender's statements were expressions of his contemporaneous state of mind – in particular, of his intentions. His state of mind was relevant, of course, because that was what was being investigated by the court hearing the conspiracy charge. Admittedly, the statements might have been false, but so might any other expression of intention. The authorities before *Callender* do not support either the concession made by his counsel, or the view of the Court of Appeal that the *Andrews* test applies to all categories of *res gestae*.[81] This was certainly not the view of the Law Commission, which referred to this exception as having 'four separate strands to it, *each with its own precondition for admissibility* and individual justifications for its existence'.[82]

STATEMENTS IN FURTHERANCE OF A COMMON ENTERPRISE

Where defendants are charged with conspiracy, or simply charged jointly in relation to an alleged common enterprise, evidence of acts done or statements made by one defendant in furtherance of the enterprise will be admissible against other defendants, even though the other defendants were not present at the time when the act was done or the statement made. The reason for this is that a combination of persons for the purpose of committing a crime is regarded as implying an authority in each to act or speak in furtherance of the common enterprise on behalf of the others.[83]

There must always be some evidence other than the hearsay evidence of a party to the alleged common enterprise to prove that a particular defendant *is* a party to that enterprise,[84] but evidence of the acts, including verbal acts, of the defendants can establish this.[85]

It has been suggested[86] that if what was said by one defendant is no more than a

---

80   See above.

81   See the commentary on *Callender* in [1998] Crim LR 338–39.

82   Law Commission No 245, 1997, para 8.114, emphasis added.

83   *R v Gray and Others* [1995] 2 Cr App R 100.

84   *R v Murray and Others* [1997] 2 Cr App R 136.

85   See Smith, 1996; Smith, 1997.

86   *Tripodi v R* (1961) 104 CLR 1, approved in *R v Gray and Others* [1995] 2 Cr App R 100.

narrative of an event that has already taken place, this principle is unlikely to apply because such a statement would only rarely be *in furtherance* of the common enterprise. This would certainly be true of a confession, made by one of the defendants to the police, that referred to the actions of other defendants. But an account of events narrated by one party to another in order to bring him up to date while the common enterprise was continuing would be likely to be seen as made in furtherance of the enterprise, and so admissible against all those referred to.[87] The exclusion of what is described as 'mere narrative' applies only to narrative after the conclusion of the conspiracy. Statements made during the conspiracy will be admissible if they are part of the arrangements to carry out the conspiracy. A useful test for admissibility is to be able to say of what was said or written, 'This is the enterprise in operation'.[88]

An example of the operation of this exception to the hearsay rule can be seen in *R v Devonport and Pirano*.[89] The appellants were two of five defendants convicted of conspiracy to defraud a bank. One of the items of evidence in the case was a document found in the possession of a girlfriend of one of the defendants. The prosecution's case was that it had been dictated to her by her boyfriend and that it showed the proposed division of the proceeds of the conspiracy. It referred to all five defendants. There was no suggestion that either of these two appellants had prepared the document himself or been a party to its preparation, and no link between either of them and the document could be established. The only conspirator with any knowledge of, or connection with, the document was the one who had dictated it. Was the document evidence against all the conspirators?

The Court of Appeal held that it was, provided: (a) it constituted an act or declaration by the conspirator who brought it into existence in furtherance of the conspiracy; and (b) there was some further evidence beyond the document itself that the persons to whom it referred were parties to the conspiracy alleged against them. In fact, such evidence was available. Since the document appeared to be *not a record of distribution after the conspiracy* but an indication of the *intended distribution* of the proceeds of the conspiracy when it had been fulfilled, it was prima facie prepared in furtherance of the conspiracy and so admissible against all those named in it.

THE 'SAFETY-VALVE'

By s 114(1)(d) of the CJA 2003, a hearsay statement is admissible if 'the court is satisfied that it is in the interests of justice for it to be admissible'. By sub-s (2), in

---

87   *R v Jones and Others* [1997] 2 Cr App R 119, pp 128–29.

88   *R v Platten* [2006] EWCA Crim 140, paras 35–36.

89   [1996] 1 Cr App R 221.

deciding whether a statement should be admitted under this provision the court must have regard to the following factors:

(a) how much probative value the statement has (assuming it to be true) in relation to a matter in issue in the proceedings, or how valuable it is for the understanding of other evidence in the case;

(b) what other evidence has been, or can be, given on the matter or evidence mentioned in para (a);

(c) how important the matter or evidence mentioned in para (a) is in the context of the case as a whole;

(d) the circumstances in which the statement was made;

(e) how reliable the maker of the statement appears to be;

(f) how reliable the evidence of the making of the statement appears to be;

(g) whether oral evidence of the matter stated can be given and, if not, why it cannot;

(h) the amount of difficulty involved in challenging the statement; and

(i) the extent to which that difficulty would be likely to prejudice the party facing it.

The court must also have regard to any other factors that it considers relevant. The list is intended to focus attention on whether the circumstances surrounding the making of the hearsay statement show that it can be treated as reliable enough to admit it as evidence, despite the fact that its maker cannot be cross-examined.[90] The obligation to 'have regard to' the factors set out in s 114(2) does not require the judge to embark on an investigation so as to reach a conclusion in relation to each one of them. What is required is the exercise of judgment after giving consideration to those factors, and to any others that the judge considers relevant. Indeed, the judge is not required to reach a specific conclusion in relation to even one of them.[91]

Sub-section (3) provides that hearsay statements may still be excluded on other grounds, even if they fulfil the requirements of this Chapter of the Act. So, for example, confessions can be excluded under s 76 or 78 of the Police and Criminal Evidence Act 1984.

The safety-valve is available to both prosecution and defence. It can extend to multiple hearsay, but in that case it seems that the condition contained in s 121(1)(c) would have to be satisfied.[92]

---

90   Explanatory Notes to the CJA 2003, para 398.

91   *R v Taylor (Stuart)* [2006] EWCA Crim 260, [2006] 2 Cr App R 14; followed in *R v Williams (Dion Mark)* [2007] EWCA Crim 211.

92   See below.

SUPPLEMENTARY PROVISIONS

MULTIPLE HEARSAY

As noted above, hearsay is said to be 'multiple', or 'second hand', 'third hand' and so on, where information presented to a court is at more than one remove from the person making the original observation. Additional requirements have to be satisfied before the court will admit multiple hearsay. Section 121(1) provides as follows:

A hearsay statement is not admissible to prove the fact that an earlier hearsay statement was made unless –

(a) either of the statements is admissible under section 117, 119 or 120;

(b) all parties to the proceedings so agree; or

(c) the court is satisfied that the value of the evidence in question, taking into account how reliable the statements appear to be, is so high that the interests of justice require the later statement to be admissible for that purpose.[93]

As noted earlier, the effect is to limit significantly the occasions when multiple hearsay can be given of a statement made by a witness who is unavailable.

CAPABILITY TO MAKE A STATEMENT

By s 123, a hearsay statement cannot be admitted under s 116 (unavailability) unless the person who made it had the 'required capability' for making a statement at the time when it was made. A hearsay statement cannot be admitted under s 117 (business and other documents) if any person who supplied or received the information, or created or received the document, did not have the 'required capability' at the relevant time. If individuals in the chain through which the information passed cannot be identified, it is enough if they can reasonably be assumed to have had the required capability. A similar rule almost certainly applies to the preserved common law exceptions.[94]

The capability test is satisfied if the person in question was able to understand questions put to him about the matters stated, and to give answers that could be understood to such questions.[95] Where an issue as to capability arises, the burden of proof lies on the party seeking to adduce the statement, and the standard of proof for both prosecution and defence is the balance of probabilities.[96]

---

93   For ss 117 (business and other documents), 119 (inconsistent statements) and 120 (other previous statements of witnesses), see above.

94   It was held in *R v Pike* (1829) 3 C&P 598 that the maker of a dying declaration, one of the former common law exceptions, had to satisfy the test for witness competence when the declaration was made.

95   Cf the test for competence in the Youth Justice and Criminal Evidence Act 1999, s 53.

96   CJA 2003, s 123(4).

CREDIBILITY

It was provided under the Criminal Justice Act 1988 that where documentary hearsay was admitted, there should also be admissible any evidence that would have been admissible to attack the credibility of the maker of the statement if he had given oral evidence. With leave of the court, evidence of any collateral matter that could have been put to him in cross-examination, but in relation to which his denial would have been 'final',[97] was also admissible. Evidence of any statement made by him that was inconsistent with something in the hearsay statement was admissible without leave.[98] These provisions are now applied to both oral and written hearsay by s 124 of the CJA 2003. It should be noted that s 124 covers inconsistent statements made at any time,[99] and that such statements are, like any other inconsistent statements, evidence of the truth of their contents.[100] Where hearsay is admitted under s 117 (business and other documents), the rules in s 124 apply to all those in the chain of communication by treating them, for the purposes of this section, as 'the maker of the statement'.[101]

By s 124(3), if, as a result of evidence admitted under this section, an allegation is made against the maker of a hearsay statement, the court may permit additional evidence 'of such description as the court may specify' to be led for the purpose of denying or answering the allegation.

STOPPING THE CASE WHERE EVIDENCE IS UNCONVINCING

Section 125(1) is a new exception to the general rule[102] that, in a Crown Court trial, questions of law are for the judge and questions of fact for the jury. The sub-section provides as follows:

If on a defendant's trial before a judge and jury for an offence the court is satisfied at any time after the close of the case for the prosecution that –

(a) the case against the defendant is based wholly or partly on a statement not made in oral evidence in the proceedings; and

(b) the evidence provided by the statement is so unconvincing that, considering its importance to the case against the defendant, his conviction of the offence would be unsafe,

the court must either direct the jury to acquit the defendant of the offence or, if it considers that there ought to be a retrial, discharge the jury.

This provision applies only to jury trials, because in summary trials the magistrates or district judge would be bound to find in such circumstances that there was no case to answer.

---

97 See above, Chapter 6.
98 Criminal Justice Act 1988, s 28 and Sched 2, para 1.
99 Section 124(2)(c).
100 Section 119(2).
101 Section 124(4).
102 See above, Chapter 1.

GENERAL DISCRETION TO EXCLUDE EVIDENCE

The court has a common law discretion to exclude prosecution evidence where its prejudicial effect is likely to outweigh its probative value.[103] There is also a statutory discretion to exclude evidence on which the prosecution proposes to rely where the admission of the evidence would have such an adverse effect on the fairness of the proceedings that the court ought not to admit it.[104] Both discretions are preserved in relation to hearsay evidence by s 126(2) of the CJA 2003. Section 126(1) provides a further discretion to exclude a hearsay statement if 'the court is satisfied that the case for excluding the statement, taking account of the danger that to admit it would result in undue waste of time, substantially outweighs the case for admitting it, taking account of the value of the evidence'.

HEARSAY AND HUMAN RIGHTS

Among the 'minimum rights' of a defendant in criminal proceedings referred to in Art 6(3) of the European Convention on Human Rights is the right 'to examine or have examined witnesses against him'.[105] In broad terms, this provision gives a defendant the right to have a witness who gives evidence against him called to give evidence and be subjected to cross-examination. It amounts to a prima facie prohibition on the admission of hearsay evidence to support the prosecution case. The considerations that support this prohibition also justify the exclusion of hearsay evidence that supports the defence case.[106]

The principle expressed in Art 6(3)(d) is, however, limited in its application. In the first place, the Strasbourg court has frequently said that the admissibility of evidence is a matter for national law, and that the role of the court is to assess the overall fairness of the criminal proceedings in question. The rights set out in Art 6(3) are 'specific' or 'particular' aspects of the right to a fair trial, but they are not themselves absolute. Secondly, the Strasbourg court has recognised the need for a fair balance between the general interest of the community and the personal rights of the individual; indeed, it has described the search for this balance as inherent in the whole Convention.[107] Unsurprisingly, the Court of Appeal has said that there is no merit in the argument that s 114 CJA 2003 is incompatible with Art 6.[108]

---

103   *R v Sang* [1980] AC 402.

104   Police and Criminal Evidence Act 1984, s 78(1). See further Chapter 11.

105   Article 6(3)(d).

106   *Thomas v United Kingdom* (2005) 41 EHRR SE 11.

107   *Grant v The Queen* [2006] UKPC 2, [2007] 1 AC 1, para 17.

108   *R v Xhabri* [2005] EWCA Crim 3135, [2006] 1 All ER 776, para 42; *R v Cole* [2007] EWCA Crim 1924, para 7.

There is a suggestion in Strasbourg jurisprudence that where a conviction is based solely, or to a decisive degree, on statements made by a person whom the accused has had no opportunity to examine or have examined, 'the rights of the defence are restricted to an extent that is incompatible with the guarantees provided by Art 6.'[109] Nevertheless, a line of English appellate authority supports the proposition that even where hearsay evidence is the sole, or the decisive, evidence against a defendant, it is possible for it to be admitted without infringing the defendant's right to a fair trial under Art 6. For example, in *Grant v The Queen* Lord Bingham said that it would be intolerable if a defendant could intimidate a witness so that he refused to give evidence, and then rely on Art 6 to exclude hearsay evidence from that witness. Where a witness was unavailable because of death or illness, or any of the other reasons in s 116, the argument for admitting hearsay was 'less irresistible'. But, Lord Bingham said, there might still be a compelling argument for admitting it, provided this does not unfairly disadvantage the defendant.[110]

In *R v Sellick*[111] the Court of Appeal said that where a court was sure that a witness had been kept from giving evidence by the defendant, or by persons acting for him, there would be no infringement of Art 6 because the defendant would have denied himself the opportunity of cross-examining the witness. It was said that more difficulty arose where the case was not quite so clear cut, but the court believed there was a high degree of probability that the witness had been intimidated on behalf of the defendant. Nevertheless, having regard to the rights of victims, their families, and to the safety of the public in general, it still could not be right for there to be some absolute rule that where hearsay evidence was the sole or decisive evidence for the prosecution, it must automatically be excluded on the basis that to admit it would infringe the defendant's right to a fair trial.

In *R v Al-Khawaja*[112] the appellant had been charged with two counts of indecent assault. By the time of the trial, one of the complainants had died. Her statement was admitted under earlier legislation providing for the admissibility of hearsay evidence in cases of unavailability.[113] On appeal it was argued that this violated Art 6(3)(d). The Court of Appeal dismissed the appeal. It said that where a witness who is the sole witness of a crime has made a statement to be used by the prosecution and has later died, Art 6 would not necessarily be infringed by admitting the statement in evidence. The public interest in enabling the prosecution to proceed must not be allowed to outweigh the defendant's right to a fair trial, but the right to cross-examine a prosecution witness was only one element in a fair trial. In this case the appellant had been able to attack the accuracy of the deceased complainant's

---

109   *Luca v Italy* (2003) 36 EHRR 46, para 40.
110   [2006] UKPC 2, [2007] 1 AC 1, para 17.
111   [2005] EWCA Crim 651, [2005] 1 WLR 3257.
112   [2005] EWCA Crim 2697, [2006] 1 WLR 1078.
113   Criminal Justice Act 1988, s 23.

statement by exploring the inconsistencies between it and the evidence of recent complaints that she had made. He had been able to adduce expert evidence to counter her allegations. Finally, the trial judge had directed the jury on the difficulties presented by loss of the opportunity to cross-examine. The proceedings as a whole had been fair.

The direction to the jury about hearsay evidence is of considerable importance. In *Al-Khawaja* Jack J, delivering the judgment of the court, quoted an example from *R v McCoy*.[114] In this case the Court of Appeal had said that if a statement of a critical witness is to be read to the jury, the trial judge must ensure that the jury realise the drawbacks which are imposed on the defence if the prosecution statement is read to them. It is not enough simply to say that defence counsel has not had the opportunity of cross-examining the witness. The judge must at least explain that the jury may feel quite unable to attach anything like as much weight to the evidence in the statement as they might have done if it had been tested in cross-examination. It might be desirable for the judge to indicate, by way of illustration, the sort of matters that could have been dealt with in cross-examination. According to the specimen direction recommended by the Judicial Studies Board,[115] the judge should direct the jury to examine the statement that has been read with particular care, having regard to certain limitations:

- They have not had the opportunity of seeing and hearing the witness. He should point out that when jurors see and hear a witness they may get a much clearer idea of whether the evidence is honest and accurate.
- The witness's statement was not made or verified on oath.
- The evidence has not been tested by cross-examination.
- The statement forms only a part of the evidence, and must be considered in the light of all the other evidence in the case. The judge should point out any discrepancies between the statement and the oral evidence from other witnesses.

The judge should also refer to any particular matters that might affect the jury's view of the witness's evidence, such as any matters referred to during the trial that are relevant to the witness's reliability.

So far, the House of Lords has not considered the compatibility of s 114 with Art 6, but it is inconceivable that, if they have to do so, they will find incompatibility. The status of hearsay evidence that is the sole, or the decisive, evidence for the prosecution is slightly less certain, but the decision of the Privy Council in *Grant v The Queen* suggests that such evidence will not inevitably be excluded. It remains possible that a UK decision will one day reach Strasbourg and that a more inflexible approach will be adopted.

---

114   [1999] All ER (D) 1410.
115   June 2007 revision, para 35.

CASE STUDY: *MAHER v DPP*[116]

No new law emerges from this decision, but it is a useful example of the operation of some of the hearsay provisions in the 2003 Act. Those principally concerned are ss 114(1)(d), 117 and 121.

The case arose from a minor collision in a supermarket car park. The appellant had parked her BMW Mini, which was light blue in colour and with registration number YF51 SYR, in a Sainsbury's car park. Mr Huddlestone had parked his Vauxhall Astra nearby in the same car park and was inside the store with his girl-friend, Miss McDonough. The appellant, in the course of leaving the car park, reversed her Mini into the Astra, got out, looked at the damage, and then drove off. Her actions were observed by Mr and Mrs Dennis, who were also in the car park.

The Dennises made a note of the appellant's registration number, added their own contact details, and left the paper on the windscreen of the damaged Astra under the wiper. When Mr Huddlestone and Miss McDonough returned to the Astra they found the note. Miss McDonough telephoned the police and recited the number of the vehicle that had done the damage. The police recorded the details in the Police Incident Log. A subsequent check of the registration number led to the appellant, who admitted being the driver of a BMW Mini, registration number YF51 SYR, and to being in the car park at the relevant time, but she denied being involved in a collision.

By the time of the appellant's trial before the magistrates for careless driving and failing to stop and report the accident, the note that had been left on the windscreen had been either lost or destroyed. But the magistrates admitted the Police Incident Log in evidence, despite objection by the appellant's representative. They convicted the appellant. She appealed, arguing that the magistrates had been wrong to admit the police log, as it was hearsay and the only evidence fully implicating the appellant.

The Divisional Court held that the entry in the police log was multiple hearsay of the identity of the vehicle that had damaged the Astra. The court's analysis was as follows. Mrs Dennis had identified the number of the offending vehicle, had written it on a piece of paper, which she had then placed on the windscreen of Mr Huddlestone's car. When Mr Huddlestone returned to the car with Miss McDonough, the latter took the paper, telephoned the police, and read the number to someone who recorded it in the Log. The transmission of the relevant information (namely, the number of the offending car) was therefore from Mrs Dennis to Miss McDonough, via the note; from Miss McDonough to the clerk in the police station;

---

116   [2006] EWHC 1271 (Admin).

and from the clerk to the police log. The first hand hearsay was Mrs Dennis's written statement to Miss McDonough to the effect that the offending vehicle was the one with registration number YF51 SYR.

Focusing initially on the first hand hearsay, the only route for that to be admitted was s 114(1)(d). Assuming for the moment that the first hand hearsay would have been admitted under that provision, it was then necessary to look at the police log. At this stage s 121 came into play. Was the police log admissible under s 117, as required by s 121(1)(a)? (It clearly could not have been admitted under s 119 or s 120.) The entry in the police log was obviously created by a person in the course of a trade or business, profession or other occupation, or as the holder of a paid or unpaid office. So it satisfied s 117(2)(a).

By s 117(2)(b), it is necessary that the person who supplied the information contained in the statement ('the relevant person') had or may reasonably be supposed to have had personal knowledge of the matters dealt with. The statement was the registration number of the offending vehicle. The document in which it was contained was the police log. Who supplied the information about the registration number? It was Mrs Dennis. What happened afterwards was the transmission of the supplied information via Miss McDonough and the police clerk to the police log. Mrs Dennis plainly had personal knowledge of the registration number of the offending vehicle when she recorded it. So s 117(2)(b) was satisfied.

But an insuperable difficulty arose when the court reached s 117(2)(c). This requires that each person (if any) through whom the information was supplied from the relevant person to the person mentioned in paragraph (a) – in this case, the person who created the entry in the police log – received the information in the course of a trade, business, profession or other occupation, or as the holder of a paid or unpaid office. The police clerk satisfied this condition, but Miss McDonough, the first link in the chain of transmission, did not. The situation would have been entirely different if the information had been given to the car park attendant, but that was not what had happened.

Returning to s 121, since neither of gateways (a) and (b) in sub-s (1) was available, the only possibility that remained was gateway (c). Could the court have been satisfied that the value of the evidence in question, taking into account how reliable the statement appeared to be, was so high that the interests of justice required the later statement (the statement in the police log) to be admissible?

Bearing in mind the admissions made by the appellant about the presence of her car in the car park at the relevant time, the only issue under (c) could be whether, for some inexplicable reason, Mrs Dennis wrote down the number of the appellant's car in mistake for some other car, or whether there had been some misstatement of the number further down the line of transmission of that information. It would be extraordinary if there had been a mistake in transmission and the number recorded in the police log just happened to coincide precisely with the number of a vehicle that was in the car park at the time.

The magistrates would inevitably have concluded that the evidence ought to be admitted had they relied on ss 114(2) and 121(1)(c), rather than on s 117, as they had mistakenly done.

As Leveson J said, 'it is important to underline that care must be taken to analyse the precise provisions of the legislation and ensure that any route of admissibility is correctly identified. In any case of multiple hearsay, this should be done in stages so that each link in the multiple chain can be tested'.[117]

FURTHER READING

—Birch, 'Criminal Justice Act 2003: (4) Hearsay – Same Old Story, Same Old Song?' [2004] Crim LR 556.

—Choo, *Hearsay and Confrontation in Criminal Trials*, 1996, pp 112–39.

—Law Com No 245, *Evidence in Criminal Proceedings: Hearsay and Related Topics*, 1997.

—Ormerod, 'Redundant *Res Gestae*?' [1998] Crim LR 301.

EXERCISES

1. Andrew wrote a letter to Bella containing information that Bella wishes to use at her forthcoming trial for handling. Andrew has died since writing the letter. What conditions must be satisfied before Bella can use the letter in her defence?

2. Clarence gave a written statement to the police describing what he saw when a fight broke out in his local wine bar. Clarence now says that he is too frightened to give evidence at the trial of those taking part in the fight. Can the prosecution get Clarence's information before jury? If so, how?

3. What rules were established by *Andrews* (1987) for admitting evidence of 'excited utterances'?

4. What conditions must be satisfied before admitting evidence of a statement relating to the maker's performance of an act?

5. Why is it difficult to predict whether someone's statement of intention will be admitted in a criminal trial?

6. In what circumstances, if any, can narrative statements be admitted as statements in furtherance of a common enterprise?

7. What is 'multiple hearsay'? When, if at all, is it admissible?

8. Where a hearsay statement is read to the jury in the course of a trial, what directions should the judge give to the jury in his summing-up?

---

117   Paragraph 26.

10
HAZARDOUS EVIDENCE

All evidence, without exception, is hazardous because it is inherently liable to mislead. There are several reasons for this. The first is that all evidence emerges as a result of some kind of selection. One kind may be loosely described as 'natural selection'. Not all the evidence that is relevant to a particular inquiry will have survived. Witnesses may have died; documents may have been destroyed; the physical features of a building may have been altered. Another kind of selection is human selection. In any investigation someone has to gather the evidence that *has* survived; but to gather effectively, you have to be intelligent enough to recognise what may be significant, and honest enough to do the job without preconceived ideas of what the outcome of the investigation should be. These conditions are not always satisfied in police investigations. According to a former Scientific Support Manager for the West Midlands Police:

> There is a tendency to settle early on a particular hypothesis and then to set out to find evidence to substantiate it rather than seeking evidence that either proves or disproves the hypothesis – or for that matter, evidence that generates a new hypothesis.[1]

Natural selection and human frailty between them ensure that no court ever sees more than a part of the whole picture, and that part may be a very small, misleading one.[2]

---

1   Leary, 2004, p 32.
2   Cf Carr, 1987, pp 7–30.

Another reason for the hazardous nature of evidence is that too much has to be taken on trust. It is not always appreciated that the only direct experience on which a tribunal of fact can rely in a legal inquiry is its perception of witnesses testifying in the witness box, and sometimes the perceptions resulting from its own examination of items of real evidence. In relation to a testifying witness two difficulties arise. The first comes from uncertainty about whether the witness can trust the evidence of his own senses. He may believe that he saw the defendant stab the victim, but what guarantee has he that things were not otherwise? The second difficulty comes from the fact that the court has to rely on the witness for an insight into what happened on the occasion under investigation. But all the triers of fact can perceive is the witness giving evidence: what is their justification for inferring from the witness's testimony that the defendant did in fact stab the victim?

A third reason for the hazardous nature of evidence is that, save for some items of real evidence, it is presented through the medium of language. But language is notoriously ambiguous. Words, it has been said:

> ... may be easily misunderstood by a dull man. They may be easily misconstrued by a knave. What was spoken metaphorically may be apprehended literally. What was spoken ludicrously may be apprehended seriously. A particle, a tense, a mood, an emphasis, may make the whole difference between guilt and innocence.[3]

But more than this, the adversary system adopted in our courts tends to perpetuate ambiguity. One of the earliest lessons learned by the student of advocacy is how to avoid giving the witness whom he is cross-examining a chance to explain his testimony. Closed, leading questions requiring a 'yes' or 'no' answer are recommended. These may be good trial tactics, but they are ill-designed for the discovery of truth.[4]

Politicians and lawyers have usually turned a blind eye to these defects. Attempts to make verdicts a little more reliable have been made only erratically and on a piecemeal basis, but there have been attempts to remove the hazards involved in the selection by police and prosecuting authorities of evidence to be used against defendants in criminal trials. There have also been attempts to control the way in which juries think about kinds of evidence that at various times have been considered particularly unreliable.

There developed from the first of these attempts a duty on the prosecution to disclose to the defence matters coming to light during their investigations that might assist the defence case.[5] The second kind of attempts gave rise to law compelling

---

3   Lord Macaulay, 1880 [1849–55], Vol 2, Chapter 5, p 161.
4   See, eg, Stone, 1988, p 107; Boon, 1993, pp 113–14. Cf McEwan, 1992, pp 16–19; Law Commission Consultation Paper 138, 1995, paras 6.42–6.49.
5   For further information about the prosecution's duty of disclosure, see the standard works on criminal procedure.

judges to warn juries in a particular way when they had to consider certain types of evidence, or evidence from certain types of witness.

In the 18th century, when the beginnings of our modern law of evidence can be seen, both prosecution and defence in criminal proceedings were often unrepresented by counsel, and the judge played a much larger part than in the 19th century and later. In particular, judges had greater control over juries' deliberations. Summings up could contain much more of the judge's opinion than would now be thought proper. Where it appeared that a deliberation was likely to be short, the jury would often not leave the jury box. Either then or in the course of testimony itself there was opportunity for informal dialogue with the judge about the evidence.[6]

This informal procedure, with its strong inquisitorial element, in time gave way to a system more like the one we are used to today, although there was one major difference: there was no general right for a defendant to testify in his own defence until 1898. Prosecution and defence were increasingly represented by counsel, probably in part because of an increase in the size of the Bar, and the judge lost some of his control over the jury's deliberations. However, because jurors were free to weigh the evidence without judicial intervention, it became more necessary to warn them during summing up about the weight to be attached to certain types of witnesses and testimony and of the danger of convicting on the basis of such evidence without some independent support. Warnings were thought to be necessary in three main cases: those involving the evidence of children; those involving the evidence of accomplices; and those involving complaints of a sexual crime. In these cases, juries were generally invited to look for evidence that supported, or, to use the technical expression, 'corroborated' the evidence regarded as hazardous, and were warned of the danger of convicting solely on uncorroborated evidence.

For a long time the content of the warning, and even whether a warning was given at all, was a matter solely for the trial judge's discretion. The mechanism for converting judicial discretion into rules of law did not exist: Parliament was an unsuitable institution to deal with the minutiae of criminal law reform, and there was no effective system of criminal appeals until the Court of Criminal Appeal was established in 1907. Only then did discretionary practices begin to harden into rules of law. It was not until 1916 that the law of corroboration began to be clearly formed. From that time, however, it was settled that what was needed was some independent evidence implicating the accused in a material particular.[7]

Before long, a highly complex body of law developed, the effect of which was that in the absence of an accurate warning, a conviction was very likely to be quashed. Reform came about only when fashionable opinion began to take a more trusting

---

6   See above, Chapter 2.

7   *R v Baskerville* [1916] KB 658. For the development of corroboration law generally, see Langbein, 2003, pp 158–65, 203–17, and Allen, 1997, pp 43–49.

view of children's evidence and to regard as unconvincing the suggestion that some women might, for malicious reasons or for no reasons at all, concoct allegations against men of sexual offences. Corroboration law has now been very largely abolished by s 34(2) of the Criminal Justice Act 1988[8] and s 32 of the Criminal Justice and Public Order Act 1994.[9]

Alongside the strict law of corroboration there had grown up a less formal body of law about warnings that should be given to a jury where a witness might be unreliable, even though he did not fall within the limited classes to which corroboration law applied. For example, it was held that an informal warning should be given where witnesses had a purpose of their own to serve in giving evidence, or where they suffered from a mental disorder.[10] This body of law was not expressly abolished by the reforming legislation, but it is clear that it now has no independent existence.[11]

DISCRETIONARY CARE WARNINGS

The narrow, prescriptive law of corroboration had been very largely abolished. What, if anything, was to replace it? The answer from the Court of Appeal was that discretionary care warnings were to replace the former system. In *R v Makanjuola* Lord Taylor CJ outlined the new approach as follows:

■ Parliament has abolished the requirement to give a corroboration direction in respect of particular categories of witness. It is now a matter for the trial judge's discretion what, if any, warning should be given in respect of *any* witness in whatever type of case. Whether he chooses to give a warning, and in what terms, will depend on the circumstances of the case, the issues raised, and the content and quality of the witness's evidence.

■ In some cases it may be appropriate for the judge to warn the jury to exercise

---

8   In relation to the evidence of children.

9   In relation to evidence of complainants of sexual offences and evidence of accomplices. There was no pressure of opinion to change the law concerning accomplices' evidence, but it was presumably felt that the fewer opportunities judges had to get things wrong, the better it would be for criminal trials. There remain three cases where a conviction cannot be secured without corroboration: high treason, perjury and speeding. See the Treason Act 1785, s 1; Perjury Act 1911, s 13; the Road Traffic Regulation Act 1984, s 89(2). See, generally, Criminal Law Revision Committee, 11th Report, 1972, para 183; Law Commission No 202, Cm 1620, 1991; Dennis, 1995b; Mirfield, 1995.

10   *R v Beck* [1982] 1 WLR 461; *R v Spencer* [1987] AC 128. See also Law Commission No 202, Cm 1620, 1991, Appendix C.

11   *R v Stone (MJ)* [2005] EWCA Crim 105, para 89.

caution before acting on the unsupported evidence of a particular witness. But this will not be appropriate simply because the witness falls into one of the categories where formerly a corroboration direction was required. There must be an evidential basis for suggesting that the evidence of a witness may be unreliable.

■ If any question arises as to whether the judge should give a special warning in respect of a witness, it is desirable that the question be resolved by discussion with counsel in the absence of the jury before final speeches.

■ Where some warning is required, it will be for the judge to decide the strength and terms of the warning. He is not bound in any way to follow the directions given under the former corroboration law. 'Attempts to re-impose the straitjacket of the old corroboration rules are strongly to be deprecated.'

■ The Court of Appeal is unlikely to interfere with the exercise of a trial judge's discretion, except on the basis of *Wednesbury* unreasonableness.[12]

There remain several categories of evidence where a warning governed by rules, rather than by a discretion, is required. In *R v Jones and Jenkins*[13] the Court of Appeal said that where there are 'cut-throat' defences, in which each defendant disclaims liability and blames a co-defendant for the alleged offence, the jury should be directed that when considering one defendant's evidence against a co-defendant, they should bear in mind that the defendant giving evidence may have an interest to serve.[14]

In *R v Benedetto*[15] the Privy Council, distinguishing *Makanjuola*, held that a caution should always be given where the prosecution relies on evidence that the defendant made a confession to another prisoner while remanded in custody. The danger of such 'cell confessions' is that the evidence of the informers is inherently unreliable because of the personal advantage they think they may obtain from providing information to the authorities. Further, the prisoner against whom the evidence is given is always at a disadvantage. He has none of the usual Code C protections against invention or inaccurate recording, and it may be difficult for him to obtain all the information that is needed to expose fully the informer's bad character. The judge in such a case must draw the jury's attention to matters that may justify an inference that the informer's evidence is tainted, and advise the jury to be cautious before accepting it.

Since then, however, the Court of Appeal has again asserted that the judge's discretion under *Makanjuola* is not to be confined by fixed rules. Any case involving a cell confession will prompt the most careful consideration by the judge, but not

---

12   [1995] 1 WLR 1348, pp 1351–52. On the final point, see *Associated Provincial Picture Houses Ltd v Wednesbury Corporation* [1948] 1 KB 223.

13   [2004] 1 Cr App R 5; followed in *R v Petkar* [2004] 1 Cr App R 22.

14   It had earlier been held in *R v Warwick Muncaster* [1999] Crim LR 409 that co-defendants could be the subject of a *Makanjuola* discretionary warning.

15   [2003] UKPC 27, [2003] 1 WLR 1545.

every case requires such a warning. A summing-up should be tailored by the judge to the circumstances of the particular case. If, for example, a particular confession would not have been easy to invent because of its detail, it would be absurd to require the judge to tell the jury that invention of confessions is often easy. If the defendant has deliberately avoided cross-examining the informer on the basis that his evidence was prompted by hope of advantage, the judge is not required to tell the jury that, merely because the informer was a prisoner, there may have been such a motive.[16]

Evidence of lies told by a defendant either inside or outside court will often require a judicial warning to ensure that the jury approaches such evidence correctly. In addition, identification evidence falling within the rules set out in *R v Turnbull*[17] and subsequent cases must be the subject of a particular type of judicial warning in the summing up. These two topics require more detailed consideration.

DEFENDANTS' LIES

As Sir Jeffrey Gilbert wrote in the 18th century, a defendant's falsehood creates a presumption against him, 'for truth is the proper shield of the guiltless'.[18] The presumption was later explained in this way:

> [E]xperience teaches that commonly in matters of moment a lie is not uttered without a sufficient motive; and therefore from the lie a just inference is, there was a motive for it; and, allowing a motive, it is not unreasonable to conclude it sprang from a consciousness of guilt. And in this way the falsehood becomes a fact, that is, evidence against the accused; and, put into the scale against him, must have its due weight allotted to it.[19]

However, courts now recognise that, without a warning from the judge, a jury may jump immediately from a conclusion that a defendant has told a lie to the conclusion that he is guilty of the offence charged. As Judge LJ said in *R v Middleton*:

> People do not always tell the truth. Laudable as it may be to do so, whatever the circumstances, they do not, or cannot, always bring themselves to face up to reality. Innocent people sometimes tell lies even when by doing so they create or reinforce the suspicion of guilt. In short, therefore, while lying is often resorted to by the guilty to hide and conceal the truth, the innocent can sometimes misguidedly react to a problem, or postpone facing up to it or attempt to deflect ill-founded suspicion, or fortify their defence by telling lies.[20]

---

16 *R v Stone (MJ)* [2005] EWCA Crim 105, [2005] Crim LR 569, paras 82–84.

17 [1977] QB 224; *Sourcebook*, 1996, p 174.

18 Gilbert, 1791, Vol II, p 898.

19 Ram, 1861, p 81.

20 [2001] Crim LR 251.

In appropriate cases, therefore, a judge must provide the necessary warning when summing up. This is often called a '*Lucas* direction' after the name of a case[21] where the problem was discussed in the context of the old corroboration law. A more recent case, *R v Burge and Pegg*,[22] has restated the law in the following way.

The gist of the direction contains two points:

(a)   the lie must be admitted by the defendant, or the jury must find it proved beyond reasonable doubt, before it can be taken into account; and

(b)   the jury must be warned that the mere fact that the defendant has lied is not in itself evidence of guilt, because defendants may lie for innocent reasons. Only if the jury is sure that the defendant did *not* lie for an innocent reason can a lie support the prosecution case.

This cannot mean that the jury must find that the defendant lied *because he was guilty of the offence charged* before they can take the lie into account, for then they would already have come to the conclusion that the prosecution had proved its case and it would be unnecessary to refer to the lie at all. What it must mean is that the prosecution has to disprove any innocent explanation for the lie given by the defendant before the jury can take the lie into account.

According to *R v Burge and Pegg*, a direction on these lines is usually required in four circumstances:

(a)   Where the defendant relies on an alibi.

(b)   Where the judge, in exercise of the wide discretion that he now has as a result of s 32 of the Criminal Justice and Public Order Act 1994, suggests that the jury look for something to support a hazardous item of prosecution evidence and points to an alleged lie by the defendant as potential support.

(c)   Where the prosecution try to show that the defendant has told a lie, either in or out of court, about a matter separate and distinct from the offence charged, but which points to the guilt of the defendant on that charge. For example, suppose George is charged with the murder, by shooting, of a bank clerk. He tells the police that he has never handled a gun in his life; in fact he has won several prizes in shooting competitions. The prosecution would argue that George lied to try to get out of trouble because he knew he was guilty.

(d)   Where, although the prosecution have not used an argument like the one in (c), the judge thinks that the jury might adopt such an argument independently.

---

21   *R v Lucas* [1981] QB 720.

22   [1996] 1 Cr App R 163.

A direction is not required in every case where a defendant gives evidence merely because the jury might conclude that some of his evidence contained lies. There may be occasions where a full *Lucas* direction will do more harm than good to a defendant's case; for example, by drawing the jury's attention to a discrepancy in his evidence and emphasising the possibility that it might have been the result of a lie instead of a mistake. In such a case a judge would be justified in giving a modified direction or no direction at all.[23] A direction is not required if rejection by the jury of the defendant's evidence leaves them no choice but to convict. This will be the case where the prosecution witnesses' evidence is in direct and irreconcilable conflict with the evidence of the defendant and his witnesses. In such a case, a direction about lies would be unnecessary and confusing. If the jury comes to the conclusion that the prosecution witnesses are telling the truth, the outcome of the case is settled. For a direction to be appropriate, the lie generally has to be about a *subsidiary* matter so as to provide *additional* evidence of the defendant's guilt. Where there is no distinction between the issue of guilt and the issue of lies, a direction on the lines indicated in *R v Burge* will usually only confuse.[24]

Some examples from decided cases may help to show when a *Lucas* direction is likely to be needed, and when it would only confuse the jury and should not be given.

In *R v Patrick*[25] the defendant was charged with arson. It was said that he had set fire to the complainant's pigeon loft in order to intimidate the complainant, who was due to give evidence against the defendant in relation to an earlier burglary committed at his premises. At the trial for arson there were two main but related issues: the identification of the defendant by the complainant and the defendant's alibi defence. In the course of his evidence the complainant first described the earlier burglary. He said that he had disturbed the burglar and pursued him. He had not caught him, but had been able to describe him to the police. Among the features he had mentioned was the fact that the burglar was wearing a baseball cap. Later, the complainant had picked out the defendant at an identification parade.

On the second occasion, the complainant said, he returned home in response to a telephone call from his wife, who had heard someone trying to break into the house. Close by his house he encountered the defendant, who was wearing the same clothes as before, including a baseball cap. The defendant apparently went away, but some time later the complainant saw that his pigeon loft was ablaze. About two weeks before this incident the police had investigated another matter, and in the course of doing so had observed and photographed a baseball cap in the defendant's car. In the

---

23   *R v Nyanteh* [2005] EWCA Crim 686, [2005] Crim LR 651.

24   *R v Harron* [1996] 2 Cr App R 457.

25   18 March 1999, unreported.

interview concerning suspected arson, the defendant denied all knowledge of such a cap and said that he had never owned one.

At his trial for arson the defendant gave evidence of an alibi. He said that at his interview he had forgotten the baseball cap because it belonged to his brother-in-law. He added that currently his brother-in-law was not talking to him, and that was why he was not appearing as a witness for the defendant.

There were therefore at least two matters about which the jury could have concluded that the defendant was lying. The first was about ownership of the baseball cap. If they concluded that he was lying about that, they could have inferred that he was doing so in order to establish that he was not the person seen by the complainant on the evening when the fire broke out. From that they might have inferred that he was indeed the person seen by the complainant, and that his alibi evidence was false. In relation to the evidence about the cap the trial judge did give a *Lucas* direction, and the Court of Appeal held that he had been right to do so.

But in relation to the alibi evidence itself he gave no *Lucas* direction, and this was one of the grounds relied upon by the defendant in his appeal against conviction for arson. It was argued on his behalf that the jury should have been told that an alibi may sometimes be invented to bolster a genuine defence. It was argued for the prosecution that the direction was not essential. Relying on *Harron*, counsel argued that the complainant's evidence of identification on the evening of the fire was in direct and irreconcilable evidence with the defendant's alibi. The jury, as a matter of common sense and logic, had to decide which witnesses were telling the truth. If they accepted the evidence of the complainant, that necessarily involved a conclusion that the evidence of the defendant was untrue and that the defendant was therefore lying. There was therefore no distinction between the issue of guilt and the issue of lies, and a *Lucas* direction was unnecessary.

The Court of Appeal accepted the prosecution's argument. As a matter of logic, there may have been room for the possibility that the alibi was false, but the complainant was mistaken in identification of the defendant. As a matter of practical reality and common sense, however, given the way in which the case was presented, the only basis on which the jury could have rejected the alibi was that they were satisfied that the complainant's identification was correct. On the evidence, there was no danger of the jury rejecting the alibi for reasons other than the correctness of the complainant's identification.

The difference between the evidence about the baseball cap and the alibi evidence should be understood. The jury might legitimately have concluded that the defendant had lied about ownership of the baseball cap. But this was not a central feature of the prosecution case as presented at trial. A lie about this peripheral matter might have been prompted by consciousness of guilt. But it might also have been prompted by the desire of an innocent man to explain away apparently incriminating evidence. But the complainant's identification had been absolutely central to the prosecution case. The only basis on which the jury could have rejected the possibility that the alibi might have been true was that they were sure of the correctness of this identification. If they were sure of that, a conviction inevitably followed. There was no realistic distinction between the issue of guilt and the issue of lies.[26]

Another case where the Court of Appeal held that a *Lucas* direction had been unnecessary was *R v Barnett*.[27] The defendant was charged with handling stolen goods. He was a dealer in second-hand electrical goods who had been found with a painting valued at £40,000 under his bed. When questioned under caution immediately after his arrest, he said that he had found the painting whilst walking his dog. When interviewed later in the presence of a solicitor, he said that a friend, whom he had met in a public house, had produced the painting and had asked him to find a purchaser for it. In evidence at his trial he said that a friend had entrusted the painting to him for safe keeping while the friend tried to find a purchaser. It was not contested that the painting had been stolen; the question was whether the defendant knew or believed it to have been stolen. The prosecution relied, amongst other things, on the fact that the defendant had told three different stories about the circumstances in which he had acquired it. Should the judge have given a *Lucas* direction in relation to those stories?

The Court of Appeal held that the judge had been right not to do so. The fact that inconsistent statements were made did not in itself call for a *Lucas* direction. The prosecution had not been relying as evidence of guilt on any specific lies which the defendant had told. Instead, they were relying on the defendant's constant changes of story as evidence that he was trying to escape from the obvious inference, namely, that he must have realised that the painting was stolen. The specific lie that the prosecution had relied on was the statement in evidence by the defendant that he had not known or believed the painting was stolen. But, as the court pointed out:

> In almost every contested handling case, the defendant denies knowing or believing that the relevant goods were stolen, and the prosecution assert that that evidence is a lie. It would be absurd to suggest that every handling case requires a *Lucas* direction.[28]

It would be absurd because in such cases there is an exact overlap between the issue of guilt and the issue of lies.

---

26   It seems, from reading the transcript of the judgment, logically possible that the identification was correct but that someone else was responsible for the fire. That, of course, was not an argument put forward at trial on behalf of the defendant. Whether a *Lucas* direction will be appropriate or not depends very much on what are the live issues in any particular trial.

27   [2002] EWCA Crim 454, [2002] 2 Cr App R 11.

28   Paragraph 30.

IDENTIFICATION AND *TURNBULL* GUIDELINES

It has been recognised for many years that evidence of identification presents particular difficulties for any tribunal of fact. In its 11th Report, the Criminal Law Revision Committee stated: 'We regard mistaken identification as by far the greatest cause of actual or possible wrong convictions.'[29] A similar view was taken in the Devlin Report.[30] The reason is that evidence of identification is exceptionally difficult to assess. As the Devlin Report put it, there are two ways of testing a witness. The first is by the nature of his story: is it probable and coherent? The second is by the demeanour of the witness: does he appear to be honest and reliable? Eye witnesses of an event can differ widely about the details of it. Normally, when a court has to reach a conclusion about an incident or event, it does not have to make a finding on each detail. It is enough if, out of the evidence as a whole, there can be extracted as much of the story as is necessary to know in order to determine the point in issue. But with identification evidence there is no story. The issue rests on a single piece of observation:

> The state of the light, the point of observation and the distance from the object are useful if they can show that the witness must be using his imagination; but otherwise where there is a credible and confident assertion, they are of little use in evaluating it. Demeanour in general is quite useless. The capacity to memorise a face differs enormously from one man to another . . . If a man thinks he is a good memoriser and in fact is not, that fact will not show itself in his demeanour.[31]

English law now tries to protect defendants from wrongful convictions that are based on mistaken identification evidence in two ways: by a system of judicial warnings to juries, and by a Code of Practice governing identification procedures.

In *R v Turnbull*,[32] the Court of Appeal acknowledged that evidence of visual identification presented special difficulties in criminal cases and had led to miscarriages of justice. To deal with this problem, the court laid down guidelines for judges summing up in cases where the prosecution relies on contested identification evidence. Failure to follow the guidelines is likely to lead to the quashing of a conviction as unsafe. Two questions arise: (a) When do the guidelines apply? (b) What do they require the judge to do?

---

29   Criminal Law Revision Committee, Cmnd 4991, 1972, para 196.

30   *Report to the Secretary of State for the Home Department of the Departmental Committee on Evidence of Identification in Criminal Cases*, 1976, para 8.1.

31   Devlin Report, 1976, para 4.25.

32   [1977] QB 224. The dangers inherent in identification evidence may also have to be considered in a civil context: *R v Cardinal Newman's School Birmingham ex p S* (1997) *The Times*, 26 December, DC.

WHEN DO THE GUIDELINES APPLY?

They apply whenever the prosecution case depends 'wholly or substantially' on the correctness of one or more identifications of the defendant, and the defence allege that the identifying witnesses are mistaken. The words 'wholly or substantially' were used by Lord Widgery CJ in *R v Turnbull*. On the face of it, they suggest that a *Turnbull* direction would *not* be required where identification evidence was only a small item in a mass of other evidence against the defendant. But it is unlikely that a judge would invite an appeal by omitting the direction in a case where the prosecution placed *any* reliance on disputed identification evidence.

A *Turnbull* direction must be given in cases where identification is based on *recognition*, as well as in other situations where it might be thought that the risk of error was greater: for example, where there has been a mere fleeting glimpse by the identifying witness.[33] Failure to direct the jury about the possibility of mistake in a case of recognition can lead to quashing of the conviction.[34] Of course, as Lord Lowry pointed out in *Beckford v The Queen*, no rule is absolutely universal. If, for example, the witness's evidence of identification is that he saw the defendant commit the offence, and that immediately beforehand he and the defendant, whom he had known for many years, had been talking together face to face for about half an hour, a *Turnbull* direction would be pointless. But such cases will be rare exceptions to the general rule that, even in a recognition case, a *Turnbull* direction should always be given.[35]

The full direction does not have to be given where the jury itself is asked to make the identification. In *R v Blenkinsop*,[36] the jury were asked to identify the defendant, whom they had seen in court, as the person shown in a video film and various 'still' photographs taken at the scene of a demonstration. The Court of Appeal held that a full *Turnbull* warning was not required because the jury did not need to be told things such as whether the photograph was of good or poor quality, or whether the person alleged to be the defendant was shown in close up or not: they could see for themselves. But a jury should still be warned of the risk of mistaken identification and the need to exercise particular care in any identification which they make for themselves.

The need for a *Turnbull* direction arises generally where the issue is whether the defendant was present at a particular place or not. Where his presence at the scene is not disputed, but his participation in the offence is, the direction does not have to be given automatically. It *will* be necessary where there is the possibility that a witness has mistaken one person for another: for example, because of similarities of clothing,

---

33   *Shand v The Queen* [1996] 1 WLR 67, p 72.
34   See, eg, *R v Torme (D)* [2003] EWCA Crim 2322; *Langford v Dominica* [2005] UKPC 20.
35   (1993) 97 Cr App R 409 (PC), p 415. See also *Capron v The Queen* [2006] UKPC 34, para 16.
36   [1995] 1 Cr App R 7.

colour or build,[37] or because of confused action, such as a fight during a wedding reception.[38]

The *Turnbull* direction came into existence to deal with the problem posed by the honest but mistaken witness. Suppose, however, the defence is that the prosecution witnesses who purport to have identified the accused as being present are lying. In *Shand v The Queen*,[39] the Privy Council stated the position in this way. There may be exceptional cases where a *Turnbull* direction is unnecessary, or where it is sufficient to give it more briefly than where honest mistake is alleged, but the cases in which the warning can be wholly dispensed with must be exceptional. Even where the defence say that there has been perjury rather than an honest mistake, the judge should normally tell the jury to consider whether they are satisfied that the witness was not mistaken.

However, there are cases where the Court of Appeal has recognised that, on the facts and because of the nature of the defence, the *Turnbull* warning *could* be omitted altogether. A recent case was *R v Cape and Others*[40] where the defendants were charged with violent disorder in a public house. The prosecution case depended solely on the evidence of the licensee, who knew the defendants. Each defendant said that, although he had been in the public house at the relevant time, he had not been involved in violence. Two said that the licensee was lying as the result of a grudge. The Court of Appeal said that, in relation to those two defendants, no issue of identification arose, because the allegation was that the licensee was framing them. Accordingly, no *Turnbull* direction had been required.[41]

It seems that a *Turnbull* warning is not required where a witness does not identify the suspect, but merely gives evidence of aspects of someone seen that point to the suspect as the person guilty of an offence. In *R v Byron*,[42] the defendant was charged with assaulting four children of the woman with whom he was living. Evidence was given by a witness who had seen a man with a large tattoo on his upper left arm striking two of the children. The defendant was one of only two adult males living in the house. He had such a tattoo, whereas the other did not. The Court of Appeal said that the evidence was 'descriptive' and was evidence of 'elimination' rather than of 'identification'.

The distinction was more fully considered in *R v Gayle*,[43] where the defendant was charged with burglary. The case for the prosecution was that he had entered a

---

37   *R v Slater* [1995] 1 Cr App R 584.

38   *R v Thornton* [1995] 1 Cr App R 578.

39   [1996] 1 WLR 67. See also *R v Beckford* (1993) 97 Cr App R 409.

40   [1996] 1 Cr App R 191.

41   See also *R v Courtnell* [1990] Crim LR 115.

42   (1999) *The Times*, 10 March. See also *D v DPP* (1998) *The Times*, 7 August; *R v Doldur* [2000] Crim LR 178.

43   [1999] 2 Cr App R 130.

school classroom and there had stolen a handbag. The bag, without the money that it had contained, was found in the rubbish bin of a nearby public house in the following circumstances. Between 3.00 pm and 3.10 pm on the same day, a cook in the public house was preparing food for a customer whom she had not, at that stage, seen. While doing so, she saw a man by the rubbish bins in the yard. She described him as a black man, who was wearing a black nylon jacket with a brightly coloured capital 'K' on the back. She saw him put something in one of the bins. When she took the food that she had been preparing to the customer, she recognised him as the man she had seen in the yard. After serving him, she went to look in the rubbish bin. There she found the stolen handbag. The defendant, when interviewed by the police, admitted that he had been the man in the yard, but he said that he had gone to urinate there and had found the bag on the ground. He said that he had never seen it before and had put it in the bin.

There were certain internal difficulties with this account, but it was clearly desirable to establish some link between the defendant and the school. A possible link was the evidence of the school caretaker. He said that he had seen a man at about the relevant time on the school premises, going towards the exit that led to the public house, but that the man had been too far away for him to see his actual features. He was able to say, however, that it had been a black man in his late 20s to early 30s, six feet tall, stocky in build, wearing a black bomber jacket with the 'Kangol' logo on the back. Thus, it was possible for the jury to infer from this evidence that the man he had seen was the defendant. He had accurately described the jacket, he had seen the man walking towards the public house, and he had given a good general description that fitted the defendant.

No identification parade was held, and at trial the question arose whether there should have been a parade. The defence relied on Code D, para 2.3, of the Codes of Practice issued under the Police and Criminal Evidence Act 1984. This stated that whenever a suspect disputed *an identification*, an identity parade should be held, save in certain exceptional cases.[44] The trial judge held that a parade would have been inappropriate because the caretaker had not *identified* the defendant as the burglar. It was argued on appeal that the trial judge had been wrong, but the Court of Appeal disagreed. The caretaker had not identified as the defendant the person whom he had seen and described. Henry LJ said that there was a qualitative difference between identification evidence and 'evidence of description'.

He added:

The special need for caution before conviction on identification evidence is because, as experience has often shown, it is possible for an honest witness to make a mistaken identification. But the danger of an honest witness being mistaken as to distinctive clothing, or the general

---

44   For a discussion of the provisions contained in the revised Code D, which is now in force, see below.

description of the person he saw . . . [is] minimal. So the jury can concentrate on the honesty of the witness, in the ordinary way.[45]

If, where there is evidence that is merely evidence of description, the jury can 'concentrate on the honesty of the witness, in the ordinary way', it follows not only that an identification parade is inappropriate, but that a *Turnbull* warning is inappropriate also. This is consistent with the decision of the Court of Appeal in *R v Browning*,[46] where it was said that *Turnbull* warnings are inappropriate in cases involving the identification of motor cars.

Where identification is by voice, there is no obligation to hold a 'voice identification parade',[47] but evidence obtained in this way is not inadmissible.[48] Where evidence of identification by voice is relied on, the judge should direct the jury on suitably adapted *Turnbull* lines.[49] If the identification of a voice is disputed, the jury should not be asked to make comparisons of voices heard on a tape without the help of expert evidence. Where the prosecution does not rely on expert evidence, but on the evidence of someone who claims to recognise the voice, evidence should be given of the circumstances relied on in support of the witness's ability to recognise the voice. The court should then decide whether the evidence of recognition is sufficiently reliable to be admitted.[50]

WHAT DOES A *TURNBULL* DIRECTION REQUIRE?

When a judge has to give a *Turnbull* direction he must do three things:

(a) He must warn the jury of the special need for caution before convicting the accused in reliance on the evidence of identification.

(b) He must tell the jury the reason for needing such a warning. Some reference should be made to the possibility that a mistaken witness can be a convincing one, and that a number of such witnesses can all be mistaken. In *R v Pattinson and Exley*,[51] the Court of Appeal allowed appeals and criticised a direction on identification for failing to make adequate reference to the risk of miscarriages of justice resulting from mistaken identification evidence. In *R v Nash*[52] the Court of Appeal

---

45   *R v Gayle* [1999] 2 Cr App R 130, p 135.

46   (1992) 94 Cr App R 109, pp 121–23.

47   *R v Deenik* [1992] Crim LR 578; *R v Gummerson and Steadman* [1999] Crim LR 680.

48   *R v Hersey* [1998] Crim LR 281. Home Office Circular 057/2003 contains advice on the procedure to be followed if it is decided to hold a voice identification parade.

49   *Ibid; R v Gummerson and Steadman* [1999] Crim LR 680. See also *R v Roberts* [2000] Crim LR 183, where the Court of Appeal appeared to acknowledge that there are even greater difficulties with voice identification than with visual identification. See Ormerod, 2001; Ormerod, 2002.

50   *R v Chenia* [2003] 2 Cr App R 83, pp 118–19.

51   [1996] 1 Cr App R 51.

52   [2004] EWCA Crim 2696, [2005] Crim LR 232.

quashed a conviction in a case where the trial judge had, among other things, failed to tell the jury that the need for special caution was 'rooted in the courts' actual experience of miscarriages of justice', and commented that the jury must be exposed to 'the full impact' of the *Turnbull* direction in cases where identification is the central issue.

(c)   He must direct the jury to examine closely the circumstances in which each identification came to be made.

The court in *R v Turnbull* suggested the following as possible subjects of judicial comment, and they can be used as a checklist, provided it is remembered that it is not an *exclusive* list:

(a)   *Previous sightings.* Had the accused been seen by the witness before? Recognition may be more reliable than a fleeting glance, but the jury should still be reminded that mistakes in recognising relations and close friends are sometimes made.

(b)   *Impediments.* Was observation impeded, for example, by passing traffic or people?

(c)   *Distance.* How far away from the person identified was the identifying witness?

(d)   *Discrepancies.* Is there a match between the witness's first description of the suspect to the police and the defendant's actual appearance?

(e)   *Light.*

(f)   *Extents of time.* How long did the observation last? How much time passed between the original observation and the witness's subsequent identification of the defendant to the police at an identification parade or by some other means?

(g)   *Specific weaknesses.* Is the identification evidence weakened by any special circumstances: for example, because the identifying witness had been drinking or had weak sight?

In *R v Stanton*[53] the Court of Appeal quashed a conviction because the trial judge had failed to specify in his summing-up the particular weaknesses of the identification evidence in that case. In doing so, the court observed that to do so was 'a specific obligation on a judge in even the shortest case which involves identification evidence'.[54] In some earlier decisions the Court of Appeal said that it was not always necessary for a trial judge to specify such weaknesses in his summing-up.[55] But in a number of other appeals, convictions have been quashed because the trial judge failed

---

53   [2004] EWCA Crim 490.

54   Paragraph 12.

55   See, eg, *R v Pattinson and Exley* [1996] 1 Cr App R 51; *R v Qadir* [1998] Crim LR 828.

to do so.[56] It seems that a judge will be wise to do so in all cases, at least where the defence has raised arguments during the trial about specific weaknesses. Having warned the jury in accordance with the guidelines, the judge should go on to direct them to consider if the identification evidence is supported by any other evidence. At this stage he should identify for them the evidence that is capable and incapable of providing such support. Supporting evidence might include a rejected defence alibi,[57] or the defendant's silence, either under police questioning or at trial.[58]

It was said in *R v Turnbull* that where the quality of the identification evidence is good, the jury can safely be left to assess it even without any supporting evidence, subject to an adequate warning. But where the quality is poor, the judge should withdraw the case from the jury at the end of the prosecution case unless there is other evidence to support the correctness of the identification.

A witness may be able to make only a qualified identification, for example, by saying that he is '80–85% sure' that the person he has picked out was the person whom he saw near the scene of the crime. A defendant cannot be convicted on the evidence of a qualified identification alone, but in *R v George*[59] the Court of Appeal said that identifications of this kind can be admitted in at least two situations:

- where the qualified identification supports, or is at least consistent with, other evidence indicating the defendant's guilt;
- where the explanation for having to qualify the identification, or even for having been unable to make any identification, might help to place that part of the witness's evidence in its proper context, so as to show, for example, that his or her evidence about other matters might nevertheless be reliable.

In each case it is for the judge to decide whether the evidence in question is more prejudicial than probative, and so ought to be excluded.

IDENTIFICATIONS INSIDE AND OUTSIDE COURT

The law concerning identifications made inside and outside court is inevitably a compromise. On the one hand, it tries to ensure by the Code of Practice that such evidence is reliable. On the other hand, there is reluctance to exclude evidence of

---

56   See, eg, *R v Popat (No 2)* [2000] 1 Cr App R 387; *R v Nash* [2004] EWCA Crim 2696, [2005] Crim LR 232; *Langford v Dominica* [2005] UKPC 20.

57   But in that case the jury should be warned that a false alibi is sometimes invented to bolster a true defence: see *R v Lesley* [1996] 1 Cr App R 39.

58   Criminal Justice and Public Order Act 1994, ss 34 and 35.

59   [2003] Crim LR 282.

identification on technical grounds where there is little danger of unreliability. This can be seen, for example, in cases where the hearsay rule has either been ignored or treated in a cavalier fashion.

DOCK IDENTIFICATION

The rule here is often misunderstood. Identification of an accused person *for the first time* when he is in the dock at trial is to be avoided.[60] But once there has been an out-of-court identification, there can be no objection to asking a witness to identify the accused in court as part of the background to his account of events. The same would be true where identification was not an issue: for example, in a shoplifting case where the defendant does not deny being in the shop or taking the goods but says that he forgot to pay.[61]

EVIDENCE OF PREVIOUS IDENTIFICATIONS

It has long been settled that evidence of a previous out-of-court identification of the defendant can be given by the person who made the identification. The reason is that it shows that the witness was able to identify the accused at a time nearer to the events under investigation, so reducing the chance of mistake.[62] Evidence of a previous out-of-court identification is now given by virtue of s 120(4) and (5) of the Criminal Justice Act 2003. The effect of these provisions appears to be that, provided the person making the identification gives some evidence, he need not himself remember or give evidence about making the identification.[63]

IDENTIFICATION FROM VIDEOS AND PHOTOGRAPHS

It sometimes happens that a photographic image of the commission of the crime is available. In *AG's Reference (No 2 of 2002)*[64] the Court of Appeal summarised four ways in which such material can be used:

■ Where the image is sufficiently clear, the jury can compare it with the defendant sitting in the dock.[65]

---

60   *R v Cartwright* (1914) 10 Cr App R 219. But see *Barnes v Chief Constable of Durham* [1997] 2 Cr App R 505 (dock identifications customary in magistrates' courts). In *Karia v DPP* (2002) 166 JP 753, the Divisional Court followed *Barnes*, holding the decision in that case to be compatible with the defendant's right to a fair trial under Art 6 of the European Convention on Human Rights.

61   Typically, the questioning would go somewhat as follows where the store detective is being examined: Where were you on such and such a date? Did you see anybody on that occasion? Do you see that person here in court today?

62   See the speech of Viscount Haldane in *R v Christie* [1914] AC 545.

63   The position was the same at common law; see *R v Osbourne and Virtue* [1973] 1 QB 678.

64   [2003] 1 Cr App R 321, p 327.

65   They should be warned of the risk of mistaken identification and of the need to exercise particular care in any identification that they make for themselves. See *R v Blenkinsop* above, p 186.

- Where a witness knows the defendant well enough to recognise him as the offender in the photographic image, he can give evidence to that effect.[66]
- Where a witness who does not know the defendant spends substantial time viewing photographic images of the scene of the crime, he can thereby acquire special knowledge not possessed by the jury. He can later give evidence of identification based on a comparison between those images and a reasonably contemporary photograph of the defendant, provided that the images and the photograph are available to the jury.
- A witness who is an expert in facial mapping can give evidence of identification based on a comparison between images from the scene of the crime and a reasonably contemporary photograph of the defendant, provided both are available to the jury.

CODE D OF THE PACE CODES OF PRACTICE

Section 66 of the Police and Criminal Evidence Act 1984 (PACE) provides that the Secretary of State shall issue Codes of Practice in connection with various matters, including the identification of persons. By s 67(11), any Code shall be admissible in evidence, and if any provision of such a Code appears to the court to be relevant to any question, it shall be taken into account in determining that question. Code D of the current Codes of Practice made under PACE is likely to be relevant to any problem involving identification.[67] The whole of the Code is important, but special attention should be paid to Annex A (video identification), Annex B (identification parades) and Annex E (showing photographs). The importance of the Code lies in the fact that evidence obtained in breach of its provisions is likely to be unreliable, and so likely to be excluded under s 78(1) of PACE. This provides:

> In any proceedings the court may refuse to allow evidence on which the prosecution proposes to rely to be given if it appears to the court that, having regard to all the circumstances, including the circumstances in which the evidence was obtained, the admission of the evidence would have such an adverse effect on the fairness of the proceedings that the court ought not to admit it.

This provision is more fully discussed in Chapter 11, but it should be noted here that s 78(1) gives only a discretion to exclude evidence to a trial judge. It follows, therefore, that even if a breach of Code D can be established, the identification

---

66   This is so even where the image is no longer available for the jury to see. In *Taylor v Chief Constable of Cheshire* [1986] 1 WLR 1479 a thief was recorded on video film as he stole from a store. The video was seen by three police officers, who recognised the thief as the defendant. The recording was later accidentally erased. The Divisional Court held, however, that the police officers could give evidence of having seen the defendant on the video recording of the theft.

67   The latest version of Code D came into effect on 1 January 2006.

evidence obtained in this way will not inevitably be excluded. However, where a breach of Code D has been established, but the trial judge has nevertheless decided to admit the identification evidence, he should explain in his summing-up that there has been a breach of the Code, and how it has arisen. He should also invite the jury to consider the possible effect of that breach. For example, if the breach is a failure to hold an identification parade, the jury should ordinarily be told that this procedure enables a suspect to put the reliability of an eyewitness's identification to the test, that the suspect has lost the benefit of that safeguard, and that the jury should take account of that fact in its assessment of the whole case, giving it such weight as it thinks fair.[68] After an introduction and some general provisions, Code D deals with identification by witnesses. By para 3.1, a record has to be made of the description of the suspect as first given by a potential witness. This must be done before the witness takes part in any formal identification. A copy of the record shall 'where practicable' be given to the suspect or his solicitor before any identification procedures are carried out.

In a case that involves disputed identification evidence, and where the identity of the suspect is known to the police and he is available, there are three main formal identification procedures. These are a video identification, an identification parade, or a group identification. The rules for the conduct of these procedures are set out in Annexes A, B and C to the Code. The responsibility for arranging and conducting an identification procedure is given to an officer who is not below the rank of inspector, and who is not involved with the investigation.[69]

The preferred method of identification was initially an identification parade.[70] The general rule now is that where an identification procedure is required, the suspect shall initially be offered either a video identification or an identification parade, at the option of the police. A video identification will normally be more suitable if it can be arranged and completed sooner than an identification parade.[71] The offer of a group identification can be made if it is practicable and would be more satisfactory than either a video identification or a parade.[72] If none of the three main formal procedures is practicable, identification can be made by a confrontation between suspect and witness, in accordance with the provisions of Annex D. This does not require the suspect's consent,[73] but force may not be used to make the suspect's face visible to the witness.[74] The confrontation should normally take place in the police station, either

---

68   *R v Forbes* [2001] 1 AC 473, para 27.

69   D: 3.11.

70   This should be kept in mind when reading earlier cases on Code D, where references are usually to an 'identification parade' rather than to an 'identification procedure'.

71   D: 3.14.

72   D: 3.16.

73   D: 3.23.

74   Annex D, para 3.

• 260 •

in a normal room or in one equipped with a screen permitting the witness to see the suspect without being seen himself.[75]

In a video identification the witness is shown moving images of a known suspect, together with similar images of others who resemble the suspect.[76] Only one witness may see the set of images at a time. The witness can ask at any point to see a particular part of the set, or to have a particular image frozen so that it can be studied. There is no limit on the number of times a witness is allowed to view the whole or a part of the set of images. However, the witness should be asked not to make any decision until he has seen the whole set at least twice.[77]

In an identification parade the witness sees the suspect in a line of other persons who resemble the suspect.[78] In both a video identification and an identification parade, the suspect must be shown at least eight other people 'who, so far as possible, resemble the suspect in age, height, general appearance and position in life'.[79] Neither the Code nor the Annex says how this resemblance 'so far as possible' is to be achieved, but it has been held that artificial means can be used to enable volunteers to resemble the suspect more closely.[80] In both procedures, only one suspect may be shown at a time, unless there are two suspects of roughly similar appearance. In that case they may be shown together with at least 12 other people.[81]

In a group identification the witness sees the suspect in an informal group of people. For example, the group might consist of people leaving an escalator, walking through a shopping centre, or waiting in queues or groups in other public places.[82] In such a procedure the number of others present in addition to the suspect cannot, obviously, be controlled; nor can features such as age, sex, race or the general style of clothing. In selecting a location for the group identification, however, the general appearance and numbers of people likely to be present must be considered. In particular, the officer conducting the procedure must reasonably expect that, over the period during which the witness observes the group, it will be possible from time to time to see a number of others whose appearance is broadly similar to that of the suspect.[83]

By D: 3.12, whenever a suspect disputes being the person a witness claims to have seen, 'an identification procedure shall be held unless it is not practicable or would serve no useful purpose in proving or disproving whether the suspect was the person involved in committing the offence'. This provision raises two questions.

---

75   Annex D, para 6.
76   D: 3.5. See D: 3.21 for circumstances in which still images may be used.
77   Annex A, para 11.
78   D: 3.7.
79   Annex A, para 2; Annex B, para 9.
80   *R v Marrin (KI)* [2002] EWCA Crim 251.
81   *Ibid.*
82   D: 3.9; Annex C, para 4.
83   Annex C, para 6.

First, in what circumstances will it be 'not practicable' to hold an identification procedure? Secondly, in what circumstances would an identification procedure 'serve no useful purpose'?

Earlier versions of Code D provided that, 'Whenever a suspect disputes an identification, an identification parade shall be held unless paragraphs 2.4 or 2.7 or 2.10 apply'. Paragraphs 2.7 and 2.10 dealt simply with situations where other forms of identification procedure were thought to be preferable to an identification parade. Paragraph 2.4 provided, 'A parade need not be held if the identification officer considers that, whether by reason of the unusual appearance of the suspect or for some other reason, it would not be practicable to assemble sufficient people who resembled him to make a parade fair'. Does the new version of the Code extend the scope of impracticability? It is possible that it does, though it is not easy to imagine circumstances that would not be covered by the old provision.

The second question may be more important. As will be seen below, it is possible to adduce evidence of an identification made by a witness at or near the scene of the crime and shortly after the commission of the offence. The provisions of Code D do not apply to such identifications. If a witness has made a full and complete identification in such circumstances, could it be said that a formal identification procedure would serve no useful purpose? An example given in the text of D: 3.12 in the current version is 'when it is not disputed that the suspect is already well known to the witness who claims to have seen them [sic] commit the crime'. There was no corresponding provision in earlier versions of Code D, but the courts had settled that D: 2.3 did not impose an obligation to hold an identification parade where to do so would be futile, because, for example, the witness who saw the commission of the offence said that he would not be able to recognise the culprit if he saw him again, or where the suspect had been informally identified by someone who knew him well and recognised him.[84] It seems likely that the new provision does no more than recognise this development. It could, however, be argued that its effect is wider. Before being rejected by the House of Lords in *R v Forbes*[85] there was a line of Court of Appeal authority on the interpretation of the former D: 2.3, which held that the provision did not apply where a suspect had previously been 'properly and adequately' identified by the witness, or where there had been an 'actual and complete' identification by the witness.[86] According to this line of authority, a purposive approach was to be taken to D: 2.3. A parade was not required where it would serve no useful purpose, and that would be the case where it added nothing to an identification that had already been made informally.[87] Has the reference to 'no useful purpose' in the

---

84   *R v Forbes* [2001] 1 All ER 686, p 697.

85   *Ibid.*

86   See, eg, *R v Popat* [1998] 2 Cr App R 208.

87   *Ibid*, pp 223–24.

current D: 3.12 revived the approach that *Forbes* rejected? It seems unlikely. It could be argued that the example given in D: 3.12 limits the scope of the new provision. More fundamentally, if it were otherwise, the sort of problems perceived by the House of Lords in *Forbes* would arise again. First, a reversion to pre-*Forbes* law would force the police to make difficult judgments about the adequacy of an earlier identification, which would be challenged at trial and might form the basis of a subsequent appeal. Secondly, to give such decisions to the police would be invidious, since their primary concern is to promote the investigation and prosecution of crime, not to protect the interests of suspects. Thirdly, the pre-*Forbes* approach overlooked the fact that grave miscarriages of justice have in the past resulted from identifications which were thought at the time to be satisfactory, but which were later proved to be wrong.[88]

The Code does not prevent an initial street identification shortly after the commission of the offence. For example, in *R v Kelly*,[89] the defendant was charged with attempted rape. The offence took place in a street and the attacker was disturbed before he could complete the full offence. The victim called for the police, who arrived shortly afterwards. As she was talking to the police, she saw the accused in the street and said, 'I think it's him'. One of the officers questioned, but did not arrest, the defendant. Meanwhile the victim was brought nearer to him, where the light was better, in a police car. She was asked to look hard and confirm that the man she saw was her attacker. She said she was sure and the accused was arrested.

On appeal, it was argued that the defendant should have been arrested as soon as the victim had pointed him out on the first occasion. The defendant would then have had the benefit of a properly conducted identification parade. The second stage of her identification had amounted to a confrontation, which according to the Code should not have taken place unless other forms of identification were impracticable. The Court of Appeal dismissed the appeal. It said that when a complainant made a tentative identification within minutes of her ordeal, but in a situation where distance and lack of light made the task difficult, the natural and sensible reaction was to take her closer for a better look. Where a suspect was found within minutes of the crime, and close to the scene, it might well be that the provisions of the Code did not apply.

In *R v Hickin and Others*,[90] the Court of Appeal took a similar view, saying that Code D catered largely for formal identification procedures and should not be interpreted so as to require the police to behave in a way that was an affront to common sense. In that case, the defendants were charged with violent disorder. The offence had been committed at night. Two men had been seriously injured in the disorder, and shortly after the police learned of this they arrested a large group of suspects. Two members of the public saw the assaults and reported them to other police officers who, within minutes of the assaults, took the witnesses to the large group of suspects

---

88   [2001] 1 All ER 686, p 696.
89   [1992] Crim LR 181.
90   [1996] Crim LR 584. See also *R v Malashev* [1997] Crim LR 587.

to see if they could identify participants. There were no identification parades. The Court of Appeal approved of the course taken. It was clearly impracticable to set up that night the large number of identification parades that would have been required under Code D. It would have been undesirable to postpone the attempts at identification because recollections might become weaker, and later identifications would deprive the witnesses of the opportunity to see the suspects' clothing, which could be a valuable aid. The court observed, however, that where there was more than one witness it might be advisable to reserve one or more for an identification parade – thus in effect providing a filter for suspects picked out by the informal procedure.

Where the identity of the suspect is not known, a police officer may take a witness to a particular neighbourhood or place to see whether he can identify the person he saw on the relevant occasion. If this happens, the principles applicable to formal identification procedures are to be followed so far as practicable. For example, a record should be made of the witness's description of the suspect before asking the witness to make an identification, and care must be taken not to direct the witness's attention to any individual, though the witness may be asked to look towards a group or in a particular direction if this appears necessary.[91]

A witness must not be shown photographs, computerised or artist's composite likenesses, or similar likenesses or pictures, if the identity of the suspect is known to the police and the suspect is available to take part in one of the three main formal identification procedures. If the suspect's identity is not known, a witness may be shown photographs in order to obtain identification evidence. This must be done in accordance with Annex E.[92] In particular, it should be noted that only one witness should be shown the photographs at any one time. He should be given as much privacy as is practicable, and should not be allowed to communicate with any other witness in the case.[93] He should be shown not fewer than 12 photographs at a time, which should, as far as possible, all be of a similar type.[94] If a witness makes a positive identification from photographs, then, unless the person identified is eliminated from inquiries or is not available, other witnesses must not be shown photographs. Instead, they and the identifying witness should be asked to attend one of the three main formal identification procedures, at which the person whose photograph was picked out will also be present.[95]

The fact that photographs have been used at some stage in the identification process will not usually be brought out at trial by the prosecution. The reason, of course, is that to disclose their use shows that the defendant has a criminal record.

---

91   D: 3.2.
92   D: 3.3.
93   Annex E, para 3.
94   *Ibid*, para 4.
95   *Ibid*, para 6.

Where photographs have been used, the defence should be informed and left to decide for themselves whether any reference to this fact should be made.[96]

FURTHER READING

— Ashworth and Redmayne, *The Criminal Process*, 3rd edn, 2005, sections 5.3, 5.4.

— Coates, *The Strange Story of Adolf Beck*, 1999.

— Devlin Report: *Evidence of Identification in Criminal Cases*, 1976.

— Lewis, 'A Comparative Examination of Corroboration and Caution Warnings in Prosecutions for Sexual Offences' [2006] Crim LR 889.

— Ormerod, 'Sounds Familiar? Voice Identification Evidence' [2001] Crim LR 595.

— Ormerod, 'Sounding Out Expert Voice Identification' [2002] Crim LR 221.

— Roberts, 'The Problem of Mistaken Identification' (2004) 8 E&P 100.

EXERCISES

1. What are discretionary care warnings? When will they be given?

2. What should a *Lucas* direction contain? When should it be given?

3. What should a *Turnbull* direction contain? When is it *not* necessary for it to be given?

4. Where a photographic image of the commission of a crime is available, in what ways can it be used to assist identification?

5. In what ways can a breach of Code D be used by the defence?

---

96   *R v Lamb* (1980) 71 Cr App R 198. But there is no absolute ban on reference by the prosecution to photographs: see *R v Allen* [1996] Crim LR 426. The best justification for this is that such evidence, though it may be probative, will normally be outweighed by the prejudicial effect on the jury when they hear something that shows the defendant to have a criminal record. But, as with all evidence, prejudicial effect is capable of being outweighed in a particular case by probative value: see the commentary on this case at p 427.

11

CONFESSIONS AND ILL-GOTTEN EVIDENCE

Although confessions are out-of-court statements adduced to prove the truth of their contents, they are admissible under s 76(1) of the Police and Criminal Evidence Act 1984 (PACE) as an exception to the hearsay rule.[1] This provision put on a statutory basis an exception long recognised by the common law. Its justification was the supposed reliability of such statements. As Wills wrote:

> A voluntary confession of guilt, if it be full, consistent and probable, is justly regarded as evidence of the highest and most satisfactory nature. Self-love, the mainspring of human conduct, will usually prevent a rational being from making admissions prejudicial to his interest and safety, unless when caused by the promptings of truth and conscience.[2]

However, it is recognised that considerations of fairness or reliability may make it undesirable to admit evidence of a particular confession, or other items of evidence on which the prosecution proposes to rely. The law on these matters reflects a tension between the need to ensure the conviction of the guilty and the need to ensure that

---

1   This exception is preserved by the Criminal Justice Act 2003, s 118(1).
2   Wills, 1902, p 91.

people are not convicted on evidence that is unreliable, or as a result of proceedings that are unfair.

To try to ensure reliability and fairness, Codes of Practice have been brought into existence under ss 60(1)(a) and 66 of PACE. They are aimed, among other things, at controlling the way in which certain kinds of evidence are obtained. It is important to be familiar with their provisions, especially in relation to police questioning and identification, because breaches *may* lead to the exclusion of evidence under either s 76 or s 78 of PACE. It is also important to be aware of the right to legal advice, granted by PACE, that is reflected in some of the provisions of the Codes. But it is not enough merely to be able to point to a breach, either of a provision in PACE or of the Code: the breach must be used as part of a more complex argument. It is arguments of this kind that are the subject of this chapter.

Sections 76 and 78 of PACE deal respectively with confessions and with a discretion to exclude, for reasons of fairness, evidence on which the prosecution proposes to rely. These sections are very often relied on in the alternative. It was decided in *R v Mason*[3] that s 78 applies to confessions just as much as to any other evidence. The cases, therefore, cannot be read on the basis that one group is relevant to s 76 and another to s 78, and some overlap is inevitable in what follows. However, if you want to exclude a confession, s 76(2) is the better instrument. The reason for this, explained in more detail below, is that exclusion under this provision is mandatory if the prosecution fail to satisfy the judge beyond reasonable doubt that the defence's contentions are wrong. By contrast, s 78(1) provides only a discretionary power of exclusion, and the law about where the burden of proof lies is less clear.

A preliminary warning is necessary. In reading cases where evidence has been excluded under either section, but particularly under s 78, you are not reading precedents that will have to be followed in later cases; you cannot step twice into the same river. No situation is ever exactly repeated, no defendant is exactly like another, and the effect of acts or omissions by the police is likely to vary greatly from case to case. Knowledge of some previous decisions is helpful because they give some idea of the ways in which courts have behaved, but such knowledge is no substitute for careful thought about the facts of your own particular case, including the nature of your particular defendant. You cannot avoid the struggle to work out a satisfactory argument which will bring *your particular facts* within the scope of either s 76 or s 78. It is clear that the effect of s 76(2)(b) is to require the court to take into account the particular circumstances of the defendant who relies on the sub-section. In *R v Wahab* Judge LJ said, 'In our view it is inappropriate for the question of reliability under s 76(2), when it arises, to be decided by reference, directly or by analogy, to circumstances which have arisen and been decided in different appeals. The question is

---

3   [1988] 1 WLR 139.

always fact specific, and in particular, defendant specific . . .'.[4] In relation to s 78, it has been said that the decision of a judge whether or not to exclude evidence is made as a result of the exercise by him of a discretion based upon the particular circumstances of the case and upon his assessment of the adverse effect, if any, it would have on the fairness of the proceedings. Judges may well take different views in the proper exercise of their discretion, even where the circumstances of two cases are similar. This is not an apt field for hard case law and well founded distinctions between cases.[5]

It is in relation to a confession that an argument for exclusion will very often have to be made. By s 76(2):

> . . . if in any proceedings where the prosecution proposes to give in evidence a confession made by an accused person it is represented to the court that the confession was or may have been obtained –
>
> (a)   by oppression of the person who made it; or
>
> (b)   in consequence of anything said or done which was likely, in the circumstances existing at the time, to render unreliable any confession which might be made by him in consequence thereof,
>
> the court shall not allow the confession to be given in evidence against him except in so far as the prosecution proves to the court beyond reasonable doubt that the confession (notwithstanding that it may be true) was not obtained as aforesaid.

This puts the burden of showing that a confession was *not* obtained in the vitiating circumstances referred to in (a) and (b) on the prosecution. By sub-s (3), the court may 'of its own motion' (that is, without the point being taken on the defendant's behalf) require the prosecution to satisfy it that a confession was not made in the vitiating circumstances.

By sub-s (4), the fact that a confession is wholly or partly excluded under sub-s (2) shall not affect the admissibility in evidence of any facts discovered as a result of the confession. Suppose Charlie confesses to stealing some jewellery and tells the police that he hid it under the floor in his bedroom. The police search his bedroom and recover the jewellery. The fact that the stolen jewellery was found in that place is admissible as evidence against Charlie, even if his confession is excluded under sub-s (2). What the police cannot say, if Charlie's confession is excluded, is that they found the jewellery in his bedroom *as the result of what he told them*.

By the same sub-section, where a confession has a relevance that goes beyond the truth of its contents because it shows that the defendant speaks, writes or expresses himself in a particular way, so much of the confession as is necessary to

---

4   [2003] 1 Cr App R 232, p 241.

5   *R v Jelen and Katz* (1989) 90 Cr App R 456, pp 464–65; approved in *R v Roberts* [1997] 1 Cr App R 217, CA, p 231.

show that he does so will be admissible. Suppose Bertha has been raped. She tells the police that her attacker spoke English poorly, with a strong German accent. Hans is interviewed by the police and makes several damaging admissions. The interview is subsequently ruled inadmissible under sub-s (2). In principle, the prosecution should be able to adduce enough of the tape containing neutral questions and answers to show that Hans speaks English poorly, with a strong German accent.

When a confession appears in a set of prosecution statements you must be able to do three things:

(a) recognise it when you see it;

(b) assess its impact on the case as a whole; and

(c) work out what arguments are available to you to get it excluded.

RECOGNISING THE CONFESSION

There is a partial definition of a confession in s 82(1) of PACE. 'Confession' includes any statement wholly or partly adverse to the person who made it, whether made to a person in authority or not and whether made in words or otherwise. Note that a statement only *partly* adverse to its maker comes within this definition. Thus, 'I admit I was at the robbery with Fred, but I only went with him because he threatened to shoot me if I didn't help' is a confession. It must be a question of fact whether a particular statement contains something that is adverse to its maker, and borderline cases could arise. What would be the effect, for example, of an admission that the defendant was in the area where a crime was committed, even though he denied having anything to do with its commission? Almost certainly the size of the area would be crucial. A defendant who admitted being in the same house as the deceased at the time of the murder would have made a statement that was partly adverse, but what of a defendant who admitted being only in the same city?

It is important to remember that a 'mixed' statement, containing partly favourable and partly adverse matters, is evidence of the truth of *all* its contents.[6] This means that in the unlikely event of the defendant's failure to testify, there will still be evidence of the favourable matters for the jury to consider, because those matters will have been referred to by the police witnesses. It is the duty of the prosecution to present the case fairly; to exclude answers that were favourable to the defendant while admitting those that were unfavourable would be misleading.[7]

If a defendant does not give evidence, his advocate may wish to argue that a statement made by his client contains inculpatory as well as exculpatory matters so

---

6   *R v Sharp* (1988) 86 Cr App R 274, HL; followed *R v Aziz* [1996] AC 41, HL.

7   *R v Pearce* (1979) 69 Cr App R 365.

as to have the whole statement admitted as evidence of the truth of its contents. The prosecution may then argue that the statement is purely exculpatory, because such a statement, though admissible as evidence of the accused's reaction to incriminating facts, is not admissible as evidence of the truth of its contents.[8] This is likely to be a hard distinction for a jury to appreciate, but the practical significance is that if the statement of a defendant who gives no evidence is mixed, and the defendant is of good character, the judge must direct the jury that his good character is relevant both to disposition and to credibility.[9] Further, such a statement is likely to satisfy any evidential burden that the defendant may have: for example, in relation to self-defence.

A situation of this kind arose in *Western v DPP*,[10] where the defendant was charged with using threatening behaviour, contrary to s 4 of the Public Order Act 1986. Police had found the defendant fighting with another man in an alley. When interviewed, he admitted that he had hit the other man, but said that he had done so in self-defence. At trial, the defendant gave no evidence, but it was argued that what he had said when interviewed raised the issue of self-defence. The magistrates took the view that it had not, on the basis that it was a purely exculpatory statement. The defendant was convicted. On appeal, it was argued that the magistrates had been wrong, because the defendant had admitted his presence in the alley and his participation in fighting. That was sufficient to make the statement mixed. The prosecution argued that a statement is mixed only if the prosecution relies on inculpatory parts of it. In this case, it was argued, the prosecution was not relying on admissions about presence in the alley or participation in fighting: there was ample evidence of those matters from police witnesses. But the Divisional Court observed that there had been no finding by the magistrates that the prosecution did not rely on the defendant's admissions. 'Indeed,' said Butterfield J, 'it is highly likely that the prosecution did rely on those admissions. Not only had the defendant admitted presence at the scene and fighting, but had also admitted a series of earlier exchanges with the other man that could have given rise to an inference that he was angry, ready and willing to fight, and was far from acting in self-defence.'

On that narrow ground, the Divisional Court was prepared to allow the appeal, but the court added that it had grave doubts about the correctness of the prosecution's argument. Whether a statement is mixed or not should not depend on whether other evidence is available to the prosecution, but on an examination of the statement itself. This view seems, tacitly at least, to have been adopted in *R v Garrod*,[11] in which the Court of Appeal said that where a statement contains an

---

8   *R v Storey and Anwar* (1968) 52 Cr App R 334.
9   See below, Chapter 12.
10   [1997] 1 Cr App R 474.
11   [1997] Crim LR 445.

admission of fact that is *capable* of adding *some* degree of weight to the prosecution case, the statement must be regarded as mixed.[12]

Suppose a statement appears to be *purely* exculpatory; then, later, it can be shown to be a lie and thus incriminating. Will this make it a confession? In two cases, the Court of Appeal has said that this will not make a confession out of an apparently wholly exculpatory statement. In *R v Sat-Bhambra*,[13] the court had to consider the admissibility of a number of tape recorded interviews between customs officers and the defendant. Defence counsel admitted that the answers given by his client were exculpatory, but he argued that they had a damaging effect because they showed the defendant to be evasive and prevaricating, and because many of the statements which he made proved eventually to be false. The court took the view, *obiter*, that purely exculpatory statements were not within the scope of s 82(1). Section 76 was aimed at excluding confessions obtained by words or deeds likely to render them unreliable, that is, admissions or partial admissions contrary to the interests of the defendant and welcome to the interrogator. The section 'can hardly have been aimed at statements containing nothing which the interrogator wished the defendant to say and nothing apparently adverse to the defendant's interests'. As Lord Lane observed, to hold otherwise would mean that the statement 'I had nothing to do with it' might in due course become a 'confession', which, he thought, would be surprising.[14]

This interpretation was adopted by the Court of Appeal in *R v Park*.[15] The defendant had been stopped by police while driving a car with defective rear lights. During a roadside conversation the police came to suspect that he was carrying stolen goods, and a conversation then took place in which the defendant made only exculpatory statements, some of which were later shown to be false. The court held that these statements did not amount to confessions, because s 82(1) was not aimed at statements that the maker intended to be exculpatory, that were exculpatory on their face, but that could later be shown to be false or inconsistent with the maker's evidence on oath.

In *R v Z*[16] the Court of Appeal reconsidered *Sat-Bhambra* and *Park* in the light of the Human Rights Act 1998 and Art 6 of the European Convention on Human Rights. The European Court of Human Rights had said that the right not to incriminate oneself, which is part of the concept of fairness contained in Art 6, cannot be confined to admissions of wrongdoing or to remarks that are directly incriminating. Exculpatory remarks or mere information on questions of fact can

---

12   Emphasis added. See Birch, 1997.

13   (1989) 88 Cr App R 55.

14   (1989) 88 Cr App R 55, p 61.

15   (1994) 99 Cr App R 270.

16   [2003] 2 Cr App R 173.

later be used to support the prosecution case, for example, by contradicting or casting doubt on the accused's evidence.[17] In *R v Z*, Rix LJ noted that the definition of a confession as 'a statement wholly or partly adverse to the person who made it' left open the question of the time at which the statement was to be judged adverse. *Sat-Bhambra* and *Park* had indicated that the relevant time was that at which the statement was made, but in *R v Z* the Court of Appeal preferred the approach taken in *Saunders v UK*, saying that the better view is that it is the time when the statement is to be given in evidence. It followed in that case that assertions in a defendant's confidential interview with the police about a third party, referred to as 'X', which happened to cast doubt on his defence of duress by X in respect of an offence with which he had already been charged, amounted to a confession within s 82(1). The assertions, though not on their face inculpatory, were adverse to the defendant at the time of the trial in which he raised the defence of duress. It followed that, in the absence of Code C protections, the defendant's assertions at the confidential interview should have been excluded.[18]

The prosecution appealed to the House of Lords, which approved *Sat-Bhambra* and reversed the decision of the Court of Appeal.[19] Lord Steyn, with whose opinion on this point the other Law Lords agreed, found it 'wholly impossible' that the draftsman of s 82 of PACE would have made express reference only to wholly or partly adverse statements if he had also had in mind statements that were wholly exculpatory. Such a wide interpretation was unnecessary, because s 78 was wide enough to exclude wholly exculpatory statements relied on by the prosecution if they had been obtained by unfairness. *Saunders* had been concerned solely with evidence obtained under compulsion or under threat of a legal penalty. The decision in that case had not attempted to define what might amount to a confession for the purposes of s 76 and was of no assistance in the present context.

Section 82(1) establishes that a confession can be made 'in words or otherwise' and whether or not the person to whom it is made is 'a person in authority'. The definition thus assumes that a statement can be made by non-verbal means. While this clearly includes a gesture intended to acknowledge guilt, such as a nod of the head when an accusation is put, it might also include an action that was not so intended, but from which a confession is capable of being *inferred*. So a potentially incriminating act of the defendant, such as running away or attempting to bribe witnesses, might amount to a confession.

In *R v Hazy and Collins*, the defendants' flight when detected in the act of lopping a tree was held to be capable of showing that they were acting without

---

17 *Saunders v UK* (1996) 23 EHRR 313, para 71.

18 The court left open the question of whether a statement that was obviously exculpatory on its face, such as 'I did not do it', could amount to a confession. See generally Munday, 2003.

19 [2005] UKHL 22; [2005] 2 AC 467, *sub nom R v Hasan*.

authorisation.[20] In *Moriarty v London, Chatham and Dover Railway Co*,[21] a plaintiff's attempts to persuade several persons to give false evidence in support of his claim was held to be evidence of an admission by conduct that the case he was putting forward was untrue. More recently, in *Parkes v R*,[22] a girl had been stabbed to death and the defendant was charged with murdering her. The mother of the girl testified that when she found that her daughter had been injured, she accused the defendant to his face. He made no reply, whereupon she threatened to detain him until the police could arrive. He then attempted to stab her. The Privy Council held that the defendant's reaction to the accusation was evidence from which the jury could infer that he acknowledged the truth of the accusation.[23]

It was emphasised in *Parkes v R* that the defendant's reaction had not been one of *mere* silence, and thus the Privy Council appeared to leave undecided the effect of silence alone in the face of an accusation. But if silence could be interpreted as an adoption of an allegation made against a suspect, it could in principle amount to a confession, since by s 82(1) a confession may be made 'in words or otherwise'. Whether silence is capable of amounting to an adoption of an accusation will be a question of fact in each case. But old civil cases dealing with admissions show that this is possible, and 'confessions' are just admissions (partial or complete) made by the defendant in a criminal case.[24]

Two cases often contrasted are *Bessela v Stern*[25] and *Wiedemann v Walpole*.[26] The first of these was an action for breach of promise of marriage. The plaintiff testified that the defendant had seduced her, had made her pregnant, and had repeatedly promised to marry her. Her sister gave evidence that she had overheard a conversation between the plaintiff and the defendant after the child had been born. During this encounter, the plaintiff had said to the defendant, 'You always promised to marry me and you don't keep your word'. The defendant's response was to say that he would give her some money to go away. Statute required that in a breach of promise case there had to be material evidence in support of the promise, apart from that of the plaintiff, and the question arose of whether the evidence of the defendant's response satisfied this requirement.

---

20   (1826) 2 C&P 458. But the decision was of a trial judge on assize and the defendant was unrepresented.

21   (1870) LR 5 QB 314.

22   [1976] 1 WLR 1251.

23   See also *Preece and Others v Parry* [1983] Crim LR 170, where the Divisional Court held that the defendants' violent and abusive behaviour to the police when arrested for committing criminal damage and assault in a public house earlier that evening was capable of constituting an admission to those offences.

24   Stone and Wells, 1991, pp 345–46.

25   (1877) 2 CPD 265.

26   (1891) 2 QB 534.

The Court of Appeal held that it did. Cockburn CJ pointed out that the defendant had made no answer to the allegation. True, he had offered her money to go away, and that might have been done even if there had been no promise to marry. But on the other hand, the jury could infer from his silence that he admitted the promise. Bramwell LJ said: 'If a statement is such that a denial of it is not to be expected, then silence is no admission of its truth; but if two persons have a conversation, in which one of them makes a statement to the disadvantage of the other, and the latter does not deny it, there is evidence of an admission that the statement is correct.'[27]

In *Wiedemann v Walpole*, the Court of Appeal was concerned with another breach of promise case. Here the plaintiff claimed that she and the defendant had had sexual intercourse at a hotel in Constantinople and that he had promised to marry her. The plaintiff produced at trial copies of three letters that she and others on her behalf had later sent to the defendant alleging his promise of marriage. The defendant had not answered any of these letters and the question arose of whether his silence was capable of being construed as an admission of the allegation.

Lord Esher MR said that the context was not the same as a commercial one, where silence following an allegation in correspondence that a promise had been made might amount to an admission. Such cases as those were 'wholly unlike the case of a letter charging a man with some offence or meanness'. According to the ordinary practice of mankind, an admission of guilt could not be inferred from failure to answer:

> If it were so, life would be unbearable. A man might day by day write such letters, which, if they were not answered, would be brought forward as evidence of the truth of the charges made in them. The ordinary and wise practice is not to answer them – to take no notice of them.[28]

However, Lord Esher emphasised the importance of the circumstances; the effect might be different if the allegation were contained in one letter which went unanswered as part of a continuing correspondence between a man and a woman.

A comparison of *Bessela v Stern* and *Wiedemann v Walpole* suggests that silence in the face of an *oral* accusation will be more readily interpreted as acknowledgment of its truth than silence in the face of a written accusation. The reason for this is probably that the greater immediacy of an accusation made face to face is thought to make failure to respond more suspicious than failure to reply to a letter. A recent case has shown that an oral assertion need not even be made in circumstances where one person accuses another for silence to be interpreted as acknowledgment of guilt. In *R v Batt*,[29] the failure by one defendant to dissociate himself from something said to him by another defendant in a conversation was interpreted as acknowledging an allegation of a criminal offence to be true. Ashley and Kerry Batt were charged

---

27   (1877) 2 CPD 265, p 272.
28   [1891] 2 QB 534, p 538.
29   [1995] Crim LR 240.

with robbery. There was evidence that one of the robbers had been holding a gun concealed by some material. While they were on remand in custody, the two men shared a cell at the police station. A policeman reported a lot of shouting. He said he heard Kerry say, 'They'll fuck themselves if they show that gun in court. It's not the one used'. Kerry added, 'I've got a friend ID'ing [identifying] me. He is very frightened. He won't pick me out. He knows better than that'.

At trial the judge, when summing up, merely observed that there was nothing recorded of anything said by Ashley in that conversation. It was argued on appeal for Ashley that the judge should have directed the jury that anything Kerry might have said was not evidence against Ashley. But the prosecution argued that the evidence was admissible against Ashley as well as Kerry because Ashley had been present when the words were shouted, had heard what was said, and had failed to dissociate himself from it. The Court of Appeal upheld the prosecution's argument.

IMPACT OF A CONFESSION ON THE CASE AS A WHOLE

The impact is obvious where a defendant has said something that incriminates him in relation to the offence charged, but suppose a defendant says something that incriminates not only himself but also his co-defendant. Where such a statement was made in the presence of the co-defendant, it may be possible to argue that the latter, by his own words or actions or by his silence, adopted what was said so as to make the statement his own. But if what was said was not in the presence of the co-accused, this is not possible. Then, because of the hearsay rule, what was said outside court will be evidence against the speaker only and not against the co-defendant.[30] This does not mean that the statement will inevitably be excluded at trial, either wholly or in part. Sometimes in the past the judge has agreed to 'edit' a record of a statement or interview so as to omit references to co-defendants. But it is clear that this practice will not be adopted where the defendant who made the remarks does not agree to editing.

The leading authority is now the decision of the Privy Council in *Lobban v The Queen*.[31] Three robbers had entered a house with guns and had killed three victims

---

30   *R v Gunewardene* [1951] 2 KB 600. Of course, the same is also true of a statement which is wholly exculpatory in relation to its maker and in which all the blame is put on a co-defendant. Note, however, that where the guilt of D1 is a condition precedent to the guilt of D2, the guilt of D1 can be established by D1's confession without infringing the principle that what is said outside court will be evidence against the speaker alone, provided D1's confession is not used to confront any part of D2's defence (*R v Hayter* [2003] 2 Cr App R 435; dist'd *Persaud v State of Trinidad and Tobago* [2007] UKPC 51; [2007] 1 WLR 2397). For the effect of CJA 2003, see *R v Y* [2008] EWCA Crim 10.

31   [1995] 2 Cr App R 573.

during the robbery. Lobban and another man named Russell were charged with their murder. About six weeks after the killings, Russell made a statement to the police in which he admitted being the driver of the car in which the robbers had made their journey, but he said that he had not known what the men intended to do. He had seen the guns only when his passengers came out of the house to which they had told him to drive. He added that they had forced him to drive them away. In the final paragraph of his statement, he explained that some time later he had seen a photograph of Lobban in a newspaper and had then recognised him as one of the men involved. The prosecution tendered this statement as part of the evidence against Russell. Counsel for Lobban asked the trial judge to exclude the final paragraph implicating his client. Counsel for Russell objected and the judge refused to exclude it. His refusal was the basis of subsequent appeals after Lobban's conviction.

The Privy Council held that the final part of the statement was relevant to Russell's defence because it might have helped to explain the gap of six weeks between the murders and Russell's report to the police. His reference to Lobban was an integral part of that explanation and was put forward as a sign of frankness. It was therefore relevant. Given its relevance, the judge had no discretion to exclude it. The discretionary power to exclude relevant evidence applies only to evidence on which the *prosecution* proposes to rely. It exists to ensure a fair trial to the defendant or, in a joint trial, to each defendant. But it does not extend to the exculpatory part of a mixed statement on which one of the *defendants* proposes to rely. Any suggestions to the contrary in earlier cases were wrong.

So far I have been concerned with what one defendant says *outside court* concerning another. What one defendant says *in court* about another is treated differently. Evidence given by one defendant in his own defence at trial is evidence against co-defendants whom it implicates just as much as the evidence from prosecution witnesses.[32] Suppose a defendant (D1) makes a statement outside court to a policeman (P) about another defendant (D2). D1's statement cannot be evidence against D2, when repeated by P in court, because of the hearsay rule. But if D1 makes the same allegation against D2 from the witness box at trial, the evidence of D1 will not be hearsay. D1 may, of course, be cross-examined on it by counsel for D2 and it is for this reason that a distinction is drawn between a statement by one defendant about another made *outside court* and a similar statement made by that defendant from the witness box *in court*.

EXCLUDING THE CONFESSION

A confession can be open to attack under s 76(2)(a) or (b). Section 76(2)(a) provides for exclusion where the confession was, or may have been, obtained by oppression.

---

32   *R v Rudd* (1948) 32 Cr App R 138.

Under s 76(2)(b), a confession will be excluded where it was, or may have been, obtained 'in consequence of anything said or done which was likely, in the circumstances existing at the time, to render unreliable any confession which might be made by [the defendant] in consequence thereof'.

SECTION 76(2)(a) OF PACE

There are two principal reasons underlying the rule that a confession obtained by oppression should not be admitted in evidence. One is that such a confession may well be unreliable. A second reason, stated in more recent years, is that 'in a civilised society a person should not be compelled to incriminate himself, and a person in custody should not be subjected by the police to ill treatment or improper pressure in order to extract a confession'.[33] It follows that since s 76(2) of the 1984 Act was based on these considerations, it is inconsistent with the purpose of that provision that the jury should rely on a confession that was not made voluntarily. Accordingly, where a trial judge admits a confession in evidence, he must, where the issue has been raised, direct the jury that if they consider that the confession was, or might have been, obtained by oppression, they should disregard it.[34]

Oppression is partially defined in s 76(8) to include 'torture, inhuman or degrading treatment, and the use or threat of violence (whether or not amounting to torture)'. The meaning of oppression was discussed in *R v Fulling*,[35] where Lord Lane CJ said that the word should be given its ordinary dictionary meaning. He cited a definition from the *Oxford English Dictionary*: 'Exercise of authority or power in a burdensome, harsh or wrongful manner; unjust or cruel treatment of subjects, inferiors, etc; the imposition of unreasonable or unjust burdens.' He also cited an illustrative quotation from the dictionary entry: 'There is not a word in our language which expresses more detestable wickedness than oppression.' Lord Lane thereby emphasised the seriousness of the conduct envisaged and added that the court found it hard to think of circumstances in which there would be oppression without some impropriety on the part of the interrogator.[36]

However, the case of *R v Paris and Others*[37] shows that even in the absence of physical violence an interview can be oppressive. The Lord Chief Justice said that, on hearing one of the interview tapes, each member of the court had been horrified. The defendant Miller, the admissibility of whose confessions was in issue, had been

---

33   *R v Mushtaq* [2005] UKHL 25, [2005] 1 WLR 1513, paras 7, 45. See also *A v Secretary of State for the Home Department (No 2)* [2005] UKHL 71, [2006] 2 AC 221.

34   *R v Mushtaq*, above.

35   [1987] QB 426.

36   So it is clear that not everything in Lord Lane's dictionary definition will be 'oppression' for these purposes. The exercise of power might be wrongful (because, eg, of an honest mistake) but not oppressive.

37   (1993) 97 Cr App R 99.

'bullied and hectored'. The officers were not questioning him so much as shouting at him what they wanted him to say. Short of physical violence, it was hard to conceive of a more hostile and intimidating approach by officers to a suspect. The court said that the tapes made it clear that for extended periods Miller was crying and sobbing, yet he was not given any respite.

The court had no doubt that there had been oppression. A confession obtained in such circumstances would have been unreliable even with a suspect of normal mental capacity. In fact, Miller was on the borderline of mental handicap with an IQ of 75, a mental age of 11 and a reading age of eight. There had been a solicitor present, but he had scarcely intervened at all. The Lord Chief Justice pointed out that Law Society guidelines for solicitors advising a suspect in the police station had apparently been ignored and added, 'We can only assume that, in the present case, the officers took the view that unless and until the solicitor intervened, they could not be criticised for going too far. If that is so, they were wholly wrong'.[38] Although the court did not expressly say so, it seems clear from these words that police officers conducting an interrogation have a duty of fairness to suspects which they break at their peril. The presence of a legal adviser does not diminish this duty one jot, let alone extinguish it. The appeal was allowed and the court ordered that copies of the relevant tape be sent to the DPP.

It is sometimes assumed that *any* police impropriety amounts to oppression, but this is not so. Counsel for the appellant in *R v Parker*[39] relied on the dictionary definition quoted in *Fulling* and argued that the exercise of authority in a wrongful manner amounted to oppression. The Court of Appeal rejected this argument, saying that the word 'wrongful' should be understood in the context of the rest of the definition, particularly the words 'burdensome' and 'harsh' which preceded it, and the words 'unjust or cruel treatment' which followed. If it were otherwise, any breaches of Code C, however trivial, could be said to be wrongful, and would therefore amount to oppression.

SECTION 76(2)(b) OF PACE

The test that has to be applied under this provision is not a test of *actual* reliability. Instead, the question the court has to ask is a *hypothetical* one: might what was said or done have been likely, in the circumstances, to make *any* confession by that defendant unreliable?

The hypothetical nature of this question can be seen in *R v Cox*.[40] The defendant, who was mentally handicapped, was interviewed by police in the absence of an 'appropriate adult', in breach of Code of Practice C. During the interview,

---

38   (1993) 97 Cr App R 99, p 110.

39   [1995] Crim LR 233.

40   [1991] Crim LR 276.

he admitted being a party to two burglaries. The defence applied to exclude his confession under s 76(2)(b), but when the defendant gave evidence on the *voir dire* as part of this application, he admitted his involvement in one of the burglaries. This led the judge to conclude that the confession was reliable and should therefore be admitted. The Court of Appeal held that the judge had applied the wrong test. The essential question was not whether the confession was true, but whether the breach of the Code was likely in the circumstances to produce an unreliable confession. In *R v Bow Street Magistrates' Court ex p Proulx*,[41] the Divisional Court held that 'any confession' referred to *any such a confession as the defendant had made*. Thus, the subject matter of the confession cannot be disregarded when applying the test. Were it otherwise, it would always be possible to think of some confession by the defendant that would be likely to be unreliable as a consequence of what was said or done. For example, a trivial breach of Code C might make a confession to a trivial offence unreliable because the defendant might have thought that a conviction for such an offence did not matter. However, the same would not be true of a confession to a much graver offence.

For sub-s (2)(b) to apply, it must be shown, as with sub-s (2)(a), that the matters complained of *did in fact cause the confession to be made*. It is particularly important to remember this when considering sub-s (2)(b) because a confession that may very well be unreliable is not covered by that sub-section unless it was made as a result of something 'said or done' by a person other than the suspect. In *R v Goldenberg*,[42] it was argued that a defendant's confessions ought to have been excluded because he was a heroin addict who had been in custody for some weeks, so that it might have been expected that he would say anything to get bail and feed his addiction. No submission had been made at trial to exclude under s 78, but there had been a submission under s 76(2)(b). It was argued that 'anything said or done' could include things said or done by the suspect. Here the suspect had requested an interview. In the court's view, however, the language of the statute did not extend so far. The words were limited to something external to the person making the confession.[43]

Once you can show that an external factor may have caused the confession, the purely personal circumstances of the defendant *can* be taken into account to determine whether that external factor was likely to render unreliable any confession that the accused might make in consequence. This is so because the accused's personal

---

41   [2001] 1 All ER 57.

42   (1989) 88 Cr App R 285.

43   In similar circumstances s 78 should be used: see *R v Anderson* [1993] Crim LR 447 (chronic alcoholism). But see *R v Walker* [1998] Crim LR 211, where the Court of Appeal appears to have taken the view that the mere interviewing of the suspect is capable of being something 'said or done'.

circumstances are *at that stage* part of what s 76(2)(b) refers to as 'the circumstances existing at the time', in the light of which reliability has to be tested.[44]

For example, in *R v McGovern*,[45] the appellant relied on four grounds for saying that a confession had been made in consequence of things said or done which were likely in the circumstances existing at the time to make any confession unreliable:

(a) The appellant had unlawfully been denied access to a solicitor.

(b) There had been a breach of Code C in relation to notes of the interview.

(c) The appellant was peculiarly vulnerable because of her low IQ and mental age.

(d) The physical condition of the appellant at the time of her interview. She was six months pregnant and had been vomiting in her cell before the interview.

The Court of Appeal remarked that although items (c) and (d) were not within the scope of 'anything said or done', they did form the background upon which the submission was made that the confession was unreliable.

This was another of those cases where the police evidence itself lifts the curtain slightly so that we get a glimpse of another world. This was one of the officers giving evidence on the *voir dire*:

> The lady [meaning the defendant] didn't understand all the questions. She didn't even know why she was in the police station. In the last part of the interview she was crying; she was clearly upset; she was crying heavily. Yes, I carried on questioning her. She was not offered a break to compose herself, not even a glass of water. I never offered her a solicitor until she confessed.[46]

In *R v McGovern*, there was a second interview the following day. This was conducted in accordance with the provisions of Code C and in the presence of a solicitor. The defendant made a full confession. Could the prosecution rely on *that* interview, even if they could not rely on the first? The Court of Appeal said they could not. When an accused person has made a series of admissions at a first interview, the very fact that those admissions have been made is likely to have an effect on the second interview. The second interview must therefore be tainted if the first was.

However, what was said on this point has to be read in the light of *R v Neil*,[47] where the Court of Appeal considered earlier decisions and said that whether a later,

---

44 Because the court will be concerned with the reliability of the confession, which can be affected without improper behaviour by the police, these personal circumstances need not have been known to the police. If they were known and advantage was taken of them there would have been impropriety as well as possible unreliability, and in a serious case there might even have been oppression.

45 (1991) 92 Cr App R 228.

46 (1991) 92 Cr App R 228, 1996, p 233.

47 [1994] Crim LR 441. See also *R v Nelson* [1998] 2 Cr App R 379.

unobjectionable, interview should be excluded is a matter of fact and degree. The answer will depend, first, on whether the matters that led to the exclusion of the earlier interview were of a 'fundamental and continuing nature'. The meaning of this expression is unclear. An example might be where an officer who had used oppression in the first interview also conducted the second. If the matters that led to the exclusion of the earlier interview were not of a fundamental and continuing nature, admissions in the second interview would presumably be admitted. If they were of such a nature, a second question has to be asked: did the arrangements for the later interview give the accused sufficient opportunity to exercise an informed and independent choice about whether to adopt or retract what he had said earlier, or to say nothing?

An argument frequently found in connection with both s 76 and s 78 is that the challenged item of evidence was obtained by breach of the defendant's right to legal advice. There is no doubt that a breach of this right, or of some provision under one of the Codes, counts as something 'said or done' for the purposes of s 76. The right in question is set out in s 58 of PACE.

The fundamental provision, contained in s 58(1), is that a person arrested and held in custody in a police station or other premises shall be entitled, if he so requests, to consult a solicitor privately at any time. By sub-s (4), if a person makes such a request, he must be permitted to consult a solicitor as soon as is practicable unless delay is permitted. In any case, he must be permitted to consult a solicitor within 36 hours from 'the relevant time', which is likely to be the time of arrival at the police station.[48]

Delay is usually permitted only in the case of a person who is in police detention for an indictable offence, and if an officer of at least the rank of superintendant authorises it.[49] The grounds on which delay can be authorised are set out in sub-ss (8) and (8A) as follows:

(8)   Subject to subsection (8A) below an officer may only authorise delay where he has reasonable grounds for believing that the exercise of the right conferred by subsection (1) above at the time when the person detained desires to exercise it –

(a)   will lead to interference with or harm to evidence connected with an indictable offence or interference with or physical injury to other persons; or

(b)   will lead to the alerting of other persons suspected of having committed such an offence but not yet arrested for it; or

(c)   will hinder the recovery of any property obtained as a result of such an offence.

(8A)   An officer may also authorise delay where he has reasonable grounds for believing that –

---

48   See PACE, ss 58(5) and 41(2).

49   Section 58(6). By sub-s (12), nothing in s 58 applies to a person arrested or detained under anti-terrorist legislation. In such cases, other statutory provisions apply.

(a)   the person detained for the indictable offence has benefited from his criminal conduct, and

(b)   the recovery of the value of the property constituting the benefit will be hindered by the exercise of the right conferred by subsection (1) above.

Sub-section (8A) could apply, for example, where a suspect was thought to have committed a fraud to obtain money, which he had subsequently placed in a bank account.

Code C, Annex B, para 3 summarises earlier decisions of the Court of Appeal and provides that authority to delay an arrested person's right to consult privately with a solicitor can be given only if the authorising officer has reasonable grounds to believe that the solicitor the arrested person wants to consult will, inadvertently or otherwise, pass on a message from the arrested person, or act in some other way which will have any of the consequences specified in sub-ss (8) or (8A). In such a case, the arrested person must be allowed to choose another solicitor.

The importance of the right to consult a solicitor was emphasised in *R v Samuel*,[50] where it was described in the judgment of the Court of Appeal as 'one of the most important and fundamental rights of a citizen'. Breach is therefore very likely to lead to the exclusion of a confession, either under s 76 or s 78. An exceptional case is *R v Alladice*.[51] The defendant was convicted of robbery. The prosecution relied on admissions which, according to the defence, should have been excluded because he had been wrongfully denied a solicitor. The Court of Appeal agreed that there had been a breach of s 58, but said that the question then arising was whether the confession had been obtained *as a result of that breach*[52] and, if so, whether that was likely in all the circumstances to render the confession unreliable. The defendant had given evidence on the *voir dire*. He had said that he was well able to cope with interviews, that he had been given the appropriate caution before each of them, that he had understood the caution and had been aware of his rights. His reason for wanting a solicitor had been to have some sort of check on the conduct of the police during the interview. The trial judge concluded that the only difference the presence of a solicitor would have made would have been to provide additional advice as to the appellant's right to say nothing. This right the defendant knew and understood and, at times during the interview, had exercised. The Court of Appeal commented that 'it may seldom happen that a defendant is so forthcoming about his attitude towards the presence of a legal adviser'.[53]

Not surprisingly, the court concluded on these facts that there was no case for exclusion, either under s 76 because of the absence of causation, or under s 78 on the

---

50   [1988] QB 615.

51   (1988) 87 Cr App R 380. See also *R v Gerald* [1999] Crim LR 315.

52   See the wording of s 76(2)(b). There was no suggestion of oppression.

53   (1988) 87 Cr App R 380, p 386.

fairness principle but this kind of situation is rare. It certainly does not follow that a suspect with previous convictions can safely be denied a solicitor because he is supposed to know his rights.[54]

CODES C AND E OF THE PACE CODES OF PRACTICE

These are the Codes most likely to be relevant when considering the admissibility of a confession. Code C is the Code of Practice that governs the detention, treatment and questioning of persons by police officers. Code E governs the procedure to be followed when recording interviews with suspects.[55] These Codes, with others, are issued pursuant to powers conferred by s 66 of PACE. By s 67(9), persons 'who are charged with the duty of investigating offences or charging offenders' and who are not police officers are bound by relevant provisions of the Codes. So, for example, Customs & Excise officers and special compliance officers from the Inland Revenue's investigation branch must conduct their interviews in accordance with the provisions of Code C.[56] This category of persons is not limited to those whose duties are prescribed by statute or who occupy some official position. The question whether or not a particular person comes within s 67(9) can be a question of fact, to be determined by evidence at trial. Where the court has to construe a statute or some other document, such as a contract of employment, it can become a question of law.[57] It may be necessary to have regard to the provisions of Code C even where a particular person is not 'charged with the duty of investigating offences or charging offenders'. In *R v Ristic (RJ)*[58] the Court of Appeal held that a support officer in a prison, who had no investigative role and whose sole duty was to search visitors to the prison on their way in and to assist their departure, should have complied with the provisions of the Code in relation to a conversation that he had overheard between two visitors, even though he was not technically bound by the Code.

The whole of Code C is important, but there are some provisions to which special attention should be given.

By para 1.1, all persons in custody must be dealt with expeditiously, and released as soon as the need for detention no longer applies. Paragraph 8 contains rules governing the physical circumstances of detention. Paragraph 10 deals with the

---

54   The right to legal advice must also be considered in the light of the European Convention on Human Rights, but the impact of the Convention has so far been almost entirely on special provisions contained in anti-terrorist legislation. See *Magee v UK* [2000] Crim LR 681 and *Averill v UK* [2000] Crim LR 682. It also led to the passing of s 34(2A) of the Criminal Justice and Public Order Act 1994: see below, Chapter 11.

55   The current version of Code C (essentially the same as the version that came into force on 1 January 2006, but without references to persons detained under the Terrorism Act 2006) came into force on 25 July 2006. The current version of Code E came into force on 1 January 2006.

56   *R v Sanusi* [1992] Crim LR 43; *R v Gill and Gill* [2003] Crim LR 883.

57   *R v Bayliss* (1993) 98 Cr App R 235.

58   [2004] EWCA Crim 2107.

circumstances in which a caution must be given to a suspect. Paragraphs 11 and 12 are particularly important, as they contain general rules for the conduct of interviews. Note particularly para 11.4 which requires that 'any significant statement or silence' on the part of the suspect which occurred before an interview began should be put to him at the beginning of the interview, so that he can confirm or deny it, or add anything that he wishes. By para 11.13, a written record must be made of any comments of a suspect which are made outside an interview and might be relevant to the offence under investigation. The suspect should, where practicable, be given the opportunity to read this record and sign it as correct, or to indicate how he considers it to be inaccurate. By para 12.2, in any period of 24 hours a suspect must generally be allowed a continuous period of at least eight hours for rest. By para 12.6, suspects must not be required to stand while being questioned and, by para 12.8, there should be breaks from interviewing at recognised meal times, and short refreshment breaks approximately every two hours. There are special provisions for juveniles, mentally disordered persons, and some disabled persons. Annex B, concerning the power to delay access to legal advice, is also particularly important.

SECTION 78(1) OF PACE

Section 78(1) provides:

> In any proceedings the court may refuse to allow evidence on which the prosecution proposes to rely to be given if it appears to the court that, having regard to all the circumstances, including the circumstances in which the evidence was obtained, the admission of the evidence would have such an adverse effect on the fairness of the proceedings that the court ought not to admit it.

INTERPRETATION

There are several points to be made about the interpretation of this provision:

(a) 'In any proceedings': 'proceedings' means criminal proceedings, whether in the Crown Court or in magistrates' courts.[59]

(b) 'The court may refuse to allow evidence . . . to be given': the idea of discretion appears at first sight to be expressed in two ways. Section 78(1) provides that, in the circumstances subsequently set out, 'the court *may* refuse to allow evidence on which the prosecution proposes to rely to be given . . .' (emphasis added). Those circumstances are where 'the admission of the evidence would have such an adverse effect on the fairness of the proceedings *that the court ought not to admit it*' (emphasis

---

59   See s 82(1) and *R v King's Lynn JJ ex p Holland* (1993) 96 Cr App R 74.

added). It seems curious that, if the court decides that these circumstances exist, there should remain any room for the exercise of further discretion. On this view, in the opening words of the sub-section, 'may' means 'shall'. This approach has now been adopted by the Court of Appeal.[60]

(c) 'Evidence on which the prosecution proposes to rely': the evidence must not have been admitted already. In *R v Sat-Bhambra*,[61] it was only after evidence of a confession had been given, and further evidence had been heard, that application was made for the confession to be excluded. The Court of Appeal held that at that stage it was too late for either s 76 or s 78 to apply; the wording of both sections shows that the court's power exists only where the evidence in question has not yet been given. Section 76 contemplates a situation where 'the prosecution *proposes to give in evidence* a confession by an accused person', and s 78 contemplates a situation where evidence on which the prosecution '*proposes to rely*' has yet to be given.[62] But even if ss 76 and 78 are unavailable because the evidence has already been admitted, a judge still has the common law powers, preserved by s 82(3), to exclude evidence where the prejudicial effect exceeds its probative value.[63]

(d) 'Such an adverse effect on the fairness of the proceedings that the court ought not to admit it':

■ It is not enough that the admission of the evidence will have *some* adverse effect; the adverse effect must be so great that the court ought not to admit the evidence. So you can have an adverse effect on the fairness of the proceedings that is not substantial enough to lead to exclusion.[64]

■ In some cases the suggestion has been made that the 'fairness of the proceedings' refers only to that part of the criminal proceedings taking place in court.[65] But in *R v Looseley*[66] Lord Nicholls, while allowing

---

60   *R v Middlebrook* (1994) unreported; *R v Chalkley and Jeffries* [1998] 2 All ER 155, p 178.

61   (1989) 88 Cr App R 55.

62   In *R v Sat-Bhambra*, the problem was solved by relying on s 82(3), which preserves the common law power to exclude prosecution evidence. See below.

63   This was the solution adopted in *R v Sat-Bhambra* (1989) 88 Cr App R 55. In *R v Parris (MA)* [2003] EWCA Crim 3734, para 13, the Court appears to have taken a broader view of the availability of s 78, saying that it is the judge's continuing duty under that provision to exclude any evidence if it is unfair, whatever stage may have been reached in the trial. *Sat-Bhambra* was not referred to, and there appears to have been no argument on the matter.

64   *R v Walsh* (1990) 91 Cr App R 161.

65   *R v Mason* (1988) 86 Cr App R 349, p 354; *DPP v Marshall* [1988] 3 All ER 683, p 688.

66   [2001] 4 All ER 897, p 902.

that the expression was 'directed primarily at matters going to fairness in the actual conduct of the trial', such as the reliability of the evidence, said that 'rightly, the courts have been unwilling to limit the scope of this wide and comprehensive expression strictly to procedural fairness'. In the same case, Lord Scott acknowledged that 'the fairness of a trial may be compromised if the prosecution is allowed to rely on evidence obtained by unfair means'.[67]

■ It is fairness of the *proceedings* that the judge has to consider. Fairness to the defendant is part of this, but the section is not directed solely towards fairness to the defendant. Fairness of the proceedings requires the judge to take into account fairness to the prosecution as well as to the defence. In *R v O'Loughlin*,[68] Kenneth Jones J said in relation to s 78(1): 'I therefore have to balance matters having regard, on the one hand, to the interests of the defendant; on the other hand, to the interests of the public as represented by the prosecution.'[69] This conveys something of the right idea, but is misleading in that it ranges public interest solely on the side of the prosecution. It is obvious today, even if in 1987 it was not, that the public has a significant interest in the avoidance of wrongful convictions.

EXERCISE OF THE DISCRETION

The Court of Appeal has given trial judges a very free hand in their operation of s 78(1) and subjects their decisions to a minimum of review. In *R v Samuel*,[70] the Court of Appeal said that it was undesirable to attempt any general guidance as to the way in which a judge's discretion under s 78 should be exercised because circumstances varied infinitely. In *R v Jelen and Katz*,[71] the Court of Appeal made the same point, saying that this was not an apt field for hard case law and well founded distinctions between cases. More recently, in *R v Sanghera*,[72] Lord Woolf said that it was important to consider each particular case on its facts and to make no broad generalisations about the application of s 78.

It is now clear that a judge's exercise of discretion under this provision can be faulted only on the basis of '*Wednesbury* unreasonableness'.[73] This is a concept drawn from administrative law and is based on the decision in *Associated Provincial Picture*

---

67   [2001] 4 All ER 897, pp 931–32.

68   (1987) 85 Cr App R 157. See also, eg, *R v Cooke* [1995] 1 Cr App R 318, p 328.

69   *Ibid, O'Loughlin*, p 163.

70   [1988] QB 615.

71   (1989) 90 Cr App R 456, pp 464–65; approved in *R v Roberts* [1997] 1 Cr App R 217, p 231.

72   [2001] Crim LR 480.

73   *R v Christou* [1992] 1 QB 979, p 989; *R v Rankin* (1995) *The Times*, 5 September; *R v McCarthy* [1996] Crim LR 818; *R v McEvoy* [1997] Crim LR 887.

Houses v Wednesbury Corp.[74] This case decided that where an authority had a discretion, the courts, in the absence of error in law or fact, could interfere with its exercise only if the decision made in exercise of the discretion was so unreasonable that no reasonable authority could ever have made it. Under this principle, 'the court does not decide what the reasonable authority *would* do, but only what no reasonable authority *could* do. In other words, a court should not strike down a decision . . . on substantive grounds just because it does not agree with it'. In practice, however, in the field of administrative law 'it seems clear that even when a court purports to quash a decision because it is "*Wednesbury* unreasonable", it may be applying a standard of unreasonableness less stringent than that specified'.[75] Michael Zander has noted that 'as a matter of impression' the Court of Appeal seems readier to take a different view from that adopted by the trial judge than in some other areas of law where the *Wednesbury* principle is relevant.[76] In practice, therefore, it may be slightly easier to overturn a trial judge's decision than the words of the judges in the Court of Appeal suggest.

Different considerations apply where the judge fails to exercise his discretion at all: for example, where he takes the view that there has been no breach of the Code when in fact there has. The Court of Appeal can then exercise the discretion in his place.[77]

Perhaps a good way of explaining the concept of unfairness embodied in s 78(1) is to compare it with a similar provision in a different area of law. In the administration of a company under the Insolvency Act 1986 a judge may have to decide in an application under s 27(1) of that Act whether the company's affairs are being managed 'in a manner which is unfairly prejudicial' to the interests of some part of its creditors. In *Re Charnley Davies Ltd (No 2)*, Millett J said that the concept of unfairly prejudicial management was a matter of perspective. The appropriate metaphor was 'not a supermarket trolley but a hologram'.[78] This metaphor fits the concept of unfairness under s 78 as well.

What Millett J meant was that there are at least two radically different ways of determining whether a particular legal state of affairs exists. With some you have a shopping list of items, and when you have collected them all you have a particular state of affairs. Has there been theft? You apply the checklist contained in s 1 of the Theft Act 1968. Has there been an appropriation of property belonging to another? Was it dishonest? Was there an intention to deprive permanently? To establish negligence in a civil action you push your trolley round the supermarket in a similar

---

74   [1948] 1 KB 223.
75   Cane, 1992, pp 208–09.
76   Zander, 1995, p 245.
77   *R v Samuel* [1988] QB 615.
78   [1990] BCLC 760, p 783. I am indebted to Mark Phillips QC for this reference.

way, taking a duty of care from one shelf, breach from another, causation from a third and loss and damage from a fourth.

However, a court that is looking to see if there has been unfairly prejudicial management in an application under the Insolvency Act, or a sufficiently adverse effect on the fairness of the proceedings under s 78(1) of PACE, approaches the problem in quite a different way. Now there is no shopping list to be checked or supermarket trolley to be filled. Instead, there are all the circumstances, which, like a hologram, have to be viewed from one point and then another. It is, as Millett J said, all a matter of perspective. From the standpoint of one set of creditors, there will appear to have been unfairly prejudicial management, but if you take the standpoint of other creditors there will not. From the standpoint of a defendant in a criminal trial, the admission of some evidence may well appear to have such an adverse effect on the fairness of the proceedings that it ought to be excluded. From the standpoint of others with an interest in the proceedings, things may appear very differently.

Having said that, there are some general points that can still be made about the exercise of the discretion under s 78(1):

(a) According to the Court of Appeal in *R v Anderson*,[79] it is not entirely clear where the burden of proof lies on all the issues raised by the sub-section. But at least it seems clear from the decision of the Divisional Court in *Vel v Owen*[80] that the prosecution does not have a burden to disprove unfairness in the way that it has a burden to disprove matters relied on by the defence under s 76. However, in *R v Stagg*,[81] very experienced prosecuting counsel accepted that it was for the prosecution to demonstrate either that there was no unfairness, or that its degree did not warrant the exclusion of the evidence.

(b) Although the sub-section would not be one's *first* choice for the exclusion of a confession (because of the burden placed on the prosecution by s 76), it has frequently been relied on by the courts in connection with this sort of evidence. It may be particularly helpful where you want to exclude a confession for unreliability but cannot point to anything said or done by someone other than the defendant so as to trigger s 76.

A good example is *R v Brine*.[82] In that case, the defendant, who suffered from stress, was accused of indecent assault on a child. He was interviewed with his solicitor present for five hours and made no admissions. After the solicitor had left, he did make some admissions and

---

79   [1993] Crim LR 447.
80   [1987] Crim LR 496.
81   (1994) unreported, 14 September. See further *R (Saifi) v Governor of Brixton Prison and Another* [2001] 1 WLR 1134.
82   [1992] Crim LR 122.

was interviewed further. The total interview time was eight hours. There had been breaches of Code C because of insufficient breaks in questioning and the provision of insufficient meals, but none of these breaches was attributed to deliberate misconduct by the police and, in any case, there was no causal link between these breaches and the defendant's confessions.

The defence called a psychologist on the *voir dire* who said that the defendant, when making his admissions, had been suffering from a mild form of paranoid psychosis. The effect of this condition was that the defendant would have felt very threatened and would have been likely to tell lies and make untrue admissions. In his opinion the confession was unreliable, but the police had not known of the defendant's condition, and the trial judge took the view that because there was no improper conduct which had caused the defendant to make his admissions, there was no room for exclusion under s 76, or, apparently, under s 78.

The Court of Appeal, however, said that s 78 was certainly available in circumstances where, although the police had behaved properly, the defendant's psychological condition made his confession unreliable. For this reason, to admit evidence of the confession would have had such an adverse effect on the fairness of the proceedings that the court ought not to have admitted it. Thus, no external element is *essential* to trigger the operation of the sub-section; in this respect it differs importantly from s 76.

(c) A breach of one of the Codes may *help* to get evidence excluded under s 78(1). The importance of the Codes was emphasised by the Court of Appeal in *R v Elson*:[83] they are there to protect the individual against the might of the State. The individual, the court added, is at a great disadvantage when arrested by the police, and this is so whether or not the police behave with the utmost propriety.

But Code breach will not lead to *automatic* exclusion.[84] This was made clear in *R v Keenan*[85] where there had been breaches of provisions of Code C in relation to recording and authenticating interviews. Hodgson J said in the Court of Appeal that, in cases where there had been 'significant and substantial' breaches of the 'verballing' provisions of the Code, evidence would frequently be excluded, but not every breach, or combination of breaches, of the Code would justify exclusion. The courts

---

83   (1994) *The Times*, 30 June.

84   It would be absurd, eg, to argue that evidence should be excluded because the suspect's period of rest lasted seven hours and 55 minutes instead of eight hours. (See Code C, para 12.2.)

85   [1989] 3 All ER 598. See also *R v Kelly* (1998) *The Times*, 23 February, in relation to breaches of Code D.

should not undertake the task of punishing the police for failure to observe the Codes. This approach was reflected in *R v Senior*,[86] where the Court of Appeal held that there had been a 'significant and substantial' breach of Code C: 10.1 in relation to the cautioning of suspects, but held also that on the facts there had been no unfairness that required exclusion under s 78 of the suspects' answers to questions.

An argument for exclusion based on Code breach may have to consider whether the provision relied on did in fact apply. The position of the person who has not been arrested, but who is 'assisting the police with their inquiries', is problematic.

Note 1A of Code C states:

> Although certain sections of this Code apply specifically to people in custody at police stations, those there voluntarily to assist with an investigation should be treated with no less consideration, eg, offered refreshments at appropriate times, and enjoy an absolute right to obtain legal advice or communicate with anyone outside the police station.

Two questions arise here:

- Does 'should' govern 'enjoy an absolute right', so that it expresses a mere wish? Or does 'should' govern only 'be treated with no less consideration', so that the note appears to be declaratory of an existing right to obtain legal advice or communicate with someone outside the police station?
- In either case, what is the status of a note for guidance in the Code?

The answer to the second question appears clearly at para 1.3, which says that the notes are *not* provisions of the Code. However, there are parts of the Code that must apply to persons not yet arrested as well as to those who have been: para 10 (dealing with the caution) is an obvious example. Paragraphs 3.21 and 3.22 deal specifically with persons attending a police station voluntarily to assist with an investigation.

In *R v Christou*,[87] there are *dicta* supporting an argument that a person not yet arrested has the protection of the Code. Lord Taylor said:

> In our view, although the Code extends beyond the treatment of those in detention, what is clear is that it was intended to protect suspects who are vulnerable to abuse or pressure from police officers or who may believe themselves to be so. Frequently, the suspect will be a detainee. But the Code will also apply where a suspect, not in detention, is being questioned about an offence by a police officer

---

86   [2004] 3 All ER 9, p 19. See also *R v Armas-Rodriguez* [2005] EWCA Crim 1081.
87   [1992] 1 QB 979.

acting as a police officer for the purpose of obtaining evidence. In that situation, the officer and the suspect are not on equal terms. The officer is perceived to be in a position of authority; the suspect may be intimidated or undermined.[88]

EVIDENCE OBTAINED BY A TRICK

In addition to these general points about the operation of s 78(1), one particular topic requires consideration: the application of the sub-section where evidence has been obtained by a trick.[89] For example, in *R v Bailey*,[90] two suspects, who had exercised their rights to silence in police interviews, were placed together in a bugged police cell after the police had pretended to be unwilling to leave them together. Their subsequent incriminating conversation was recorded and later held admissible in evidence. The judge's decision was upheld by the Court of Appeal, which observed, however, that such methods were to be used only in grave cases, and where there was no suggestion of oppression or unreliability. In *R v Mason*,[91] however, the police trick was too much for the Court of Appeal. In that case, a police officer had lied to a suspect and to his solicitor about the existence of incriminating evidence. It was held that the suspect's subsequent confession should have been excluded.

The use of intrusive surveillance devices, such as telephone tapping or bugging, has sometimes given rise to submissions based on s 78(1). Here again the European Convention may be relevant. Article 8 provides as follows:

1   Everyone has the right to respect for his private and family life, his home and his correspondence.

2   There shall be no interference by a public authority with the exercise of this right except such as is in accordance with the law and is necessary in a democratic society in the interests of national security, public safety or the economic wellbeing of the country, for the prevention of disorder or crime, for the protection of health or morals, or for the protection of the rights or freedoms of others.

In *Khan v UK*,[92] the European Court had to consider the case of an applicant in the following circumstances. The applicant had been sentenced to imprisonment for drug dealing on the basis of evidence improperly obtained by a listening device attached by police to a private house without the knowledge of the owners or occupiers. The applicant's appeal against conviction was ultimately dismissed by the House of Lords.[93] Lord Nolan said that there were two separate issues involved in

---

88   [1992] 1 QB 979, p 991.
89   See Birch, 1994; Noorlander, 1998; Ashworth, 2002.
90   [1993] 3 All ER 513.
91   [1988] 1 WLR 139.
92   [2000] Crim LR 684.
93   *R v Khan (Sultan)* [1997] AC 558.

the appeal. First, was the evidence admissible at all? Secondly, if it was, should it have been excluded, either under the judge's common law discretion or under s 78(1)?[94] On the first issue, the House of Lords held that there was no right to privacy in English law. Even if there had been, the common law rule was that evidence obtained improperly, or even unlawfully, could still be admitted. On the second issue, it was held that the fact that evidence had been obtained in breach of Art 8 of the Convention was *relevant* to the exercise of the judge's discretion under s 78(1), but did not *determine* the way in which that discretion should be exercised. On the facts, the trial judge had been entitled to conclude that s 78(1) did not require exclusion. In due course, it was argued for the applicant before the European Court that there had been a breach of his right to a fair trial under Art 6(1) of the Convention in that there had been a breach of his rights under Art 8.

The European Court held that his rights under Art 8 had been violated because UK domestic law did not at the relevant time regulate the use of covert listening devices. The interference with the applicant's rights had thus not been 'in accordance with the law', as required by Art 8(2), but a majority of the Court held that a violation of Art 6(1) had not been established. The Court relied on earlier decisions[95] to the effect that it would not decide as a matter of principle that unlawfully obtained evidence should never be admissible. Although, in this case, the recording was in effect the only evidence against the applicant, there was no risk of its being unreliable. The need for supporting evidence was therefore weaker. The central question was whether the proceedings as a whole were fair. The applicant had had ample opportunity to challenge both the authenticity and the use of the recording. He had not challenged its authenticity and the evidence could have been excluded under s 78(1).

The use of covert surveillance devices is now regulated by Pt III of the Police Act 1997 and the Regulation of Investigatory Powers Act 2000, but neither statute deals with the admissibility of evidence obtained in breach of its provisions. Such breaches are likely also to entail breaches of Art 8 of the European Convention, but it does not follow that evidence thereby obtained will inevitably be excluded. As appears from *Khan v UK*,[96] the European Court has taken a broad approach to Art 6(1), and this is reflected in the Court of Appeal's approach to s 78(1).[97]

Other problems have arisen in connection with evidence obtained by 'entrapment'. The leading common law authority on this subject before the Police and

---

94 *R v Khan (Sultan)* [1997] AC 558, p 573. For the common law discretion, see the reference to *R v Sang* [1980] AC 402 below.

95 Such as *Schenk v Switzerland* (1988) 13 EHRR 242 and *Teixeira de Castro v Portugal* [1998] 4 BHRC 533.

96 [2000] Crim LR 684.

97 See also *R v Mason and Others* [2002] 2 Cr App R 628; *PG and JH v UK* [2002] Crim LR 308; *Perry v UK* [2003] Crim LR 280.

Criminal Evidence Act 1984 was the decision of the House of Lords in *R v Sang*.[98] The defendant had been charged with conspiring to utter counterfeit American bank notes. He pleaded not guilty and, in the absence of the jury, alleged through his counsel that he had been induced to commit the offence by an informer, who had been acting on police instructions. In the absence of that inducement, he would not have committed any offence of the kind with which he was charged. His counsel acknowledged that the trial judge was bound by recent decisions of the Court of Appeal to the effect that entrapment was not a defence to a criminal charge. But he went on to submit that if the judge was satisfied at a 'trial within a trial' that the facts relied on by the defendant were true, he would have a discretion to exclude prosecution evidence that had been obtained in such a way. The trial judge ruled that even if the facts were as alleged, he had no such discretion. The House of Lords reaffirmed the rule that entrapment was not a defence under English law. On the judicial discretion to exclude prosecution evidence, Lord Diplock stated the law in this way:

(1) A trial judge in a criminal trial has always a discretion to refuse to admit [prosecution] evidence if in his opinion its prejudicial effect outweighs its probative value.

(2) Save with regard to admissions and confessions and generally with regard to evidence obtained from the accused after the commission of the offence, he has no discretion to refuse to admit relevant admissible evidence on the ground that it was obtained by improper or unfair means. The court is not concerned with how it was obtained. It is no ground for the exercise of discretion to exclude that the evidence was obtained as the result of the activities of an *agent provocateur*.[99]

Although a more liberal approach to the use of discretion can be seen in the speech of Lord Scarman, *R v Sang* was generally regarded as authority for the propositions stated by Lord Diplock.[100]

It remains the case that entrapment is not a defence to a criminal charge, but English criminal law developed in important respects during the period after *Sang*.[101] First came s 78(1) of PACE. In *R v Smurthwaite*[102] the Court of Appeal, though holding on the facts of that case that there had been no entrapment, clearly took the view that s 78(1) had widened the judicial discretion to exclude prosecution evidence, and that there might be cases where evidence obtained by entrapment should be excluded. The court suggested relevant considerations, some of which were clearly

---

98   [1980] AC 402.

99   *Ibid*, p 437.

100   But see Polyviou, 1981, pp 226–47.

101   See the speech of Lord Nicholls in *R v Looseley* [2001] 4 All ER 897, pp 902–03.

102   (1994) 98 Cr App R 437, p 440.

concerned with the reliability of evidence obtained in this way, but others of which were concerned with ensuring that the integrity of the criminal process was not damaged by executive abuse of power. Next, the common law was developed when the House of Lords, in *Bennett v Horseferry Road Magistrates' Court*,[103] held that courts have jurisdiction to stay proceedings for abuse of process, and to order the defendant's release, where there has been a serious abuse of power by the executive from which the prosecution wants to take an advantage. In *R v Latif and Shahzad*[104] the House of Lords held that the principle established in Bennett was applicable where there had been entrapment.

These statutory and common law developments were reinforced by the Human Rights Act 1998. It is clear that evidence obtained by entrapment is capable of depriving a defendant of his right to a fair trial under Art 6 of the European Convention. In *Teixeira de Castro v Portugal*,[105] the European Court of Human Rights had to consider the application of a person who had been convicted of drug dealing in the following circumstances. The applicant had no previous criminal record and had been previously unknown to the police. A third party introduced him to two undercover police officers, who told him that they wanted to buy a quantity of heroin. The applicant bought the drugs for them. He was convicted on the evidence of the undercover officers.

The Court held that, in these circumstances, there had been a violation of the applicant's right to a fair trial under Art 6(1). The public interest could not justify the use of evidence obtained as a result of police incitement. There had been no evidence that the applicant was predisposed to crime, nor were the police acting in the course of an officially authorised investigation. The officers had incited the commission of an offence that would not have been committed without their intervention. The Court distinguished the facts of this case from the situation where an undercover officer tries to buy drugs from someone known to be already engaged in selling.

The leading case on entrapment is now the decision of the House of Lords in *R v Looseley*.[106] In this case the appellant had been convicted of supplying a class A drug on the basis of evidence which, it was argued, should have been excluded because it had been obtained by entrapment. In the course of their speeches, the Law Lords discussed the circumstances in which entrapment could lead to the exclusion of evidence or a stay of proceedings.

Entrapment occurs when an agent of the State, usually a law enforcement officer or an informer under his control, causes someone to commit an offence in

---

103   [1994] 1 AC 42.
104   [1996] 2 Cr App R 92.
105   [1998] Crim LR 751.
106   [2001] 4 All ER 897.

order that he should be prosecuted.[107] Entrapment is to be discouraged for two principal reasons. First, the courts have a duty 'to stand between the state and its citizens' in order to prevent oppression of the latter.[108] Secondly, the courts have a duty not to allow their own proceedings to be abused by executive agents of the State, because to permit such abuse would bring the administration of justice into disrepute,[109] or would constitute an affront to the public conscience.[110] However, in competition with the need to avoid this kind of abuse of process is the need to convict and punish those who have committed crimes. The two needs have to be balanced, and this means that in deciding whether there has been entrapment it will be necessary to take various factors into account in each case. The weight given to each factor will depend on the particular facts under consideration.[111]

How is the line to be drawn between legitimate undercover investigation and entrapment? Some have suggested that the answer lies in the role adopted by the police.[112] If the defendant has already formed the general intention to commit a crime of the same or of a similar kind, it is unobjectionable if undercover police do no more than give him the opportunity to carry out his intention. It is otherwise if the defendant lacked that intention initially, and developed it only as a result of police inducement. But a general intention on the part of a defendant to commit an offence of a certain type will not always be decisive; there can be misuse of State power even where such an intention exists.[113] Just as the question of entrapment cannot be resolved simply by asking whether the defendant was given the opportunity to commit an offence, of which he freely took advantage, so it is not helpful to apply a test that attempts to distinguish between 'active' and 'passive' conduct on the part of the police. For example, in cases in which the offence involves the purchase of goods or services it would be absurd to expect the test purchaser to wait silently for an offer. He must do what an ordinary purchaser would do, and the fact that his actions are technically unlawful (as counselling, procuring, or inciting the commission of an offence) is not of itself a ground for treating them as an abuse of power.[114]

A useful guide is to consider whether the police did no more than present the defendant with an ordinary opportunity to commit an offence. Was the police conduct that preceded the offence no more than might have been expected from others in the circumstances? But the greater the inducement held out by the police, and the more forceful or persistent their overtures, the more likely will be a finding of

---

107   [2001] 4 All ER 897, p 907, *per* Lord Hoffmann.

108   *Ibid,* pp 889–90, *per* Lord Nicholls.

109   *Ibid,* p 910, *per* Lord Hoffmann.

110   *Ibid,* p 910, *per* Lord Hoffmann; p 924, *per* Lord Hutton; p 931, *per* Lord Scott.

111   *Ibid,* p 910, *per* Lord Hoffmann; p 924, *per* Lord Hutton.

112   References to the police in this context should be taken to include informers acting as their agents.

113   *Ibid,* p 904, *per* Lord Nicholls; pp 910–11, *per* Lord Hoffmann.

114   *Ibid,* p 915, *per* Lord Hoffmann.

entrapment. Regard must be given in this connection to the particular defendant's circumstances, including his vulnerability. What is a significant inducement to one person may not be so to another.[115] Thus in *Nottingham CC v Amin*,[116] where the defendant had been charged with plying for hire as a taxi driver without a licence, the Divisional Court held that it had been proper for plainclothes police to have flagged him down, to have asked to be taken to a named destination, and to have paid when the journey ended. It might have been different if they had waved £50 notes or pretended to be in distress. But the difficulty with applying this test to all cases is that while ordinary members of the public become involved in regulatory offences, such as plying for hire without a taxi driver's licence, selling liquor in unlicensed quantities, or selling videos to children who are under age, they do not become involved in more serious offences such as large scale drug dealing or conspiracy to rob. The appropriate standards of behaviour for undercover officers in such cases are therefore more difficult to assess.[117]

In the case of some regulatory offences, the law could not be effective unless enforcement officers are able to make random tests. But normally it will not be proper for police to provide people not suspected of being engaged in any criminal activity with the opportunity to commit crimes. The only proper purpose of police participation is to obtain evidence of criminal acts which they suspect someone is about to commit, or in which he is already engaged; it is not to tempt people to commit crimes in order to expose their bad characters and punish them. So, for example, it would be wrong for an officer who wanted to increase his record of successful arrests to plant a wallet with money in an obvious location in a park, hoping to catch someone weak enough to steal it. But the requirement of reasonable suspicion does not mean that there must always be suspicion of the particular person who happens to commit the offence. A decoy, human or inanimate, can properly be used in the course of the detection of crime that has been prevalent in a particular place. For example, it would be legitimate for police to plant a handbag in a bus terminal where numerous thefts have recently taken place. The fact that the defendant who is caught may not previously have been suspected, or even have thought of offending, is immaterial.[118]

The fact that a suspect has previous convictions for the type of offence being investigated will not by itself justify the use of covert operations against him.

---

115   [2001] 4 All ER 897, pp 905–06, *per* Lord Nicholls.

116   [2000] 2 All ER 946.

117   *R v Looseley* [2001] 4 All ER 897, p 912, *per* Lord Hoffmann.

118   *Ibid*, pp 905, 912–14. Lord Hoffmann gives *Williams v DPP* [1993] 3 All ER 365 as an example of the legitimate use of a decoy. Police were investigating thefts from vehicles in Essex. They left an unattended van with the back door open and cartons of cigarettes visible. When the appellants stole the cigarettes, they were arrested. According to Lord Hoffmann, if the trick had been the individual enterprise of a policeman in an area where such crime was not prevalent, it would have been an abuse of State power. It was justified because it was an authorised investigation into actual crime.

Additional material pointing to his involvement will be needed. The fact that a person is a drug addict, and therefore likely to know a supplier, will not by itself be a sufficient ground for tempting him to move altogether outside his usual way of life and act as intermediary in the supply of a substantial quantity of drugs. It may be possible to justify such tactics for the purpose of securing the prosecution and conviction of the supplier, but not of the intermediary.[119]

Whether the undercover action was supervised is an important consideration. 'To allow policemen or controlled informers to undertake entrapment activities unsupervised carries great danger, not merely that they will try to improve their performances in court,[120] but of oppression, extortion and corruption.'[121]

The justification of entrapment will depend partly on the nature of the offence being investigated. The fact that the offence is a serious one is not by itself sufficient, but where it is difficult to obtain evidence because of the nature of the offence, entrapment methods are likely to be justified. Examples are consensual offences, such as dealing in drugs; offences with no immediate victim, such as bribery; and offences which victims are reluctant to report.[122]

THE RATIONALE OF S 78(1)

A submission about the application of a statutory provision is always helped if it can be shown that the rationale of the provision is relevant to the facts in question. Unfortunately, the rationale of s 78(1) and cases involving its application show that judicial attitudes to the discretion have been intuitive: there has been little if any attempt to apply analysis to the operation of the sub-section. At this stage I want to suggest an approach that may be helpful in argument.

At the root of s 78(1) is the idea that the admission of certain evidence is capable of adversely affecting the fairness of the proceedings. It is clear from the sub-section that the court is required to assume that the fairness of the proceedings is not an all-or-nothing affair, but something that may be affected by degrees. The court is directed to attend to 'all the circumstances', but specifically to 'the circumstances in which the evidence was obtained', when considering the exercise of the discretion. Some guidance about ideas of fairness that can be used in interpreting the sub-section can be obtained from these directions.

It is beyond controversy that one of the objects of our criminal trials is to secure rectitude of decision – the right answer – and a criminal trial will therefore cease to be fair to the extent that the likelihood of attaining this end diminishes. So one way in which the fairness of the proceedings can be adversely affected is by inviting the jury

---

119   *R v Looseley* [2001] 4 All ER 897, p 906, *per* Lord Nicholls; p 914, *per* Lord Hoffmann.
120   By boosting their record of achieving convictions.
121   *R v Looseley* [2001] 4 All ER 897, p 913, *per* Lord Hoffmann.
122   *Ibid,* p 905, *per* Lord Nicholls; p 914, *per* Lord Hoffmann.

to convict on the basis of unreliable evidence. Many cases show the significance of reliability when considering the s 78(1) discretion.

In *R v O'Connor*,[123] for example, the Court of Appeal held that the trial judge ought to have excluded, under s 78(1), evidence of a former co-accused's conviction for conspiring with the defendant. The reason was that the effect of admitting this evidence had been to enable the prosecution to put before the jury a statement, made by the former co-accused in the absence of the defendant, without having the maker of the statement available for cross-examination. Similarly, in *R v O'Loughlin*,[124] it was held that had the depositions of certain absent witnesses been admissible, they should have been excluded under s 78(1) because, although they were probative of guilt, the jury would have had little or no guidance in deciding what weight should be attached to them.

Evidence that might ordinarily be reliable may be made unreliable by the way in which it has been obtained, and s 78(1) has been used to exclude it in these circumstances. In *R v Keenan*,[125] for example, it was said that the provisions of Code C, ensuring that interviews were fully recorded and the suspect given an opportunity to check the record, should be strictly followed, and that the courts should not be slow to exclude evidence following substantial breaches by the interrogator. The importance of the reliability of evidence in exercising the power under s 78(1) can be seen from many cases. It was highly significant, as we have seen, in *R v Khan*.

It may be difficult to present an argument based on fairness where evidence has been improperly obtained but is nevertheless reliable. Some cases appear to suggest that, provided reliability has not been impaired by the impropriety, any unfairness will not be substantial enough to lead to exclusion. *R v Khan*[126] is an example. Other cases besides *R v Khan* suggest that the courts regard drug dealing as an offence that threatens the fabric of society,[127] and in such cases it is not surprising to find crime control values winning in any struggle with process values. A similar approach was taken in *R v Cooke*.[128] In this case, rape and kidnapping were alleged, and the question arose whether s 78(1) should be used to exclude evidence of a sample of hair, because it might have been improperly taken from the defendant. The Court of Appeal agreed with the trial judge's decision to admit the evidence, regardless of any possible assault on the defendant. The court pointed out that the vast majority of cases under s 78(1) concerned confessions obtained in breach of Code C. In such cases, the impropriety involved in obtaining the confession affected its reliability as an incriminating item of evidence. But in this case, the evidence was of a different nature. The reliability of

---

123   (1987) 85 Cr App R 298.
124   (1987) 85 Cr App R 157.
125   [1989] 3 All ER 598.
126   [1996] 2 Cr App R 440.
127   See also, eg, *R v Latif and Shahzad* [1996] 2 Cr App R 92.
128   [1995] 1 Cr App R 318.

the DNA tests, which strongly supported the prosecution case, was unaffected by the impropriety of the way in which the sample had been obtained.

In both these cases, a serious crime was alleged and, once it was clear that any impropriety had not affected reliability, the evidence was admitted. But the importance of reliability for admissibility has been shown in far less serious cases. In *R v Stewart*,[129] the defendant was convicted of abstracting electricity and stealing gas. Electricity company officials, accompanied by police, entered the defendant's house in circumstances that were arguably unlawful. There they found a mechanical apparatus used to bypass the meters. The Court of Appeal held that it was unnecessary to decide about the lawfulness of the entry. Even assuming there had been breaches of Code B, the admission of the evidence had not had any effect on the fairness of the proceedings because the apparatus had been there for all to see, whether the entry had been unlawful or not. It was quite a different case from one involving evidence of admissions where there had been a breach of Code C. The basis of the distinction was clearly that in this case, unlike the case of an admission obtained through a breach of Code C, there was no doubt about the reliability of the evidence.

So is reliability the *sole* consideration under s 78? A significant number of decisions show that it is not, and that the operation of s 78(1) can best be understood if 'fairness of the proceedings' takes into account justifiability as well. Rectitude of decision is necessary, but it is also necessary to be able to justify the decision to the defendant and to the public at large. This cannot be done if the verdict rests on reliable evidence that has been obtained by iniquitous means. 'Apparently reliable evidence may need to be excluded if it carries significant risks of impairing the moral authority of the verdict.'[130]

An obstacle, though not an insuperable one, in the way of this approach is the unfortunate decision of the Court of Appeal in *R v Chalkley and Jeffries*.[131] The defendants had been charged with conspiracy to rob. At trial, the prosecution wished to rely on covertly obtained tape recordings of conversations between them. To obtain these recordings, the police had arrested Chalkley and his partner in connection with another matter, and in their absence had entered their house and planted a listening device. The Court of Appeal later found that this other matter was not a 'trumped up' allegation, although neither Chalkley nor his partner was ever charged in respect of it. At the trial of Chalkley and Jeffries for conspiracy to rob, the judge was asked to exclude the taped conversations under s 78(1). He looked for guidance to cases relating to the dismissal of prosecutions for abuse of process, and concluded that he should conduct a balancing exercise with the circumstances. Did the balance come down in favour of the effective prosecution of crime? Or did it

---

129   [1995] Crim LR 500.

130   Dennis, 1989, pp 35–44. See also Duff, 1986, pp 99–143.

131   [1998] 2 All ER 155.

favour instead the public interest in discouraging abuse of police power? Having conducted this exercise, he decided to admit the evidence. The defendants, solely as a result of this ruling, changed their pleas to guilty. They then appealed. The primary question that the Court of Appeal had to consider was whether it had power to quash a conviction based on a plea of guilty in these circumstances. The court held that it had not.

That was enough to decide the appeal. Nevertheless, the court went on to consider the arguments that had been put forward in relation to s 78(1). It concluded that there was no basis for the submission that admitting the tapes would have had such an adverse effect on the fairness of the proceedings that they ought to have been excluded. Accordingly, the appeals were dismissed on that ground also. However, the court also disapproved of the way in which the trial judge had reached the same conclusion, and made further observations about the scope and effect of s 78(1). In particular, the court said that the reference to 'the circumstances in which the evidence was obtained' was not intended to widen the common law rule stated by Lord Diplock in *R v Sang*.[132] Save in the case of admissions and confessions and generally as to evidence obtained after the commission of the offence, there was no discretion to exclude evidence unless its quality was or might have been affected by the way in which it was obtained. The trial judge had therefore been wrong to apply the balancing process that was appropriate to abuse of process cases when considering the operation of s 78(1).

Shortly after s 78(1) had become law there were suggestions that it had not altered the common law as stated in *R v Sang*.[133] But this narrow construction was rejected in other decisions,[134] and several decisions of the Divisional Court and Court of Appeal have shown that s 78(1) can be used in circumstances lying outside the scope defined in *R v Sang*. For example, in *Matto v Wolverhampton Crown Court*,[135] the Divisional Court held that evidence of breath specimens should have been excluded under s 78(1) because they had been obtained in bad faith and as the result of oppression.[136]

R v Smurthwaite,[137] which was not referred to in *R v Chalkley and Jeffries*,

---

132 [1980] AC 402.

133 See, eg, *R v Mason* (1988) 86 Cr App R 349, p 354.

134 See, eg, *R v Fulling* (1987) 85 Cr App R 136, p 141; *R v O'Leary* (1988) 87 Cr App R 387, p 391.

135 [1987] RTR 337.

136 See also *Sharpe v DPP* [1993] RTR 392. And in *R v Khan and Others* [1997] Crim LR 508, the Court of Appeal accepted that s 78(1) was capable of being used to exclude evidence obtained by an illegal search, though on the facts it upheld the trial judge's decision to admit the evidence. In *R v Shannon* [2001] 1 Cr App R 168 the Court of Appeal referred to s 78(1) as having 'superseded' *Sang*: see *per* Auld LJ at p 183. And in *R v Looseley* [2001] 4 All ER 897, Lord Nicholls said that the decision in *R v Sang* on the admissibility of unfairly obtained evidence had been reversed by s 78 (p 902).

137 [1994] 1 All ER 898.

considered arguments based on entrapment in connection with s 78(1). Among factors relevant to the reliability of evidence obtained by entrapment were factors that were relevant to *the degree of impropriety* involved in collecting the evidence. Had the police enticed a defendant to commit a crime that he would not otherwise have committed? Had the police *abused their role* by asking questions that ought properly to have been asked only at a police station and in accordance with the Codes?[138]

Further, although the Court of Appeal has said on several occasions that it is not the function of the court to discipline the police, it is clear that the presence of bad faith on their part will make exclusion more likely. Thus, in *R v Walsh*,[139] it was said that bad faith might make 'substantial or significant' a breach that might not otherwise be so. In *R v Alladice*,[140] the Court of Appeal said that a distinction was to be drawn when considering the effect of refusing access to a solicitor between cases where the police had acted in good faith and cases where they had acted in bad faith. But bad faith is irrelevant if the court is concerned solely with reliability.

Thus, *R v Chalkley and Jeffries* is at odds, on this point, with many other decisions of the Court of Appeal and Divisional Court. More recently, the House of Lords in *R v Khan*[141] accepted that a breach of the defendant's right to privacy under Art 8 of the European Convention on Human Rights was at least a *relevant* consideration under s 78(1); yet how could it be, if the sole concern of the court is with the reliability of evidence, however improperly obtained? A further consideration is that in *R v Looseley*[142] two of the Law Lords clearly took the view that the scope of s 78 was wider than that suggested in *R v Chalkley*. Lord Hoffmann, with whom Lord Hutton agreed on this point, said that sometimes an application to exclude evidence under s 78 is in substance a belated application to stay the proceedings for abuse of process.[143] In those circumstances the court should apply the principles applicable to the grant of a stay. It is thus assumed that s 78 is wide enough to take into account matters that go far beyond the mere reliability of evidence.[144]

---

138 In *R v Lin* [1995] Crim LR 817, the Court of Appeal said that there would be a strong reason for exclusion if a judge found that the use of undercover officers had been purely in order to get round the requirements of the Code.

139 (1990) 91 Cr App R 161. See also *R v Sanghera* [2001] Crim LR 480.

140 (1988) 87 Cr App R 380.

141 [1997] AC 558.

142 [2001] 4 All ER 897, pp 909, 926.

143 This remedy is appropriate where there has been improper conduct by police or prosecutors which is so grave that it threatens to undermine the rule of law itself. See, eg, *R v Allan* [2004] EWCA Crim 2236 (breach of defendant's right against self-incrimination under Art 6 ECHR by causing a police 'stooge' to share the defendant's cell); *Grant v The Queen* [2006] QB 60 (interception and recording of privileged conversations between suspects and legal advisers).

144 Cf p 902, *per* Lord Nicholls.

That the courts do in practice exclude evidence under s 78(1), despite its reliability, is illustrated by *R v Veneroso*,[145] a decision at first instance where the defendant was charged with possession of drugs with intent to supply. The trial judge excluded evidence of the discovery of drugs because the police had entered his house unlawfully, albeit in good faith. He held that the public interest in bringing the defendant to trial did not outweigh the need to protect his right to privacy under Art 8. The result, he said, might have been different if explosives had been found.

Finally, if s 78(1) merely restates the common law, it is difficult to account for s 82(3) of the Act (see below). It is submitted that on a correct view of the law, despite the approval of *R v Chalkley* by the Court of Appeal in *R v Shannon*,[146] judges are entitled to take process values into consideration under s 78(1), and that reliability, though important, is not the only factor to be taken into consideration.[147]

THE COMMON LAW DISCRETION TO EXCLUDE

Section 82(3) of the Police and Criminal Evidence Act 1984 provides as follows:

> Nothing in this Part of this Act shall prejudice any power of a court to exclude evidence (whether by preventing questions being put or otherwise) at its discretion.

The effect of this provision is to retain the common law discretion to exclude evidence on the ground that its probative value is outweighed by its likely prejudicial effect.[148] It is submitted that this common law discretion remains, despite the provisions of the Criminal Justice Act 2003.[149]

USE OF CONFESSIONS BY A CO-DEFENDANT

Where a defendant's confession has been excluded under s 76 or s 78(1), it is no longer available to the prosecution. But by s 76A(1) of PACE,[150] a confession made by one defendant may be given in evidence for a co-defendant, provided it is not excluded by further provisions of s 76A. Section 76A(2) provides that:

---

145   [2002] Crim LR 306.

146   [2001] 1 Cr App R 168.

147   See also Choo and Nash, 1999.

148   See, eg, *R v O'Leary* (1988) 87 Cr App R 387, p 391.

149   See below, Chapter 12.

150   An amendment made by s 128 of the Criminal Justice Act 2003.

If, in any proceedings where a co-accused proposes to give in evidence a confession made by an accused person, it is represented to the court that the confession was or may have been obtained –

(a) by oppression of the person who made it; or

(b) in consequence of anything said or done which was likely, in the circumstances existing at the time, to render unreliable any confession which might be made by him in consequence thereof,

the court shall not allow the confession to be given in evidence for the co-accused except in so far as it is proved to the court on the balance of probabilities that the confession (notwithstanding that it may be true) was not so obtained.

The effect of this provision is that rules relating to the admissibility of confessions are the same for the prosecution and defence, except that a co-defendant has only the civil standard of proof in respect of the matters referred to in s 76A(2).[151]

FAILURE TO ANSWER QUESTIONS OR MENTION FACTS

The initial part of this chapter included a discussion of circumstances in which a suspect's silence might amount to a confession. Under the Criminal Justice and Public Order Act 1994, there may be circumstances in which a suspect's silence, though not amounting to a confession, may be used by magistrates or juries as the basis for making inferences at trial. I have already dealt, in Chapter 5, with the effect of s 35 on a defendant's failure to testify at trial, but three other sections need consideration here.

By s 34, a court or jury may draw such inferences as appear proper from evidence that the defendant failed, on being questioned under caution or on being charged with the offence, to mention any fact relied on in his defence if it was a fact which, in the circumstances existing at the time, he could reasonably have been expected to mention. Inferences may be drawn when determining either whether there is a case to answer or the question of guilt.

A judge can leave to the jury the possibility of drawing an inference from silence at interview, or an inference from silence at the time of charge, or both, provided no unfairness is caused to the defendant. In *R v Dervish*[152] the defendant gave 'no comment' interviews to the police. Evidence of these was excluded by the trial judge for breaches of Code C, but the prosecution wanted to rely on the defendant's silence

---

151 Note also s 76A(4), which applies the same rules as those contained in s 76(4).

152 [2002] 2 Cr App R 105.

when he was subsequently charged. The trial judge found that at the time of the charge he was in a position to understand clearly what was being alleged against him, and that he was in a situation that called for an explanation. She therefore instructed the jury that they could draw an inference under s 34. It was argued on appeal that adverse inferences could never be drawn in circumstances where the defendant had said nothing during an interview that had been excluded. If it were otherwise, the police would always have a 'back-up' inference available, which would nullify the safeguards in Code C. The Court of Appeal nevertheless upheld the trial judge's decision, and held that the Act did not exclude the possibility of drawing an inference from silence at each stage. The only question was whether, on the facts of any particular case, it would be fair to draw such an inference. A judge should not permit an inference if it would nullify the safeguards of the Act and the Codes, or if the police had acted in bad faith, deliberately breaching the Codes in the knowledge that an inference could be drawn from the defendant's silence on being charged even if the interview were to be excluded. But the trial judge had not found those circumstances to exist in this case.

Section 36 deals with situations where a suspect is arrested and cautioned and fails to answer questions about apparently incriminating circumstantial evidence. If the constable who arrests him, or another constable investigating the case, reasonably believes that the presence of an 'object, substance or mark' may be attributable to participation in the offence specified, he may tell the suspect of his belief and ask him to account for its presence. If the suspect fails to do so, the court or jury may draw such inferences as appear proper in determining either whether there is a case to answer or the question of guilt. By s 36(1), the provision is applicable only where the object, substance or mark is on his person, or in or on his clothing or footwear, or otherwise in his possession, or in any place in which he is at the time of arrest.

Example

A country house has been burgled. Entry was gained by breaking a window; a safe has been blown open and antique silver taken. Charlie is arrested for the burglary. The arresting officer finds him carrying a bag containing antique silver. In his pocket is a stick of gelignite and there are recent cuts to his fingers. Charlie's failure to account for any or all of these may allow proper inferences to be drawn.

Section 37 deals similarly with failure by an accused to account for his presence at a particular place at or about the time of the alleged commission of the offence for which he has been arrested.

Example

As above; Charlie is found hiding in the grounds of the house shortly after the burglary took place, and fails to account for his presence.

There has been a tendency, not always maintained, to interpret s 34 restrictively.[153] There are two reasons for this. First, there is the view taken by many judges that the sections should not be construed more widely than necessary, because they restrict common law rights that were designed to protect defendants from injustice.[154] Secondly, judges have been influenced by the view of the European Court of Human Rights that a defendant's right to silence, though not absolute,[155] lies at the heart of a notion of fair procedure under Art 6, and that particular caution is required before a court can invoke a defendant's silence against him.[156]

THE OPERATION OF S 78(1) OF PACE

In relation to ss 34–37 inclusive, the accused's failure will form an item of evidence on which the prosecution proposes to rely. There will accordingly be a discretion to exclude it under s 78 of PACE. It follows that the court may have to consider whether the circumstances are such that to admit the evidence of silence would have such an adverse effect on the fairness of the proceedings that it ought to be excluded. What might such circumstances be? One suggestion is that since silence is going to be used for purposes *similar* to a confession, the principles developed by the courts in relation to confessions should apply here as well.[157]

Suppose that, at trial, the accused relies on certain facts for his defence. He says he mentioned them to the police in an interview that was not taped. The officer's notebook records that questions under caution were put to which the accused made no reply. The accused did not sign this record, nor was it shown to him. There has been a breach of para 11.11 of Code C, which provides that, unless it is impracticable, the person interviewed shall be given the opportunity to read the interview record and to sign it as correct or to indicate the respects in which he considers it inaccurate. The breach is significant and substantial, because it affects the reliability of the evidence against the accused. There is a strong case for exclusion under s 78.[158]

An important amendment to s 34, prompted by concerns that the section might be incompatible with the implied right to silence contained in Art 6 of the European Convention on Human Rights, is sub-s (2A). This provides that where

---

153 There has been virtually no case law on ss 36 and 37, and the discussion is therefore confined to s 34.

154 See, eg, *R v Bowden* [1999] 2 Cr App R 176, p 181, *per* Lord Bingham CJ.

155 The European Court has frequently stated that it may be permissible to draw inferences from a defendant's silence, provided the evidence adduced is such that the only commonsense inference to be drawn, given a convincing prima facie case, is that the defendant has no answer to the case against him. See, eg, *Telfner v Austria* [2001] Crim LR 821.

156 See, eg, *Beckles v UK* (2003) 36 EHRR 13.

157 Dennis, 1995b, pp 14–15.

158 Note *R v Dervish* [2002] Cr App R 105, above, where the interviews were excluded, but inferences could be drawn from the defendant's silence on being charged.

the accused is not at an authorised place of detention at the time of his silence, no inference can be drawn under s 34 unless he has been allowed an opportunity to consult a solicitor before being questioned.

THE CONDITIONS FOR ALLOWING AN INFERENCE TO BE DRAWN

Sections 34, 36 and 37 set out conditions that have to be satisfied before an inference can be made. The conditions in s 34 were discussed by the Court of Appeal in *R v Argent*.[159] Most were referred to without comment, but the court did expand on the requirement that the unmentioned fact must be one which, in the circumstances existing at the time, the defendant could reasonably have been expected to mention when questioned. When considering reasonableness, the court must take into account all relevant circumstances at the time of questioning: for example, the time of day and personal characteristics of the defendant such as age, experience, mental capacity, state of health, sobriety, tiredness, and his personality generally. Consideration has to be taken, not of some hypothetical reasonable defendant of ordinary fortitude, but of the actual defendant, with such qualities, knowledge, apprehensions and advice as he is shown to have had at the time.

Whether the defendant knew the grounds of suspicion against him when questioned must also be important. A person cannot be expected to mention a fact when he has no means of telling whether it is relevant or not. In practice, the police voluntarily provide some disclosure in order to counter an argument at trial that no adverse inferences should be drawn under s 34.[160] But there are no rules or established procedures about such disclosure. The 'quality and quantity' of disclosure will depend on the case,[161] but it is not necessarily wrong for the police to hold back some part of their case before interviewing a suspect.[162] So, for example, in *R v W*[163] it was held proper for the first interview of a rape suspect, in which he denied having had intercourse with the complainant, to take place before the police revealed that there was DNA evidence to show that intercourse had in fact taken place between the suspect and the complainant. The Court of Appeal recognised that such 'sequential disclosure' was standard practice.

In *R v Mountford*[164] and *R v Gill*,[165] the Court of Appeal developed a restriction on the use of s 34. According to these decisions, where the truth of an unmentioned fact is the central issue in the trial, so that its resolution will determine the verdict, a

---

159   [1997] 2 Cr App R 27.

160   See *R v Roble* [1997] Crim LR 449. This informal, voluntary, disclosure should not be confused with the statutory rules of disclosure under the Criminal Procedure and Investigations Act 1996.

161   *R v Nottle* [2004] EWCA Crim 599, para 14.

162   *R v Farrell* [2004] EWCA Crim 597, para 22.

163   [2006] EWCA Crim 1292.

164   [1999] Crim LR 575.

165   [2001] 1 Cr App R 160.

s 34 direction should not be given. The reason is that in these circumstances the s 34 issue cannot be resolved as an independent one, and therefore cannot amount to additional support for the prosecution case. For example, in *R v Gill*, the defendant was charged, together with a man called Taylor, with possession of heroin with intent to supply. The police had visited Gill's flat, where he and Taylor were present. As the police entered, Taylor threw a bag of heroin out of a window. It was the prosecution case that both men were in possession of all the heroin with the intention of supplying it to others. When interviewed, Gill said that the heroin was for his own use. He said that he was using four or five bags each week and that he had bought four bags earlier that day. He declined to say who the supplier was, and later he refused to answer any further questions. In evidence, Gill said that it was Taylor who had supplied him. He added that during the interview he had been prepared to answer only questions about his own use of drugs. He had refused to answer any more questions because he did not want to implicate anyone else, including Taylor. The trial judge gave a direction under s 34 in respect of his silence, but the Court of Appeal held this to have been wrong. In deciding whether Gill could reasonably have been expected to mention during interview that Taylor was his supplier, the jury could only be sure that he was lying, and so reject his explanation for silence, if they concluded, independently of s 34, that Gill was a dealer.

However, the Court of Appeal has not consistently imposed this limitation on s 34. In *R v Gowland-Wynn*[166] a differently constituted court disapproved of the decisions in *Mountford* and *Gill*, saying that they had the effect of 'emasculating and defeating' the very purpose of s 34, and that that provision has the largest and most significant part to play where a defendant says nothing about something that goes right to the heart of his defence. In *R v Chenia*[167] the Court of Appeal said that the approach taken in *Mountford* and *Gill* would be appropriate rarely, and only in the simplest and most straightforward of cases.

The Court of Appeal has, however, made it clear that s 34 does not give the police a right to test the defendant's story by cross-examination before trial. That would be a greater intrusion on the right to silence than the wording of the section warrants. It follows that it would be wrong for a judge to invite inferences under s 34 where at the police interview the defendant presents, but refuses to answer questions about, a written statement that sets out all the facts on which he later relies at trial.[168] But a prepared statement will not always enable the defendant to avoid s 34 inferences. If it is not presented at interview, but only later, the facts contained in it will not have been mentioned 'on being questioned' by the police. It may, in important respects, be incomplete in comparison with the defendant's later evidence, or even inconsistent with it. In the latter event a trial judge could, depending on the

166   [2002] 1 Cr App R 569.
167   [2003] 2 Cr App R 83.
168   See *R v Ali and Others* (2001) 151 NLJ 1321; *R v Knight* [2004] 1 Cr App R 117.

circumstances, direct the jury to treat that part of the statement as a lie, rather than as the foundation for a s 34 inference.[169]

WHEN DOES A DEFENDANT RELY ON A FACT?

For s 34 to apply, the defendant must have failed to mention some fact that he relies on in his defence, but it may not always be easy to determine whether this basic condition has been satisfied. In *R v Milford*[170] 'fact' was said to have its ordinary meaning of 'something that is actually the case', but the court in *Milford* was not concerned with admissions, and in *R v Betts and Hall*[171] it was held that a bare admission at trial of part of the prosecution case does not constitute a 'fact' for s 34 purposes.[172] The court said that were it otherwise, the defendant would be obliged to make admissions at interview, and this would conflict with the right to silence given by Art 6 of the European Convention. There was good reason to limit the right of silence where positive assertions were to be made at trial, so that they could be investigated and tested, but no similar considerations could apply to a bare admission.[173] A completely different line was taken by the Court of Appeal in *R v Daly*,[174] where it was held that an admitted fact was 'just as much a "fact relied on" for the purposes of the section as a fact which is extraneous to the prosecution case'.[175]

In *R v Moshaid*,[176] the defendant gave a 'no comment' interview, and at trial he gave no evidence and called no witnesses. The Court of Appeal held that the trial judge should not have allowed the jury to consider the possibility of drawing an inference under s 34. The section did not apply because there were no facts relied on by the defendant. So if the defence do no more than put the prosecution to proof of its case, s 34 will not apply. However, because there are no *witnesses* for the defence it will not always follow that there are no *facts relied on* by the defence. In most trials, evidence of such facts will, of course, come from the defendant and perhaps from other defence witnesses, but they can also come from prosecution witnesses, either during cross-examination or even during examination-in-chief.[177] If a defendant who gives no evidence relies in his defence on facts established in this way, s 34 could apply as well as s 35.

---

169   *R v Turner (Dwaine)* [2004] 1 Cr App R 305.

170   [2001] Crim LR 330.

171   [2001] 2 Cr App R 257.

172   Where an explanation for the admitted fact is advanced by reliance on other facts, it would be possible for those facts to give rise to a s 34 inference if they were not referred to in the interview.

173   [2001] 2 Cr App R 257, pp 264–65.

174   [2002] 2 Cr App R 201.

175   *Betts and Hall* was cited, but only, it seems, in connection with a different point.

176   [1998] Crim LR 420.

177   *R v Bowers and Others* [1998] Crim LR 817; *R v Chenia* [2003] 2 Cr App R 83.

In *R v Nickolson*[178] the Court of Appeal emphasised the distinction between facts and theories. Section 34 applies to facts alone. In that case, a child claimed that the defendant had sexually abused her in the premises where they both lived. The police took a nightdress that belonged to her which, when analysed, was shown to have been stained by semen. The defendant was interviewed before this was discovered. He denied any indecency with the child, but told the police that he habitually masturbated in his bedroom and in the bathroom. He was asked during cross-examination if he could think of any way in which semen stains might have appeared on the nightdress. He suggested that the child could have gone to the bathroom after he had masturbated there and have come into contact with semen on the lavatory seat. The trial judge gave a s 34 direction on the basis that this explanation had not been put forward at the interview. The Court of Appeal held that this was wrong. The defendant had not asserted *as a fact* that the stains had been caused in this way. What he said had been more in the nature of a theory, or a speculation.[179]

It is for the jury to decide whether the defendant has relied on a particular fact and, if so, whether he failed to mention it. But there may be some trials where it is proper for the judge to decide, as a matter of law, whether there is any evidence on which a jury could conclude that these conditions have been satisfied. If a judge rules that there is no such evidence, he ought to direct the jury that they should not draw any inferences from the defendant's silence.[180]

THE EFFECT OF LEGAL ADVICE ON SILENCE

In *R v Argent*, the Court of Appeal said that legal advice was something the court might have to consider when deciding whether a suspect could reasonably have been expected to mention a particular fact. The significance of legal advice was more fully discussed by the Court of Appeal in *R v Condron*,[181] a case where the defendants had refused to answer questions on the advice of their solicitor. The court gave the following guidance to cover similar cases.

If the defendant says that he failed to answer questions on legal advice, that bare assertion is unlikely to be regarded as a sufficient reason for failure to mention matters relevant to the defence. In practice, therefore, the defendant will have to go further and provide, either through his own testimony or that of the legal adviser, the reasons

---

178   [1999] Crim LR 61.

179   But theories are based on facts, and there may be circumstances where a theory put forward at trial is so dependent on specific facts that both facts and theory might reasonably be expected to be mentioned. See the Commentary on *R v Nickolson* and *R v B(MT)* [2000] Crim LR 181.

180   *R v McGarry* [1998] 3 All ER 805.

181   [1997] 1 Cr App R 185.

for the advice.[182] The prosecution will then be able to cross-examine the relevant witness with a view to discovering whether there were any merely tactical reasons for the advice.[183]

Silence on legal advice was discussed further in *R v Betts and Hall*.[184] In that case the Court of Appeal said that where silence at an interview is alleged to be on legal advice, the judge must make it clear to the jury that they can draw inferences only if they are sure that the failure to mention facts subsequently relied on was because the defendant had not at that stage any explanation to offer, or none that he believed could stand up to questioning or investigation, so that the legal advice was no more than a convenient shield behind which to hide. In particular, the jury are not concerned with whether the advice was good or bad, but only with the defendant's state of mind. As Kay LJ said, 'If it is a plausible explanation that the reason for not mentioning facts is that [the defendant] acted on the advice of his solicitor and not because he had no, or no satisfactory, answer to give, then no inference can be drawn'.[185]

A different approach was taken in *R v Howell*.[186] In that case, in a judgment delivered by Laws LJ, the Court of Appeal said that the police interview and the trial are to be seen as part of a continuous process in which the suspect is engaged from the beginning. There is a public interest in reasonable disclosure by a suspect of what he has to say when faced with incriminating facts. This interest is thwarted if currency is given to the belief that a suspect can avoid adverse comment at his trial if he remains silent on legal advice. Such a belief may even encourage solicitors 'to advise silence for other than good objective reasons'. Laws LJ continued:

> We do not consider, *pace* the reasoning in *Betts and Hall*, that once it is shown that the advice (of whatever quality) has genuinely been relied on as the reason for the suspect's remaining silent, adverse comment is thereby disallowed. The premise of such a position is that in such circumstances it is in principle not reasonable to expect the suspect to mention the facts in question. We do not believe that is so. What is reasonable depends on all the circumstances . . .

He went on to suggest circumstances that would be likely to justify silence, such as the suspect's ill health or mental disability; his state of confusion, intoxication or

---

182   A defendant who gave evidence of what his solicitor said to him would not, of course, infringe the rule against hearsay. He would not be relying on the truth of what the solicitor said to him. He would be relying on the effect of the solicitor's words on his own decision whether or not to answer questions. See *R v Davis* [1998] Crim LR 659; *R v Daniel* [1998] 2 Cr App R 373.

183   The advice given by a solicitor to a client could not normally be the subject of questioning in court because of the client's 'legal professional privilege': see below, Chapter 15. But this privilege would have been 'waived' by a defendant who chose to give evidence about the advice he had received.

184   [2001] 2 Cr App R 257.

185   *Ibid*, p 270.

186   [2003] EWCA Crim 1; [2003] Crim LR 405.

shock; or his inability to remember events in the absence of documents or persons to assist him. Laws LJ continued, 'There must always be soundly based objective reasons for silence, sufficiently cogent and telling to weigh in the balance against the public interest in an account being given by the suspect to the police'.[187]

Two criticisms, one minor and one major, can be made of this. The minor criticism is that Laws LJ failed to appreciate what was said in *Betts and Hall* about the burden of proof on this point. That case did not decide that a defendant *must show* that he genuinely relied on his solicitor's advice to remain silent before adverse comment is prohibited. It is clear from the judgment that so long as genuine reliance on legal advice is a *plausible explanation* for silence, no inferences can be drawn. In other words, the jury must be satisfied before beginning to consider whether to draw any inferences that the defendant *did not* genuinely rely on the advice given to him, but was using it, in Kay LJ's words, only as a shield behind which to hide. The major criticism is that Laws LJ rejected the significance, apparent in s 34, spelled out in *Argent*, and emphasised in *Betts and Hall*, of the suspect's personal characteristics. Further, as the law stands at present, a judge who directs a jury about the possibility of drawing inferences under s 34 must tell them that they can draw an adverse inference only if satisfied that the defendant was silent because he had no answers, or none that could stand up to cross-examination.[188] If *Howell* is to be followed, this direction will no longer be correct, because even if a jury is satisfied that a defendant was silent because he genuinely accepted the advice given by his solicitor, they could still draw an adverse inference if, somehow, they came to believe that the solicitor had no 'good objective reasons' for advising silence.[189] In *R v Hoare*[190] an attempt was made to close the gap between *Betts and Hall* and *Howell*. The Court of Appeal said that the question for the jury in the end is whether, regardless of advice given and accepted, an accused has remained silent not because of that advice, but because he had no, or no satisfactory, explanation to give.[191] In observations on the rationale of s 34, the Court said that the whole basis of the section is an assumption that 'an innocent defendant – as distinct from one who is entitled to require the prosecution to prove its case – would give an early explanation to demonstrate his innocence'. If he is advised by his solicitor to remain silent, Auld LJ remarked, why on earth should he do so unless

---

187   [2003] EWCA Crim 1, EWCA, paras [23] and [24].

188   See *R v Gill* [2001] 1 Cr App R 160 and *R v Petkar* [2003] EWCA Crim 2668, referred to below.

189   In *R v Robinson* [2003] EWCA Crim 2219, the Court of Appeal drew from previous decisions a number of propositions of law relating to s 34. Unfortunately, while confirming the statement of the law contained in *Betts and Hall*, it failed to draw out the incompatibility with that decision of what was said in *Howell*, which was also cited. In *R v Knight* [2004] 1 Cr App R 117 Laws LJ, in delivering the judgment of the Court of Appeal, stated *obiter* that *Howell* (in which he had delivered the judgment) was good law.

190   [2004] EWCA Crim 784; [2005] 1 WLR 1804.

191   Paragraphs 54, 55.

there is a danger that he might wrongly inculpate himself for the sort of reasons referred to in *Howell*.[192]

DIRECTIONS TO THE JURY UNDER S 34 OF THE 1994 ACT

The leading case on this subject is *R v Gill*.[193] The Court of Appeal, influenced by the decision of the European Court of Human Rights in *Condron v UK*,[194] set out the duties of a judge giving a s 34 direction as follows:

- He must identify the fact on which the defendant relies.
- He must direct the jury that: (a) it is for them to decide whether in the circumstances it was something that the defendant could reasonably have been expected to mention; and (b) if they think it was, that they are not *obliged* to draw any inferences but that they have a *discretion* to do so.

The Court went on to cite *R v Cowan*[195] and to summarise the essential elements of a direction under s 35 set out in that decision.[196] It seems clear from this that the safeguards provided by *R v Cowan* are to be applied also to directions under s 34. Accordingly, in giving a direction under that section, a judge must also tell the jury that a suspected person is not bound to answer police questions, and that an inference from silence cannot on its own prove guilt. Further, the jury must be satisfied that the prosecution has shown that there is a case to answer before drawing any adverse inference from silence. Finally, they should be directed that they can draw an adverse inference only if they are satisfied that the defendant was silent because he had no answers, or none that would stand up to cross-examination.

The Court of Appeal said, in *R v Petkar*,[197] that the inferences which it is suggested might be drawn from failure to mention the facts relied on should be identified, to the extent that they may go beyond the standard inference of late fabrication. The jury should be told that, if an inference is drawn, they should not convict wholly *or mainly* on the strength of it; and that an inference should be drawn only if they think it is a fair and proper conclusion. In addition, the jury should be reminded of the evidence on the basis of which they are invited *not* to draw any conclusion from the defendant's silence.

---

192 Paragraphs 51, 53. In *Howell* Laws LJ gave examples of circumstances that could justify silence and mentioned a suspect's ill health, mental disability, confusion, intoxication, shock, or inability to recall matters in the absence of documents or persons to assist him.

193 [2001] 1 Cr App R 160. See also *R v Milford* [2001] Crim LR 330.

194 [2000] Crim LR 679.

195 [1996] QB 373.

196 See Chapter 5.

197 [2004] 1 Cr App R 270.

PRESERVATION OF SOME EXISTING COMMON LAW

Section 34 has no effect on any common law principles that already allow inferences to be drawn from silence under accusation or questioning. It remains the law that a failure to deny an accusation or answer questions about an offence *may* amount to an acknowledgment of the truth of the accusations.[198] If situations like those in *Parkes v R* or *R v Batt*[199] were to recur, the result in each case would be the same.

THE *VOIR DIRE*

Where the admissibility of a confession or other item of prosecution evidence is disputed, the judge will often hear evidence in the absence of the jury before deciding the question. This procedure is known as a '*voir dire*' after the type of oath administered to witnesses who give evidence during it.[200] Where the admissibility of a confession is disputed, the defendant will usually give evidence about the circumstances which led him to make it. If he also gives evidence later in front of the jury, the prosecution may want to cross-examine him about discrepancies between what he said on the *voir dire* and what he said to the jury. It was decided by the Privy Council in *Wong Kam-Ming v R*[201] that this was permissible only where the judge had decided on the *voir dire* that the confession was *admissible*. It was also decided in *Wong Kam-Ming v R* that:

(a) since the *voir dire* was concerned with the *admissibility* of a confession and not with its *truth*, a defendant giving evidence on the *voir dire* should not be cross-examined about whether his confession was true or not; and

(b) in order to maintain the distinction between the issue of admissibility, which has to be decided on the *voir dire*, and the issue of guilt, which has to be decided in the main part of the trial, the prosecution may not call evidence before the jury of anything said by the defendant on the *voir dire*.

Wong Kam-Ming v R was decided before PACE, and it is possible that it no longer represents the law, because the effect of ss 76(1) and 82(1) of that Act is to make admissible any statements by the defendant on the *voir dire* that are wholly or partly adverse to him. The fact that there has been no decision on this point after some 20 years suggests either that the problem does not arise in practice or that, if it does,

---

198   See above.

199   [1976] 1 WLR 1251; [1995] Crim LR 240.

200   See above, Chapter 1. It is improper for the judge to tell the jury about his ruling during a *voir dire* on the admissibility of a confession: *Mitchell v The Queen* [1998] 2 Cr App R 35, PC. 194

201   [1980] AC 247.

judges are willing to preserve the distinction between the issue on the *voir dire* and the issues in the rest of the trial by using their exclusionary discretion under s 78(1).

FURTHER READING

—Ashworth, 'Redrawing the Boundaries of Entrapment' [2002] Crim LR 161.
—Birch, 'Suffering in Silence: A Cost-Benefit Analysis of Section 34 of the Criminal Justice and Public Order Act 1994' [1999] Crim LR 769.
—Choo and Nash, 'What's the Matter with Section 78?' [1999] Crim LR 929.
—Gudjonsson, *The Psychology of Interrogations, Confessions and Testimony*, 1992, Chapter 8.
—Donagan, 'The Right Not to Incriminate Oneself', in Malpas, (ed), *Philosophical Papers of Alan Donagan*, 1994, Vol 2, pp 248–61.
—Hartshorne, 'Defensive Use of a Co-Accused's Confession and the Criminal Justice Act 2003' (2004) E&P 165.
—Jennings, 'Silence and Safety: The Impact of Human Rights Law' [2000] Crim LR 879.
—Ormerod, 'ECHR and the Exclusion of Evidence' [2003] Crim LR 61.
—Ormerod and Birch, 'Evolution of the Discretionary Exclusion of Evidence, [2004] Crim LR 138.
—Redmayne, 'Rethinking the Privilege against Self-Incrimination' (2007) 27 OJLS 209.
—Squires, 'The Problem with Entrapment' (2006) 26 OJLS 351.

EXERCISES

1. What is the meaning of 'oppression' in s 76(2)(a) of PACE?
2. Why would defence counsel use s 76 rather than s 78 to exclude a confession?
3. What is the origin of the word 'exculpatory'? What, in evidence law, is a wholly exculpatory statement, and what is its evidential status?
4. What is a 'mixed' statement, and what is its evidential status?
5. Suppose a statement appears to be wholly exculpatory, but later it can be shown to be a lie, and thus incriminating. Can s 76(2) be used to exclude it? Give your reasons.
6. Can silence amount to a confession?
7. Where a confession made by one defendant before trial implicates a co-defendant, what is its evidential status in relation to that co-defendant? How, if at all, could the co-defendant have the references to him excluded?
8. Fiona makes a confession after wrongly being denied access to a solicitor. The prosecution do not wish to rely at trial on that confession. But they do want to rely on a second confession, made by her during an interview the next day, after she had seen a solicitor. Can they do so?
9. In what circumstances can a suspect's access to a solicitor ordinarily be delayed?
10. Gerald is arrested on suspicion of murdering his wife. While he is being driven to the police station, he is heard to say, 'I can't live with this. I killer her, and now I must face up to it'. What should the police do to ensure that Gerald's statement is admissible at his trial?

11. In what circumstances will the Court of Appeal interfere with a trial judge's decision not to exclude evidence under s 78 of PACE?

12. Harry refused to answer questions at his police interview on the advice of his solicitor. How should the jury be directed in the summing-up if the prosecution relies at trial on s 34 of the Criminal Justice and Public Order Act 1994?

12

CHARACTER EVIDENCE

INTRODUCTION

The common law recognised two different ways in which evidence of character could be relevant. First, it could make allegations against a defendant more likely to be true. Evidence of a defendant's bad character was admissible in order to support the allegations made against him, whether in civil or criminal proceedings, if it could be said to fall within the scope of what was called 'similar fact evidence'. Conversely, at least in criminal proceedings, evidence of a defendant's good character could be adduced in order to show that the allegations made against him were less likely to be true.[1] Secondly, in relation to *any* witnesses in either civil or criminal trials, evidence of bad character could be relevant to credibility; so also could the good character of a defendant in a criminal trial. The theory behind this was that a conviction for *any* offence was relevant to the credibility of a witness because of what it was supposed to reveal about the moral character of that person. For example, in *Clifford v Clifford*,[2]

---

1   There is old authority for the proposition that, in civil proceedings, evidence of a party's good character is inadmissible because it is irrelevant: see, eg, *AG v Radloff* (1854) 10 Exch 84, p 97. However, such evidence might very well be considered relevant in civil cases where the act complained of is a crime as well as a tort.

2   [1961] 1 WLR 1274, p 1276.

Cairns J said, 'It has never, I think, been doubted that a conviction for any offence could be put to a witness by way of cross-examination as to credit, even though the offence was not one of dishonesty'. Witnesses in civil and criminal proceedings could therefore be cross-examined about their previous convictions in order to show that they should not be believed on their oath. This rule gave rise to special problems when defendants in criminal trials were given a general right to give evidence in their own defence by the Criminal Evidence Act 1898.[3]

Such a cut and dried distinction between the two types of relevance – relevance to 'issue' and relevance to 'credit' – was not always easy to maintain. Nevertheless, the common law did its best, and came in for some criticism in consequence.

There were two restrictions that applied to witnesses generally in respect of cross-examination about previous convictions. The first was judge-made; the second was statutory.[4] The judge-made restriction was set out in *Hobbs v CT Tinling and Co Ltd*.[5] In brief, a question would be proper only if the information about bad character that it was designed to elicit would seriously affect the court's opinion as to the credibility of the witness on the matter to which he had testified. A question would be improper if designed to elicit information about matters so remote in time, or of such a character, that the truth of the imputation would not affect, or would affect only slightly, the opinion of the court about the witness's credibility on the matter to which he was testifying. For example, as Sir James Stephen had said earlier:

> The fact that a woman had an illegitimate child at eighteen is hardly a reason for not believing her at forty, when she swears that she locked up her house safely when she went to bed at night, and found the kitchen window broken open and her husband's boots gone when she got up in the morning.[6]

This principle remains applicable in civil trials. The common law governing the admissibility of evidence of bad character in criminal proceedings is abolished by s 99(1) of the Criminal Justice Act (CJA) 2003, but the provisions of that Act retain the principle.

---

3   Before this Act, defendants in nearly all the most serious criminal trials had been barred from testifying in their own defence. There were various reasons for this. One frequently relied on was that to allow a defendant to testify would be to leave him open to oppressive questioning, which might compel him to convict himself unless he chose to commit perjury. A more sophisticated argument was that if defendants were allowed to testify, the jury would ask themselves the wrong question: not whether the prosecution had proved its case, but whether they believed the defendant. For the history of this legislation, see Allen, 1997, Chapter 5.

4   For the statutory restriction, see the Rehabilitation of Offenders Act 1974, referred to below in the section on 'Spent convictions'.

5   [1929] 2 KB 1.

6   Stephen, 1973 [1883], Vol I, p 435.

SIMILAR FACT EVIDENCE

'Similar fact evidence' was evidence adduced by one party against another, which showed that other party to be guilty of some other misconduct than that primarily alleged, or which showed him to have some discreditable propensity or interest. Such evidence was generally adduced in criminal, rather than civil, proceedings. As already stated, the purpose of the evidence was to show that the defendant was likely to have been guilty of whatever was currently alleged against him. Evidence of bad character or conduct that was not itself criminal could be admitted. For example, in *R v Barrington*[7] evidence was given that the defendant possessed indecent photographs; in *R v Lewis*[8] evidence was given that the defendant possessed literature from a paedophile society. In neither case did the prosecution attempt to rely on the fact that the possession of the material in itself constituted a criminal offence.[9] The expression 'similar fact evidence' was adopted because the question of admissibility typically arose where an offence had been committed in an idiosyncratic way, and the defendant could be shown to have indulged in similar previous behaviour. But admissibility was not confined to such situations and could also arise, for example, where articles of an incriminating nature were found in the defendant's possession, or where the defendant admitted interests, such as paedophilia, that were relevant to the case alleged against him.

Similar fact evidence could be adduced of matters not referred to in the indictment, but problems associated with this type of evidence could also arise where such evidence related to other counts in the same indictment. Where an indictment contains more than one count, the usual rule is that each count has to be separately considered; evidence on one count is inadmissible in relation to another. But where similar fact features could be found among the counts, evidence on one count could be admitted in relation to others.

The law governing similar fact evidence went through various stages of development. After the decision of the House of Lords in *DPP v P*,[10] it was clear that admissibility in criminal trials was determined by asking in each case whether the probative worth of such evidence outweighed any improper prejudicial effect that it might have on the jury. Similar fact problems rarely arose in civil trials. There were probably two reasons for this. The first was the belief that judges sitting alone were not prone to the prejudices that might affect members of a jury. Secondly, because of their experience in trying cases, judges were thought far more likely than juries to be

---

7   [1981] 1 WLR 419.

8   (1983) 76 Cr App R 33.

9   See also *R v Butler* (1987) 84 Cr App R 12, where evidence was given of consensual sexual acts between the defendant and his former girlfriend similar to those alleged to have been forced on a rape victim.

10   [1991] 2 AC 447.

able to assess the proper weight to be attached to evidence of a potentially prejudicial nature. The approach to similar fact evidence in civil cases was therefore more flexible. In *Mood Music Publishing Co Ltd v De Wolfe Publishing Ltd*,[11] the Court of Appeal said that civil courts will admit similar fact evidence wherever it is relevant in determining the matters in issue, provided it would not be oppressive or unfair to the other side to do so. The stricter approach of the criminal courts will, however, be found on the rare occasions when a civil action is tried by a jury.[12] More recently, in *O'Brien v Chief Constable of South Wales Constabulary*,[13] the Court of Appeal said that in civil trials the court must have regard to the matters listed in r 1.2 of the Civil Procedure Rules, and, in the absence of countervailing arguments based on probative force, should have a tendency to exclude similar fact evidence if it would be likely to lengthen the proceedings and add to their cost or complexity. Added complexity would be a particularly important consideration if there were to be a jury trial.

As we shall see, the common law of similar fact evidence has been abolished for criminal trials by the CJA 2003, but that Act has no bearing on civil proceedings, which will continue to be governed by the rules and guidelines set out in the cases to which reference has just been made.

CRIMINAL EVIDENCE ACT 1898

Section 1 of this Act made the defendant a competent witness for the defence in all criminal trials, but to have put the defendant in the same position as any other witness would have created problems. We have already noted the general rule that a witness could be cross-examined about his bad character, and in particular about any previous convictions, with a view to weakening his credibility. A defendant with previous convictions would have been deterred from testifying if this rule had been applied to him. There was another rule for the protection of witnesses generally. This allowed them to claim a 'privilege against self-incrimination'[14] and refuse to answer any questions tending to show that they had committed a criminal offence. If a defendant in the witness box had been allowed to take advantage of this privilege, the prosecution's task of cross-examination would have been made impossible.

Special provisions were therefore necessary for defendants called as witnesses. These were contained in s 1(2) and (3).[15] Section 1(2) removed the privilege against self-incrimination from a defendant who gave evidence by providing that he could be

---

11   [1976] 1 Ch 119.

12   *Thorpe v Chief Constable of Greater Manchester Police* [1989] 1 WLR 665.

13   (2003) *The Times*, 22 August.

14   See further Chapter 15.

15   Originally s 1(e) and (f).

asked any question in cross-examination 'notwithstanding that it would tend to incriminate him as to the offence charged'. Section 1(3)(ii) restricted the prosecution's right to cross-examine a defendant about his previous convictions to circumstances where he had put his own character in issue, or where the nature or conduct of his defence was such as to involve an imputation on a prosecution witness. Where a defendant (D1), while giving evidence in his own defence, supported the prosecution case against a co-defendant (D2) or undermined D2's defence, s 1(3)(iii) gave D2 a right to cross-examine D1 about D1's bad character, including any previous convictions. The right of the prosecution under s 1(3)(ii) was subject to a judicial discretion to exclude cross-examination, but D2's right to cross-examine under s 1(3)(iii) was absolute.

These provisions of the 1898 Act have been repealed and replaced by provisions contained in Pt 11, Chapter 1, of the CJA 2003.

SPENT CONVICTIONS

Section 1(1) of the Rehabilitation of Offenders Act 1974 allows a person's convictions to be 'spent' after a certain period of time has gone by.[16] Where this is the case, there is a general prohibition under s 4(1) against referring to the spent convictions in judicial proceedings, but this prohibition is limited by s 7(2), which in effect gives free scope for reference to spent convictions in criminal proceedings. An attempt to maintain the spirit of the Act was made in a Practice Direction[17] to the effect that no one should refer in open court to a spent conviction without the authority of the judge, who should not give authority unless the interests of justice require it.

The general prohibition under s 4(1) is also subject to s 7(3) of the Act. This provides:

> If at any stage in any proceedings before a judicial authority in Great Britain . . . the authority is satisfied, in the light of any considerations which appear to it to be relevant . . . that justice cannot be done in the case except by admitting or requiring evidence relating to a person's spent convictions . . . that authority may admit . . . the evidence in question . . .

One effect of this sub-section is that in a civil trial spent convictions can be admitted, subject to the judge's discretion, when credit is in issue and the convictions are relevant to credit. For example, in *Thomas v Commissioner of Police for the Metropolis*,[18] the plaintiff claimed damages against the defendant for assault, false imprisonment and malicious prosecution. The case was heard by a judge and jury, and the judge allowed the plaintiff to be cross-examined about his spent convictions under

---

16   For particulars of the various lengths of time that must elapse before a conviction is spent, see s 5 of the Act.

17   See now *Practice Direction (Criminal: Consolidated)* [2002] 3 All ER 904, 909, Part I, para 6.

18   [1997] 2 WLR 593.

s 7(3). A majority of the Court of Appeal upheld his decision on the basis that it was a case where the credibility of the plaintiff on the one hand, and two police officers on the other, was crucial.

The provisions of this Act remain in force in criminal as well as civil cases, and may be relevant when considering provisions of the CJA 2003.[19]

EVIDENCE OF GOOD CHARACTER IN CRIMINAL PROCEEDINGS

A defence advocate will wish, where possible, to give evidence of a client's good character in order to show the improbability of his having committed the alleged offence. However, it is not always appreciated that there are limitations on the evidence that can be adduced for this purpose.

THE NATURE OF THE EVIDENCE

The rule is that only evidence of general reputation is admissible as evidence of good character; evidence of the opinions of specific persons, or evidence of specific acts performed by the accused, is inadmissible. This rule was laid down in *R v Rowton*.[20] In that case, evidence had been called of the defendant's good character, and the prosecution had been allowed to rebut this by proving that the accused was in fact of bad character. The witness called for this purpose was asked what was the accused's general character for decency and morality. The answer was as follows: 'I know nothing of the neighbourhood's opinion, because I was only a boy at school when I knew him; but my opinion, and the opinion of my brothers who were pupils of his, is that his character is that of a man capable of the grossest indecency and the most flagrant immorality.'

A majority of the Court for Crown Cases Reserved[21] held that this testimony should not have been admitted. Two points in particular emerge from the majority judgments:

- ▓ Character evidence is confined to evidence of general reputation; the accused may not give evidence of particular facts for the purpose of showing that he is not the sort of person to commit the offence charged.

---

19   See in particular ss 100(3)(b) and 101(4), which direct the court to have regard to the time when previous offences were committed.

20   (1865) Le&Ca 520. The rule originally applied to evidence of bad character as well, but the effect of the Criminal Evidence Act 1898 was to make evidence of disposition admissible in addition to evidence of reputation in order to show bad character. See *Stirland v DPP* [1944] AC 315, p 325.

21   A criminal appellate court that preceded the Court of Criminal Appeal. The latter was established in 1907 and reconstituted as the Criminal Division of the Court of Appeal in 1966.

■ It is quite true that character evidence is most cogent when accompanied by evidence showing that the witness has had opportunities of acquiring information beyond what the man's neighbours in general would have acquired. In practice, the admission of such evidence is often carried beyond the letter of the law in the accused's favour.

Evidence of bad character called to rebut evidence of good character was at that time subject to the same restrictions. Since the witness had disclaimed all knowledge of the defendant's general reputation, his answer was inadmissible.

The rule in *Rowton* has been much criticised. It was based on a practice, current at the time, which was justified in at least two ways. First, it was said that evidence of particular facts lacked weight, because even the worst criminal could perform acts of generosity. Secondly, it was argued that to allow such evidence to be given would raise issues of which the prosecution had no notice, and on which they could not enter into argument. A third justification may have been that to allow such evidence could unduly prolong trials.

Rowton indicated that some flexibility was, in practice, shown in admitting evidence of good character. But the practice is not reliable, as appears from R *v Redgrave*.[22] The defendant was charged with an offence involving homosexual activity in a public lavatory. As part of his defence he wished to adduce evidence, including love letters, Valentine cards and photographs, to show that he had been very actively involved in relationships with women. The trial judge held this evidence inadmissible.[23] The defendant was convicted and appealed. Lawton LJ emphasised, relying on *Rowton*, that it was not open to the defendant to call evidence of particular facts to show that he had a disposition to make his commission of the offence unlikely. Counsel for the appellant had brought to the court's attention the fact that defendants accused of homosexual offences were often allowed in practice to say that they were happily married and having a normal sexual relationship with their wives. Lawton LJ recognised this practice, but said that it was 'an indulgence on the part of the court'. Defendants did not have a *right* to give such evidence.

THE SIGNIFICANCE OF GOOD CHARACTER

Where evidence of good character is given,[24] its significance must be explained to the jury. Such evidence was originally relevant to guilt or innocence alone. It could not have been relevant to the defendant's credibility as a witness, because the defendant was not competent to give evidence in his own defence. But once the defendant was

---

22 (1981) 74 Cr App R 10.

23 It appears to have been accepted that the evidence was relevant.

24 Typically, this will be by establishing that the defendant has no previous convictions. Character witnesses can also be called, provided they restrict themselves to the evidence allowed by *Rowton*.

allowed to testify, it was clear that good character could have a double function: not only did it make it less likely that the defendant had done what the prosecution alleged, but it meant that he was a more credible witness than someone who was not of good character.

For a long time there were no binding rules about what a judge should say to a jury in summing up on these matters. But wide judicial discretion led to anomalies, and in 1993 the Court of Appeal laid down rules in *R v Vye*.[25] In this case the court recognised two 'limbs' in any direction about good character: the first dealt with the relevance of good character to credibility, and the second with the relevance of good character to the question of whether the defendant was likely to have behaved as alleged by the prosecution. The court then proceeded to consider three problems.

The first problem was whether a direction under the first limb (relevance to credibility) needed to be given in a case where the defendant did not give evidence, but at an earlier stage in the investigation had made exculpatory statements to the police or others.

Evidence of what any defendant has said to the police will generally be admissible in one of three ways. A wholly inculpatory statement will be admissible as a confession. A mixed statement, containing both inculpatory and exculpatory parts, will be admissible as evidence of the truth of all those things that were said.[26] A wholly exculpatory statement will be admissible, not as evidence of the truth of the matters contained in it, but as evidence of the accused's reaction to incriminating facts.[27] In *Vye* the Court of Appeal said that when a defendant has not given evidence at trial, but relies in support of his defence on a mixed statement made to the police or others, the judge should direct the jury to have regard to the defendant's good character when considering its credibility.[28] The reason for this is, as we have seen, that such a statement (unlike a wholly exculpatory statement) is evidence of the truth of its contents. It is therefore evidence in relation to which an issue of credibility arises.

The second problem considered was whether the second limb of the direction (relevance of good character to guilt or innocence) was mandatory or discretionary. The court concluded that this direction *must* be given where the defendant is of good character. No distinction should be made between cases where the defendant has given evidence and those where he has not. The judge should indicate that good character is relevant to propensity, but the actual words used should be a matter for the judge in each case.

The third problem was the position where some defendants in a trial were of good character, but others were not. The court's decision was that a defendant of

---

25   (1993) 97 Cr App R 134.

26   *R v Sharp* (1988) 86 Cr App R 274; *R v Aziz* [1996] AC 41.

27   *R v Storey and Anwar* (1968) 52 Cr App R 334.

28   A direction about the significance of a wholly exculpatory statement is unnecessary, because such a statement is not evidence of the truth of its contents. See above.

good character is entitled to a full direction, even if jointly tried with someone of bad character. In dealing with the co-defendant with bad character, the judge has two choices. In some cases it will be best to grasp the nettle and tell the jury that they have heard nothing about the co-defendant's character, and that they must not speculate or take the absence of information as evidence against him. In other cases it might be better to make no reference to the subject.

DOUBTFUL CASES OF GOOD CHARACTER

In *R v Aziz*,[29] the House of Lords said that a person with no previous convictions was generally to be treated as being of good character. Sometimes, however, a defendant will admit as part of his defence, to *some* wrongdoing, though not that alleged by the prosecution. For example, one of the defendants in *Aziz* admitted making a false mortgage application in connection with a matter that was not the subject of the indictment. The House of Lords ruled that in such cases the *Vye* directions should still be given, accompanied by some appropriate qualification to present a fair and balanced picture to the jury. Exceptionally, it was said, a judge may dispense with the *Vye* directions where it would be an insult to common sense to give them. This might be the case, for example, where a defendant with no previous convictions was shown to have committed a serious crime similar to the offence charged, but not the subject of the indictment.

When a defendant has already pleaded guilty to one or more counts on the indictment, but is contesting others, the earlier pleas will generally mean that he is no longer of good character. What direction, if any, should be given about character is a matter for the judge's discretion.[30]

In giving a *Vye* direction, a trial judge is entitled to take into account the fact that the defendant has been formally cautioned by the police, instead of being charged, in connection with another matter. For a formal caution to be given, the suspect must admit his guilt of the offence in question. Accordingly, it would be proper to direct the jury that such a defendant's lack of previous convictions was relevant to his credibility, but to refuse to give the second limb of the direction in relation to propensity.[31]

SPENT CONVICTIONS AND GOOD CHARACTER

Can a defendant with spent convictions hold himself out to the jury as a person of good character? The answer appears to be that he can, with the leave of the judge, provided the jury is not lied to or misled;[32] so a jury cannot be told that a defendant

---

29   [1996] AC 41.

30   *R v Challenger* [1994] Crim LR 202; cf *R v Teasdale* [1993] 4 All ER 290.

31   *R v Martin* [2000] 2 Cr App R 42.

32   *R v Nye* (1982) 75 Cr App R 247; *R v Bailey* [1989] Crim LR 723.

has no previous convictions when he has,[33] but it is considered legitimate to say that the defendant is 'a man of good character with no relevant convictions'.[34] Even if a conviction is not spent, it may be similarly overlooked if it is minor and of no special significance in the context of the current charge.[35] In *R v Gray*[36] the Court of Appeal said that where the previous conviction can only be regarded as irrelevant in relation to the offence charged, that discretion ought to be exercised in favour of treating the defendant as of good character. Further, where a defendant of previous good character, 'whether absolute or, we would suggest, effective', has been shown at trial to be guilty of some criminal conduct, though not that charged, the prima facie rule of practice is to deal with this by qualifying a *Vye* direction rather than by withdrawing it. If an earlier conviction is ignored or, though mentioned, is treated as irrelevant, the judge should give the *Vye* directions on good character.[37]

EVIDENCE OF BAD CHARACTER IN CRIMINAL PROCEEDINGS

This topic is now almost wholly governed by the CJA 2003. There are some other statutory provisions, the most important of which is s 27(3) of the Theft Act 1968.

DEFINITION OF 'BAD CHARACTER'

Section 98 of the CJA 2003 provides as follows:

References in this Chapter to evidence of a person's 'bad character' are to evidence of, or of a disposition towards, misconduct on his part, other than evidence which –

(a) has to do with the alleged facts of the offence with which the defendant is charged; or

(b) is evidence of misconduct in connection with the investigation or prosecution of that offence.

In several cases the court has had to consider whether evidence had to do with the alleged facts of the offence. In *R v Machado*[38] the defendant was charged with robbery. He wanted to adduce evidence that, during his encounter with the complainant, the latter offered to supply drugs to him and told him that he, the

---

33   *R v O'Shea* [1993] Crim LR 951.

34   May and Powles, 2004, para 7.26.

35   *R v Timson* [1993] Crim LR 58; *R v H* [1994] Crim LR 205.

36   [2004] EWCA Crim 1074, [2004] 2 Cr App R 498, para 57.

37   *R v H* [1994] Crim LR 205.

38   [2006] EWCA Crim 837.

complainant, had taken an ecstasy tablet. The prosecution argued that this evidence should not be admitted as it was evidence of bad character and was excluded by s 100 CJA 2003. The trial judge excluded the evidence on this basis, but the Court of Appeal held that he had been wrong to do so. The evidence related to the very circumstances in which the offence was alleged to have occurred. They were therefore matters 'to do with the alleged facts of the offence' and did not constitute evidence of bad character under s 98.

There must be some nexus in time between the offence charged and the evidence that is said to have to do with the alleged facts of the offence.[39] But a fact that is not exactly contemporaneous with the offence can still fall into this category. For example, in *R v Brummit (Lee)*[40] the Court of Appeal held that the trial judge had been right to admit matters that had occurred half an hour or less before the offence was committed. The defendant was charged with causing death by dangerous driving. As part of the evidence adduced to establish that the defendant's driving had been dangerous, the prosecution wanted to prove certain events that had taken place not more than half an hour earlier, when there had been an altercation and some violence with a shop manager over a stolen fish tank. The defendant had driven the van away in some haste immediately after this incident. The trial judge ruled all these matters admissible as evidence that had to do with the alleged facts of the offence, not as evidence of bad character. The jury, he said, was entitled to know that the defendant had been involved in an emotionally charged incident within half an hour or less of the fatal accident. It was relevant to his state of mind, and might shed some light on his manner of driving afterwards. The Court of Appeal upheld his decision.

Events occurring after the offence can also fall within s 98(a). In *R v McNeill (Tracy)*[41] the defendant was charged with making threats to kill. It was alleged that she damaged a neighbour's front door with a hammer and shouted through the hole that she had made in the door, 'I will burn you and kill you all'. The prosecution was allowed to adduce evidence from a local council housing officer that, two days after this incident, the defendant came to the housing office and asked for temporary accommodation. When told that the office could not help her, she threatened to go home and burn her neighbour's flat down, declaring, 'They'll come out in body bags'. This evidence was admitted, not as evidence of bad character but as evidence that had to with the alleged facts of the offence. The Court of Appeal upheld this decision, observing that the words 'has to deal with' are of broad application.

'Misconduct' is defined in s 112(1) as 'the commission of an offence or other reprehensible behaviour'. The Law Commission's recommendation was that evidence of a person's bad character should be defined as evidence showing or tending to show

---

39   *R v Tirnaveanu* [2007] EWCA Crim 1239, para 23.
40   [2006] EWCA Crim 1629.
41   [2007] EWCA Crim 2927.

either that that person had committed an offence, or had behaved, or was disposed to behave, 'in a way of which a reasonable person might disapprove'.[42] The Commission's aim was to define bad character, as far as possible, according to objective criteria. It recognised that the question of whether a reasonable person would disapprove of particular conduct would sometimes be a matter of opinion, but concluded that a court should be capable of deciding, in a judicial manner, whether disapproval was *within the range of responses open to a reasonable person*. The Commission did not think it would be sensible to draw a distinction between evidence of conduct and evidence of a disposition which had not, or could not be shown to have, manifested itself in conduct.[43] These recommendations may throw light on the way in which s 98 is likely to be interpreted. Section 98 follows the recommendation that evidence of disposition by itself should come within the scope of bad character. According to the Explanatory Notes accompanying the CJA 2003, the definition of misconduct in s 112(1) is intended to be a broad one, and it is suggested that evidence not related to criminal proceedings 'might include, for example, evidence that a person has a sexual interest in children or is racist'.[44] It is likely that courts, in deciding whether there is a disposition towards misconduct, will look at the particular facts of each case and avoid laying down general rules. For example, if there is evidence that a man had admitted having a sexual interest in children, while denying ever having acted on that interest, that could, but need not inevitably, be treated as evidence of disposition towards misconduct.

The requirement that misconduct should consist of the commission of an offence *or other reprehensible behaviour* appears to set a more rigorous standard than that proposed by the Law Commission. Reprehensible behaviour is treated as something capable of objective assessment. If something is said to be reprehensible, the fundamental idea is that it is blameworthy in a moral sense.[45] Often this is unlikely to give rise to difficulty, but problem cases could arise, particularly where sexual morality is concerned. However, if evidence of a certain type of behaviour is not evidence of bad character, the bars to admissibility provided in Chapter 1 of the CJA 2003 will not apply, so defendants will be unlikely to argue that their behaviour is outside the definition.[46]

According to the Explanatory Notes, the definition of bad character is intended to include evidence of previous convictions, evidence on charges being tried concur-

---

42   Law Commission No 273, 2001, para 8.19.

43   Law Commission No 273, paras 8.16–8.18.

44   Explanatory Notes, paras 353, 355. In *R v Donnelly (Anthony Patrick)* [2006] EWCA Crim 545, the Court of Appeal said it was certainly arguable that evidence of a defendant's heroin addiction came within the definition of 'bad character' for the purposes of s 98.

45   As an example of usage, *The New Shorter Oxford English Dictionary* gives, 'It's . . . reprehensible to cheat the grocer' (AS Neill). Cf the earlier *Shorter Oxford English Dictionary*, which gives, 'In a meane man prodigalitie and pride are faultes more reprehensible than in Princes' (Puttenham).

46   An argument for exclusion is more likely to be based on relevance.

rently, and also evidence relating to offences for which a person has been charged, but where either the charge was not prosecuted or the prosecution led to an acquittal.[47] In *R v Mustapha (Mohammed Amadu)*[48] the Court of Appeal held that there is no bar to receiving evidence of bad character despite the fact that the evidence relates to an offence of which the defendant has been acquitted. This is in line with the law before CJA 2003. In *R v Z*[49] the House of Lords held that similar fact evidence could be adduced where it was evidence of circumstances that had led to a criminal charge, in respect of which the defendant was later acquitted. In that case there had been a series of attacks on women. The defendant had been charged in respect of four of them, and had been acquitted on three of the charges. When he was tried in respect of yet another attack, it was held that the evidence supporting the earlier charges on which he had been acquitted could be used to assist in proving his guilt on the current charge. However, Lord Hobhouse observed that while such evidence is in principle admissible, the facts of each case will need to be examined with special care. A wide variety of circumstances is possible. At one end of the spectrum there may be a man who has had to face a series of similar allegations of rape made by different women. Suppose that on each occasion his defence was consent, or a belief that the woman consented. Such defences might well succeed at first, but later become implausible through repetition. If he is charged again with rape and raises the same defence as before, it is likely that the earlier occasions could be used in rebuttal. But suppose the earlier acquittals had come about in a variety of ways. For example, at one trial there might have been a successful submission of no case to answer; at another, a defence of consent succeeded; at yet another, a defence of mistaken identity. The probative worth, at his fourth trial for rape, of the circumstances leading to those acquittals is by no means clear. Another relevant consideration is likely to be the number of previous acquittals; one alone, in the absence of other similar fact evidence, would almost certainly be insufficient, yet another consideration could be the distance in time between the earlier alleged offences and the current one.[50]

NON-DEFENDANT'S BAD CHARACTER

As we have seen, at common law, a defendant was, in principle, entitled to shake the credit of any prosecution witnesses by showing that they had previous convictions, and the prosecution had a free hand to do the same with any defence witnesses who were not themselves defendants.[51]

Section 100(1) sets out the limited circumstances in which evidence of the bad character of a person other than the defendant can now be given. The words 'a person

---

47   Explanatory Notes, para 354.

48   [2007] EWCA Crim 1702, para 23.

49   [2000] 3 All ER 385.

50   *R v Z* [2000] 3 All ER 385, pp 407–08.

51   See above.

other than the defendant' will include prosecution witnesses and defence witnesses other than defendants. It is not clear whether the words include a person who has died, such as a deceased victim of the alleged offence. However, it is necessary to remember the definition of bad character in s 98. It does not include matters that have to do with the offence with which the defendant is charged, or with misconduct in connection with the investigation or prosecution of that offence. So a defendant is free, for example, to allege that the offence was committed by one of the prosecution witnesses and not by himself, or that the police planted evidence on him. But evidence of a non-defendant's bad character falling within s 98 can be given only if it meets one of three conditions: (a) it is important explanatory evidence; (b) it has substantial probative value in relation to a matter in issue in the proceedings, and that issue is one of substantial importance in the context of the case as a whole; or (c) all parties to the proceedings agree that the evidence should be admitted. Where reliance is placed on (a) or (b), the leave of the court is required,[52] but no guidance is given as to how this discretion is to be exercised. (The exercise of *discretion* pre-supposes a *judgment* that one of the conditions is satisfied.)

The nature of important explanatory evidence is dealt with below in connection with the defendant's bad character, because it is in that context that it is most likely to be considered by a court. In respect of non-defendants, evidence of bad character is most likely to have substantial probative value where the honesty as a witness of the non-defendant is questioned. Where this is the case, will previous convictions have to be for offences of dishonesty in order to satisfy the test under s 100(1)(b)? Almost certainly not. Suppose it is alleged that a prosecution witness is deliberately giving false evidence against the defendant. The witness has a recent conviction for assault. When tried for that offence, he pleaded not guilty and gave evidence in his own defence. It must follow from his conviction that he was then disbelieved on his oath, and that fact could be held to have substantial probative value in relation to his honesty as a witness in the current trial.

Sub-section (3) directs the court to have regard to various factors, and to any others it considers relevant, in assessing whether the value of evidence is 'substantial' for the purposes of sub-s (1)(b). These are:

(a) the nature and number of the events, or other things, to which the evidence relates;

(b) when those events or things are alleged to have happened or existed;

(c) where –

    (i)   the evidence is evidence of a person's misconduct, and

    (ii) it is suggested that the evidence has probative value by reason of similarity between that misconduct and other alleged misconduct,

---

52 Section 100(4). Although cross-examination is not expressly mentioned, it cannot be doubted that leave is necessary to cross-examine about bad character (*R v V* [2006] EWCA Crim 1901, para 23).

the nature and extent of the similarities and the dissimilarities between each of the alleged instances of misconduct;

(d)   where –

(i)   the evidence is of a person's misconduct,

(ii)   it is suggested that that person is also responsible for the misconduct charged, and

(iii)   the identity of the person responsible for the misconduct charged is disputed,

the extent to which the evidence shows or tends to show that the same person was responsible each time.

Finally, it should be noted that nothing in s 100 affects the rule whereby a party is not allowed to impeach the credit of his own witness by general evidence of bad character. Nor does the section affect the exclusion of evidence under s 41 of the Youth Justice and Criminal Evidence Act 1999.[53]

DEFENDANT'S BAD CHARACTER

Section 101(1) of CJA 2003 provides seven 'gateways' through which evidence of a defendant's bad character can be admitted:

(a)   all parties to the proceedings agree to the evidence being admissible,

(b)   the evidence is adduced by the defendant himself or is given in answer to a question asked by him in cross-examination and intended to elicit it,

(c)   it is important explanatory evidence,

(d)   it is relevant to an important matter in issue between the defendant and the prosecution,

(e)   it has substantial probative value in relation to an important matter in issue between the defendant and a co-defendant,

(f)   it is evidence to correct a false impression given by the defendant, or

(g)   the defendant has made an attack on another person's character.

In *R v Highton (Edward Paul)*[54] the Court of Appeal said that a distinction must be drawn between the *admissibility* of bad character evidence, which depends on getting it through one of the gateways, and the *use* to which it can be put once it is admitted. The use depends on matters to which it is relevant rather than to the gateway through which it is admitted. For example, in the case of gateway (g), admissibility depends on the defendant's having made an attack on another person's character. But once the evidence is admitted it may, depending on the facts, be relevant not only to credibility but also to propensity to commit offences of the kind with which the defendant is charged. Similarly, evidence admitted under gateway (d) to show propensity may also have relevance to credibility.[55]

---

53   CJA 2003, s 112(3)(a) and (b).

54   [2005] EWCA Crim 1985, [2005] 1 WLR 3472, para 10.

55   *R v Campbell* [2007] EWCA Crim 1472, [2007] 1 WLR 2798.

The warning of the Court of Appeal in *R v Renda*[56] should be remembered when studying the gateways. Judgments in these cases are 'fact specific', and the trial judge's 'feel' for the case is usually critical. It follows that decisions in other cases do not constitute a body of 'authority' from which precedents can be cited, and argument must concentrate on the facts of the particular case. The Court of Appeal will not interfere with a trial judge's decision just because each member of the Court would have decided differently had he or she been the trial judge. An appellant must show *Wednesbury* unreasonableness on the part of the trial judge before the Court will interfere.

Gateways (a) and (b): all parties consent; evidence from the defendant

Gateway (a) requires no comment. Under sub-s (1)(b), evidence of the defendant's bad character is admissible where it is adduced by the defendant himself. The view taken by the Law Commission was that a defendant should always have the right to adduce such evidence if it would be helpful to him to do so. An obvious example would be where the defendant had an alibi because he was in prison at the time when the offence was committed.[57] There may also be occasions where a defendant's bad character is bound to be the subject of cross-examination. His counsel may wish to anticipate this by bringing out the details during examination-in-chief, in the hope that this will reduce the effect of the information on the jury. Under the same sub-section, evidence of the defendant's bad character is also admissible where it is 'given in answer to a question asked by [the defendant] in cross-examination and intended to elicit it'. This envisages the situation where a prosecution witness, such as a police officer, does not give evidence-in-chief of the defendant's bad character, but defence counsel believes that it is bound to come out when the defendant is cross-examined, and so, for the same tactical reason, wishes to bring this information before the jury at the earliest possible stage. The sub-section allows him to do so by cross-examining an appropriate prosecution witness on the subject.

A problem arose under the Criminal Evidence Act 1898 in *Jones v DPP*.[58] A defendant gave evidence admitting that he had at first given a false alibi to the police. He said the reason was that he had previously been in trouble with the police and did not want to be in trouble with them again. The House of Lords interpreted the 1898 Act as prohibiting cross-examination that would tend to show *for the first time* that the defendant was of bad character. The defendant's reference to previous trouble with the police had been imprecise, but a majority thought that it would have been reasonable for the jury to infer from that expression that the defendant had a previous conviction. This opened the way for the prosecution to cross-examine in detail about

---

56   [2005] EWCA Crim 2826, para 3.

57   Law Commission No 273, 2001, para 8.30.

58   [1962] AC 635.

events leading to an earlier conviction for rape, because that cross-examination did not reveal to the jury *for the first time* that the defendant was of bad character; the defendant himself had revealed that fact. Would the result be the same today? Arguably, the defendant would have adduced evidence of his bad character within s 101(1)(b) and, having done so, would have left the prosecution free to cross-examine so as to provide the jury with a complete picture.[59]

Important explanatory evidence: s 101(1)(c)

Section 101(1)(c) allows evidence of the defendant's bad character to be admitted where it is 'important explanatory evidence'. To understand this concept it is necessary to look at an area of the common law, now abolished by s 99, which admitted what came to be known as 'background evidence'. According to the Law Commission, background evidence might be admissible in any of four ways:

■ The evidence was close in time, place or circumstances to the facts or circumstances of the offence charged.
■ The evidence was necessary to complete the account of the circumstances of the offence charged so as to make it comprehensible to the jury.
■ The accused had had a relationship with the victim of the offence charged, and the evidence was of the defendant's previous conduct in relation to the victim.
■ The evidence helped to establish motive.[60]

The Commission said that there were two different reasons for admitting such evidence. One was that it was inextricably linked to the facts of the offence charged. Evidence of this kind was part of the narrative of the offence and should be automatically admissible:

> It would, for example, be very strange if evidence of an assault committed in the course of a rape, but not separately charged, were to be treated as *prima facie* inadmissible; or if, on a charge of murder by firing a bullet through a window, the prosecution had to seek leave to adduce evidence that the defendant had not only killed the deceased but also broken the window; or if, on a charge of burning down a hostel for ex-prisoners, leave were required to prove that the defendant was a resident of that hostel.[61]

Evidence of this kind would not be regarded as falling within s 98, because it has to do with the alleged facts of the offence with which the defendant is charged, and so would not be evidence of 'bad character' for the purposes of this Chapter of Pt 11 of the CJA 2003.

---

59 But this part of the decision in *Jones v DPP* attracted criticism, and a court today might say that cases decided under the earlier legislation were of no assistance in interpreting s 101(1)(b).
60 Law Commission No 273, 2001, para 10.1.
61 Law Commission No 273, 2001, para 10.4.

The second reason for admitting background evidence was that although it did not form part of the alleged facts of the offence, it was linked to those facts because it made them comprehensible. The origin of this idea was often traced to *R v Pettman*, an unreported decision of the Court of Appeal in 1985.[62] This was authority for the proposition that evidence showing the defendant's commission of the offence could be admitted if it was necessary to place it before the jury in order to complete, or make comprehensible, the facts alleged in support of the charge. So, for example, in *R v M(T) and Others*,[63] in which *Pettman* was applied, evidence that M had from a young age been taught by a member of his family to abuse his sisters sexually was held admissible to explain, among other things, why one of M's sisters had made no attempt to obtain help when M had abused her on later occasions that were the subject of the indictment.

The problem with the *Pettman* test was that there appeared to be two possible forms. One permitted background evidence where, without it, the account placed before the jury would be *incomprehensible*; the other appeared to admit such evidence where, without it, the account would be merely *incomplete*. The test, therefore, had a potential for admitting evidence that might be only minimally probative, but was substantially prejudicial to a defendant. For example, although not specifically referred to, the *Pettman* principle seems to have been relied on in *R v Underwood*.[64] In that case, the defendant was charged with offences of violence against the woman with whom he was living. The prosecution was allowed to adduce, as part of the background history, evidence of another act of violence not covered by the indictment, evidence that the defendant had prevailed on the complainant to have an abortion, and evidence of the defendant's knowledge of the effect of his violence after the complainant had suffered a stroke. The Court of Appeal upheld the admissibility of all three items of evidence as part of the essential background to the relationship between the parties, and also as rebutting the defence of accident raised by the defendant in relation to one of the counts.[65]

Because of this defect, the Law Commission recommended that, to be admitted, such evidence should have substantial explanatory value, and that the interests of justice should require it to be admitted, even taking account of its potentially prejudicial effect.[66] Section 102 now provides that evidence is 'important explanatory evidence' if without it the court or jury would find it *impossible* or *difficult* to understand properly other evidence in the case, *and* its value for understanding the case as a whole is substantial. There is no requirement that the prosecution show that the interests of justice require the evidence to be admissible. But the

---

62   (1985) unreported, 2 May.
63   [2000] 1 All ER 148.
64   [1999] Crim LR 227.
65   For another example of the potential scope of *Pettman*, see *R v Fulcher* [1995] 2 Cr App R 251.
66   Law Commission No 273, 2001, paras 10.7–10.12.

common law discretion to exclude prosecution evidence where prejudicial effect exceeds probative worth almost certainly remains.[67]

Relevant to important matter in issue between defendant and prosecution: s 101(1)(d)

Sub-section (1)(d) concerns evidence of a defendant's bad character to be given, but only by the prosecution,[68] where 'it is relevant to an *important* matter in issue between the defendant and the prosecution'.[69] By s 103(1):

For the purposes of section 101(1)(d) the matters in issue between the defendant and the prosecution include –

(a) the question whether the defendant has a propensity to commit offences of the kind with which he is charged, except where his having such a propensity makes it no more likely that he is guilty of the offence;

(b) the question whether the defendant has a propensity to be untruthful, except where it is not suggested that the defendant's case is untruthful in any respect.

Where sub-s (1)(a) applies, the propensity may, without prejudice to any other way of doing so, be established by evidence that the defendant has been convicted of an offence of the same description, or of the same category, as the one with which he is charged.[70]

Several points need attention. First, under s 101(1)(d) there is no requirement that the probative value of such evidence should be substantial. Indeed, it seems that even the mere making of an allegation against a defendant on an earlier occasion is capable of amounting to evidence of bad character.[71] In this respect it differs from provisions relating to the bad character of both non-defendants,[72] and co-defendants.[73] It also differs from the recommendations of the Law Commission that

---

67   See the discussion of *R v Sang*, below, in relation to sub-s (1)(d). Arguably, if the evidence satisfies the s 102 test it would be bound to satisfy an interests of justice test, and its probative worth would be bound to exceed any prejudicial effect that the evidence might have.

68   Section 106(3).

69   Section 101(1)(d), emphasis added.

70   Section 103(2). Offences are of the same description as each other if the statement of the offence in the charge or indictment would be in the same terms; eg, both are offences of theft, both are offences of assault occasioning actual bodily harm, or both are offences of rape. Categories of offences are to be prescribed by statutory instrument. The only restriction is that they must consist of offences 'of the same type'. See s 103(4), (5). Foreign convictions, if properly proved, can be relied on (*R v Kordasinski* [2006] EWCA Crim 2984).

71   *R v Edwards* [2005] EWCA Crim 3244, paras 1, 81. But see the doubt expressed in *R v Bovell* [2005] EWCA Crim 1091, para 21.

72   Section 100(1)(b).

73   Section 101(1)(e).

such evidence should have 'substantial probative value in relation to a matter in issue (other than whether the defendant has a propensity to be untruthful) which is itself of substantial importance in the context of the case as a whole' and that the interests of justice should require its admission, even taking account of its potentially prejudicial effect.[74]

Secondly, the question of propensity is as important where the defence is a complete denial of what is alleged as where a defendant relies on mistaken identity, or an innocent explanation for an ambiguous action. In *R v Wilkinson (Thomas McBride)*[75] the defendant was charged with attempting to rape a female under the age of sixteen. The prosecution was allowed, under gateway (d), to adduce in evidence his previous convictions for sexual offences against children. The defence case was that the complainant's allegation was a complete fabrication. He was convicted. On appeal it was argued that the important matter in issue between the defendant and the prosecution was whether an attempted rape had taken place at all, and the previous convictions were not relevant to that. They *would* have been relevant if the defendant had committed some minor sexual offence against the complainant but had denied the more serious charge. The Court of Appeal rejected this argument, saying that it could not make any difference to the question of admissibility whether the defendant denied any physical contact with the girl, or whether he admitted some lesser physical contact.

Thirdly, convictions *after* the commission of the offence for which the defendant is being tried are capable of amounting to evidence of propensity.[76]

Fourthly, under s 103(1), matters in issue between the defendant and the prosecution include both propensity to commit offences of the kind with which he is charged, and propensity to be untruthful. The view of the Law Commission was that the defendant's general propensity to be untruthful was not a matter that it would be fair to allow the prosecution to assert as part of its case. As was said:

> Where the defendant simply denies the truth of some or all of the prosecution's evidence in relation to the offence charged, and makes no attempt to attack anyone *else's* credibility, we think it virtually inconceivable that evidence of the defendant's general untruthfulness could ever have sufficient probative value to outweigh the risk of prejudice.[77]

Section 101(1)(g) allows evidence of the defendant's bad character to be given where he attacks someone else's credibility. It is plain, therefore, that there may now be circumstances where evidence of the defendant's propensity to be untruthful could

---

74   Law Commission No 273, 2001, para 11.46.

75   [2006] EWCA Crim 1332.

76   *R v Adenusi (Oladele)* [2006] EWCA Crim 1059. (Defendant tried for using a false instrument and attempting to obtain a money transfer by deception; convictions admitted for two offences of using a false instrument on a date five days after that of the offences being tried.)

77   Law Commission No 273, 2001, para 11.32.

be given regardless of the fact that no such attack has been made. The Explanatory Notes suggest that s 103(1)(b) 'is intended to enable the admission of a limited range of evidence such as convictions for perjury or other offences involving deception (for example, obtaining property by deception), as opposed to the wider range of evidence that will be admissible where the defendant puts his character in issue by, for example, attacking the character of another person'.[78] Without some limitation, the effect of s 103(1)(b) could be very wide because potentially it would allow the prosecution to adduce evidence that the defendant has been found guilty in the past in any trial in which he had pleaded not guilty and given evidence in his defence. Such evidence would be particularly damning where the defence unsuccessfully raised on an earlier occasion was of the same nature as the one raised in the current trial; for example, where the defence was an alibi, or involved an allegation that incriminating articles had been 'planted'. Support for this wide interpretation can be found in *R v Hanson*,[79] where the Court of Appeal said that propensity to untruthfulness is not the same as propensity to dishonesty. Previous convictions, *whether for offences of dishonesty or otherwise*, are likely to be capable of showing a propensity to be untruthful where, in earlier cases, either there was a plea of not guilty and the defendant gave an account in evidence which the jury must have disbelieved, or the way in which the earlier offence was committed showed a propensity for untruthfulness, for example, by the making of false representations.

An example of this broad interpretation can be seen in *R v Alobaydi (Mohand Stephen)*.[80] The defendant was charged with rape. His defence was that sexual intercourse with the complainant had been consensual. There was therefore what the Court of Appeal described as 'a stark issue of credibility' for the jury to determine. The prosecution applied for evidence of the defendant's bad character to be admitted on the basis that it showed a propensity to be untruthful. On one previous occasion he had been convicted on an indictment containing counts of aggravated burglary, damaging property, making threats to kill, and assault occasioning actual bodily harm. On that occasion he had pleaded not guilty, and had given evidence in his own defence which, because of their guilty verdict, the jury must have disbelieved. Before being charged with those offences he had made statements in a police interview which reflected what he later said in evidence. By inference, therefore, these earlier statements had also been false. The judge in the rape trial concluded that he had not told just one or two lies, but had given an entirely false account in all respects. He was convicted and appealed.

His counsel argued that if s 103(1)(b) were to be applied across the board, every person who has pleaded not guilty on a previous occasion and has been convicted is at risk of having evidence of his bad character given in a later trial. The Court of Appeal

---

78   Explanatory Notes, para 374.

79   [2005] EWCA Crim 824, [2005] 1 WLR 3169, para 13.

80   [2007] EWCA Crim 145.

appears to have recognised this, while trying to avoid the full impact of the argument by saying that decisions made under s 101(1)(d) 'are very fact sensitive', and that the approach of the trial judge is all important. The conviction was upheld.

However, a wide application of s 103(1)(b) may be less likely in view of the decision of the Court of Appeal in *R v Campbell*.[81] According to Lord Phillips of Worth Matravers CJ, who delivered the judgment of the Court, it will be comparatively rare for the case of a defendant who denies the charge not to involve some element that the prosecution suggests is untruthful. But just because there is an issue as to whether the defendant's case might be true, it does not follow that evidence can be admitted to show that he has a propensity to be untruthful. The reason for this, according to Lord Phillips, is that the question whether the defendant has a propensity for being untruthful will not normally be capable of being described as being an *important* matter in issue between the defendant and the prosecution so as to fall within s 101(1)(d). A propensity for untruthfulness will not, by itself, go very far towards establishing the guilt of the defendant:

> To suggest that a propensity for untruthfulness makes it more likely that a defendant has lied to the jury is not likely to help them. If they apply common sense they will conclude that a defendant who has committed a criminal offence may well be prepared to lie about it even if he has not shown a propensity for lying, whereas a defendant who has not committed the offence charged will be likely to tell the truth, even if he has shown a propensity for telling lies. In short, whether or not a defendant is telling the truth to the jury is likely to depend simply on whether or not he committed the offence charged. The jury should focus on the latter question rather than on whether or not he has a propensity for telling lies.
>
> For these reasons, the only circumstance in which there is likely to be an *important* issue as to whether a defendant has a propensity to tell lies is where telling lies is an element of the offence charged. Even then, the propensity to tell lies is only likely to be significant if the lying is in the context of committing criminal offences, in which case the evidence is likely to be admissible under section 103(1)(a).[82]

Evidence of propensity will not be available under sub-s (1)(d) if having the propensity 'makes it no more likely that [the defendant] is guilty of the offence'.[83]

---

81   [2007] EWCA Crim 1472, [2007] 1 WLR 2798, paras 29–31.

82   Lord Phillips's observations seem to make s 103(1)(b) a 'dead letter'; see Mirfield, 2008, where their extension to gateway (g) is also considered. At present it is unclear how far previous convictions can be used on the basis that they are relevant to a defendant's credibility. Matters in issue between the defendant and the prosecution *include*, but are not *confined to*, those set out in s 103(1). The credibility of a defendant could well be another matter in issue, and perhaps an important one. In *R v Stephenson (David)* [2006] EWCA Crim 2325, para 27, the Court of Appeal said that previous convictions which do not involve either the making of false statements or the giving of false evidence can have substantial probative value in relation to credibility.

83   See s 103(1)(a).

The Explanatory Notes cautiously suggest that this might be the case where the question is whether facts that are agreed constitute an offence.[84] Before the 2003 Act, courts took the view that the earlier commission of commonplace offences in a commonplace way was not of sufficient probative worth to be admitted when a defendant was later charged with the same commonplace offence committed in the same commonplace way.[85] It seems clear, however, that such evidence can now be admitted. For example, in *R v Hanson*[86] the defendant was charged with theft of cash from the private quarters of a public house. Evidence was held admissible under gateway (d) of a considerable number of previous convictions for burglary and theft from a dwelling. And in *R v Gilmore*[87] the defendant had been charged with theft of property on the basis that it had been taken either from a garden shed or from a nearby alleyway. Although the mode of commission of the current offence was different, three shoplifting offences committed within a six-week period ending three months before the date of the offence charged were held to have been properly admitted through gateway (d). The Court of Appeal concluded that the trial judge had been fully entitled to conclude that these offences showed a recent persistent propensity to steal.

The fact that a defendant's previous convictions are of the same description or category[88] as the offence with which he is charged does not mean that they are automatically admissible. In *R v Tully (Stephen) and Wood (Kevin)*[89] the defendants were charged with robbery. Wood had eight previous convictions for robbery and 18 other convictions for offences of dishonesty. Tully had five previous convictions for robbery and 23 other convictions for offences of dishonesty. The prosecution had intended to put in only the convictions of both for robbery, but the trial judge urged that all the other offences of dishonesty should be put in as well, on the basis that they were convictions for offences of the same category as robbery. This was done. The Court of Appeal said that the judge had been wrong to hold, in effect, that a propensity to obtain other people's property by one means or another made it more likely that the defendants committed the offence of robbery with which they were charged. The Court said that it is not possible to define the degree of similarity which must be shown between previous convictions and the offence being tried. That must be for the judge's discretion and judgment in each individual case. But the judge must strike a balance, bearing in mind s 101(3).

---

84   Explanatory Notes, para 371.
85   See, eg, *R v Brown* (1963) 47 Cr App R 204; *DPP v Boardman* [1975] AC 421, p 454.
86   [2005] EWCA Crim 824, [2005] 1 WLR 3169.
87   Reported with *R v Hanson*.
88   See s 103(2).
89   [2006] EWCA Crim 2270.

By s 101(3), the court *must not* admit evidence under sub-s (1)(d)[90] if, on an application by the defendant to exclude it, it appears to the court that the admission of the evidence would have such an adverse effect on the fairness of the proceedings that the court ought not to admit it. On an application to exclude evidence under s 101(3) the court must have regard, in particular, to the length of time between the matters to which that evidence relates and the matters which form the subject of the offence charged.[91] For example, a court could decide that evidence of a spent conviction should not be given, but the exception is not confined to spent convictions.

Where the prosecution wishes to rely on s 103(1)(a) and (2) to show propensity to commit offences of the kind with which the defendant is charged, account must be taken of the restriction contained in s 103(3). This provides that sub-s (2), which permits proof of previous convictions to establish propensity, *does not apply* in the case of a particular defendant 'if the court is satisfied by reason of the length of time since the conviction *or for any other reason*, that it would be unjust to apply it in his case'.[92]

Either under s 101(3) or s 103(3), it will therefore be open to the defence to argue that evidence admissible under s 101(1)(d) ought to be excluded because its prejudicial effect exceeds its probative value. The concept is a familiar one. It was the guiding principle in the law against the admission of similar fact evidence, as finally formulated in *DPP v P*.[93] Before that decision, it had been held by the House of Lords in *R v Sang*[94] that a judge in a criminal trial has always a discretion to refuse to admit prosecution evidence if in his opinion its prejudicial effect outweighs its probative value. Section 99(1) of the CJA 2003 provides that 'the common law rules governing the admissibility of evidence of bad character in criminal proceedings are abolished'. But it is most unlikely that this has the effect of abolishing the *general* common law rule established by *Sang*. Further, s 101(3) adopts the test for exclusion contained in s 78(1) of the Police and Criminal Evidence Act 1984, and it seems clear that this test can be satisfied where the prejudicial effect of an item of evidence exceeds its probative value.[95] In addition, s 103(3) refers expressly to the length of time since the previous conviction, and this indicates that a court should be concerned with prejudicial effect and probative worth. Even if this were not so, the very broad expression 'any other reason' in the sub-section must make such a consideration relevant. It seems likely that, in considering whether to admit evidence under

---

90   Or under sub-s (1)(g); see below.

91   Sub-section (4).

92   Emphasis added.

93   [1991] 2 AC 447.

94   [1980] AC 402.

95   See, eg, *R v Boyson* [1991] Crim LR 274; *R v Lee* [1996] Crim LR 825; and *R v Mahmoud and Manzur* [1997] 1 Cr App R 414, where this was taken to be a proper consideration under s 78(1). Section 78 of PACE is almost certainly available as an additional protection for a defendant (*R v Highton (Edward Paul)* [2005] EWCA Crim 1985, para 13).

s 101(1)(d), the reasoning of the court will be very similar to that adopted in relation to similar fact evidence after *DPP v P*.[96] It may be useful to illustrate this reasoning by reference to two examples: cases where similar fact evidence was admitted to prove identification, and where it was admitted to rebut a defence put forward by the accused.

In *R v Lee*,[97] the Court of Appeal emphasised that the test of admissibility for similar fact evidence in identification cases was, as in other types of case, the balancing of probative weight against prejudice to the defendant in the particular circumstances of the case. The court said that similar fact evidence could be used to identify the defendant as the wrongdoer by means of a 'signature' (that is, an unusual feature of the way in which the offence was committed), *or by some other special feature*. Sometimes another special feature has been the discovery of incriminating articles in the defendant's possession.

One of the earliest examples is *Thompson v R*.[98] The defendant was charged with committing an act of gross indecency in a public lavatory with two boys. The prosecution said that the acts in question had been committed on 16 March, and that the person who committed them had made an arrangement to see the boys again at the same place on 19 March. Police officers kept watch with the boys on 19 March. In due course the defendant arrived. After he had been identified by the boys and arrested, he claimed to be the victim of mistaken identification. Evidence was given at trial that, when arrested, the defendant had been in possession of powder puffs, and that when his rooms were searched indecent photographs of boys had been found. The House of Lords held that this evidence showed the defendant to be a homosexual, and was admissible to support the boys' identifications. If their identifications had not been accurate, it was an unbelievable coincidence that the man they mistakenly identified was also a homosexual.

Where discovery of incriminating articles is relied on to support the prosecution case, there is clearly a danger that, without some limitation on the type of articles admissible, the defendant will be convicted merely because the articles suggest that he is likely to commit offences of the type in question. It used to be said that the articles found must have had some connection with the offence charged. In *R v Taylor*,[99] the defendant was charged with shopbreaking. A police officer gave evidence that, at about midnight, he had seen the defendant and another man outside a shop, had heard the door being forced open, and had seen the defendant and another man run out. On arrest, the defendant told the officer that the affair was a drunken escapade, and that he and the other man had charged one another against the door and broken it. There were no marks of any kind on the door and nothing had been stolen, but at

---

96   [1991] 2 AC 447.
97   [1996] Crim LR 825; see also *R v W (John)* [1998] 2 Cr App R 289.
98   [1918] AC 221.
99   (1923) 17 Cr App R 109.

trial evidence was given that when the defendant's house was later searched, a jemmy had been found. It was argued on appeal that no connection had been shown between the jemmy and what the defendant was alleged to have done. For this reason as well as for others his appeal was allowed.

Similarly, in the Australian case of *Thompson v The Queen*,[100] the defendants were charged with burglary from two safes, which had been blown open by explosives. The prosecution was allowed to call evidence to show that the accused had in their possession a collection of instruments for opening safes by blowing, by drilling, or by picking the locks. The court held that evidence of possession of articles that *might* have been used in the commission of the offence was admissible, but the extent of the evidence that had been admitted was too wide, and the appeal was allowed.

Even in the absence of an apparent connection between the incriminating articles and the offence, evidence of their discovery could be given if it had some bearing on a defence put forward by the defendant. In *R v Da Silva*,[101] for example, the defendant was charged with armed robbery. Two masked men had entered the bedroom of a hotel owner at about 1 am and had made off with about £8,500 in cash. The prosecution alleged that the defendant was one of those involved, and relied, among other evidence, on what had been found during a search of the defendant's room. Police had discovered one of the hotel's brochures, £1,200 in cash and a dagger, which the hotel owner said resembled one with which he had been threatened by the robbers. The police also found a meat cleaver, a knife and a truncheon hidden under the floorboards. Were these items admissible? There was no evidence that they had been used in the robbery. But the defendant had provided an explanation for his possession of the dagger: according to him, it was part of his equipment for martial arts training. The trial judge held that evidence of the discoveries under the floorboards could be given, because that evidence tended to show that the explanation for possession of the dagger was untrue. How it was meant to do so is unclear, but the judge's decision was upheld by the Court of Appeal.

R v Da Silva was an example of a case where similar fact evidence was admitted because of the nature of the defence. A similar line of reasoning was adopted in several cases of drug importation. For example, in *R v Sokialiois*,[102] the defendant was charged with importing cocaine. A packet had been posted from Holland to an address in Dover. It was intercepted, and a co-defendant who attempted to retrieve it from the post office was arrested. The defendant was arrested a little later. In his possession was a piece of paper containing the Dover address where the packet was to be delivered, and a diary with a note of the same address and the words 'Uncle Charlie' (a slang expression for cocaine). When interviewed, the defendant denied

---

100   (1968) 117 CLR 313.
101   [1990] 1 WLR 31.
102   [1993] Crim LR 872.

any knowledge of the address and said, 'I am not a drug dealer. I don't deal in drugs. I don't even take drugs'. His holdall was later recovered from a hotel and found to contain a further quantity of cocaine of similar purity. His defence was that the paper containing the address and the drugs in the holdall had been planted on him by one of his co-accused.

The judge admitted the evidence of the holdall on the ground that it was relevant to the defendant's replies given in the interview. On appeal it was argued that the discovery of the second quantity of cocaine was relevant only to propensity, and in effect amounted merely to evidence of bad character, which on ordinary principles would have been inadmissible. The Court of Appeal, however, rejected this argument, saying that the evidence rebutted what had been said in the interview, which itself had been designed to bolster the defence that the defendant had been framed.

A more difficult case was *R v Peters*.[103] The defendant was charged with importing amphetamines by concealing them in his car. In police interviews he denied any knowledge of the presence of the drugs, and said that he had no connection with drugs in any form. A search of his home revealed small quantities of cannabis and some drug-related equipment. Was this evidence admissible? The Court of Appeal held that it was, because it showed that his denial of any connection with drugs was untrue. But the court added that it would have been admissible even if in the interview he had merely denied knowledge of how the amphetamines had come to be concealed in his car. In effect, the defendant was saying that he was the innocent victim of someone who had used his car to smuggle drugs. According to the court, the defendant's own connection with drugs – even of a different kind – was relevant and admissible to rebut this defence. But the court noted that it was 'clear, of course', that evidence of previous convictions for drug offences could not have been given for this purpose.[104]

Similar fact evidence was often admitted to rebut a defence that the defendant had no criminal intent. An old but vivid example is *R v Mortimer*.[105] The defendant was charged with the murder of a woman cyclist. The case for the prosecution was that on the morning of 8 August 1935, he had deliberately driven his car at a woman riding a bicycle and had knocked her down, with fatal results. His defence was accident. In the light of this, the prosecution was allowed to prove that on two occasions during the previous evening he had knocked down two other women

---

103   [1995] 2 Cr App R 77.

104   The reasoning is obscure. What generalisations about the way things are in the world were tacitly assumed when the court said that the chances of the defendant's being an innocent victim of a drug smuggler must depend greatly on whether he had any contact, even if only as a customer, with persons who handled unlawful drugs? (*R v Peters* [1995] 2 Cr App R 77, pp 81–82. See also *R v Yalman* [1998] 2 Cr App R 269; *R v Groves* [1998] Crim LR 200. For a commentary on *Yalman*, see Redmayne, 1999.)

105   (1936) 25 Cr App R 150.

cyclists in a similar way, and had stopped his car to assault them. Evidence was also admitted to show that on the afternoon of 8 August, he had knocked down another woman cyclist and had stolen her handbag, and that later he had driven directly at three different parties of police officers who had tried to stop his car. The Court of Criminal Appeal held that all this evidence had been properly admitted, because it was of crucial importance to show that what had been done to the murder victim was deliberate.

More recently, similar fact evidence was used to rebut a defence in *R v Kidd*.[106] The defendant, charged with going equipped for theft, was seen lying face down in a field which was protected under legislation designed to preserve ancient monuments and archaeological sites. He had with him a metal-detector. His defence was that he had been drinking, had decided to walk to a friend's house, and had taken the metal-detector with a view to selling it. In the field he had stopped for a cigarette and fallen asleep. The trial judge admitted evidence of his previous convictions for theft from archaeological sites where a metal-detector had been used. The defendant's appeal was dismissed; the previous convictions were highly relevant to rebut the defence that the defendant had been innocently sleeping.

R v Lewis[107] shows the difficulties that could arise where an indictment contained several counts and there were different defences in respect of them. The defendant was tried in connection with four incidents involving himself and the children of a woman with whom he was living. In relation to one of the incidents, the defence was a complete denial that the action alleged had taken place. The defences in relation to the other three counts were either accidental touching of a child, or touching for the proper purpose of drying the child after a bath.

The prosecution was allowed to call evidence to show that the defendant possessed magazines, letters and posters from a paedophile society; that in interviews with police he referred to himself as a paedophile; and that he had asked the children's mother if she could live with a paedophile. The evidence tended to show, therefore, not that he was guilty of other criminal acts, but that his disposition was such that he was likely to have committed the offences for which he was being tried. The Court of Appeal held that this evidence was inadmissible in relation to the count where there was a straight denial of the action alleged, but was admissible in relation to the other three counts because it tended to rebut the defences of accident or innocent behaviour. This distinction was criticised, but was maintained in later cases. Thus, where allegations of buggery and gross indecency were made by schoolboys against their headmaster and his defence was simply that the allegations had been fabricated, the Court of Appeal held that evidence should not have been admitted of

---

106   [1995] Crim LR 406.

107   (1983) 76 Cr App R 33.

articles found in his possession tending to show that he had homosexual inclinations.[108]

The Law Commission, in its discussion of the effect of bad character evidence, took 'prejudicial effect' to mean, 'that a verdict is reached, not as a valid conclusion from a logical line of reasoning, but either by giving too much weight to the evidence of bad character ("reasoning prejudice"), or by convicting otherwise than on the evidence ("moral prejudice")'. There is an obvious danger that a jury will exaggerate the likelihood that someone who has been convicted will re-offend, or of assuming that individuals cannot change.[109] There is a further danger that a jury may form such a low opinion of the defendant when they hear about his bad character that they will be tempted to convict, regardless of the other evidence in the case.[110] In this connection it should be remembered that the CJA 2003, like any other statute, must be interpreted in the light of the European Convention on Human Rights, Art 6(2) of which provides that everyone charged with a criminal offence shall be presumed innocent until proved guilty according to law. Moral prejudice, at least, erodes that presumption, since 'factfinders view the accused with suspicion because of the evidence of discreditable incidents, and are more likely to be inclined to convict unless he or she can produce some convincing exculpatory evidence'.[111]

It will already be clear that, in any particular case, whether and to what extent gateway (d) will be used is likely to be a matter of considerable uncertainty. Some guidelines were laid down in *R v Hanson*,[112] when the Court of Appeal considered for the first time some of the provisions in CJA 2003 relating to evidence of a defendant's bad character. Before considering the particular cases for each appellant, the Vice President (Rose LJ), in delivering a judgment to which all members of the Court had contributed, made a number of general observations about the way in which some of these provisions should be applied. The main points in relation to gateway (d) are as follows:

1. The starting point should be for judges and practitioners to bear in mind that Parliament's purpose in the legislation was 'to assist in the evidence-based conviction of the guilty, without putting those who are not guilty at risk of conviction by prejudice'. An application to adduce such evidence should not be made routinely, merely because a defendant has previous

---

108   *R v Wright* (1990) 90 Cr App R 325. See also *R v B(RA)* [1997] 2 Cr App R 88.

109   Law Commission Consultation Paper 141, 1996, paras 7.7–7.9.

110   *Ibid*, paras 7.10–7.15. This is most likely to be the case, of course, where previous convictions for sexual offences are revealed, but there are other sensitive areas as well. A previous conviction for dealing in drugs or for causing death by dangerous driving could well set up resonances in the minds of some jurors that would make it difficult for them to try the defendant impartially.

111   *Ibid*, para 7.14.

112   [2005] EWCA Crim 824, [2005] 1 WLR 3169.

convictions, but should be based on the particular circumstances of each case.

2. Where propensity to commit the offence is relied on as the basis for admitting evidence of a defendant's bad character under s 101(1)(d), there are essentially three questions to be considered:

   (i)   Does the history of convictions establish a propensity to commit offences of the kind charged?

   (ii) Does that propensity make it more likely that the defendant committed the offence charged?

   (iii) Is it unjust to rely on the convictions;[113] and, in any event, will the proceedings be unfair if they are admitted?[114]

3. There is no minimum number of events necessary to demonstrate propensity. A single previous conviction for an offence of the same description or category will often not show propensity. But it may do so where, for example, it shows a tendency to unusual behaviour, such as child molestation or fire raising.

   So, for example, the Court of Appeal held in *R v M (Michael)*[115] that an isolated instance of possessing a sawn-off shotgun when the defendant was 28 was not capable of establishing a propensity to commit firearms offences when he was 48. However, the Court said that just one conviction, even 20 years earlier, *might* be relevant to propensity, but such cases would be rare, and would be ones where the earlier conviction showed some very special and distinctive feature, such as 'a highly unusual form of sexual activity, or some arcane or highly specialised knowledge relevant to the present offence'. Where there were less distinctive features in common, there would have to be some evidence of the propensity manifesting itself during the intervening period in order to make the earlier evidence admissible as evidence of continuing propensity.[116]

   But the need for very special and distinctive features where only one previous conviction is relied on should not be exaggerated. In *R v Bernasconi (Grant Christopher)*[117] the Court of Appeal took the view that waving an imitation gun in the face of a stranger was sufficiently unusual to be admitted at a later trial for possessing an imitation firearm where there was evidence that a stranger had been threatened in the same

---

113   See s 103(3).
114   See s 101(3).
115   [2006] EWCA Crim 3408, [2007] Crim LR 637.
116   Paragraph 16.
117   [2006] EWCA Crim 1052.

way. A similar decision was *R v Hassan (Abdullah Saleh)*.[118] The defendant was charged with robbing a female victim of her mobile telephone as she was walking home in the early hours of the morning. The trial judge allowed the prosecution to adduce evidence through gateway (d) of a conviction for robbery seven years earlier. On that occasion the victim was also a woman who had been walking home by herself late at night. The judge said that the earlier conviction showed not just a propensity to commit robbery, but to do so at night against women who were alone. The Court of Appeal said that the judge had been entitled to admit the evidence on that basis.[119]

4. When considering what is just under s 103(3), and the fairness of the proceedings under s 101(3), the judge may, among other factors, take into consideration the degree of similarity between the previous convictions and the offence charged, always remembering that striking similarity is not an essential requirement for admissibility. The judge may also take into account the respective gravity of the past and present offences.[120]

5. The judge must always consider the strength of the prosecution case. 'If there is no or very little other evidence against a defendant, it is unlikely to be just to admit his previous convictions, whatever they are.'[121]

6. The age of a previous conviction may be a relevant consideration in deciding whether to admit it. But it is clear that a spent conviction can be admitted to show propensity. In *R v Pickstone*[122] the defendant was charged with several offences of indecent assault and rape on a girl aged about eleven. He had pleaded guilty twelve years earlier to indecent assault on another girl aged eleven. The trial judge took into account the lapse of time, but concluded that 'a defendant's sexual mores and motivations are not necessarily affected by the passage of time'.[123] The Court of Appeal concluded that he had been right to admit the conviction.

---

118   [2007] EWCA Crim 1287.

119   Yet it was a commonplace offence, and surely committed in commonplace circumstances. The trial judge's decision seems odd, and the Court of Appeal's reluctance to interfere is likely to be attributed to a desire to discourage appeals from decisions under s 101, especially where gateway (d) has been used.

120   Although in what way is not discussed. Probably the idea is that where a defendant is charged with a serious offence, previous minor offences in the same category will have little probative weight but could be prejudicial. Perhaps the reverse might be true also.

121   The application of this guideline in cases depending wholly or largely on identification may be particularly difficult. Previous convictions can be adduced on the basis that they support an identification made in difficult circumstances. Alternatively, they can be excluded on the basis that the only other evidence is weak.

122   Reported with *R v Hanson* [2005] EWCA Crim 824, [2005] 1 WLR 3169.

123   Paragraph 51.

7. In any case in which evidence of bad character is admitted to show propensity, whether to commit offences or to be untruthful, the judge in summing up should make these points:

    (i)   They should not place undue reliance on previous convictions. In particular, they should not conclude that the defendant has been untruthful or has committed the offence with which he has been charged merely because he has these convictions.

    (ii) Whether the convictions do in fact show propensity is for them to decide.[124]

    (iii) If they do find propensity, they are entitled to take this into account when determining guilt. But it is only one relevant factor, and they must assess its significance in the light of all the other evidence in the case.[125]

The contents of a summing-up where bad character evidence has been adduced was considered further by the Court of Appeal in *R v L*.[126] The defendant was charged with rape. Evidence of previous incidents in his relationship with the complainant were adduced by the prosecution under s 101(1)(c) and (d). The defendant denied these incidents, and he had not been convicted of any offence arising from them. The judge did not give any direction to the jury about how this evidence was to be used, on the basis that it did not constitute evidence of previous convictions. The Court of Appeal held that this was wrong. There should have been a 'bad character direction', comprising the following elements in relation to each incident relied on:

- The potential significance of the evidence should be explained to the jury.
- The jury should decide whether the facts as alleged by the prosecution had been proved to the criminal standard.
- Any incident not proved to that standard should be put aside and given no significance.
- The jury should be warned against attaching too much weight to the evidence of bad character. They should also be warned against giving the incidents any significance if an alternative construction of those incidents cast doubt on the construction contended for by the prosecution.

---

124   The judge must, of course, already have decided that they are *capable* of doing so, or they would not have been admitted.

125   In *R v Edwards* [2005] EWCA Crim 1813, [2006] 1 Cr App R 3, para 3, the Court of Appeal emphasised that this guidance on the contents of a summing-up was not intended to be a blueprint, departure from which would lead to the quashing of a conviction. What the summing-up must contain is a clear warning to the jury against placing undue reliance on previous convictions, which cannot, by themselves, prove guilt.

126   [2007] All ER (D) 213 (Dec).

Substantial probative value in relation to an important matter in issue between defendant and co-defendant: s 101(1)(e)

By s 101(1)(e), in criminal proceedings evidence of a defendant's bad character is admissible where 'it has *substantial* probative value in relation to an *important* matter in issue between the defendant and a co-defendant'.[127] In other words, evidence with only marginal or trivial value will not be admissible, nor will evidence be admissible if the issue to which it relates is marginal or trivial in the case as a whole.[128] The test is a more demanding one than under s 101(1)(d), but once it is satisfied, the court has no power to exclude the evidence. There is no common law discretion to exclude evidence adduced by a co-defendant, as opposed to the prosecution, under *R v Sang*,[129] and s 78(1) of the Police and Criminal Evidence Act 1984 applies only to evidence on which the *prosecution* proposes to rely.[130]

A defendant may wish to adduce evidence of a co-defendant's bad character if it is his case that it was the co-defendant, and not himself, who committed the offence. A good example of this situation arose in *R v Miller*.[131] Three defendants, Miller, Mercado and Harris, were charged with conspiracy to evade customs duties on the importation of nylon stockings. Mercado's defence was that he had not been concerned in the illegal importations. He said that Harris, one of his employees, had posed as Mercado and had used Mercado's office for the illegal transactions. In order to establish that it was Harris, and not Mercado, who had been involved, counsel for Mercado wanted to prove that Harris had been in prison during a period when the illegal importations had been suspended. The trial judge, Devlin J, held that, in the light of Mercado's defence, the evidence was relevant and admissible.

Another example is *R v Bracewell*.[132] Two men, Lockwood and Bracewell, were charged with the murder of a man in a house where they had committed burglary. Neither denied the burglary, but each blamed the other for the murder. Lockwood was allowed to give evidence that he was an experienced burglar of a strictly non-violent type, with a cool head in emergencies, whereas Bracewell was inexperienced, nervous, excitable, and possibly under the influence of alcohol (and so, by implication, the man more likely to have panicked and committed the murder). The Court of Appeal held that this evidence entitled Bracewell to cross-examine Lockwood about occasions when Lockwood had been violent to his mistress, and to call evidence in rebuttal of any denial.

---

127 Emphasis added.

128 Explanatory Notes, para 375. See also *R v Musone* [2007] EWCA Crim 1237, para 46.

129 [1980] AC 402.

130 So evidence that is in principle admissible for the prosecution under gateway (d), but is excluded by the judge under s 101(3), can nevertheless be admitted for a co-defendant under gateway (e). See, eg, *R v De Vos (Dick Theodoris)* [2006] EWCA Crim 1688.

131 [1952] 2 All ER 667.

132 (1978) 68 Cr App R 44.

Evidence of a co-defendant's bad character can be based on matters leading to a criminal charge that has not yet been tried. In *R v Rafiq*[133] three men were tried on counts of murder and conspiracy to rob. Two of them had entered a shop to commit robbery, while a third had waited for them in a car. One of those who entered the shop fatally stabbed a manager. Each one of the three denied any part in the stabbing and blamed his co-defendants. When Rafiq gave evidence he denied stabbing the manager, and said that he did not commit robberies with weapons. His co-defendants wanted to adduce evidence to show that he had been charged with another robbery, which had not yet come to trial, in which he had sprayed a can of chemicals in a shop assistant's face. The trial judge admitted this evidence. Rafiq was convicted of the murder as well as the conspiracy. He appealed.

It was argued on his behalf that evidence of the second offence was inadmissible as it had not yet been tried. Rafiq was to be treated as innocent of it until he had been proved guilty. But the Court of Appeal, following the decision of the House of Lords in *R v Randall*,[134] rejected this submission. The fact that Rafiq had not been convicted of the second offence was irrelevant. What the court was concerned with were the particular circumstances of the other offence, if it had been committed by Rafiq. Those circumstances were relevant in the trial for murder and conspiracy because they tended to disprove Rafiq's claim that he never used weapons in robberies, and to make it more likely that it was he who had delivered the fatal blow. The Court pointed out that even if he had been tried and acquitted of the other robbery, its facts could have been admissible in a later trial on the authority of *R v Z*.[135]

It seems that the position would be different were such an application to be made by the prosecution. In that case, the principle in *R v Smith*[136] would be applied, namely, that where a defendant has other charges hanging over him, it is wrong to bring matters relating to them before the court. To be able to do so would circumvent safeguards to prevent a defendant's being questioned about matters on which he was entitled to remain silent. The reason for this disparity between the position of the prosecution and that of a co-defendant is that it would be wrong to favour one defendant over another by denying a co-defendant's right to adduce relevant evidence in support of his defence. But if the prosecution wishes to rely on matters that are the

---

133   [2005] EWCA Crim 1423, [2005] Crim LR 963.

134   [2003] UKHL 69, [2004] 1 WLR 56.

135   [2000] 2 AC 483. It was obviously sensible that Rafiq should be in no better position before trial than he would have been after trial and acquittal. But it is interesting to consider what the situation would be after *R v L*, above. Presumably, the jury would now be told that, before taking the facts of the other robbery into account, they would have to be satisfied that the prosecution had proved those facts beyond reasonable doubt; and that if what Rafiq said about them while giving evidence in the current trial might reasonably be true, the prosecution would not have proved those facts, and they should be entirely rejected from consideration from that point onwards.

136   [1989] Crim LR 900, CA.

subject of other charges, it has the power to ensure that they are either tried first, or jointly with the current offence.

In other cases, however, a defendant may wish to attack the credibility of a co-defendant simply because the nature or conduct of his defence is such as to undermine his own defence. Evidence that is relevant to the question whether the co-defendant has a propensity to be untruthful is admissible in these, although not in any other, circumstances.[137]

The question whether evidence given by one defendant undermined the defence of a co-defendant arose under the Criminal Evidence Act 1898. By s 1(3)(iii), evidence of a defendant's bad character was admissible where he had 'given evidence against any other person charged in the same proceedings'.[138] In *Murdoch v Taylor*,[139] the House of Lords held that the provision that later became s 1(3)(iii) would apply where the evidence of a co-defendant, taken in the context of the whole case, supported the prosecution's case or undermined a co-defendant's defence. Murdoch and his co-defendant, Lynch, were tried together on an indictment which alleged that they had received three cameras, knowing that they had been stolen. Both pleaded not guilty. The prosecution alleged that both Murdoch and Lynch had been involved in an attempt to sell the cameras at a watchmaker's shop. Murdoch gave evidence in his own defence. In examination-in-chief he stated that he had seen a box in Lynch's possession, but had discovered that it contained cameras only when Lynch had called him into the watchmaker's shop after first entering and spending some time there himself. Under cross-examination by counsel for Lynch, he asserted that he had had nothing to do with the stolen cameras and that they had been entirely Lynch's responsibility. Counsel for Lynch claimed to be entitled to cross-examine Murdoch under s 1(3)(iii). The trial judge permitted this, and his decision was ultimately upheld by the House of Lords. The Law Lords discussed what amounted to 'evidence against' a co-defendant under the exception contained in the 1898 Act. They concluded that evidence which does no more than contradict something that a co-defendant has said, without further advancing the prosecution case to any significant degree, would not bring a defendant within the exception. But any evidence which, taken in the context of the whole case, supported the prosecution case or undermined the co-defendant's defence would do so. On the facts of this case, the evidence given by Murdoch was evidence against Lynch. It put Lynch in sole possession and control of property which, according to the rest of the evidence, had been stolen the day before, and which Lynch had tried to sell for a fraction of its true value.

---

137 Section 104(1). The kind of evidence that would be relevant to a defendant's propensity to be untruthful has already been discussed in relation to s 101(1)(d).

138 This referred not to a defendant who had turned Queen's Evidence and was appearing as a prosecution witness, but to one who, in giving evidence in his own defence, harmed the case of a co-defendant.

139 [1965] AC 574.

A similar situation occurred in *R v Varley*.[140] Varley and a man named Dibble were jointly charged with robbery. At trial, Dibble's defence was that he had taken part in the robbery with Varley, but that he had done so only under duress because of threats made against his life by Varley. Varley gave evidence that he had not been present at the commission of the crime at all. The trial judge held that Varley had brought himself within the 1898 Act exception. Varley appealed, arguing that he had not given evidence against Dibble.

Clearly, Dibble had given evidence against Varley. But was the converse true? The Court of Appeal laid down these further guidelines:

■ Inconvenience to, or inconsistency with, a co-defendant's defence is not itself sufficient for the exception to apply. In particular, mere denial of participation in a joint venture is not in itself sufficient to rank as evidence against a co-defendant.

■ For the exception to apply, the denial must lead to the conclusion that if the witness did not participate, then it must have been the other defendant who did.

On the facts of this case, Varley *had* given evidence against Dibble. Varley was saying that he had not gone with Dibble, and had not forced Dibble to go. The effect of this evidence was not only that Dibble was telling lies, but that Dibble was left as a participant on his own, and not acting under duress.

Varley appeared to have laid down a strictly limited definition of evidence that supported the prosecution case or undermined a co-defendant's defence, and this was illustrated by *R v Bruce*.[141] Bruce, another man named McGuinness, and some others were charged with robbery. The prosecution said that they had frightened a passenger in a train into giving them money. McGuinness's evidence supported the prosecution case that there had been an agreement to rob. According to him, they had all gone to Hampstead that night to look for a Pakistani to rob. On failing to find anyone who appeared to fit that description, they had boarded a train and found a victim there. McGuinness said, however, that he had played no part in the robbery. Bruce said in his evidence that there had never been a plan to rob anyone. The trial judge ruled that he had thereby given evidence against McGuinness, and so had brought himself within the exception.

The Court of Appeal disagreed. The evidence of Bruce that there had been no conspiracy to rob certainly contradicted part of McGuinness's evidence and damaged his credibility. But it did not contradict McGuinness's evidence that he had taken no part in the robbery. Moreover, Bruce's evidence undermined the case for the prosecution, because what he said made it not more, but less, likely that there had

---

140   [1982] 2 All ER 519.
141   [1975] 1 WLR 1252.

been a robbery for which McGuinness could be convicted. In one way Bruce had given evidence against McGuinness, but in another he had not. The court concluded that, on balance, what Bruce said exculpated McGuinness from the robbery and did not incriminate him.

A similar conclusion was reached in *R v Kirkpatrick*.[142] In that case, two defendants, K and B, were charged with indecently assaulting a woman. A third man, L, who was charged with them, pleaded guilty. It was alleged that the complainant had been indecently assaulted in a bedroom by K, B, L and another man who was not tried. B was the first defendant to give evidence. He said that L, after kissing and cuddling the complainant, had gone into a bedroom with her. He himself had fallen asleep, but had been woken up by screams. He denied participating in the indecent assault. K gave evidence that B and another man were indecently assaulting the complainant, and that he, K, intervened to stop them. Obviously, K had given evidence against B, but had B, by his evidence, given evidence against K? The trial judge held that he had not, and was upheld by the Court of Appeal. B's defence was inconsistent with that of K, but this did not amount to undermining K's defence. Even if the jury accepted what B said, that did not prevent them from acquitting K.

But a less rigorous line was taken in *R v Crawford*.[143] The victim alleged that she had been robbed in the lavatory of a restaurant by the two defendants and a third woman, who was not traced. Crawford gave evidence in her own defence and said that she had not been present during the robbery. The co-defendant's case was that Crawford and the third woman had committed the robbery, while the co-defendant was merely an innocent bystander. The co-defendant had clearly given evidence against Crawford. But had Crawford's evidence undermined the case for the co-defendant, so as to allow the co-defendant to cross-examine her about her previous convictions? The trial judge ruled that it had, and was upheld by the Court of Appeal. If, as Crawford asserted, she was not in the lavatory at all when the robbery occurred, and the jury accepted that evidence, that made it much less likely that the co-defendant simply stood by while Crawford and the third woman committed the robbery. *Varley* was not to be read as if it were a statute. For the exception under the 1898 Act to apply, it was enough for the evidence of one defendant to jeopardise the credibility of a co-defendant, and so make the prosecution case against that co-defendant more likely to be true.

The CJA 2003 does not provide a formula for a ready decision about whether, in any particular case, the evidence of one defendant has undermined a co-defendant's defence. The different approaches shown, on the one hand, by *Varley*, *Bruce* and *Kirkpatrick*, and, on the other, by *Crawford*, will have to be kept in mind when interpreting the new legislation. What is likely to happen is that the Court of

---

142   [1998] Crim LR 63.
143   [1998] 1 Cr App R 338.

Appeal will say that the question is essentially one of fact in each case. In this way a line of potentially conflicting 'precedents' will be avoided, but at the expense of certainty in applying the law.

To correct a false impression given by the defendant: s 101(1)(f)

Under s 101(1)(f), evidence of a defendant's bad character is admissible 'to correct a false impression given by the defendant'. The essence of this exception is to allow such evidence to be adduced for its *corrective* value. By s 105(1):

> For the purposes of section 101(1)(f) –
>
> (a)   the defendant gives a false impression if he is responsible for the making of an express or implied assertion which is apt to give the court or jury a false or misleading impression about the defendant;
>
> (b)   evidence to correct such an impression is evidence which has probative value in correcting it.

Section 105(2) lists the circumstances in which a defendant is to be treated as being responsible for an assertion. An obvious instance is where the assertion is made by the defendant in the proceedings.[144] A problem is likely to occur where a defendant gives evidence as part of his defence that has the effect of showing good character. Such a problem would not be new. It arose under the 1898 Act, which allowed cross-examination about a defendant's previous convictions or bad character where he had given evidence of his good character.[145] The essential test under that provision appeared to be the nature of the connection between the assertion, express or implied, of good character, and the prosecution allegations. The defendant had to counter the prosecution's version of events, but in doing so he might give evidence that had the incidental effect of showing his character in a good light.

A case in which this situation arose was *Malindi v R*.[146] The defendant was charged with conspiracy to commit arson. The prosecution relied on evidence from co-conspirators, who had been present at a meeting with the defendant when a political campaign of arson was allegedly discussed and approved by him. The defendant gave evidence. He admitted that he had met the co-conspirators. He said

---

144   Section 105(2)(a).

145   Criminal Evidence Act 1898, s 1(3)(ii), formerly s 1(f)(ii). In *R v Renda* [2005] EWCA Crim 2826, the Court of Appeal discouraged the citation of 'authorities' that were no more than factual examples of occasions when an individual defendant had put his character in issue under the Criminal Evidence Act 1898. For the purposes of s 101(1)(f) CJA 2003, the question whether a defendant has given a false impression about himself is 'fact-specific'. While the anxiety of the Court of Appeal to avoid having to listen to lengthy submissions on the former law is understandable, some reference to pre-2003 cases can be helpful to a student in understanding the kind of questions that may arise under this provision.

146   [1967] AC 439.

that they had proposed an arson campaign to him, but he had declined to participate. He had pointed out the illegality of what they suggested and had recommended a political procession instead. This had angered the others, who had accused him of being a moderate and a police informer, and had walked out. The trial judge ruled that the defendant had thereby given evidence of his own good character, which allowed him to be cross-examined under the 1898 Act. By his evidence he had put himself forward as a person who was, and was regarded by others, as being a moderate and a man of peace. The Privy Council rejected this view. All the defendant had done was to give a narrative of what he said took place at the meeting; he had given his version of events and conversations but had done no more. He had not made any independent assertion of good character, and so had not brought himself within the exception.

So if what the defendant said went beyond his need to meet the prosecution version of the facts in issue, so as to raise the issue of his good character independently, he would be caught, but not otherwise. Had he given direct evidence of good character, from which it might be inferred that he did not do what the prosecution alleged? If so, he could be cross-examined. Or had he given evidence that he did not do what was alleged, from which it might be inferred that he was of good character? In that case he could not be cross-examined.

The distinction can be illustrated by a story of two defendants charged on different occasions with theft from a supermarket. Charlie says, 'I put the gin in my own holdall because I didn't want it to roll about and break the eggs in the supermarket's basket. I had forgotten it was there by the time I reached the checkout because I was worrying about my wife who was due to have an operation that day'. Charlie cannot be cross-examined about his previous convictions. The prosecution relies on the facts that the gin did not go into the wire basket and was not produced at the checkout. Charlie produces a neutral explanation for putting the gin in his holdall. He meets his failure to produce it at the checkout by saying that he forgot it was there, and he explains this by describing what was dominating his mind at the time. The fact that it happens to be something showing him in a good light is subsidiary to his defence.

Compare this case with that of Ronald, who finds himself in a very similar situation. His reasons for putting the gin in his own holdall and for failing to produce it at the checkout are the same as those given by Charlie. But he also adds, 'I would never do a thing like that. It's forbidden in the Ten Commandments'. Ronald has given an *additional* reason, based on his character, for the jury to acquit him: he respects the Ten Commandments and is the sort of person who would never break any of them. A person like that is unlikely to have committed theft. He *has* given evidence of his own good character, which will allow him to be cross-examined about his previous convictions.

It seems very likely that these considerations, stemming from *Malindi*, will be adopted in the interpretation of s 105(2)(a).

An assertion that is apt to give a false or misleading impression about the defendant does not have to be expressly made: it can be implied. In particular, s 105(4) provides:

> Where it appears to the court that a defendant, by means of his conduct (other than the giving of evidence) in the proceedings, is seeking to give the court or jury an impression about himself that is false or misleading, the court may if it appears just to do so treat the defendant as being responsible for the making of an assertion which is apt to give that impression.

By sub-s (5), 'conduct' includes appearance or dress. As the Law Commission expressed it, '[I]f a defendant is to lose the shield if he tells the court he is a vicar he should nonetheless be liable to do so where he makes the same assertion in non-verbal form, such as by appearing in court [in] a dog collar'.[147] The legitimacy of the claim need not be challenged. It is the claim to good character associated, whether rightly or not, with certain types of occupation at which sub-ss (4) and (5) are aimed. Another example would be a defendant who appears in court wearing the uniform of a security company. Borderline cases will inevitably arise. What, for example, of the professional burglar who appears in court dressed in a dark, three-piece suit, or in a regimental blazer?[148]

The express or implied assertion referred to in s 105(1) can be made by the defendant whether or not evidence is given by him.[149] So, for example, if the assertion is made by his advocate, or if the defendant makes it by way of an interruption while sitting in the dock, s 101(1)(f) will apply. It also includes, if used in evidence, an assertion made by the defendant on being questioned under caution or on being charged, where evidence of that assertion is given in the proceedings,[150] or if the assertion is made by a witness called by the defendant.[151] A defendant will be treated as being responsible for the making of an assertion if 'the assertion is made by any witness in cross-examination in response to a question asked by the defendant that is intended to elicit it, or is likely to do so',[152] or where the assertion was made by any person out of court, and the defendant adduces evidence of it in the proceedings.[153]

The only escape for a defendant who is held to have given a false impression in any of these ways is by s 105(3). This provides that a defendant who would otherwise

---

147   Law Commission No 273, 2001, para 13.19. The expression 'dog collar' is colloquial and refers to the clerical collar worn by many Christian priests and ministers.

148   As Colin Tapper once observed, such a defendant can hardly be expected to appear dressed in a striped T-shirt and mask, with a bag labelled 'swag' slung over his shoulder.

149   Section 105(2)(a).

150   Section 105(2)(b). It would be usual for the prosecution to edit out such evidence if the defendant did not wish to rely on it; see also sub-s (3).

151   Section 105(2)(c).

152   Section 105(2)(d).

153   Section 105(2)(e).

be treated as responsible for the making of an assertion shall not be so treated 'if, or to the extent that, he withdraws it or disassociates himself from it'. In *R v Renda*[154] the question arose whether the defendant had successfully withdrawn assertions made during examination-in-chief when he admitted their falsity during subsequent cross-examination. The trial judge ruled that he should *not* be treated as having done so, and this decision was upheld by the Court of Appeal. A concession extracted in cross-examination that the defendant was not telling the truth during examination-in-chief will not normally amount to a withdrawal of, or disassociation from, the original assertion for the purposes of s 105(3). It could be otherwise where the defendant's decision to withdraw or disassociate is unprompted.

In the Law Commission's proposals the prosecution, in order to introduce evidence to correct a false or misleading impression about the defendant, needed to prove that the evidence had substantial probative value in correcting that impression. It was also necessary to prove either that the evidence was unprejudicial, or that it had such corrective value that, even taking account of the risks of prejudice, the interests of justice *required* it to be admissible. These express safeguards have not survived, but the common law discretion to exclude prosecution evidence on the basis that its probative value is exceeded by its prejudicial effect[155] could, presumably, be relied on. Arguably, s 78(1) of the Police and Criminal Evidence Act 1984 would also be available. But a doubt is created by s 101(3), which provides what is in effect the s 78(1) test in relation to gateways (d) and (g) only.

It should be noted that evidence is admissible under s 101(1)(f) only if it goes no further than is necessary to correct the false impression.[156] At common law there was a rule that character was 'indivisible'. This meant that if a defendant put his character in issue in any respect, the prosecution was entitled to refer to the *whole* of his character; a defendant could not say that he had a good character in some respects without exposing himself to inquiry about the rest of his character. In *R v Winfield*,[157] for example, the defendant was charged with committing an indecent assault on a woman. He called a witness and asked her questions designed to establish his good character with regard to sexual morality. However, he had previous convictions for dishonesty. The trial judge held that he could be cross-examined about them under the 1898 Act. The Court of Criminal Appeal upheld this decision. As Humphreys J said, '[T]here is no such thing known to our procedure as putting half your character in issue and leaving out the other half'.[158] But it is possible that the common law rule about the indivisibility of character has been abolished, with the rest of the common law rules governing the admissibility of evidence of bad character, by s 99(1) of the

---

154   [2005] EWCA Crim 2826.

155   *R v Sang* [1980] AC 402.

156   Section 105(6).

157   [1939] 4 All ER 164.

158   *Ibid*, p 165. The principle was approved by the House of Lords in *Stirland v DPP* [1944] AC 315.

CJA 2003. It may be, therefore, that if the facts in *Winfield* were to be repeated today, the cross-examination about convictions for dishonesty would be held inadmissible, not because it went further than necessary to correct a false impression, but because the evidence given on behalf of the defendant would be held not to have given a false impression.[159]

Finally, it should be noted that, by s 105(7), only the prosecution can use s 101(1)(f).

Counters defendant's attack on another person's character: s 101(1)(g)

By s 101(1)(g), evidence of a defendant's bad character is admissible, but only for the prosecution,[160] if the defendant 'has made an attack on another person's character'. Ordinarily, the other person is likely to be a prosecution witness, but it could also include any person who is alleged by the defendant to have committed the offence rather than himself.[161] This can include a co-defendant.[162] It is unclear from the statute whether the person whose character is attacked must be alive. Under the Criminal Evidence Act 1898 an 'imputation' on the character of the deceased victim of an alleged crime exposed the defendant to cross-examination about his own bad character, but only because an amendment was inserted to that effect. It might be argued that if it was intended that this protection for deceased persons and their relations should continue, the statute would have said so expressly. On the other hand, the Court of Appeal has observed *obiter* in relation to gateway (g) that a defendant's attack on another person will often be on the victim of the alleged crime, 'whether alive or dead'.

An attack is made for the purposes of this gateway even though it is a necessary part of the defendant's case. For example, in *R v Singh (James Paul)*[163] it was a necessary part of the defence that the complainant had invited the defendant to his flat, and that they had spent several hours there smoking crack cocaine. The trial judge held that this evidence had opened gateway (g), and the Court of Appeal

---

159 This assumes, of course, that the defendant's only previous convictions were for offences of dishonesty, and did not include other convictions for sexual offences. In the latter event, he would be subject to cross-examination about the sexual offences, but not about the convictions for dishonesty, because these would be regarded as going further than necessary to correct the false impression that he behaved properly in relation to sexual matters.

160 Section 106(3).

161 Section 106(2)(a). There seems to be no reason why a co-defendant should not be 'another person' for the purpose of this provision, unless it could be argued that because co-defendants are covered by s 101(1)(e) they are excluded from the scope of this provision. But there is no certainty that such an argument would succeed. Section 101(1)(e) is available only to a co-defendant, so if s 101(1)(g) does not include co-defendants, a prosecutor would be powerless if a co-defendant for some reason chose not to exercise his right.

162 See, eg, *R v Dowds*, reported in *R v Bovell* [2005] EWCA Crim 1091.

163 [2007] EWCA Crim 2140.

agreed. The Court also said that the purpose of gateway (g) is to enable the jury to know from what kind of source the allegations have come. This gateway does not depend on being able to show any propensity in the defendant to offend as charged or to be untruthful.

What constitutes an attack for the purposes of gateway (g)? The Court of Appeal has said cases decided under the Criminal Evidence Act 1898 about what amounted to an 'imputation' on the witnesses for the prosecution or the deceased victim of the alleged crime will continue to apply, to the extent that they are compatible with s 106 of the 2003 Act, when assessing whether an attack has been made on another person's character. By s 106(1), a defendant makes an attack if he adduces evidence attacking the other person's character; or asks questions in cross-examination that are intended to elicit such evidence, or are likely to do so; or where evidence is given of an imputation about the other person made by the defendant on being questioned or charged.

It was held, in interpreting the Criminal Evidence Act 1898, that a defendant charged with rape who gave evidence of the complainant's consent did not expose himself to cross-examination under s 1(3)(ii) on the basis that the nature or conduct of his defence was such as to involve an imputation on a witness for the prosecution.[164] This was justified either on the theory that lack of consent was an element that the prosecution had to prove, or that such cases simply stood on their own. This rule probably remains unchanged. In *R v Ball*[165] the defendant was charged with rape. He gave evidence of the complainant's consent and said that she had fabricated the rape allegation. But in the course of a police interview he said that the complainant was 'easy', and added, 'She's a bag really, you know what I mean, a slag'. The trial judge ruled that this evidence had probative worth in relation to the prosecution case and should therefore be admitted.[166] But he also decided on the strength of this evidence, following s 106(1)(c)(i), that the defendant had made an attack on the complainant's character and should be cross-examined about his previous convictions. The Court of Appeal upheld this ruling, but noted with approval that the judge had not allowed cross-examination on the convictions simply on the basis of the defendant's assertion that the allegation of rape had been fabricated.[167]

---

164   *Selvey v DPP* [1970] AC 304.

165   Reported with *R v Renda* [2005] EWCA Crim 2826.

166   The reason appears to have been that the expressions reflected to some extent what the defendant was alleged to have said to the complainant immediately after he had raped her: 'Look at you, you're nowt but a slag.'

167   So it's safe, apparently, for a rape suspect with previous convictions to tell the police in his interview that the complainant consented, but he moves into very dangerous territory if he elaborates on this by explaining why she was likely to have done so. It is, of course, at this early stage in the proceedings that an innocent suspect, through shock and panic, is most likely to exaggerate the bad character of the complainant.

Evidence attacking another person's character is evidence to the effect that the other person has committed an offence (whether the one with which the defendant is charged or a different one), or has behaved, or is disposed to behave, 'in a reprehensible way'.[168] A suggestion that a witness is mistaken, as opposed to lying, is not intended to activate this exception.[169]

A distinction developed under the 1898 Act that is also likely to persist is between occasions when the suggestion of lying amounts to no more than an emphatic denial of what is alleged against the defendant, and occasions when such a suggestion is that of a lie in the strict sense. Two old cases illustrate the distinction. In *R v Rouse*,[170] the defendant, while giving evidence, said of the chief prosecution witness's evidence, 'It is a lie, and he is a liar'. The Court of Criminal Appeal held that this was not an imputation; it was simply 'a plea of not guilty put in forcible language such as would not be unnatural in a person in the defendant's rank in life'. But in *R v Rappolt*,[171] the allegation made in evidence by the defendant was that a prosecution witness was such a horrible liar that not even his brother would speak to him. The Court of Criminal Appeal agreed with the trial judge that this *was* an imputation.

Students have interpreted these decisions in various ways. Some have thought that they are in conflict. Others have thought that *R v Rappolt* is authority for the proposition that it is never an imputation to allege, without any elaboration, that a prosecution witness is lying. Both interpretations are wrong; they result from attaching too much importance to the form of words used, and not enough to their context and the speaker's intention. What happened in *R v Rouse* was that, on the facts of that case, the Court of Criminal Appeal recognised that the defendant did not intend to make an imputation on the prosecution witness, because he did not intend to assert that the witness was a person who had *knowingly* said something untrue.[172] But in *R v Rappolt* the court had to interpret different words uttered in a different context; not surprisingly, it reached a different conclusion. The reference to the brother's behaviour was clearly intended to support an allegation of habitual untruthfulness on the part of the witness. That *was* an imputation.

Unfortunately, it was not always *easy* to predict whether a defendant would expose himself to cross-examination by references to 'lying' or by the use of similar language, and this difficulty is likely to continue under the CJA 2003. In *R v Desmond*,[173] a prosecution witness gave an account of events that differed significantly from that in his witness statement and, in doing so, implicated the

---

168 Section 106(2).
169 Explanatory Notes, para 379.
170 [1904] 1 KB 184.
171 (1911) 6 Cr App R 156.
172 A lie consists in speaking a falsehood *with the intention of deceiving*.
173 [1999] Crim LR 313.

defendant further in the robbery that was alleged. In cross-examination, defence counsel suggested to him that he was lying under oath. The trial judge allowed cross-examination of the defendant about his previous convictions on the basis that an imputation had been made against the prosecution witness, but the Court of Appeal held that the matters put did not go beyond an emphatic denial of the charge.[174] A solution to the problem was in one respect made more difficult by the judgment of the Court of Appeal in *R v Britzman*.[175] In that case Lawton LJ, in a discussion of how a judge should exercise his discretion to exclude cross-examination under the 1898 Act, said that where there was nothing more than a denial, however emphatic or offensively made, of an act or short series of acts amounting to a single incident, or of what was said to have been a short interview, the discretion should be exercised in favour of the defendant. But to be able to exercise a discretion to exclude cross-examination, a situation permitting cross-examination must already have arisen, and on facts such as those suggested it might not have done.

A good point made in *R v Britzman* was that if what was alleged amounted *in effect* to an allegation of lying in the proper sense, a defendant would be caught even if the allegation was put politely by avoiding words such as 'lie' or 'lying'. So, for example, a suggestion made in cross-examination of a police officer that he was mistaken in his recollection of an incident occurring during a long period of observation would not attract the exception, because such a mistake could have been honestly made. But a suggestion that the officer was 'mistaken' or 'wrong' in saying that he had made any observation at all would be caught, because that is something about which it is inconceivable that an honest mistake could have been made. Suppose that a police officer gives evidence that, from an upper floor at 11 Hilldrop Crescent, he observed the defendant trafficking in drugs in the street. If it is put to the officer that he might be mistaken when he says that he saw the defendant pass a small packet to another person, that would not bring the defendant within the exception. It would be otherwise, however, if it were put to the officer that he had not been keeping watch from 11 Hilldrop Crescent at all, but from some other location, from which he could not have seen the defendant at all. This distinction is likely to be followed under the new legislation.

What amounts to an 'attack on another person's character' is likely to be governed by interpreting what a defendant says in its context, and by trying to take into account current opinion. The latter may be difficult, because what is an attack in one section of society, or at one period of time, might not be so in another section of

---

174   See also *R v Wignall* [1993] Crim LR 62. Defence counsel alleged that a prosecution witness was concocting her evidence, telling an untruth, and making up her evidence as she went along so as to bolster the case against the defendant. The Court of Appeal held that all this amounted to no more than an emphatic denial of the charge.

175   [1983] 1 All ER 369.

society, or at a different time. The new legislation does nothing to solve the problem, because s 106(2)(b) refers only to evidence that another person 'has behaved, or is disposed to behave, in a reprehensible way'. For this reason, caution is needed when reading earlier cases. In *R v Bishop*,[176] for example, the defendant, charged with burglary, accounted for the presence of his fingerprints in the bathroom of the complainant's premises by saying that he had had a homosexual relationship with the complainant. This was at that time held to involve an imputation on the character of a prosecution witness,[177] but would the decision be the same today? Might the answer depend on the character of the witness?[178] Sometimes it may be possible to avoid the problem because the clash of testimony will mean that one of the witnesses must be lying,[179] but this solution may not always be available.

Finally, it should be noted that evidence admissible under s 101(1)(g) must be excluded if it appears to the court that its admission would have such an adverse effect on the fairness of the proceedings that it ought not to be admitted.[180]

MISCELLANEOUS PROVISIONS UNDER THE CJA 2003

By s 107, if on a defendant's trial before a judge and jury for an offence evidence of bad character has been admitted under any of paras (c) to (g) of s 101(1), and the court is satisfied at any time after the close of the case for the prosecution that that evidence is so 'contaminated' that, considering its importance to the case against the defendant, his conviction would be unsafe, the court must either direct the jury to acquit the defendant or order a retrial before a different jury. By s 107(5), a person's evidence is 'contaminated' where it is false or misleading in any respect or is different from what it would otherwise have been, either as a result of an agreement or understanding between that person and one or more others, or as a result of that person being aware of anything alleged by one or more others whose evidence may be, or has been, given in the proceedings.

By s 108, in proceedings for an offence alleged to have been committed by the defendant when aged 21 or over, evidence for his conviction for an offence when under the age of 14 is not admissible unless both offences are triable only on indictment, and the court is satisfied that the interests of justice require evidence of the earlier offence to be given.

By s 109, the relevance or probative value of evidence adduced under Chapter 1 of Pt 11 of the CJA 2003 is to be assessed on the assumption that it is true, unless it

---

176   [1975] QB 274.

177   The relevant test under Criminal Evidence Act 1898, s 1(3)(ii).

178   An allegation of an active homosexual relationship with a single man who was open about his sexual orientation would not be an attack. However, it would almost certainly amount to an attack in the case of a married clergyman. But would a court want to undertake this sort of assessment?

179   See *R v Britzman*, referred to above.

180   Section 101(3).

appears on the basis of any material before the court, including any evidence it decides to hear on the matter, that no court or jury could reasonably find it to be true.

By s 110, the court must give reasons for its rulings on whether an item of evidence is evidence of bad character, on whether such evidence is admissible, and for any rulings made under s 107.

By s 112(2), where a defendant is charged with two or more offences in the same proceedings, Chapter 1 of Pt 11, with the exception of s 101(3), has effect as if each offence were charged in separate proceedings. The effect of this is that evidence of bad character can be admissible in relation to one charge but not others,[181] but that where the question is whether an item of evidence should be excluded under s 101(3), the court has to look at the effect of the admission of the evidence on the fairness of the proceedings as a whole, and not just at its effect on the charges in relation to which it is admissible.

SECTION 27(3) OF THE THEFT ACT 1968

The Law Commission recommended the repeal of this provision, but this was not followed in the 2003 Act, and it remains part of the current law. Where a person is being proceeded against for handling stolen goods (but not for any offence other than handling stolen goods),[182] then at any stage of the proceedings, if evidence has been given of his having or arranging to have in his possession the goods which are the subject of the charge, or of his undertaking or assisting in, or arranging to undertake or assist in, their retention, removal, disposal or realisation, the following evidence is admissible for the purpose of proving that he knew or believed the goods to be stolen:

(a)   evidence that he has had in his possession, or has undertaken or assisted in the retention, removal, disposal or realisation of, stolen goods from any theft taking place not earlier than 12 months before the offence charged;[183]

(b)   (provided that seven days' notice in writing has been given to him of the intention to prove the conviction) evidence that he has within the five years preceding the date of the offence charged been convicted of theft or handling stolen goods.

The sub-section can be used solely for the purpose of proving guilty knowledge on a handling charge. What happens where the defendant is charged with several counts of handling, and in relation to some he denies guilty knowledge, but in relation to

---

181   As was the case, eg, in *R v Lewis* (1983) 76 Cr App R 33.

182   So the sub-section cannot be used where a charge of handling is joined with another charge, such as theft.

183   Note that the sub-section allows evidence to be given of a possession later than the offence charged: *R v Davies* [1972] Crim LR 431. Under the sub-section the mere fact of possession is enough; there is no need for the possessor to have been prosecuted.

others he denies possession? In such a case the trial judge should consider excluding altogether the evidence allowed by the sub-section so as to avoid any misuse of it by the jury. If he does allow such evidence to be admitted, the jury must be clearly warned of the limited use that can be made of it.[184]

It has been held that the sub-section should be restrictively interpreted. In particular, sub-s (3)(a) does not permit evidence to be given of the transaction which led to stolen property coming into the possession of the defendant on the earlier occasion,[185] but sub-s (3)(b) is to be read subject to s 73(2) of the Police and Criminal Evidence Act 1984. This provides that a certificate of conviction on indictment of an offence must give the substance and effect of the indictment and conviction. It follows that the details of the previous conviction appearing on the certificate are admissible under sub-s (3)(b).[186]

Although the sub-section makes no provision for balancing prejudicial effect against probative worth, it is clear that a judge is entitled to take this into account because evidence permitted by this provision can be excluded, either at common law,[187] or under s 78(1) of the Police and Criminal Evidence Act 1984.

FURTHER READING
—Ho, 'Similar Facts in Civil Cases' (2006) 26 OJLS 131.
—Law Com No 273, *Evidence of Bad Character in Criminal Proceedings*, 2001.
—Mirfield, 'Character, Credibility and Truthfulness' [2008] LQR 1.
—Munday, 'Cut-Throat Defences and the "Propensity to be Untruthful" ' [2005] Crim LR 624.
—Redmayne, 'The Relevance of Bad Character' [2002] CLJ 684.
—Spencer, *Evidence of Bad Character*, 2006.
—Tapper, 'The Criminal Justice Act 2003: (3) Evidence of Bad Character' [2004] Crim LR 533.
—Waterman and Dempster, 'Bad Character: Feeling Our Way One Year On' [2006] Crim LR 614.

EXERCISES
1. When can spent convictions be referred to in court?
2. What did *Rowton* (1865) decide about the admissibility of good character evidence?
3. Would the result in *Redgrave* (1981) be the same today?
4. What are the contents of a *Vye* (1993) direction?
5. What is evidence of a person's 'bad character' for the purposes of Part 11, CJA 2003?

---

184   *R v Wilkins* (1975) 60 Cr App R 300.
185   *R v Bradley* (1979) 70 Cr App R 200.
186   *R v Hacker* [1994] 1 WLR 1659.
187   *R v Perry* [1984] Crim LR 680.

6. What is 'important explanatory evidence' for the purposes of Part 11, CJA 2003?

7. How could the defence use *Campbell* (2007) to argue against a prosecution application to adduce evidence of the defendant's previous convictions because they show a propensity to be untruthful?

8. What guidelines are given in *Hanson* (2005) in relation to gateway (d)?

9. Can a defendant cross-examine a co-defendant under gateway (e) about matters that have not yet come to trial? If he does so, how should the judge direct the jury in the summing-up?

10. Tristan is charged with murder. He relies on provocation as a partial defence, and gives evidence that the deceased solicited him for homosexual purposes in a public park, whereupon he 'saw red' and stabbed him. Can Tristan's previous convictions be introduced under gateway (g)?

13
OPINION EVIDENCE

WHEN IS OPINION EVIDENCE ADMISSIBLE?

The fundamental rule is that witnesses testify about facts and not about the opinions they have formed from facts. The reason for this is that it is the job of the 'tribunal of fact' (a judge or, very occasionally, a jury in a civil case, and magistrates or a jury in a criminal case) to hear the evidence, find facts, and make inferences from them. It is thought that the tribunal may be misled and hindered in its work if opinion evidence is too freely received. The pervasiveness of the rule can sometimes be forgotten in cross-examination. A witness should not generally be asked to give his opinion about what another witness has said. For example, in *R v Windass*[1] an appeal against conviction was allowed where a defendant had been asked during cross-examination to interpret entries that his girlfriend had made in her diary without any contribution from him.

A distinction between fact and opinion lies at the heart of the rule and its rationale. Arguably, the distinction cannot be sustained. Believing that something is the case involves making a judgment – an assent to a proposition. Sense awareness involves us in being receptive to objects and events in our surroundings, but belief that something is, or was, the case involves more than just receptivity: it involves acts

---

1   (1989) 89 Cr App R 258. See also *R v Gray and Evans* [1998] Crim LR 570.

of mind, in which the material provided by sense awareness is interpreted.[2] If an opinion is an inference from facts, there may be difficulty in finding a fact that is untainted by any element of opinion. Suppose I say that I saw my neighbour Mary in the supermarket. There lurks behind this apparent statement of fact an opinion based on my knowledge of Mary and comparisons I have made between her characteristics and those of the person whom I saw in the supermarket. Sometimes an expression of opinion may be a shorthand way of stating perceived facts. If, at the scene of a motor accident, a bystander who observed what happened says, 'That pedestrian never gave the driver a chance to stop', he probably intends to convey his perception that the pedestrian walked into the road quickly and without paying any attention to the traffic. The fundamental rule is not pressed too far; in the example given, the witness would probably be allowed to state the opinion, but would be required afterwards to state, so far as he could, the facts on which his opinion was based.[3]

Fortunately, the problem of classification is not one that bothers the courts much in practice. What they are mainly concerned with is the exception to the rule against opinion evidence which allows an expert to give evidence of his opinion in certain circumstances. This exception allows an expert to give the court the benefit of his expertise, including his opinion, where the matters on which he testifies are likely to be outside the experience of judge or jury. In each case it is for the judge to decide:

(a)   whether the issue is one on which the court could be assisted by expert evidence; and

(b)   whether the expert tendered has the expertise to provide such evidence.[4]

R v Land[5] is one of many cases illustrating the rule that expert evidence must be directed to matters that are outside the normal experience and knowledge of a judge or jury. The defendant was charged with the offence of possessing indecent photographs of a child. A child for the purposes of this offence was a person under the age of 16. There was no direct evidence of the age of the youths in the photographs. The trial judge directed the jury that in relation to two of the charges they could use their own experience to decide whether it was proved that the persons depicted were under 16. The Court of Appeal held that he had been right to do so, and that expert evidence on the matter from either prosecution or defence would have been

---

2   Cf Landesman, 1997, pp 6–7.

3   Cf *R v Davies* [1962] 3 All ER 97, where the Courts Martial Appeal Court held that, on a charge of drunken driving, a witness who is not medically qualified can give his general impression as to whether a driver has taken drink but must describe the facts on which he relies. The common law rule allowing such 'shorthand' expressions of opinion remains applicable in criminal cases, but received statutory recognition so far as civil proceedings were concerned in s 3(2) of the Civil Evidence Act 1972.

4   *R v Stockwell* (1993) 97 Cr App R 260, p 264, *per* Lord Taylor CJ.

5   [1999] QB 65.

inadmissible. The members of the jury were as well placed as experts to determine the question.

In an age in which professional experts of all kinds proliferate, it is almost inconceivable that an expert witness should be called who is an amateur. But the possibility remains, and perhaps if the area of expertise is sufficiently recondite it might be necessary to rely on one. In *R v Silverlock*,[6] the Court for Crown Cases Reserved had to consider whether a witness giving his opinion about samples of handwriting needed to be a professional expert, or at least a person whose ordinary business led him to have special experience in questions of handwriting, or whether the evidence of any person who had merely studied handwriting for some years would suffice. The court held that while a witness giving such evidence should be skilled in the subject, there were no restrictions on the *manner* in which that skill had to be acquired. The evidence of a person without professional qualifications could be admitted, provided the judge was satisfied that the witness was sufficiently skilled.

A witness who has acquired his expertise in the course of his daily work may certainly give expert evidence, even though he lacks paper qualifications. In *R v Murphy*,[7] for example, a police constable who was a traffic accident expert was allowed to give evidence of his opinion as to the nature of a collision, the course of one of the vehicles involved and other matters said to be deducible from marks in the road and damage to the vehicles. The Court of Appeal upheld the judge's ruling. Provided the judge was satisfied that these matters were within his expertise, his evidence was admissible. In *Southwark LBC v Simpson*[8] the Divisional Court held that the question whether premises are 'prejudicial to health' within s 79(1) of the Environmental Protection Act 1990 requires expert evidence, and this can be provided by a surveyor with some experience or expertise on this subject, even though he lacks a medical qualification.

A witness who is otherwise not specially qualified may be an 'expert ad hoc' where he has special knowledge acquired by study of materials that are relevant in a particular case, such as video recordings or photographs. In *R v Clare and Peach*,[9] a police officer had made a special study of video recordings showing people arriving at a football match and later scenes of disorder in a town centre. He was permitted to give evidence identifying the defendants as persons shown on the film committing offences. The appellants argued that his evidence was inadmissible, because he was in no better position than the members of the jury to make identifications from the video recordings. The Court of Appeal rejected this argument. It held that, as a result of his study, the officer had special knowledge which the jury did not possess. To give

---

6   [1894] 2 QB 766.

7   [1980] 1 QB 434.

8   (1999) 31 HLR 725.

9   [1995] 2 Cr App R 333; appvd *Attorney General's Reference (No 2 of 2002)* [2002] EWCA Crim 2373, [2003] 1 Cr App R 21.

the jury similar time and facilities to conduct the same research would have been utterly impracticable. It was therefore legitimate for the officer to assist them in his evidence by pointing to what he believed to be happening in scenes shown on the film.

A similar decision was reached in *R v Abnett (Gary)*.[10] In this case there was CCTV footage of an incident in which a firearm had been discharged into rear of a parked car. The defendant was arrested and interviewed by a police officer, who later studied the CCTV footage and identified the defendant as a man who was shown carrying a sawn-off shotgun as he left the scene of the incident. On appeal it was argued that the officer's evidence of identification should not have been admitted. The Court of Appeal took into account the fact that the officer had spent a whole day with the defendant when he was arrested and interviewed, had watched the CCTV footage several times and had created stills from it. The Court concluded that his acquaintance with the appearance of the man in the footage and the appearance of the defendant was 'inevitably deeper or greater or more considered' than that which the jury could have obtained. This gave him sufficient special knowledge to enable him to give evidence of identification that had a 'particular objective value'. Although the expression was not used, he, like the officer in *Clare and Peach*, had made himself an ad hoc expert for the purpose of identification.

The witness's area of expertise must be one that the court is prepared to recognise. For example, in *R v Stagg*[11] Ognall J expressed a strong doubt whether evidence obtained from the technique known as 'psychological profiling' was expert evidence of a kind recognised by the courts. In *R v Gilfoyle*[12] the Court of Appeal held that evidence of a 'psychological autopsy' of a deceased person was not expert evidence of a kind that can be placed before a court. But new areas of expertise are accepted from time to time. For example, in *R v Dallagher*[13] the Court of Appeal held expert evidence of ear prints to be admissible, as was the evidence of a lip-reading expert in *R v Luttrell*.[14] Where the question is admittedly one for an expert, and the court is satisfied that the witness is qualified as an expert, the employment of an unorthodox technique is more likely to affect weight than admissibility. Thus, in *R v Robb*[15] a phonetician was allowed to express an opinion on voice identification, although he relied on a technique that had only minority support within his profession.

In *Liverpool Roman Catholic Archdiocesan Trustees Inc v Goldberg (No 3)*[16] it was

---

10   [2006] EWCA Crim 3320.
11   Unreported, 14 September 1994.
12   [2001] Crim LR 312.
13   [2003] 1 Cr App R 195.
14   [2004] EWCA Crim 1344. This case also accepted that a skill or expertise can be the subject of expert evidence, even though it cannot be said to be a scientific discipline.
15   (1991) 93 Cr App R 161.
16   [2001] 1 WLR 2337.

held at first instance that the relationship between a proposed expert witness and the party calling him might render the expert evidence inadmissible. The claim was for professional negligence in respect of advice given by a barrister specialising in taxation. Another tax barrister was called on behalf of the defendant as an expert witness. He and the defendant had known each other for 28 years, were good friends, and were members of the same set of barristers' chambers. The judge held that he should disregard the expert's evidence because of the witness's close relationship with the defendant. The expert had said in his report that although he did not believe the relationship would have affected his evidence, his personal sympathies were engaged to a greater degree than would probably be normal with an expert witness. The judge held that this admission rendered his evidence unacceptable because of the public policy that justice must be *seen* to be done, as well as done in fact. Where it was shown that a relationship existed between the expert and the party calling him, which a reasonable observer might think capable of affecting the expert's views so as to make them unduly favourable to that party, his evidence should not be admitted, however unbiased his conclusions might probably be.

However, these observations were later disapproved by the Court of Appeal in *Regina Factortame Limited and Others v Secretary of State for Transport, Local Government and the Regions (No 8)*,[17] and in *Armchair Passenger Transport Limited v Helical Bar Plc*[18] Nelson J, after considering the authorities, laid down the following principles:

1. It is always desirable that an expert should have no actual or apparent interest in the outcome of the proceedings.

2. The existence of such an interest, whether as an employee of one of the parties or otherwise, does not automatically render the evidence of the proposed expert inadmissible. It is the nature and extent of the interest or connection which matters, not the mere fact of the interest or connection.

3. The decision as to whether an expert should be permitted to give evidence in such circumstances is a matter of fact and degree. The test of apparent bias is not relevant to the question of whether or not an expert witness should be permitted to give evidence.

4. The questions which have to be determined are whether (a) the person has relevant expertise; and, (b) he is aware of his primary duty to the Court if he gives expert evidence, and is willing and able, despite the interest or connection with the litigation or a party, to carry out that duty.

5. If the expert has an interest which is not sufficient to preclude him from giving evidence the interest may nevertheless affect the weight of his evidence.

---

17   [2002] 3 WLR 1104.
18   [2003] EWHC 367 (QB), para 29.

THE BASIS OF THE OPINION

An expert gives his opinion on the basis of facts in a particular case, but those facts must themselves be proved by admissible evidence. However, if the rule against hearsay were strictly applied, an expert would often be prevented from giving an opinion because his reasoning and conclusions will be governed by matters that he has learned in the course of his training and experience, either from what he has read or from others who share his specialisation. The courts have therefore relaxed the hearsay rule to take this into account. So, for example, an expert in property valuations is not confined to giving evidence based on comparables of which he has first hand knowledge. Of course, a surveyor who is asked to express a view on the open market value of a particular property will have regard to any relevant personal experience. He will also have regard to the sales experience of his office, whether that is within his own first hand knowledge or not, and to all sources from which information can be obtained about market trends and conditions.[19]

Experts may support their opinions by referring to articles, letters to journals and other materials, whether published or not, when giving their testimony.[20] An example of this practice can be seen in *R v Abadom*.[21] The appellant had been convicted of robbery, and his appeal raised a question about the materials that could be used by expert witnesses when giving evidence. The main evidence against him was that a pair of his shoes had fragments of glass embedded in them; it was the prosecution's case that the glass came from a window broken during the robbery. One of the prosecution expert witnesses relied, in support of this contention, on statistics collated by the Home Office Central Research Establishment in relation to the refractive index of broken glass.[22] The point taken on appeal was that the evidence of this expert was inadmissible hearsay because the expert had no personal knowledge of the analyses whose results were collated in these statistics. The Court of Appeal rejected this contention on the ground that experts must be entitled to draw on material produced by others in their field of expertise. Indeed, it is part of their duty to consider any material that might be available and not to draw conclusions based solely on their own experience, which will inevitably be limited. The court emphasised that the primary facts on which an expert's opinion is based must be proved by admissible evidence. So here, for example, it was necessary to show by admissible evidence that glass from the broken window and glass from the appellant's

---

19 *Abbey National Mortgages plc v Key Surveyors Nationwide Ltd* [1996] 3 All ER 184, p 189, *per* Sir Thomas Bingham MR. This Court of Appeal decision shows a greater readiness to accept hearsay than the decision of Megarry J in *English Exporters (London) Ltd v Eldonwall Ltd* [1973] Ch 415.

20 *H v Schering Chemicals Ltd* [1983] 1 WLR 143.

21 [1983] 1 All ER 364. See also *R v Hodges and Walker* [2003] 2 Cr App R 247.

22 The refractive index is a measure of the extent to which light is bent when it passes into a particular piece of glass.

shoes had the same refractive index. But once the primary facts have been proved, experts are entitled to draw on the work of others, whether published or unpublished, as part of their own experience in that field. Where they have done so, however, this should be mentioned in their evidence so that it can be taken into account when considering the probative worth of their opinion as a whole. This common law exception to the rule against hearsay is preserved by s 118(1) of the Criminal Justice Act 2003.

Sometimes the primary facts of a case are not established by the expert himself, but by other members of a team, which the expert leads. In such a case, the evidence of the other relevant team members must be available (in the absence of formal admissions),[23] so that the primary facts can all be proved by admissible evidence.[24] The distinction between primary facts and other facts relied on by an expert to interpret primary facts (which may be called 'expert's facts') is that only primary facts are peculiar to the investigation being carried out. For example, in *R v Abadom*, primary facts included the location of the glass fragments and the refractive index of those fragments, and in *R v Jackson*, they included the location of blood stains and their blood groupings. Expert's facts come from other factual situations. Often they are facts about experiments used to test and substantiate a particular hypothesis. So, in *R v Abadom*, the Home Office statistics, based on tests carried out in different situations, were expert's facts, and could be relied on without formal proof by the expert when interpreting primary facts of that case, namely, the location and refractive index of the glass fragments. But in *R v Jackson*, the facts about the blood stains were primary, because it was the blood that was being investigated for the purpose of the trial. So those facts had to be formally proved, in the absence of admissions.

By s 30(1) of the Criminal Justice Act 1988, an 'expert report' (that is, a written report by a person dealing wholly or mainly with matters on which he is, or, if living, would be, qualified to give expert evidence)[25] shall be admissible as evidence in criminal proceedings, whether or not the person making it attends to give oral evidence. If it is proposed that the person making the report shall not give oral evidence, the report shall be admissible only with leave of the court. It seems most unlikely that a court would allow an expert report to be adduced without calling the maker if the opposing party had a genuine desire to cross-examine on it. The effect of this provision is that if an expert gives evidence, his report is admissible as evidence of the facts and opinions that it contains. The jury can therefore be given copies, and the expert does not have to read it aloud, or cover all the matters contained in it

---

23   See above, Chapter 4.

24   *R v Jackson* [1996] 2 Cr App R 420. By the Criminal Justice Act 2003, s 127, such evidence can be given as an exception to the rule against hearsay, unless the court orders that it is not in the interests of justice for it to be given in this way.

25   Criminal Justice Act 1988, s 30(5).

during examination-in-chief. There are provisions, affecting the defence as well as the prosecution, for advance disclosure of expert evidence.

In its report on hearsay and related topics, the Law Commission considered the problem that very often an expert's opinion will be based on the investigation of primary facts by members of his team. In order to save time and money, the Commission recommended that the present disclosure requirements should be extended. The advance notice would include a list of any persons who had supplied information on which the expert relied, and a brief description of the information that each person had supplied. Any other party to the proceedings could apply for a direction that a person named in this way should give oral evidence, but a direction could be made only if the applicant satisfied the court that there was a real issue that could be pursued better with the assistant than with the expert. In the absence of any application in relation to a named assistant, a new hearsay exception would operate. This would allow the expert to base his evidence on any information supplied by that assistant on matters of which that assistant had (or might reasonably be supposed to have had) personal knowledge. Any information relied on in this way would be admissible as evidence of its truth. If a direction were made that the assistant should give evidence in person, the exception would not apply.[26]

EVIDENCE FROM PSYCHIATRISTS AND PSYCHOLOGISTS

According to Lord Campbell, '[H]ardly any weight is to be given to the evidence of what are called scientific witnesses; they come with a bias on their minds to support the cause in which they are embarked . . .'.[27] Judicial attitudes have not greatly changed where the witnesses are experts in psychiatry or psychology. To some extent, judges recognise that a psychiatrist or psychologist may be able to provide useful testimony about matters that are outside the experience of judge or jurors.[28] At the same time, they tend to think there is a danger that mental experts will usurp the role of the jury or other triers of fact unless a clear line is drawn between abnormal

---

26   Law Commission No 245, 1997, paras 9.23–9.29.

27   *The Tracy Peerage* (1839) 10 Cl&F 154, p 191.

28   For an example of psychiatric evidence that was of assistance to the court, see *DPP v A & BC Chewing Gum Ltd* [1968] QB 159; *Sourcebook*, 1996, p 395, where the Divisional Court held that magistrates hearing an information under the Obscene Publications Act 1964 should have heard the expert evidence of psychiatrists who had been available at trial to give their opinion about the tendency of certain articles to deprave and corrupt children. Lord Parker CJ observed that while the effect of a publication on an adult might well be capable of being assessed without expert evidence, where the effect on children was in issue the justices needed all the help they could get.

and normal mental states. The latter are taken to include lust, anger, and other undesirable emotions which, judges believe, are perfectly capable of being understood by ordinary people without expert assistance. The attempt to make such a distinction has led to some unhappy compromises, the most unhappy being the distinction drawn between expert evidence relevant to the reliability of a confession, and expert evidence relevant to *mens rea*.

In *R v Raghip and Others*,[29] the Court of Appeal acknowledged that it was the regular practice of judges to admit psychiatric or psychological evidence when considering submissions about the admissibility of confessions. The reason for this is that the mental condition of the defendant at the time of interview is one of the circumstances to be considered by the trial judge on a submission under s 76(2)(b) of the Police and Criminal Evidence Act 1984. It was previously thought that expert evidence could be admitted about a propensity to make false confessions only where the defendant suffered from a recognised mental illness. It is now accepted that evidence can be admitted if it shows that the defendant is suffering from a personality disorder tending to affect the reliability of the confession. The test for admissibility is not whether the condition comes within a recognised category of disorder, it is whether the disorder can render the confession unreliable.[30] But such evidence is admissible only when it shows a substantial deviation from normality, and there must be a history of abnormality that predates the confession.[31]

The Court in *Raghip* also said that a distinction must be made between psychiatric or psychological evidence directed towards the admissibility of a confession, and the admission of such evidence because it is relevant to the defendant's *mens rea*. Following this distinction, the Court of Appeal in *R v Coles*[32] held that expert evidence is inadmissible to enable a jury to reach a decision about the existence of *mens rea, unless related to the mental health or psychiatric state of the defendant*. The defendant was charged with arson. After he had given evidence himself, his counsel applied for leave to call the expert evidence of a psychologist. The trial judge held the evidence inadmissible because it was not evidence of any mental abnormality, merely that the defendant was of low average mental capacity. The Court of Appeal upheld his decision, observing that, 'Adolescents of varying stages of maturity and brightness are all within the common experience of jurors'.

There are limitations where the defence want to call the evidence of a psychologist or psychiatrist because of its relevance to *mens rea*. In *R v Masih*[33] the defendant and two co-defendants were charged with rape. There was a possibility that the defendant might have been persuaded to act as he did by his co-defendants. He was

---

29   (1991) *The Times*, 9 December.

30   *R v Ward* [1993] 1 WLR 619, p 690.

31   *R v O'Brien (Michael Alan)* [2000] Crim LR 676.

32   [1995] 1 Cr App R 157.

33   [1986] Crim LR 395.

neither insane nor psychiatrically ill. But, in relation to *mens rea*, the defence wanted to call expert evidence to the effect that he had an IQ placing him on the boundaries of dull-normal and subnormal intelligence, was extremely immature, limited in his understanding of people, likely to judge events at face value, be confused as to willingness or unwillingness, and had a strong desire to please and to conform to others' expectations. The trial judge refused to admit this evidence and was upheld by the Court of Appeal, which stated, however, that where a defendant had an IQ of 69 or less, this should be admitted as being relevant to *mens rea*. But the Court said that expert evidence about a defendant's state of mind should not generally be admitted where a defendant was within the scale of normality, albeit at the lower end. This should be contrasted with medical evidence about a defendant's ability to form an intention where he is affected by drugs or hypoglycaemia. These are matters outside the ordinary experience of jurors.[34]

There can be other occasions when a jury may be assisted by expert evidence about matters usually within ordinary experience. In *R v X (Childhood Amnesia)*[35] the defendant was convicted of indecently assaulting his daughter when she was aged four or five. She made a statement to the police about this for the first time when she was 19. The Criminal Cases Review Commission later referred the case to the Court of Appeal, which heard evidence from a psychologist who was an expert in memory formation and development. The object was to decide whether the psychiatrist could have given expert evidence at the defendant's trial, had he then been available.

He said that memories of early childhood were qualitatively different from memories of later events. Adults were usually unable to remember early childhood events to the extent of being able to give a coherent narrative. The period covered by this 'childhood amnesia' lasted until about the age of seven. It followed that evidence of an event taking place before a child had reached that age, which contained detail and surrounding facts, might be unreliable although apparently credible.

The Court held that this would have been admissible as expert evidence. It provided information likely to be outside the knowledge and experience of the jury. But the Court added that evidence on these lines would be admissible in child abuse cases only in the most unusual circumstances: where the complainant provided a description of events very early in life, which appeared to contain an unrealistic amount of detail. A witness's ability to remember events will ordinarily be well within the experience of jurors.

The 'common experience of jurors' had been established in *R v Turner*[36] as a key concept in determining the admissibility of psychiatric or psychological evidence on the issue of *mens rea*. The defendant was charged with the murder of his girlfriend, and the defence was provocation. It was said that the defendant had been deeply in

---

34   *R v Toner* [1991] 93 Cr App R 382.
35   [2005] EWCA Crim 1828, [2006] 1 Cr App R 10.
36   [1975] QB 834.

love with the girl and had believed her to be pregnant by him. One day he was sitting in a motor car with her when she told him, with a grin, that while he had been in prison she had been sleeping with two other men, that she could make money in that way, and that the child she was carrying was not his. The defendant claimed that he had been very upset by what she told him. His hand had come across a hammer by the side of the seat and he had hit her with it. He said, 'It was never in my mind to do her any harm. I did not realise what I had in my hand. I knew it was heavy . . . When I realised it was a hammer I stopped'.

The psychiatrist would have said that the defendant's relationship with his girlfriend was such as to make him likely to be overwhelmed by anger as a result of what she had said to him. In his opinion, the defendant's personality was such that he could have killed her in an explosive release of blind rage. He added, however, that the defendant showed no signs of mental illness. While he would obviously benefit from psychotherapeutic counselling, there was no need for psychiatric treatment.

In the Court of Appeal, Lawton LJ referred to the well established rule[37] that an expert's opinion is admissible to furnish the court with scientific information which is likely to be outside the experience and knowledge of a judge or jury. But he said that the opinion of an expert is unnecessary if a judge or jury can form their own conclusions on the facts without help. In particular, they do not need the help of experts 'on matters of human nature and behaviour within the limits of normality'. In relation to the evidence in this case, Lawton LJ said:

> We all know that both men and women who are deeply in love can, and sometimes do, have outbursts of blind rage when discovering unexpected wantonness on the part of their loved ones . . . Jurors do not need psychiatrists to tell them how ordinary folk who are not suffering from any mental illness are likely to react to the stresses and strains of life.[38]

It followed that the psychiatrist's evidence was not admissible to establish that the defendant was likely to have been provoked.

In the course of argument, *Lowery v The Queen*[39] was cited as part of the appellant's submission. This case, which the court in *R v Turner* said was 'decided on its special facts', involved two defendants, Lowery and King, who were convicted of the sadistic and otherwise motiveless murder of a girl aged 15. At trial they ran 'cut-throat' defences, each saying that the other was solely responsible for the crime. King called in his defence a psychologist whose testimony supported King's evidence against Lowery. In the event, both defendants were convicted. Lowery appealed, arguing that the psychologist's evidence should not have been admitted. The Privy Council upheld the trial judge's decision to admit the evidence and dismissed Lowery's appeal.

---

37   See the decision of Lord Mansfield in *Folkes v Chadd* (1782) 3 Doug KB 157.
38   [1975] QB 834, p 841.
39   [1974] AC 85.

The evidence on behalf of King had been given by a Professor Cox, a psychologist. He had had interviews in turn with both Lowery and King, and in each case he had applied certain tests. These were partly intelligence tests, but in the main were tests as to the general personality of the person interviewed. Among other things, he had found a callousness and a sadistic tendency in Lowery that were not present in King.

The main reason why the Privy Council held this evidence admissible for King seems to have been that the situation was analogous to one where there was a relevant physical disparity between two co-defendants. Evidence would have been admissible to show that one defendant had greater physical capacity to commit the crime than the other. The Privy Council held in effect that no logical distinction could be drawn between physical capacities and mental ones. Professor Cox had provided scientific evidence as to the respective personalities of the two accused. That kind of information was not within the knowledge of judges or jurors and it was therefore appropriate to admit expert evidence on the subject. The opinion of the Privy Council shows that it was *influenced* by the fact that Lowery had put his own character in issue both by attacking King, and by claiming that he was less likely by reason of his character and circumstances to have committed the crime than his co-defendant. But however relevant and necessary that evidence might have been to King's defence, this consideration could not have been conclusive of *admissibility*.[40] For the evidence to be admissible, the Privy Council had to accept the argument that expert evidence about relevant characteristics of a defendant's personality could be received by analogy with expert evidence about relevant physical characteristics. In both cases the evidence was necessary, and so admissible, to assist the jury in matters beyond their own experience.

Another argument in *R v Turner* was that the psychiatrist's evidence was relevant and admissible to help the jury in relation to the credibility of the defendant's evidence. The Court of Appeal rejected this on the basis that the defendant was not mentally disordered. This test was followed in *R v Mackenney and Pinfold*,[41] in which the Court of Appeal said that if a witness is suffering from some defect or abnormality of mind it may well be permissible to call *psychiatric* evidence to show that the witness is incapable of giving reliable evidence.[42] The mental illness need not be such as to

---

40   In *R v Theodosi* [1993] RTR 179, the Court of Appeal emphasised that a trial judge had no discretion to admit inadmissible opinion evidence merely because the defendants were running cut-throat defences.

41   (1981) 76 Cr App R 271.

42   The evidence of a psychologist is inappropriate because it is psychiatry, not psychology, that is the branch of medical science dealing with diseases and disorders of the mind: *ibid*, p 275. Mackenney and Pinfold finally had their convictions quashed in 2003 after a reference to the Court of Appeal by the Criminal Cases Review Commission. On this occasion the court adopted a slightly more flexible approach, and held that the evidence of a psychologist as to the credibility of a witness whom he had observed in court, but had not otherwise examined, was admissible in the circumstances of that particular case. See *R v Pinfold and Mackenney* (2004) *The Times*, 9 January.

make the witness totally incapable of giving accurate evidence, but it must substantially affect the witness's capacity to do so. This is very different from calling psychiatric evidence with a view to warning a jury that a witness who is capable of giving reliable evidence may be choosing not to do so. If a witness is mentally capable of giving reliable evidence, it is for the jury to decide whether that evidence is reliable, and they do not need the assistance of a psychiatrist.[43] Similarly, in *R v Browning*[44] it was held that evidence from a psychologist about the deterioration of memory was inadmissible because the subject matter of the proposed testimony was within the jury's experience.

In *R v Deighton (Richard)*[45] the Court of Appeal warned against 'the temptation to medicalise normality'. The defendant was convicted of cheating the public revenue by failing to account for the tax due on a disposal of shares, and for income tax and national insurance contributions for a period of eight years. He admitted his failure but denied dishonesty, saying that he had had no intention to defraud. He had 'buried his head in the sand' with regard to overwhelming debts that had accumulated after his call to the Bar. At trial, the defence wanted to call the evidence of two psychiatrists and a psychologist. These experts had not found him to be suffering from mental illness, but two of them had diagnosed a condition called 'Avoidant Personality Disorder'. A third expert had rejected that diagnosis, but said that the defendant had anxious avoidant personality traits. It was argued that this evidence was relevant to the question whether the defendant was suffering from a psychiatric abnormality that could have predisposed him to avoid thinking about what he was doing and its effect, and that this was relevant to the broader questions of dishonesty and intent to defraud.

The trial judge ruled that the matters to which the evidence was directed were not outside the knowledge or experience of the jury, and the evidence was therefore inadmissible. The Court of Appeal held that he had been right. As Longmore LJ said, 'Any juror knows people who have a disposition of being unable to face up to awkward situations and thus have a disposition . . . to deny or repress problems.' The expert evidence was part of a 'trend to medicalise normality', which the courts should resist.[46]

The question sometimes arises whether the prosecution can call evidence to boost the credibility of a prosecution witness who suffers from some sort of mental abnormality. In *R v Robinson (Raymond)*[47] the Court of Appeal said that the Crown cannot call a witness and then, without more, call a psychologist or psychiatrist to say

43   (1981) 76 Cr App R 271, p 276.
44   [1995] Crim LR 227.
45   [2005] EWCA Crim 3131, para 14.
46   Paragraphs 13–14. See also *R v Weightman* (1991) 92 Cr App R 291 (jurors would know that there are people who are histrionic and likely to draw attention to themselves).
47   [1994] 98 Cr App R 370, pp 374–75.

why the jury should regard that witness as reliable. However, if the defence call an expert witness to say that a prosecution witness should be considered unreliable because of some mental abnormality outside the jury's experience, it may be open to the Crown to call an expert in rebuttal. It may even be open to the Crown to rebut by expert evidence an allegation put in cross-examination that a prosecution witness is unreliable in some respect because of mental abnormality. And in *R v VJS*[48] the Court of Appeal, while refusing to lay down any principle of general application, held that a trial judge had been right to allow the prosecution to call expert evidence about the general nature of a neurological illness (autism) suffered by one of the prosecution witnesses, with the object of trying to ensure that the jury were not misled about the weight to attach to that witness's evidence.

Whether an expert could give his opinion on what has been called 'the ultimate issue' – that is to say, the very question to be decided by the court – was a vexed question for a long time. So far as civil proceedings are concerned, the question is now answered by s 3 of the Civil Evidence Act 1972, which provides that where a person is called as a witness in civil proceedings, his opinion on any relevant matter, including an issue in the proceedings, shall be admissible if he is qualified to give expert evidence on it. In criminal cases, evidence of an expert on a particular matter is sometimes excluded on the ground that it would be providing an opinion on the ultimate issue.[49] However, the rule is frequently ignored. The rationale behind the supposed prohibition is that the expert should not usurp the functions of the jury, but the rule is of little use, because counsel can bring a witness so close to giving his opinion on the ultimate issue that the inference as to his view is obvious. In *R v Stockwell*,[50] the Court of Appeal said that an expert is called to give his opinion and should be allowed to do so. What is important is that the judge should make it clear to the jury that they are not bound by an expert's opinion.

CONFLICTS OF EXPERT EVIDENCE

What is a finder of fact to do, particularly in a criminal trial, in the face of conflicting expert evidence? For example, pathologists may disagree about the cause of death in cases of alleged strangulation. An argument whether the hyoid bone[51] was fractured before death (supporting the conclusion of strangulation), or whether it occurred after death, perhaps during the post mortem itself (discounting strangulation), is commonplace. The general principle is that it is for the jury to decide between the

---

48   [2006] EWCA Crim 2389.

49   See, eg, *R v Theodosi* [1993] RTR 179.

50   (1993) 97 Cr App R 260. See also *R v Ugoh and Others* [2001] EWCA Crim 1381, para 19.

51   A bone in the neck.

experts, by reference to all the available evidence, and that it is open to the jury to accept or reject the evidence of experts on either side.[52] The Court said that dicta in *R v Cannings*[53] relating to a situation where two or more sudden, unexplained infant deaths occurred in the same family, and where there was a serious disagreement between reputable experts about the cause of death, were not to be taken as authority for the proposition that whenever there is a conflict between expert witnesses the case for the prosecution must fail, unless a conviction can be justified by evidence other than that of the experts.[54]

FURTHER READING

—Mackay and Colman, 'Excluding Expert Evidence' [1991] Crim LR 800.

—Mackay and Colman, 'Equivocal Rulings on Expert Psychological and Psychiatric Evidence' [1996] Crim LR 88.

—Pattenden, 'Conflicting Approaches to Psychiatric Evidence in Criminal Trials' [1986] Crim LR 92.

—Redmayne, *Expert Evidence and Criminal Justice*, 2001, Chapters 5, 6 and 7.

—Roberts, 'Towards the Principled Reception of Expert Evidence of Witness Credibility in Criminal Trials' (2004) 8 E&P 215.

—Spencer, 'Court Experts and Expert Witnesses' (1992) 45(2) CLP 213.

EXERCISES

1. What is an 'expert ad hoc'? Give an example from a decided case.

2. You are defending a surgeon in a civil action for professional negligence. He wants to call his sister, a distinguished surgeon, to testify as an expert witness on his behalf. What would you advise?

3. When can expert psychiatric or psychological evidence be called as to the unreliability of a defendant's confession?

4. When can expert psychiatric or psychological evidence be called on the basis that it is relevant to a defendant's *mens rea*?

5. What do you understand by 'the temptation to medicalise normality' in the context of the admissibility of expert psychiatric or psychological evidence?

6. Is there a conflict between the decisions in *Turner* (1975) and *Lowery v The Queen* (1974)?

7. To what extent is an expert's opinion on the 'ultimate issue' admissible?

8. How far is the rule against hearsay relaxed for expert witnesses?

---

52   *R v Kai-Whitewind* [2005] EWCA Crim 1092, [2005] 2 Cr App R 31, para 89.

53   [2004] EWCA Crim 1, [2004] 1 WLR 2607.

54   *R v Kai-Whitewind*, para 84. See also *R v Anthony (Donna)* [2005] EWCA Crim 952, para 81.

14

JUDICIAL FINDINGS AS EVIDENCE

INTRODUCTION

The rule at common law is that a judicial finding in one case is inadmissible, in another case between different parties, to prove the facts on which the first decision was based. The reason for this is that it would be unjust for someone to have his rights affected by litigation to which he was not a party and in which, therefore, he could not be heard. This appears from the unanimous opinion of all the judges in *The Case of the Duchess of Kingston*,[1] that:

> . . . as a general principle . . . a transaction between two parties in judicial proceedings ought not to be binding upon a third; for it would be unjust to bind any person who could not be admitted to make a defence, or to examine witnesses, or to appeal from a judgment he might think erroneous; and therefore the depositions of witnesses in another cause in proof of a fact, the verdict of the jury finding the fact, and the judgment of the court upon the facts found, although evidence against the parties and all claiming under them, are not, in general, to be used to the prejudice of strangers.

---

1   (1776) 20 St Tr 355, col 538.

As a general principle, this is obviously sound. Unfortunately, the principle was applied in such a way that criminal convictions had to be ignored in cases where common sense would have acknowledged them to be both relevant and weighty. Reform in civil cases was achieved by statute in 1968, and in criminal cases in 1984.

CONVICTIONS AS EVIDENCE IN CIVIL CASES

The commission of an offence often gives rise to civil as well as criminal liability. For example, assaults are torts as well as crimes, and acts or omissions constituting the offences of careless or dangerous driving can give rise to actions for damages in negligence, or to claims under the Fatal Accidents Act 1976. Criminal proceedings are usually completed more quickly than civil proceedings. Where this has happened, what is the status at the subsequent civil trial of an earlier criminal conviction relating to the same facts? The answer given by the common law was that it had no status at all, despite the fact that there might be a defendant common to both proceedings, and this was confirmed in the leading case of *Hollington v F Hewthorn and Co Ltd*.[2] The case arose from a collision between two motor cars in which the plaintiff's son sustained fatal injuries. The plaintiff brought an action under the Fatal Accidents Acts against the defendants on behalf of his son's estate. However, because of his son's death, he had no evidence of the defendant's negligence available except the conviction for careless driving of the second defendant, for whose tort the first defendants were alleged to be vicariously liable. It was argued on his behalf (by AT Denning KC, as he then was) that the conviction was admissible as at least prima facie evidence of negligence, but this argument was rejected by the Court of Appeal. In giving judgment, Lord Goddard CJ stated:

> [T]he conviction is only proof that another court considered that the defendant was guilty of careless driving. Even were it proved that it was the accident that led to the prosecution, the conviction proves no more than what has just been stated. The court which has to try the claim for damages knows nothing of the evidence that was before the criminal court. It cannot know what arguments were addressed to it, or what influenced the court in arriving at its decision . . . It frequently happens that a bystander has a complete and full view of an accident. It is beyond question that, while he may inform the court of everything he saw, he may not express any opinion on whether either or both of the parties were negligent . . . [O]n the trial of the issue in the civil court, the opinion of the criminal court is equally irrelevant.[3]

---

2   [1943] KB 587.

3   [1943] KB 587, pp 594–95.

He also referred to the impossibility of determining what weight should be given to a conviction without, in effect, re-trying the criminal case. The father's claim therefore failed. Doubts were expressed about the justice of this result, and these were reflected in the 15th Report of the Law Reform Committee on the subject of what had come to be known as 'the rule in *Hollington v Hewthorn*'.[4] In their report, the Committee stated:

> Rationalise it how one will, the decision in the case offends one's sense of justice. The defendant driver had been found guilty of careless driving by a court of competent jurisdiction. The onus of proof of culpability in criminal cases is higher than in civil; the degree of carelessness required to sustain a conviction for careless driving is, if anything, greater than that required to sustain a civil cause of action in negligence. Yet the fact that the defendant driver had been convicted of careless driving at the time and place of the accident was held not to amount even to *prima facie* evidence of his negligent driving at that time and place. It is not easy to escape the implication in the rule in *Hollington v Hewthorn* that, in the estimation of lawyers, a conviction by a criminal court is as likely to be wrong as right. It is not, of course, spelt out in those terms in the judgment of the Court of Appeal, although, in so far as their decision was based mainly upon the ground that the opinion of the criminal court as to the defendant driver's guilt was as irrelevant as that of a bystander who witnessed the accident, the gap between the implicit and the explicit was a narrow one.[5]

The Committee's criticisms were followed by the enactment of ss 11–13 of the Civil Evidence Act 1968.[6] Section 11 provided, amongst other things, as follows:

(1) In any civil proceedings the fact that a person has been convicted of an offence by or before any court in the United Kingdom or by a court-martial there or elsewhere shall (subject to sub-section (3) below) be admissible in evidence for the purpose of proving, where to do so is relevant to any issue in those proceedings, that he committed that offence, whether he was so convicted upon a plea of guilty or otherwise and whether or not he is a party to the civil proceedings; but no conviction other than a subsisting one shall be admissible in evidence by virtue of this section.

(2) In any civil proceedings in which by virtue of this section a person is proved to have been convicted of an offence by or before any court in the United Kingdom or by a court-martial there or elsewhere –

    (a) he shall be taken to have committed that offence unless the contrary is proved; and

    (b) without prejudice to the reception of any other admissible evidence for the purpose of identifying the facts on which the conviction was based, the contents of any

---

4   Law Reform Committee, Cmnd 3391, 1967.

5   Law Reform Committee, Cmnd 3391, 1967, para 3.

6   These are contained in Pt II of the 1968 Act, which remains unaffected by the Civil Evidence Act 1995.

> document which is admissible as evidence of the conviction, and the contents of
> the information, complaint, indictment or charge sheet on which the person in
> question was convicted, shall be admissible in evidence for that purpose.

(3) Nothing in this section shall prejudice the operation of section 13 of this Act or any other
enactment whereby a conviction or a finding of fact in any criminal proceedings is for the
purposes of any other proceedings made conclusive evidence of any fact.

Similar provisions relating to findings of adultery and paternity as evidence in civil
proceedings are contained in s 12.

The Law Reform Committee took the view that in actions other than those for
defamation, the relevance of the conviction is to prove that the convicted person's
conduct was such as to give rise to a civil liability, either on the part of the convicted
person himself or on the part of another person, such as an employer or insurer.
Because this liability is additional to the penal consequences of the conviction and
may fall on someone other than the convicted person, the Committee concluded that
the person on whom civil liability would fall should not be completely precluded
from showing that the convicted person's conduct on the occasion in question was
not such as the criminal court had found it to be. But the Committee thought that
in actions for defamation the only issue, other than that of damages, was whether a
person who had been tried for a criminal offence was guilty of that offence. The real
purpose of the action was to obtain a re-trial of the criminal proceedings upon
different evidence by a court which lacked jurisdiction to try criminal cases, and
which applied a procedure and standard of proof regarded by the law as inappropriate
in criminal proceedings. As it happened, a few years before the report there had been
a much publicised case where the plaintiff had been convicted of robbery and had had
the conviction upheld by the Court of Criminal Appeal. Several years later, he
brought an action for libel against a defendant who had published a statement that
the plaintiff was guilty of the robbery of which he had been convicted. As the law
then stood, the defendant had the burden of proving that the plaintiff had in fact
been guilty. He failed to discharge it and the plaintiff's claim succeeded.[7]

Accordingly, s 13(1) of the 1968 Act provided:

> In an action for libel or slander in which the question whether a person did or did not commit a
> criminal offence is relevant to an issue arising in the action, proof that, at the time when that
> issue falls to be determined, that person stands convicted of that offence shall be conclusive
> evidence that he committed that offence; and his conviction thereof shall be admissible in
> evidence accordingly.

Nothing more will be said about s 13(1), but several points need to be made in
relation to s 11.

---

7   *Hinds v Sparks* (1964) *The Times*, 28, 30 July.

THE SCOPE OF THE SECTION

Section 11(1) refers to proof of 'the fact that a person has been convicted of an offence by or before any court in the United Kingdom . . .'. It follows that the rule in *Hollington v Hewthorn* continues to apply to convictions by foreign courts, and they therefore remain irrelevant, and so inadmissible.[8] Nor does the section extend to adjudications of guilt in police disciplinary proceedings.[9] Sub-section (1) provides that 'no conviction other than a subsisting one shall be admissible in evidence'. If a person has been convicted, but there is an appeal pending, the court will not rely on the section. Instead, the civil hearing will be adjourned until the criminal appeal has been determined.[10]

PLEADING THE SECTION

If the claimant intends to rely on a criminal conviction as evidence under s 11, he must include in his pleading a statement of that intention, with particulars of the conviction and its date, the court that made the conviction, and the issue in the action to which the conviction is relevant. An appropriate paragraph in a particulars of claim would follow particulars of the negligence alleged, and would read something like this:

> Further, the defendant was convicted on 1 April 2008 by the magistrates' court sitting at Barchester of the offence of driving his motor car on the road without due care and attention contrary to s 3 of the Road Traffic Act 1988. The said conviction is relevant to the issue of negligence and the claimant intends to rely on it as evidence in this action.

THE EFFECT OF THE SECTION

Broadly, there are two views about the effect of the section. One is that a conviction merely operates to raise a *presumption* that the facts on which it was based are true.[11] On this view, the conviction itself has no weight as an item of evidence. The other view is that the conviction is in itself an item of evidence to be weighed in the scales against the defendant. Both views found expression in the decision of the Court of Appeal in *Stupple v Royal Insurance Co Ltd*.[12] In that case Buckley LJ said that no weight was to be given to the mere fact of conviction. He was chiefly influenced by the difficulty of assessing weight in such a situation. After saying that weight could not depend on such considerations as the status of the court that convicted, or whether the verdict was unanimous or by a majority, he concluded: 'It remains, I think, as true today as before the Act that mere proof of conviction proves nothing

---

8   This was confirmed by the Court of Appeal in *Union Carbide Corp v Naturin Ltd* [1987] FSR 538.
9   *Thorpe v Chief Constable of Greater Manchester Police* [1989] 1 WLR 665.
10   *In Re Raphael (Decd)* [1973] 1 WLR 998.
11   On presumptions generally, see above, Chapter 7.
12   [1971] 1 QB 50.

relevant to the plaintiff's claim.'[13] In other words, a conviction is only a trigger that activates the presumption under sub-s (2), so as to place a burden of proof on the defendant to show that he did not commit the offence relied on.

Lord Denning MR took a different view. He said:

> I think that the conviction does not merely shift the burden of proof. It is a weighty piece of evidence of itself. For instance, if a man is convicted of careless driving on the evidence of a witness, but that witness dies before the civil action is heard . . . then the conviction itself tells in the scale in the civil action. It speaks as clearly as the witness himself would have done, had he lived. It does not merely reverse the burden of proof. If that was all it did, the defendant might well give his own evidence negativing want of care, and say: 'I have discharged the burden. I have given my evidence and it has not been contradicted.' In answer to the defendant's evidence, the plaintiff can say to him: 'But your evidence is contradicted. It is contradicted by the very fact of your conviction.'[14]

Lord Denning's example is a persuasive argument in favour of his interpretation of the section. The editors of *Phipson* have produced further arguments in support, based on the wording of s 11.[15] They point to the fact that sub-s (1) expressly provides: '. . . the fact that a person has been convicted of an offence . . . shall . . . be admissible in evidence for the purpose of proving . . . that he committed that offence.' The presumption of the correctness of the conviction is not referred to until sub-s (2). They argue that s 11(1) could exist perfectly well in the absence of s 11(2). In that case, its meaning would clearly be the one favoured by Lord Denning. Given that that is so, it is hard to see why the addition of sub-s (2) should change that meaning. Further, 'the fact' of a conviction is, by sub-s (1), admissible '*in evidence*'; the interpretation of Buckley LJ would deprive it of any evidential effect as a fact. They argue that their view is supported by Lord Diplock's approach in *Hunter v Chief Constable of West Midlands Police*, where he said, 'The burden of proof of "the contrary" that lies upon a defendant under s 11 is the ordinary burden in a civil action: proof on a balance of probabilities; although in the face of a conviction after a full hearing this is likely to be an uphill task'. If the conviction was not an item of evidence, but merely a trigger, a distinction could not have been made between convictions based on a guilty plea and convictions 'after a full hearing'.[16]

In *Stupple v Royal Insurance Co Ltd*,[17] Lord Denning accepted that a distinction could be made. He thought that the weight to be given to a conviction would depend

---

13   [1971] 1 QB 50, p 76.

14   *Ibid*, p 72. Do not be misled by Lord Denning's references to shifting or reversing the burden of proof. There is more than one issue in the case. The effect of s 11(2) is to place the burden of proof in relation to one of those issues (the commission of the offence) on the defendant, once the plaintiff has proved the fact of conviction. See above, Chapter 7.

15   *Phipson on Evidence*, 14th edn, 1990, p 918.

16   [1982] AC 529, p 544.

17   [1971] 1 QB 50.

on the circumstances, and that a plea of guilty might have less weight than a conviction after a full trial because sometimes defendants pleaded guilty in error, or to save time and expense where the offence was minor, or to avoid some embarrassing fact coming out. The Law Reform Committee took the same view. They stated in their 15th Report that a conviction after a contested trial, a conviction on a plea of guilty, and an acquittal did not have the same probative value in relation to the question in issue in a civil action.[18] Later, when dealing with the defendant's burden of proof, they drew a distinction between convictions after a contested trial and convictions on a plea of guilty. In the former case, they said, the burden was unlikely to be discharged by the testimony of the convicted person alone; in the latter case they suggested that it could, if he produced a convincing explanation for his plea. Support for Lord Denning's views can also be found in the decision of the Court of Appeal in *Taylor v Taylor*, where Davies LJ said that it was 'obvious that, when a man has been convicted by 12 of his fellow countrymen and countrywomen at a criminal trial, the verdict of the jury is a matter which is entitled to very great weight when the convicted person is seeking, in the words of the statute, to prove the contrary'.[19]

No doubt it may be difficult to assess the weight of a particular conviction, for example, where it was by a majority verdict, or where for some reason the defendant was unrepresented. However, it does seem possible to say that some convictions will carry less weight than others, and the arguments in favour of Lord Denning's position are strong.[20]

CONVICTIONS AS EVIDENCE IN CRIMINAL CASES

Some offences presuppose the commission of an earlier offence by someone else. For example, handling presupposes that the property handled has already been stolen. Sometimes the easiest way to prove that goods have been stolen is to prove that someone else has been convicted of their theft. But if the person charged with handling was tried separately from the thief, the handler would not have been a party in the trial for theft, would therefore not have been heard in it, and so would have been powerless to affect its outcome. It was this sort of powerlessness that the common law took into account in the general principle that a judicial finding in one case was inadmissible in another case, between different parties, to prove the facts on

---

18   Law Reform Committee, Cmnd 3391, 1967, para 10.

19   [1970] 1 WLR 1148, p 1152.

20   See, further, the note by Zuckerman, 1971. For brief arguments in favour of Buckley LJ's view, see Tapper, 2007, p 121; Carter, 1990, p 433.

which the first decision was based. The application of that principle in the kind of situation just described led courts to treat the earlier conviction as no more than non-expert evidence of opinion,[21] and so inadmissible to establish the fact that the goods were stolen.[22] Similarly, where a defendant was charged with permitting betting on licensed premises, evidence that a bookmaker had been convicted of using the premises on the occasion in question was inadmissible to prove that betting had been taking place there;[23] and where a defendant was charged with living on the earnings of prostitution, evidence that a particular woman had been convicted of practising as a prostitute was inadmissible to prove that she was a prostitute.[24] In cases where two persons were indicted for a criminal offence and one pleaded guilty but the other did not, the judge had to direct the jury that they must pay no attention to the fact that one of the defendants had pleaded guilty. A man's confession was evidence only against himself and not against anyone else.[25]

In 1972, the Criminal Law Revision Committee criticised the state of the law in this respect, saying that it was quite wrong that the prosecution should be required to prove again the guilt of the earlier defendant. It appears, however, that the Committee thought that the amended law would apply in only limited circum-stances, for they added that their proposed amendment would 'be helpful to the prosecution in various cases where the guilt of the accused depends on another person's having committed an offence', such as handling stolen goods, harbouring offenders and offences under ss 4 and 5 of the Criminal Law Act 1967 of assisting offenders and concealing offences.[26] In fact, when the law in this respect was changed by the Police and Criminal Evidence Act 1984, the scope of the legislation was far wider. Section 74 provided as follows:

(1) In any proceedings the fact that a person other than the accused has been convicted of an offence by or before any court in the United Kingdom or by a Service court outside the United Kingdom shall be admissible in evidence for the purpose of proving, where to do so is relevant to any issue in those proceedings, that that person committed that offence, whether or not any other evidence of his having committed that offence is given.

(2) In any proceedings in which by virtue of this section a person other than the accused is proved to have been convicted of an offence by or before any court in the United Kingdom or by a Service court outside the United Kingdom, he shall be taken to have committed that offence unless the contrary is proved.

---

21   *R v Shepherd and Shepherd* (1980) 71 Cr App R 120.

22   *R v Turner* (1832) 1 Mood CC 347.

23   *Taylor v Wilson* (1911) 76 JP 69.

24   *R v Hassan* [1970] 1 QB 423.

25   *R v Moore* (1956) 40 Cr App R 50, pp 53–54.

26   Criminal Law Revision Committee, 1972, paras 217–20.

(3)   In any proceedings where evidence is admissible of the fact that the accused has committed an offence, in so far as that evidence is relevant to any matter in issue in the proceedings for a reason other than a tendency to show in the accused a disposition to commit the kind of offence with which he is charged, if the accused is proved to have been convicted of the offence –

    (a)   by or before any court in the United Kingdom; or

    (b)   by a Service court outside the United Kingdom,

he shall be taken to have committed that offence unless the contrary is proved.

(4)   Nothing in this section shall prejudice –

    (a)   the admissibility in evidence of any conviction which would be admissible apart from this section; or

    (b)   the operation of any enactment whereby a conviction or a finding of fact in any proceedings is for the purposes of any other proceedings made conclusive evidence of any fact.

Section 75(1) applies where evidence that a person has been convicted of an offence is admissible by virtue of s 74. This sub-section provides that, among any other admissible evidence for the purpose of identifying the facts on which the conviction was based, reliance may be placed on the contents of any document which is admissible as evidence of the conviction, and the contents of the information, complaint, indictment or charge sheet on which the person in question was convicted.

Before I turn to a more detailed consideration of the scope of s 74 and its interaction with s 78, which provides a general exclusionary discretion in relation to evidence on which the prosecution proposes to rely, some general points need to be made about these provisions:

(a)   The reference to 'proceedings' in s 74 is a reference to criminal proceedings, and the reference to a 'Service court' is a reference to a court-martial or standing civilian court.[27]

(b)   It should be noted that under s 74(2) and (3), the burden of proving that a person did not commit the offence for which he has been convicted rests on a defendant who asserts that fact. Proof will be to the civil standard of a balance of probabilities, because that is the standard always applicable where a defendant in a criminal trial bears a burden of proof in relation to any issue.[28]

(c)   Section 74(3) would apply, for example, where the prosecution needs to prove that the defendant committed some other offence for which he has been convicted, because that provides an element of the later offence

---

27   Police and Criminal Evidence Act 1984, s 82(1).

28   *R v Carr-Briant* [1943] KB 607.

with which he is charged. For example, suppose that after a defendant's conviction for assault, his victim dies. If the defendant were then charged with murder or manslaughter, the fact of the assault could be established merely by proof of the conviction. The sub-section could also apply if a defendant who was being cross-examined under s 1(3)(ii) or (iii) of the Criminal Evidence Act 1898 denied the fact of conviction or any admissible details of the offences.

(d) The way to prove convictions is governed by s 73(1) and (2) of the Act. Whether the conviction was at a summary trial or on indictment, proof may be made (a) by producing a certificate of conviction duly signed by the clerk of the appropriate court; and (b) by proving that the person named in the certificate is the person whose conviction is to be proved. A document purporting to be a duly signed certificate shall be taken to be such unless the contrary is proved.

(e) Proof of previous convictions in criminal proceedings may also be required as proof of bad character under the Criminal Justice Act 2003. Foreign convictions can be relied on for this purpose if they are properly proved under s 7 of the Evidence Act 1851.[29]

(f) It is a precondition of the admissibility of any evidence that it should be relevant, and care should be taken to establish the relevance of any previous convictions tendered under s 74. For example, in *R v T (AB)*[30] the defendant was charged with indecently assaulting his niece. The niece also alleged that she had been sexually assaulted in separate incidents by her step-grandfather. Before the defendant's trial, the step-grandfather pleaded guilty to the charges against him. The Court of Appeal held that the trial judge should not have allowed evidence of these convictions to be adduced at the defendant's trial. There was no suggestion that the defendant had taken part in the step-grandfather's activities, and no application had been made to admit his convictions as explanatory evidence under s 100(1)(a) CJA 2003. The Court of Appeal held that the convictions could not possibly have been relevant to the issue of whether or not the defendant had assaulted his niece, and should therefore have been excluded.

THE SCOPE OF S 74(1) OF PACE

Clearly, proof of the commission of an earlier offence will be 'relevant to any issue' in the current proceedings if it establishes an element of the offence now charged. So, for

---

29   *R v Kordasinski* [2006] EWCA Crim 2984.
30   [2006] EWCA Crim 2006, [2007] 1 Cr App R 4.

example, in *R v Pigram*,[31] where two men were charged with handling stolen goods, the plea of guilty made by one of the defendants was held admissible at the trial of the other for the purpose of proving that the goods were stolen. In *DPP v P*[32] the defendant was charged with allowing himself to be carried in a motor car that had been taken without the consent of the owner. The driver had already pleaded guilty to taking the car without consent, and evidence of his conviction for that offence was given at the defendant's trial. There was no evidence from the owner of the vehicle to prove that it had been taken without consent, and the magistrates therefore ruled that there was no case to answer. The Divisional Court held that this was wrong. The driver's conviction was prima facie evidence that the car had been taken without consent. None of the cases decided under the old law that were referred to at the beginning of this section would now be decided in the same way. But the Court of Appeal has held that a wide interpretation should be applied to 'issue', so as to allow it to cover not just essential ingredients of an offence, but evidentiary matters also. In *R v Castle*,[33] for example, C and others, including F, were charged with robbery. F pleaded guilty. The victim had picked out C and F at identification parades, saying 'Yes' when identifying C and 'Possibly' when identifying F. The trial judge admitted evidence of F's guilty plea under s 74(1) and was upheld by the Court of Appeal, on the basis that the plea of guilty by F was relevant to the reliability of the identification of C, which was the 'issue' for the purposes of the sub-section. F had, as it were, confirmed an identification made by the victim that had been no more than tentative. If that was correct, then the probability was that the more certain identification of C was correct also.

While the Court of Appeal has said that it does not approve of allowing evidence to go before a jury that is irrelevant, inadmissible, prejudicial or unfair simply on the basis that it is convenient for the jury to have 'the whole picture',[34] it has also been said that 'anything which enables a jury better to understand the relevant factual background against which the issue arises is properly to be described as relevant to that issue within the terms of s 74'. So in a case where defendants were charged with conspiracy to pervert the course of justice by obtaining the false evidence of witnesses at an earlier trial, it was held proper to have proved that the earlier trial had resulted in a conviction, and that at a later trial others had already been convicted of conspiracy to pervert the course of justice in relation to the earlier trial.[35] Where there was strong circumstantial evidence linking two defendants to a third in the commission of a burglary, the guilty plea of the third defendant was admissible to show that the other

---

31   [1995] Crim LR 808.

32   [2006] EWHC 1270 (Admin).

33   [1989] Crim LR 567.

34   *R v Boyson* [1991] Crim LR 274.

35   *R v Buckingham and Others* (1993) 99 Cr App R 303; see particularly the *dicta* of McCowan LJ at p 307.

defendants were also involved in its commission.[36] Even the previous convictions of persons other than the co-accused may be relevant to an issue. In *R v Warner and Jones*,[37] the defendants were charged with conspiracy to supply heroin. The prosecution case was based in part on police observations at the address of one of the defendants. These revealed that a great many people had visited the house. Eight of the visitors observed by the police had previous convictions for the possession or supply of heroin. The trial judge allowed evidence of these convictions to be adduced under s 74 and was upheld by the Court of Appeal. The previous convictions of the visitors were relevant to the characters of the people that the defendants were letting into the house, and this had a bearing on the nature of the transactions going on there.

It would be possible for a defendant to use s 74(1). Suppose A is charged alone with a particular offence. His defence is that the offence was committed not by him, but by B, who has previous convictions for committing the same type of offence in a similar way. It seems that there would be nothing to stop A from proving this by relying on s 74(1), which does not have the limitation to be found in s 74(3) excluding evidence that is relevant only because it has a tendency to show disposition. If the defendant were not A, but B, the prosecution could not rely on s 74(3) to prove the previous convictions and would have to prove the similar facts by other evidence. But if A and B were charged together, A should be in no worse position because of that and ought to be able to rely on s 74(1). Moreover, the judge would have no discretion to exclude the evidence under s 78, because that section applies only to evidence upon which the *prosecution* proposes to rely, nor are there any other sources of discretion that would enable a judge to exclude relevant evidence which a defendant wished to call.[38]

INTERACTION WITH S 78(1)

It has already been shown how s 78 provides a judicial discretion to exclude evidence upon which the prosecution proposes to rely if the admission of that evidence would have such an adverse effect on the fairness of the proceedings that the court ought not to admit it. This section, as well as providing some remedy where evidence has been unfairly obtained, has also been used to mitigate the potential for unfairness contained in s 74(1). It is now settled that once a judge is satisfied that the evidence tendered under s 74(1) has some probative force, careful consideration should be given to s 78(1) to see whether the discretion to exclude should be exercised.[39] It was emphasised above, in Chapter 11, that the wording of s 78(1) does not refer to a

---

36   *R v Grey* (1988) 88 Cr App R 375.

37   (1992) 96 Cr App R 324.

38   See the commentary on *R v Hendrick* [1992] Crim LR 427.

39   *R v Boyson* [1991] Crim LR 274; *R v Skinner and Others* [1995] Crim LR 805; *R v Lee* [1996] Crim LR 825; *R v Mahmoud and Manzur* [1997] 1 Cr App R 414.

balance of prejudicial over probative value to determine exclusion. However, it has to be said that in connection with s 74(1) this is the test that has been assumed to apply by virtue of the section.[40] There is a suggestion in *R v Lee*, at least in relation to conspiracy charges, that the greater the probative value of the conviction, the more prejudice will be caused to the defendant by admitting it in evidence, because to adduce evidence in this way denies an opportunity for cross-examination which the defendant would have had if evidence of the commission of an offence had been called in the ordinary way. If evidence is admitted under s 74(1), the jury must always be told to what issues it is relevant, and to what issues it is *not* relevant.[41]

In several cases, the court has suggested that the discretion to exclude ought to be exercised where the earlier conviction was obtained as the result of a guilty plea, rather than a contested trial. Thus, in *R v Kempster* Staughton LJ said:

> It may well be true that the other person is unlikely to have pleaded guilty unless he was in fact guilty; but the defence will be deprived of any opportunity to cross-examine him, in particular as to the complicity of the defendant. No doubt such cross-examination may in itself be unlikely in some cases, or else turn out to be a disaster . . . But one cannot always assume that.[42]

Further, the use of s 74(1) may give rise to a problem that has not yet been openly considered by the courts. What is the position where the plea may have been the result of plea bargaining? Suppose A, B and C are charged with a joint offence. B and C plead not guilty, but A, as part of a plea bargain involving other outstanding allegations against him, pleads guilty. The weight of the guilty plea as evidence of the commission of the offence is almost bound to be reduced, yet the court trying the case will be in no position to discover whether this has happened or not, nor, in most cases, will the defendants who plead not guilty. It may be particularly tempting for a prosecutor to use s 74(1), because the Court of Appeal has said that in principle the prosecution should be very careful before deciding to call as a witness an accomplice in the crime in respect of which the defendant is standing trial. Before doing so, there should be a clear indication from the accomplice of willingness to give evidence for the prosecution.[43]

However, the Court of Appeal has not been consistent in its application of s 78(1) where there has been an earlier guilty plea. Thus, in *R v Grey*[44] the argument based on lack of opportunity to cross-examine was disregarded. Turner J said that the

---

40   See, eg, *R v Boyson* [1991] Crim LR 274; *R v Lee* [1996] Crim LR 825; *R v Mahmoud and Manzur* [1997] 1 Cr App R 414.

41   *R v Kempster* [1989] 1 WLR 1125; *R v Boyson* [1991] Crim LR 274; *R v Skinner and Others* [1995] Crim LR 805; *R v Mahmoud and Manzur* [1997] 1 Cr App R 414.

42   [1989] 1 WLR 1125, p 1134. See also *R v Humphreys and Tully* [1993] Crim LR 288; *R v Lee* [1996] Crim LR 825; *R v Mahmoud and Manzur* [1997] 1 Cr App R 414.

43   *R v Moran* (1985) 81 Cr App R 51, p 52; *R v Sinclair* (1989) *The Times*, 18 April.

44   (1988) 88 Cr App R 375.

man whose conviction had been proved under s 74(1) could have been called to give evidence for the Crown: 'Had he done so, no sensible objection could have been raised to evidence by [him] that he had been convicted of that offence or, for that matter, that he had pleaded guilty to it.' However, the admissibility of a witness's evidence was not the point; what Turner J ought to have been considering was the potential for unfairness to a defendant where there was no witness whom he could cross-examine, especially where the commission of the offence had been established merely by a guilty plea. A similarly blithe approach appears to have been taken in *R v Turner*.[45] In that case, T and another man, L, were in separate cars driving at night down a hill towards a bend in the road. The road was slightly greasy. Both were driving at a slightly excessive speed. L overtook T, cut in sharply on the corner, losing control of his car and colliding with an oncoming vehicle. As a result, L's passenger died. The prosecution alleged that L and T were racing, though not by any previous arrangement. L pleaded guilty to causing death by reckless driving. T was tried on the same charge. His defence was that he was not racing, not reckless, and not contributing to any recklessness by L. The trial judge allowed L's guilty plea to be admitted under s 74(1) to prove that L had been driving recklessly. The Court of Appeal said that provided the judge made it clear, as he had, that L's plea did not amount to an admission that he was racing, but only that he was reckless, there was nothing unfair in admitting the evidence. It was true, the court acknowledged, that since L was not called as a witness it was impossible to cross-examine him as to the basis of his plea, but such a result, they said, was inevitable in cases of this sort.

From time to time, the Court of Appeal does appear to have recognised the potential for unfairness that s 74(1) can create. In *R v Hillier and Farrar*,[46] Watkins LJ said, 'It is the widely held view, which we share, that Parliament cannot have appreciated how wild an animal it was prepared to let loose upon the field of evidence when it enacted s 74'. It has been said that the sub-section should be 'sparingly' used[47] and, in *Warner v Jones*,[48] it was suggested that it might have been wiser not to use it since it added little to an already strong case against the defendants.[49] More importantly, in *R v Kempster*,[50] Staughton LJ, in delivering the judgment of the Court of Appeal, drew attention to an observation of that court in the earlier unreported case of *R v Curry*[51] to the effect that where the evidence that the prosecution wish to adduce

45   [1991] Crim LR 57.

46   (1992) 97 Cr App R 349.

47   *R v Robertson* (1987) 85 Cr App R 304; *R v Chapman* [1991] Crim LR 44; *R v Boyson* [1991] Crim LR 274; *R v Humphreys & Tully* [1993] Crim LR 288; *R v Skinner and Others* [1995] Crim LR 805; *R v Mahmoud and Manzur* [1997] 1 Cr App R 414.

48   (1988) 88 Cr App R 375.

49   See also *R v Humphreys and Tully* [1993] Crim LR 288.

50   [1989] 1 WLR 1125.

51   28 April 1988.

under s 74(1) expressly or by necessary inference imports the complicity of the person on trial in the offence with which he is charged, the sub-section should not be used.

It cannot be said that in all cases the Court of Appeal has followed the maxim referred to by Staughton LJ, but the cases on conspiracy show that in that area at least it has very largely done so. In *R v O'Connor*,[52] a case in which conspiracy between only two persons was alleged, the Court of Appeal held that the trial judge should have used s 78(1) to exclude evidence of the co-accused's conviction, because the effect of admitting this evidence had been to allow the prosecution to put before the jury a statement made by the co-accused in the absence of the defendant, without the co-accused being before the court to be cross-examined about the admission that he had made. By contrast, in *R v Robertson*,[53] the conspiracy was alleged to have been between the defendant, two other named men, and other unknown persons. The Court of Appeal held that evidence of the convictions of the other named men had been rightly admitted. In this case, also, it was true that the prosecution had been enabled to put to the jury statements made by the co-accused in the absence of the defendant, without the opportunity for cross-examination. The different conclusions are explicable if one looks at what the evidence in each case was likely to prove. In *R v O'Connor*, where the conspiracy was alleged to have been between the defendant and the co-accused, and no other person, the conviction of the co-accused on his own admission did not just prove the existence of a conspiracy: it proved also that the defendant was a conspirator. This was the very matter that the prosecution had to establish, and it is not surprising that the Court of Appeal appears to have taken the view that the absence of safeguards usually surrounding testimony made the evidence unsafe for consideration by the jury, even after judicial guidance.[54] In *R v Robertson*, however, the co-accused's pleas and convictions did not on their face involve the defendant. Even if the co-accused had given evidence at the defendant's trial in accordance with their pleas, defence counsel would almost certainly not have cross-examined them.[55] The co-accused's pleas were put forward for the limited purpose of establishing the fact that a conspiracy had existed; the defendant's involvement in it had been proved by other means.

R v O'Connor and *R v Robertson* can be seen as standing at opposite ends of a scale of cases concerning the use of s 74(1) in cases of conspiracy. At a point somewhere between them lies *R v Lunnon*.[56] In this case the prosecution set out to prove that on a particular date the defendant had conspired with S Lake, J Lake and Perrey

---

52   (1987) 85 Cr App R 298.

53   (1987) 85 Cr App R 304.

54   For a similar case that did not involve conspiracy, see *R v Mattison* [1990] Crim LR 117.

55   (1987) 85 Cr App R 304, p 312.

56   (1989) 88 Cr App R 71.

to steal from shops in Watford. Two propositions appear to have been involved: (a) there had been such a conspiracy between the Lakes and Perrey; (b) Lunnon also had been a party to it. The prosecution wanted to prove the first proposition by using s 74(1), but the situation differed in an important respect from that in *R v Robertson*. In the latter case, the defendant had not been mentioned in the counts to which the co-accused had pleaded guilty. Here, however, the position was that S Lake had pleaded guilty to a count, the particulars of which alleged that on the date in question he had conspired with J Lake, Perrey and Lunnon to steal from shops in Watford. If the prosecution could prove the conspiracy by establishing this conviction, with the details of the conspiracy that the indictment would have revealed, would there not be the same danger of insufficiently tested evidence directly implicating the defendant that had existed in *R v O'Connor?*

The trial judge thought not, and the Court of Appeal agreed with him. The court pointed to the fact that the conviction had been adduced only for the purpose of proving the existence of a conspiracy; other evidence had been relied on to show that the defendant had been a party to it. Substantial reliance was placed on the warnings given by the trial judge to the jury about the way in which this evidence could be used. In particular, he had been careful to tell them the limited purpose for which the evidence had been adduced. He had emphasised that the jury could find any of the defendants, or all of them, not guilty of being a part of it. It seems that unless there are only two persons involved in the conspiracy, then, provided a sufficient warning is given to the jury that the evidence can be used solely to show that there was a conspiracy, and not that the defendant was part of it, evidence under s 74(1) is likely to be admitted, in the absence of any other reason to exclude it.

In *R v Smith (Derk Nathan)*[57] the Court of Appeal referred with approval to the judgment of Staughton LJ in *R v Kempster*,[58] and held that evidence of a former co-defendant's plea of guilty should not have been admitted. The defendant and a prostitute called Zoe were jointly charged with robbing one of the prostitute's clients. The case against them was that when Zoe and the victim were together, the defendant had burst into the room with a gun, which he then held at the victim's throat while Zoe stole £260 from the victim's wallet. Zoe pleaded guilty. The defendant's case was that he came to Zoe's assistance when he heard her call for help, and that he had nothing to do with the theft. The trial judge admitted Zoe's plea of guilty under s 74.

The Court of Appeal observed that evidence of her plea was admissible in the defendant's trial to show that she had committed the offence. It was an integral part of proving that what had been committed was a joint offence by Zoe and the defendant. The real question in the case was whether this conviction ought nevertheless to have been excluded under s 78 because of its adverse effect on the fairness of

---

57   [2007] EWCA Crim 2105.
58   [1989] 1 WLR 1125.

the proceedings. The Court referred to the line of cases reviewed by Staughton LJ in *R v Kempster*,[59] which showed that s 74 should be sparingly applied, and commented:

> The reason is because the evidence that a now absent co-accused has pleaded guilty may carry in the minds of the jury enormous weight, but it is nevertheless evidence which cannot properly be tested in the trial of the remaining defendant. That is particularly so where the issue is such that the absent co-defendant who has pleaded guilty could not, or scarcely could, be guilty of the offence unless the present defendant were also. In both those situations the court needs to consider with considerable care whether the evidence of the conviction would have a disproportionate and unfair effect upon the trial. With those cases can be contrasted the kind of case in which there is little or no issue that the offence was committed, and the real live issue is whether the present defendant was party to it or not. In those circumstances, commonly, the pleas of guilty of other co-defendants can properly be admitted to reinforce the evidence that the offence did occur, leaving the jury independently to consider whether the guilt of the present defendant is additionally proved.[60]

The issue for the jury in the defendant's trial was whether there had been a robbery. The fact that Zoe had admitted this went a long way towards closing off this issue as a live one. The judge should have excluded the evidence of her conviction under s 78. Once it had been given, the jury was likely to consider it extremely powerful evidence against the defendant. But there was no opportunity to test Zoe's evidence, and no one was in a position to address possible reasons why she might have pleaded guilty when she was not. As Hughes LJ said when delivering the judgment of the Court:

> Defendants do sometimes admit what is not true. There is perhaps a special risk of that in persons such as this girl, who was a drug addict and a prostitute. She was likely to have frequent contact with the police. She was in need of a quiet life. Her case was no doubt going to be . . . that she was but the merest pawn in the hands of the appellant. She might well have expected that she would be dealt with comparatively leniently.[61]

If evidence of the conviction of another person is admitted, it is important that the judge should give an accurate direction to the jury on its significance. In particular, he must be careful to direct the jury that evidence of a former co-defendant's conviction is not evidence that the defendant is guilty,[62] and although the

---

59   [1990] 90 Cr App R 14.

60   [2007] EWCA Crim 2105, para 16.

61   Paragraph 22. See also *R v Miell (Richard)* [2007] EWCA Crim 3130, para 52, where the Court of Appeal said, *obiter*, that when the use of s 74 would effectively shift the burden of proof onto the defendant, evidence of the conviction should be excluded under s 78. (The defendant had been convicted on his own admission of perjury at his earlier trial for murder, and the prosecution wanted an order under s 76 CJA 2003 for his retrial on the murder charge, at which evidence could be adduced under s 74 PACE of his perjury conviction.)

62   See *R v Stewart* [1999] Crim LR 746.

conviction is evidence that the offence in question took place, it is not conclusive evidence; it can be rebutted. The issue is one for the jury to decide, and a judge should not by his comments appear to withdraw that issue from them.[63]

EVIDENCE OF PREVIOUS ACQUITTALS

Evidence of previous acquittals will only rarely be admitted in either civil or criminal proceedings. The main reason for this is that an acquittal is not conclusive evidence of innocence. A jury may return a verdict of not guilty because it is unsure of the defendant's guilt rather than convinced of his innocence. In *R v Terry*[64] the police had, with proper authority, covertly installed a listening device in a car used by the defendant, members of his family, and customers of the family business. The recorded conversations suggested that thefts of cars and computer equipment had been planned and carried out. The defendant and others were later charged with offences of burglary, theft and handling. The prosecution relied in part on the evidence of an expert in voice recognition in their case against all the defendants. Four of the counts in the indictment related to alleged offences in respect of which this defendant's guilt depended entirely on the expert's identification of his voice. The trial judge held that the expert's evidence was inadmissible against the defendant on these counts, and consequently verdicts of not guilty were recorded in relation to him in respect of them.

During the defendant's trial on the remaining counts, the defence wanted to adduce evidence of the four acquittals as conclusive proof that the defendant had not been in the car at the times when the conversations had been recorded. The judge ruled that evidence of the acquittals could show that the car was being used by other persons at the relevant times, and that it was one of them speaking in the recordings made on those occasions. But he said that the defence were not entitled to a ruling that the acquittals were conclusive proof that the defendant was not in the car at the relevant times.

The Court of Appeal upheld this ruling on the basis that an acquittal is not conclusive evidence of innocence. Nor does it mean that all relevant issues, such as those affecting the defendant in this case, have been resolved in favour of the acquitted person.[65]

Quite apart from this, the different standards of proof in civil and criminal trials will usually have the effect of making a defendant's acquittal on a criminal

---

63   See *R v Dixon (Sarah Louise)* [2001] Crim LR 126.

64   [2004] EWCA Crim 3252, [2005] QB 996.

65   Paragraph 43.

charge irrelevant in subsequent civil proceedings arising from the same facts. It remains the case that even where what amounts to a serious crime is alleged, the standard in civil proceedings is proof on a balance of probabilities.[66] The defendant's earlier acquittal because the prosecution failed to prove its case *beyond reasonable doubt* will have no effect one way or the other in later civil proceedings. So, for example, where insurers were sued on an insurance policy and claimed that they were not liable because the company insured had been responsible through its principle shareholder and director for itself causing the destruction by fire of the property insured, the trial judge held evidence of the director's earlier acquittal on a charge of arson arising from the same facts irrelevant, and so inadmissible.[67]

As in civil proceedings, so in criminal; the position is that a previous acquittal remains subject to the rule in *Hollington v Hewthorn*: it is irrelevant and inadmissible. A good example of the application of this rule can be found in the decision of the Privy Council in *Hui Chi-Ming v The Queen*.[68] A man named Ah Po, who was carrying a length of water pipe, went to 'look for someone to hit', accompanied by the defendant and four other youths. Ah Po found a victim and hit him with the pipe, thereby causing injuries that proved fatal. In due course, Ah Po was charged with murder. The jury found him not guilty of murder, but guilty of manslaughter. The prosecution had done some plea bargaining with most of the other defendants, but Hui Chi-Ming would not plead guilty to manslaughter. He was therefore tried for the murder of Ah Po's victim, the prosecution arguing that Ah Po had in fact murdered the man and that Hui Chi-Ming had been participating in a joint enterprise. The defence wanted to adduce evidence of Ah Po's acquittal on the charge of murder, but the prosecution objected to its admissibility and was upheld by the trial judge. The Privy Council concluded that the trial judge had been right. Citing *R v Turner*[69] and *Hollington v F Hewthorn and Co Ltd*,[70] Lord Lowry said that the verdict of a different jury at the earlier trial was irrelevant since it was no more than evidence of their opinion.

A previous acquittal *will* be admissible if it is possible to argue that it is relevant to any of the issues that the court has to decide, and sometimes a court will be satisfied that it is relevant to an issue of credibility. Take the illustration of Parker LJ in *R v Cooke*.[71]

> Suppose a police officer says that he has obtained admissions from seven defendants to a group of offences in a series of interviews conducted over a short period. Suppose all of them say that

---

66   See above, Chapter 7.

67   *TD Radcliffe and Co v National Farmers' Union Mutual Insurance* [1993] CLY 708.

68   [1992] 1 AC 34.

69   (1832) 1 Mood CC 347.

70   [1943] KB 587.

71   (1987) 84 Cr App R 286, p 293.

the interviews never took place. Suppose that six of the seven are all tried separately and that all six are acquitted. Suppose the seventh is then tried. It offends against common sense to say that on the trial of the seventh it is not relevant [to] credibility for the jury to know that the officer's evidence has not been accepted by six separate juries.

That, of course, is an extreme example. As Parker LJ said in the same case, whether evidence of acquittals will be admissible because of relevance to credibility is a matter of degree. One case where such evidence was admitted was *R v Hay*.[72] Hay had signed a statement admitting charges of arson and burglary. Separate trials of the two charges took place. At the first trial, on a count of arson, Hay said that his statement had been fabricated by the police. In due course the jury acquitted him. The judge at the later trial for burglary, at which the prosecution again relied on Hay's statement, refused to allow evidence of Hay's earlier acquittal to be given. The Court of Appeal disagreed with this decision. They held that because the confession to arson had been shown to be untrue by the verdict of the first jury, the whole of the statement was suspect. The acquittal on the arson charge had therefore been relevant in assessing the weight to be given to the confession of burglary.

In another case an acquittal became relevant because of the way in which the prosecution conducted its case. In *R v Doosti*,[73] the defendant was charged with conspiracy to supply heroin. At a trial six months earlier he had been charged with a drug offence and with obstructing the police; these offences were alleged to have taken place at the same premises as those involved in the conspiracy count. At both trials the same police officer gave evidence about the seizure of drugs. At the first trial the defendant had been acquitted on the drugs charge, but convicted of obstruction. At the later trial his counsel wanted to cross-examine the police officer about the earlier acquittal, but the trial judge refused leave. When the defendant came to give evidence, he was cross-examined under s 1(3)(ii) of the Criminal Evidence Act 1898 about his previous convictions, including the conviction for obstruction. He was not allowed to give evidence on re-examination of his acquittal on the drugs charge at the earlier trial.

The Court of Appeal said that the earlier acquittal did not necessarily mean that the police officer had been lying or was unreliable; it was consistent with the jury's not being sure that the prosecution case had been made out. Thus, the trial judge had been right to stop cross-examination about the previous acquittal because it had not been directed to any relevant issue, but since the prosecution had chosen to cross-examine about the previous conviction for obstruction, the defence ought to have been allowed to adduce evidence of the defendant's acquittal on the drugs charge. The court emphasised that the conviction and acquittal had resulted from the same trial, that the trial had concerned a similar charge in similar circumstances,

---

72   (1983) 77 Cr App R 70. Cf *R v Joseph (Robert H)* [1990] 90 Cr App R 440.
73   (1985) 82 Cr App R 181.

and that it had involved the same police officer as the chief prosecution witness in the current case. Ewbank J said:

> The prosecution are not obliged to bring out a defendant's conviction. If they choose to do so they, in our judgment, incur the risk that in such circumstances as obtained in this case a defendant will be permitted to refer to an acquittal on another charge which may throw doubt on the reliability of the prosecution witness.[74]

Where an acquittal is too ambiguous, however, it will not be admitted. This was the case in *R v Henri*.[75] The defendant was charged with buggery, attempted rape and indecent assaults on two girls aged eight and nine, the daughters of the woman with whom he cohabited. At the first trial he was acquitted on some counts and the jury failed to agree on others. He was retried on six counts of buggery and indecent assault in respect of which the first jury had failed to agree. Both girls gave evidence at the retrial. Defence counsel asked leave to adduce evidence of the earlier acquittals as being relevant to the reliability of one of the girls. The trial judge refused, and the Court of Appeal upheld his decision on the basis that there could have been several reasons, apart from the witness's unreliability, why the first jury had acquitted on some counts. The trial judge had rightly held that to allow the evidence to be given would have encouraged the jury to speculate about why the first jury had reached the decision they had, rather than concentrating on the evidence in the trial before them. As the commentary in the *Criminal Law Review* states, the case is 'a neat illustration of the principle that the relevance of evidence in law is determined not simply by the dictates of logic, but is affected by other factors such as fairness, and the need to avoid the proliferation of side issues which may serve to confuse the jury'.[76]

FURTHER READING

—Law Reform Committee, 15th Report, Cmnd 3391, 1967.

—Munday, 'Proof of Guilt by Association under Section 74 of the Police and Criminal Evidence Act 1984' [1990] Crim LR 236.

EXERCISES

1. What was the rule in *Hollington v Hewthorn* (1943), and what criticisms were levelled against it?

2. What is the effect under the Civil Evidence Act 1968 of proving a person's conviction?

---

74   (1985) 82 Cr App R 181, p 185.

75   [1990] Crim LR 51.

76   See also above, Chapter 1, and the discussion of cross-examination on previous acquittals, above, Chapter 6, pp 86–88.

3. Rose was convicted of stealing by a Spanish court. Can this conviction, if relevant, be adduced against her (a) in English civil proceedings; and, (b) in English criminal proceedings?
4. Why will evidence of acquittals generally be irrelevant in later civil proceedings?
5. Give an account of the decision in *Smith (Derk Nathan)* (2007). What is its significance for the operation of s 74 of PACE?

15

PRIVILEGE AND PUBLIC INTEREST IMMUNITY

INTRODUCTION

This chapter deals with reasons for excluding evidence that are unlike any previously encountered. Other exclusionary rules or principles have as the reason for their existence the need to secure a fair trial. Relevant evidence can be excluded because it is likely to mislead the jury[1] or because it would have an adverse effect on the fairness of the proceedings.[2] The justification for the rules relating to privilege and public interest immunity has nothing to do with the fairness of the trial but with some other benefit that is thought to be more important. The rules about privilege and public interest immunity acknowledge that the public have interests that must occasionally be allowed to prevail over their interest in securing fair trials at which all relevant and otherwise admissible evidence can be heard. Although these topics have this understanding in common, they operate differently. A *privilege* is a *right which the law gives to a person* allowing him to refuse to testify about a particular matter or to withhold a document. Effect is given to *public interest immunity* by means of a *power which the*

---

1   See, eg, the law relating to hearsay, similar fact evidence or the exclusion of confessions under the Police and Criminal Evidence Act 1984 (PACE), s 76(2)(b).

2   See, eg, PACE, s 78(1) or the common law discretion to exclude evidence whose prejudicial effect outweighs its probative value.

courts have to exclude evidence on the ground that disclosure of information would be damaging to the general good.

PRIVILEGE

There are three main privileges: privilege against self-incrimination; legal professional privilege; and the privilege arising from statements made 'without prejudice'.

PRIVILEGE AGAINST SELF-INCRIMINATION

Section 14(1) of the Civil Evidence Act 1968, which is declaratory of the common law,[3] describes the privilege as the right of a person in any legal proceedings, other than criminal proceedings, to refuse to answer any question, or produce any document or thing, if to do so would tend to expose that person to proceedings for an offence or for the recovery of a penalty. The privilege is designed to protect a person from being compelled by the State to convict himself out of his own mouth. This protection is given where a person has a reasonable ground for apprehending a real and appreciable danger of incrimination.[4] There is ample authority for the proposition that the privilege does not apply in relation to offences under foreign law.[5] But the Court of Appeal has said that this rule may have to be revisited in the light of Art 6 of the European Convention on Human Rights, and in the context of extradition proceedings.[6] A person may be exposed to proceedings for the recovery of a penalty through the imposition of a fine by the European Commission. Such penalties are recoverable under English law by virtue of the European Communities Act 1972.[7] Section 14 extends the privilege in civil proceedings to protect a person's spouse. At common law the privilege was restricted to the person claiming it.[8]

---

3   *Rio Tinto Zinc Corp v Westinghouse Electric Corp* [1978] AC 547, p 636.

4   *R v Khan (Mohammed Ajmal)* [2007] EWCA Crim 2331, para 29.

5   See, eg, *Re Westinghouse Electric Corporation Contract* [1978] AC 547, p 636; *Brannigan v Davison* [1997] AC 238 (PC).

6   *R v Khan (Mohammed Ajmal)* [2007] EWCA Crim 2331, para 25.

7   *Rio Tinto Zinc v Westinghouse Electric Corporation* [1978] AC 547, pp 565, 612.

8   The origins of the privilege were traditionally said to be the reaction of common lawyers against the prerogative courts of Star Chamber and High Commission during the time of the Civil Wars and Commonwealth in the mid-17th century. More recently it has been argued that the privilege developed at a later stage as the result of the rise of adversary procedure at the end of the 18th century: see Langbein, 1997, Chapter 4. Another view is that the privilege came into English law via European and canon law: see Macnair, 1990.

The consequences of exercising the privilege may be considerable. As Templeman LJ said:

> Where a defendant in a civil action relies on the doctrine against self-incrimination and insists on remaining silent and on concealing documents and other evidence relevant to the action, he is relying on his own wrongdoing or on his own apparent or possible wrongdoing to hamper the [claimant] in the proof of his just claims in the suit.[9]

Statutes have abolished the privilege in certain cases. Sometimes that has been done by providing that a person may be questioned, but that only a limited use may be made of his answers. For example, by s 31 of the Theft Act 1968, the privilege may not be claimed in proceedings for the recovery or administration of any property on the ground that to answer questions would expose the person questioned to proceedings under the Theft Act. But the section goes on to provide that no statement or admission made by anyone answering questions in such proceedings shall be admissible in evidence against that person in proceedings for an offence under the Act.[10] At one time it was thought that the scope of the privilege could be cut down by the courts in a similar way, but it is now accepted that where statute has not limited the use to which such evidence can be put, the civil courts have no power to impose a limit of their own devising.[11] The Youth Justice and Criminal Evidence Act 1999 amends various statutory provisions so as to restrict the use that may be made in criminal proceedings of answers and statements given under compulsion by virtue of those provisions.[12]

As well as cases where the privilege has been expressly removed by statute, there are cases where statutes have impliedly removed it. For example, in *Re London United Investments plc*,[13] the Court of Appeal held that the privilege was not available to persons who were being examined by inspectors appointed by the Department of Trade and Industry under s 432 of the Companies Act 1985, and in *Bank of England v Riley*,[14] the Court of Appeal held that it was not available to persons being examined under the Banking Act 1987. In the *Bishopsgate*[15] case, the Court of Appeal held that

---

9   *Rank Film Distributors v Video Information Centre* [1980] 2 All ER 273, p 291.

10   The section also covers questioning in proceedings for the administration of any property, for the execution of any trust or for an account of any property or dealings with property. Provisions of a similar kind can be found under the Criminal Damage Act 1971, s 9, the Children Act 1989, s 98 (in relation to proceedings relating to the care, supervision and protection of children), the Supreme Court Act 1981 (proceedings for the infringement of intellectual property rights), s 72, and in various statutes relating to the investigation of fraud.

11   *Bishopsgate Investment Management Ltd v Maxwell* [1992] 2 All ER 856, pp 866–67.

12   Youth Justice and Criminal Evidence Act 1999, s 59 and Sched 3.

13   [1992] 2 All ER 842.

14   [1992] 1 All ER 769.

15   See above.

the privilege was not available where inquiries were being conducted by persons such as liquidators under s 235 of the Insolvency Act 1986, or by the court under s 236. The right not to incriminate oneself is guaranteed by Art 6(1) of the European Convention on Human Rights, but it has been held by the European Court that this provision does not have the effect of prohibiting completely the use of compulsory powers to provide information.[16]

The privilege has to be claimed on oath by the person who wishes to rely on it. Thus, where the privilege was claimed by a solicitor on his client's behalf, it was held that the claim had not been properly made. But a person who claims the privilege does not have to show in detail why disclosure might incriminate him, because such a requirement might expose him to the peril against which the privilege is designed to protect him.[17]

LEGAL PROFESSIONAL PRIVILEGE

It has been said that legal professional privilege is a fundamental human right and 'a necessary corollary of the right of any person to obtain skilled advice about the law'. The reason is that such advice cannot be effectively obtained unless the client is able to put all the facts before the adviser, without fear that they may afterwards be disclosed and used to his prejudice.[18]

The scope of legal professional privilege at common law is reflected in s 10 of the Police and Criminal Evidence Act 1984.[19] There are three categories:

(a)   *Legal advice privilege* Communications between a professional legal adviser and his client, or any person representing his client, made in connection with the giving of legal advice to the client. Here the communication is a two-way system and can be thought of in the form of a straight line, with the client or his agent at one end and the legal adviser at the other. The legal advice can be of any kind and does not have to be connected with litigation or the prospect of it. The protection is available even where the lawyer is an 'in-house' lawyer advising his employers.[20] In

---

16   But it is not easy to draw a line between cases where Art 6(1) can be relied on and those where it cannot. See *JB v Switzerland* [2001] Crim LR 748; *Allen v UK* [2003] Crim LR 280.

17   *Downie v Coe* [1997] EWCA Civ 2648.

18   *R (on the Application of Morgan Grenfell and Co Ltd) v Special Commr of Income Tax* [2002] 3 All ER 1, pp 4–5, *per* Lord Hoffmann. It has been held by the European Court of Human Rights to be part of the right to privacy guaranteed by Art 8 of the Convention.

19   *R v Central Criminal Court ex p Francis and Francis* [1988] 3 WLR 989. The section defines 'items subject to legal privilege' in the context of powers of entry, search and seizure.

20   *Alfred Crompton Amusement Machines Ltd v Customs & Excise* [1972] 2 QB 102, p 129. The decision of the Court of Appeal on this point was not challenged in the subsequent appeal to the House of Lords.

Balabel v Air India,[21] Taylor LJ said that, although the test for a privileged communication was whether it had been made confidentially for the purpose of obtaining legal advice, this purpose was not to be narrowly construed and should be taken to include practical advice about what should be done in the relevant legal context. In line with this approach, Colman J, in *NRG v Bacon and Woodrow*,[22] observed that a solicitor's duty frequently includes advising on the commercial wisdom of entering into a transaction in relation to which legal advice has been sought. The scope of legal advice privilege was, however, thrown into doubt by the decision in *Three Rivers District Council v Bank of England (No 6)*.[23] In this decision the Court of Appeal held that for the privilege to apply, the dominant purpose of the communication between solicitor and client must be the obtaining of advice in relation to legal rights and obligations. It followed that the privilege did not apply to material submitted to solicitors where the dominant purpose of the submission was to obtain advice about the presentation of evidence at a public inquiry in the way least likely to attract criticism. The Court of Appeal acknowledged that the traditional role of a solicitor had expanded, but said that it was necessary to keep the privilege within justifiable bounds. The fact that the work done was within the ordinary business of a solicitor did not mean that it was automatically privileged.

This decision was, however, reversed by the House of Lords,[24] which held that legal advice covers what should prudently and sensibly be done in a relevant legal context. This included the presentation of a case to an inquiry by someone whose conduct might be criticised by it. But how is a legal context to be identified, and how is legal advice to be defined? According to Baroness Hale:

> There will always be borderline cases in which it is difficult to decide whether there is or is not a 'legal' context. But much will depend upon whether it is one in which it is reasonable for the client to consult the special professional knowledge and skills of a lawyer, so that the lawyer will be able to give the client sound advice as to what he should do, and just as importantly what he should not do, and how to do it.[25]

In relation to legal advice, the House of Lords unanimously approved the

---

21   [1988] Ch 317.

22   [1995] 1 All ER 976.

23   [2004] QB 916.

24   [2005] 1 AC 610.

25   Paragraph 62.

statement of Taylor LJ, in *Balabel v Air India*,[26] that 'legal advice is not confined to telling the client the law; it must include advice as to what should prudently and sensibly be done in the relevant legal context'. A typical situation where the courts might be persuaded that advice was commercial rather than legal would be where advice is given to a company by its employed lawyer, and that person also holds another office in the company.[27] And if a solicitor becomes the client's 'man of business', responsible for advising the client on all matters of business, including investment policy, finance policy and other business matters, the advice may be given outside a relevant legal context.[28]

(b) *Litigation privilege* Communications between lawyer, client *and third parties* for the purpose of pending or contemplated litigation. It is enough if the litigation is contemplated only by the party asking for advice; the other prospective party to the litigation can be totally ignorant of the fact that litigation might arise.[29] The lines of communication can be seen as forming a triangle so as to involve three parties instead of two. Here the communications with the third parties – often other professionals such as surveyors, doctors or accountants – will be protected only if the *dominant purpose* is for use in litigation, pending or contemplated.

The 'dominant purpose' test was settled by the House of Lords in *Waugh v British Railways Board.*[30] The appellant's husband was employed by the British Railways Board. A train that he was driving collided with another and he died as a result. His widow brought an action under the Fatal Accidents Acts 1846–1959. This appeal arose from an interlocutory application by the plaintiff for disclosure by the Board of a report, called 'the joint inquiry report', made by officers of the Board two days after the accident. The Board had resisted, claiming legal professional privilege for it. The document had been prepared for a dual purpose: for railway operation and safety purposes and for the purpose of obtaining legal advice in anticipation of litigation. Both purposes were of equal weight. The House of Lords held that this was not enough to support a claim for privilege. For privilege to be available, the purpose of preparing for litigation had to be the sole or dominant purpose of the document under consideration. Since the purposes in this case were of equal weight, there was no dominant purpose and the report was ordered to be disclosed.

(c) Items enclosed with or referred to in communications of types (a) or (b),

---

26   [1988] Ch 317, p 330.
27   Thanki, 2006, para 2.118.
28   *Three Rivers (No 6)*, para 38, *per* Lord Scott.
29   *Plummers Ltd v Debenhams plc* [1986] BCLC 447, Ch D.
30   [1980] AC 521.

provided the items came into existence in connection with the giving of legal advice and are in the possession of a person who is entitled to possession of them. The point here is that the privilege exists to protect communications between client, legal adviser and, sometimes, third parties. It does not exist to protect evidence from production. To take an obvious example, suppose Charlie murders Bertie after planning the crime carefully on paper. He cannot prevent the police from obtaining this document by handing it to his solicitor. Even if an object or document is placed in a solicitor's hands for the legitimate purpose of obtaining advice in connection with the defence case, privilege will not protect it. In *R v King*[31] the defendant had been charged with conspiracy to defraud. He sent some documents to his solicitors so that they could obtain the opinion of a handwriting expert on them. The defence later decided not to call the expert, but the prosecution served him with a subpoena compelling him to produce in court the documents that he had received from the defence solicitors.[32] The Court of Appeal upheld the trial judge's decision that legal professional privilege did not protect them. *They had not been brought into existence for the purpose of the solicitor and client relationship.*

Copies of original documents are, of course, frequently brought into existence in the course of this relationship. Whether *their* disclosure can be compelled depends on whether the *originals* would have been privileged or not. If the originals would not, the copies will not attract privilege just because they are part of a set of instructions to enable the client to obtain legal advice.[33]

Legal professional privilege will not protect a communication to facilitate crime or fraud. The principle is easy to state but not always easy to apply. 'Fraud' is very widely defined to include, in addition to the tort of deceit, 'all forms of fraud and dishonesty such as fraudulent breach of contract, fraudulent conspiracy, trickery and sham contrivances'.[34] It may be difficult in a particular case to determine whether a client was obtaining advice to *facilitate* a fraud in this wide sense or to *avoid* one. A solicitor, of course, can quite properly be asked for advice about the effect of a proposed transaction by a client who wishes to avoid prosecution or civil litigation. In

---

31   [1983] 1 WLR 411.

32   There was, of course, no attempt to get him to disclose the instructions he had received from the defence solicitors or his own advice to them.

33   *Dubai Bank Ltd v Galadari* [1989] 3 All ER 769.

34   *Crescent Farm (Sidcup) Sports Ltd v Sterling Offices Ltd* [1972] Ch 553, p 565, *per* Goff J. Cf s 10(2) of PACE, which provides that items held with the intention of furthering a criminal purpose are not subject to legal professional privilege. Perhaps surprisingly, this has been interpreted to include items that were the subject of a third party's intention to further a criminal purpose: *R v Central Criminal Court ex p Francis and Francis* [1989] AC 346.

a doubtful case it will be easier to argue that the communication was not to facilitate a crime or fraud where the lawyer is asked to explain the effect of what has already been done, rather than to advise about the structuring of a transaction that has yet to be carried out.[35]

This exception to the scope of legal professional privilege has more recently been expressed by saying that for the privilege to apply there must be 'absence of iniquity'.[36] The breadth of this concept is illustrated by *Barclays Bank plc v Eustice*.[37] In that case 'iniquity' was held to include obtaining advice about how to structure a series of transactions at an undervalue that would have had the effect of prejudicing the interests of creditors.[38] The Court of Appeal held that it made no difference that neither the solicitor nor even the client realised that this would be the effect of what was proposed.[39] It has been held at first instance that criminal or fraudulent conduct undertaken by private investigators in the conduct of litigation can also cause the privilege to be lost. In *Dubai Aluminium Co Ltd v Al Alawi*,[40] Dubai sued the defendant in respect of his conduct while he was its sales manager and obtained a worldwide Mareva, or 'freezing', injunction against him. The defendant applied to have the injunction discharged on the ground that, while investigating his finances and assets, Dubai's agents had contravened the Data Protection Act 1984 and Swiss laws on banking secrecy. In pursuit of his claim to discharge the injunction, he applied for an order requiring Dubai to disclose the documents relating to their investigation. He accepted that these were prima facie subject to legal professional privilege, but he argued that the privilege did not attach to them because they were part of, or relevant to, iniquitous acts by Dubai. Rix J found on the facts that there was a strong prima facie case of criminal or fraudulent conduct in the obtaining of information about the defendant's accounts. He held that such conduct constituted 'crime, fraud or iniquity' so as to remove the protection of legal professional privilege, saying that if investigative agents employed by solicitors for the purpose of litigation were permitted to indulge in criminal or fraudulent conduct without any consequence for the conduct of the litigation, the courts would be going far towards sanctioning such conduct. The defendant had also complained that his dustbins had been searched, and documents taken from them and copied before being put back, but Rix J held that such civil wrongs did not amount to 'crime, fraud or iniquity'.

---

35   *Barclays Bank plc v Eustice* [1995] 1 WLR 1238, pp 1249–50, *per* Schiemann LJ; *Sourcebook*, 1996, p 417.

36   *Ventouris v Mountain* [1991] 1 WLR 607, p 611, *per* Bingham LJ; *ibid, Barclays Bank plc v Eustice*, p 1252, *per* Schiemann LJ.

37   [1995] 1 WLR 1238.

38   See the Insolvency Act 1986, s 423.

39   If it were otherwise, the communications between a client and an incompetent solicitor might be protected, while those between a client and a competent one would not.

40   [1999] 1 All ER 703.

Expert reports prepared for the purpose of current litigation will normally be covered by legal professional privilege, but reports from experts such as doctors and psychiatrists brought into existence by parties to cases involving the welfare of children are an exception. The overriding duty to regard the welfare of a child as paramount in such cases will not allow the parties to suppress 'unfavourable' reports. However, only reports of third parties are affected by this rule. Privilege continues to apply to communications between legal advisers and their clients in actions of this kind.[41]

Duration of the privilege

The general rule is, 'once privileged, always privileged'.[42] So documents prepared for one action will continue to be privileged in subsequent litigation, even though the subject matter or the parties may be different. A good example of this is *The Aegis Blaze*.[43] The defendants were the owners of the vessel *The Aegis Blaze*. In December 1980, a cargo was damaged while being carried in that vessel. In March 1981, proceedings in respect of that loss were in contemplation and the defendants' solicitors instructed surveyors to inspect the vessel (which lay at Sibenik in Yugoslavia) for the purpose of obtaining evidence. The surveyors reported to the solicitors in the same month. It was common ground that their report ('the Sibenik Report') was privileged from production, at least in the litigation then contemplated.

In July 1981, another cargo was damaged while being carried in the vessel on another voyage. Two lots of different cargo owners sued to recover in respect of this loss. They knew of the Sibenik Report and wanted it to be disclosed to them. It was agreed that it was relevant to their case, but the defendants claimed that because it was privileged in relation to the first proceedings it was privileged in relation to the second also.

The Court of Appeal upheld the defendants' argument. Parker LJ said that if a party claiming privilege in a second action is the party entitled to privilege in an earlier action, but there is no connection of subject matter whatever, it is most improbable that a question of privilege will arise, because in such circumstances the document will not be relevant, and so not disclosable. If there is a sufficient connection for the document to be relevant, then the party entitled to the privilege will be able to assert it in the second action. If this were not the case, the court would again and again have to become involved on discovery in balancing the interests of the public in protecting access to legal advice against the interests of the public in having all relevant information available at the trial of actions.

---

41   *Oxfordshire County Council v M* [1994] Fam 295.
42   *Calcraft v Guest* [1898] 1 QB 759, p 761, *per* Lindley MR.
43   [1986] 1 Lloyd's Rep 203.

Another example of the maxim 'once privileged, always privileged' is the rule whereby documents concerning property rights that are privileged in the hands of one owner are privileged in the hands of that person's successors in title.[44]

It used to be thought that where the holder of a privilege could derive no further benefit from its exercise, the privilege could be defeated by the interest of another person who needed to have access to the information, particularly where this was needed to defeat a criminal charge.[45] However, since the decision of the House of Lords in *R v Derby Magistrates' Court ex p B*,[46] it is clear that this is not the case. The problem in this case stemmed from the murder, in April 1978, of a girl of 16. Shortly afterwards, the applicant, B, was arrested. At first he denied involvement, but subsequently admitted sole responsibility. He was charged with murder. Preparations for trial were well advanced when, in October 1978, he was seen by a psychiatrist. Following that interview, he changed his story and made a statement to the effect that his stepfather had killed the girl. He admitted being present at the time and to taking some part, but he said that he had been under duress. At his trial in November, he relied on this account and was acquitted.

In July 1992, the stepfather was arrested and charged with the murder. Committal proceedings were begun, and the applicant was called on behalf of the prosecution to give evidence. In the course of cross-examination on behalf of his stepfather, he was asked about instructions that he had given the solicitors acting for him in 1978. The question arose whether he could still maintain the legal professional privilege attaching to those communications. The magistrate, following earlier cases, decided that he had to balance the two public interests[47] and decided in favour of disclosure. But the House of Lords said that earlier decisions had been wrong. The principle remains that a man must be able to consult his lawyer in confidence, since otherwise he might hold back half the truth. The client must be sure that what he tells his lawyer will never be revealed without consent. Legal professional privilege is much more than an ordinary rule of evidence; it is a fundamental condition on which the administration of justice rests.

Bypassing the privilege via secondary evidence

Legal professional privilege prevents facts *from having to be disclosed*. It does not prevent the facts *from being proved* if any other means of doing so can be found. For example, in *Calcraft v Guest*,[48] the appellant had obtained copies of certain privileged

---

44   *Minet v Morgan* (1873) 8 Ch App 361.

45   *R v Barton* [1973] 1 WLR 115; *R v Ataou* [1988] QB 798.

46   [1995] 3 WLR 681.

47   In protecting access to legal advice and in having all relevant and admissible evidence available at trial.

48   [1898] 1 QB 759.

documents and so was in a position to prove the contents of the originals by means of secondary evidence. Was he entitled to do so? The Court of Appeal held that he was, and approved an earlier *dictum* of Parke B to the effect that even if the original had been stolen, a correct copy of it could be admitted.

It may be possible to block this escape route if the party who stands to lose the benefit of the privilege can obtain an injunction to restrain the use of the copies. This is what happened in *Ashburton (Lord) v Pape*,[49] in which Cozens-Hardy MR explained the decision as follows:

(a) *Calcraft v Guest* establishes only that if a litigant wants to prove a particular document whose original he cannot produce because of privilege, he may produce a copy as secondary evidence even though the copy has been obtained by improper, even criminal, means. The reason why he can do so is that in the main action, in which the copy is to be used, the court is not concerned with the circumstances in which the evidence was obtained.

(b) The situation is different where proceedings are brought that have those circumstances as their central concern, such as proceedings for an injunction to restrain the use of the copy document. In other words, the question is one of *relevance*.

In *Ashburton (Lord) v Pape*, Swinfen Eady LJ said that the basis of the remedy is the principle, on which the Court of Chancery acted for many years, that allows a court to restrain the publication of confidential information improperly or surreptitiously obtained, or of information imparted in confidence that ought not to be divulged. The fact that an original or copy document is *admissible* according to evidence law is no answer to the demand of the lawful owner for delivery up of the document, and no answer to the application of the lawful owner of confidential information to restrain it from being published or copied.[50] However, in *Goddard v Nationwide Building Society*,[51] Nourse LJ took the view that the basis of relief was not the confidential nature of the communications but the legal professional privilege attaching to them. The importance of this distinction may lie in the fact that on the more recent view there appears to be less scope for a judge to exercise his discretion when deciding whether to grant the injunction. It had been suggested that a judge should conduct a balancing exercise, taking into account, for example, the way in which the information had been obtained and its importance to the issues being tried.[52] But in

---

49   [1913] 2 Ch D 469.

50   See the judgment of Swinfen Eady LJ in *Calcraft v Guest*. Separate proceedings are not necessary and an application can be made at any time up to the point when the copies are used by the party who has obtained them: *Webster v James Chapman and Co* [1989] 3 All ER 939.

51   [1986] 3 All ER 264.

52   *Webster v James Chapman and Co* [1989] 3 All ER 939 (Scott J).

Derby and Co Ltd v Weldon (No 8),[53] the Court of Appeal held that such an exercise was inappropriate where the court was being asked for an injunction in support of legal professional privilege.

Where a privileged document, or a copy, has been obtained by trickery or by some other improper means, a party wishing to prevent its use must apply for an injunction. But sometimes, privileged documents are accidentally included among documents that a party has a duty to disclose to his opponent under r 31 of the Civil Procedure Rules. Where this happens, the party who has seen the document may use its contents only with the court's permission.[54] In deciding whether to grant permission the court will be guided by cases decided before the Civil Procedure Rules came into force.[55] The principle formerly applied was that where it was obvious that the document had been disclosed by mistake the privilege continued to apply. But if the person examining the document might reasonably have concluded that the privilege was being waived, it would be lost.[56]

In *Butler v Board of Trade,*[57] it was held that public policy would prevent an injunction of this kind from being granted where its effect would be to restrain the prosecution from adducing admissible evidence in criminal proceedings. In cases where the prosecution obtained a privileged communication by accident rather than improperly, the Court of Appeal has held that it can be used during the cross-examination of the defendant. For example, in *R v Tomkins*[58] a note written by the defendant to his counsel was found on the floor of the court during the course of the trial. It was handed to prosecuting counsel by his instructing solicitor. The note was inconsistent with the testimony that the defendant had just given. When cross-examination was continued, the defendant was handed the note and asked whether he stood by his earlier evidence. He then effectively withdrew that evidence. The Court of Appeal decided that the note, although privileged, was admissible in evidence once it had come into the possession of the prosecution. Legal professional privilege did not determine issues of admissibility; the privilege was a privilege against production.

This principle was applied in *R v Cottrill.*[59] Solicitors acting for the defendant accidentally sent a copy of the defendant's proof of evidence to the prosecution. The defendant knew nothing of this, and gave evidence at trial that was inconsistent with his earlier proof. The judge permitted prosecuting counsel to use the earlier proof

---

53   [1990] 3 All ER 762.
54   Civil Procedure Rules r 31.20.
55   *Al Fayed and Others v Commr of Police of the Metropolis and Others* [2002] EWHC 1734.
56   Cf *IBM Corp v Phoenix International (Computers) Ltd* [1995] 1 All ER 413 and *Pizzey v Ford Motor Co Ltd* [1994] PIQR 15.
57   [1971] Ch 680.
58   (1977) 67 Cr App R 181.
59   [1997] Crim LR 56.

during the defendant's cross-examination, and the Court of Appeal upheld this decision.[60]

Journalists' sources

There are no other types of communication protected by privilege, but there is a special provision for the protection of journalists' sources in s 10 of the Contempt of Court Act 1981. This provides:

> No court may require a person to disclose, nor is any person guilty of contempt of court for refusing to disclose, the source of information contained in a publication for which he is responsible, unless it be established to the satisfaction of the court that disclosure is necessary in the interests of justice or national security or for the prevention of disorder or crime.

The burden is on the party who wishes to obtain disclosure to prove that one or more of the conditions is satisfied.[61] In order to show that an order for disclosure is necessary, a claimant must show that all other reasonable means have been employed to identify the source, but without success.[62]

The meaning of 'necessary' has been considered in several cases. In *Re An Inquiry Under the Company Securities (Insider Dealing) Act 1985*,[63] Lord Griffiths said:

> I doubt if it is possible to go further than to say that 'necessary' has a meaning that lies somewhere between 'indispensable' on the one hand, and 'useful' or 'expedient' on the other, and to leave it to the judge to decide towards which end of the scale of meaning he will place it on the facts of any particular case. The nearest paraphrase I can suggest is 'really needed'.[64]

In *Camelot Group plc v Centaur Communications Ltd*,[65] there was a continuing threat that further information would be improperly disclosed by an employee, and the unease and suspicion that the leaks had caused was inhibiting good working relationships. Schiemann LJ said that in such cases, the following legal principles applied:

- There is an important public interest in the press being able to protect the anonymity of its sources.
- The law does not enable the press to protect that anonymity in all circumstances.
- When assessing whether a disclosure order should be made, a relevant but not conclusive factor is that an employer may wish to identify the employee so as to exclude him from future employment.

---

60   See also *R v Willis (Clayton Clyde)* [2004] EWCA Crim 3472.
61   *Secretary of State for Defence v Guardian Newspapers Ltd* [1985] AC 339.
62   *Ashworth Hospital Authority v MGN Ltd* [2001] 1 All ER 991, p 1011, *per* Lord Phillips MR.
63   [1988] AC 660.
64   *Ibid*, p 704.
65   [1998] 1 All ER 251.

■ Whether sufficiently strong reasons are shown in a particular case will depend on the facts.

■ Great weight will be given to judgments in cases, especially if they are recent, where the facts were similar.[66]

Since these decisions, however, the Court of Appeal has emphasised the significance of the European Convention on Human Rights, and it remains to be seen if disclosure would be ordered if similar situations were to recur. Section 10 must be read in the light of Art 10 of the Convention. This provides:

1   Everyone has the right to freedom of expression. This right shall include freedom to hold opinions and to receive and impart information and ideas without interference by public authority and regardless of frontiers . . .

2   The exercise of these freedoms, since it carries with it duties and responsibilities, may be subject to such formalities, conditions, restrictions or penalties as are prescribed by law and are necessary in a democratic society, in the interests of national security, territorial integrity or public safety, for the prevention of disorder of crime, for the protection of health or morals, for the protection of the reputation or rights of others, for preventing the disclosure of information received in confidence, or for maintaining the authority and impartiality of the judiciary.

In *Ashworth Hospital Authority v MGN Ltd,*[67] the Court of Appeal held that the interpretation of s 10 of the Contempt of Court Act 1981 should, so far as possible, equate the specific purposes for which an order for disclosure of sources is permitted under the Act with the legitimate aims in Art 10 of the Convention, and should apply the same test of necessity as that applied by the European Court of Human Rights when interpreting that Article. The court also held that, by analogy with Art 10, 'the interests of justice' is not confined to the administration of justice in courts of law, but covers all interests that are justiciable. Thus where, as in the *Ashworth Hospital Authority* case, there have been leaks of information from confidential hospital records, the health authority can argue that its claim for identification of the source is in the interests of the protection of health, the protection of the rights of others and the prevention of the disclosure of information received in confidence.

However, the Court of Appeal pointed out that the approach of the European Court to the question whether an order for disclosure should be made involves

---

66   *Ibid*, pp 257–60. See also *Michael O'Mara Books Ltd v Express Newspapers plc* (1998) *The Times,* 6 March, where a court at first instance ordered disclosure because suspicions about the leak of information had affected the reputation of two innocent companies, and where there remained the threat of further leaks.

67   [2001] 1 All ER 991; affirmed [2002] 4 All ER 193, HL.

something more than deciding whether, on the facts, it is necessary for the achievement of a legitimate aim. It must also be considered whether the achievement of the legitimate aim is, on the facts, so important that it overrides the considerable public interest in protecting journalists' sources. Protecting journalists' sources protects free communication of information to and through the press; orders for source disclosure have a 'chilling effect' on the exercise of that freedom. Lord Phillips MR, in a judgment with which the other members of the court agreed, acknowledged that the decisions of the European Court showed that freedom of the press had in the past carried greater weight in Strasbourg than in the UK.[68]

In *Mersey Care NHS Trust v Ackroyd (No 2)* Sir Anthony Clarke MR, delivering the judgment of the Court, said, 'It is now clear that the approach of the English courts to both s 10 of the 1981 Act and Art 10 of the Convention should be the same'. Before the court will order a journalist to disclose the name of his source, the claimant must show that (1) an order for disclosure is necessary, in the sense of there being an overriding interest in disclosure amounting to a pressing social need; and, (2) an order for disclosure is proportionate. Whether under the Convention or the Act, the judge must balance the interests of the claimant, who relies on a right to privacy, and the journalist, who relies on a right to freedom of expression.[69]

Without prejudice statements[70]

This head of privilege is founded partly on the public policy of encouraging litigants to settle their differences rather than pursuing them to the bitter end. It is founded also on the express or implied agreement of the parties that communications in the course of their negotiations should not be admissible in evidence if the negotiations break down.[71] The rule applies to exclude from evidence all negotiations genuinely aimed at settlement, whether oral or in writing. The application of the rule does not depend on the use of the expression 'without prejudice', though it is no doubt safer to use it. If the circumstances make it clear that the parties were trying to settle a claim, evidence of the negotiations will not generally be admissible to establish an admission. Conversely, the use of the 'without prejudice' label will be of no effect where there is no attempt at settlement.[72]

Evidence of the negotiations will be admissible if it is necessary to show the terms of a settlement that was ultimately reached: for example, where one of the

---

68   [2001] 1 All ER 991, pp 1010–12.

69   [2007] EWCA Civ 101, paras 12, 17–20.

70   Statements that are 'without prejudice' to their maker if the terms proposed are not accepted. See *Walker v Wilsher* (1889) 23 QBD 335, p 337.

71   *Unilever plc v The Proctor & Gamble Co* [2001] 1 All ER 783, pp 789–90, 796, *per* Robert Walker LJ.

72   *Paddock v Forrester* (1842) 3 Man&G 903; *Oliver v Nautilus SS Co* [1903] 2 KB 639; *Re Daintrey ex p Holt* [1893] 2 QB 116.

parties wants to sue on that agreement.[73] But it does not follow that the privilege no longer applies just because a settlement has been reached. For example, where several parties are engaged in building construction works, there is a risk that at some stage there will be litigation between two or more of them. Suppose the main contractor makes certain admissions in an attempt to settle a dispute with one of the sub-contractors. If those admissions could be used against him by other sub-contractors with whom he was also in dispute, this would discourage settlements with *any* of the sub-contractors. The House of Lords decided, therefore, in *Rush & Tompkins Ltd v GLC*[74] that generally the without prejudice rule makes evidence of negotiations inadmissible in any subsequent litigation connected with the same subject matter. *Instance v Denny Bros Printing Ltd*,[75] a decision of Lloyd J, suggests that the privilege may apply between the same parties even in relation to future litigation that is not connected with precisely the same subject matter. Lloyd J said that the reference to subsequent litigation connected with the same subject matter was a reference to the facts of *Rush & Tompkins Ltd v GLC*, and was not intended to define exhaustively the scope of the protection.

PUBLIC INTEREST IMMUNITY

Public interest immunity (PII), formerly called 'Crown privilege', is a rule of law that requires the withholding of documents on the ground that it would be harmful to the public interest to disclose them. A convenient starting point for examining this rule is the decision of the House of Lords in *Duncan v Cammell Laird and Co Ltd*.[76] That action was brought by the dependants of men who had died when a submarine sank during trials. It was alleged that the defendants, who built the submarine, had been negligent. Among the documents that the plaintiffs wanted to obtain on discovery were contracts between the defendants and the Admiralty, and salvage reports. The Admiralty resisted disclosure on the ground of national security. The House of Lords held that the court was bound to accept the minister's certificate that disclosure of these documents would be harmful to the public interest. The effect of this decision was that a court could never question a claim of Crown privilege, if made in the proper form, regardless of the nature of the documents that the government wished to keep secret. The House of Lords said that claims to Crown privilege could be put on two alternative grounds:

---

73   *Tomlin v Standard Telephones and Cables Ltd* [1969] 1 WLR 1368. For other exceptions, see *Unilever plc v The Proctor & Gamble Co* [2001] 1 All ER 783, pp 792–93.
74   [1989] AC 1280. Cf *Gnitrow Ltd v Cape plc* [2000] 3 All ER 763.
75   [2000] FSR 869, p 885.
76   [1942] AC 264.

(a) Disclosure of the *contents* of the particular documents would harm the public interest, for example, by endangering national security or prejudicing diplomatic relations.

(b) The documents belonged to a *class* of documents that had to be withheld in the interests of 'the proper functioning of the public service'.

In 1956, the Lord Chancellor, Viscount Kilmuir, made a statement in the House of Lords indicating that the class of documents routinely withheld to protect 'the proper functioning of the public service' would be narrowed by excluding those categories of documents that appeared to be particularly relevant to litigation, and for which the highest degree of confidentiality was not required in the public interest. These included road accident reports, ordinary contractual documents, and medical records and reports. He added, 'We also propose that if medical documents, or indeed other documents, are relevant to the defence in criminal proceedings, Crown privilege should not be claimed'. In this statement, Kilmuir explained that the reason for claiming Crown privilege on a class, as opposed to a contents basis, was that it was needed to secure 'freedom and candour of communications with and within the public service', so that government decisions could be taken on the best advice and with the fullest information. People advising the government must be able to know that they were doing so in confidence, and that any document containing their advice would not subsequently be disclosed.[77]

The beginning of the modern approach to PII can be seen in the decision of the House of Lords in *Conway v Rimmer*.[78] The plaintiff, who had been a probationary police officer, brought an action against his former superintendent for malicious prosecution. (He had been prosecuted for theft from a fellow probationer and acquitted.) His legal advisers wanted to obtain on discovery a number of confidential reports which had been made on the plaintiff during his probationary period. These were likely to be relevant to the issue of malice, and both sides wanted them to be produced. The Home Secretary objected. The House of Lords took the opportunity to reverse its earlier ruling in *Duncan v Cammell Laird*, and held that in such cases it was for the court to decide where the balance of public interest lay: in protecting a government claim for secrecy, or in upholding a litigant's right to have all relevant materials available for the proper adjudication of his claim. But the idea that PII might be based on a class rather than a contents claim was still accepted, and it was said that the reason for supporting a class claim was that disclosure 'would create or fan ill-informed or captious public or political criticism', or would be 'inimical to the proper functioning of the public service'.[79]

---

77   *HL Deb*, col 741–48, 6 June 1956.

78   [1968] AC 910.

79   *Ibid*, [1968] AC 910, pp 952, 993–94.

PII can operate in cases not involving the government. In *R v Lewes JJ ex p Secretary of State for the Home Department*,[80] it was said that the old expression 'Crown privilege' was wrong and misleading. While a minister was always an appropriate, and often the most appropriate, person to assert the public interest, it is open to any person to raise the question, and there may be cases where the trial judge should do so if no one else has. So, for example, in *D v NSPCC*,[81] the House of Lords protected the anonymity of an informer who had reported suspicions of child cruelty to the NSPCC.

An important distinction between PII and the sort of privilege that might be claimed by a private litigant, such as legal professional privilege or the privilege against self-incrimination, used to be that a privilege might be waived, but a claim to PII could not. As Lord Scarman said in *Air Canada v Secretary of State for Trade*,[82] 'The Crown, when it puts forward a public interest immunity objection, is not claiming a privilege but discharging a duty'. Similarly, in *Makanjuola v Metropolitan Police Commissioner*,[83] Bingham LJ said that, 'public interest immunity is not a trump card vouchsafed to certain privileged players to play when and as they wish'.[84] It cannot 'in any ordinary sense' be waived, because although rights can be waived, duties cannot. It follows that where a litigant holds documents in a class prima facie immune, he should (save in a very exceptional case) assert that they are immune, and decline to disclose them, since the ultimate decision about where the balance of public interest lies is not for him, but for the court. This approach, coupled with a class claim rather than a contents claim, led to undesirably wide PII claims being made by ministers in a number of trials. The practice was criticised in the Scott Report,[85] and the central government has now effectively abandoned class claims.[86]

Further, in *R v Chief Constable of West Midlands Police ex p Wiley*,[87] the House of Lords held that a class claim cannot be made in respect of documents compiled as part of the investigation of a complaint against the police, and it seems likely that class claims generally will be much reduced in future. In *ex p Wiley*, Lord Woolf acknowledged that Bingham LJ's *dicta* in *Makanjuola* had provided 'a very clear statement as to the nature of public interest immunity', but suggested that the *dicta*

---

80   [1973] AC 388, p 400.
81   [1978] AC 171.
82   [1983] 2 AC 394, p 446.
83   [1992] 3 All ER 617.
84   *Ibid*, p 623.
85   Scott, 1996a.
86   Attorney General's statement to the House of Commons, *HC Deb*, Vol 287, cols 949–57, and Lord Chancellor's statement to the House of Lords, *HL Deb*, Vol 576, cols 1507–17, 18 December 1996.
87   [1995] 1 AC 274.

had been applied subsequently in a manner beyond what Bingham LJ had intended.[88] As was shown above, Bingham LJ was not referring to something new when he used the 'trump card' analogy: in *Air Canada*, Lord Scarman had spoken similarly of a duty rather than a right. But after *ex p Wiley*, it is clear that if a minister believes that the overriding public interest requires government documents to be *disclosed*, he is not obliged to request immunity for them. It appears that ministers must now consider, before making a claim for PII, whether the public interest is better served by disclosure than by concealment. It looks very much as if they are expected to exercise a discretion in deciding whether or not to claim PII.

In recent decades, the leading cases on PII in the House of Lords have been concerned with civil claims, and it seems that the judges in those cases did not regard themselves as expressing principles that were equally applicable in criminal trials.[89] In *R v Governor of Brixton Prison ex p Osman*,[90] Mann LJ said that he thought they should apply, although he acknowledged that great weight should be attached in such cases to the need to do justice to the defendant. Sir Richard Scott has argued, however, that this view is contradicted by *dicta* in both old and modern criminal cases.[91]

In *R v H and Others*[92] the House of Lords said that the starting point for consideration of PII in relation to criminal cases is the principle that a person charged with a criminal offence should receive a fair trial, and that if he cannot be tried fairly he should not be tried at all. Fairness ordinarily requires that any material held by the prosecution which weakens its case, or strengthens that of the defendant, should be disclosed to the defence. The golden rule is that full disclosure of such material should be made.

But circumstances may arise in which material held by the prosecution and tending to undermine the prosecution or assist the defence cannot be disclosed to the defence, fully or even at all, without the risk of serious prejudice to an important public interest. The public interest most regularly engaged is interest in the effective investigation and prosecution of serious crime. This may involve the use of informers and undercover agents, or the use of scientific or operational techniques, details of which cannot be disclosed without exposing individuals to risk, or jeopardising the success of future operations. In such circumstances some derogation from the golden rule of full disclosure may be justified, but there must always be the minimum necessary to protect the public interest in question, and the overall fairness of the trial must never be put at risk.

---

88   [1995] 1 AC 274, p 296.
89   Scott, 1996b, pp 430–32.
90   [1991] 1 WLR 281, DC.
91   Scott, 1996b, pp 432–35.
92   [2004] UKHL 3, [2004] 2 AC 134, paras 10, 14, 18.

The withholding of evidence on the basis of PII has been recognised as permissible by the European Court of Human Rights, which acknowledged that there may be competing interests to be weighed against the rights of a defendant to disclosure of all material evidence in the hands of the prosecution.[93] By s 3(1)(a) of the Criminal Procedure and Investigations Act 1996 (CPIA), as amended, the prosecution is required to make an initial disclosure of material if it 'might reasonably be considered capable of undermining the case for the prosecution against the accused or of assisting the case for the accused'.[94] This is a wider duty than that originally laid down in the Act. Now it is the *possible* effect of the material that matters; formerly it was the *likely* effect. This may be significant for the operation of PII. Under the earlier law, there was a line of authority to the effect that if the material satisfied the CPIA test, it should be disclosed, and this approach was reflected in Crown Prosecution Service guidelines. But another line of authority was to the effect that even where the test was satisfied, PII could still justify non-disclosure, and the Act itself in s 3(6) contemplates this possibility.[95] With the wider duty of disclosure, it may be that PII will be claimed in more cases where the test is satisfied.

Suppose a defendant in a criminal case requests information from the prosecution, such as the name of an informer, relating to the methods by which offences are investigated. The prosecution claims PII. This is a good example of a situation where no real balancing of interests is done by a criminal court. While the relevance of such information in a particular case is not uncritically accepted, the line taken is that, if such information is in fact relevant to the conduct of the defence, it must be disclosed. The basic rule is that in public prosecutions witnesses may not be asked, and will not be allowed to disclose, the names of informers or the nature of the information given. Thus, in *Marks v Beyfus*,[96] an action for malicious prosecution, the Director of Public Prosecutions was called as a witness by the plaintiff but refused on grounds of public policy to give the names of his informers or to produce the statement on which he had acted in directing the earlier unsuccessful prosecution of the plaintiff. His objection was upheld by the trial judge and by the Court of Appeal. The reason for the rule is that informers need to be protected, both for their own safety and to ensure that the supply of information about criminal activities does not dry up.

However, in *Marks v Beyfus*, Lord Esher qualified this basic rule by stating that it could be departed from if the disclosure of the name of the informant was necessary to show the defendant's innocence. In such a case one public policy would be in conflict with another, and the policy that an innocent man should not be condemned

---

93   Parkinson, 2003. See also *Chief Constable of Greater Manchester Police v McNally* [2002] 2 Cr App R 617, CA.

94   The same test governs the prosecution's continuing duty of disclosure under s 7A.

95   Parkinson, 2004.

96   (1890) 25 QBD 494.

when his innocence could be proved had to prevail. But it is for the defendant to show that there is a good reason for disclosure.[97]

An example of a case where disclosure was considered appropriate is *R v Agar*.[98] In that case, a prosecution for possession of drugs, the Court of Appeal said that the trial judge should have ordered the informer's name to be disclosed. The accused's defence was that the informer and the police had acted together to frame him. The information was necessary for a proper presentation of the defence case because disclosure of the informer's identity might have given weight to the defendant's testimony. But disclosure will not be ordered in the usual case, where knowledge of the informer will not affect the defence. An example is *R v Slowcombe*.[99] Following a tip off, the defendant had been arrested in possession of a shotgun outside a sub post office. He claimed to have been recruited by V and to have been told by him that there was an accomplice working in the post office who would hand over the money, but that the gun was necessary for the sake of appearances. The defendant argued that he was not guilty of conspiracy to rob, but only of conspiracy to steal. The judge refused a defence application to ask a police officer whether the informer had been V. The Court of Appeal upheld this decision. If V had not been the informer, the defendant's story could still have been true. If V *had* been the informer, that would not establish that only a theft had been planned. V could have conspired with the defendant to commit the robbery but then have turned informer. Disclosing the name of the informer could therefore contribute little or nothing to the issue the jury had to consider, which was whether the defendant's explanation might reasonably have been true.[100]

The rule in *Marks v Beyfus*[101] also protects the identity of persons who have allowed their premises to be used for police observation, as well as the identity of the premises from which observation was kept. But even if the defendant argues that identification of the premises is necessary to establish his innocence (because, for example, it has a bearing on the accuracy of witness observations), the judge may still refuse to allow the question to be put. In *R v Johnson*,[102] where the defendant was charged with supplying drugs, the only evidence against him was supplied by police officers who had kept observation from private premises. The defence applied to cross-examine about the exact location in order to test whether the officers could have

---

97   *R v Hennessey* (1978) 68 Cr App R 419. See also *R v Keane* [1994] 1 WLR 746; *R v Menga and Marshalleck* [1998] Crim LR 58.

98   [1990] 2 All ER 442.

99   [1991] Crim LR 198.

100   In *R v Turner* [1995] 1 WLR 264 Lord Taylor CJ said that judges should scrutinise applications for disclosure of informers with very great care and should ensure that the information requested was essential to the running of the defence.

101   (1890) 25 QBD 494.

102   [1989] 1 All ER 121.

seen what they said they did. The trial judge ruled that the exact location should not be revealed, and the Court of Appeal upheld his decision. However, the prosecution must first provide a proper evidential basis to support its claim for protection of identity. In *R v Johnson*, Watkins LJ stated the following as minimum requirements:

(a) the police officer in charge of the observations must testify that he visited all the observation places to be used and ascertained the attitude of their occupiers, both as to the use to be made of them and to possible subsequent disclosure; and

(b) a police officer of at least the rank of chief inspector must testify that immediately prior to the trial he visited the places used for observation and ascertained whether the occupiers were the same as when the observation took place and, whether they were or not, the attitude of those occupiers to possible disclosure of their use as observation points.

The object of keeping the identity of premises secret is to protect the owner or occupier. Where this consideration does not apply, cross-examination may be permitted on the details of surveillance. Thus, in *R v Brown*,[103] where officers gave evidence that they had kept observation from an unmarked police vehicle, it was held that the defence were entitled to information relating to the surveillance and to the colour, make and model of the vehicle.

FURTHER READING

—Forsyth, 'Public Interest Immunity: Recent and Future Developments' [1997] CLJ 51.

—Langbein, 'The Privilege and Common Law Criminal Procedure: the Sixteenth to the Eighteenth Centuries', in Helmholz, *The Privilege against Self-Incrimination*, 1997.

—McGrath, 'Without Prejudice Privilege' (2001) 5 E&P 213.

—Macnair, 'The Early Development of the Privilege against Self-Incrimination' (1990) 10 OJLS 66.

—Sandy and Passmore, 'Refining Legal Advice Privilege' (2004) 154 NLJ 588.

—Scott, 'The Acceptable and Unacceptable Use of Public Interest Immunity' [1996] PL 427.

—Supperstone and Coppel, 'A New Approach to Public Interest Immunity' [1997] PL 211.

—Thanki, *The Law of Privilege*, 2006.

EXERCISES

1. Explain the scope of:

(a) the privilege against self-incrimination,

(b) legal advice privilege, and

(c) litigation privilege.

---

103   (1987) 87 Cr App R 52.

2. When are copies of original documents privileged?
3. What is referred to by 'absence of iniquity' in the context of legal professional privilege?
4. Give an example of a case where the maxim, 'Once privileged, always privileged' was applied.
5. Can the decisions in *Calcraft v Guest* (1898) and *Ashburton v Pape* (1913) be reconciled?
6. What does a claimant have to show before a court will order a journalist to disclose his sources?
7. When will evidence of negotiations be admissible?
8. What is the rule in *Marks v Beyfus* (1890)?

16

ESTOPPEL

INTRODUCTION

An 'estoppel' exists when, *in consequence of some previous act or statement to which he is either a party or a privy,*[1] a person is precluded from afterwards showing the existence of a different state of affairs than that indicated by the previous act or statement.[2] The rule is based on considerations of justice and public policy. It would be *unjust* to allow someone to do or say something, yet afterwards try to obtain an advantage by denying the validity of what he did earlier, or the truth of what he said earlier. It would be *contrary to public policy* to allow identical claims to be repeatedly litigated. However, estoppel cannot be used to authorise illegality.[3] For example, if powers that are *ultra vires* are assumed by a person or body, estoppel cannot be used to authorise what has been done.[4] Similarly, the courts have refused to allow an estoppel to prevent the application of the Moneylenders Acts.[5] It is a matter of interpretation in each case

---

1   A 'privy' is someone who has a type of legal connection to another person; for example, for some purposes an agent is the privy of his principal, and vice versa.

2   The definition of estoppel by Diplock LJ in *Thoday v Thoday* [1963] P 181, p 197, is too wide to differentiate this rule of exclusion from others.

3   *Re A Bankruptcy Notice* [1924] 2 Ch 76, p 97, *per* Lord Atkin.

4   See, eg, *Ministry of Agriculture and Fisheries v Matthews* [1950] 1 KB 148.

5   *Hoare v Adam Smith (London) Ltd* [1938] 4 All ER 283.

whether a statute has made a transaction absolutely illegal or void, or merely voidable; in the latter case, it may be possible to plead estoppel successfully.[6]

It has been a matter of some controversy whether estoppel forms part of adjective or substantive law. Some judges have insisted that it is merely a rule of evidence, and so belongs exclusively to adjective law.[7] Others have pointed out that while a party cannot found a cause of action on an estoppel, he may, as a result of being able to rely on an estoppel, succeed in a cause of action where otherwise he would have failed; for this reason, it is said, estoppel is more correctly viewed as a substantive rule of law.[8] The truth of the matter is that in some contexts estoppel will appear to operate more as a rule of substantive law; in others it will appear predominantly to be a rule of evidence, and so part of adjective law. This chapter is concerned only with those features that belong to adjective law. In particular, no reference is made to 'equitable estoppel', which is more appropriately seen as part of substantive law.

In accordance with my aim of covering estoppel only to the extent that it operates as a rule of evidence, I have divided this chapter into three parts. The first, and largest, part deals with estoppels that arise from previous judicial proceedings. This is followed by shorter sections on estoppel by deed and estoppel by conduct.

ESTOPPEL BY PREVIOUS JUDICIAL PROCEEDINGS

A judgment is conclusive against everyone in relation to the *legal state of affairs* that it produces. This is of special importance where the judgment affects the status of a person or thing (a 'judgment *in rem*'): for example, a judgment to the effect that a person is divorced, or that a ship seized in wartime is not a neutral vessel. A judgment also has the effect of preventing the parties to an action, or their privies,[9] from *denying*

---

6   *Western Fish Products Ltd v Penwith DC* [1981] 2 All ER 204, p 221, *per* Megaw LJ. A party relying on estoppel must plead it; failure to do so may amount to a waiver of the estoppel: *Vooght v Winch* (1819) 2 B&Ald 662.

7   See, eg, *Low v Bouverie* [1891] 3 Ch 82, p 105, *per* Bowen LJ; *Maritime Electric Co Ltd v General Dairies Ltd* [1937] AC 610, p 620, *per* Lord Maugham.

8   See, eg, *Canada and Dominion Sugar Co Ltd v Canadian National (West Indies) Steamships Ltd* [1947] AC 46, p 56, *per* Lord Wright; *Amalgamated Investment and Property Co Ltd v Texas Commerce International Bank Ltd* [1982] 1 QB 84, pp 131–32, *per* Brandon LJ.

9   See fn 1 above.

the facts on which it is based. This form of estoppel may operate either as 'cause of action estoppel' or as 'issue estoppel', and is based on two policy considerations. The first is that litigation should be final; the second, that nobody should be harassed twice in respect of the same cause of action.[10]

CAUSE OF ACTION ESTOPPEL

This prevents a party to an action from asserting or denying, as against the other party, the existence of a particular cause of action, the existence of which has already been determined in a final judgment on the merits in previous litigation between the same parties. If judgment was given for the plaintiff in the earlier action, the cause of action no longer exists (and so cannot be sued on again) because the judgment has taken its place. If judgment was given for the defendant in the earlier action, the effect is that the earlier court has found the cause of action not to exist. As a result, the unsuccessful plaintiff can no longer assert that it does. Suppose, for example, that Alice sues Bertie for repayment of a loan of £10,000, which she alleges was made to Bertie on 1 April 2001. Bertie, by his defence, denies the fact of the loan and says that the money was a gift. In due course, the county court judge hears the action, decides that the transaction was a gift rather than a loan, and gives judgment for Bertie. Alice cannot later sue Bertie again to recover the same sum on the basis that it was a loan. If she tries to do so, Bertie will apply successfully to have her action struck out as an abuse of the process of the court, on the ground that she is estopped by the judgment in the first action from making the allegation that she loaned him the money.[11]

Originally, this form of estoppel was known as 'estoppel by record' (the record being that of the court delivering the judgment), but it is now immaterial whether the judicial decision has been pronounced by a tribunal that is required to keep a written record of its decisions or not.[12] A final judgment 'on the merits' means a judgment on the cause of action that cannot be varied, re-opened or set aside by the court delivering it, or by any other court of co-ordinate jurisdiction, although it may be subject to appeal to a court of higher jurisdiction.[13] There will be no judgment on the merits when an action is dismissed for want of prosecution.[14] Default judgments and judgments by consent, however, are treated as judgments

---

10   See, eg, *Carl Zeiss Stiftung v Rayner & Keeler Ltd (No 2)* [1967] AC 853, p 946, *per* Lord Upjohn; *C (A Minor) v Hackney London BC* [1996] 1 WLR 789, p 792, *per* Simon Brown LJ. Some judges and writers refer to these policies in their Latin forms: '*Interest republicae ut sit finis litium*' and '*Nemo debet bis vexari pro una [et eadem] causa*'.

11   Civil Procedure Rules, r 3.4(2) and PD, para 1.5.

12   *Carl Zeiss Stiftung v Rayner & Keeler Ltd (No 2)* [1967] AC 853, p 933, *per* Lord Guest.

13   *The Sennar (No 2)* [1985] 1 WLR 490, p 494, *per* Lord Diplock.

14   *In Re Orrell Colliery and Fire-Brick Co* (1879) Ch D 681.

'on the merits'.[15] A judgment obtained by fraud or collusion will not give rise to an estoppel.[16]

Cause of action estoppel applies also to 'privies' of (or to persons who are 'in privity with') the parties to the original action.[17] The term 'privity' refers to a type of relation between two or more parties that is recognised by the law, and is said to be either of blood (for example, between ancestor and heir), of title (for example, between vendor and purchaser), or of interest.[18] The difficulty with this description is the potentially wide concept of 'interest'. It is clear that privity for this purpose is not established merely by having some interest, in the sense of mere curiosity or concern, in the outcome of the original litigation. The sense of 'interest' is narrower than that, and is governed by the fundamental principle that nobody should be harassed twice in respect of the same cause of action. This principle requires some degree of identity between the successful defendant in the first action and the party who is being sued in the later action. For example, in an action relating to trust property, there will normally be sufficient privity between the trustees and the beneficiaries to make a decision that is binding on the trustees binding on the beneficiaries, and vice versa. In deciding whether or not privity exists, it is important to remember that privity with a party to earlier proceedings will apply whether that party won or lost. This consideration requires a narrow construction of 'interest', because:

> Any contention which leads to the conclusion that a person is liable to be condemned unheard is plainly open to the gravest of suspicions. A defendant ought to be able to put his own defence in his own way, and to call his own evidence. He ought not to be concluded by the failure of the defence and evidence adduced by another defendant in other proceedings unless his standing in those other proceedings justifies the conclusion that a decision against the defendant in them ought fairly and truly to be said to be in substance a decision against him. Even if one leaves on one side collusive proceedings and friendly defendants, it would be wrong to enable a plaintiff to select the frailest of a number of possible defendants, and then to use the victory against him not merely *in terrorem* of other and more stalwart possible defendants, but as a decisive weapon against them.[19]

ISSUE ESTOPPEL

There are many causes of action that can be established only by proving that two or more different conditions are fulfilled. Such causes of action involve as many separate issues between the parties as there are conditions to be fulfilled by the plaintiff in

---

15   *In Re South American and Mexican Co ex p Bank of England* [1895] 1 Ch 37; *Kinch v Walcott* [1929] AC 482; *Kok Hoong v Leong Cheong Kweng Mines Ltd* [1964] AC 993, pp 1010–12, *per* Lord Radcliffe.

16   *The Duchess of Kingston's* case (1776) 20 St Tr 355, cols 478–81.

17   *C (A Minor) v Hackney London Borough Council* [1996] 1 WLR 789, p 792, *per* Simon Brown LJ.

18   *Ibid; Carl Zeiss Stiftung v Rayner & Keeler Ltd (No 2)* [1967] AC 853, p 910, *per* Lord Reid.

19   *Gleeson v J Wippell and Co Ltd* [1977] 1 WLR 510, p 516, *per* Megarry VC.

order to establish his cause of action. If, in litigation on one cause of action, any of the separate issues as to whether a particular condition has been fulfilled is determined by a court of competent jurisdiction, neither party can, in subsequent litigation between one another on *any* cause of action that depends on the fulfilment of the identical condition, assert that the condition was fulfilled if the court in the first action determined that it was not. Nor can either party subsequently deny that such a condition was fulfilled if the court in the first action determined that it was.[20] In order to see whether issue estoppel applies, the facts established and reasons given by the judge, his judgment, the pleadings, the evidence, and even the history of the matter may be taken into account.[21] For issue estoppel to apply, three conditions must be satisfied:

(a)   the same issue must have been decided in the earlier case;
(b)   the judicial decision in the earlier case must have been final; and
(c)   the parties to the decision, or their privies, must be the same persons as the parties to the proceedings in which the estoppel is raised, or their privies.[22]

The difference between cause of action estoppel and issue estoppel is that in cause of action estoppel, the cause of action has merged in the judgment and no longer has any independent existence. In issue estoppel, for the purpose of some *other* claim or cause of action, a state of fact or law is alleged or denied, the existence of which is a matter necessarily decided by the prior judgment, and it cannot afterwards be raised between the same parties or their privies. It has been suggested that one test for the operation of issue estoppel is that a party will be estopped from bringing an action which, if it succeeds, will result in a judgment conflicting with an earlier judgment.[23]

Issue estoppel, like cause of action estoppel, is a feature of adversary procedure. Where proceedings have an inquisitorial element, therefore, issue estoppel will not be strictly applied. So, for example, issue estoppel could rarely, if ever, apply to proceedings for divorce, or to children's cases.[24] Another example occurred in *The European Gateway*.[25] In this case, Steyn J held that a court set up to conduct a formal investigation into a collision at sea under the Merchant Shipping Act 1894 was a court of competent jurisdiction in exercising its powers to order a master's certificate to be suspended or cancelled. But he held that in other matters its role was purely investigatory, with the result that it was not a court of competent jurisdiction in

---

20   *Thoday v Thoday* [1963] P 181, p 198, *per* Diplock LJ.
21   *Carl Zeiss Stiftung v Rayner & Keeler Ltd (No 2)* [1967] AC 853, p 946, *per* Lord Upjohn.
22   *Ibid*, p 935, *per* Lord Guest.
23   *Port of Melbourne Authority v Anshun Proprietary Ltd* (1981) 147 CLR 589, pp 597, 603, *per* Gibbs CJ, Mason and Aickin JJ.
24   See, eg, *Thoday v Thoday* [1964] P 181; *B v Derbyshire County Council* [1992] 1 FLR 538; *In Re B* [1997] 3 WLR 1.
25   [1987] QB 206.

relation to the shipowners' civil liability. Matters litigated before the court of formal investigation could accordingly be litigated again in High Court Admiralty proceedings, and were not barred by issue estoppel.

Issue estoppel has been extended to cover not only the case where a particular point has been raised and specifically determined in the earlier proceedings, but also the case where a party later attempts to raise a point that might have been, but was not, raised in the earlier proceedings. This extension is based on *dicta* in *Henderson v Henderson*, where Wigram VC said:

> I believe I state the rule of the court correctly when I say that, where a given matter becomes the subject of litigation in, and of adjudication by, a court of competent jurisdiction, the court requires the parties to that litigation to bring forward their whole case, and will not (except under special circumstances) permit the same parties to open the same subject of litigation in respect of matter which might have been brought forward as part of the subject in contest, but which was not brought forward, only because they have, from negligence, inadvertence, or even accident, omitted part of their case. The plea of *res judicata* applies, except in special cases, not only to points upon which the court was actually required by the parties to form an opinion and pronounce a judgment, but to every point which properly belonged to the subject of litigation, and which the parties, exercising reasonable diligence, might have brought forward at the time.[26]

Although the court in *Henderson* was considering cause of action estoppel, it is clear that Wigram VC's observations apply to issue estoppel also.[27] They were spoken of as 'settled law' by Lord Shaw when delivering the opinion of the Privy Council in *Hoystead v Commissioner of Taxation*.[28] The importance of the rule for ensuring that court time is not wasted by dealing with litigation that could have been dealt with earlier was emphasised by the Court of Appeal in *Sanctuary Housing Association v Baker (No 2)*.[29]

The rule in *Henderson* thus falls into two parts. The first relates to those points actually decided by the court. Secondly, the rule extends to those points which might have been brought forward at the time, but were not. This is founded on the principle of public policy in preventing multiplicity of actions.[30] Thus, in *Greenhalgh v Mallard*,[31] it was held that if, in one action for damages for conspiracy, acts done in combination are alleged, a plaintiff cannot bring a second action on the same facts, even though in the first action the claim was formulated on the basis of an unjustified ultimate purpose only, without reliance on the means by which it was to be achieved,

26   (1843) 3 Hare 100, pp 114–15.

27   *Arnold v National Westminster Bank plc* [1991] 2 AC 93, p 107, *per* Lord Keith of Kinkel.

28   [1926] AC 155, p 170.

29   (1999) 31 HLR 746, pp 751–52.

30   *Talbot v Berkshire County Council* [1994] QB 290, p 296, *per* Stuart-Smith LJ.

31   [1947] 2 All ER 255.

and in the second action the means were alleged to be unlawful, but no challenge was made to the legitimacy of the ultimate purpose.

A further example of the operation of the rule can be seen in the decision of the High Court of Australia in *Port of Melbourne Authority v Anshun Proprietary Ltd.*[32] Under an agreement for the hire of a crane, Anshun agreed to indemnify the Port Authority against any claims that might be made against the Authority arising from the use of the crane. A workman suffered injury arising from Anshun's use of the crane, and he sued Anshun and the Authority for damages. The defendants served contribution notices on each other, but the Authority's notice was confined to a claim for contribution. Damages were awarded against both defendants, and between them it was ordered that the Authority pay 90% and Anshun 10%. The Authority then brought a separate action against Anshun, claiming an indemnity under the agreement in respect of all amounts that it had paid to the workman as damages and costs. The judge ordered that the action be stayed on the ground that the claim under the agreement should have been raised in the original action, with the result that the Authority was estopped from raising it in the current litigation. The majority of the High Court[33] held that this reasoning was correct. The Authority had been unreasonable in failing to raise the indemnity agreement in the first action, as that agreement was a defence to Anshun's claim for contribution, and was so closely connected with the subject matter of that action that it was to be expected that the Authority would raise it as a defence and as a basis of recovery from Anshun. A decision that the Authority was not entitled to an indemnity against Anshun had not been a necessary step to the judgment in the first action that Anshun was entitled to contribution, and the judgment did not, therefore, effect an issue estoppel in the strict sense, but it did in the extended sense based on the rule in *Henderson*. The High Court noted that the application of the rule to issue estoppel was to be treated with caution, and said that there should be no estoppel unless it appeared that the matter relied upon as a defence in the second action was so relevant to the subject matter of the first that it would have been unreasonable not to rely on it.[34]

The English Court of Appeal has held that the rule in *Henderson* should apply in actions for personal injury. A classic problem was presented in *Talbot v Berkshire County Council.*[35] A was a passenger in a motor car driven by B, which was involved in a collision caused partly by the fault of B and partly by the fault of C, the local authority, which was responsible for the maintenance of the highway. A and B were both injured in the collision. A sued B for damages for personal injury. B issued third party proceedings against C, claiming a contribution in respect of A's claim, but making no claim against C in respect of B's own injuries. Judgment was given in A's

---

32   (1981) 147 CLR 589.
33   Gibbs CJ, Mason and Aickin JJ.
34   (1981) 147 CLR 589, p 602.
35   [1994] QB 290.

favour against both B and C, who were each held partly to blame. B subsequently brought a fresh action against C in respect of his own personal injuries. The Court of Appeal held that he was estopped from doing so. The court said that the rule in *Henderson* was valuable, because it avoided unnecessary expense to the parties and the waste of court time that could be available to other litigants. A further argument in its favour was that it had the advantage, particularly important in personal injury claims, of preventing stale claims from being brought long after the event; it enabled a defendant to know the extent of his potential liability in respect of any one event, which was important for insurance companies, who had to make provision for claims; it might also affect their conduct of negotiations, their defence and any question of appeal. The court said that the *Henderson* rule should not be restricted to those cases where points could have been taken, but were not, in relation to one particular cause of action and defence. B's own personal injury claim should have been brought at the time of the original action. A safeguard to prevent injustice existed in that the court would not apply the rule in its full rigour if there were special circumstances why it should not do so. But no such circumstances existed in this case:

> The mere fact that a party is precluded by the rule from advancing a claim will inevitably involve some injustice to him, if it is or may be a good claim; but that cannot of itself amount to a special circumstance, since otherwise the rule would never have any application. The court has to consider why the claim was not brought in the earlier proceedings. The plaintiff may not have known of the claim at that time . . . or there may have been some agreement between the parties that the claim should be held in abeyance to abide the outcome of the first proceedings; or some representation may have been made to the plaintiff on which he has relied, so that he did not bring the claim earlier. These would be examples of special circumstances, though of course they are not intended to be an exhaustive list.[36]

The court acknowledged that the negligence or inadvertence of which Wigram VC had spoken would often be that of legal advisers rather than of the party himself, but added that 'the action or inaction of the agent is that of the principal'.[37]

In reaching this decision, the Court of Appeal dealt with one aspect of a problem that had arisen from the requirement that for issue estoppel to operate, there must be an identity of issues as well as parties. The question whether there is identity of issues depends on whether the issues are analysed broadly or minutely. In road accident cases, the issue may be seen as, 'Who caused the collision?'. Alternatively, it may be argued that because negligence requires a breach of duty owed to a particular

---

36   [1994] QB 290, p 299.

37   *Ibid.* See also *Wain v F Sherwood and Sons Transport Ltd* (1998) *The Times*, 16 July. But the rule in *Henderson v Henderson* has been held not to extend to prevent a defendant from bringing a subsequent action when he could have claimed an indemnity or contribution in earlier proceedings in which he was sued with a co-defendant. See *Sweetman v Shepherd and Others* (2000) *The Times*, 29 March, CA.

individual[38] there are different issues for each particular duty of care, so that identity of issues will be rare. Several cases at first instance show different approaches to the problem.[39] So far as personal injury cases are concerned, it appears that the Court of Appeal favours the use of the rule in *Henderson* to bypass undesirable effects of minute analysis. But in other types of litigation this approach may not be possible. For example, in *New Brunswick Railway Co v British and French Trust Corp Ltd*,[40] the House of Lords held that a judgment delivered on the construction of one bond would not operate as an estoppel to prevent one of the parties to that action raising a defence as to the construction of another bond in a different action, even though the two bonds were in identical terms. The House was of the opinion that if in an action the question of the construction of a particular document had been decided, each party to that action was estopped from subsequently litigating the same question of construction of that particular document, but the parties would not be estopped from subsequently litigating the question of construction of another document, even though the second one was in substantially identical words: 'For the documents are two distinct documents, and the questions of their construction are two distinct questions.'[41]

The parties to the earlier decision must not only have been the *same persons* as the parties to the later action in which the estoppel is raised. They must also be suing or being sued in the later action in the *same capacities* as in the first. In *Marginson v Blackburn Borough Council*,[42] the plaintiff was a passenger in a motor car owned and driven by his wife. The car was involved in a collision with a bus driven by an employee of the defendants. As a result of the collision, the plaintiff suffered personal injuries, his wife was killed, and two nearby houses were damaged. The owners of the houses sued both Marginson and the council, alleging that the damage to their houses had been caused by the negligence of both drivers, Marginson being vicariously liable (as the law then stood) for the negligence of his wife, and the council for that of its employee. There were third party proceedings between Marginson and the council. The county court judge held Marginson and the council equally liable. Subsequently, Marginson brought a High Court action against the council. He claimed in two capacities. First, he claimed damages in his own right for the injuries that he had suffered. He also claimed as the administrator of his wife's estate for the benefit of her estate, and on his own and his daughter's behalf as dependants of his deceased wife. The Court of Appeal held that Marginson was estopped from pursuing his personal

---

38 *Bourhill v Young* [1943] AC 92.
39 See, eg, *Randolph v Tuck* [1962] 1 QB 175; *Wood v Luscombe* [1966] 1 QB 169; *Wall v Radford* [1991] 2 All ER 741.
40 [1939] AC 1.
41 [1939] AC 1, p 43, *per* Lord Romer.
42 [1939] 2 KB 426.

claim by virtue of the county court judgment (the law then being that contributory negligence was a complete defence to a claim in negligence), but the court held that he was not estopped from pursuing the claims that he was making in a representative capacity, as administrator of his wife's estate.

Identity of parties was a crucial factor in *C (A Minor) v Hackney London Borough Council*,[43] in which the Court of Appeal distinguished *Talbot v Berkshire County Council*.[44] The plaintiff, a minor, lived in a council house where her mother was the tenant. The house was damp and in a state of disrepair. An action by the plaintiff's mother against the council, based on these facts, was disposed of by way of a consent order specifying the works necessary to put the house into repair and providing for payment of damages. Afterwards, the plaintiff brought proceedings against the council by her stepfather as next friend, claiming damages for negligence and breach of statutory duty under the Defective Premises Act 1972. She alleged ill health from the disrepair. It was argued for the council that she was estopped from bringing the action by virtue of the consent order made in the earlier action brought by her mother. The court rejected this argument. It could not be right, it said, that her dependence on her mother created such a nexus between them that they should be regarded effectively as the same party. If that were so, it would be right equally in the context of a road accident case where a mother and infant child were both injured by the defendant's negligence. If the mother sued and obtained judgment on her own behalf, it could not be the case that her child would be thereby barred from making a subsequent claim. The court said that the critical difference between this case and the *Talbot* case was that in the latter the parties were the same; in this case they were not.

Does the fact that the first judgment was obtained by default make any difference to the application of the rule in the *Henderson* case? There are various *dicta* to suggest that it does. In *New Brunswick Railway Co v British and French Trust Corp Ltd*, Lord Maugham LC said:

> In my opinion we are at least justified in holding that an estoppel based on a default judgment must be very carefully limited. The true principle in such a case would seem to be that the defendant is estopped from setting up in a subsequent action a defence which was necessarily, and with complete precision, decided by the previous judgment . . .[45]

In the same case, Lord Wright said that all necessary effect was given to a default judgment by treating it as conclusive of what it directly decided; a further effect by way of estoppel would be an illegitimate extension of the doctrine.[46]

---

43   [1996] 1 WLR 789.
44   [1994] QB 290.
45   [1939] AC 1, p 21.
46   *Ibid*, p 38.

A similarly cautious approach was suggested by Lord Radcliffe when delivering the opinion of the Privy Council in *Kok Hoong v Leong Cheong Kweng Mines Ltd.*[47] After stating that there was no doubt that a default judgment could give rise to an estoppel, he said that the question was not whether there could be such an estoppel, but rather what the judgment should be treated as deciding. 'There is obvious and, indeed, grave danger in permitting such a judgment to preclude the parties from ever reopening before the court on another occasion, perhaps of very different significance, whatever issues can be discerned as having been involved in the judgment so obtained by default.' From one point of view, a default judgment was like a judgment by consent, but from another, it 'speaks for nothing but the fact that a defendant, for unascertained reasons, negligence, ignorance or indifference, has suffered judgment to go against him in the particular suit in question'. In his opinion, when judgment had been obtained by default, it would be wrong to apply the full rigour of any principle as widely formulated as that in *Henderson*; a much more restricted operation should be given to any estoppel arising from a default judgment. In *Arnold v National Westminster Bank plc* Lord Keith of Kinkel suggested that, where the earlier proceedings had resulted in a default judgment, this might amount to special circumstances that would prevent the rule in *Henderson* from applying.[48]

It is plain from *Henderson* that the discovery of new material will not by itself suffice to avoid issue estoppel. The point was further explained by Lord Cairns LC in *Phosphate Sewage Co Ltd v Molleson*, where he said that a party who had been unsuccessful in litigation could not be allowed to reopen that litigation merely by saying that, since the former case, there had emerged another fact going in exactly the same direction as the facts stated before, leading up to the same relief asked for before, but additional to facts already relied on. The only way litigation could be reopened was if the new fact entirely changed the aspect of the case, and it could not by reasonable diligence have been discovered before.[49] In *Arnold v National Westminster Bank plc*, Lord Keith of Kinkel suggested that it should be easier to overcome an issue estoppel than a cause of action estoppel where a party relies on further relevant material which he could not by reasonable diligence have adduced in the earlier proceedings. The underlying principles on which estoppel is based – public policy and justice – have, he said, greater force in cause of action estoppel, where the subject matter of the two proceedings is identical, than they do in issue estoppel, where the subject matter is different.[50]

---

47   [1964] AC 993, pp 1010–12.

48   [1991] 2 AC 93, p 107.

49   (1879) 4 App Cas 801, p 814. Lord Cairns's test was applied by the Court of Appeal in *Ashmore v British Coal Corp* [1990] 2 QB 338, and in *Smith v Linskills* [1996] 1 WLR 763, and by the House of Lords in *Hunter v Chief Constable of West Midlands Police* [1982] AC 529.

50   [1991] 2 AC 93, p 108.

There are signs that the rule in *Henderson v Henderson* may now be applied more flexibly. In *Johnson v Gore Wood and Co*,[51] the House of Lords held that the raising of a matter in later proceedings will not necessarily be an abuse of process just because it could have been raised in earlier proceedings. Whether there is an abuse of process will not depend on a dogmatic approach, but on a broad, merits-based judgment. It is preferable to ask whether in all the circumstances, a party's conduct was an abuse of process than to ask whether it was an abuse and then, if it was, whether it was excused or justified by special circumstances. It remains to be seen whether this approach will in practice produce different results.

ANALOGOUS PROVISIONS IN CRIMINAL PROCEEDINGS

We have seen that, in civil cases, cause of action estoppel will prevent a defendant from being sued twice in respect of the same cause of action. A similar principle operates in criminal law, in which the pleas of *autrefois acquit* and *autrefois convict* are available to prevent a defendant's being put in what is sometimes called 'double jeopardy'. The leading authority on the scope of these pleas at common law is the speech of Lord Morris of Borth-y-Gest in *Connelly v DPP*.[52] In this speech, Lord Morris laid down a number of propositions, of which the following are the most important:

(a) A man cannot be tried for a crime in respect of which he has previously been acquitted or convicted.

(b) A man cannot be tried for a crime in respect of which he could on some previous indictment have been convicted.

(c) The same rule applies if the crime in respect of which he is being charged is in effect the same, or substantially the same, as a crime in respect of which he has been acquitted, or could have been convicted, or has been convicted.

(d) One test as to whether the rule applies is whether the evidence that is necessary to support the second indictment, or whether the facts that constitute the second offence, would have been sufficient to procure a conviction on the first indictment, either in relation to the offence charged, or in relation to an offence of which, on that indictment, the accused could have been found guilty.

A substantial inroad on the common law has been made in ss 54–57 of the Criminal Procedure and Investigations Act 1996. These sections introduce the concept of 'tainted acquittals' and apply to acquittals in respect of offences alleged to have been

---

51   [2000] 2 WLR 72.

52   [1964] AC 1254.

committed on or after 15 April 1997.[53] In the event of a successful appeal against conviction, the Court of Appeal may order the appellant to be retried if the interests of justice so require.[54] See also provisions for the retrial of serious offences in Pt 10, CJA 2003.

The provisions apply where (a) a person has been acquitted of an offence, and (b) a person has been convicted of an 'administration of justice offence' involving interference with or intimidation of a juror or a witness, or potential witness, in any proceedings that led to the acquittal.[55] Where it appears to the court before which the person was convicted that there is a real possibility that, but for the interference or intimidation, the acquitted person would not have been acquitted, the court shall certify that it so appears, unless it would be contrary to the interests of justice to take proceedings against the acquitted person for the offence of which he was acquitted, whether because of lapse of time, or for any other reason.[56] Where a court has certified under these provisions, an application may be made to the High Court for an order quashing the acquittal. Where such an order is made, proceedings may be taken against the acquitted person for the offence in respect of which he was acquitted.

The High Court shall not make an order quashing an acquittal unless four conditions are satisfied:

(a) it appears to the High Court likely that, but for the interference or intimidation, the acquitted person would not have been acquitted;

(b) it does not appear to the court that, because of lapse of time or for any other reason, it would be contrary to the interests of justice to take proceedings against the acquitted person for the offence of which he was acquitted;

(c) it appears to the court that the acquitted person has been given a reasonable opportunity to make *written* representations to the court; and

(d) it appears to the court that the conviction for the administration of justice offence will stand. In determining whether this condition is satisfied, the court shall take into account all the information before it, but shall ignore the possibility of new factors coming to light.[57]

A further substantial inroad on the common law has been made by Pt 10 of the Criminal Justice Act 2003, which provides for a retrial where a defendant has been

---

53   Criminal Procedure and Investigations Act 1996 (Appointed Day No 4) Order 1997 (SI 1997/ 1019).

54   Criminal Appeal Act 1968, s 7.

55   Criminal Procedure and Investigations Act 1996, s 54(1). The definition of an 'administration of justice offence' is contained in s 54(6).

56   Criminal Procedure and Investigations Act 1996, s 54(2) and (5).

57   *Ibid*, s 55.

acquitted of a serious offence,[58] but where there is 'new and compelling evidence' against the acquitted person,[59] and in all the circumstances it is in the interests of justice for the acquittal to be quashed and a re-trial ordered.[60]

The pleas of *autrefois acquit* and *autrefois convict* provide in a criminal context something analogous to cause of action estoppel in civil proceedings. Is there anything analogous to issue estoppel?[61] Some authorities suggest that the prosecution may be estopped from adducing evidence that either contradicts, or is at least inconsistent with, a defendant's innocence of an earlier offence for which he has been tried and acquitted. The principal authority was formerly the decision of the Privy Council in *Sambasivam v Public Prosecutor*.[62] In that case, the Privy Council held that the effect of an acquittal was not just that the person acquitted could not be tried again for the same offence. In addition, the verdict was binding and conclusive in all subsequent proceedings between the parties to the adjudication. The defendant had originally been charged on two counts, one in relation to possession of a firearm and the other in relation to possession of ammunition. He had signed a statement admitting both offences, but repudiated this at trial. He was acquitted of the charge relating to ammunition, but the court disagreed on the other charge, and a re-trial was ordered. At the re-trial, the whole confession was once again put in evidence. The parts dealing with possession of ammunition were, of course, inconsistent with the defendant's previous acquittal, but the court was not told of the acquittal, and it convicted the defendant on the firearms charge. The Privy Council held that the conviction should be set aside. Lord MacDermott said:

> Here, the appellant having been acquitted at the first trial on the charge of having ammunition in his possession, the prosecution was bound to accept the correctness of the verdict, and was precluded from taking any step to challenge it at the second trial. And the appellant was no less entitled to rely on his acquittal in so far as it might be relevant in his defence.[63]

The *Sambasivam* rule was unlike issue estoppel because it was one-sided. An accused person is not prevented from denying that he committed an offence for which he has been convicted; he has only to overcome a presumption of guilt under s 74 of the Police and Criminal Evidence Act 1984. By contrast, a true estoppel is mutual: it binds both parties.

However, the rule was capable of leading to difficulties, as Andrews and Hirst pointed out:

---

58   The offences, referred to as 'qualifying offences', are listed in Sched 5.

59   Section 78.

60   Section 79. The sort of evidence that might qualify would be DNA evidence, not available at the time of trial, which incriminates the acquitted person.

61   See Mirfield, 1980; Hirst, 1991.

62   [1950] AC 458.

63   [1950] AC 458, p 479.

Imagine that D has been charged with a murder, and acquitted in controversial circumstances; imagine then that some months later a similar offence is committed, and that it is clear for various reasons that whoever committed the first offence also committed the second. Moreover, D seems to be the only person who could have been involved in both incidents. The *Sambasivam* rule would preclude use of that crucial similar fact evidence.[64]

This hypothetical problem arose in *R v Z*.[65] The defendant was charged with rape. His defence was that the complainant had consented to intercourse; alternatively, that he believed that she had consented. In order to rebut these defences, the prosecution wished to call four women who had made previous complaints of rape against the defendant. Each complaint had given rise to a separate trial. In one, the defendant had been convicted, but in the other three, he had been acquitted. At a preparatory hearing, the judge ruled that the one conviction was insufficient to be admitted as similar fact evidence, and the prosecution did not challenge that. The judge also ruled that the four sets of circumstances, taken together, shared enough common features to be admissible as similar fact evidence, but that evidence of the circumstances surrounding allegations that had led to acquittals was inadmissible because of the rule in *Sambasivam*. On an interlocutory appeal by the prosecution, the Court of Appeal reluctantly upheld this ruling, but that court's decision was subsequently reversed by the House of Lords, which held that the principle of double jeopardy does not render relevant evidence inadmissible merely because that evidence tends to show that a defendant was in fact guilty of an offence of which he was earlier acquitted. Such evidence is admissible because the defendant is not being put on trial again for the offence of which he has been acquitted, nor does he stand in jeopardy of being punished for it on some other ground.

ESTOPPEL BY DEED

Where an action is brought on a deed, the parties to the deed and those claiming through them, such as successors in title, are estopped from denying the truth of the facts stated in the deed. An early example of the application of this rule is *Bowman v Taylor*.[66] The plaintiff claimed as patentee the rent under a licence to use certain looms for weaving, called 'power looms', which had been granted to the defendants. The licence had been granted by a deed, which recited that the plaintiff had invented power looms, for which he had obtained a patent. The defendants by their plea

---

64   Andrews and Hirst, 1997, p 517.
65   [2000] 3 All ER 385. See Roberts, 2000; Mirfield, 2001.
66   (1834) 4 LJKB 58.

denied, amongst other things, that the plaintiff was the inventor, or that the power loom was a new invention. The plaintiff alleged that those pleas were bad, because the defendants were estopped by the recitals in the deed to which they were parties. The Court of King's Bench held that where a person has entered into a deed, by which, in express terms, he has admitted certain facts to exist, he is estopped from afterwards disputing those facts. The recitals were so bound up in the deed that they were essentially part of the deed itself. Accordingly, the defendants were estopped from denying either that the power loom was a new invention, or that the plaintiff was its inventor.

However, in *Greer v Kettle*,[67] Lord Maugham said that while he did not doubt the correctness of the result in *Bowman v Taylor*, he did doubt whether the recital considered in that case could properly be taken to be a statement on behalf of the licensee, who could have had little knowledge of the matters contained in it. The decision was better explained on the ground that the deed was entered into on the footing that the recital, whether true or not, must be taken during the continuance of the licence as true. Thus, the licensee of a patent right was bound on the same principle and in the same way as a tenant who has taken a lease of lands from another, and who is estopped during the lease from denying his landlord's title.[68]

Recitals will not always bind both parties to a deed. The law was explained by Patteson J in *Stroughill v Buck* as follows:

> When a recital is intended to be a statement which all the parties to the deed have mutually agreed to admit as true, it is an estoppel upon all. But, when it is intended to be the statement of one party only, the estoppel is confined to that party, and the intention is to be gathered from construing the instrument.[69]

This statement of the law was approved by the House of Lords in *Greer v Kettle*.

For recitals to be binding, they must relate to specific facts, and be certain, clear and unambiguous.[70] Estoppel by deed will not operate so as to prevent a party from relying on fraud, duress, illegality, or any other fact entitling him to rescission or rectification of the deed.[71] An example of such a case is *Wilson v Wilson*.[72] The defendant, Lascelles Wilson, wanted to buy a house with the help of a building society loan. His personal earnings did not meet the society's requirements, so he invited his brother, Donald Wilson, to become a co-purchaser. The transfer, by which

---

67   [1938] AC 156.
68   *Ibid*, pp 169–70.
69   (1850) 14 QB 781, p 787.
70   *Greer v Kettle* [1938] AC 156, p 170, *per* Lord Maugham.
71   *Ibid*, p 171.
72   [1969] 1 WLR 1470.

the vendor transferred his interest in the property to the two brothers, stated that the transferees should stand possessed of the property as joint tenants upon trust for sale, with a power to postpone sale. The title was registered in the brothers' joint names subject to a registered charge to the building society, both brothers being joined as mortgagors. The plaintiff later served a notice purporting to sever the joint tenancy and began an action claiming that, pursuant to the transfer, he was entitled to an undivided share in half the property.

Buckley J held that the common intention of the brothers at the time of purchase was that the beneficial ownership should be vested solely in the defendant, and that the plaintiff had joined in the transaction merely in order to help his brother to obtain a mortgage. The two brothers had not appreciated the effect of the declaration of beneficial interest, or had even appreciated that it was in the deed at all. Accordingly, he concluded that there should be rectification of the transfer, and the parties were not estopped by the declaration of beneficial interest that it contained.

ESTOPPEL BY CONDUCT

An estoppel may arise where it would be unconscionable for a person to deny a representation of fact that is implicit in his conduct. Such an estoppel may arise from agreement, from an express or implied representation, or from negligence. For there to be estoppel by conduct, the representation must relate to an existing fact and be unambiguous.

AGREEMENT

An old example is *Cooke v Loxley*.[73] This was an action for use and occupation of land let to the defendant by the plaintiff's predecessor in title. The defendant had paid rent not only to the plaintiff's predecessor in title, but also to the plaintiff. At trial, the defendant wanted to call evidence that the plaintiff had no title to the land. The evidence was rejected, and the trial judge's decision was upheld by the Court of King's Bench. Lord Kenyon CJ said that in an action for use and occupation, a tenant who occupies land by agreement with another, ought not, as a matter of convenience and public policy, to be permitted to call upon that other person to show the title under which he let the land.

For similar reasons, bailees, licensees and agents cannot deny the title of their bailors, licensors or principals after having effectively acknowledged them in the transactions carried out on their behalf.[74]

---

73 (1792) 5 TR 4.
74 See, eg, *Gosling v Birnie* (1831) 7 Bing 399; *Crossley v Dixon* (1863) 10 HL Cas 293.

EXPRESS OR IMPLIED REPRESENTATION

In *Pickard v Sears*,[75] the rule was laid down that where a person by words or conduct wilfully causes another to believe in a certain state of things, and thereby induces him to act or to alter his own previous position, the representor will be estopped from alleging that a different state of affairs existed at the time when the representation was made. By 'wilfully', it is meant either that the representor alleges something to be true that he knows to be false, or that he means his representation to be acted upon, and it is acted upon accordingly. 'If, whatever a man's meaning may be, he so conducts himself that a reasonable man would take the representation to be true, and believe that it was meant he should act upon it, and did act upon it as true, the party making the representation would be equally precluded from contesting its truth.'[76]

In *Greenwood v Martins Bank Ltd*,[77] for example, the plaintiff's wife had forged her husband's signature on cheques drawn on the defendant bank. The husband discovered that his wife had been forging his signature, but at first said nothing about it to the bank. Eventually, he threatened to do so, and the wife killed herself. The husband then sued the bank for the amounts that it had paid out of his account on the authority of the forged cheques, but it was held by the House of Lords that he was estopped from relying on the fact of the forgery. It was acknowledged that mere silence could not amount to a representation. When, however, there was a duty of disclosure, deliberate silence might become significant and amount to a representation. A bank's customer had a duty to disclose the fact of forgery to his bank, if he discovered it. The plaintiff's silence in this case therefore amounted to a representation that the forged cheques were in order. Assuming that detriment to the bank followed, all the elements essential to estoppel were present.

NEGLIGENCE

To establish estoppel by negligence, it has to be proved that a duty of care was owed to the person who has suffered loss,[78] and that there has been a breach of that duty. In *Coventry, Sheppard and Co v Great Eastern Railway*,[79] both conditions were satisfied. A railway company had negligently issued two delivery orders in respect of one consignment of wheat. This had enabled a swindler to obtain two advances of money, as if there had been two separate consignments. It was held that the railway company's negligence estopped it from denying that there had been two consignments.[80]

---

75   (1837) 6 A&E 469.

76   *Freeman v Cooke* (1848) 18 LJ Ex 114, pp 119–20, *per* Parke B.

77   [1933] AC 51.

78   For a case where this could not be established, see *Moorgate Mercantile Co Ltd v Twitchings* [1977] AC 890.

79   (1883) 11 QBD 776.

80   Cf *Mercantile Bank of India Ltd v Central Bank of India Ltd* [1938] AC 287, where a plea of estoppel failed because there had been no breach of a duty of care.

FURTHER READING

——Mirfield, '*Res Judicata* Rejected' [2001] 117 LQR 194.

——Roberts, 'Acquitted Misconduct Evidence and Double Jeopardy Principles, from *Sambasivam* to *Z*' [2000] Crim LR 952.

EXERCISES

1. What is the legal meaning of a 'privy'?
2. What is 'cause of action estoppel'?
3. How does issue estoppel differ from cause of action estoppel?
4. What is the rule in *Henderson v Henderson* (1843)? Give an example of a case where the rule was applied.
5. What exceptions are there to the principles of *autrefois acquit* and *autrefois convict*?

BIBLIOGRAPHY

Alexander, L, 'Are Procedural Rights Derivative Substantive Rights?' (1998) 17 *Law and Philosophy*, 19.

Allan, T, 'Journalists' Sources and Disloyal Employees: Discretion, Fact and Judgment' [1998] CLJ 235.

Allan, TRS, 'Abuse of power and public interest immunity' (1985) 101 LQR 200.

Allan, TRS, 'Privilege and confidentiality' [1987] CLJ 43.

Allen, C, *Sourcebook on Evidence*, 1996, London: Cavendish Publishing.

Allen, C, *The Law of Evidence in Victorian England*, 1997, Cambridge: Cambridge University Press.

Allen, C, 'Judicial notice extended' (1998) 2 E&P 37.

Allen, CK, *Law in the Making*, 7th edn, 1964, Oxford: Clarendon.

Anderson, T, Schum, D, and Twining, W, *Analysis of Evidence*. 2nd edn, 2005, Cambridge: Cambridge University Press.

Andrews, JA, 'Public interest and criminal proceedings' (1988) 104 LQR 410.

Andrews, JA, and Hirst, M, *Criminal Evidence*, 3rd edn, 1997, London: Sweet & Maxwell.

Andrews, JA, and Hirst, M, *Criminal Evidence*, 4th edn, 2001, London: Jordans.

Andrews, NH, 'Privileged documents' [1989] CLJ 43.

Anon, 'Old Bailey experience' (1833) 10 *Law Magazine* 259, pp 276–77.

Archbold: Criminal Pleading, Evidence and Practice 2008, London: Sweet & Maxwell.

Ashworth, A, 'The self-incrimination saga' [2001] 5 Archbold News 5.

Ashworth, A, 'Redrawing the boundaries of entrapment' [2002] Crim LR 161.

Ashworth, A, and Redmayne, M, *The Criminal Process*. 3rd edn, 2005, Oxford: Oxford University Press.

Austin, JL, *How to Do Things with Words*, 2nd edn, 1975, Oxford: Clarendon.

Austin, JL, *Philosophical Papers*, 3rd edn, 1979, Oxford: Oxford University Press.

Baker, JH, 'Criminal courts and procedure at common law 1550–1800', in Cockburn, JS (ed), *Crime in England 1550–1800*, 1977, London: Methuen.

Baker, JH, *An Introduction to English Legal History*, 3rd edn, 1990, London: Butterworths.

Baldwin, J and McConville, M, *Jury Trials*, 1979, Oxford: Clarendon.

Beattie, J, 'Scales of justice: defence counsel and the English criminal trial in the eighteenth and nineteenth centuries' (1991) 9 Law and History Review 221.

Bentham, J, 'Rationale of Judicial Evidence', in Bowring, J (ed), *The Works of Jeremy Bentham*, 1838–43, Vol 6, Edinburgh: William Tait.

Bentham, J, 'Anarchical Fallacies', in Waldron, J (ed), *Nonsense Upon Stilts: Bentham, Burke and Marx on the Rights of Man*, 1987, London: Methuen, Article II.

Benn, SI, 'Rights' in Edwards, P (ed), *The Encyclopedia of Philosophy*, 1967, London: Collier-Macmillan.

Best, WM, *Principles of the Law of Evidence*, 5th edn, 1870, London: H Sweet.

Birch, D, 'Hunting the snark: the elusive statutory exception' [1988] Crim LR 221.

Birch, D, 'Children's evidence' [1992] Crim LR 262.

Birch, D, 'Excluding evidence from entrapment' (1994) 47(2) CLP 73.

Birch, D, 'The sharp end of the wedge: use of mixed statements by the defence' [1997] Crim LR 416

Birch, D, 'Suffering in silence: a cost-benefit analysis of section 34 of the Criminal Justice and Public Order Act 1994' [1999] Crim LR 769.

Birch, D, 'A better deal for vulnerable witnesses' [2000] Crim LR 223.

Birch, D, 'Rethinking sexual history evidence: proposals for fairer trials' [2002] Crim LR 531.

Birch, D, 'The Criminal Justice Act 2004: (4): Hearsay: same old story, same old song?' [2004] Crim LR 556.

Birch, D, and Leng, R, *Blackstone's Guide to the Youth Justice and Criminal Evidence Act 1999*, 2000, London: Blackstone.

Blackstone, Sir W, *The Commentaries on the Laws of England*, Kerr, RM (ed), 1876, London: John Murray.

Boon, A, *Advocacy*, 1993, London: Cavendish Publishing.

Brennan, M, 'The battle for credibility' [1993] NLJ 623.

Brown, The Rt Hon Lord Justice S, 'Public interest immunity' [1994] PL 579.

Cairns, DJA, *Advocacy and the Making of the Adversarial Criminal Trial 1800–1865*, 1998, Oxford: Clarendon.

Campbell, J (1st Baron Campbell), *The Lives of the Chief Justices of England*, 1849–57, London: John Murray.

Campbell, K, 'Offence and defence', in Dennis, I (ed), *Criminal Law and Justice*, 1987, London: Sweet & Maxwell.

Cane, P, *An Introduction to Administrative Law*, 2nd edn, 1992, Oxford: Clarendon.

Carr, EH, *What Is History?*, 2nd edn, 1987, Harmondsworth: Penguin.

Carter, PB, 'Judicial notice: related and unrelated matters', in Campbell, E, and Waller, L (eds), *Well and Truly Tried: Essays on Evidence in Honour of Sir Richard Eggleston*, 1982, Sydney: The Law Book Co.

Carter, PB, 'Hearsay, relevance and admissibility' (1987) 103 LQR 106.

Carter, PB, *Cases and Statutes on Evidence*, 2nd edn, 1990, London: Sweet & Maxwell.

Carter, PB, 'Evidence obtained by use of a covert listening device' (1997) 113 LQR 468.

Charge of the Lord Chief Justice of England in the Case of The Queen against Thomas Castro . . . printed from the shorthand writer's notes, 1874, London: Vacher and Sons.

Choo, AL-T, 'Confessions and corroboration: a comparative perspective' [1991] Crim LR 867.

Choo, AL-T, 'The notion of relevance and defence evidence' [1993] Crim LR 114.

Choo, AL-T, *Hearsay and Confrontation in Criminal Trials*, 1996, Oxford: Clarendon.

Choo, AL-T, and Nash, S, 'What's the matter with section 78?' [1999] Crim LR 929.

Cottu, C, *On the Administration of Criminal Justice in England; and the Spirit of the English Government*, translated from the French, 1822, London: Richard Stevens.

Creighton, P, 'Spouse competence and compellability' [1990] Crim LR 34.

Criminal Justice Act 2003: Explanatory Notes, 2003, London: The Stationery Office.

Criminal Law Revision Committee, 9th Report, *Evidence: Written Statements, Formal Admissions and Notices of Alibi*, 1966, Cmnd 3145, London: HMSO.

Criminal Law Revision Committee, 11th Report, *Evidence (General)*, Cmnd 4991, 1972, London: HMSO.

Cross, Sir R, *Cross on Evidence*, 4th edn, 1974, London: Butterworths.

Cullen, T, *Crippen: The Mild Murderer*, 1988, Harmondsworth: Penguin.

Damaska, MR, *The Faces of Justice and State Authority: A Comparative Approach to the Legal Process*, 1986, New Haven, CT and London: Yale University Press.

Daniel, WTS, *The History and Origin of the Law Reports*, undated, London: Wildy & Sons.

Darbyshire, P, 'An essay on the importance and neglect of the magistracy' [1997a] Crim LR 627.

Darbyshire, P, 'Previous misconduct and magistrates' courts – some tales from the real world' [1997b] Crim LR 105.

Davis, KC, 'Judicial notice' (1955) 55 Col LR 945.

Dennis, I, 'Reconstructing the law of criminal evidence' (1989) CLP 21.

Dennis, I, 'Miscarriage of justice and the law of confessions' [1993] PL 291.

Dennis, I, 'Instrumental protection, human right or functional necessity?' [1995a] CLJ 342.

Dennis, I, 'The Criminal Justice and Public Order Act 1994: the evidence provisions' [1995b] Crim LR 4.

Dennis, I, 'Silence in the police station: the marginalisation of section 34' [2002a] Crim LR 25.

Dennis, I, *The Law of Evidence*. 3rd edn, 2007, London: Sweet & Maxwell.

Devlin, P, *Easing the Passing: The Trial of Dr John Bodkin Adams*, 1986, London: Faber & Faber.

Duff, RA, *Trials and Punishments*, 1986, Cambridge: Cambridge University Press.

Duman, D, 'Pathway to professionalism: the English Bar in the eighteenth and nineteenth centuries' (1980) Journal of Social History 615.

Dworkin, R, 'Is law a system of rules?', in Dworkin, R (ed), *The Philosophy of Law: Oxford Readings in Philosophy*, 1977a, Oxford: Oxford University Press.

Dworkin, R, *Taking Rights Seriously*, 1977b, London: Duckworth.

Dworkin, R, 'Principle, policy, procedure', in *A Matter of Principle*, 1986, Oxford: Clarendon.

Easton, S, 'Legal advice, common sense and the right to silence' (1998) 2 E&P 109.

Edwards, P (ed), *The Encyclopedia of Philosophy*, 1967, London: Collier-Macmillan.

Eggleston, Sir R, *Evidence, Proof and Probability*, 2nd edn, 1983, London: Weidenfeld & Nicolson.

Evans, J, 'Change in the doctrine of precedent in the nineteenth century', in Goldstein, L (ed), *Precedent in Law*, 1987, Oxford: Oxford University Press.

Fielding, H, *The History of Tom Jones*, Signet Classics Series, 1963 [1749], London: The New English Library.

Forsyth, C, 'Public interest immunity: recent and future developments' [1997] CLJ 51.

Friedman, RD, 'Thoughts from across the water on hearsay and confrontation' [1998] Crim LR 697.

Gilbert, Sir J, *The Law of Evidence*, Lofft, C (ed), 4th edn, 1791, London: A Strahan and W Woodfall.

Gooderson, RN, '*Res gesta* in criminal cases' [1956] CLJ 199; [1957] CLJ 55.

Grevling, K, 'Fairness and the exclusion of evidence under section 78(1) of the Police and Criminal Evidence Act' (1997) 113 LQR 667.

Hale, Sir M, *The History of the Pleas of the Crown*, Wilson, G (ed), 1778, London: for T Payne *et al*.

Hart, HLA, *Essays on Bentham*, 1982, Oxford: Clarendon.

Healy, P, 'Proof and policy: no golden threads' [1987] Crim LR 355.

Helmholz, RH *et al*, *The Privilege Against Self-Incrimination: Its Origins and Development*, 1997, London and Chicago: University of Chicago Press.

Heydon, JD, 'Statutory restrictions on the privilege against self-incrimination' (1971) 87 LQR 214.

Hirst, M, 'Contradicting previous acquittals' [1991] Crim LR 510.

Hirst, M, 'Conduct, relevance and the hearsay rule' (1993) 13 LS 54.

Ho, H, 'Similar Facts in Civil Cases' (2006) 26 OJLS 131.

Hoffmann, LH, 'Similar facts after *Boardman*' (1975) 91 LQR 193.

Holdsworth, Sir WS, *A History of English Law*, 1903–72, London: Methuen and Sweet & Maxwell.

Hoyano, L, 'Variations on a theme by Pigot: special measures directions for child witnesses' [2000] Crim LR 250.

Hunter, M, 'Judicial discretion: section 78 in practice' [1994] Crim LR 558.

Imwinkelried, EJ, 'The worst evidence principle: the best hypothesis as to the logical structure of evidence law' (1992) U Miami L Rev 1069.

Jack, A, 'Lord Woolf and expert evidence' (1994) 144 NLJ 1099.

Jackson, JD, 'Silence and proof: extending the boundaries of criminal proceedings in the United Kingdom' (2001) 5 E&P 145.

James, GF, 'Relevancy, probability and the law' (1941) 29 Cal L Rev 689.

Jennings, A *et al*, 'Silence and safety: the impact of human rights law' [2000] Crim LR 879.

Kant, I, *Foundations of the Metaphysics of Morals*, Beck, LW (trans), *The Library of Liberal Arts*, 2nd edn, 1990 [1785], London: Macmillan.

Kean, AWG, 'The history of criminal liability of children' (1937) 53 LQR 364.

Keane, A, *The Modern Law of Evidence*. 6th edn, 2006, Oxford: Oxford University Press.

Kenny, A, 'The expert in court' (1983) 99 LQR 197.

Kibble, N, 'The sexual history provisions . . .' [2000] Crim LR 274.

Landesman, C, *An Introduction to Epistemology*, 1997, Oxford: Blackwell.

Landsman, S, 'From Gilbert to Bentham: the reconceptualization of evidence theory' (1990a) 36 Wayne L Rev 1149.

Landsman, S, 'The rise of the contentious spirit: adversary procedure in eighteenth-century England' (1990b) 75 Cornell L Rev 497.

Langbein, JH, 'The criminal trial before the lawyers' (1978) 45 U Chi L Rev 236.

Langbein, JH, 'Shaping the eighteenth-century criminal trial: a view from the Ryder sources' (1983) 50 U Chi L Rev 1.

Langbein, JH, 'Historical foundations of the law of evidence: a view from the Ryder sources' (1996) 96 Columbia L Rev 1168.

Langbein, JH, 'The privilege and common law criminal procedure: the sixteenth to the eighteenth centuries', in Helmholz, RH *et al*, *The Privilege Against Self-Incrimination*, 1997, London and Chicago: University of Chicago Press.

Langbein, JH, *The Origins of Adversary Criminal Trial*, 2003, Oxford: Oxford University Press.

Laudan, L, *Truth, Error, and Criminal Law: An Essay in Legal Epistemology*. 2006, Cambridge: Cambridge University Press.

Law Commission No 29, *Offences of Damage to Property*, 1970, London: HMSO.

Law Commission No 202, *Corroboration of Evidence in Criminal Trials*, 1991, London: HMSO.

Law Commission No 216, *The Hearsay Rule in Civil Proceedings*, 1993, London: HMSO.

Law Commission No 245, *Evidence in Criminal Proceedings: Hearsay and Related Topics*, 1997, London: The Stationery Office.

Law Commission No 273, *Evidence of Bad Character in Criminal Proceedings*, 2001, London: The Stationery Office.

Law Commission Consultation Paper 138, *Evidence in Criminal Proceedings: Hearsay and Related Topics*, 1995, London: HMSO.

Law Commission Consultation Paper 141, *Evidence in Criminal Proceedings: Previous Misconduct of a Defendant*, 1996, London: HMSO.

Law Commission Consultation Paper 145, *Legislating the Criminal Code: Corruption*, 1997, London: The Stationery Office.

Law Reform Committee, 15th Report, *The Rule in Hollington v Hewthorn*, Cmnd 3391, 1967, London: HMSO.

Law Reform Committee, 16th Report, *Privilege in Civil Proceedings*, Cmnd 3472, 1967, London: HMSO.

Law Reform Committee, 17th Report, *Evidence of Opinion and Expert Evidence*, Cmnd 4489, 1970, London: HMSO.

Leary, R, 'Evidential reasoning and analytical techniques in criminal pre-trial investigation', 2004, University College London PhD thesis.

Lieberman, D, *The Province of Legislation Determined: Legal Theory in Eighteenth-Century Britain*, 1989, Cambridge: Cambridge University Press.

Lobban, M, *The Common Law and English Jurisprudence 1760–1850*, 1991, Oxford: Clarendon.

Lowndes, J, *A Few Brief Remarks on Lord Denman's Bill for Improving the Law of Evidence*, 1843, London: Saunders and Benning.

Macaulay, TB (Lord Macaulay), *The History of England from the Accession of James II*, 1880 [1849–55], London: Longmans, Green.

McConville, M, 'The doctrine of judicial notice and its relation to evidence' (1979) 1 Liverpool LR 62.

McEwan, J, 'In defence of vulnerable witnesses: the Youth Justice and Criminal Evidence Act 1999' (2000) 4 E&P 1.

McGrath, D, 'Without prejudice privilege' (2001) 5 E&P 213.

Mackay, RD, and Colman, AM, 'Excluding expert evidence' [1991] Crim LR 800.

Mackay, RD, and Colman, AM, 'Equivocal rulings on expert psychological and psychiatric evidence' [1996] Crim LR 88.

Macnair, MRT, 'The early development of the privilege against self-incrimination' (1990) 10 OJLS 66.

Malpas, J. (ed), *The Philosophical Papers of Alan Donagan*. 2 vols. 1994, Chicago and London: University of Chicago Press.

Manchester, C, 'Judicial notice and personal knowledge' (1979) 42 MLR 22.

May, R, and Powles, S, *Criminal Evidence*. 5th edn, 2004, London: Sweet & Maxwell.

Megarry, Sir R, *A Second Miscellany-at-Law: A Further Diversion for Lawyers and Others*, 1973, London: Stevens.

Milsom, SFC, *Historical Foundations of the Common Law*, 2nd edn, 1981, London: Butterworths.

Mirfield, P, 'Shedding a tear for issue estoppel' [1980] Crim LR 336.

Mirfield, P, 'Expert evidence and unreliable confessions' (1992) 108 LQR 528.

Mirfield, P, ' "Corroboration" after the 1994 Act' [1995] Crim LR 448.

Mirfield, P, *Silence, Confessions and Improperly Obtained Evidence*, 1997, Oxford: Clarendon.

Mirfield, P, '*Res judicata* rejected' (2001) 117 LQR 194.

Mirfield, P, 'Character, credibility and truthfulness.' [2008] LQR 1.

Morgan, EM, *Some Problems of Proof Under the Anglo-American System of Litigation*, 1956, New York: Columbia University Press.

Munday, RJC, 'What constitutes a good character?' [1997] Crim LR 247.

Munday, RJC, 'Admitting acquittals as similar fact evidence of guilt' [2000] 59 CLJ 468.

Munday, RJC, 'Adverse denial and purposive confession' [2003] Crim LR 850.

Murphy, P, *Murphy on Evidence*, 5th edn, 1995, London: Blackstone.

Murphy, P, 'Character evidence: the search for logic and policy continues' (1998) 2 E&P 71.

Murphy, P, *Murphy on Evidence*. 9th edn, 2005, Oxford: Oxford University Press.

Nance, DA, 'The best evidence principle' (1988) 73 Iowa L Rev 227.

Nokes, GD, 'Real evidence' (1949) 65 LQR 57.

Nokes, GD, 'Professional privilege' (1950) 66 LQR 88.

Nokes, GD, '*Res gestae* as hearsay' (1954) 70 LQR 370.

Nokes, GD, 'The limits of judicial notice' (1958) 74 LQR 59.

Nokes, GD, *An Introduction to the Law of Evidence*, 4th edn, 1967, London: Sweet & Maxwell.

Noorlander, P, 'Covert policing and the Convention: entrapment' (1998) 148 NLJ 511.

Ormerod, D, 'The hearsay exceptions' [1996] Crim LR 16.

Ormerod, D, 'Redundant *res gestae*?' [1998] Crim LR 301.

Ormerod, D, 'A prejudicial view' [2000] Crim LR 452.

Ormerod, D, 'Sounds familiar? – voice identification evidence' [2001] Crim LR 595.

Ormerod, D, 'Sounding out expert voice identification' [2002] Crim LR 771.

Osborne, C, 'Hearsay and the European Court of Human Rights' [1993] Crim LR 255.

Packer, HL, 'Two models of the criminal process' (1964) 113 U of Pa L Rev 1.

Parkinson, GRH (ed), *An Encyclopaedia of Philosophy*, 1988, London: Routledge.

Parkinson, S, 'Exposing the informer and other secrets of the prosecution' (2003) 153 NLJ 1910.

Parkinson, S, 'Fairness and public interest immunity: inconsistent concepts?' (2004) 154 NLJ 46.

Passmore, C, 'The future of legal professional privilege' (1999) 3 E&P 71.

Pattenden, R, 'Conflicting approaches to psychiatric evidence in criminal trials' [1986] Crim LR 92.

Pattenden, R, 'Should confessions be corroborated?' (1991) 107 LQR 317.

Pattenden, R, 'Similar fact evidence and proof of identity' (1996) 112 LQR 446.

Pattenden, R, 'Litigation privilege and expert opinion evidence' (2000) 4 E&P 213.

Phillipps, SM, *A Treatise on the Law of Evidence*, 7th edn, 1829, London: William Benning.

Phipson on Evidence, 13th edn, 1982, London: Sweet & Maxwell.

Phipson on Evidence, 14th edn, 1990, London: Sweet & Maxwell.

Polyviou, PG, 'Illegally obtained evidence and *R v Sang*', in Tapper, CFH (ed), *Crime, Proof and Punishment: Essays in Memory of Sir Rupert Cross*, 1981, London: Butterworths.

Post, JB, 'The admissibility of defence counsel in English criminal procedure' (1984) 5 J Leg Hist 23.

Postema, GJ, *Bentham and the Common Law Tradition*, 1986, Oxford: Clarendon.

Ram, J, *A Treatise on Facts as Subjects of Inquiry by a Jury*, 1861, London: William Marshall.

Redmayne, M, 'Drugs, money and relevance' (1999) 3 E&P 128.

Redmayne, M, *Expert Evidence and Criminal Justice*, 2001, Oxford: Oxford University Press.

Report to the Secretary of State for the Home Department of the Departmental Committee on Evidence of Identification in Criminal Cases, 1976, London: HMSO.

Roberts, A, 'Questions of "who was there?" and "who did what?": the application of Code D in cases of dispute as to participation but not presence' [2003] Crim LR 709.

Roberts, P, 'Taking the burden of proof seriously' [1995] Crim LR 783.

Roberts, P, 'Acquitted misconduct evidence and double jeopardy principles, from *Sambasivam* to *Z* [2000] Crim LR 952.

Roberts, P, 'Towards the principled reception of expert evidence of witness credibility in criminal trials' (2002) 8 E&P 215.

Robertson, G, 'Entrapment evidence' [1994] Crim LR 793.

Royal Commission on Criminal Justice Report, Cm 2263, 1993, London: HMSO.

Royal Commission on Criminal Procedure Report, Cmnd 8092, 1981, London: HMSO.

Sandy, D, and Passmore, C, 'Redefining legal advice privilege' (2004) 154 NLJ 588.

Schiff, S, 'The use of out-of-court information in fact determination at trial' (1963) 41 Can Bar Rev 335.

Scott, KE, 'Two models of the civil process' (1974–75) 27 Stanford L Rev 937.

Scott, the Rt Hon Sir R, *Report of the Inquiry into the Export of Defence Equipment and Dual-Use Goods to Iraq and Related Prosecutions*, HC 115, 1996a, London: HMSO.

Scott, the Rt Hon Sir R, 'The acceptable and unacceptable use of public interest immunity' [1996b] PL 427.

Scruton, R, *Kant*, 1982, Oxford: Oxford University Press.

Shapin, S, *A Social History of Truth: Civility and Science in Seventeenth-Century England*, 1994, Chicago and London: University of Chicago Press.

Sharpe, S, 'Covert police operations and the discretionary exclusion of evidence' [1994] Crim LR 793.

Sharpe, S, 'Judicial discretion and investigative impropriety' (1997) 1 E&P 149.

Simpson, AWB, 'The rise and fall of the legal treatise: legal principles and the forms of legal literature' (1981) 45 U Chi L Rev 632.

Smith, JC, 'The presumption of innocence' (1987) 38 NILQ 223.

Smith, JC, 'Proving conspiracy' [1996] Crim LR 386.

Smith, JC, 'More on proving conspiracy' [1997] Crim LR 333.

Spencer, J, *Evidence of Bad Character*, 2006, Oxford and Portland, Oregon: Hart Publishing.

Spencer, J, and Flin, R, *The Evidence of Children: The Law and the Psychology*, 2nd edn, 1993, Oxford: Oxford University Press.

Spencer, JR, 'Court experts and expert witnesses' (1992) 45(2) CLP 213.

Squires, D, 'The Problem with Entrapment' (2006) 26 OJLS 351.

Starkie, T, *A Practical Treatise on the Law of Evidence*, 3rd edn, 1842, London: V and R Stevens and GS Norton.

Stein, A, 'After Hunt: the burden of proof, risk of non-persuasion and judicial pragmatism' (1991) 54 MLR 570.

Stein, A, *Foundations of Evidence Law*, 2005, Oxford: Oxford University Press.

Stephen, Sir JF, *A Digest of the Law of Evidence*, 3rd edn, 1877, London: Macmillan.

Stephen, Sir JF, *A Digest of the Law of Evidence*, 12th edn, 1936, London: Macmillan.

Stephen, Sir JF, *A History of the Criminal Law of England*, 1973 [1883], New York: Burt Franklin.

Stone, J, '*Res gesta reagitata*' (1939) 55 LQR 66.

Stone, D, 'The presumption of death: a redundant concept?' (1981) 44 MLR 516.

Stone, J, and Wells, WAN, *Evidence: Its History and Policies*, 1991, Sydney: Butterworths.

Stone, M, *Cross-Examination in Criminal Trials*, 1988, London: Butterworths.

Stone, M, 'Instant lie detection? Demeanour and credibility in criminal trials' [1991] Crim LR 821.

Sugarman, D, 'Legal theory, the common law mind and the making of the textbook tradition', in Twining, W (ed), *Legal Theory and Common Law*, 1986, Oxford: Blackwell.

Sullivan, R, *An Introduction to Kant's Ethics*, 1994, Cambridge: Cambridge University Press.

Supperstone, M, and Coppel, J, 'A New Approach to Public Interest Immunity' [1997] PL 211.

Tapper, C, 'Privilege and policy' (1974) 37 MLR 92.

Tapper, C, 'The open society and its enemy' (1978) 41 MLR 192.

Tapper, C, 'Prosecution and privilege' (1996) 1 E&P 5.

Tapper, C, 'Clouded acquittal' (2001) 117 LQR 1.

Tapper, C, 'The Criminal Justice Act 2003: (3) Evidence of bad character' [2004] Crim LR 533.

Tapper, C, 'Privilege, Policy and Principle' [2005] 121 LQR 181.

Tapper, C, *Cross and Tapper on Evidence*. 11th edn, 2007, Oxford: Oxford University Press.

Taylor, JP, *Treatise on the Law of Evidence*, 6th edn, 1872, London: William Maxwell.

Temkin, J, 'Sexual history evidence' [1993] Crim LR 3.

Temkin, J, 'Sexual history evidence – beware the backlash' [2003] Crim LR 217.

Thanki, B, *The Law of Privilege*, 2006, Oxford: Oxford University Press.

Thayer, JB, 'Judicial notice and the law of evidence' (1890) 3 Harv LR 285.

Thayer, JB, *A Preliminary Treatise on Evidence at the Common Law*, 1898, Boston: Little, Brown.

Trautman, HL, 'Logical or legal relevancy – a conflict in theory' (1952) 5 V and L Rev 385.

Tribe, LH, 'Triangulating hearsay' (1974) Harv LR 957.

Twining, W, *Theories of Evidence: Bentham and Wigmore*, 1985, London: Weidenfeld & Nicolson.

Twining, W, *Rethinking Evidence: Exploratory Essays*, 2nd edn, 2006, Cambridge: Cambridge University Press.

Waldron, J (ed), *Theories of Rights: Oxford Readings in Philosophy*, 1984, Oxford: Oxford University Press.

Waldron, J, 'The philosophy of rights', in Parkinson, GRH (ed), *An Encyclopedia of Philosophy*, 1998, London: Routledge.

Weyrauch, WO, 'Law as mask – legal ritual and relevance' (1978) 66 Cal L Rev 699.

Wigmore, JH, *The Principles of Judicial Proof*, 2nd edn, 1931, Boston: Little, Brown.

Wigmore, JH, *The Science of Judicial Proof*, 3rd edn, 1937, Boston: Little, Brown.

Wigmore, JH, *Treatise on Evidence in Trials at Common Law*, 3rd edn rev, 1940, Boston: Little, Brown.

Wigmore, JH, *A Treatise on the System of Evidence in Trials at Common Law*, Tillers, P (ed), 1983, Boston: Little, Brown.

Williams, CR, 'The problem of similar fact evidence' (1979) Dalhousie LJ 281.

Williams, CR, 'Offences and defences' (1982) 2 LS 233.

Williams, G, *Criminal Law: The General Part*, 2nd edn, 1961, London: Stevens.

Williams, G, 'Evidential burdens on the defence' (1977a) 127 NLJ 182.

Williams, G, 'The evidential burden: some common misapprehensions' (1977b) 127 NLJ 156.

Williams, G, 'The logic of "exceptions" ' [1988] CLJ 261.

Wills, W, *An Essay on the Principles of Circumstantial Evidence*, Wills, A (ed), 5th edn, 1902, London: Butterworths.

Winder, WHD, 'The courts of requests' (1936) 52 LQR 369.

Woffinden, B, *Miscarriages of Justice*, 1989, London: Coronet.

Wolchover, D, and Heaton-Armstrong, A, *Wolchover and Heaton-Armstrong on Confession Evidence*, 1996, London: Sweet & Maxwell.

Witting, C, '*Res ipsa loquitur*: some last words?' (2001) 117 LQR 392.

Zuckerman, AAS, 'Previous convictions as evidence of guilt' (1971) 87 LQR 21.

Zuckerman, AAS, 'Privilege and public interest', in Tapper, CFH (ed), *Crime, Proof and Punishment: Essays in Memory of Sir Rupert Cross*, 1981, London: Butterworths.

Zuckerman, AAS, *The Principles of Criminal Evidence*, 1989, Oxford: Clarendon.

INDEX